DATA FILES FOR STUDENTS

To complete the activities in this book, students will need data files, which are available online.

To access the data files, follow these instructions:

1. Open your browser and access the companion website at NGL.Cengage.com/AdobeId

2. For data files to complete each activity within a chapter, select the chapter number from the drop-down box (below the book title), then click "Student Downloads" in the Book Overview section on the left panel.

3. For ACP Prep Guide data files, select "Student Downloads" in the Book Resources section on the left panel.

T0130992

Adobe
InDesign
REVEALED

CHRIS BOTELLO

NATIONAL GEOGRAPHIC LEARNING | CENGAGE

Acknowledgments

Grateful acknowledgment is given to the authors, artists, photographers, museums, publishers, and agents for permission to reprint copyrighted material. Every effort has been made to secure the appropriate permission. If any omissions have been made or if corrections are required, please contact the Publisher.

Cover Image Credit:

Krystal Wright/National Geographic

Adobe® Photoshop®, Adobe® InDesign®, Adobe® Illustrator®, Adobe® Flash®, Adobe® Dreamweaver®, Adobe® Edge Animate®, Adobe® Creative Suite®, and Adobe® Creative Cloud® are trademarks or registered trademarks of Adobe Systems, Inc. in the United States and/or other countries. Third party products, services, company names, logos, design, titles, words, or phrases within these materials may be trademarks of their respective owners.

Adobe product screenshot(s) reprinted with permission from Adobe Systems Incorporated.

Copyright © 2023 Cengage Learning, Inc.

ALL RIGHTS RESERVED. No part of this work covered by the copyright herein may be reproduced or distributed in any form or by any means, except as permitted by U.S. copyright law, without the prior written permission of the copyright owner.

"National Geographic","National Geographic Society" and the Yellow Border Design are registered trademarks of the National Geographic Society ® Marcas Registradas

For product information and technology assistance, contact us at Customer & Sales Support, 888-915-3276

For permission to use material from this text or product, submit all requests online at **www.cengage.com/permissions**

Further permissions questions can be emailed to **permissionrequest@cengage.com**

National Geographic Learning | Cengage
200 Pier 4 Boulevard, Suite 400
Boston, MA 02210

National Geographic Learning, a Cengage company, is a provider of quality core and supplemental educational materials for the PreK–12, adult education, and ELT markets. Cengage is a leading provider of customized learning solutions with employees residing in nearly 40 different countries and sales in more than 125 countries around the world. Find your local representative at **NGL.Cengage.com/RepFinder.**

Visit National Geographic Learning online at **NGL.Cengage.com.**

ISBN: 978-0-357-54176-0

Printed in the United States of America.

Print Number: 01
Print Year: 2022

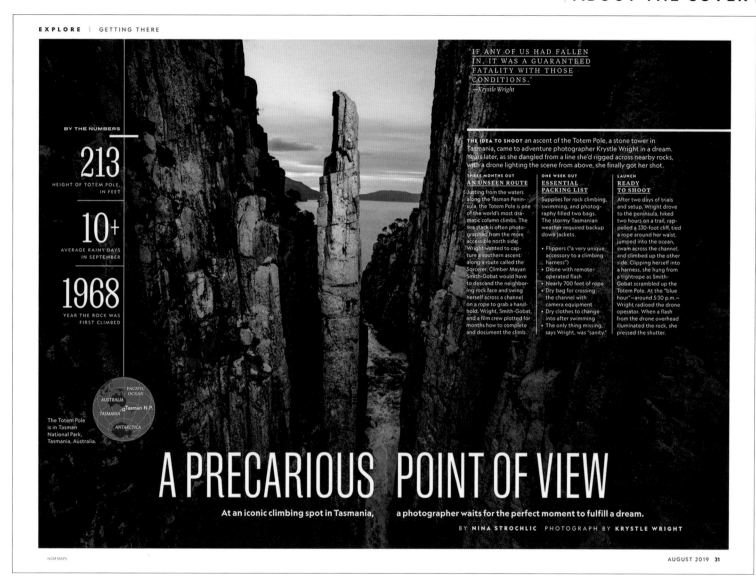

'IF ANY OF US HAD FALLEN IN, IT WAS A GUARANTEED FATALITY WITH THOSE CONDITIONS.'
—*Krystle Wright*

THE IDEA TO SHOOT an ascent of the Totem Pole, a stone tower in Tasmania, came to adventure photographer Krystle Wright in a dream. Years later, as she dangled from a line she'd rigged across nearby rocks, with a drone lighting the scene from above, she finally got her shot.

THREE MONTHS OUT
AN UNSEEN ROUTE
Jutting from the waters along the Tasman Peninsula, the Totem Pole is one of the world's most dramatic column climbs. The sea stack is often photographed from the more accessible north side; Wright wanted to capture a southern ascent along a route called the Sorcerer. Climber Mayan Smith-Gobat would have to descend the neighboring rock face and swing herself across a channel on a rope to grab a handhold. Wright, Smith-Gobat, and a film crew plotted for months how to complete and document the climb.

ONE WEEK OUT
ESSENTIAL PACKING LIST
Supplies for rock climbing, swimming, and photography filled two bags. The stormy Tasmanian weather required backup down jackets.

- Flippers ("a very unique accessory to a climbing harness")
- Drone with remote-operated flash
- Nearly 700 feet of rope
- Dry bag for crossing the channel with camera equipment
- Dry clothes to change into after swimming
- The only thing missing, says Wright, was "sanity."

LAUNCH
READY TO SHOOT
After two days of trials and setup, Wright drove to the peninsula, hiked two hours on a trail, rappelled a 330-foot cliff, tied a rope around her waist, jumped into the ocean, swam across the channel, and climbed up the other side. Clipping herself into a harness, she hung from a tightrope as Smith-Gobat scrambled up the Totem Pole. At the "blue hour"—around 5:30 p.m.—Wright radioed the drone operator. When a flash from the drone overhead illuminated the rock, she pressed the shutter.

BY THE NUMBERS

213
HEIGHT OF TOTEM POLE, IN FEET

10+
AVERAGE RAINY DAYS IN SEPTEMBER

1968
YEAR THE ROCK WAS FIRST CLIMBED

PACIFIC OCEAN
AUSTRALIA
TASMANIA — Tasman N.P.
ANTARCTICA

The Totem Pole is in Tasman National Park, Tasmania, Australia.

A PRECARIOUS POINT OF VIEW

At an iconic climbing spot in Tasmania, a photographer waits for the perfect moment to fulfill a dream.

BY **NINA STROCHLIC**   PHOTOGRAPH BY **KRYSTLE WRIGHT**

Krystle Wright hiked, rappelled, and swam to get this shot of the Totem Pole, one of the world's most dramatic column climbs.
Photo location: Tasman National Park, Tasmania, Australia.

CONTENTS

UNIT 2 INCORPORATING IMAGES AND ILLUSTRATIONS

CONTENTS

UNIT 2 PROJECT

NATIONAL GEOGRAPHIC CREATIVE
BREAK DOWN THE STORY

UNIT 3 UTILIZING ADVANCED FEATURES

CHAPTER 9 WORKING WITH TABS AND TABLES

CHAPTER 10 MAKING BOOKS, TABLES OF CONTENTS, AND INDEXES

CHAPTER 11 PREPARING, PACKAGING, AND EXPORTING DOCUMENTS FOR PRINT AND THE WEB

ABOUT THE AUTHOR

Chris Botello began his career as a print production manager for *Premiere* magazine. He designed and produced movie and TV campaigns for numerous Los Angeles-based studios and agencies, including Miramax Films and NBC Television, and was the art director for Microsoft's launch of sidewalk.com/boston. Chris is the author of the *Revealed* series of books on Photoshop, Illustrator, and InDesign, and the co-author of *YouTube for Dummies*. He lives in Los Angeles where he teaches graphic design and Adobe software classes. Chris uses his own Revealed books as the text for his classes.

REVIEWERS

Eric Cornish
Miami Dade College
Miami, Florida

Linda Dickeson
Adobe Certified Instructor
Lincoln, Nebraska

Beverly Houwing
Adobe Certified Instructor,
Squid Gallery
Los Angeles, California

Dr. Marilyn Proctor-Givens
Lincoln High School
Tallahassee, Florida

Jessica Salas
George Jenkins High School
Lakeland, Florida

Natasha Smith
Union High School
Tulsa, Oklahoma

CREATIVE STORYTELLING | *THE REVEALED SERIES VISION*

The Revealed Series is your guide to today's best-selling multimedia applications. These comprehensive books teach the skills behind the application, showing you how to apply smart design principles to multimedia products such as dynamic graphics, animation, and websites.

A team of design professionals including multimedia instructors, students, authors, and editors worked together to create this series. We recognized the unique learning environment of the multimedia classroom and produced a series that:

- Gives you comprehensive step-by-step instructions.

- Offers in-depth explanation of the "Why" behind a skill.

- Includes creative projects for additional practice.

- Explains concepts clearly using full-color visuals.

- Keeps you up-to-date with the latest software upgrades so you can always work with cutting-edge technology.

It was our goal to create a book that speaks directly to the multimedia and design community—one of the most rapidly growing computer fields today. We think we've done just that, with a sophisticated and instructive book design.

AUTHOR'S VISION

I am thrilled to present this book on Adobe InDesign Creative Cloud. For me, it's been a pleasure to watch InDesign evolve into the smart, strategic layout package it is today. Whether you are producing layouts for print or interactive uses, InDesign remains a powerhouse application to help you achieve your goals. As new media continues to evolve across devices, InDesign remains positioned with a central role in that evolution, and that's exciting.

Thank you to Ann Fisher for your intelligence, dedication, and friendship as the developmental editor on this title. Thank you to Karen Caldwell for guiding this project to completion and always keeping us informed and on track. Thank you to the reviewers for their invaluable real-world feedback. Thank you to Chris Jaeggi for your clarity and consistent leadership. Thank you to Raj Desai for your vision and commitment to imagine what is possible. And thank you to Allison Katen Lim for creating the National Geographic features that compliment this book so well.

—Chris Botello

INTRODUCTION TO
ADOBE® INDESIGN CREATIVE CLOUD

Welcome to *Adobe InDesign Creative Cloud—Revealed*. This book offers creative projects, concise instructions, and complete coverage of basic to advanced InDesign skills, helping you to create polished, professional-looking layouts. The book is designed to be used as content for the classroom and as a general reference for the software.

This text is organized into 11 chapters. These chapters cover a spectrum of basic to intermediate to advanced InDesign skills. You will explore the many options InDesign provides for creating comprehensive layouts, including formatting text and body copy, designing display headlines, setting up a document, working with process and non-process colors, placing graphics from Adobe Illustrator and Adobe Photoshop, working with tabs and tables, and preparing an InDesign layout for output. By the end of the book, you'll be able to create professional-looking layouts that incorporate illustrations and bitmap graphics, as well as sophisticated presentations of text and typography.

Chapter Opener

Each chapter opens with an impactful, full-page image to engage students visually with what they will be learning. The lesson topics and the Adobe Certified Professional Exam Objectives covered in the chapter are clearly laid out so students and instructors can easily track their progress in acquiring skills and preparing for the exam.

What You'll Do

A What You'll Do figure begins every lesson. This figure gives you an at-a-glance look at what you'll do in the chapter, either by showing you a reference figure from the project or a feature of the software.

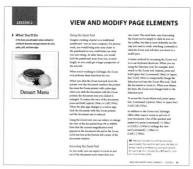

Comprehensive Conceptual Lessons

Before jumping into instructions, in-depth conceptual information tells you "why" skills are applied. This book provides the "how" and "why" through the use of clear and concise narrative instruction. Also included in the text are tips and sidebars to help you work more efficiently and creatively, or to teach you a bit about the history or design philosophy behind the skill you are learning.

PREVIEW

Step-by-Step Instructions

This book combines in-depth conceptual information with concise steps to help you learn InDesign Creative Cloud. Each set of steps guides you through a lesson where you will create, modify, or enhance an InDesign Creative Cloud file. Steps reference large colorful images and quick step summaries round out the lessons.

Skills Review

A Skills Review at the end of each chapter contains hands-on practice exercises that mirror the progressive nature of the lesson material.

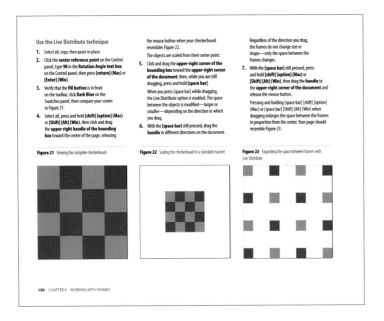

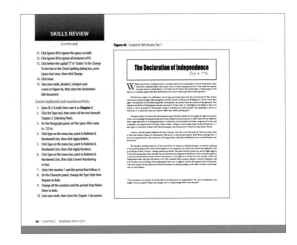

Chapter Projects

This book contains a variety of end-of-chapter materials for additional practice and reinforcement. Each chapter concludes with at least two Project Builders and one or two Design Projects. Together, these projects provide a valuable opportunity for students to practice and explore the concepts and techniques learned in the chapter. For the instructor, they are an opportunity to evaluate students' abilities to utilize taught skills as they work independently.

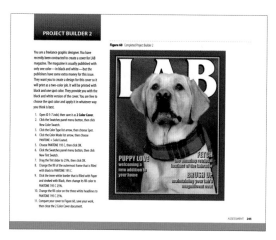

PROJECT BUILDER 2

Figure 60 Completed Project Builder 2

You are a freelance graphic designer. You have recently been contracted to create a cover for LAB magazine. The magazine is usually published with only one color—in black and white—but the publishers have some extra money for this issue. They want you to create a design for this cover so it will print as a two-color job. It will be printed with black and one spot color. They provide you with the black and white version of the cover. You are free to choose the spot color and apply it in whatever way you think is best.

1. Open ID 5-7.indd, then save it as **2 Color Cover**.
2. Click the Swatches panel menu button, then click New Color Swatch.
3. Click the Color Type list arrow, then choose Spot.
4. Click the Color Mode list arrow, then choose PANTONE + Solid Coated.
5. Choose PANTONE 195 C, then click OK.
6. Click the Swatches panel menu button, then click New Tint Swatch.
7. Drag the Tint slider to 25%, then click OK.
8. Change the fill of the outermost frame that is filled with black to PANTONE 195 C.
9. Click the inner white border that is filled with Paper and stroked with Black, then change its fill color to PANTONE 195 C 25%.
10. Change the fill color on the three white headlines to PANTONE 195 C 25%.
11. Compare your cover to Figure 60, save your work, then close the 2 Color Cover document.

ASSESSMENT **349**

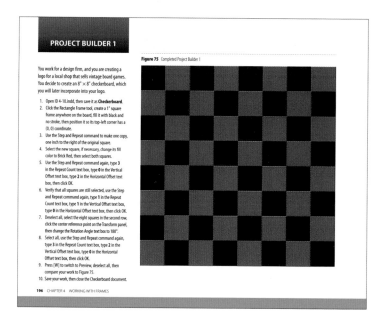

PROJECT BUILDER 1

Figure 75 Completed Project Builder 1

You work for a design firm, and you are creating a logo for a local shop that sells vintage board games. You decide to create an 8" × 8" checkerboard, which you will later incorporate into your logo.

1. Open ID 4-10.indd, then save it as **Checkerboard**.
2. Click the Rectangle Frame tool, create a 1" square frame anywhere on the board, fill it with black and no stroke, then position it so its top-left corner has a (0, 0) coordinate.
3. Use the Step and Repeat command to make one copy, one inch to the right of the original square.
4. Select the new square, if necessary, change its fill color to Brick Red, then select both squares.
5. Use the Step and Repeat command again, type **3** in the Repeat Count text box, type **0** in the Vertical Offset text box, type **2** in the Horizontal Offset text box, then click OK.
6. Verify that all squares are still selected, use the Step and Repeat command again, type **1** in the Repeat Count text box, type **1** in the Vertical Offset text box, type **0** in the Horizontal Offset text box, then click OK.
7. Deselect all, select the eight squares in the second row, click the center reference point on the Transform panel, then change the Rotation Angle text box to 180°.
8. Select all, use the Step and Repeat command again, type **3** in the Repeat Count text box, type **2** in the Vertical Offset text box, type **0** in the Horizontal Offset text box, then click OK.
9. Press [W] to switch to Preview, deselect all, then compare your work to Figure 75.
10. Save your work, then close the Checkerboard document.

196 CHAPTER 4 WORKING WITH FRAMES

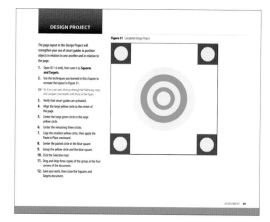

DESIGN PROJECT

Figure 31 Completed Design Project

The page layout in this Design Project will strengthen your use of smart guides to position objects in relation to one another and in relation to the page.

1. Open ID 1-6.indd, then save it as **Squares and Targets**.
2. Use the techniques you learned in this chapter to recreate the layout in Figure 31.

TIP Try it on your own, then go through the following steps, and compare your results with those in the figure.

3. Verify that smart guides are activated.
4. Align the large yellow circle to the center of the page.
5. Center the large green circle in the large yellow circle.
6. Center the remaining three circles.
7. Copy the smallest yellow circle, then apply the Paste in Place command.
8. Center the pasted circle in the blue square.
9. Group the yellow circle and the blue square.
10. Click the Selection tool.
11. Drag and drop three copies of the group at the four corners of the document.
12. Save your work, then close the Squares and Targets document.

ASSESSMENT **39**

PREVIEW

NATIONAL GEOGRAPHIC | CREATIVES

This edition of *Adobe InDesign Creative Cloud—Revealed* provides five opportunities for students to discover the work of National Geographic Creatives and be inspired to pursue their own artistic careers.

Two mid-unit features are based on in-depth interviews and images designed by the Creatives. These features give students a window into their career development, creative processes, and passion for their work. Students learn firsthand how accomplished creative professionals use their skill and talent to create impactful, meaningful works that bring their projects to life. The projects encourage students to create their own work based on the design featured in the career profile they have just studied. Students are guided to create pieces that relate to their lives, and to incorporate photographs or copy that tie directly to their school, community, and interests.

Three end-of-unit features incorporate longer creative projects that allow students to explore designing for impact. The emphasis of these projects is on creating layouts, while noting the relationship between imagery and text, and the use of color and font, as inspired by the featured National Geographic examples.

UNIT 1 PROJECT VISUAL DISPLAY OF INFORMATION

THE SUN IS STILL HIGH IN THE ALASKAN SUMMER SKY WHEN THE CALL COMES IN AT 9:47 P.M.

Layout/design by Tim Nartz. From "Into the Fire," National Geographic Magazine, Vol. 205, No. 5, May, 2019.

| DESIGN PROJECT |

PROJECT DESCRIPTION

In this project, you will explore the relationship between imagery and text using a model spread from *National Geographic*. You will then study the differences between various magazine spread layouts and work with a peer to create the layout for your own spread. Your group will choose an impactful photograph and write accompanying text to describe it. The goal of this project is to create a layout that is balanced in its imagery and text placement.

SKILLS TO EXPLORE

- Format Text
- Format Paragraphs
- Create and Apply Styles
- Edit Text
- Create Bulleted and Numbered Lists
- Create a New Document and Set Up a Master Page
- Create Text on Master Pages
- Apply Master Pages to Document Pages
- Modify Master Pages and Document Pages

SOFT SKILLS CHALLENGE

In print publishing, a "Wall Walk" is an opportunity to view all pages of a product before it goes to print. During this event, large format, full-color spreads are taped to the wall, so team members can view all pages in the book or magazine in one plane and discuss changes that need to be made to the design or layout.

In this challenge, you and your partner will engage in a Wall Walk. The goal of this project is to help refine your idea of what a balanced spread looks like. To prepare, look through old magazines or conduct an Internet search. Do not choose the first spreads you see. Instead, allow yourself to peruse different styles. Look for layouts, images, text placements, and font changes that capture your eye. Then select four or more full-color spreads that grab your attention. Lay the spreads on a table or tape them to the wall.

Then observe each element of the spreads carefully. Notice the details that differentiate the spreads from one another. During your Wall Walk, discuss the relationship between text and imagery, changes in font size or style, use of white space, and the balance on each of the spreads.

WALL WALK CHECKLIST

1. Partner
2. Four or more magazine spreads
3. Safe space to facilitate respectful conversation

◄ Alaskan smokejumpers parachute into remote forested areas to fight fires.

The end-of-unit features also incorporate a "Soft Skills Challenge" that provides an opportunity to collaborate and engage with peers about each project.

- **Design Projects** give students hands-on practice creating their own artifacts, inspired by the featured theme or topic. Using their own research, students build their own composition, illustration, or layout. Design Projects include examples of pre-work to encourage student planning and preparation.

- **Portfolio Projects** allow students to build on the design project, to create a more complex piece, and incorporate more advanced skills from the current unit. Students have the freedom to be creative and choose from a list of recommended skills and tools to use in their projects. These projects encourage students to provide information about a given topic, incorporating both visual and textual elements.

INTO THE FIRE

EACH SUMMER, ELITE TEAMS KNOWN AS SMOKEJUMPERS PARACHUTE INTO ALASKA'S BACKCOUNTRY IN A DANGEROUS RACE TO FIGHT REMOTE FIRES.

Layout&Design by Tim Fellis. From "Into the Fire." *National Geographic Magazine* Vol. 215, No. 5, May, 2010.

PROJECT DESCRIPTION

In this project, you will create a comprehensive spread based on the layout from your Design Project. Consider experimenting with font size and style, and using text elements such as bulleted lists, numbered lists, or captions. Play with graphic and text frames, and add color as you see fit. The goal of this project is to create a magazine-style spread that engages the reader using a balance of imagery and text.

SKILLS TO EXPLORE

- Place and Thread Text
- Create New Sections and Wrap Text
- Align and Distribute Objects on a Page
- Stack and layer Objects
- Work with Graphics Frames
- Work with Text Frames
- Working with Color
- Work with Process Colors

SOFT SKILLS CHALLENGE

Working with a partner in a creative project can present its challenges. Often, both people bring differing views and perspectives to the project. In order to create a project you are both proud of, you will need to work together. Be honest as you discuss your strengths and weaknesses with each other. Decide how to break up the work. Will you make every decision together, or will each partner have the opportunity to use their own creative skills? Look over your layout and the Skills to Explore. Work together to come up with a list of tasks for each person in your group. Practice your speech so you are confident while presenting. You want your audience to view you as an expert on the topic.

◀ Alaskan smokejumpers parachute into remote forested areas to fight fires.

GETTING STARTED

It's often challenging to start with a blank screen. Allow your Design Project to guide you.

1. Look at the balance on your page. Should the image take up the whole spread with just a bit of text? Or would it make more sense to have a single-page image with text on either the right or the left? Should the text come before the image, or the image before the text? These small decisions greatly influence the visual feel of the spread.

2. Compare the two *National Geographic* spreads. Both use a feature image to capture the reader's attention, but one has much more text than the other. Which one are you more drawn to and why? Think about how you might have designed these spreads differently. For example, imagine the "Into the Fire" spread had more text. What would be lost? How might this impact the spread as a whole?

3. Challenge yourself to enhance the layout with text and graphic frames. Link text blocks together in interesting ways and experiment with placing text in different positions on the page. Think outside the box by arranging the text in a way that shows its importance. For example, you may be able to reduce a larger text block to three sentences and instead use small caps to convey the importance of the words.

4. Think about how best to include color in your spread, either through font, background, or a feature callout. Remember, the text and images should work together for the ultimate visual impact.

RESOURCES

A FULL SUITE OF SUPPORTING RESOURCES

Instructor Companion Site
Everything you need for your course in one place! This collection of product-specific lecture and class tools is available online via the instructor resource center. You'll be able to access and download materials such as PowerPoint® presentations, data and solution files, Instructor's Manual, Industry-Aligned Credential correlations, and more.

- Download your resources at **companion-sites.cengage.com**.

Instructor's Manual
The Instructor's Manual includes chapter overviews and detailed lecture topics for each chapter, with teaching tips.

Syllabus
A sample Syllabus includes a suggested outline for any course that uses this book.

PowerPoint® Presentations
Each chapter has a corresponding PowerPoint® presentation to use in lectures, distribute to your students, or customize to suit your course.

Solutions to Exercises
Solution files are provided to show samples of final artwork. Use these files to evaluate your students' work or distribute them electronically so students can verify their work.

Test Bank and Test Engine
Cognero®, Customizable Test Bank Generator is a flexible, online system that allows you to import, edit, and manipulate content from the text's test bank or elsewhere, including your own favorite test questions; create multiple test versions in an instant; and deliver tests from your LMS, your classroom, or wherever you want.

- K12 Teachers, log on at **nglsync.cengage.com** or **companion-sites.cengage.com**.

- Higher Education Teachers, log on at **www.cengage.com**.

 CENGAGE | MINDTAP

 SYNC

THE ONLINE SOLUTION FOR CAREER AND TECHNICAL EDUCATION COURSES

MindTap for *Adobe Revealed Creative Cloud* is the online learning solution for career and technical education courses that helps teachers engage and transform today's students into critical thinkers. Through paths of dynamic assignments and applications that you can personalize, real-time course analytics, and an interactive eBook, MindTap helps teachers organize and engage students. Whether you teach this course in the classroom or in hybrid/e-learning models, MindTap enhances the course experience with data analytics, engagement tracking, and student tools such as flashcards and practice quizzes. MindTap for Adobe Illustrator also includes:

- an Adobe Professional Certification Prep Guide
- Career Readiness Module for the Arts, A/V Tech & Communications Career Cluster

K-12 teachers and students who have adopted MindTap can access their courses at **nglsync.cengage.com**.

Don't have an account? Request access from your Sales Consultant at **ngl.cengage.com/repfinder**.

Higher education teachers and students can access their courses at **login.cengage.com**.

ACCESS RESOURCES ONLINE, ANYTIME

Accessing digital content from National Geographic Learning, a part of Cengage, has never been easier. Through our new login portal, NGLSync, you can now easily gain access to all Career & Technical Education digital courses and resources purchased by your district, including: MindTap, Cognero Test Bank Generator, and Teacher/Student Companion Sites.

Log on at **nglsync.cengage.com** or **www.cengage.com**.

SUBJECT MATTER EXPERT CONTRIBUTORS

Adobe Certified Professional Test Prep Guide
Debbie Keller
Director Career & Technical Education
Adobe Education Leader
Medina Valley Independent School District
Castroville, Texas

Chana Messer
Artist, Designer, Educator
Adobe Education Leader
University of Southern California (USC), FIDM
Los Angeles, California

INTENDED AUDIENCE

This text is designed for the beginner or intermediate user who wants to learn how to use Adobe InDesign Creative Cloud. The book provides comprehensive, in-depth material that not only educates, but also encourages you to explore the nuances of this exciting program.

APPROACH

The text allows you to work at your own pace through step-by-step tutorials. A concept is presented, and the process is explained, followed by the actual steps. To learn the most from the use of the text, you should adopt the following habits:

- Proceed slowly: Accuracy and comprehension are more important than speed.
- Understand what is happening with each step before you continue to the next step.
- After finishing a skill, ask yourself if you could do it on your own, without referring to the steps. If the answer is no, review the steps.

GENERAL

Throughout the initial chapters, students are given precise instructions regarding saving their work. Students should feel they can save their work at any time, not just when instructed to do so.

Students are also given precise instructions regarding magnifying/reducing their work area. Once the student feels more comfortable, he/she should feel free to use the Zoom tool to make their work area more comfortable.

ICONS, BUTTONS, AND POINTERS

Symbols for icons, buttons, and pointers are shown in the step each time they are used. Once an icon, button, or pointer has been used on a page, the symbol will be shown for subsequent uses on that page *without* showing its name.

FONTS

The data files contain a variety of commonly used fonts, but there is no guarantee these fonts will be available on your computer. If any of the fonts in use are not available on your computer, you can make a substitution, realizing that the results may vary from those in the book.

WINDOWS AND Mac OS

Adobe Illustrator CC works virtually the same on Windows and Mac OS operating systems. In those cases where there are significant differences, the abbreviations (Win) and (Mac) are used.

SYSTEM REQUIREMENTS

For a Windows operating system:

- Processor: Intel® Pentium® 4 processor or AMD Athlon® 64 processor (2 GHz or faster)

- Operating System: Microsoft® Windows 7 (with Service Pack 1), 8, or 8.1

- Memory: 1 GB of RAM

- Storage space: 2.5 GB of available hard-disk space

- Monitor: 1024 × 768 resolution (1280 × 800 recommended)

- Video: 16-bit or higher OpenGL 2.0 video card; 512 MB RAM (1 GB recommended)

- Broadband Internet connection required for activation, Creative Cloud membership validation, and access to online services

For a MacOS operating system:

- Processor: Multicore Intel® processor with 64-bit support

- Operating System: Mac OS X 10.7, v10.8, or v10.9

- Memory: 1 GB of RAM

- Storage space: 3.2 GB of available hard-disk space

- Monitor: 1024 × 768 or greater monitor resolution (1280 × 800 recommended)

- Video: 16-bit or greater OpenGL 2.0 video card; 512 MB of VRAM (1 GB recommended)

- Broadband Internet connection required for software activation, Creative Cloud membership validation, and access to online services

As the sun ri
above the Ti
Plateau, Pasa
Sherpa (fron
Lhakpa Tenj
pass 28,700
Mount Ever
big question
George Mal
Sandy Irvin
far—or perh
the top—in

THE
ROOF
OF
THE
WORLD
ISSUE

PAGE

42

JULY
2020

THE GREAT MYSTERY OF
EVEREST

BY **MARK SYNNOTT**   PHOTOGRAPHS BY **RENAN OZTURK**

| UNIT 1 |

WORKING WITH TEXT AND COLOR

This dramatic photograph is paired with a visually engaging layout, compelling typography, and bold color to add intrigue to the article.

Photograph by Renan Ozturk. From "The Great Mystery of Everest." *National Geographic Magazine*, Vol. 238, No. 1, July, 2020

Bradbury's Bistro

Dessert Menu

Bradbury's Bistro

$7.95

Lemon-poppyseed
vacherin, huckleberries
and lemon curd

Bradbury's Bistro

$6.50

Orange tea cakes with
honey, pine nut brittle ice
cream and figs

Bradbury's Bistro

$7.95

Chocolate Genoise cake
with a truffle center and
cocoa nutmeg glaze

CHAPTER 1

GETTING TO KNOW INDESIGN

1. Explore the InDesign Workspace
2. View and Modify Page Elements
3. Navigate Through a Document
4. Work with Objects and Smart Guides

Adobe Certified Professional in Print & Digital Media Publication Using Adobe InDesign

2. Project Setup and Interface

This objective covers the interface setup and program settings that assist in an efficient and effective workflow, as well as knowledge about ingesting digital assets for a project.

2.2 Navigate, organize, and customize the application workspace.

  A Identify and manipulate elements of the InDesign interface.

  B Organize and customize the workspace.

  C Configure application preferences.

2.3 Use nonprinting design tools in the interface to aid in design or workflow.

  A Navigate a document.

  B Use rulers.

  C Use guides and grids.

  D Use views and modes to work efficiently.

4. Creating and Modifying Document Elements

This objective covers core tools and functionality of the application, as well as tools that affect the visual appearance of document elements.

4.3 Make, manage, and edit selections.

  A Make selections using a variety of tools.

  B Modify and refine selections using various methods.

4.4 Transform digital graphics and media within a publication.

  A Modify frames and frame content.

  B Rotate, flip, and transform individual frames or content.

EXPLORE THE INDESIGN WORKSPACE

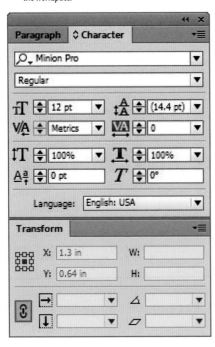

Looking at the InDesign Workspace

The arrangement of windows and panels that you see on your monitor is called the **workspace**. The InDesign workspace features the following areas: the document window, the pasteboard, the menu bar, the Control panel, the toolbar, and a stack of collapsed panels along the right side of the pasteboard. Figure 1 shows the default workspace, which is called Essentials, along with the Control panel along the top. The Control panel lists available options when you click a tool on the toolbar.

InDesign offers many predefined workspaces that are customized for different types of tasks. Each workspace is designed so panels with similar functions are grouped together. For example, the Typography workspace shows the many type- and typography-based panels that are useful for working with type. You can switch from one workspace to another by clicking Window on the menu bar, pointing to Workspace, and then clicking one of the available workspaces. Or you can use the workspace switcher on the menu bar.

You can (and should) customize the workspace to suit your working preferences. For example, you can open and close whatever panels you want and group them as you like and in a way that makes sense for you and your work. You can save a customized workspace by clicking Window on the menu bar, pointing to Workspace, then clicking New Workspace. Once the new workspace is named, it will appear in the Workspace menu.

TIP You can restore the default arrangement of a given workspace by clicking Window on the menu bar, pointing to Workspace, then clicking the Reset command for that workspace's name.

You determine the size of the document, or the page size, when you create the file. A document page is displayed as a white rectangle with a black border and shadow. The **pasteboard** is the area surrounding the document. The pasteboard provides space for extending objects past the edge of the page (known as "creating a bleed"), and it also provides space for storing objects that you may or may not use in the document. Objects that are positioned wholly on the pasteboard do not print, but they are there if you choose to use them in the future.

Figure 1 The Essentials workspace with the Control panel

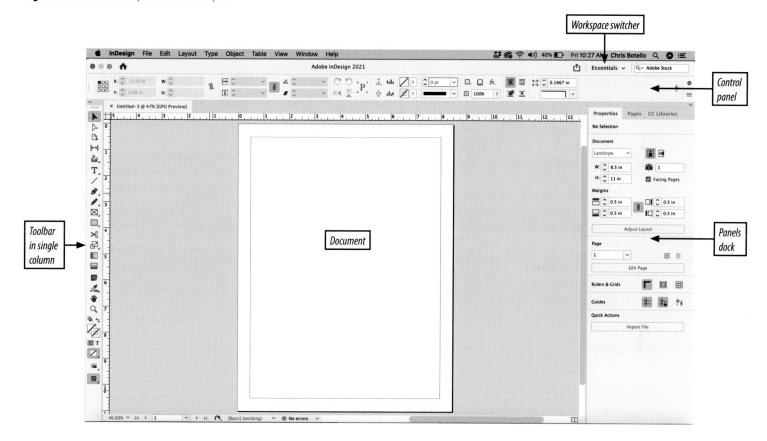

Workspace switcher

Control panel

Toolbar in single column

Document

Panels dock

Exploring the Toolbar

As its name implies, the toolbar houses all the tools that you will work with in InDesign. Simply click a tool to access it.

The first thing that you should note about the toolbar is that not all tools are visible; many are hidden. Look closely and you will see that some tools have small black triangles beside them. These triangles indicate that other tools are hidden behind them. To access hidden tools, point to the visible tool on the toolbar, then press and hold the mouse button; this will reveal a menu of hidden tools. The small black square to the left of a tool name in the menu indicates the tool that is currently visible on the toolbar, as shown in Figure 2.

You can choose to view the toolbar as a single column, a double column, or even a horizontal row of tools. Simply click the two black carats ▸▸ at the top of the toolbar to toggle between the different setups. We recommend that you work with the toolbar in two columns of tools, so that is how we will display the toolbar in this book.

Light gray horizontal lines divide the toolbar into five sections. The top section contains the selection tools. The section beneath that contains item creation tools, such as the drawing, shape, and type tools. Next is a section that contains transform tools, such as the Rotate and Scale tools. The next section contains navigation tools. Here you can find the Hand tool—used to scroll through a document, and the Zoom tool, used to magnify your view of a document.

The bottom-most sections of the toolbar contain functions for applying colors and gradients to objects and choosing different modes for viewing documents, such as the commonly used Preview mode.

To choose a tool, simply click it; you can also press a shortcut key to access a tool. For example, pressing [P] selects the Pen tool. You can have some fun learning the shortcut key for tools you use; some of them are predictable, and some are unexpected. To learn the shortcut key for each tool, point to a tool until a tooltip appears with the tool's name and its shortcut key in parentheses.

Figure 2 Hidden tools on the toolbar

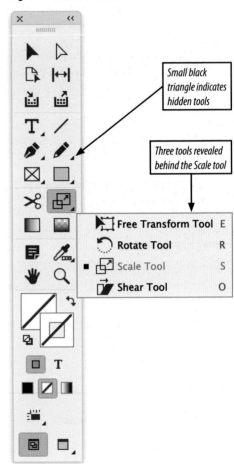

Small black triangle indicates hidden tools

Three tools revealed behind the Scale tool

Free Transform Tool	E
Rotate Tool	R
■ Scale Tool	S
Shear Tool	O

Working with Panels

Many InDesign functions are housed on panels. For example, the Paragraph panel contains paragraph editing functions such as text alignment, space before and after paragraphs, and indents. The Character panel, shown in Figure 3, offers controls for changing the font, font size, and leading. Note the panel menu button. Panels contain not only the functions that are displayed; there's also a menu of options you can access. Be sure to investigate panel menus, especially on the Character and Paragraph panels, which offer many type formatting choices.

All panels can be accessed on the Window menu. This is such an important fact that we will repeat it: All panels can be accessed on the Window menu. This means that you never have to wonder how to find a panel; it's on the Window menu.

Some panels are placed within categories on the Window menu. For example, all the text- and table-related panels, such as the Character panel and the Table panel, are listed in the Type & Tables category. The Swatches, Gradient, and Color panels are all categorized under Color. Make note of the Object & Layout category, which contains three powerful panels: Align, Pathfinder, and Transform.

When you choose a panel from the Window menu, the panel appears in its expanded view. To reduce the size of a panel, click the two black carats, which collapses the panel to a named icon.

To better manage available workspace, it's a good idea to group panels; do so strategically, based on their function. Figure 4 shows the Character and Paragraph panels grouped together. The Paragraph panel is the active panel—it is in front of the others in the group and available for use. The Character panel appears as a tab; click it to make it active.

Figure 3 Character panel

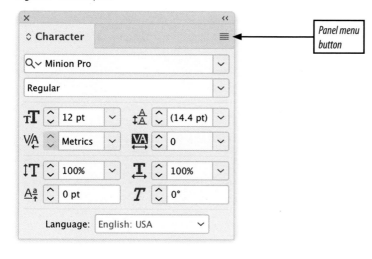

Panel menu button

Figure 4 Two grouped panels

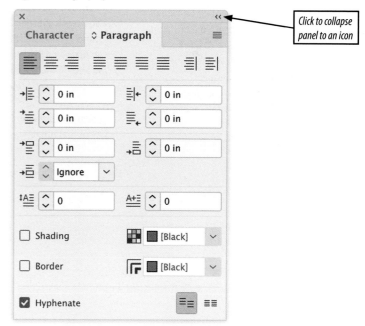

Click to collapse panel to an icon

To group panels, drag one panel by its name onto another panel's name. Ungroup panels by dragging a panel's name tab away from the other panels in the group.

Grouping panels is not the same as docking panels. Docking panels is a different function. When you **dock** panels, you connect the bottom edge of one panel to the top edge of another panel so both move together. To dock panels, drag a panel's name tab to the bottom edge of another panel. When the bottom edge of the other panel is highlighted in bright blue, release the mouse button and the two panels will be docked. To undock a panel, simply drag it away from the other panels.

RESPONDING TO LINKS AND FONT WARNINGS

InDesign documents often contain support files, such as graphics created in other programs like Photoshop and Illustrator. In creating this book, we included all such support files in the same folder as the InDesign data files with which you will be working. By doing so, InDesign will be able to locate those files and update the InDesign document when you open it. When you open a document, however, you will often see a warning about missing or modified links. Unless you are instructed otherwise, you should always click Update Links when you see this warning. Likewise, we have used common fonts in the data files to minimize warnings about missing fonts. However, if you encounter a layout that uses a font not currently loaded on your computer, you can accept the replacement font InDesign offers as an automatic replacement, or if you prefer, you can use the Find Font command on the Type menu to choose another font.

OPENING INDESIGN CC FILES IN EARLIER VERSIONS OF INDESIGN

InDesign CC documents cannot be opened in earlier versions of InDesign, such as CS5 or CS6. To open an InDesign CC document in an earlier version of InDesign, you must export the CC document in the InDesign Markup Language (IDML) format. Click File on the menu bar, click Export, then choose InDesign Markup (IDML) as the file format. The exported document can be opened in earlier versions of InDesign. Note, however, that any new CC features applied to your document will be lost when the file is converted to the older version.

Explore the toolbar

1. Launch Adobe InDesign.
2. Click **File** on the menu bar, click **Open**, navigate to the drive and folder where your Chapter 1 data files are stored, click **ID 1-1.indd**, then click **Open**.

   TIP If you see a warning about missing or modified links, click Update Links. If you see the Missing Fonts dialog box, you can use the font chosen by InDesign by clicking OK, or you can click Find Font and choose another font in the Find Font dialog box. For more information, see the Sidebar titled *Responding to Links and Font Warnings*.

3. Click **Window** on the menu bar, point to **Workspace**, then click **[Typography]**.
4. Click **Window** on the menu bar, point to **Workspace**, then click **Reset Typography** to load the default Typography workspace settings.

5. Point to the **Type tool** T, then press and hold the mouse button to see the **Type on a Path tool**.
6. Using the same method, view the **hidden tools** behind the other tools with small black triangles, shown in Figure 5.

   Your visible tools may differ from the figure.

7. Position your mouse pointer over the **Selection tool** until its tooltip appears.
8. Press the following keys, and note which tools are selected with each key: **[A]**, **[P]**, **[V]**, **[T]**, **[I]**, **[H]**, **[Z]**.
9. Press **[tab]** to temporarily hide all open panels, then press **[tab]** again.

   The panels reappear.

10. Continue to the next set of steps.

You explored the toolbar, revealed hidden tools, used shortcut keys to access tools quickly, hid the panels, then displayed them again.

Figure 5 Tools that conceal hidden tools

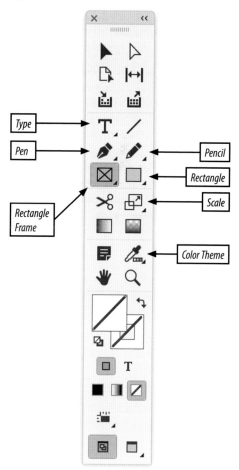

Type

Pen

Rectangle Frame

Pencil

Rectangle

Scale

Color Theme

Create a custom workspace

1. Click **Window** on the menu bar, point to **Workspace**, then click **[Essentials Classic]**.

2. Click **Window** on the menu bar, point to **Workspace**, then click **[Reset Essentials Classic]**.

    The Essentials Classic workspace is a practical workspace with many core panels showing. However, it's missing some other important panels, which you will now open.

3. Press and hold **[command] (Mac)** or **[Ctrl] (Win)**, then press the **letter [T]** on your keypad.

    The Character panel appears.

4. Press and hold **[command] [option] (Mac)** or **[Ctrl] [Alt] (Win)**, then press the **letter [T]** on your keypad.

    The Paragraph panel appears.

5. Drag the **Paragraph panel** by its name onto the name of the **Character panel**.

    The two panels are grouped.

6. Click the ▸▸ **button** at the top-right corner of the grouped panel.

    The panel is minimized.

7. Drag the **minimized panel** by the **gray bar** at the top below the Swatches panel in the panels dock at the right edge of the window.

    The Character and Paragraph panels are listed on the dock.

8. Using the Window menu, open the **Align**, **Pathfinder**, and **Transform panels**.

    Align, Pathfinder, and Transform are submenus under the Object & Layout menu.

9. Group the Align, Pathfinder, and Transform panels.

10. Drag the grouped panels into the panels dock below the Character and Paragraph panels.

    Your panels dock should resemble Figure 6. To access any of the panels, simply click on its name.

11. Click **Window** on the menu bar, point to **Workspace**, then click **New Workspace**.

    The New Workspace dialog box opens.

12. Verify that both **Capture options** are checked, type your **last name** in all caps in the **Name text box**, then click **OK**.

    The customized workspace is saved and available on the Window menu under Workspace. You should use this workspace for the remainder of the book.

13. Save your work, then continue to the next lesson.

You grouped panels, minimized them, and added them to the panels dock. You then created a new workspace based on the new arrangement of panels.

Figure 6 The panels dock

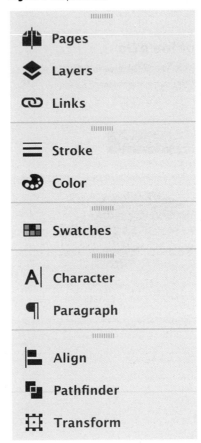

VIEW AND MODIFY PAGE ELEMENTS

▶ What You'll Do

In this lesson, you will explore various methods for viewing the document and page elements like rulers, guides, grids, and frame edges.

Using the Zoom Tool

Imagine creating a layout on a traditional pasteboard—not on your computer. For precise work, you would bring your nose closer to the pasteboard so you could better see what you were doing. At other times, you would hold the pasteboard away from you, at arm's length, so you could get a larger perspective of the artwork.

When you're working in InDesign, the Zoom tool performs these functions for you.

When you click the Zoom tool and move the pointer over the document window, the pointer becomes the Zoom pointer with a plus sign; when you click the document with the Zoom pointer, the document area you clicked is enlarged. To reduce the view of the document, press and hold [option] (Mac) or [Alt] (Win). When the plus sign changes to a minus sign, click the document with this Zoom pointer, and the document size is reduced.

Using the Zoom tool, you can reduce or enlarge the view of the document from 5% to 4000%. Note that the current magnification level appears in the document tab and in the Zoom Level text box at the bottom-left corner of the document window.

Accessing the Zoom Tool

As you work, you can expect to zoom in and out of the document more times than you

can count. The most basic way of accessing the Zoom tool is simply to click its icon on the toolbar, but that is most definitely not the way you want to work: switching constantly to click the Zoom tool will slow you down to a snail's pace.

A better method for accessing the Zoom tool is to use keyboard shortcuts. When you are using the Selection tool, for example, don't switch to the Zoom tool. Instead, press and hold [space bar] [command] (Mac) or [space bar] [Ctrl] (Win) to temporarily change the Selection tool into the Zoom Plus tool. Click the document to zoom in. When you release the keys, the Zoom tool changes back to the Selection tool.

To access the Zoom Minus tool, press [space bar] [command] [option] (Mac) or [space bar] [Ctrl] [Alt] (Win).

In addition to the Zoom tool, InDesign offers other ways to zoom in and out of your document. One of the quickest and easiest is to press [command] [+] (Mac) or [Ctrl] [+] (Win) to enlarge the view and [command] [-] (Mac) or [Ctrl] [-] (Win).

TIP Note that if you press the Zoom tool access keys simultaneously, they sometimes won't access the Zoom tool. Instead of pressing simultaneously, press [space bar] first, then add in the one or two other keys. With practice, you'll learn to do this very quickly.

Using the Hand Tool

When you zoom in on a document—when you make it appear larger—the document eventually will be too large to fit in the window. Therefore, you will need to scroll to see other areas of it. You can use the scroll bars along the bottom and the right sides of the document window, but using the Hand tool is quicker.

The best way to understand the concept of the Hand tool is to think of it as your own hand. Imagine that you could put your hand up to the document on your monitor; then move the document left, right, up, or down, like a paper on a table or against a wall. This is analogous to how the Hand tool works.

The Hand tool is a better choice for scrolling than the scroll bars because you can access the Hand tool using a keyboard shortcut. Simply press and hold [space bar] to access the Hand tool. Release [space bar] to return to the tool you were using, without having to choose it again.

TIP A word of caution: You can't use the [space bar] to access the Zoom tool or the Hand tool if your Type tool is active on the toolbar. If you press the [space bar], the software will behave as if you are typing a space.

Working with Rulers, Grids, and Guides

Designing and working with page layouts involves using measurements to position and align elements in your documents.

You will find that InDesign is well-equipped with many features that help you with these tasks.

Figure 7 shows various measurement utilities. **Rulers** are positioned at the top and left side of the pasteboard to help you align objects. Click Show Rulers/Hide Rulers on the View menu to access rulers.

Rulers (and all other measurement utilities in the document) can display measurements in different units, such as inches, picas, or points. You determine the units and increments with which you want to work in the Preferences dialog box. On the Edit menu, point to Preferences, then click Units & Increments to display the dialog box shown.

Figure 7 Various measurement utilities

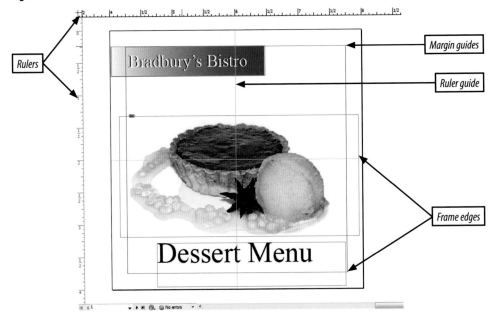

Ruler guides are horizontal and vertical rules that you can position anywhere in a layout as a reference for positioning elements. **Margin guides** are guides you can specify to appear at a given distance within the page, usually to maintain visual consistency from page to page or as a reminder to keep text or other important elements from getting too close to the edge of the page. In addition to guides, InDesign offers a **document grid** for precise alignment. With the "snap" options on, objects that you move around on the page automatically align themselves with guides or with the grid quickly and easily.

Choosing Screen Modes

Screen modes are options for viewing your documents. The two basic screen modes in InDesign are Normal and Preview. You'll work in Normal mode most of the time. In **Normal mode**, you can see all page elements, including margin guides, ruler guides, frame edges, and the pasteboard.

Preview mode shows you what your page would look like with all nonprinting elements removed. When you switch to Preview mode, all guides, grids, and frame edges become invisible to give you an idea of what your document would look like printed or as a PDF file. Even the pasteboard is hidden and becomes gray; thus, any objects on the pasteboard—or any objects that extend off your document page—become invisible. You can think of Preview mode as showing you a "cropped" view of your page—only that which is on the page is visible. However, Preview mode does not hide panels or the menu bar.

TIP The View menu offers commands for switching between Normal and Preview modes, but it's much faster and easier to press the [W] key on your keypad to toggle between the two modes.

Presentation mode presents a view of your document as though it were being showcased on your computer monitor. To toggle Presentation mode on and off, press [shift] [W] on your keypad.

In Presentation mode, your document goes full screen against a black background and is centered and sized so the entire document fits in your monitor window. All other InDesign elements, including panels and the menu bar, disappear. It's a great way to see a "clean" view of the current state of your document and when you think you're done working, a great way to see a "final" view.

When in Presentation mode, you'll have no tools or menus whatsoever to navigate through a multipage document. Instead, use the arrow keys on your keypad to move from page to page. You can also use the [esc] key to leave presentation mode.

Working with Multiple Open Documents

On many occasions, you'll find yourself working with multiple open documents. For example, let's say you're into scrapbooking. If you were designing a new document to showcase a recent trip to Italy, you might also have the file open for the scrapbook you created last year when you went to Hawaii. Why? For any number of reasons. You might want to copy and paste layout elements from the Hawaii document into the new document. Or you might want the Hawaii document open simply as a reference for typefaces, type sizes, image sizes, and effects like drop shadows that you used. When you're working with multiple open documents, you can switch from one to the other simply by clicking on the title bar of each document.

InDesign offers a preference for having multiple open documents available as tabs in the document window. With this preference selected, a tab will appear for each open document showing the name of the document. Simply click the tab and the document becomes active. This can be useful for keeping your workspace uncluttered. However, at times, it might be inhibiting because when working with multiple documents, the tabbed option allows you to view only one document at a time.

You indicate in the Interface Preferences dialog box whether you want open documents to appear as tabs. Click InDesign (Mac) or Edit (Win) on the menu bar, point to Preferences, then click Interface. Click the Open Documents as Tabs check box to select it, as shown in Figure 8, then click OK.

Figure 8 Interface Preferences dialog box

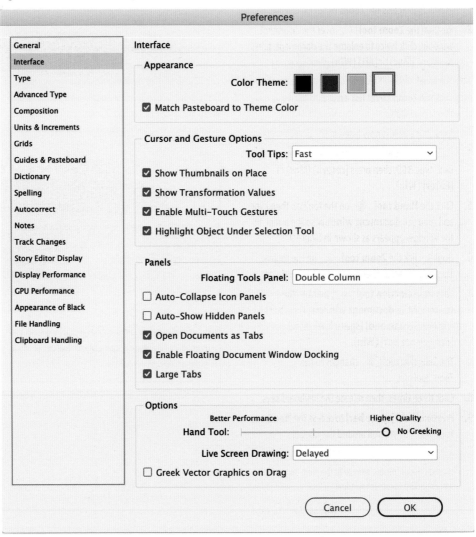

Use the Zoom tool and the Hand tool

1. Press **[Z]** to access the **Zoom tool** 🔍 .

2. Position the **Zoom tool** 🔍 over the document window, click twice to enlarge the document, press **[option] (Mac)** or **[Alt] (Win)**, then click twice to reduce the document.

3. Click the **Zoom Level list arrow** on the status bar, then click **800%**.

   Note that 800% is now listed in the document tab.

4. Double-click **800%** in the **Zoom Level text box**, type **300**, then press **[return] (Mac)** or **[Enter] (Win)**.

5. Click the **Hand tool** 🖐 on the toolbar, then click and drag the **document window** so the image in the window appears as shown in Figure 9.

6. Double-click the **Zoom tool** 🔍 on the toolbar. The magnification changes to 100% (actual size).

7. Click the **Selection tool** ▶, point to the **center of the document window**, then press and hold **[command] [space bar] (Mac)** or **[Ctrl] [space bar] (Win)**.

   The Selection tool ▶ changes to the Zoom tool 🔍 .

8. Click three times, then release the keyboard keys.

9. Press and hold **[space bar]** to access the **Hand tool** 🖐 , then scroll around the image.

TIP Double-clicking the Hand tool 🖐 on the toolbar changes the document view to fit the page (or the spread) in the document window.

Continued on next page

Figure 9 Scrolling with the Hand tool

Bradbury's Bistro

Dessert Menu

The Hand tool will become a fist when you click and drag.

10. Press and hold **[option] [command] [space bar] (Mac)** or **[Ctrl] [Alt] [space bar] (Win)**, then click the **pasteboard** multiple times to reduce the view to 25%.

Your document window should resemble Figure 10.

11. Save your work, then continue to the next set of steps.

You explored various methods for accessing and using the Zoom tool for enlarging and reducing the document. You also used the Hand tool to scroll around an enlarged document.

Figure 10 A reduced view of the document

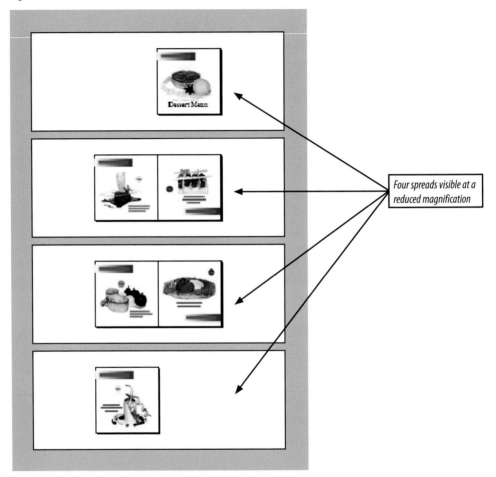

Four spreads visible at a reduced magnification

Hide and show rulers and set units and increments preferences

1. Click **View** on the menu bar, note the shortcut key for the **Fit Page in Window command**, then click **Fit Page in Window**.

   The most commonly used commands in InDesign list a shortcut key beside the command name. Shortcut keys are useful for quickly accessing commands without stopping work to go to the menu. Make a mental note of helpful shortcut keys and incorporate them into your work. You'll find that using them becomes second nature.

2. Click **View** on the menu bar, then note the **Rulers command** and its shortcut key.

   The Rulers command is set to either Hide Rulers or Show Rulers, depending on whether they are showing or not. Click the **pasteboard** to escape the View menu, then press **[command] [R] (Mac)** or **[Ctrl] [R] (Win)** several times to hide and show rulers, finishing with rulers showing.

3. Note the units on the rulers.

   Depending on the preference you have set, your rulers might be showing inches, picas, or another unit of measure.

4. Click **InDesign (Mac)** or **Edit (Win)** on the menu bar, point to **Preferences**, then click **Units & Increments**.

5. In the **Ruler Units section**, click the **Horizontal list arrow** to see the available measurement options.

6. Set the **Horizontal** and **Vertical fields** to **Inches** as shown in Figure 11, then click **OK**.

   The horizontal and vertical rulers change to inches for measurements. Note that when you create a new document, you can specify measurements in the New Document dialog box. It's important to understand that the unit of measure you set in the Preferences dialog box is a global choice. It will affect all measurement utilities in the application, such as those on the Transform panel, in addition to the ruler increments.

   TIP Prior to the advent of using computers for layout, graphic designers and layout artists used specific measurements called picas as industry-standard measurements for layouts. (A pica equals ⅙ of an inch.) Those days are long in the past, however. We advise you to use inches as your measurements simply because they are standard and easily understood. (If you're in Europe or anywhere else that uses the metric system, you are advised to use centimeters.) In this book, page measurements will be in inches. Note, however, that it remains standard to use points as the measurement for type size. One point is equal to $1/72$ of an inch. To give you an example, most body copy in books and magazines use type that is 12 points, or ⅙ of an inch.

7. Save your work, then continue to the next set of steps.

   You used shortcut keys to hide and show rulers in the document. You used the Units & Increments Preferences dialog box to change the unit of measure for the document.

Figure 11 Ruler Units set to Inches

Hide and show ruler guides and the document grid

1. Click **View** on the menu bar, point to **Grids & Guides**, then note the **Show/Hide Guides command** and its shortcut key.

   The command is set to either Hide Guides or Show Guides depending on whether they are showing or not.

2. Click the **pasteboard** to escape the View menu, then press **[command] [;] (Mac)** or **[Ctrl] [;] (Mac)** several times to toggle between hiding and showing guides, finishing with guides showing.

   Showing and hiding guides is easy when you use the shortcut keys. Figure 12 identifies ruler guides and margin guides, which you will learn to create and modify in Chapter 3.

3. Click **View** on the menu bar, point to **Grids & Guides**, then note the **Show/Hide Document Grid** command and its shortcut key.

   The Document Grid command is set to either Hide Document Grid or Show Document Grid depending on whether it is showing or not.

Figure 12 Viewing frame edges and guides

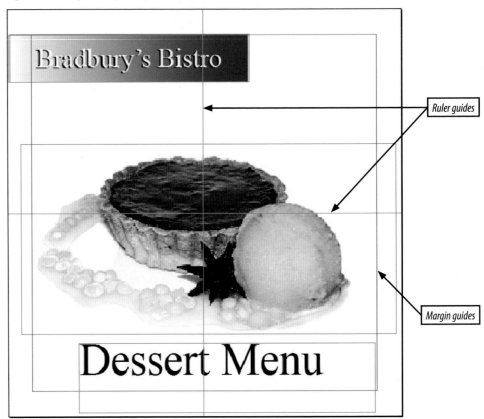

Ruler guides

Margin guides

4. Click the **pasteboard** to escape the View menu, then press **[command] ['] (Mac)** or **[Ctrl] [']** **(Win)** several times to toggle between hiding and showing the document grid.

   Table 1 includes frequently used viewing command shortcut keys.

TIP Make note of the difference between the Hide/Show Guides shortcut key and the Hide/Show Document Grid shortcut key—they're just one key away from each other.

5. Click **View** on the menu bar, point to **Grids & Guides**, then note the **Snap to Guides** and **Snap to Document Grid commands**.

   The Snap to Guides and Snap to Document Grid commands are on/off commands. When they're active, a check mark is visible to the left of the command.

6. Click the **pasteboard** to escape the View menu.

You used shortcut keys to hide and show frame edges, ruler guides, and the document grid. You noted the location of the Snap to Guides and Snap to Document Grid commands in the View menu.

TABLE 1: SHORTCUT KEYS FOR VIEW COMMANDS		
	Mac	**Windows**
Hide/Show Guides	[command] [;]	[Ctrl] [;]
Hide/Show Edges	[command] [H]	[Ctrl] [H]
Hide/Show Rulers	[command] [R]	[Ctrl] [R]
Activate/Deactivate Smart Guides	[command] [U]	[Ctrl] [U]
Fit Page in Window	[command] [0]	[Ctrl] [0]
Fit Spread in Window	[option] [command] [0]	[Alt] [Ctrl] [0]
Toggle Normal and Preview	[W]	[W]
Toggle Presentation Mode On/Off	[shift] [W]	[Shift] [W]

SETTING UP DOCUMENT AND FRAME-BASED GRIDS

Sometimes ruler guides just aren't enough, so designers choose to work with grids. Grids are multiple guides positioned to create a grid pattern across the layout. Grids help you align objects quickly and precisely. Every InDesign file you create has a default Document Grid, which you can hide or show using the Hide or Show Document Grid command in the Guides & Grids options on the View menu. You can modify the color and spacing increments of the default document grid using the Grids command in the Preferences dialog box. Choose Snap to Document Grid in the Grids and Guides options on the View menu to force objects to align to the Document Grid.

Sometimes you'll want to use a grid in a specific text frame as opposed to across the entire document. You can set up a grid for a text frame in the Text Frame Options dialog box. Select the frame, click the Object menu, then click Text Frame Options. Click the Baseline Options tab at the top of the dialog box, then enter specifications for the frame-based grid.

Toggle between screen modes

1. Click **View** on the menu bar, point to **Screen Mode**, then click **Preview**.

    All guides and frame edges are hidden, and the pasteboard is now gray. The menu bar and panels remain visible.

2. Press the **letter [W]** on your keypad several times to toggle between Preview and Normal modes, finishing with your document in Normal mode.

3. Click **View** on the menu bar, point to **Screen Mode**, then click **Presentation**.

    The window changes to full-screen, and the full document appears against a black background. Guides, grids, frame edges, panels, and the menu bar are no longer visible.

4. Press the ↓ on your keypad to scroll through the document to the last page.

5. Press the ↑ on your keypad to scroll up to the first page.

6. Press **[esc]** to leave Presentation mode.

7. Press **[shift] [W]** to switch to Presentation mode.

8. Press **[shift] [W]** again to return to Normal mode.

You used menu commands and keyboard keys to toggle among Normal, Preview, and Presentation modes. When in Presentation mode, you used keyboard keys to navigate through the document.

Work with multiple documents

1. Click **InDesign (Mac)** or **Edit (Win)** on the menu bar, point to **Preferences**, click **Interface,** click the **Open Documents as Tabs check box** to select it if it is unchecked, then click **OK**.

2. Save ID 1-1.indd as **Dessert Menu**.

3. Open ID 1-2.indd, then click the **tabs** of each document several times to toggle between them, finishing with Dessert Menu as the active document.

4. Drag the **Dessert Menu tab** straight down approximately ½ inch.

    When you drag a tabbed document down, it becomes a "floating" document.

5. Position the **mouse pointer** over the **bottom-right corner** of the document window, then click and drag **toward the center** of the monitor window to reduce the window to approximately half its size.

6. Position the **mouse pointer** over the **title bar of the document**, then click and drag to move **Dessert Menu halfway down** toward the bottom of your monitor screen.

    A "floating" document window can be positioned so part of it is offscreen.

7. Position the **mouse pointer** over the **title bar of Dessert Menu**, click and drag to position it at the **top of the window** beside the **ID 1-2.indd tab**, then release the mouse button when you see a horizontal blue bar.

    The document is tabbed once again.

8. Close ID 1-2.indd without saving changes if you are prompted to do so.

You selected the Open Documents as Tabs option in the Preferences dialog box. You opened a second document and noted that it was tabbed. You removed the document from its tabbed position, resized it, moved it around, then returned it to its tabbed status.

NAVIGATE THROUGH A DOCUMENT

▶ What You'll Do

In this lesson, you will use various methods for navigating through a multiple-page document.

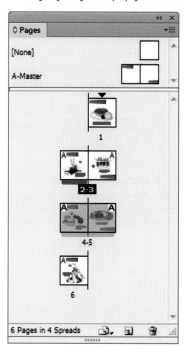

Navigating to Pages in a Document

When you create a layout for a magazine, book, or brochure, you create a document that has multiple pages. A **spread** is two pages that face each other—a left page and a right page—in a multipage document. If you imagine laying an open book on a table, you'd be looking at a spread in the book. Some documents you build will be built with spreads, while others will be just a series of single pages.

You have a variety of methods at your disposal for navigating to pages or spreads in your document. The Go to Page command in the Layout menu offers you the option to enter the page to which you want to go. You can also use the scroll bars on the bottom and right sides of the document window or choose a page from the Page menu in the lower-left corner of the document window. There are also First Page, Previous Page, Next Page, and Last Page buttons at the bottom left of the document window, which you can click to navigate to the document.

The Pages panel, shown in Figure 13, is a comprehensive solution for working with pages and for moving from page to page in your document. The Pages panel shows icons for all of the pages in the document. Double-clicking a single-page icon brings that page into view. The icon representing the currently visible page appears in blue on the panel. Click the Pages panel menu button to display the Pages panel menu. This menu contains powerful commands that you can use to control all page navigation in InDesign.

Applying Thumbnail Color Labels

You can apply one of 15 color labels to a page thumbnail on the Pages panel. Color labels can be useful for organizing your own work or for working with others on a document. For your own work, you might want to assign color labels to different types of pages. For example, you might want to assign a color label to pages in a document that contain imported Photoshop graphics. Or you might want to assign a specific color to pages that have been approved by your client. When working with others, color labels can be effective as status codes. For example, you can apply a specific color to all pages that are proofed and approved. This way, your whole team can see what is done and what needs to be done at a glance.

To apply color labels, click the Pages panel menu button, point to Page Attributes, point to Color Label, then choose a color. The color that you choose will appear as a small solid rectangle beneath the thumbnail.

Figure 13 Pages panel

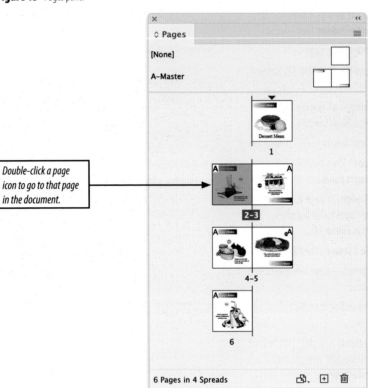

Double-click a page icon to go to that page in the document.

Navigate to pages in a document

1. Click the **Page menu list arrow** at the **bottom left of the document window**, then click **3.**

   The document view changes to page 3.

2. Click **View** on the menu bar, then click **Fit Spread in Window.**

3. At the **bottom-left corner of the document window**, click the **Next Page button** ▶ .

4. Click the **Previous Page button** ◀ twice.

5. Display the **Pages panel**, then double-click the **page 6 icon** on the Pages panel.

   The document view changes to page 6, and the page 6 icon on the Pages panel becomes highlighted, as shown in Figure 14.

6. Double-click the **page 3 icon** on the Pages panel.

   The right half of the spread—page 3—is centered in the document window.

7. Click **Layout** on the menu bar, then click **First Page.**

8. Press **[command] [J] (Mac)** or **[Ctrl] [J] (Win)** to open the Go to Page dialog box, enter **5**, then press **[return] (Mac)** or **[Enter] (Win).**

TIP Make a point of remembering this command—*J for Jump.* It is one of the fastest ways to jump to a specific page, especially in long documents with a lot of pages on the Pages panel.

You navigated to pages using the Page menu, the Next Spread and Previous Spread buttons, page icons on the Pages panel, the Layout menu, and the Go to Page dialog box.

Figure 14 Targeting page 6 on the Pages panel

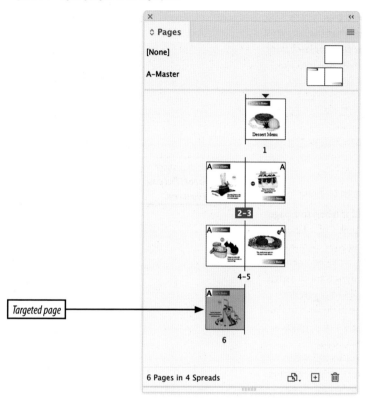

Targeted page

Apply color labels to page thumbnails

1. Click the **page 2 thumbnail** on the Pages panel.

2. Click the **Pages panel menu button** ≡ point to **Page Attributes**, point to **Color Label**, then click **Red**.

    A red bar appears beneath the page thumbnail.

3. Click the **page numbers 4–5** on the Pages panel to select both thumbnails.

4. Click the **Pages panel menu button** ≡ , point to **Page Attributes**, point to **Color Label**, then click **Green**.

    Your Pages panel should resemble Figure 15.

5. Save the file, then close the Dessert Menu document.

You applied a color label to a single page thumbnail and a spread thumbnail.

Figure 15 Color labels on the Pages panel

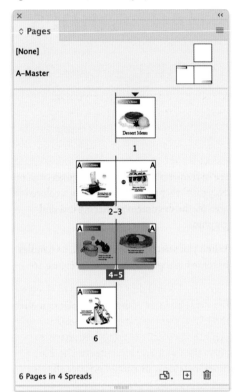

PAGES PANEL OPTIONS

To customize the Pages panel, click the Pages panel menu button, then click Panel Options. This opens the Panel Options dialog box. In the Pages and Masters sections of the dialog box, you can choose a size for page and master icons by clicking the Size list arrow. The Show Vertically and Show Thumbnails check boxes in the Pages and Masters sections control how the icons on the panel are displayed. If you remove the Show Vertically check mark, the page icons on the Pages panel will be displayed horizontally, and you will only be able to resize the width of the Pages panel, not the height. If you remove the Show Thumbnails check mark, the page icons will be blank on the Pages panel. The Icons section of the dialog box defines which additional icons appear next to the page icons. For example, if the Transparency check box is checked, a small transparency icon, that looks like a checkerboard, appears next to the page icon where transparency has been applied to master items. In the Panel Layout section, you can choose whether you want masters on top or document pages on top of the Pages panel.

WORK WITH OBJECTS AND SMART GUIDES

▶ *What You'll Do*

In this lesson, you will work with objects with smart guides.

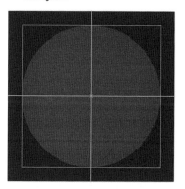

Resizing Objects

Working in InDesign, the term **object** is used to refer to any element on the page. Text, text frames, or graphic elements such as images, blocks of color, or simple lines are all objects on the page. All objects in InDesign are in frames. **Frames** are rectangular, oval, or polygonal shapes used for creating a colored area on the document or placing text and graphics.

When you select an object's frame, its handles become highlighted, as shown in Figure 16.

You can click and drag the handles to change the shape and size of the frame. InDesign offers three important keyboard combinations that you can use when dragging frame handles to affect the frame and its contents. These are listed in Table 2. Be sure to practice all three and incorporate them into your skills set.

You can resize multiple objects just as easily. Simply select multiple objects, and handles will appear around all the selected objects. You can then drag those handles to affect all the objects simultaneously.

Figure 16 Viewing frame handles on a text frame

TABLE 2: DRAGGING FRAME HANDLES WITH KEYBOARD COMBINATIONS		
Mac	**Windows**	**Result**
[shift]-drag a handle	[Shift]-drag a handle	The frame is resized in proportion; contents of the frame are not scaled.
[shift] [command]-drag a handle	[Shift] [Ctrl]-drag a handle	Both the frame and the contents of the frame are scaled.
[shift] [option] [command]-drag a handle	[Shift] [Alt] [Ctrl]-drag a handle	Both the frame and the contents of the frame are scaled from their centers.

Copying Objects

Copying and pasting an object is standard for most software packages. InDesign also offers the Paste in Place command on the Edit menu. This is useful for placing a copy of an object exactly in front of the original object. Select an object, copy it, then click the Paste in Place command.

The Paste in Place command is also useful when pasting objects from page to page. With Paste in Place, copied objects will paste in the exact same location from one page to another.

You can also copy objects while dragging them. Press and hold [option] (Mac) or [Alt] (Win), then drag to create a copy of the object.

Hiding, Locking, and Grouping Objects

The Hide, Lock, Group, and Ungroup commands on the Object menu are essential for working effectively with layouts, especially complex layouts with many objects. Hide objects to get them out of your way. They won't print, and nothing you do changes the location of them as long as they are hidden. Lock objects when you have them in a specific location and you don't want them accidentally moved or deleted. Locking an object makes it immovable—you will not even be able to select it. Don't think this is being overly cautious; accidentally moving or deleting objects—and being unaware that you did so—happens all the time in complex layouts and creates all kinds of problems.

Grouping objects is a smart and important strategy for protecting the relationships between multiple objects. When you select multiple objects and group them, clicking on one object with the Selection tool selects all the objects in the group. Thus, you can't accidentally select a single object and move or otherwise alter it independently from the group. However, you *can* select individual objects using the Direct Selection tool—that's how the tool got its name. Even if you select and alter a single object within a group, the objects are not ungrouped.

To group multiple objects, select them and click the Group command on the Object menu.

Working with Smart Guides

When aligning objects, you will find smart guides to be really effective and, yes, really smart. **Smart guides** are guides that appear automatically when objects are moved in a document and provide information to help position objects precisely in relation to the page or other objects.

For example, smart guides tell you when objects are aligned to each other or to specific areas of the page. Smart guides will tell you when the center of an object is aligned to the horizontal and vertical centers of the page.

Use the View menu to turn smart guides on and off. Figure 17 shows smart guides at work.

Figure 17 Smart guides aligning the top edges of two objects

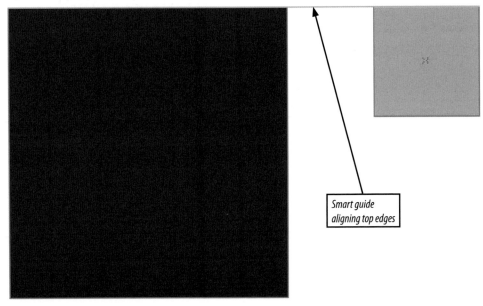

Smart guide aligning top edges

Resize a text object

1. Open ID 1-2.indd, then save it as **Objects**.
2. Click the **Selection tool** ▶ , then click the **yellow text box** to select it.
3. Click and drag **various handles** and note how the object is resized.
4. When you are done experimenting, undo all the moves you made.

   The Undo command is at the top of the Edit menu.
5. Press and hold **[shift]**, then drag the **top left corner handle** toward the top-left corner of the document.

   The object is resized proportionately. The text reflows within the resized object, but the text itself is not enlarged.
6. Undo your last step.
7. Press and hold **[option] (Mac)** or **[Alt] (Win)**, then click and drag **any corner handle**.

   The object is resized from its center. The text is not resized.
8. Undo your last step.
9. Press and hold **[shift] [command] [option] (Mac)** or **[shift] [Ctrl] [Alt] (Win)**, then drag **any corner handle**.

   As shown in Figure 18, the object and the text in the object are resized proportionately from the object's center.
10. Click **File** on the menu bar, click **Revert**, then click **Revert (Mac)** or **Yes (Win)** if you are prompted to confirm.

    Reverting a file returns it to its status when you last saved it.

You explored various options for resizing an object and its contents, then you reverted the file.

Figure 18 Resized object and contents

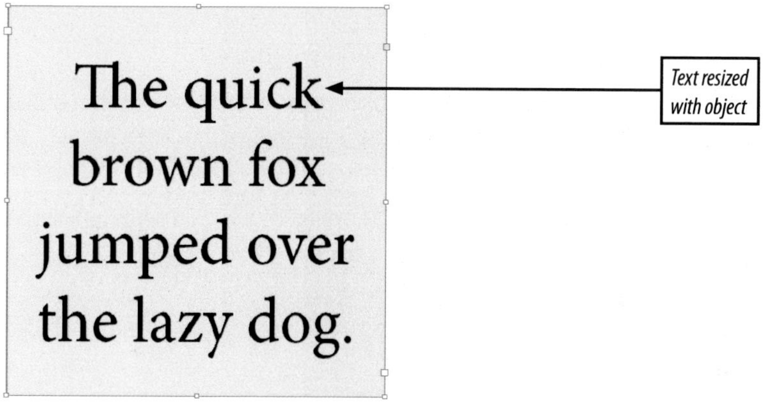

The quick brown fox jumped over the lazy dog.

Text resized with object

Copy and duplicate objects

1. Select the **text frame**, then press **[command] [C] (Mac)** or **[Ctrl] [C] (Win)** to copy it.

2. Click **Edit** on the menu bar, then click **Paste in Place**.

   A copy of the text frame is placed in front of the original in the exact location.

3. Drag the **copy** to the right so the two are side by side.

4. Select the **left object**.

5. Press and hold **[option] (Mac)** or **[Alt] (Win)**, then drag a **copy of the object** to the left so your screen resembles Figure 19.

   TIP This method for creating a copy is referred to as "drag and drop" a copy.

6. Select **all three objects**.

   Handles appear around all three objects.

7. Click and drag **various handles** to resize all three objects.

8. Click **Edit** on the menu bar, then click **Cut**.

9. Save your work, then continue to the next set of steps.

You duplicated an object in two different ways, first with the Copy and Paste in Place command combination and then with the drag-and-drop technique. You resized multiple objects, then cut them from the document.

Figure 19 Dragging a copy

The quick brown fox jumped over the lazy dog.

The quick brown fox jumped over the lazy dog.

The quick brown fox jumped over the lazy dog.

Hide, lock, and group objects

1. Click **Object** on the menu bar, then click **Show All on Spread**.

   This document was originally saved with hidden objects. Three objects appear. They are unselected.

2. Select all three objects, click **Object** on the menu bar, then click **Group**.

3. Click the **Selection tool** ▶, click the **pasteboard** to deselect all, then click the **pink circle**.

   As shown in Figure 20, all three objects are selected because they are grouped. The dotted line around the objects is a visual indication that they are grouped.

4. Click the **pasteboard** to deselect all, click the **Direct Selection tool** ▷, then click the **pink circle**.

Only the circle is selected because the Direct Selection tool ▷ selects individual objects within a group.

5. Select all, click **Object** on the menu bar, click **Ungroup**, then click the **pasteboard** to deselect all.

6. Click the **Selection tool** ▶, select **the small square**, click **Object** on the menu bar, then click **Lock**.

   The object's handles disappear, and a lock icon appears indicating that the object can no longer be selected.

7. Click **Object** on the menu bar, then click **Unlock All on Spread**.

   The small square is unlocked.

8. Select all, click **Object** on the menu bar, then click **Hide**.

All selected objects disappear.

9. Click **Object** on the menu bar, then click **Show All on Spread**.

   The three objects reappear in the same location that they were in when they were hidden.

TIP Memorize the shortcut keys for Hide/Show, Group/Ungroup, and Lock/Unlock. They are fairly easy to remember and extremely useful. You will be using these commands over and over again when you work in InDesign.

10. Hide the **pink circle** and the **small square**.

11. Save your work, then continue to the next set of steps.

You revealed hidden objects, grouped them, then used the Direct Selection tool to select individual objects within the group. You ungrouped the objects, locked them, unlocked them, and hid them.

Figure 20 Three grouped objects

Work with smart guides

1. Click **Edit** on the menu bar, point to **InDesign (Mac)** or **Preferences (Win)**, then click **Guides & Pasteboard**.

2. Verify that your **Smart Guide Options section** matches Figure 21, then click **OK**.

3. Click **View** on the menu bar, point to **Grids & Guides**, then click **Smart Guides**, if necessary, to activate it.

4. Click the **blue rectangle**, then try to center it visually on the page.

5. Release the mouse button when both the **horizontal and vertical smart guides** appear, as shown in Figure 22.

   Both the horizontal and the vertical pink smart guides appear when the object's center point is aligned with the center point of the document. By default, smart guides that show the relationship between objects and the document are pink.

   TIP The gray box beside the cursor shows the location coordinates of the object on the page. You will learn a lot more about location coordinates in Chapter 3.

6. Show the **hidden objects**, then hide the **small blue square**.

7. Using the same method, align the **center of the pink circle** with the **center of the large blue square**.

   When the center points of the two objects are aligned, your smart guides will resemble Figure 23.

Figure 21 Smart Guide Options in the Guides & Pasteboard Preferences dialog box

Figure 22 Centering the square on the page

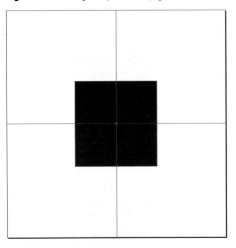

Figure 23 Centering the circle on the square

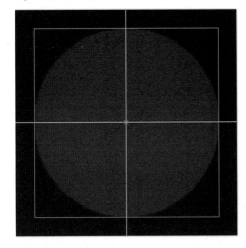

8. Show the **hidden small square**.

9. Use smart guides to align the **top of the small square** with the **top of the large square**, as shown in Figure 24.

10. "Snap" the **left edge of the small square** to the **right edge of the large square**.

11. Position the **small square** as shown in Figure 25.

12. Save your work, then close the Objects document.

You aligned an object at the center of the document and created precise relationships among three objects, using smart guides.

Figure 24 Aligning the top edges of the two squares

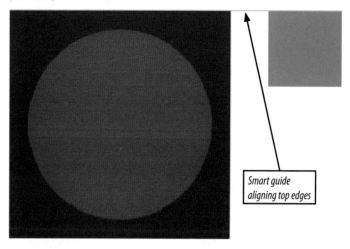

Smart guide
aligning top edges

Figure 25 Aligning the bottom edges of the two squares

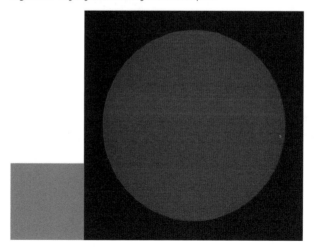

Explore the InDesign workspace

1. Launch Adobe InDesign.
2. Click File on the menu bar, click Open, navigate to the drive and folder where your Chapter 1 Data Files are stored, click ID 1-3.indd, then click Open.
3. Save the file as **Hana.indd**.
4. Click Window on the menu bar, point to Workspace, then click [Essentials Classic].
5. Click Window on the menu bar, point to Workspace, then click Reset Essentials Classic.
6. Point to the Type tool, then press and hold the mouse button to see the hidden tools behind the Type tool.
7. Using the same method, view the hidden tools behind the other tools with small black triangles.
8. Position your mouse pointer over the Selection tool until its tooltip appears.
9. Press the following keys and note which tools are selected with each key: [A], [P], [V], [T], [I], [H], [Z].
10. Press [tab] to temporarily hide all open panels, then press [tab] again.

Work with panels

1. Click the Color panel icon in the stack of collapsed panels on the right of the workspace to expand the Color panel.
2. Drag the Color panel name tab to the left so it is ungrouped from the Stroke panel.
3. Drag the Swatches panel out of the dock, then group it with the Color panel.
4. Click Window on the menu bar, point to Object & Layout, then click Transform.

5. Drag the Transform panel name tab to the bottom edge of the Swatches and Color panels group, then release the mouse button.
   The Transform panel is docked at the bottom of the Swatches and Color group.
6. Click and drag the dark gray bar at the top of the panel group, above the Color and Swatches panel tabs, to move the group of panels.
7. Click the Transform panel name tab, then drag it away from the other two panels to undock it.

Work with the Zoom tool and the Hand tool

1. Press [Z] to access the Zoom tool.
2. Position the Zoom tool over the document window, click three times to enlarge the document, press [option] (Mac) or [Alt] (Win), then click three times to reduce the document.
3. Click the Zoom Level list arrow on the menu bar, then click 1200%.
4. Double-click 1200% in the Zoom Level text box, type **350**, then press [return] (Mac) or [Enter] (Win).
5. Click the Hand tool on the toolbar, then click and drag the document window to scroll around the page.
6. Double-click the Zoom tool.
7. Click the Selection tool, point to the center of the document window, then press and hold [command] [space bar] (Mac) or [Ctrl] [space bar] (Win) to access the Zoom tool.
8. Click three times, then release [command] [space bar] (Mac) or [Ctrl] [space bar] (Win).
9. Press and hold [space bar] to access the Hand tool, then scroll around the image.

10. Press and hold [command] [option] [space bar] (Mac) or [Ctrl] [Alt] [space bar] (Win), then click the mouse button multiple times to reduce the view to 25%.
11. Click View on the menu bar, note the shortcut key for the Fit Page in Window command, then click Fit Page in Window.

Work with rulers, guides, and the document grid

1. Click View on the menu bar, then note the Rulers command and its shortcut key.
2. Click the pasteboard to escape the View menu, then press [command] [R] (Mac) or [Ctrl] [R] (Win) several times to hide and show rulers, finishing with rulers showing.
3. Note the units on the rulers.
4. Click InDesign (Mac) or Edit (Win) on the menu bar, point to Preferences, then click Units & Increments.
5. In the Ruler Units section, click the Horizontal list arrow to see the available measurement options.
6. Set the Horizontal and Vertical fields to Picas.
7. Reopen the Units & Increments Preferences dialog box, change the Horizontal and Vertical fields to Inches, then click OK.
8. Click View on the menu bar, point to Extras, then note the Frame Edges command and its shortcut key.
9. Click the pasteboard to escape the View menu, then enter [Ctrl] [H] (Mac) or [Ctrl] [H] (Win) several times to hide and show frame edges, finishing with frame edges showing.
10. Click View on the menu bar, point to Grids & Guides, then note the Guides command and its shortcut key.

11. Click the pasteboard to escape the View menu, then enter [command] [;] (Mac) or [Ctrl] [;] (Win) several times to hide and show guides, finishing with guides showing.
12. Click View on the menu bar, point to Grids & Guides, then note the Document Grid command and its shortcut key.
13. Click the pasteboard to escape the View menu, then enter [command] ['] (Mac) or [Ctrl] ['] (Win) repeatedly to hide and show the document grid.
14. Click View on the menu bar, point to Grids & Guides, then note the Snap to Guides and Snap to Document Grid commands.
15. Click the pasteboard to escape the View menu.

Toggle screen modes

1. Click the View menu, point to Screen Mode, then click Preview.
2. Press [W] on your keypad to toggle between Preview and Normal modes, finishing in Normal mode.
3. Click View on the menu bar, point to Screen Mode, then click Presentation.
4. Press the ↓ on your keypad to scroll through the document to the last page.
5. Press the ↑ on your keypad to scroll up to the first page.
6. Press [esc] to leave Presentation mode.
7. Press and hold [shift], then press [W] to switch to Presentation mode.
8. Still holding [shift], press [W] again to return to Normal mode.

Work with multiple documents

1. Click InDesign (Mac) or Edit (Win) on the menu bar, point to Preferences, click Interface, verify that Open Documents as Tabs is checked, then click OK.

2. Open ID 1-2.indd, then click the tabs to toggle between viewing both documents, finishing with Hana.indd as the active document.
3. Position your mouse pointer over the bottom-right corner, then click and drag toward the center of the monitor window to reduce the window to approximately half its size.
4. Drag the Hana document out of the group to make it a floating window on its own.
5. Float the mouse pointer over the title bar of Hana, then click and drag it to group it as a tabbed document beside ID 1-2.indd.
6. Close ID 1-2.indd without saving changes.

Navigate through a document

1. Click the Page menu list arrow at the bottom-left of the document window, then click 3.
2. Click View on the menu bar, then click Fit Spread in Window.
3. Click the Next Page button.
4. Click the Previous Page button twice.
5. Show the Pages panel.
6. Double-click the page 6 icon on the Pages panel.
7. Double-click the page 3 icon on the Pages panel.
8. Double-click the numbers 2–3 beneath the page 2 and page 3 icons on the Pages panel.
9. Click Layout on the menu bar, then click First Page.
10. Enter [command] [J] (Mac) or [Ctrl] [J] (Win) to open the Go to Page dialog box, enter 5, then press [return] (Mac) or [Enter] (Win).
11. Save your work.

Apply color labels to thumbnails on the Pages panel

1. Click the page 5 thumbnail on the Pages panel.
2. Click the Pages panel menu button, point to Page Attributes, point to Color Label, then click Blue.
3. Click the page numbers 2–3 on the Pages panel to select both thumbnails.
4. Click the Pages panel menu button, point to Page Attributes, point to Color Label, then click Orange.
5. Save your work, then close the Hana document.

Work with objects

1. Open ID 1-4.indd, then save it as **Skills Objects**.
2. Click the Selection tool, then click to select the object.
3. Click and drag various handles, and note how the object is resized.
4. Undo all the moves you made.
5. Press and hold [shift], then drag the top-left corner handle toward the left edge of the document.
6. Undo the move.
7. Press and hold [option] (Mac) or [Alt] (Win), then click and drag any corner handle.
8. Undo the move.
9. Press and hold [command] (Mac) or [Ctrl] (Win), then click and drag any corner handle.
10. Undo the move.
11. Press and hold [shift] [command] [option] (Mac) or [Shift] [Ctrl] [Alt] (Win), then drag any corner handle.
12. Click File on the menu bar, click Revert, then click Revert (Mac) or Yes (Win) if you are prompted to confirm.
13. Select the text frame, then copy it.
14. Click Edit on the menu bar, then click Paste in Place.
15. Drag the copy to the right so it is beside the original object.

(continued)

16. Select the left object.
17. Press and hold [option] (Mac) or [Alt] (Win), then drag a copy of the object to the left so your screen resembles Figure 26.
18. Select all three objects.
19. Click and drag various handles to resize all three objects.
20. Click Edit on the menu bar, then click Cut.
21. Click Object on the menu bar, then click Show All on Spread.
22. Select all three objects, click Object on the menu bar, then click Group.
23. Click the Selection tool, click anywhere on the pasteboard to deselect all, then click the green diamond.
24. Click the pasteboard to deselect all, click the Direct Selection tool, then click the green diamond.
25. Select all, click Object on the menu bar, then click Ungroup.
26. Click the Selection tool, select the small circle, click Object on the menu bar, then click Lock.
27. Click Object on the menu bar, then click Unlock All on Spread.
28. Select all, click Object on the menu bar, then click Hide.
29. Click Object on the menu bar, then click Show All on Spread.
30. Hide the green diamond and the small blue circle.
31. Save your work.

Work with smart guides

1. Click (InDesign) (Mac) or Edit (Win) on the menu bar, point to Preferences, then click Guides & Pasteboard.
2. Verify that your Smart Guide Options section shows all four options checked, then click OK.

3. Click View on the menu bar, point to Grids & Guides, then click Smart Guides, if necessary, to activate it.
4. Click the yellow circle, then try to center it visually on the page.
5. Release the mouse button when both the horizontal and vertical smart guides appear, as shown in Figure 27.

6. Show the hidden objects, then hide the small circle.
7. Using the same method, align the center of the green diamond with the center of the yellow circle.
8. Show the hidden small circle.
9. Referring to Figure 28, align the vertical center of the small circle with the right point of the green diamond.
10. Save, then close the Skills Objects document.

Figure 26 Text frame copied and duplicated

Figure 27 Horizontal and vertical smart guides

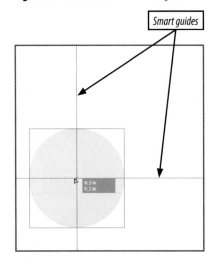

Figure 28 Completed Skills Review

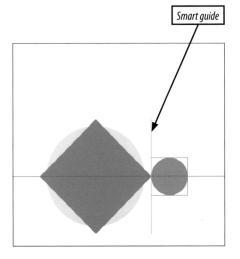

PROJECT BUILDER 1

This set of steps will give you a refresher course for grouping and docking panels. You might want to consider how you would group and dock panels for your own customized workspace.

1. Open the file named Blank Page.indd.

2. Group the Paragraph and Character panels together, then click the Paragraph panel name tab so it is the active panel.

3. Dock the Pages panel to the bottom of the Paragraph panel group.

4. Group the Layers panel with the Pages panel, then click the Layers panel name tab so it is the active panel.

5. Dock the Swatches panel below the Layers panel group.

6. Group the Color, Stroke, and Gradient panels with the Swatches panel, then click the Gradient panel name tab so it is the active panel.

7. Dock the Align panel below the Gradient panel group.

TIP The Align panel is in the Object & Layout section of the Window menu.

8. Group the Transform and the Effects panels with the Align panel, then click the Transform panel name tab so it is the active panel.

TIP The Transform panel is in the Object & Layout section of the Window menu.

9. Compare your panels with Figure 29.

10. Close the Blank Page document without saving changes.

Figure 29 Completed Project Builder 1

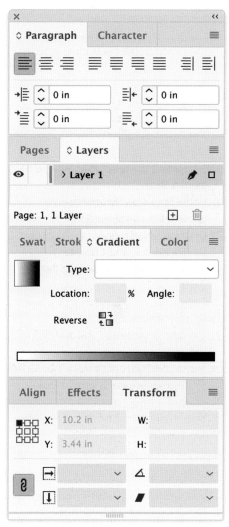

Accessing the Zoom and the Hand tools with keyboard shortcuts is one of the most important skills you need to absorb in this chapter. This Project Builder will give you more practice at that.

1. Open ID 1-5.indd.
2. Click the Selection tool if it is not active, then press [command] [space bar] (Mac) or [Ctrl] [space bar] (Win) to access the Zoom tool.
3. Position the Zoom tool slightly above and to the left of the dog's left eye, click and drag the Zoom tool pointer to draw a dotted rectangle around the eye, then release the mouse button.
4. Press [space bar], then scroll with the Hand tool to the right eye.
5. Press [option] [command] [space bar] (Mac) or [Ctrl] [Alt] [space bar] (Win), then click the Zoom tool five times on the dog's right eye.
6. Move the image with the Hand tool so both the dog's eyes and his snout are visible in the window and your screen resembles Figure 30.

    Your magnification may differ from that shown in the figure.
7. Close ID 1-5.indd without saving any changes.

Figure 30 Completed Project Builder 2

Image courtesy of Chris Botello

DESIGN PROJECT

The page layout in this Design Project will strengthen your use of smart guides to position objects in relation to one another and in relation to the page.

1. Open ID 1-6.indd, then save it as **Squares and Targets**.

2. Use the techniques you learned in this chapter to recreate the layout in Figure 31.

   TIP Try it on your own, then go through the following steps, and compare your results with those in the figure.

3. Verify that smart guides are activated.

4. Align the large yellow circle to the center of the page.

5. Center the large green circle in the large yellow circle.

6. Center the remaining three circles.

7. Copy the smallest yellow circle, then apply the Paste in Place command.

8. Center the pasted circle in the blue square.

9. Group the yellow circle and the blue square.

10. Click the Selection tool.

11. Drag and drop three copies of the group at the four corners of the document.

12. Save your work, then close the Squares and Targets document.

Figure 31 Completed Design Project

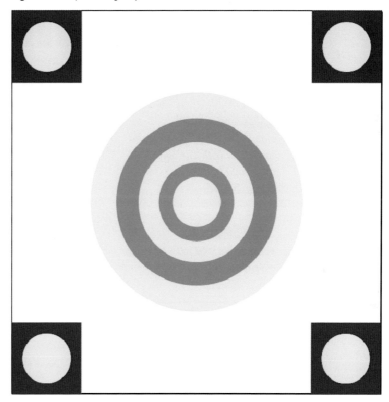

Jake's Diner

Early Bird Breakfast Menu

Eggs and Bacon

Two eggs any style, two strips of lean bacon, one biscuit with our homestyle gravy, and home fries.

$5.95

Egg Sandwich

One egg over easy, served with American or Jack cheese on a soft French croissant.

$5.25

Belgian Waffle

A golden brown buttery waffle served with fresh-picked strawberries, raspberries and blueberries. Whipped fresh cream on request.

$4.95

Silver Dollar Pancakes

A stack of eight golden pancakes served with fresh creamery butter and warm maple syrup.

$4.95

French Toast

Four triangles of thick peasant bread dipped in a cinnamon-egg batter. Served with French Fries.

$6.95

Biscuits and Gravy

Light fluffy southern biscuits served with a hearty sausage gravy.

$3.95

Eggs Hollandaise

Three eggs lightly poached served on a bed of romaine lettuce and topped with a rich Hollandaise sauce.

$6.95

Steak and Eggs

A 6 oz. strip of peppered breakfast steak cooked to your liking, served with two eggs, any style.

$7.95

CHAPTER 2

WORKING WITH TEXT

1. Format Text
2. Format Paragraphs
3. Create and Apply Styles
4. Edit Text
5. Create Bulleted and Numbered Lists

CERTIFIED PROFESSIONAL

Adobe Certified Professional in Print & Digital Media Publication Using Adobe InDesign

1. Working in the Design Industry

This objective covers critical concepts related to working with colleagues and clients as well as crucial legal, technical, and design-related knowledge.

1.4 Demonstrate knowledge of key terminology related to publications.

   C Understand and use key terms related to multipage layouts.

1.5 Demonstrate knowledge of basic design principles and best practices employed in the design industry.

   C Identify and use common typographic adjustments to create contrast, hierarchy, and enhanced readability/legibility.

2. Project Setup and Interface

This objective covers the interface setup and program settings that assist in an efficient and effective workflow, as well as knowledge about ingesting digital assets for a project.

2.2 Navigate, organize, and customize the application workspace.

   B Organize and customize the workspace.

   C Configure application preferences.

2.6 Manage paragraph, character, and object styles.

   A Load, create, apply, and modify styles.

4. Creating and Modifying Document Elements

This objective covers core tools and functionality of the application, as well as tools that affect the visual appearance of document elements.

4.2 Add and manipulate text using appropriate typographic settings.

   A Use type tools to add text.

   B Use appropriate character settings in a design.

   C Use appropriate paragraph settings in a design.

   E Manage text flow across multiple text areas.

   F Use tools to add special characters or content.

4.3 Make, manage, and edit selections.

   A Make selections using a variety of tools.

4.5 Use basic reconstructing and editing techniques to manipulate document content.

   A Use various tools to revise and refine project content.

   C Use the Story Editor to edit text within a project.

FORMAT TEXT

▶ *What You'll Do*

In this lesson, you will use the Character panel and various keyboard commands to modify text attributes.

Introducing the Min-Pin
by Christopher Smith

Creating Text

When you create text in InDesign, you do so by first creating a text frame. All InDesign text is in a text frame. Click and drag the Type tool anywhere on the page to create a text frame. You'll see a blinking cursor in the frame, prompting you to start typing.

You use the Character and Paragraph panels to format the text in the frame. You can also use the Text Frame Options command, located on the Object menu, to format the text frame itself.

Using the Character Panel

The Character panel, shown in Figure 1, is the command center for modifying text. The Character panel works hand in hand with the Paragraph panel, which is why it's wise to keep them grouped together. The Paragraph panel, as its name implies, focuses on manipulating paragraphs or blocks of text; the Character panel focuses on more specific modifications, such as font, font style, and font size.

Figure 1 Character panel

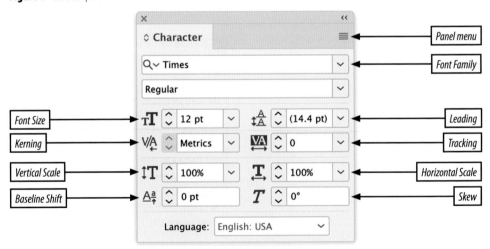

In addition to these basic modifications, the Character panel offers other controls for manipulating text. You can use the panel to modify leading, track and kern text, apply a horizontal or vertical scale to text, perform a baseline shift, or skew text. To select text quickly for editing, you can use the methods shown in Table 1: Keyboard Commands for Selecting Text.

TIP You can set the font list on the Character panel to show font names or font names and samples of each font. To enable or disable this feature, click Edit on the menu bar, point to Preferences, click Type, then click to add or remove a check mark in the Font Preview Size check box. Notice also that you can click the Font Preview Size list arrow and choose Small, Medium, or Large.

TABLE 1: KEYBOARD COMMANDS FOR SELECTING TEXT	
To select:	**Do the following:**
One word	Double-click word
One line	Triple-click any word in the line
One paragraph	Click any word in the paragraph four times
Entire story	Click any word in the story five times
Entire story	[command] [A] (Mac) or [Ctrl] [A] (Win)
One character to the right of insertion point	[shift] →
One character to the left of insertion point	[shift] ←
One line up from insertion point	[shift] ↑
One line down from insertion point	[shift] ↓
One word to the right of insertion point	[shift] [command] → (Mac) or [Shift] [Ctrl] → (Win)
One word to the left of insertion point	[shift] [command] ← (Mac) or [Shift] [Ctrl] ← (Win)
One paragraph above insertion point	[shift] [command] ↑ (Mac) or [Shift] [Ctrl] ↑ (Win)
One paragraph below insertion point	[shift] [command] ↓ (Mac) or [Shift] [Ctrl] ↓ (Win)

PASTING TEXT WITHOUT FORMATTING

When you copy text, then paste it, it is, by default, pasted with all of its formatting—its typeface, type style, type size, and any other formatting that has been applied. Sometimes, this can be undesirable. This is where the Paste Without Formatting command comes into play. It strips the copied text of all its original formatting, then formats it to match the formatting of the text frame where it is pasted.

Understanding Leading

Leading is the term used to describe the vertical space between lines of text. This space is measured from the baseline of one line of text to the baseline of the next line of text. As shown in Figure 2, the **baseline** is the invisible line on which text sits. Leading, like font size, is measured in points.

Scaling Text Horizontally and Vertically

When you format text, your most basic choices are which font you want to use and what size you want to use it. Once you've chosen a font and a font size, you can further manipulate the appearance of the text with a horizontal or vertical scale.

On the Character panel, horizontal and vertical scales are expressed as percentages. By default, text is generated at a 100% horizontal and 100% vertical scale, meaning that the text is not scaled at all. Decreasing the horizontal scale only, for example, maintains the height of the characters but decreases the width—on the horizontal axis. Conversely, increasing the horizontal scale again maintains the height but increases the width of the characters on the horizontal axis. Figure 3 shows four examples of horizontal and vertical scales.

TIP You can also control the vertical alignment of text inside a text box by selecting the text box, clicking Object on the menu bar, then clicking Text Frame Options. Click the Align list arrow, then click Top, Center, Bottom, or Justify.

Figure 2 Examples of leading

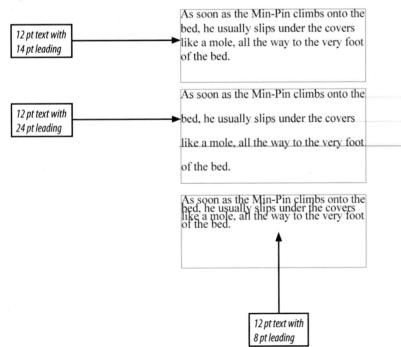

```
12 pt text with
14 pt leading
```
As soon as the Min-Pin climbs onto the bed, he usually slips under the covers like a mole, all the way to the very foot of the bed.

```
12 pt text with
24 pt leading
```
As soon as the Min-Pin climbs onto the bed, he usually slips under the covers like a mole, all the way to the very foot of the bed.

```
12 pt text with
8 pt leading
```
As soon as the Min-Pin climbs onto the bed, he usually slips under the covers like a mole, all the way to the very foot of the bed.

Figure 3 Scaling text horizontally and vertically

original text

50% horizontal scale

150% horizontal scale

50% vertical scale

150% vertical scale

Kerning and Tracking Text

Though your computer is a magnificent instrument for generating text in myriad fonts and font sizes, you will often want to manipulate the appearance of text after you have created it—especially if you have the meticulous eye of a designer. **Kerning** is a long-standing process of increasing or decreasing space between a pair of characters. Like kerning, **tracking** affects the spaces between letters, but it is applied globally to an entire word or paragraph.

Kerning and tracking are standard features in most word processing applications, but they are more about typography than word processing—that is, they are used for setting text in a way that is pleasing to the eye.

Spacing challenges with text are usually more prominent with large-size headlines than with smaller body copy—which is why many designers will spend great amounts of time tracking and kerning a headline. Figures 4 and 5 show examples of kerning and tracking applied to a headline.

The only mistake you can make regarding kerning and tracking is to ignore them. Especially when you're working with headlines, awareness of spacing is essential.

TIP Kerning and tracking are often used on body copy as a quick solution for fitting text within an allotted space. In other words, if a paragraph is taking up 12 lines and you want it to be 11 lines, tracking the text to have less space might do the trick.

InDesign measures both kerning and tracking in increments of 1/1000 em—a unit of measure that is determined by the current type size. In a 6-point font, 1 em equals 6 points; in a 12-point font, 1 em equals 12 points. It's good to know this, but you don't need to have this information in mind when kerning and tracking text. Just remember that the increments are small enough to provide you with the specificity that you desire for creating eye-pleasing text.

Creating Superscript Characters

You are already familiar with superscript characters, even if you don't know them by that term. When you see a footnote in a book or document, the superscripted character is the small number positioned to the upper-right of a word. Figure 6 shows a superscripted character.

Figure 4 Kerning text

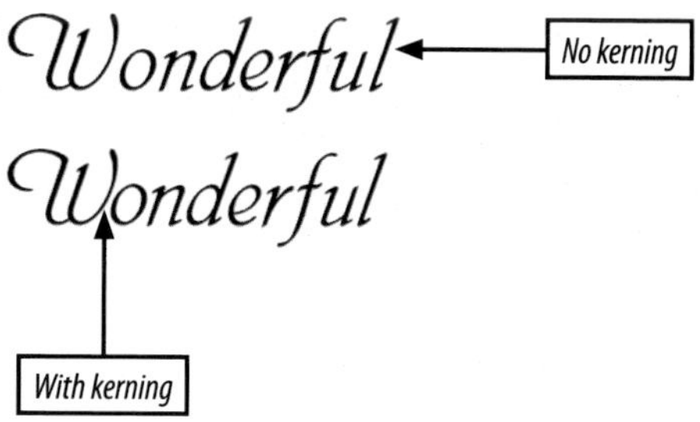

Wonderful ← No kerning

Wonderful ← With kerning

Figure 5 Tracking text

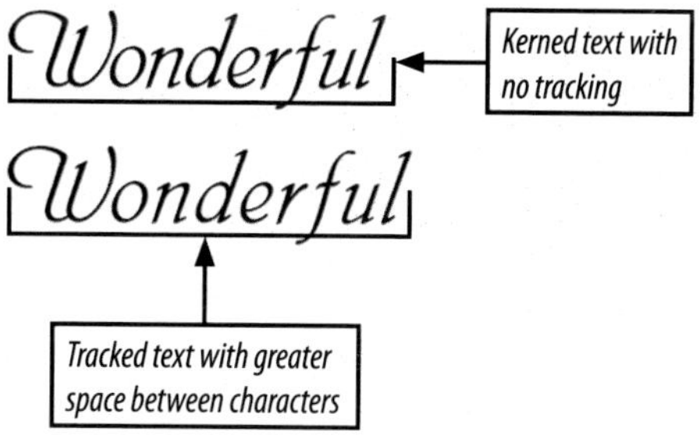

Wonderful ← Kerned text with no tracking

Wonderful ← Tracked text with greater space between characters

Figure 6 Identifying a superscripted character

Superscripted character

The Superscript command, shown in Figure 7, is listed on the Character panel menu. There's a slightly tricky thing you need to remember about superscripts. If you select a 12-point character, for example, and then apply the Superscript command, the size of the character will decrease; however, its point size will still be identified on the Character panel as 12 points.

Creating Subscript Characters

The Character panel menu also offers a command for Subscript. You can think of Subscript as the opposite of Superscript.

Instead of raising the baseline of the selected text, the Subscript command positions the text below its original baseline. As with Superscript, the Subscript command makes the selected text appear smaller.

Of the two, Subscript is used less often. Though it is seldom used for footnotes, many designers use Subscript for trademarks and registration marks.

Underlining Text

InDesign offers different methods for underlining text and for creating **rules**, which

are horizontal, vertical, or diagonal lines. When you simply want to underline selected text, the most basic method is to use the Underline command on the Character panel menu. With this command, the weight of the underline is determined by the point size of the selected text. The greater the point size, the greater the weight of the line.

Searching for Fonts on the Character Panel

Font search enhancements in Creative Cloud make working with fonts and finding the font you want to use quick and easy. Creative Cloud lets you experiment with and search for fonts in powerful ways.

The top field on the Character panel contains a magnifying glass icon on the left side. Think of this field as both the font search and current font field because you can use this field to search through the available fonts on your system. Type any font name in the field—Garamond, for example—and a scrollable font menu will appear with all the Garamond typefaces on your system, grouped and listed together. You can also search for font styles such as bold, condensed, italic, and so on.

When you click the magnifying glass, you can choose between Search Entire Font Name or Search First Word only. Search First Word only is a helpful setting if you are unsure of the complete font name that you need.

Figure 7 The Superscript command on the Character panel menu

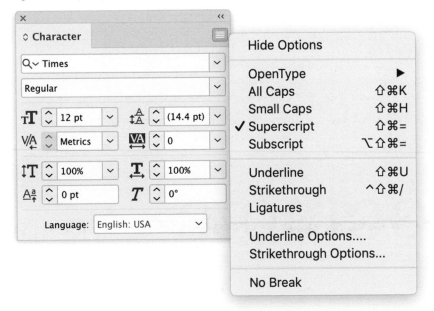

Modify text attributes

1. Open ID 2-1. indd, then save it as **Min-Pin Intro**.

2. Click **InDesign (Mac)** or **Edit (Win)** on the menu bar, point to **Preferences**, then click **Units & Increments**.

3. Verify that your settings are the same as shown in Figure 8, then click **OK**.

4. Click **Window** on the menu bar, point to **Workspace,** then click **[Typography]**.

5. Click **Window** on the menu bar, point to **Workspace,** then click **Reset Typography**.

6. Click the **Type tool** , then double-click the word **Introducing** at the top of the page.

    Double-clicking a word selects the entire word.

7. Open the **Character panel**.

    The Character panel displays the formatting of the selected text.

8. Triple-click the word **Introducing**.

    Triple-clicking a word selects the entire line of text that the word is on.

9. On the Character panel, click the **Font Family list arrow**, click **Impact,** click the **Font Size list arrow,** click **48 pt.**, then verify that the **Leading text box** reads **57.6 pt.**, as shown in Figure 9.

    The parentheses surrounding the value in the Leading text box indicate that the leading is being auto-entered as a percentage of the point size. The default auto-leading percentage in InDesign is 120%.

TIP Every function that you can perform on the Character panel can also be done on the Control panel.

Continued on next page

Figure 8 Units & Increments section of the Preferences dialog box

Figure 9 Character panel

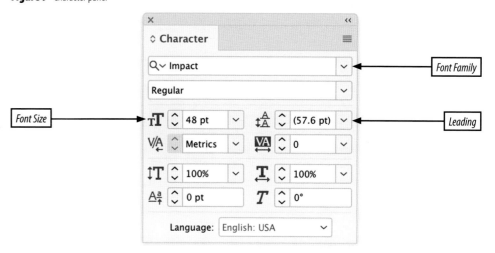

10. Press and hold **[shift] [command] (Mac)** or **[Shift] [Ctrl] (Win)**, then press **[<]** 10 times.

The point size is reduced by one point size every time you press **[<]**.

11. Press and hold **[shift] [command] (Mac)** or **[Shift] [Ctrl] (Win)**, then press **[>]** two times.

The point size is increased by two points.

12. Triple-click the word **by** on the second line to select the whole line, change the font to **Times New Roman** or a similar font, click the **Type Style list arrow**, click **Italic,** click the **Font Size list arrow**, then click **18 pt**.

13. Click the **Selection tool** ▶, then note that the **text frame** is highlighted, and the **handles** are visible.

14. Click **Object** on the menu bar, click **Text Frame Options**, click the **Align list arrow** in the Vertical Justification section, click **Center**, then click **OK**.

Your work should resemble Figure 10.

15. Save your work, then continue to the next set of steps.

You used keyboard commands and the Character panel to modify text. You then used the Text Frame Options dialog box to center the text vertically in the frame.

Track and kern text

1. Click the **Zoom tool** 🔍, click and drag the **Zoom tool** 🔍, around the **entire light green text frame**, then release the mouse button.

When you drag the Zoom tool 🔍, it creates a rectangle. When you release, the contents within the rectangle are magnified.

2. Click the **Type tool** T, then triple-click the word **Introducing**.

3. Click the **Tracking list arrow** on the Character panel, then click **200**.

The horizontal width of each word increases, and a consistent amount of space is applied between each letter, as shown in Figure 11.

4. Reduce the **Tracking value** to **25**.

Note that the space between the h and the e in the word "the" is inconsistent with the other spacing in the headline. The e is too far from the h.

5. Click **between the letters h and e in the word "the,"** click the **Kerning list arrow**, then click **−50**.

The space between the two letters decreases.

6. Click the **Selection tool** ▶ to exit type editing mode.

7. Save your work, then continue to the next set of steps.

You used the Character panel to modify tracking and kerning values.

Figure 10 Selected text frame

Introducing the Min-Pin
by Christopher Smith

Figure 11 Increasing the tracking value of selected text

I n t r o d u c i n g   t h e
M i n - P i n
by Christopher Smith

Create superscript characters

1. Click **View** on the menu bar, click **Fit Page in Window**, click the **Zoom tool** 🔍 , then drag a **selection box** that encompasses **all the body copy on the page**.

2. Click the **Type tool** T , then select the **number 1** after the words **Doberman Pinscher** at the end of the fourth paragraph.

3. Click the **Character panel menu button** ≡ , then click **Superscript**.

   The character's size is reduced and positioned higher than the characters that precede it, as shown in an enlarged view in Figure 12.

4. Select the **number 2** after the word **cows** in the last paragraph, then apply the **Superscript command**.

   TIP When the Superscript command is applied to text, its designated font size on the Character panel remains the same.

5. Select the **number 1 beside the footnote at the bottom of the page**, apply the **Superscript command**, select the **number 2** below, apply the **Superscript command** again, then deselect the text.

   Your footnotes should resemble Figure 13.

6. Save your work, then continue to the next set of steps.

   You applied the Superscript command to format selected text as footnotes.

Figure 12 Applying the Superscript command

Figure 13 Using the Superscript command to format footnotes

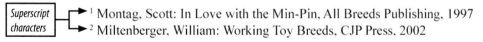

Superscript characters
¹ Montag, Scott: In Love with the Min-Pin, All Breeds Publishing, 1997
² Miltenberger, William: Working Toy Breeds, CJP Press, 2002

INSERTING FOOTNOTES AUTOMATICALLY

While you can insert footnotes using the techniques in this lesson, if you have many footnotes in a document, you can use the enhanced footnote feature to insert them quickly and easily. In InDesign, a footnote consists of a reference number that appears in document text and the footnote text that appears at the bottom of the page or column. To add a footnote, place the insertion point in the document location where you want the reference number to appear. Click Type on the menu bar, then click Insert Footnote. The insertion point moves to the footnote area at the bottom of the page or column. Type the footnote text; the footnote area expands as you type. If the text containing a footnote moves to another page, its footnote moves with it.

FORMATTING FOOTNOTES

If you use the Insert Footnote command to enter footnotes in a document, you can specify many formatting attributes. Click Type on the menu bar, then click Document Footnote Options. On the Numbering and Formatting tab, you can select the numbering style, starting number, prefix, position, character style, or separator. The Layout tab lets you set the spacing above and between footnotes, as well as the rule that appears above them. Formatting changes you make to footnotes affect all existing and new footnotes.

Underline text

1. Click **View** on the menu bar, click **Fit Page in Window,** click the **Zoom tool** 🔍 , then drag a **selection box** that encompasses **both footnotes at the bottom of the page**.

2. Click the **Type tool** T , then select **In Love with the Min-Pin** in the first footnote.

3. Click the **Character panel menu button** ≡ , then click **Underline**.

   Only the selected text is underlined.

TIP The weight of the line is automatically determined, based on the point size of the selected text.

4. Select **Working Toy Breeds** in the second footnote, then apply the **Underline command**.

5. Select the **entire first footnote** except the number 1 superscripted footnote, then reduce its size to **8 points**.

6. Select the **entire second footnote** except the number 2, then change its font size to **8 points**.

   Your footnotes should resemble Figure 14.

TIP To specify how far below the baseline the underline is positioned, click the Underline Options command on the Character panel menu, then increase or decrease the Offset value.

7. Save your work, then continue to the next lesson.

You selected text, then applied the Underline command from the Character panel menu.

Figure 14 Formatted footnotes

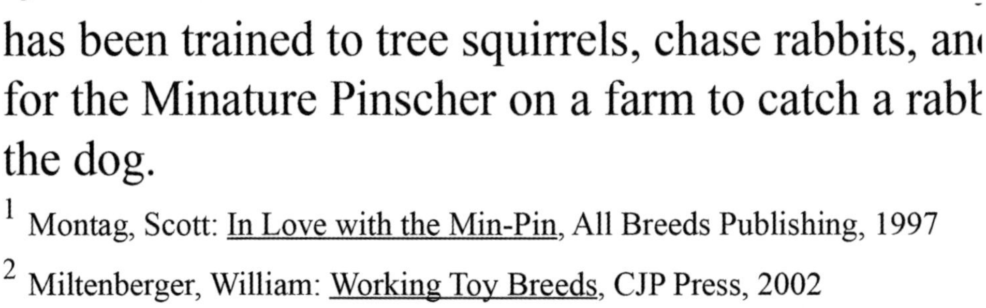

has been trained to tree squirrels, chase rabbits, and for the Minature Pinscher on a farm to catch a rabb the dog.

[1] Montag, Scott: In Love with the Min-Pin, All Breeds Publishing, 1997

[2] Miltenberger, William: Working Toy Breeds, CJP Press, 2002

FORMAT PARAGRAPHS

In this lesson, you will use the Paragraph panel and various keyboard commands to modify paragraph attributes.

Using the Paragraph Panel

The Paragraph panel, shown in Figure 15, is the command center for modifying paragraphs or blocks of text, also known as body copy.

The Paragraph panel is divided into four main sections. The top section controls alignment. Of the nine icons offering options for aligning text, the first four—Align left, Align center,

Align right, and Justify with last line aligned left—are the most common. The remaining five options include subtle modifications of justified text and two options for aligning text toward or away from the spine of a book.

The next section offers controls for indents. With these controls, you can indent the left or right sides of a paragraph, or you can indent the first or last line.

Figure 15 Paragraph panel

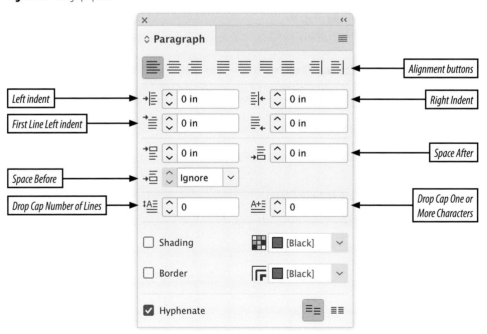

Use the First Line Left Indent when you want the first line of each paragraph to start further to the right than the other lines of text, as shown in Figure 16.

At the bottom of the figure is what is commonly referred to as a pull quote. You have probably seen these in a magazine at some point. A **pull quote** is a typographical design solution in which text is used at a larger point size and positioned prominently on the page. Note the left and right indents applied to the pull quote. They were created using the Left Indent and Right Indent buttons on the Paragraph panel.

The third section of the Paragraph panel controls vertical spacing between paragraphs and drop caps. For large blocks of text, it is often pleasing to the eye to create either a subtle or a distinct space after every paragraph. In InDesign, you create these by entering values in the Space After or the Space Before text boxes on the Paragraph panel. Of the two, the Space After text box is more commonly used. The Space Before text box is often in conjunction with the Space After text box to offset special page elements, such as a pull quote.

Figure 16 First line indent and left and right indents

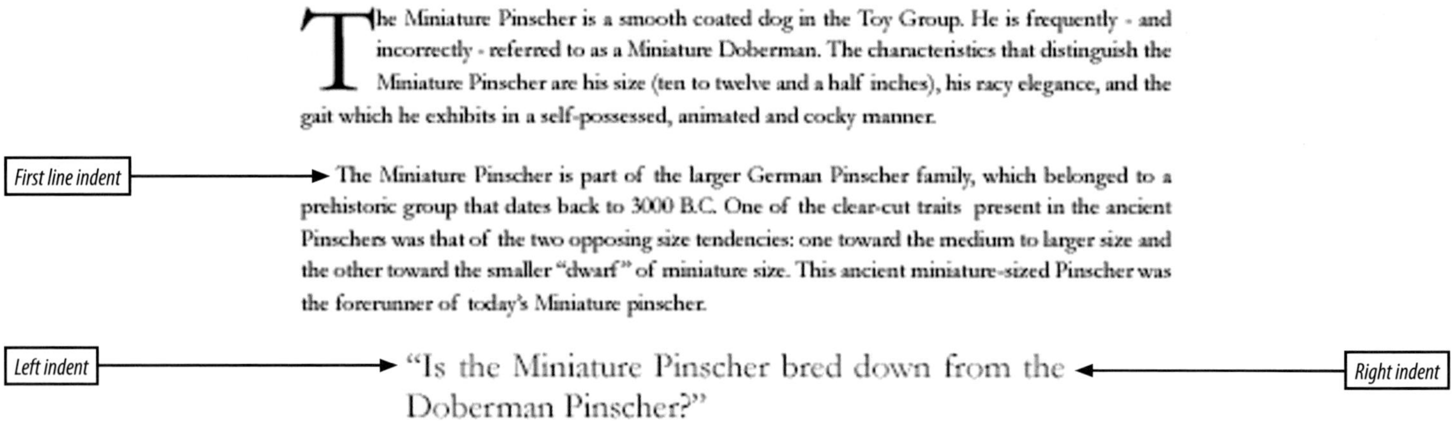

The Miniature Pinscher is a smooth coated dog in the Toy Group. He is frequently - and incorrectly - referred to as a Miniature Doberman. The characteristics that distinguish the Miniature Pinscher are his size (ten to twelve and a half inches), his racy elegance, and the gait which he exhibits in a self-possessed, animated and cocky manner.

First line indent ⟶ The Miniature Pinscher is part of the larger German Pinscher family, which belonged to a prehistoric group that dates back to 3000 B.C. One of the clear-cut traits present in the ancient Pinschers was that of the two opposing size tendencies: one toward the medium to larger size and the other toward the smaller "dwarf" of miniature size. This ancient miniature-sized Pinscher was the forerunner of today's Miniature pinscher.

Left indent ⟶ "Is the Miniature Pinscher bred down from the ⟵ Right indent
Doberman Pinscher?"

A **drop cap** is a design element in which the first letter or letters of a paragraph are increased in size to create a visual effect. In the figure, the drop cap is measured as being three text lines in height. If you click to place the cursor to the right of the drop cap and then increase the kerning value on the Character panel, the space between the drop cap and all three lines of text will be increased. Figure 17 shows a document with a drop cap and a 0.25-inch space after every paragraph.

The fourth section on the Paragraph panel allows you to highlight a paragraph and/or apply a border to a paragraph. When your cursor is positioned in any paragraph, activating the Shading or Border options will place a field of color behind the entire paragraph or a border around the paragraph. You can modify the color of each on the Paragraph panel.

At the very bottom of the Paragraph panel, the Hyphenate checkbox controls whether or not hyphens will be used to split words from line to line in a paragraph. If you uncheck Hyphenate, no words will be split with a hyphen.

USING OPTICAL MARGIN ALIGNMENT

Optical Margin Alignment is a great feature that controls the alignment of punctuation marks for all paragraphs within a block of type. Optical Margin Alignment forces punctuation marks, as well as the edges of some letters, to hang outside the text margins so that the type appears aligned. To override this feature, click the text box or type object, click the Paragraph panel menu button, then click Ignore Optical Margin. You can also click the Paragraph Styles panel menu button, click Style Options, click the Indents and Spacing category, then click the Ignore Optical Margin check box.

Figure 17 A drop cap and paragraphs with vertical space applied after every paragraph

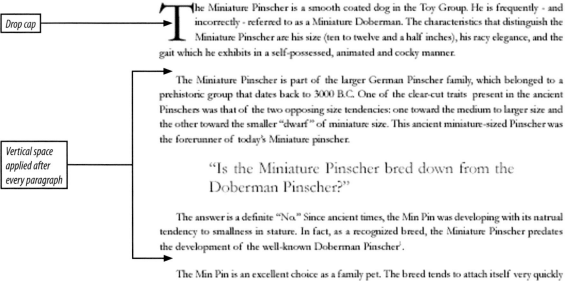

Drop cap

The Miniature Pinscher is a smooth coated dog in the Toy Group. He is frequently - and incorrectly - referred to as a Miniature Doberman. The characteristics that distinguish the Miniature Pinscher are his size (ten to twelve and a half inches), his racy elegance, and the gait which he exhibits in a self-possessed, animated and cocky manner.

The Miniature Pinscher is part of the larger German Pinscher family, which belonged to a prehistoric group that dates back to 3000 B.C. One of the clear-cut traits present in the ancient Pinschers was that of the two opposing size tendencies: one toward the medium to larger size and the other toward the smaller "dwarf" of miniature size. This ancient miniature-sized Pinscher was the forerunner of today's Miniature pinscher.

Vertical space applied after every paragraph

"Is the Miniature Pinscher bred down from the Doberman Pinscher?"

The answer is a definite "No." Since ancient times, the Min Pin was developing with its natrual tendency to smallness in stature. In fact, as a recognized breed, the Miniature Pinscher predates the development of the well-known Doberman Pinscher.

The Min Pin is an excellent choice as a family pet. The breed tends to attach itself very quickly to children and really delights in joining a youngster in bed. As soon as the Min-Pin climbs onto

Avoiding Typographic Problems

Widows and **orphans** are words or single lines of text that become separated from the other lines in a paragraph. Orphans are left alone at the bottom of a page and widows at the top of the next page or column. The Paragraph panel menu has many commands that allow you to control how text appears and flows, specifically at the end of a column or page, avoiding unsightly widows and orphans. The Keep Options command lets you highlight text that should always stay together instead of being split over two pages. The Keep Options dialog box lets you choose to keep the selected text together or choose how many lines to keep with the selected text. The Justification command opens the Justification dialog box in which you can define the percentages assigned to minimum, desired, and maximum word spacing, letter spacing, and glyph scaling. You can also change the Auto Leading value and tell InDesign how to justify a one-word line.

The Hyphenation Settings dialog box, which opens by clicking Hyphenation on the Paragraph panel menu, allows you to define how words should be hyphenated. You can turn hyphenation off completely by removing the check mark in the Hyphenation check box.

Understanding Returns

Most people think of a paragraph as a block of text, but in InDesign, a paragraph can be a block of text, a line of text, or even a single word, followed by a paragraph return. A **paragraph return**, also called a *hard return*, is inserted into the text formatting by pressing [return] (Mac) or [Enter] (Win). For example, if I type my first name and then enter a paragraph return, that one word—my first name—is a paragraph. When working with body copy, a paragraph is any block of text separated by a paragraph return.

When typing body copy, designers will often want a space after each paragraph because it is visually pleasing and helps to keep paragraphs distinct. The mistake many designers make is pressing [return] (Mac) or [Enter] (Win) twice to create that space after the paragraph. Wrong! What they've done is created two paragraphs. The correct way to insert space between paragraphs is to enter a value in the Space After text box on the Paragraph panel.

You can make a similar mistake when you want to force words from one line down to the next line. As you edit text, you may encounter a "bad line break" at the end of a line, such as an oddly hyphenated word or a phrase that is split from one line to the next. In many of these cases, you will want to move a word or phrase to the next line. Don't use a hard return to do this. Using a hard return means you are creating a new paragraph. Instead, do this by entering a soft return. A **soft return** moves words down to the next baseline but does not create a new paragraph. To enter a soft return, press and hold [shift] while pressing [return] (Mac) or [Enter] (Win).

You can avoid untold numbers of formatting problems by using correct typesetting behaviors, especially those regarding Space After and First Line Indent.

TIP When creating a first line paragraph indent, many users will press [spacebar] five or 10 times and then start typing. This is incorrect formatting. Paragraph indents are created using the First Line Left Indent setting on the Paragraph panel, not by inserting multiple spaces.

USING THE TYPE ON A PATH TOOL

Hidden behind the Type tool on the toolbar is the Type on a Path tool. The Type on a Path tool allows you to position text on any closed or open InDesign path. For example, you could draw a closed path, such as a circle, then position text on the circular path. Or you could draw a simple curved path across the page, then flow text along the path. Simply click the Type on a Path tool on the path. A blinking cursor will appear, and you can then begin typing on the path. The path itself remains visible and selectable; you can apply stroke colors and various widths to the path. You can format the size, typeface, and style of type on a path as well. Give it a try!

Use the Paragraph panel and Character panel to modify leading and alignment

1. Click **View** on the menu bar, then click **Fit Page in Window**.

2. Click the **Type tool** T , then double-click the **first word in the first paragraph**.

   Double-clicking a word selects the word.

3. Triple-click the **same word**.

   Triple-clicking a word selects the entire line of text.

4. Click the **first word in the first paragraph** four times.

Clicking a word four times selects the entire paragraph.

5. Click the **same word** five times.

   Clicking a word five times selects all the text in a text frame.

6. Click the **Leading list arrow** on the Character panel, then click **30 pt**.

   The vertical space between each line of text is increased, as shown in Figure 18. Because leading can be applied to a single selected word as well as to an entire paragraph, the Leading setting is on the Character panel (as opposed to the Paragraph panel).

7. Double-click **30** in the **Leading text box**, type **16**, then press **[return] (Mac)** or **[Enter] (Win)**.

8. Display the **Paragraph panel**, then click the **Justify with last line aligned left button** .

9. Click **Introducing** at the top of the document three times, then click the **Align center button** on the Paragraph panel.

10. Click **Edit** on the menu bar, then click **Deselect All**.

    Your document should resemble Figure 19.

You modified the leading and alignment of a block of selected text.

Figure 18 Modifying leading

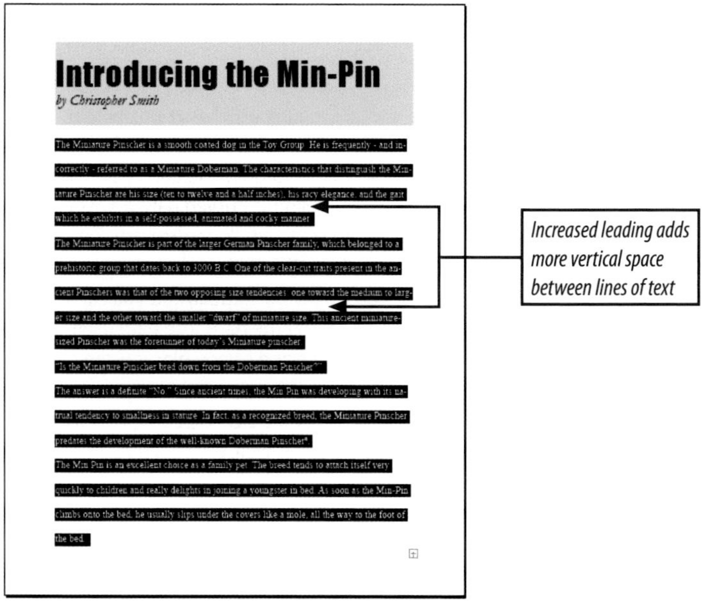

Increased leading adds more vertical space between lines of text

Figure 19 Modifying alignment

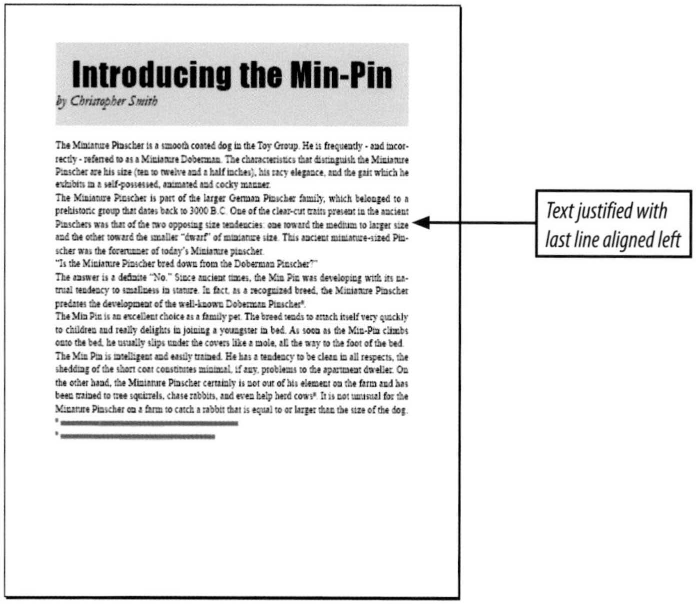

Text justified with last line aligned left

Apply vertical spacing between paragraphs

1. Click the **Type tool** T anywhere in the text frame, then enter **[command] [A] (Mac)** or **[Ctrl] [A] (Win)** to select **all the text in the text frame**.

2. Click the **Space After up arrow** ⬌ on the Paragraph panel three times so the value reads **.1875 in**, then deselect.

   As shown in Figure 20, 0.1875 inch of vertical space is applied after every paragraph.

3. Click and drag to select the **two footnotes at the bottom of the document**.

4. Double-click the **Space After text box** on the Paragraph panel, type **0**, then press **[return] (Mac)** or **[Enter] (Win)**.

5. Select only the **first footnote**, double-click the **0** in the **Space Before text box** on the Paragraph panel, type **.25**, then press **[return] (Mac)** or **[Enter] (Win)**.

   There is 0.25 inch of vertical space positioned above the first footnote.

6. **Deselect All**.

   Your document should resemble Figure 21.

7. Save your work, then continue to the next set of steps.

You used the Space After and Space Before text boxes on the Paragraph panel to apply vertical spacing between paragraphs.

Figure 20 Increasing the Space After value

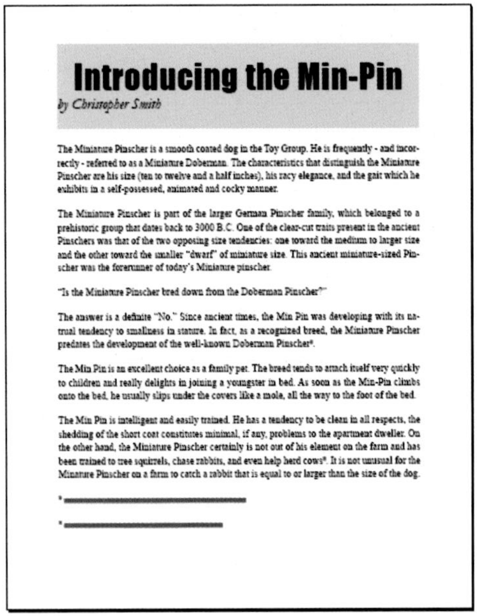

Figure 21 Increasing Space Before value to move footnotes down

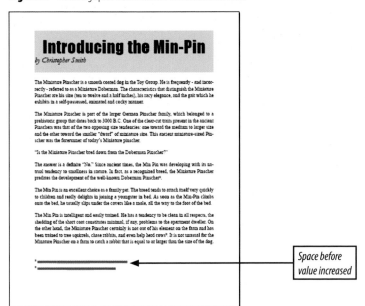

Space before value increased

Apply paragraph indents

1. Click **Type** on the menu bar, then click **Show Hidden Characters**.

   As shown in Figure 22, hidden characters appear in blue, showing blue dots for spaces, created by pressing [space bar], and paragraph marks for paragraph returns.

   TIP It's a good idea to memorize the keyboard command for hiding and showing hidden characters.

2. Select **all the body copy on the page** except the two footnotes, then click the **First Line Left Indent up arrow** on the Paragraph panel four times to change the value to **.25 in**, as shown in Figure 23.

   The first line of each paragraph is indented 0.25 in.

   Continued on next page

Figure 22 Showing hidden characters

The · characteristics · that · ← Space symbol

lf · inches), · his · racy · elegan

ocky · manner.¶ ← Paragraph return symbol

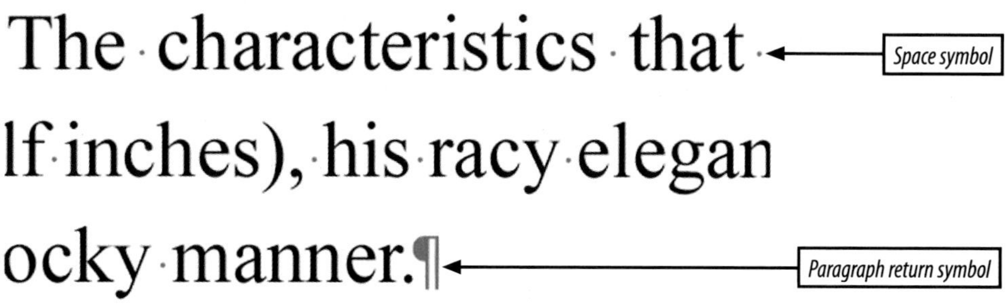

Figure 23 Applying a first line left indent

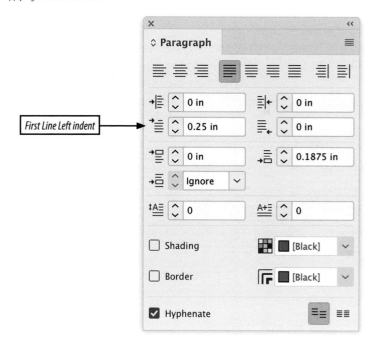

First Line Left indent

3. Select **by Christopher Smith**, then change the **Left Indent** value to **.5**.

4. Click anywhere in the **third paragraph**, then change the **First Line Left Indent** value to **0**.

5. Change the **Left Indent** value to **.75 in**, then change the **Right Indent** value to **.75 in**.

6. Click **any word in the third paragraph** three times to select the entire line, change the **font size** to **18 pt.**, change the **leading** to **20 pt.**, then deselect the paragraph.

7. Save your work, then continue to the next set of steps.

   Your document should resemble Figure 24.

You showed hidden characters so that you could better identify each paragraph. You indented the first lines of every paragraph, and then you added substantial left and right indents to a paragraph and increased its point size to create a pull quote.

Apply drop caps and soft returns

1. Click the **Paragraph panel name tab**, click anywhere in the **first paragraph**, then change the **First Line Left Indent** value to **0**.

2. Click the **Drop Cap Number of Lines up arrow** three times so the text box displays a **3**, as shown in Figure 25.

   A drop cap with the height of three text lines is added to the first paragraph.

3. Select the **entire pull quote (the third paragraph)**, then click the **Align center button** on the Paragraph panel.

   When centered, only the words Doberman Pinscher are on the second line of the pull quote. The goal now is to move more text from the first line to the second line so that the two lines are more balanced.

Figure 24 Using indents to format text as a pull quote

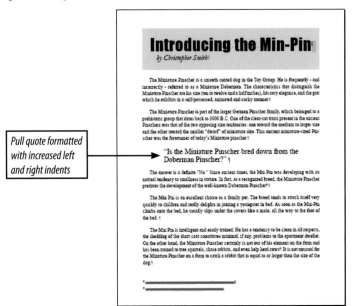

Pull quote formatted with increased left and right indents

Figure 25 Creating a drop cap

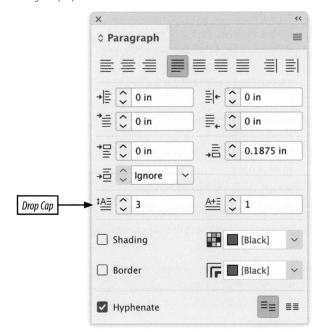

Drop Cap

4. Insert the **cursor** immediately **before the word** "**from**" in the first line of the pull quote, then press **[return] (Mac)** or **[Enter] (Win)** on your keypad.

   As shown in Figure 26, a paragraph return formatting character appears at the end of the first line, and a space is added after the first line. Entering [return] (Mac) or [Enter] (Win) on your keypad creates what's called a hard return. With a hard return, all paragraph formatting is applied. Thus, the two lines in the pull quote are now two different paragraphs, and there's a space after amount applied to the first paragraph.

5. Undo Step 4, press and hold **[shift]**, then press **[return] (Mac)** or **[Enter] (Win)** on your keypad.

   As shown in Figure 27, a soft paragraph return formatting character appears at the end of the first line. The words "from" and "the" are moved to the second line, but no space or other type of paragraph formatting is added because a soft return does not create a new paragraph; it just moves text from one line to another.

6. Use the keyboard command to hide hidden characters.

7. Press and hold **[shift]**, then press the **letter [W]** on your keypad.

   The view changes to Presentation mode.

8. Compare your document to Figure 28.

9. Press **[esc]**, save your work, then close the Min-Pin Intro document.

You created a drop cap and a soft return, which moved text to the next line without creating a new paragraph.

Figure 26 Entering a hard return creates a new paragraph.

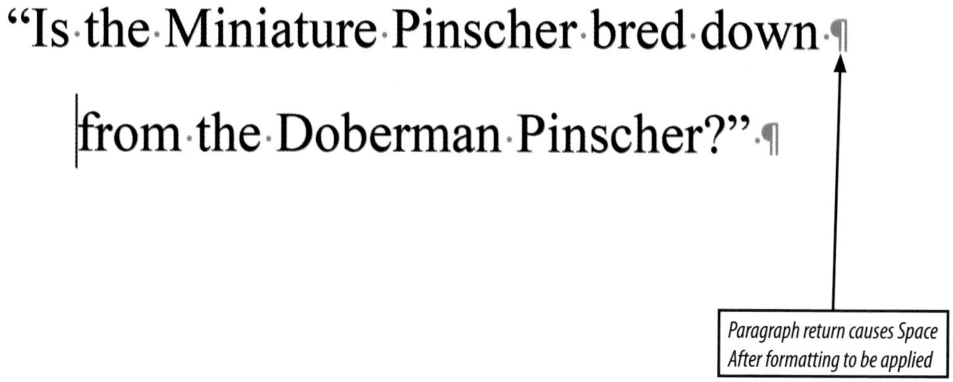

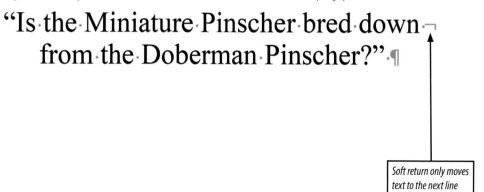

Paragraph return causes Space After formatting to be applied

Figure 27 Entering a soft return moves words to the next line but does not create a new paragraph.

Soft return only moves text to the next line

Figure 28 Final page layout with extensive formatting

Introducing the Min-Pin
by Christopher Smith

The Miniature Pinscher is a smooth coated dog in the Toy Group. He is frequently - and incorrectly - referred to as a Miniature Doberman. The characteristics that distinguish the Miniature Pinscher are his size (ten to twelve and a half inches), his racy elegance, and the gait which he exhittbits in a self-possessed, animated and cocky manner.

The Miniature Pinscher is part of the larger German Pinscher family, which belonged to a prehistoric group that dates back to 3000 B.C. One of the clear-cut traits present in the ancient Pinschers was that of the two opposing size tendencies: one toward the medium to larger size and the other toward the smaller "dwarf" of miniature size. This ancient miniature-sized Pinscher was the forerunner of today's Miniature pinscher.

"Is the Miniature Pinscher bred down from the Doberman Pinscher?"

The answer is a definite "No." Since ancient times, the Min Pin was developing with its natrual tendency to smallness in stature. In fact, as a recognized breed, the Miniature Pinscher predates the development of the well-known Doberman Pinscher[1].

The Min Pin is an excellent choice as a family pet. The breed tends to attach itself very quickly to children and really delights in joining a youngster in bed. As soon as the Min-Pin climbs onto the bed, he usually slips under the covers like a mole, all the way to the foot of the bed.

The Min Pin is intelligent and easily trained. He has a tendency to be clean in all respects, the shedding of the short coat constitutes minimal, if any, problems to the apartment dweller. On the other hand, the Miniature Pinscher certainly is not out of his element on the farm and has been trained to tree squirrels, chase rabbits, and even help herd cows[2]. It is not unusual for the Minature Pinscher on a farm to catch a rabbit that is equal to or larger than the size of the dog.

[1] Montag, Scott: In Love with the Min-Pin, All Breeds Publishing, 1997

[2] Miltenberger, William: Working Toy Breeds, CJP Press, 2002

CREATE AND APPLY STYLES

▶ *What You'll Do*

In this lesson, you will use the Character Styles and Paragraph Styles panels to create and apply styles to text.

Working with Character and Paragraph Styles

Imagine that you are writing a book. Let's say it's a user's manual for how to care for houseplants. This book will contain seven chapters. In each chapter, different sections will be preceded by a headline that is the same font as the chapter title, but a smaller font size. Within those sections, there will be subheads that, again, use the same font but in an even smaller size. Such a scenario is perfect for using styles.

A **style** is a group of formatting attributes—such as font, font size, color, and tracking—that is applied to text—whenever and wherever you want it to appear—throughout a document or multiple documents. Using styles saves you time and keeps your work consistent. Styles are given descriptive names for the type of text to which they are applied. Figure 29 shows three styles on the Character Styles panel. You use the Character Styles panel to create styles for individual words or characters, such as a footnote, which you would want in a smaller, superscript font. You use the Paragraph Styles panel to apply a style to an entire paragraph. Paragraph styles include formatting options such as indents and drop caps. The Paragraph Styles panel is shown in Figure 30.

Figure 29 Three styles on the Character Styles panel

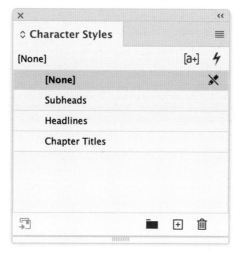

Figure 30 Two styles on the Paragraph Styles panel

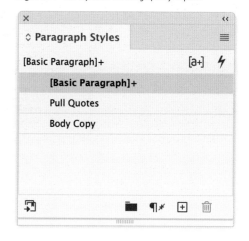

TIP You can easily import character and paragraph styles from other InDesign documents. Click the Character Styles or Paragraph Styles panel list arrow, then click Load Character Styles or Load Paragraph Styles. You'll be prompted to navigate to the documents that have the styles you wish to import.

In the scenario of the houseplant book, if you weren't using styles, you would be required to format all seven chapter headlines one at a time. You would need to remember the font size, the font style, and any tracking, kerning, scaling, or other formatting. Then you would need to do the same for every section headline, and every subheadline. For any body copy, you'd risk inconsistent spacing, indents, and other formatting options. Using styles, you define those formats one time and one time only. A much better solution, don't you think?

Another important feature about styles is that they are useful when you change your mind and want to modify text. Simply modify the style, and all the text that is assigned to that style will be automatically updated throughout the entire document.

TIP Glyphs are type characters that you won't find on your keyboard. These include characters such as arrows, boxes, and trademark, registration mark, and cents signs. InDesign makes it easy to find and use glyphs. Click Type on the menu bar, then click Glyphs to display the Glyphs panel. Click the document window with the Type tool, then double click the glyph on the Glyphs panel that you wish to insert.

Choosing the Next Style

Once you have more than one paragraph style saved on the Paragraph Styles panel, you can program which style will come next when you are currently in one style and create a new paragraph. For example, imagine you are creating a catalog and you have two styles called Item and Description. Now let's say that each time you finish typing the name of an item, you want to type the description of that item using the Description paragraph style. Then, when you finish typing the description and start a new paragraph, you want to type the next item using the Item paragraph style. You can choose which style should follow which by double-clicking a style on the Paragraph Styles panel, then clicking the Next Style list arrow in the Paragraph Style Options dialog box and choosing the name of the style that should come next.

Using Quick Apply

A quick way to apply a character or paragraph style is to use Quick Apply. The Quick Apply button is available on the Control panel, Character Styles panel, and Paragraph Styles panel. In the Quick Apply dialog box, there is a pull-down menu showing checked items, such as Character Styles. When Character Styles is checked, you can apply a character style quickly by typing its name in the Quick Apply text box. Your style will appear in a list below. Click the name in the list and your style is applied.

Quick Apply is not limited to applying styles. You can use Quick Apply to access menu commands and run scripts. Just be sure to click the Quick Apply list arrow in the Quick Apply dialog box and select Include Scripts and Include Menu Commands.

USING DATA MERGE

InDesign lets you create documents that are customized for each recipient, much like a mail merge in a word processing program, which you can use for items like letters, name labels, and postcards. In a **data merge**, you use a data source (usually a text file) that contains **fields** (labels like "First Name") and **records** (rows representing information for each recipient, such as "Bob Jones"). A **target document** is an InDesign file containing the text that will be seen by all recipients, such as a letter, as well as placeholders representing fields, such as <<First Name>>. In a data merge, InDesign places information from each record in the appropriate places in the target document, as many times as necessary. The result is a **merged document** containing the personalized letters.

To perform a data merge, click Window on the menu bar, point to Utilities, then click Data Merge. When the Data Merge panel opens, click the Data Merge panel menu button, click Select Data Source, locate the data source file, then click Open. This displays the merge fields on the Data Merge panel. Click in a text frame, and click field names to enter them in the frame. If you place placeholders on master pages, the merged document is connected to the data source, and you can automatically update the merged document with the most recent version of your data source.

To merge the document, click the Data Merge panel menu button, then click Create Merged Document. Select the records to include, then click OK.

Create character styles

1. Open ID 2-2.indd, then save it as **Jake's Diner**.

2. Display the **Character Styles panel**.

3. Click the **Character Styles panel menu button** ☰, then click **New Character Style**.

4. Type **Dishes** in the **Style Name text box** of the New Character Style dialog box, then click **Basic Character Formats** in the left column, as shown in Figure 31.

5. Click the **Font Family list arrow**, click **Impact**, click the **Size list arrow**, click **14 pt.**, click the **Leading text box**, type **16 pt.**, then click **Advanced Character Formats** in the left column.

6. Type **85** in the **Horizontal Scale text box**, then click **OK**.

   The style "Dishes" now appears on the Character Styles panel.

7. Click the **Character Styles panel menu button** ☰, click **New Character Style**, type **Descriptions** in the Style Name text box, then click **Basic Character Formats** in the left column.

8. Click the **Font Family list arrow**, click **Times New Roman** or a similar font, click the **Font Style list arrow**, click **Italic**, change the font size to **10 pt.**, change the leading to **12 pt.**, then click **OK**.

   The style "Descriptions" now appears on the Character Styles panel.

9. Click the **Character Styles panel menu button** ☰, click **New Character Style**, type **Prices** in the Style Name text box, then click **Basic Character Formats** in the left column.

10. Change the font to **Times New Roman** or a similar font, change the font style to **Bold,** change the font size to **12 pt.**, change the leading to **14 pt.**, then click **OK**.

    Your Character Styles panel should resemble Figure 32.

11. Save your work, then continue to the next set of steps.

You created three new character styles.

Figure 31 New Character Style dialog box

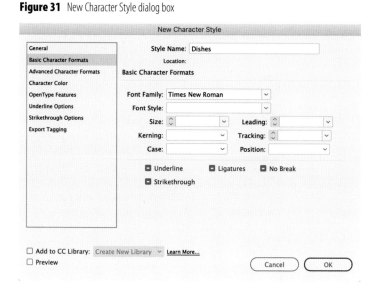

Figure 32 Character Styles panel

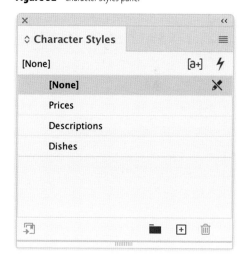

Apply character styles

1. Click the **Type tool** $\boxed{T}$, triple-click the word **Eggs** in the first title to select the entire title "Eggs and Bacon," then click **Dishes** on the Character Styles panel.

   The Dishes character style is applied to the title.

2. Select the **entire next paragraph** (beginning with the word Two), then click **Descriptions** on the Character Styles panel.

3. Select the **first price ($5.95)**, click **Prices** on the Character Styles panel, click **Edit** on the menu bar, then click **Deselect All**.

   Your first menu item should resemble Figure 33. If you used a different font, your text lines may break differently.

4. Select all the **remaining text** in the text frame, then apply the **Descriptions style**.

5. Apply the **Dishes style** to the **remaining seven dish titles**.

6. Apply the **Prices style** to the **remaining seven prices**, then deselect so that your document resembles Figure 34.

You applied character styles to format specific areas of a document.

Figure 33 Applying three different character styles

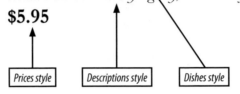

Eggs and Bacon

Two eggs any style, two strips of lean bacon, one biscuit with our homestyle gravy, and home fries.

$5.95

| Prices style | Descriptions style | Dishes style |

Figure 34 Viewing the document with all character styles applied

Jake's Diner
Early Bird Breakfast Menu

Eggs and Bacon
Two eggs any style, two strips of lean bacon, one biscuit with our homestyle gravy, and home fries.
$5.95

Egg Sandwich
One egg over easy, served with American or Jack cheese on a soft French croissant.
$5.25

Belgian Waffle
A golden brown buttery waffle served with fresh-picked strawberries, raspberries and blueberries. Whipped fresh cream on request.
$4.95

Silver Dollar Pancakes
A stack of eight golden pancakes served with fresh creamery butter and warm maple syrup.
$4.95

French Toast
Four triangles of thick peasant bread dipped in a cinnamon-egg batter. Served with French Fries.
$6.95

Biscuits and Gravy
Light fluffy southern biscuits served with a hearty sausage gravy.
$3.95

Eggs Hollandaise
Three eggs lightly poached served on a bed of romaine lettuce and topped with a rich Hollandaise sauce.
$6.95

Steak and Eggs
A 6 oz. strip of peppered breakfast steak cooked to your liking, served with two eggs, any style.
$7.95

Create paragraph styles

1. Close the **Character Styles panel**, then open the **Paragraph Styles panel**.

2. Click the **Paragraph Styles panel menu button** ☰ , then click **New Paragraph Style**.

3. Type **Prices** in the **Style Name text box**, then click **Indents and Spacing** in the left column.

   TIP Note that the New Paragraph Style dialog box contains Basic Character Formats and Advanced Character

Formats categories—the same that you find when working in the New Character Style dialog box.

4. Click the **Alignment list arrow**, then click **Center**.

5. Type **.25** in the **Space After text box**, then click **Paragraph Rules** in the left column, as shown in Figure 35.

6. Click the **list arrow** directly beneath Paragraph Rules, click **Rule Below**, then click the **Rule On check box** to add a check mark.

7. Type **.125** in the **Offset text box**, type **.25** in the **Left Indent text box**, type **.25** in the **Right Indent text box**, then click **OK**.

   The paragraph style "Prices" now appears on the Paragraph Styles panel as shown on Figure 36.

8. Save your work, then continue to the next set of steps.

You created a paragraph style, which included a center alignment, a space after value, and a paragraph rule.

Figure 35 Paragraph Rules window in the New Paragraph Style dialog box

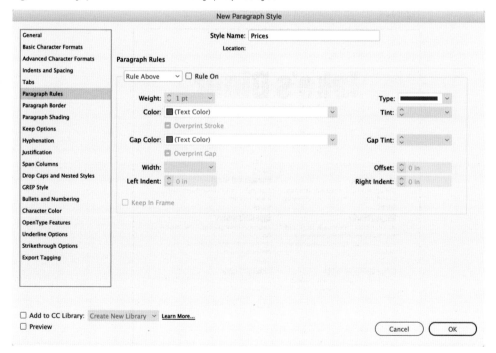

Figure 36 Paragraph Styles panel

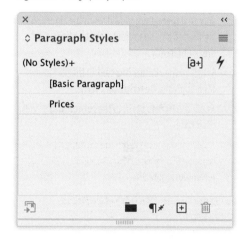

Apply paragraph styles

1. Click the **Type tool** T , then select **all the text in the document** except for the two headlines at the top of the page.

2. Click the **Align center button** ≡ on the Paragraph panel.

   For this layout, all the menu items will be aligned center. It's not necessary to create a paragraph style for all items to align center because you can simply use the Align center button ≡ on the Paragraph panel.

3. Click the **first price ($5.95)** once, click **Prices** on the Paragraph Styles panel, click the **second price ($5.25)**, then click **Prices** on the Paragraph Styles panel again.

   Your first two menu items should resemble Figure 37.

   TIP When applying paragraph styles, just place the cursor in the paragraph you want to modify.

4. Apply the **Prices paragraph style** to the remaining prices in the document except the Silver Dollar Pancakes and Steak and Eggs prices.

   You don't need to apply the paragraph style to the last two items because you don't need rules at the bottom of the menu.

5. In the **"French Toast" item**, note that the last sentence of the description is split between two lines.

6. Click **before the word "Served"** in the description text for **"French Toast,"** press and hold **[shift]**, then press **[return] (Mac)** or **[Enter] (Win)**.

   "Served" is moved to the next line. Using the same method, add soft returns to break any other lines that you think could look better, then compare your work to Figure 38.

7. Save your work, then close the Jake's Diner document.

   You applied a paragraph style to specific areas of the menu.

Figure 37 Applying a paragraph style to two prices

Eggs and Bacon

Two eggs any style, two strips of lean bacon, one biscuit with our homestyle gravy, and home fries.

$5.95

Egg Sandwich

One egg over easy, served with American or Jack cheese on a soft French croissant.

$5.25

USING THE TRACK CHANGES FEATURE

Whenever you're producing a document that involves a copy editor or more than one person making edits to copy, it becomes important that any edits made are recorded. For example, let's say you're the author of a story in a magazine. The copy editor goes through your text and makes various changes. You, as the author, will want to see what changes were made. You'll also want the option of approving or rejecting those changes, or at least the opportunity to debate whether or not the changes should be implemented.

The Track Changes feature allows for this important function within the editing process. The feature will identify each participant separately. Some of the changes that will be recorded include deleting, moving, and inserting new text. To view the changes, you use the Story Editor, accessed through the Edit menu. To accept or reject changes, use the Track Changes panel, located in the Window menu on the Editorial submenu.

Figure 38 Viewing the final document

Jake's Diner

Early Bird Breakfast Menu

Eggs and Bacon

Two eggs any style, two strips of lean bacon, one biscuit with our homestyle gravy, and home fries.

$5.95

Egg Sandwich

One egg over easy, served with American or Jack cheese on a soft French croissant.

$5.25

Belgian Waffle

A golden brown buttery waffle served with fresh-picked strawberries, raspberries and blueberries. Whipped fresh cream on request.

$4.95

Silver Dollar Pancakes

A stack of eight golden pancakes served with fresh creamery butter and warm maple syrup.

$4.95

French Toast

Four triangles of thick peasant bread dipped in a cinnamon-egg batter. Served with French Fries.

$6.95

Biscuits and Gravy

Light fluffy southern biscuits served with a hearty sausage gravy.

$3.95

Eggs Hollandaise

Three eggs lightly poached served on a bed of romaine lettuce and topped with a rich Hollandaise sauce.

$6.95

Steak and Eggs

A 6 oz. strip of peppered breakfast steak cooked to your liking, served with two eggs, any style.

$7.95

EDIT TEXT

▶ What You'll Do

In this lesson, you will use the Find/Change and Check Spelling commands to edit the text of a document.

Using the Find/Change Command

One of the great things about creating documents using a computer is the ability to edit text quickly and efficiently. Imagine the days before the personal computer. When you finished typing a document, you needed to read through it carefully, looking for any errors. If you found any, you had three options: cover it up, cross it out, or type the whole document again.

The Find/Change dialog box is a powerful tool for editing a document. With this command, you can search for any word in the document, then change that word to another word or delete it altogether with a click of the mouse button. For example, imagine that you have typed an entire document about Abraham Lincoln's early years growing up in Frankfurt, Kentucky. Then you find out that Lincoln actually grew up in Hardin County, Kentucky. You could use the Find/Change command to locate every instance of the word "Frankfurt" and change it to "Hardin County." One click would correct every instance of that error throughout the entire document.

TIP InDesign has many great features in the Find/Change dialog box. The Query menu lists predefined search options for finding (and changing) common formatting issues. For example, the Query menu has built-in searches for finding and changing dashes to en dashes and straight single or double quotes to typographer's quotes. There's a built-in search for trailing white space—useless extra spaces at the end of paragraphs or sentences—and there's even a search for telephone number formatting.

Checking Spelling

Since the earliest days of the personal computer, the ability to check and correct spelling errors automatically has been a much-promoted benefit of creating documents digitally. It has stood the test of time. The spell checker continues to be one of the most powerful features of word processing.

InDesign's Check Spelling dialog box is a comprehensive utility for locating and correcting typos and other misspellings in a document. If you've done word processing before, you will find yourself on familiar turf. The spell checker identifies words that it doesn't find in its dictionary, offers you a list of suggested corrections, and asks you what you want to do. If there is indeed a misspelling, type the correct spelling or choose the correct word from the suggested corrections list, then click Change to correct that instance or click Change All to correct all instances of the misspelling throughout the document.

Sometimes the spell checker identifies a word that is not actually a misspelling. For example, say you were typing a letter about your dog whose name is Gargantua. The spell checker is not going to find that word/name in its dictionary, and it is going to ask you what you want to do with it. You have two options. You could click Ignore, which tells the spell checker to make no changes and move on to the next questionable word. However, because in the future you will probably type the dog's name in other documents, you don't want the spell checker always asking you if this word/name is a misspelling. In this case, you'd be better off clicking the Add button. Doing so adds the name Gargantua to the spell checker's dictionary, and in the future, the spell checker will no longer identify Gargantua as a misspelling.

When you click the Add button, the word in question is added to the User Dictionary, which is InDesign's main dictionary. If you use the spell checker often, you will build up a list of words that you've chosen to ignore and a list of words that you've chosen to add to the dictionary. To see those lists and modify them, click the Dictionary button in the Check Spelling dialog box.

You can create your own user dictionary in the Dictionary section of the Preferences dialog box. Click the Language list arrow to choose the language with which you want to associate your dictionary, click the Add User Dictionary button, then select the user dictionary file. The user dictionary file is stored on the hard drive and includes a .udc or a .not extension. When you locate it, click Open. If you can't find the dictionary file, search your hard drive to locate the .udc files (try using *.udc or *.not in the search text box). The new user dictionary is added to the list under the Language menu. Then, when you are using the spell checker, click the Dictionary button, click the Target list arrow, then choose your new user dictionary from the list. You can add words to the new user dictionary using the Add button in the Check Spelling dialog box.

Using Dynamic Spell Checking

Another spell check feature is Dynamic Spelling. As you type, the program places a squiggly red line under words the spell checker thinks are misspelled. To prevent the program from flagging a proper name, you can add that name to your customized dictionary. To enable dynamic spelling, click Edit on the menu bar, point to Spelling, then click Dynamic Spelling.

Correcting Text Automatically

Autocorrect takes dynamic spell checking one step further. Instead of flagging a misspelled word, the Autocorrect feature corrects the misspelled word. For example, if you type the word "refered" and press [space bar], Autocorrect will change it to "referred."

Many commonly misspelled or easily mistyped words, such as "hte" for "the," are preprogrammed into the Autocorrect feature, and you can add words that might not already be listed. To turn on the Autocorrect feature, click Edit on the menu bar, point to Spelling, then click Autocorrect.

Use the Find/Change command

1. Open ID 2-3.indd, then save it as **Final Edit**.

2. Click **Edit** on the menu bar, then click **Find/Change**.

3. Type **Miniature Pincher** in the **Find what text box**, then type **Min-Pin** in the **Change to text box**, as shown in Figure 39.

4. Click **Find Next**.

   The first use of "Miniature Pincher" in the document is highlighted. As this is the first use of the term, you don't want to change it to a nickname.

   TIP Drag the dialog box out of the way if you cannot see your document.

5. Click **Find Next**, then click **Change**.

   The second use of "Miniature Pincher" is changed to "Min-Pin."

6. Click **Find Next** again, then click **Change**.

7. Click **Find Next** three times.

   You don't want to change all instances of Miniature Pincher to Min-Pin.

8. Click **Change**, then click **Done**.

9. Click **Edit** on the menu bar, then click **Find/Change**.

10. Type **Pincher** in the **Find what text box**, type **Pinscher** in the **Change to text box**, then click **Change All**.

    A dialog box appears stating that the search is completed, and 14 replacements were made.

11. Click **OK**, then click **Done**.

You used the Find/Change command to replace specific words in the document.

Figure 39 Find/Change dialog box

EDITING TEXT USING DRAG AND DROP

InDesign has a Drag and Drop text editing feature that allows you to move text to locations within a document without having to cut and paste. This means that you can select text and simply drag it from one text frame into another text frame. You can drag and drop text between text frames on different pages. You can even drag and drop text between documents. Dragging and dropping text is usually a lot faster and easier than cutting and pasting. You can also drag and drop a copy of selected text by pressing [option] (Mac) or [Alt] (Win) when dragging. You can turn Drag and Drop text on or off in the Type window of the Preferences dialog box. In the Drag and Drop Text Editing section, check both the Enable in Layout View and the Enable in Story Editor check boxes so the feature is activated for all your editing methods. Give it a try!

Check spelling

1. Click to the **right of the drop cap T** (between the T and the h) at the top of the page.

   Positioning your cursor at the top of a document forces the spell checker to begin checking for misspellings from the start of the document.

2. Click **Edit** on the menu bar, point to **Spelling**, then click **Check Spelling**.

   As shown in Figure 40, "refered" is listed as the first word the spell checker can't find in the dictionary. Suggested corrections are listed.

3. Click **referred** in the **Suggested Corrections list**, then click **Change**.

   The spell checker lists "racey" as the next word it can't find in the dictionary.

4. Click **racy** in the **Suggested Corrections list**, then click **Change**.

   The spell checker lists "Pinscher1" as not in the dictionary because of the number 1 footnote.

5. Click **Ignore All** for all remaining queries, click **OK**, then click **Done**.

6. Save your work, then close the Final Edit document.

TIP Never rely on the spell checker as the sole means for proofreading a document. It cannot determine if you have used the wrong word. For example, the spell checker did not flag the word "gate" in the first paragraph, which should be spelled "gait."

You used the Check Spelling dialog box to proof a document for spelling errors.

Figure 40 Check Spelling dialog box

CREATE BULLETED AND NUMBERED LISTS

Creating Bulleted and Numbered Lists

Creating numbered or bulleted lists is a common need in many types of layouts, and InDesign allows you to do so easily. The best way to start is to type the list first, without formatting. Select the list, point to the Bulleted & Numbered Lists command in the Type menu, and then choose whether you want to apply bullets or numbers to the selected text.

Bullets and numbers are like any other type of paragraph formatting. InDesign applies them to each paragraph of the selected text. At any time, you can select the text and change the marks from bullets to numbers or vice versa. You also use the same Bulleted & Numbered Lists command to remove bullets or numbers from selected text.

> **TIP** By default, InDesign applies bullets and numbers with the same typeface, type size, and color of the selected text in the paragraph.

Modifying Bulleted and Numbered Lists

You can think of bullets and numbers as being applied "virtually" to a paragraph. Let's use numbers as an example. When you

apply numbers, you can see the numbers, but you can't select them. If you select the entire paragraph of text, the numbers won't appear to be selected. This is because the numbers are applied as a format to the paragraph. For example, let's say you had a list of nine numbered entries, and then you inserted a 10th entry between numbers 5 and 6. The new entry would automatically be numbered with a "6," and the numbers on all the following entries would be automatically updated.

Once you've finished a list, you might find that you want to modify the numbers by changing the typeface, color, or size of the numbers.

To do so, you must first convert the list to text so that the numbers can be selected and modified. Click the Bulleted & Numbered Lists command, then click the Convert Bullets and Numbering to Text command, shown in Figure 41. When you do this, the numbers (or bullets) will be converted to regular text. The list will still appear to be numbered, but it will have lost the functionality of the list formatting. If you insert or remove any component of the list, the numbers won't be updated. InDesign will see it only as a block of text.

Figure 41 Convert Bullets to Text command

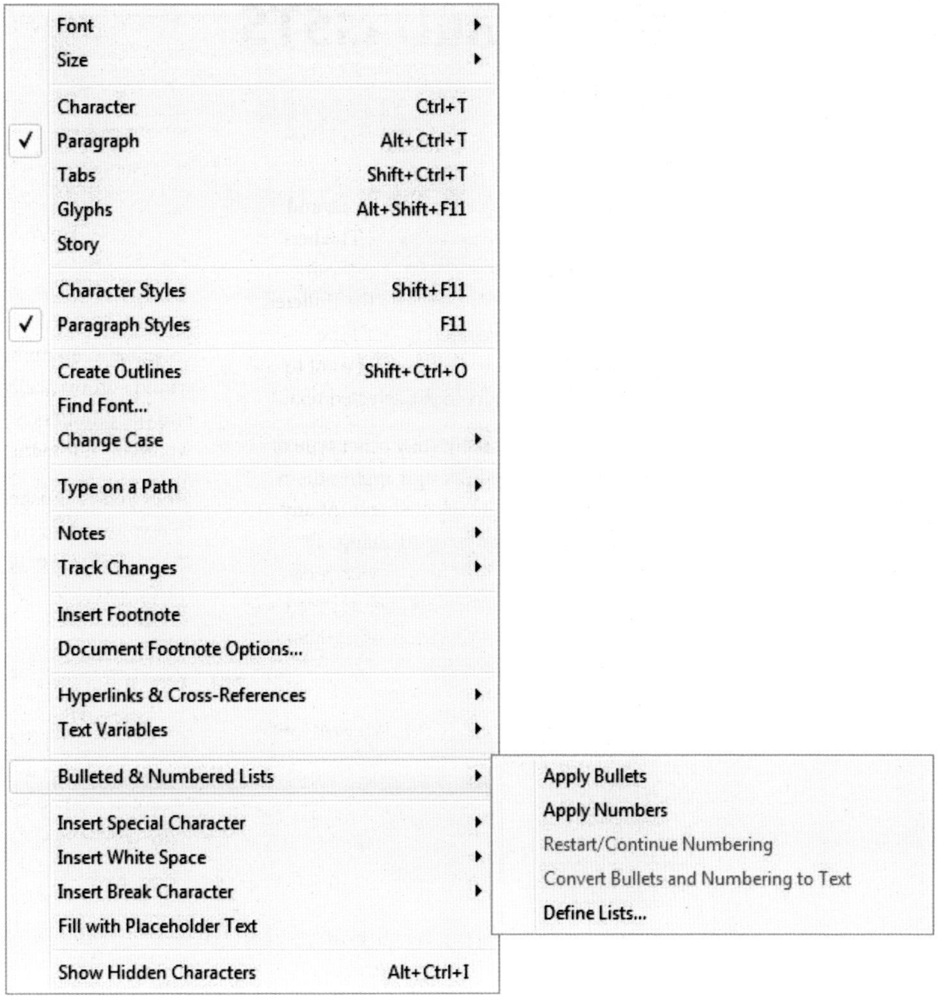

Font		▶
Size		▶
Character	Ctrl+T	
✓ Paragraph	Alt+Ctrl+T	
Tabs	Shift+Ctrl+T	
Glyphs	Alt+Shift+F11	
Story		
Character Styles	Shift+F11	
✓ Paragraph Styles	F11	
Create Outlines	Shift+Ctrl+O	
Find Font...		
Change Case		▶
Type on a Path		▶
Notes		▶
Track Changes		▶
Insert Footnote		
Document Footnote Options...		
Hyperlinks & Cross-References		▶
Text Variables		▶
Bulleted & Numbered Lists		▶
Insert Special Character		▶
Insert White Space		▶
Insert Break Character		▶
Fill with Placeholder Text		
Show Hidden Characters	Alt+Ctrl+I	

Submenu:

- **Apply Bullets**
- **Apply Numbers**
- Restart/Continue Numbering
- Convert Bullets and Numbering to Text
- **Define Lists...**

Create a bulleted and a numbered list

1. Open ID 2-4.indd, then save it as **TOC**.

2. Click the **Type tool** T, then select **all the text below Chapter 1: Getting Started**.

3. On the Paragraph panel, set the **Space After value** ⧉↕ to **.125 in**.

4. Click **Type** on the menu bar, point to **Bulleted & Numbered Lists**, then click **Apply Bullets**.

   As shown in Figure 42, bullets are applied at each paragraph in the selected text. The text remains selected, though the bullets themselves do not appear selected.

5. Click **Type** on the menu bar, point to **Bulleted & Numbered Lists**, then click **Apply Numbers**.

   The bullets change to numbers that are the same typeface, size, and color of the selected text.

6. Save your work and then continue to the next set of steps.

You applied bullets to selected text, then changed the bullets to numbers.

Figure 42 Bullets applied to text

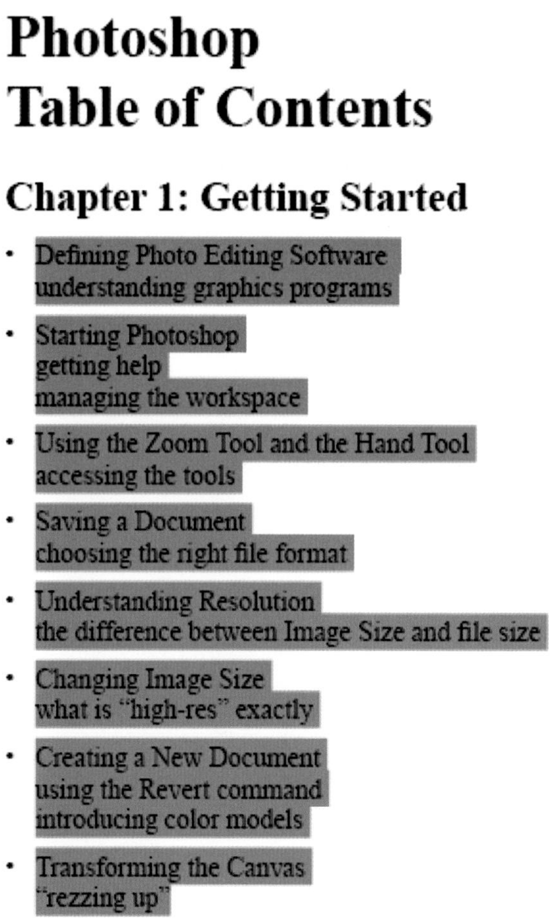

Photoshop
Table of Contents

Chapter 1: Getting Started

- Defining Photo Editing Software
  understanding graphics programs

- Starting Photoshop
  getting help
  managing the workspace

- Using the Zoom Tool and the Hand Tool
  accessing the tools

- Saving a Document
  choosing the right file format

- Understanding Resolution
  the difference between Image Size and file size

- Changing Image Size
  what is "high-res" exactly

- Creating a New Document
  using the Revert command
  introducing color models

- Transforming the Canvas
  "rezzing up"

Convert numbers to text

1. Verify that **all the numbered text** is still selected.

2. Click **Type** on the menu bar, point to **Bulleted & Numbered Lists**, then click **Convert Numbering to Text**.

3. Select the **number 8** and the **period** that follows it.

4. On the Character panel, change the **Type Style** from Regular to **Bold**.

5. Change **all the numbers** and the **periods** that follow them to bold so your list resembles Figure 43.

6. Save your work, then close the TOC document.

You converted numbering to text so you could format the numbers differently from the text in the list.

Figure 43 Reformatting the numbers in the list

Photoshop Table of Contents

Chapter 1: Getting Started

1. Defining Photo Editing Software
   understanding graphics programs

2. Starting Photoshop
   getting help
   managing the workspace

3. Using the Zoom Tool and the Hand Tool
   accessing the tools

4. Saving a Document
   choosing the right file format

5. Understanding Resolution
   the difference between Image Size and file size

6. Changing Image Size
   what is "high-res" exactly

7. Creating a New Document
   using the Revert command
   introducing color models

8. Transforming the Canvas
   "rezzing up"

Format text

1. Open ID 2-5.indd, then save it as **Independence**.
2. Click Window on the menu bar, point to Workspace, then click Reset Typography.
3. Click the Type tool, then triple-click the word Declaration at the top of the page.
4. On the Character panel, type **80** in the Horizontal Scale text box, then press [return] (Mac) or [Enter] (Win).
5. Click the Font Family list arrow, click Impact, click the Font Size list arrow, then click 36 pt.
6. Press and hold [shift] [command] (Mac) or [Shift] [Ctrl] (Win), then press [<] two times.
7. Triple-click the word July on the next line; change the typeface to Garamond, if necessary; change the Style to Italic; then click the Font Size up arrow until the font size is 18 pt.
8. Click Object on the menu bar, click Text Frame Options, change the Align setting to Center, then click OK.
9. Triple-click the word July, if necessary.
10. Type **100** in the Tracking text box, then press [return] (Mac) or [Enter] (Win).
11. Click between the letters r and a in the word Declaration, click the Kerning list arrow, then click 10.
12. Click View on the menu bar, click Fit Page in Window, if necessary, click the Zoom tool, and then drag a selection box that encompasses all the body copy on the page.
13. Click the Type tool, then select the number 1 at the end of the first paragraph.
14. Click the Character panel menu button, then click Superscript.
15. Select the number 1 at the beginning of the last paragraph, then apply the Superscript command.

Format paragraphs

1. Click View on the menu bar, click Fit Page in Window, then click the first word When in the body copy five times to select all the body copy.
2. Select (12 pt.) in the Leading text box on the Character panel, type **13.25**, then press [return] (Mac) or [Enter] (Win).
3. Display the Paragraph panel, then click the Justify with last line aligned left button.
4. Click in the word Independence at the top of the document, then click the Align center button on the Paragraph panel.
5. Click the Type tool, if necessary; click anywhere in the body copy; click Edit on the menu bar; then click Select All.
6. On the Paragraph panel, click the Space After up arrow three times so the value reads .1875 in, click Edit on the menu bar, then click Deselect All.
7. Select the footnote (last paragraph of the document), double-click the Space Before text box on the Paragraph panel, type **.5**, then press [return] (Mac) or [Enter] (Win).
8. Apply the Deselect All command.
9. Click Type on the menu bar, then click Show Hidden Characters.
10. Select all the body copy on the page except for the last paragraph (the footnote), double-click the First Line Left Indent text box on the Paragraph panel, type **.25**, then press [return] (Mac) or [Enter] (Win).
11. Select July 4, 1776, beneath the headline, then click the Align right button on the Paragraph panel.

12. Double-click the Right Indent text box on the Paragraph panel, type **.6**, then press [return] (Mac) or [Enter] (Win).

13. Click anywhere in the first paragraph, then change the First Line Left Indent value to 0.

14. Click the Drop Cap Number of Lines up arrow three times so the text box displays a 3.

15. Click the Zoom tool, then drag a selection box that encompasses the entire second to last paragraph in the body copy.

16. Click the Type tool, position the pointer before the word "these"—the second-to-last word in the paragraph.

17. Press and hold [shift], then press [return] (Mac) or [Enter] (Win).

18. Click Type on the menu bar, click Hide Hidden Characters, if necessary, click View on the menu bar, point to Grids & Guides, and then click Hide Guides.

19. Click View on the menu bar, then click Fit Page in Window.

20. Compare your document to Figure 44, click File on the menu bar, click Save, then close the Independence document.

Figure 44 Completed Skills Review, Part 1

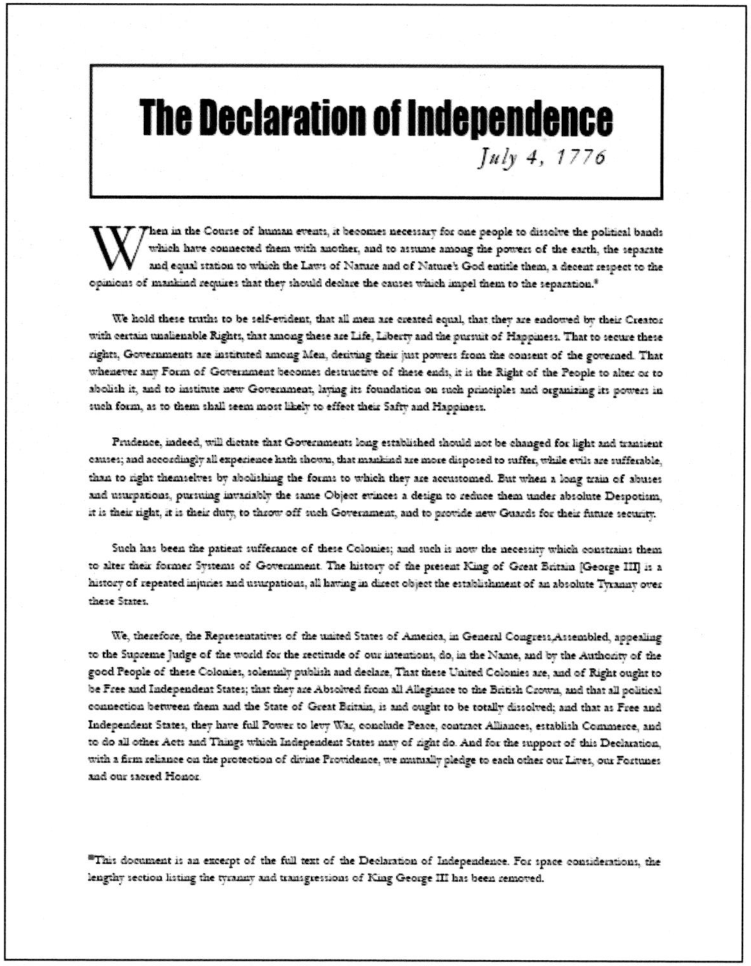

The Declaration of Independence
July 4, 1776

When in the Course of human events, it becomes necessary for one people to dissolve the political bands which have connected them with another, and to assume among the powers of the earth, the separate and equal station to which the Laws of Nature and of Nature's God entitle them, a decent respect to the opinions of mankind requires that they should declare the causes which impel them to the separation.*

We hold these truths to be self-evident, that all men are created equal, that they are endowed by their Creator with certain unalienable Rights, that among these are Life, Liberty and the pursuit of Happiness. That to secure these rights, Governments are instituted among Men, deriving their just powers from the consent of the governed. That whenever any Form of Government becomes destructive of these ends, it is the Right of the People to alter or to abolish it, and to institute new Government, laying its foundation on such principles and organizing its powers in such form, as to them shall seem most likely to effect their Safty and Happiness.

Prudence, indeed, will dictate that Governments long established should not be changed for light and transient causes; and accordingly all experience hath shown, that mankind are more disposed to suffer, while evils are sufferable, than to right themselves by abolishing the forms to which they are accustomed. But when a long train of abuses and usurpations, pursuing invariably the same Object evinces a design to reduce them under absolute Despotism, it is their right, it is their duty, to throw off such Government, and to provide new Guards for their future security.

Such has been the patient sufferance of these Colonies; and such is now the necessity which constrains them to alter their former Systems of Government. The history of the present King of Great Britain [George III] is a history of repeated injuries and usurpations, all having in direct object the establishment of an absolute Tyranny over these States.

We, therefore, the Representatives of the united States of America, in General Congress, Assembled, appealing to the Supreme Judge of the world for the rectitude of our intentions, do, in the Name, and by the Authority of the good People of these Colonies, solemnly publish and declare, That these United Colonies are, and of Right ought to be Free and Independent States; that they are Absolved from all Allegiance to the British Crown, and that all political connection between them and the State of Great Britain, is and ought to be totally dissolved; and that as Free and Independent States, they have full Power to levy War, conclude Peace, contract Alliances, establish Commerce, and to do all other Acts and Things which Independent States may of right do. And for the support of this Declaration, with a firm reliance on the protection of divine Providence, we mutually pledge to each other our Lives, our Fortunes and our sacred Honor.

*This document is an excerpt of the full text of the Declaration of Independence. For space considerations, the lengthy section listing the tyranny and transgressions of King George III has been removed.

Create and apply styles

1. Open ID 2-6.indd, then save it as **Toy Breeds**.
2. Open the Character Styles panel.
3. Click the Character Styles panel menu button, then click New Character Style.
4. Type **Breeds** in the Style Name text box, then click Basic Character Formats in the left column.
5. Change the Font to Tahoma, change the Size to 14 pt., change the Leading to 16 pt., then click OK.
6. Click the Character Styles panel menu button, click New Character Style, type **Info** in the Style Name text box, then click Basic Character Formats in the left column.
7. Change the Font to Garamond, change the Style to Italic, change the Size to 10 pt., change the Leading to 12 pt., then click OK.
8. Select all the text except for the top two lines, then click Info on the Character Styles panel.
9. Double-click the Affenpinscher headline, then click Breeds on the Character Styles panel.
10. Apply the Breeds character style to the remaining seven breed headlines, then deselect all.
11. Open the Paragraph Styles panel.
12. Click the Paragraph Styles panel menu button, then click New Paragraph Style.
13. Type **Info** in the Style Name text box, then click Indents and Spacing in the left column.
14. Click the Alignment list arrow, then click Center.
15. Type **.25** in the Space After text box, then click Paragraph Rules in the left column.
16. Click the list arrow directly below Paragraph Rules, click Rule Below, then click the Rule On check box.
17. Type **.1625** in the Offset text box, type **1** in the Left Indent text box, type **1** in the Right Indent text box, then click OK.
18. Select all the text except for the top two lines, then click the Align center button on the Paragraph panel.
19. Click in the Affenpinscher description text, then click Info on the Paragraph Styles panel.
20. Apply the Info paragraph style to all the remaining descriptions except for the Pomeranian and the Pug.
21. Click View on the menu bar, point to Grids & Guides, then click Hide Guides.
22. Click before the word "bred" in the Manchester Terrier description, press and hold [shift], then press [return] (Mac) or [Enter] (Win).
23. Click before the phrase even-tempered in the Pug description, press and hold [shift], press [return] (Mac) or [Enter] (Win), click before the word and in the "Pug" description, press and hold [shift], then press [return] (Mac) or [Enter] (Win).
    Your text may break differently. Correct any other bad breaks you see.
24. Save your work, compare your screen to Figure 45, then close the Toy Breeds document.

Edit text

1. Open ID 2-7.indd, then save it as **Declaration Edit**.
2. Select the Type tool, then click at the beginning of the first paragraph.
3. Click Edit on the menu bar, then click Find/Change.
4. Type **IV** in the Find what text box, then type **III** in the Change to text box.
5. Click Find Next.

    You want to change the IV to III in George IV, as in George III; however, the spell checker finds all instances of "IV," such as in the word "deriving."
6. Click the Case Sensitive button Aa in the middle of the Find/Change dialog box.
7. Click Find Next.
8. Click Change All, click OK in the dialog box that tells you that two replacements were made, then click Done in the Find/Change dialog box. By specifying the search to be Case Sensitive, only uppercase IV instances were found and changed.
9. Click before the drop cap in the first paragraph, click Edit on the menu bar, point to Spelling, then click Check Spelling.
10. For the query on the word "Safty," click Safety at the top of the Suggested Corrections list, then click Change.

Figure 45 Completed Skills Review, Part 2

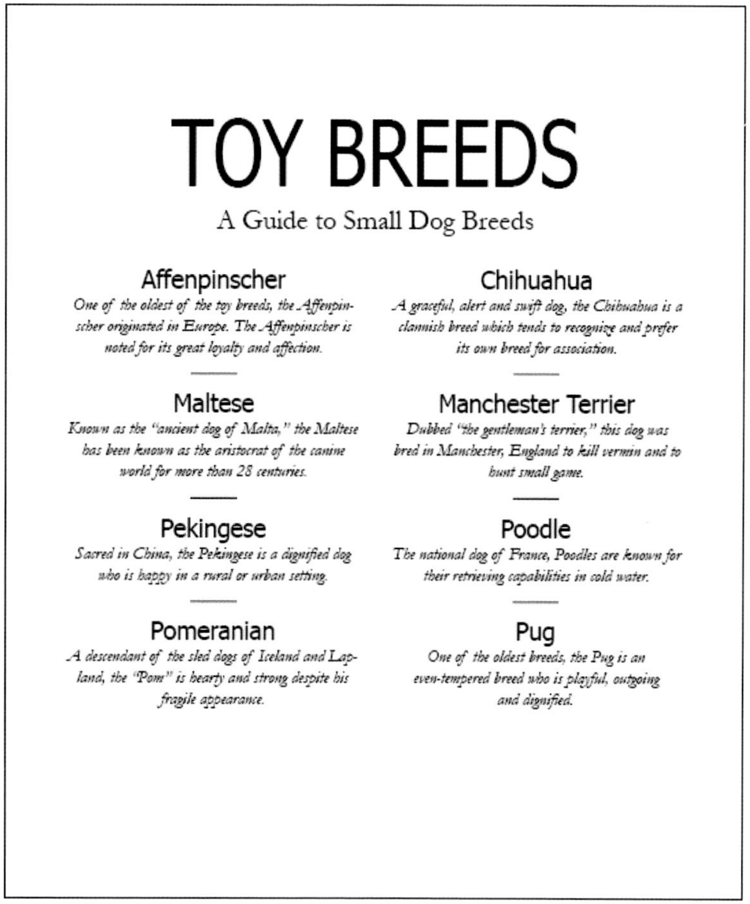

TOY BREEDS
A Guide to Small Dog Breeds

Affenpinscher
One of the oldest of the toy breeds, the Affenpinscher originated in Europe. The Affenpinscher is noted for its great loyalty and affection.

Chihuahua
A graceful, alert and swift dog, the Chihuahua is a clannish breed which tends to recognize and prefer its own breed for association.

Maltese
Known as the "ancient dog of Malta," the Maltese has been known as the aristocrat of the canine world for more than 28 centuries.

Manchester Terrier
Dubbed "the gentleman's terrier," this dog was bred in Manchester, England to kill vermin and to hunt small game.

Pekingese
Sacred in China, the Pekingese is a dignified dog who is happy in a rural or urban setting.

Poodle
The national dog of France, Poodles are known for their retrieving capabilities in cold water.

Pomeranian
A descendant of the sled dogs of Iceland and Lapland, the "Pom" is hearty and strong despite his fragile appearance.

Pug
One of the oldest breeds, the Pug is an even-tempered breed who is playful, outgoing and dignified.

11. Click Ignore All to ignore the query on hath.
12. Click Ignore All to ignore all instances of III.
13. Click before the capital "S" in "States" in the Change To text box in the Check Spelling dialog box, press [space bar] once, then click Change.
14. Click Done.
15. Save your work, deselect, compare your screen to Figure 46, then close the Declaration Edit document.

Create bulleted and numbered lists

1. Open ID 2-8.indd, then save it as **Chapter 2**.
2. Click the Type tool, then select all the text beneath Chapter 2: Selecting Pixels.
3. On the Paragraph panel, set the Space After value to .125 in.
4. Click Type on the menu bar, point to Bulleted & Numbered Lists, then click Apply Bullets.
5. Click Type on the menu bar, point to Bulleted & Numbered Lists, then click Apply Numbers.
6. Click Type on the menu bar, point to Bulleted & Numbered Lists, then click Convert Numbering to Text.
7. Select the number 1 and the period that follows it.
8. On the Character panel, change the Type Style from Regular to Italic.
9. Change all the numbers and the periods that follow them to italic.
10. Save your work, then close the Chapter 2 document.

Figure 46 Completed Skills Review, Part 3

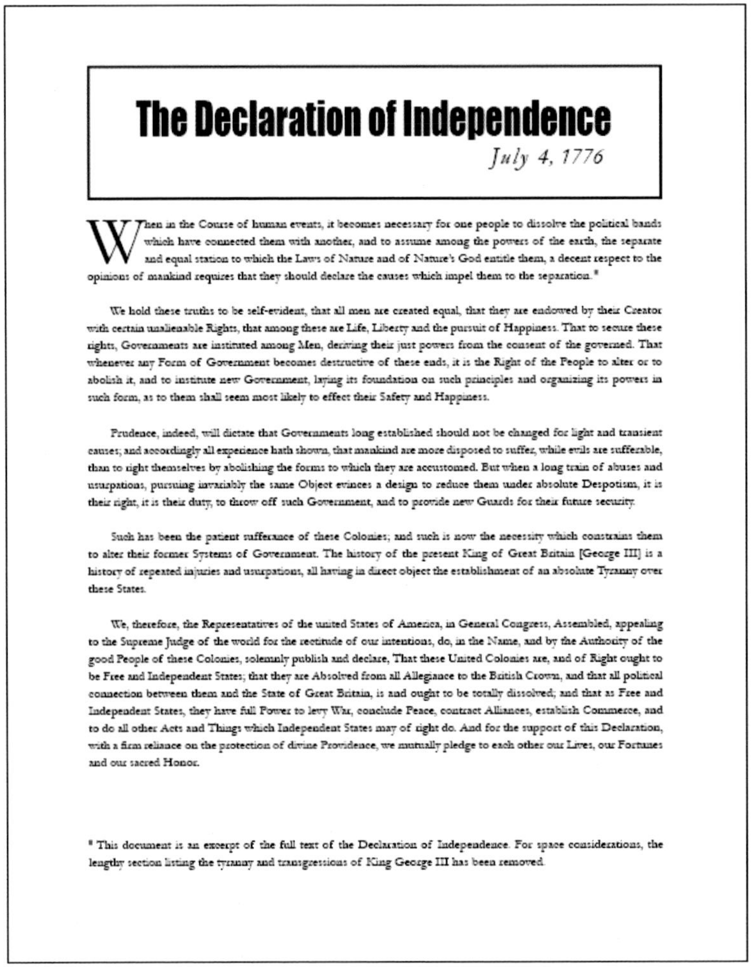

You are a freelance designer. Your client returns a document to you, telling you that she wants you to make a change to a drop cap. She wants you to format not just the first letter but the entire first word as a drop cap so it is more prominent on the page.

1. Open ID 2-9.indd, then save it as **Drop Cap Modifications**.
2. Click the Zoom tool, then drag a selection box around the first paragraph.
3. Click the Type tool, click after the W drop cap, double-click the 1 in the Drop Cap One or More Characters text box on the Paragraph panel, type **4**, and then press [return] (Mac) or [Enter] (Win).
4. Click before the word in, in the top line, then type **100** in the Kerning text box on the Character panel.
5. Select the letters HEN, click the Character panel menu button, click All Caps, click the Character panel menu button again, then click Superscript.
6. With the letters still selected, type **–10** in the Baseline Shift text box on the Character panel.
7. Click between the W and H in the word WHEN, then type **–60** in the Kerning text box.
8. Save your work, compare your screen to Figure 47, then close the Drop Cap Modifications document.

Figure 47 Completed Project Builder 1

The Declaration of Independence

July 4, 1776

WHEN in the Course of human events, it becomes necessary for one people to dissolve the political bands which have connected them with another, and to assume among the powers of the earth, the separate and equal station to which the Laws of Nature and of Nature's God entitle them, a decent respect to the opinions of mankind requires that they should declare the causes which impel them to the separation.[1]

You have designed a document about Miniature Pinschers. Your client calls you with changes. He wants to show small pictures of Miniature Pinschers in the document, one beside each paragraph. He asks you to reformat the document to create space where the small pictures can be inserted.

1. Open ID 2-10.indd, then save it as **Hanging Indents**.
2. Select the four paragraphs of body copy, then change the first line left indent to 0.
3. Change the left indent to 2 in., then change the right indent to .5 in.
4. Create a half-inch space after each paragraph.
5. Type **−1.5** in the First Line Left Indent text box, then deselect all.
6. Save your work, compare your screen to Figure 48, then close the Hanging Indents document.

Figure 48 Completed Project Builder 2

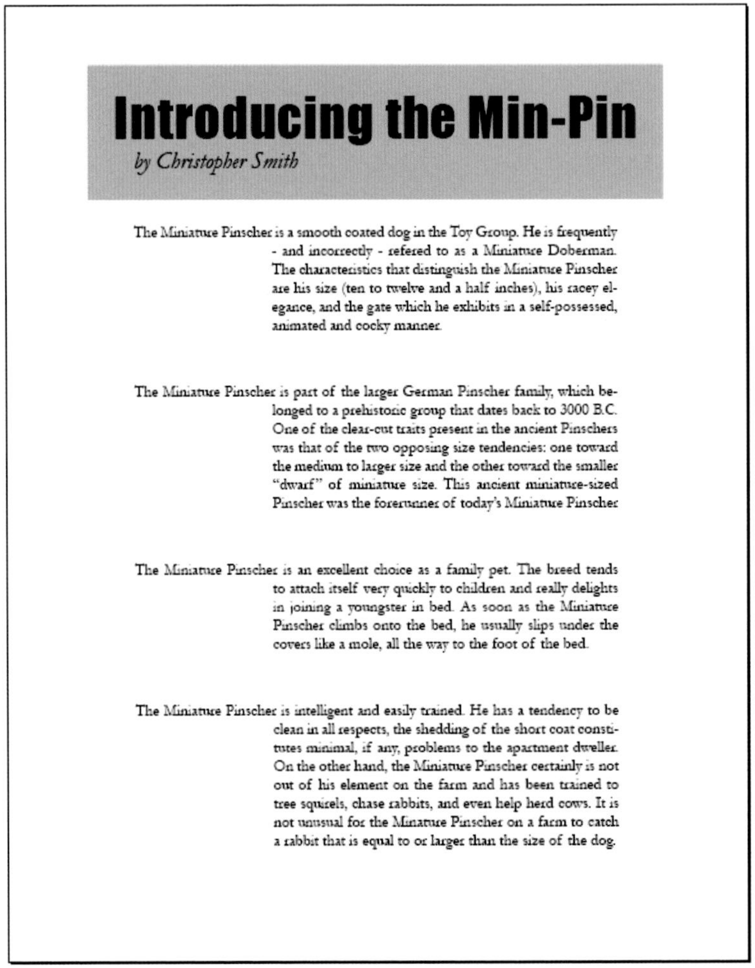

Introducing the Min-Pin
by Christopher Smith

The Miniature Pinscher is a smooth coated dog in the Toy Group. He is frequently - and incorrectly - refered to as a Miniature Doberman. The characteristics that distinguish the Miniature Pinscher are his size (ten to twelve and a half inches), his racey elegance, and the gate which he exhibits in a self-possessed, animated and cocky manner.

The Miniature Pinscher is part of the larger German Pinscher family, which belonged to a prehistoric group that dates back to 3000 B.C. One of the clear-cut traits present in the ancient Pinschers was that of the two opposing size tendencies: one toward the medium to larger size and the other toward the smaller "dwarf" of miniature size. This ancient miniature-sized Pinscher was the forerunner of today's Miniature Pinscher.

The Miniature Pinscher is an excellent choice as a family pet. The breed tends to attach itself very quickly to children and really delights in joining a youngster in bed. As soon as the Miniature Pinscher climbs onto the bed, he usually slips under the covers like a mole, all the way to the foot of the bed.

The Miniature Pinscher is intelligent and easily trained. He has a tendency to be clean in all respects, the shedding of the short coat constitutes minimal, if any, problems to the apartment dweller. On the other hand, the Miniature Pinscher certainly is not out of his element on the farm and has been trained to tree squirels, chase rabbits, and even help herd cows. It is not unusual for the Miniature Pinscher on a farm to catch a rabbit that is equal to or larger than the size of the dog.

You have been assigned the task of designing a headline for a billboard for the movie "Crushing Impact." The client has asked for a finished design in black letters on a white background. Before you design the title, you consider the following questions.

Discussion

1. Open ID 2-12.indd, then save it as **Crushing Impact**.
2. Look at the title for a full minute.
3. What font family might be best for the title?
4. Does the title demand a big, bold font, or could it work in a fine, delicate font?
5. Should the two words be positioned side by side or one on top of the other?
6. Does the title itself suggest that, visually, one word should be positioned on top of the other?

Exercise

1. Position the word IMPACT on a second line, select all the text, change the font to Impact, then change the Font Size to 64 pt.
2. Select the word IMPACT, change the Horizontal Scale to 200, then change the Vertical Scale to 80.
3. Select the word CRUSHING, change the Horizontal Scale to 50, change the Font Size to 190, then change the Leading to 190.
4. Select the word IMPACT, then change the Leading to 44.
5. Save your work, compare your screen to Figure 49, then close the Crushing Impact document.

Figure 49 Completed Design Project

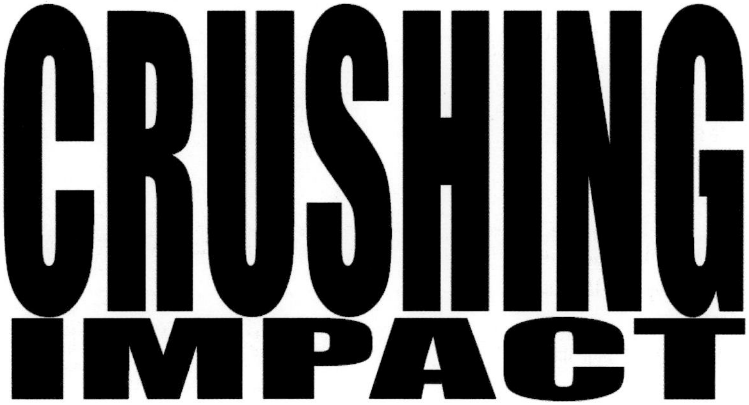

LOCATION
day/date

LOCATION
day/date

CHAPTER **3**

SETTING UP A
DOCUMENT

1. Create a New Document and Set Up a
   Master Page
2. Create Text on Master Pages
3. Apply Master Pages to Document Pages
4. Modify Master Pages and Document Pages
5. Place and Thread Text
6. Create New Sections and Wrap Text

Adobe Certified Professional in Print & Digital Media Publication Using Adobe InDesign

2. Project Setup and Interface
This objective covers the interface setup and program settings that assist in an efficient and effective workflow, as well as knowledge about ingesting digital assets for a project.

2.1 Create a document with the appropriate settings for web, print, and mobile.
   A   Set appropriate document settings for printed and on-screen images.
   B   Create a new document preset to reuse for specific project needs.

2.2 Navigate, organize, and customize the application workspace.
   A   Identify and manipulate elements of the InDesign interface.
   B   Organize and customize the workspace.
   C   Configure application preferences.

2.3 Use nonprinting design tools in the interface to aid in design or workflow.
   A   Navigate a document.
   B   Use rulers.
   C   Use guides and grids.
   D   Use views and modes to work efficiently.

2.5 Manage colors, swatches, and gradients.
   A   Set the active fill and stroke color.

3. Organizing Documents
This objective covers document structure such as layers, tracks, and managing document structure for efficient workflows.

3.2 Manage and modify pages.
   A   Create, edit, and arrange pages in a document.
   B   Edit and apply master pages.

4. Creating and Modifying Document Elements
This objective covers core tools and functionality of the application, as well as tools that affect the visual appearance of document elements.

4.2 Add and manipulate text using appropriate typographic settings.
   A   Use type tools to add text.
   C   Use appropriate paragraph settings in a design.
   E   Manage text flow across multiple text areas.
   F   Use tools to add special characters or content.

4.4 Transform digital graphics and media within a publication.
   B   Rotate, flip, and transform individual frames or content.

4.5 Use basic reconstructing and editing techniques to manipulate document content.
   B   Evaluate or adjust the appearance of objects, frames, or layers using various tools.

CREATE A NEW DOCUMENT AND SET UP A MASTER PAGE

▶ **What You'll Do**

In this lesson, you will create a new document, position guides on a master page, and position placeholder frames for text, tints, and graphics.

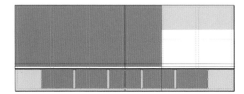

Creating a New Document

When you are ready to create a new document in InDesign, you begin in the New Document dialog box, shown in Figure 1. First you choose the type of document you need to create. Listed across the top of the dialog box are types of output categories, including Print, Web, and Mobile. When you click a category, blank document presets become available.

Figure 1 New Document dialog box

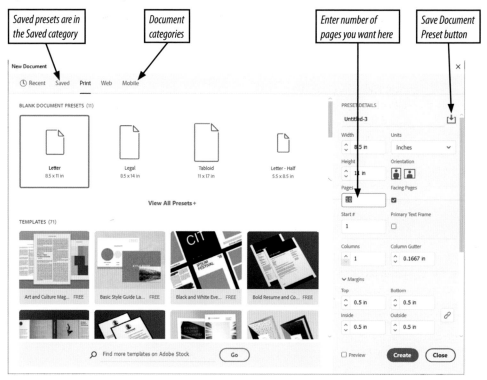

For example, if you are creating a layout for a phone, you would click the Mobile category. Blank presets including iPhone X and iPad Pro, among others, are available to choose from. After choosing a preset, you are ready to further define your document. The right side of the New Document dialog box is where you name the document and specify the number of pages the document will contain. You also specify the **page size**, or **trim size**—the width and height of the finished document. In addition, you specify whether or not the document will have **facing pages**. When you choose this option, the document is created with left and right pages that *face* each other in a spread, such as you would find in a magazine. If this option is not selected, each page stands alone, like a *stack* of pages.

The New Document dialog box also allows you to specify the width of margins on the outer edges of the page and the number of columns that will be positioned on the page. Margins and columns are useful as layout guides, and they play an important role in flowing text. When working with columns, the term **gutter** refers to the space between the columns. Figure 2 shows margins and columns on a typical page.

When creating a document with specific settings that you plan on using again and again, you can save the settings as a preset by clicking the Save Document Preset button next to the document name. Your named preset will then become available in the Saved category in the New Document dialog box.

Figure 2 Identifying margins and columns

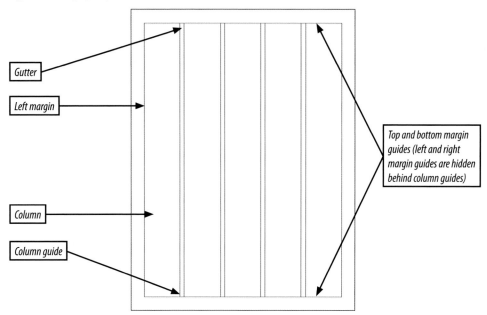

Gutter

Left margin

Top and bottom margin guides (left and right margin guides are hidden behind column guides)

Column

Column guide

Setting the Starting Page Number

Imagine that you are holding a closed book in your hands—perhaps this book—and you open the front cover. The first page of the book is a single right-hand page. If you turn the page, the next two pages are pages 2 and 3, which face each other in a spread. Now imagine closing the book and flipping it over so you are looking at the back cover. If you open it, the last page is a single left-hand page.

With this in mind, consider that whenever you create a multiple-page document with facing pages, InDesign always creates the first page on a single right-hand page and the last page on a single left-hand page. Figure 3 shows how InDesign, by default, would create a four-page document with a single right-hand page as the first page and a single left-hand page as the last page.

But what if you wanted to design those four pages as two spreads—what if you wanted the first page to be a left page?

You accomplish this in the Start # text box in the New Document dialog box. The number that you enter in this text box determines the page number of the first page and whether it is a left-hand or a right-hand page. If you enter a 2 (or any other even number), the first page will be a left-hand page. Figure 4 shows the same four-page document set up as two spreads. Note that the first page is page 2. It is a left-hand page. There is no page 1 in the document.

Modifying Margins and Columns

The New Document dialog box offers you options for specifying measurements for margins and the number of columns in the document. However, once you click OK, you cannot return to the New Document dialog box to modify those settings. The Document Setup dialog box allows you to change the page size and the number

of pages, among other choices, but it does not offer the option to modify the number of columns. But don't worry; once you've created a document, you can modify the number of columns with the Margins and Columns command on the Layout menu. Margins can be changed in the Document Setup dialog box *and* the Margins and Columns dialog boxes.

Figure 3 Four-page document set up as facing pages

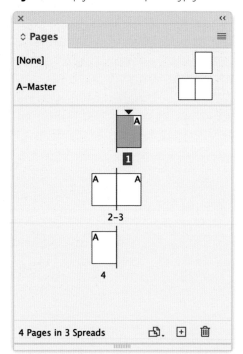

Figure 4 Four-page document set up as two spreads

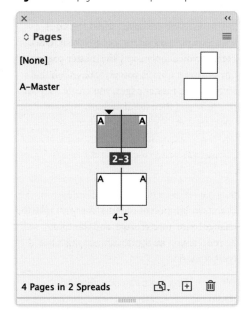

Understanding Master Pages

Imagine that you are creating a layout for a book and every chapter title page will have the same layout format. If that book had 20 chapters, you would need to create that chapter title page 20 times. And you'd need to be careful to make the layout consistent every time you created the page. Now imagine that you've finished your layout, but your editor wants you to change the location of the title on the page. That would mean making the same change—20 times!

Not so with master pages. **Master pages** are templates created for a page layout. Once created, you simply apply the master page to any document pages you want based on that layout. With master pages, you create a layout one time and then use it as many times as you like. Working with master pages spares you time-consuming repetition, and it offers consistency between document pages that are meant to have the same layout.

So what happens when your editor asks for that change in location of the title? Simply make the change to the master page, and the change will be reflected on all the document pages based on that master.

When you create a new document, one default master page is created and listed on the Pages panel, as shown in Figure 5. The Pages panel is command central for all things relating to pages and master pages. You use the Pages panel to add, delete, and apply master pages to document pages.

Figure 5 Default master page on the Pages panel

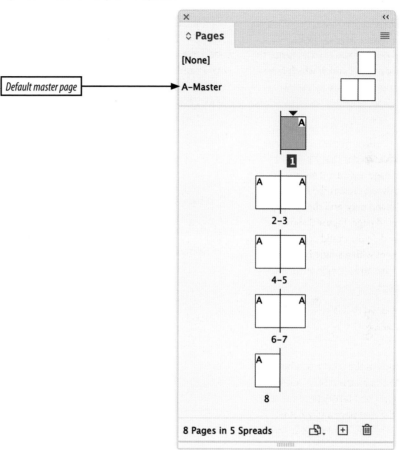

Default master page

Creating Master Items on Master Pages

In InDesign, text is positioned in text frames. **Text frames** are boxes created with the Type tool in which you type or place text. Graphics are positioned in graphics frames. **Graphics frames** are frames in which you place imported artwork. You use the Rectangle, Ellipse, or Polygon tools to create graphics frames.

When you create a frame for text or graphics on a master page, it is referred to as a **master item**. All objects on a master page are called master items and function as "placeholders" where objects on the document pages are to be positioned. For example, if you had a book broken down into chapters and you created a master page for the chapter title pages, you would create a text frame placeholder for the chapter title text. This text frame would appear on every document page that uses the chapter title master page. Working this way—with the text frame placeholder on the master page—you can feel certain that the location of the chapter title will be consistent on every chapter title page in the book.

Creating Guides

Guides, as shown in Figure 6, are horizontal or vertical lines that you position on a page. As their name suggests, guides are used to help guide you in aligning objects on the page. You have many options for creating guides. You can create them manually by "pulling" them out from the horizontal and vertical rulers. You can also use the Create Guides command on the Layout menu. Once created, guides can be selected, moved, and deleted, if necessary. You can also change the color of guides, which sometimes makes it easier to see them, depending on the colors used in your document.

TIP Press and hold [command] (Mac) or [Ctrl] (Win), then drag a guide from the horizontal ruler to create a guide that covers a spread instead of an individual page in a spread.

Figure 6 Identifying guides

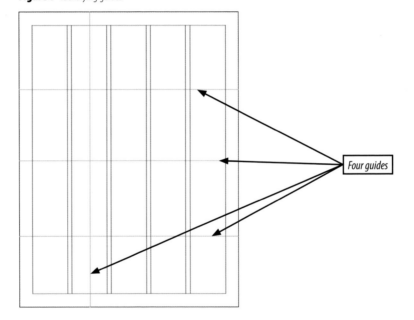

Four guides

Changing the Color of Guides, Margins, and Columns

By default, guides are cyan, column guides are violet, and margin guides are magenta. Depending on your preferences and the color of objects in the layout you are creating, you may want to change their colors.

In InDesign, you modify individual guide colors by selecting them, then clicking the Ruler Guides command on the Layout menu. Choosing a new color in the Ruler Guides dialog box affects only the selected guides. When you create more guides, they will be created in the default color.

You modify the default color of margins and columns in the Guides & Pasteboard section of the Preferences dialog box. Once you've modified the color of margins and columns, each new page you create in an existing document will appear with those colors. However, when you create a new document, the margins and columns will appear in their default colors.

Locking Column Guides

InDesign lets you lock column guides independently from any ruler guides you create. Click View on the menu bar, point to Grids & Guides, and then click Lock Column Guides to add or remove the check mark, which toggles the lock on or off. By default, column guides are locked.

Choosing Default Colors for Guides, Margins, and Columns

When you choose colors for guides, margins, and columns, you may want those choices to affect every document you create. You do so by making the color changes in the appropriate dialog boxes without any documents open. The new colors will be applied in all new documents created thereafter. Remember, if you change default colors when a document is open, the changes are only applied to that document.

Using the Transform Panel

The Transform panel identifies a selected object's width and height and its horizontal and vertical locations on the page. As shown in Figure 7, the width and height of the selected object appears in the Width and Height text boxes of the Transform panel.

When you position an object on a page, you need some way to describe that object's position on the page. InDesign defines the position of an object using X and Y Location values on the Transform panel. To work with X and Y locations, you first need to understand that the **zero point** of the page is, by default, at the top-left corner of the page. X and Y locations are made in reference to the zero point.

There are nine reference points on the Transform panel that correspond to the nine points available on a selected item's bounding box. Clicking a reference point tells InDesign that you wish to see the horizontal and vertical locations of that point of the selected object.

Figure 7 Transform panel shows location coordinates and size of selected frame

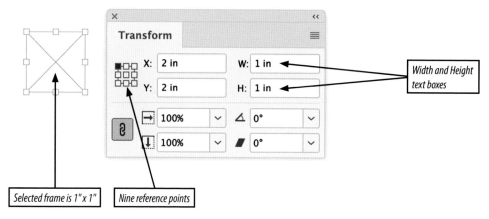

Width and Height text boxes

Selected frame is 1" x 1"   *Nine reference points*

When an object is selected, the X Location value is the horizontal location—how far it is across the page—and the Y Location value is the vertical location—how far it is down the page. The selected object in Figure 8 has an X Location of 1 inch and a Y Location of 1 inch. This means that its top-left point is 1 inch across the page and 1 inch down.

Why the top-left point? Because that is the reference point chosen on the Transform panel, also identified in Figure 8.

TIP X and Y Location values for circles are determined by the reference points of the bounding box that is placed around circles when they are selected.

Be sure to note that the text boxes on the Transform panel are interactive. For example, if you select an object and find that its X Location value is 2, you can enter 3 in the X Location text box, press [return] (Mac) or [Enter] (Win), and the object will be relocated to the new location on the page. You can also change the width or height of a selected object by changing the value in the Width or Height text boxes.

Figure 8 Identifying an object's X and Y locations

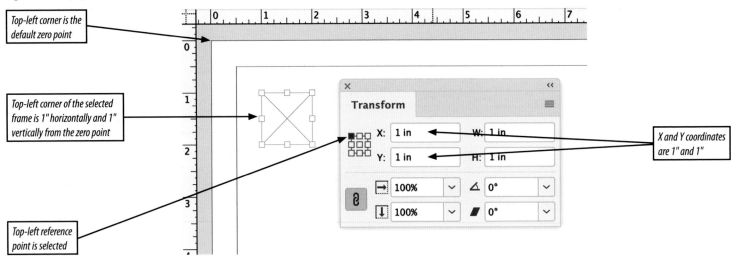

Top-left corner is the default zero point

Top-left corner of the selected frame is 1" horizontally and 1" vertically from the zero point

Top-left reference point is selected

X and Y coordinates are 1" and 1"

Using the Control Panel

You can think of the Control panel, docked at the top of the document window by default, as InDesign's "super panel." The Control panel mimics all the other panels, housing a wide variety of options for working with text and objects. Rather than always moving from one panel to another, you can usually find the option you are looking for on the Control panel.

The options on the Control panel change based on the type of object selected. For example, if a block of text is selected, the Control panel changes to show all the type-related options for modifying text, such as changing the font or font size. When any object is selected, the Control panel display is like the Transform panel. It offers X/Y coordinate reference points and text boxes and the same options for modifying a selected object. For example, you can change the width and height of a frame using the Control panel, just as you can with the Transform panel.

Unlike the Transform panel, the Control panel offers a multitude of additional options for working with frames, making the Control panel perhaps the most-used panel in InDesign. In Figure 9, the Control panel shows options for a selected graphics frame.

TIP You can perform calculations in the text boxes on the Transform panel. For example, you could select an object whose width is three inches. By typing 3 − .625 in the W text box, you can reduce the object's width to 2.375 inches. What a powerful feature!

TIP The Info panel displays information about the current document and selected objects, such as text and graphics frames. For example, if you click inside a text frame with the Type tool, the Info panel displays the number of characters, words, lines, and paragraphs in the frame. If you click the same text frame with the Selection tool, you can find out the size and location of the text frame. The Info panel is available only for viewing information. You cannot make changes to a selected object using this panel.

Using the Line Tool

The Line tool makes lines—no surprise there. Use the Line tool to make horizontal, vertical, and diagonal lines in your layouts. You can apply a fill color to a line, but generally speaking, you only want to stroke a line with color. You specify the weight of a line with the Stroke panel, and you can use the Line Length text box on the Control and Transform panels to specify the length. You can use all nine reference points on the Control and Transform panels to position a line in your layout.

Figure 9 Control panel

Transforming Objects

"Transform" is a term used to describe the act of moving, scaling, skewing, or rotating an object. You can do all of these actions on the Transform or Control panels. Figure 10 shows a rectangular frame that is 3" wide and 1.5" tall. Its center point is identified on the Transform panel because the center reference point is selected on the Transform panel. In Figure 11, the same frame has been rotated 90°—note the 90° value in the Rotation Angle text box on the Transform panel. Note also that the object was rotated at its center point. This is because the center reference point was selected when the transformation was executed. The center point of the rectangle was the point of origin for the transformation. The **point of origin** is the location on the object from which the transformation is executed. Whichever reference point is selected determines the point of origin for the transformation of the selected object.

Don't trouble yourself by trying to guess ahead of time how the choice of a point of origin and a transformation will affect an object. Sometimes it will be easy to foresee how the object will be transformed; sometimes you'll need to use trial and error. The important thing for you to remember is that the point of origin determines the point from which the transformation takes place.

Figure 10 A rectangle with its center point identified

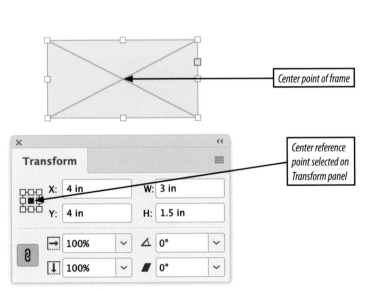

Center point of frame

Center reference point selected on Transform panel

Figure 11 Rectangle rotated 90 degrees at its center point

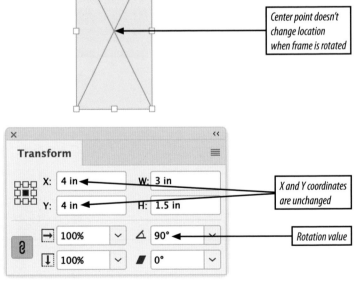

Center point doesn't change location when frame is rotated

X and Y coordinates are unchanged

Rotation value

Using the Transform Again Command

The Transform Again command is a powerful command that repeats the last transformation executed. For example, let's say you rotate a text frame. If you select another text frame and apply the Transform Again command, the same rotation will be applied to the second object. The Transform Again command is useful for creating multiple objects at specified distances.

View a multipage document

1. Open ID 3-1.indd.

TIP When you open the document, a warning stating some images are missing or need to be updated will show. Click Don't Update Links, and the file will open.

2. Press **[shift] [W]** to enter Presentation mode.

3. Use the **right** and **left arrow keys** on your computer keypad to view all the pages in the document.

The document is composed of five two-page spreads for a total of 10 pages. The document has been designed as a pamphlet for a travel company advertising destinations for a tour of Italy. Page numbers are visible at the bottom of every spread. The five spreads are based on three layout versions. The layout will be used for both a printed piece and for an interactive PDF that can be emailed.

4. Press **[esc]** to leave Presentation mode.

5. Press **[tab]** to show the panels, if necessary, then show the Pages panel.

The first page of the document is page 2, and it is a left-hand page.

6. View **spread 4–5**.

Spread 4–5, shown in Figure 12 along with other spreads, is the basis for the document you will build using master pages in this chapter.

7. Close the file without saving changes.

You viewed a finished document that will be the basis for the document you will build in this chapter.

Figure 12 Layouts used as the basis for this chapter

Set preferences and create a new document

1. Verify that no documents are open.

2. Click **InDesign (Mac)** or **Edit (Win)** on the menu bar, point to **Preferences**, then click **Units & Increments**.

3. Click the **Horizontal list arrow**, click **Inches**, click the **Vertical list arrow**, click **Inches**, then click **OK**.

4. Click **File** on the menu bar, point to **New**, then click **Document**.

5. Click the **Print category** at the top of the dialog box, then click **Letter** in the **Blank Document Presets section**.

6. On the right side of the New Document dialog box, highlight the "Untitled" text at the top, then type **Setup** for the filename.

7. Type **10** in the **Pages text box**, verify that the **Facing Pages check box** is checked, then verify that the **Start #** is set to **1**.

8. Type **6.25** in the **Width text box**, press **[tab]**, type **4.75** in the **Height text box**, then click the **Landscape Orientation button** ▤.

TIP Press [tab] to move your cursor forward from text box to text box in the New Document dialog box. Press [shift] [tab] to move backward from text box to text box.

9. In the **Columns section**, type **2**, then verify that the **Gutter text box** is set to **.1667 in**.

10. Type **.5** in the Top Margins text box, then verify that the **Make all settings the same button** ⊘ is activated.

11. Compare your dialog box to Figure 13, click **Create**, then look at the Pages panel.

    Page 1 is a single right-hand page, and page 10 is a single left-hand page.

Figure 13 Settings in the New Document dialog box

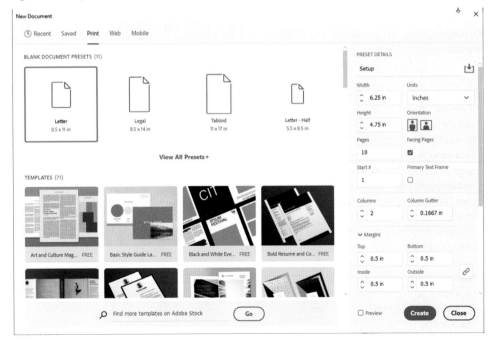

12. Click **File** on the menu bar, then click **Document Setup**.

Note that the Columns sections is not available in the Document Setup dialog box.

13. Change the **Start Page #** to **2**, click **OK**, then compare your Pages panel to Figure 14.

The document is now composed of five 2-page spreads, numbered 2–11. A reasonable question at this point would be "why create five spreads of ten 6.25" × 3.75" pages instead of as five 12.5" × 3.75" single pages?" By creating spreads, you have the option to print this as a document that folds into a 6.25" × 3.75" book or pamphlet. However, if you wanted to print it as a 12.5" × 3.75" printed book or pamphlet, the very same layout would service that choice as well. A document built as spreads can be output as single pages, folded pages, or as spreads.

14. Save your work, then continue to the next set of steps.

You set the Units & Increments preferences to specify that you will be working with inches for horizontal and vertical measurements. You then created a new document using the New Document dialog box. You specified the filename, number of pages in the document, page size for each page, and number of columns on each page. You then modified the start page number in the Document Setup dialog box to start the document on a left-hand page.

Modify margins and the number of columns on a master page

1. Set the **workspace** to **Essentials Classic**.

2. On the **Pages panel**, double-click the word **A-Master**, and note that *both* master pages in the Pages menu become blue and are targeted.

3. Note that the page menu at the lower-left corner of the document window lists A-Master.

A-Master is now the active page. You will modify the margins and the number of columns on a master page so your changes will be applied to all 10 document pages.

4. Click **Layout** on the menu bar, then click **Margins and Columns**.

The Margins and Columns dialog box opens.

5. Set the **number of columns** to **3**.

6. Reduce the **width of all four margins** to **.125 in**, then click **OK**.

Note that the width and height of the columns change to fill the area within the margins.

7. Save your work, then continue to the next set of steps.

You changed the number of columns and the width of margins on a master page.

USING THE MOVE PAGES COMMAND

If you have a multiple-page document, you can change the sequence of pages simply by moving them around on the Pages panel. Easy enough. But for documents with more pages—let's say 100 pages— dragging and dropping page icons on the Pages panel isn't so simple. Imagine, for example, trying to drag page 84 so it follows page 14. Whew! With InDesign's powerful Move Pages command, you can specify which pages you want to move and where you want to move them. Click the Pages panel menu button, click Move Pages, then specify options in the Move Pages dialog box. Be sure to check it out.

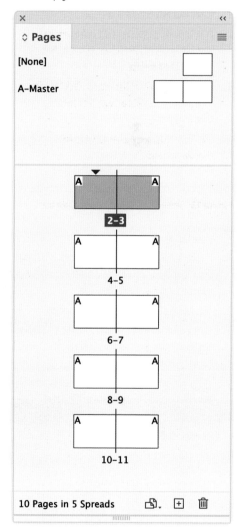

Figure 14 Pages panel showing a document starting on a left-hand page.

Add guides to a master page

1. If rulers are not visible at the top and left of the document window, click **View** on the menu bar, then click **Show Rulers**.

2. Click the **Selection tool** , position the **pointer over the horizontal ruler**, then click and slowly drag down a guide, releasing it anywhere on the page.

   A guide is positioned only on the left page of the spread.

   TIP As you drag the new guide onto the page, the value in the Y Location text box on the Control panel continually changes to show the guide's current location. See Figure 15.

3. Click **Edit** on the menu bar, then click **Undo Add New Guide**.

4. Press and hold **[command] (Mac)** or **[Ctrl] (Win)**, then drag down a **guide** from the horizontal ruler, releasing it anywhere on the page.

   The guide extends across the entire spread.

5. On the **Control panel**, type **2.5** in the **Y Location text box**, then press **[return] (Mac)** or **[Enter] (Win)**.

   The guide jumps to the specific vertical location you entered: 2.5" from the top of the page.

   TIP For this entire chapter, you can use the Transform panel interchangeably with the Control panel.

6. While pressing **[command] (Mac)** or **[Ctrl] (Win)**, drag a **second spread guide** from the horizontal ruler, drop the guide anywhere on the spread, then set its **Y Location** to **3.5 in**.

7. Click **InDesign (Mac)** or **Edit (Win)**, point to **Preferences**, then click **Units & Increments**.

8. In the **Ruler Units section**, verify that **Origin** is set to **Spread**, then click **OK**.

   With the Origin value set to Spread, the ruler and all X values are continuous across the entire spread. In other words, there's one ruler across both pages, as opposed to one ruler for the left page and another for the right page.

Figure 15 Using the Control panel to position a guide

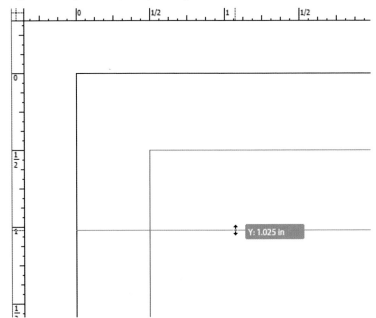

9. Drag a **guide from the vertical ruler** on the left side of the document window, then use the **Control panel** to position its **X value** at **8.35 in**.

10. Using the **Selection tool** ▶, click the **first horizontal guide** you positioned at **2.5 inches** to select it, double-click the **Y Location text box** on the Transform panel, type **3.4,** then press **[return] (Mac)** or **[Enter] (Win)**.

   The guide is moved to the new location.

TIP Selected guides appear darker blue.

11. Position a **third horizontal spread guide** at **3.25"** from the top of the page.

12. Compare your spread and guides to Figure 16, then save your work.

13. Continue to the next set of steps.

You positioned guides on the master page by dragging them from the horizontal and vertical rulers. You used the Control panel to position them at precise locations.

Figure 16 Master spread with guides in position

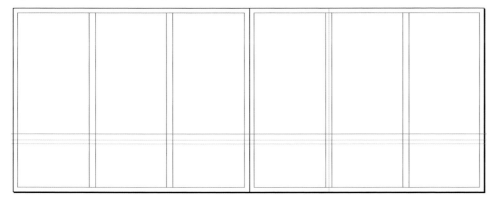

WORKING WITH CONDITIONAL TEXT

Using conditional text is a great way to create different versions of the same InDesign document. You create conditional text by first creating conditions and then applying them to text. Later, you hide or show the text that has the condition applied to it by hiding or showing conditions using the Conditional Text panel. Showing and hiding conditions works just like showing and hiding layers on the Layers panel. You assign a new condition to text, and then hide it by clicking the "Eye" (visibility) icon on the Conditional Text panel. When you have many conditions, you can create a **condition set**, which is a snapshot of the current visibility of the applied conditions. Click the Conditional Text panel menu button, then click Show Options. On the Conditional Text panel, click the Set list arrow, then click Create New Set. Name the set, then click OK. Instead of turning individual conditions on or off on the panel, you can choose a condition set to do the same job in one step.

Create placeholder text frames

1. Verify that the **fill and stroke buttons** on the toolbar are both set to **[None]**.

2. Click the **Type tool** T , then drag to create a **small text frame** anywhere in the rightmost column above the horizontal guides.

3. Click the **Selection tool** ▶ drag the **left and right handles** of the text frame so it is the full width of the column.

4. Drag the **bottom handle** down until it snaps to the topmost horizontal guide.

5. On the Control panel, click the **bottom-center reference point**, type **1.375** in the **Height text box**, then press **[return] (Mac)** or **[Enter] (Win)**.

   Your right page should resemble Figure 17.

6. Press and hold **[shift] [option] (Mac)** or **[Shift] [Alt] (Win)**, then drag and drop a **copy of the text frame** into the column to the left so your page resembles Figure 18.

   Note that the new text frames are difficult to distinguish from the ruler guides.

7. Save your work, then continue to the next set of steps.

You created two text frames, which will be used as placeholders for body copy in the document.

Figure 17 Positioning the text frame

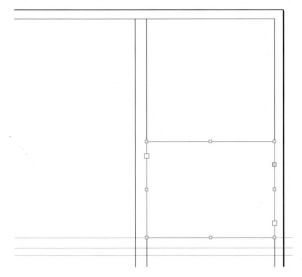

Figure 18 Duplicated text frame

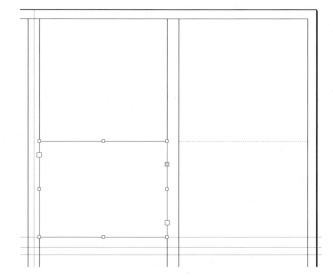

Change the color of guides, margins, and columns

1. Click **InDesign (Mac)** or **Edit (Win)** on the menu bar, point to **Preferences**, then click **Guides & Pasteboard**.

2. Verify that the **Guides in Back check box** is unchecked.

   When this option is deactivated, guides appear in front of all items on the document rather than hidden behind them.

3. In the **Color section**, click the **Margins list arrow**, then click **Light Gray**.

4. Click the **Columns list arrow**, then click **Light Gray**.

5. Click **OK**.

6. Click the **Selection tool** ▶, click the **vertical guide** to select it, press and hold **[shift]**, then click the **three horizontal guides** so all the guides you created are selected.

   All four guides appear dark blue.

7. Click **Layout** on the menu bar, then click **Ruler Guides**.

8. Click the **Color list arrow**, click **Red**, then click **OK**.

9. Click the **pasteboard** to deselect the guides, then compare your page to Figure 19.

You changed the color of margins, columns, and guides to improve your ability to distinguish text frames from page guides.

Figure 19 Viewing changed guide colors

Create color tint frames

1. Verify that the **fill and stroke buttons** on the toolbar are both set to **[None]**.

TIP You will learn much more about fills and strokes in Chapters 4 and 5.

2. Click the **Rectangle tool** 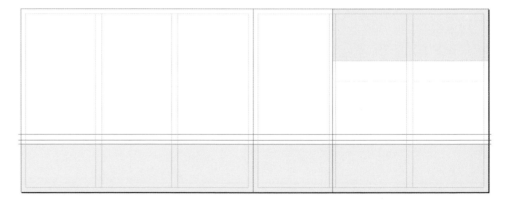, then drag a **small rectangle** anywhere **above the two text frames** in the two rightmost columns.

3. Click the **Selection tool** , click **Window** on the menu bar, point to **Object & Layout**, then click **Transform**.

The Transform panel appears.

4. Drag the **left handle** of the frame so it snaps to the red vertical guide.

TIP To verify that Snap to Guides is activated, click View on the menu bar, then point to Grids & Guides.

5. Drag the **right handle** of the frame so it snaps to the right edge of the document.

The Width text box on the Transform panel should read 4.15 in.

6. Drag the **top handle** of the frame so it snaps to the top edge of the document.

7. On the Transform panel, click the **top-center reference point**, then verify that the **Y text box** on the Transform panel reads **0**.

If the top edge of the frame is aligned to the top edge of the page, its Y coordinate must be zero.

8. On the Transform panel, change the **Height value** to **1.35 in**.

Because the Units & Increments preferences are set to Inches, you do not need to—nor should you—type the abbreviation for inches in the text box. Just type the number.

TIP Don't deselect the frame.

9. Fill the **frame** with **yellow**.

TIP Choose any shade of yellow.

10. Drag and drop a **copy of the yellow frame** straight down to the bottom of the page.

11. Drag the **top edge of the frame** down so it aligns with the bottommost of the three guides.

12. Drag the **left edge** to align with the left edge of the document.

Your spread should resemble Figure 20. The Width & Height text boxes on the Transform panel should read 12.5 in and 1.25 in, respectively.

13. Deselect all, then on the Swatches panel, click a **light blue swatch**.

14. Create a **small rectangle** anywhere in the **upper-left section** of the document.

The new rectangle is created with the light blue fill.

15. Click the **top-left reference point** on the Transform panel, enter **0** in the **X text box**, press **[tab]**, enter **0** in the **Y text box**, press **[tab]**, type **8.35** in the **Width text box**, press **[tab]**, then enter **3.4** in the **Height text box**.

16. Save your work, then continue to the next set of steps.

You created three color-filled frames on the page and used the Transform panel to position them and modify their sizes.

Figure 20 Two yellow rectangle frames positioned on the spread

Use the Line tool

1. Close the Transform panel, click **anywhere in the pasteboard** to deselect all, then click the **Line tool** / .

2. Position the **cursor** at the left edge of the document, press and hold **[shift]**, then click and drag to create a **line of any length**.

   Pressing and holding [shift] constrains the line so it is straight. Regardless of which colors are on the toolbar, once you create a line, both the fill and stroke colors change to [None]. A bounding box appears around the line.

3. Click the **stroke button** on the toolbar, then click **[Black]** on the Swatches panel.

4. Expand the **Stroke panel**, then increase the **Weight** to **4 pt**.

5. On the Control panel, click the **middle-left reference point**, type **0** in the **X text box**, press **[tab]**, type **3.5** in the **Y text box**, press **[tab]**, then type **12.5** in the **L (length) text box** so your spread resembles Figure 21.

6. Save your work, then continue to the next set of steps.

You created a line with the Line tool, specified its color and weight, then positioned it on the spread and specified its length with the Control panel.

Figure 21 Viewing the line

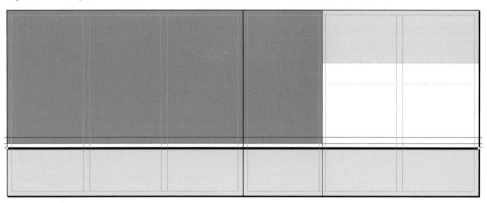

Use the Transform Again command

1. Click the **Rectangle tool** 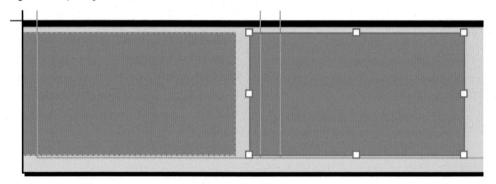, then draw a **small rectangle** in the first column anywhere at the bottom of the page.

2. On the Control panel, click the **top-left reference point**, type **0** in the **X text box**, type **3.6** in the **Y text box**, type **1.8** in the **Width text box**, then type **1** in the **Height text box**.

3. Press the **letter [I]** on your keypad to access the **Eyedropper tool**, then click the **large blue frame** at the top of the page.

   The Eyedropper tool samples the fill and stroke colors from the large frame; the small rectangle takes on the same fill and stroke color.

4. Press the **letter [V]** to access the **Selection tool** ▶ press and hold **[shift] [option] (Mac)** or **[Shift] [Alt] (Win)**, then drag a **copy** that is positioned approximately ⅛" **to the right of the original**, as shown in Figure 22.

5. Click **Object** on the menu bar, point to **Transform Again**, then click **Transform Again**.

   Step 4 is repeated, and a third frame is added.

6. Apply the **Transform Again command** two more times.

7. Select the **five small blue frames**.

8. On the Control panel, click the **center reference point**.

   With the center reference point selected, the X/Y coordinates on the Control panel now identify the center point of all five frames as a unit.

9. On the Control panel, change the **X value** to **6.25**.

As 6.25 is half of the full horizontal width of 12.5," the five frames, as a unit, are centered horizontally on the page.

10. Compare your layout to Figure 23, then save your work.

    Note that the 10 document pages on the Pages panel display an A because they are based on the A-Master by default. Their thumbnail icons reflect all the objects currently on the A-Master.

11. Continue to the next lesson.

You created a single rectangle, then changed its fill and stroke colors with the Eyedropper tool. You duplicated the rectangle with the drag-and-drop method and used the Transform Again command three times. You used the Control panel to center all five frames as a unit.

Figure 22 Duplicating the frame

Figure 23 Viewing five frames centered horizontally on the spread

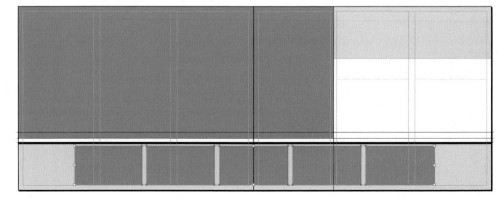

CREATE TEXT ON MASTER PAGES

▶ **What You'll Do**

In this lesson, you will position two headlines on a master page, create automatic page numbering, and create two new master pages.

Creating a New Master Page

You create new master pages by clicking the New Master command on the Pages panel menu. When you create a new master page, you have the option of giving the master page a new name. This is useful for distinguishing one master page from another. For example, you might want to use the name "Body Copy" for master pages that will be used for body copy and then use the name "Chapter Start" for master pages that will be used as a layout for a chapter title page.

When you create a new master page, you have the option of changing the values for the margins and for the number of columns on the new master page.

Loading Master Pages

You can load master pages from one InDesign document to another by clicking the Pages panel menu button, pointing to Master Pages, then clicking Load Master Pages. You will be prompted to navigate to the file that has the master pages you wish to load. Select the InDesign document, then click Open. The master pages are added to the Pages panel. You will be prompted to rename master pages that have the same name or replace the existing master pages.

Creating Automatic Page Numbering

When you create a document with multiple pages, chances are you'll want to have page numbers on each page. You could create a text frame on every page and then manually type the page number on every page, but think of what a nightmare that could turn out to be! You would have to create a text frame of the same size and in the same location on every page. Imagine what would happen if you were to remove or add a page to the middle of the document—you'd need to go back and renumber your pages!

Fortunately, InDesign offers a solution for this. You can create placeholder text frames for page numbers on your master pages. Click inside the text frame, click Type on the menu bar, point to Insert Special Character, point to Markers, then click Current Page Number. A letter will appear in the text frame, as shown in Figure 24.

That letter represents the page number. You can format it using any font, size, and alignment that you desire. On document pages based on that master, the letter in the text frame will appear as the number of the page. Page numbering is automatic. This means that the page number is automatically updated when pages are added or removed from the document.

When you work with multiple master pages, make sure that each page number placeholder is the same size, in the same location, and in the same format on each master page. This will make the appearance of page numbers consistent throughout the document, regardless of the master upon which a particular document page is based.

Inserting Space Between Characters

In Chapter 2, you learned that you should not press the space bar more than once to create extra spacing between characters. However, sometimes a single space does not provide enough space between words or characters. You may want to insert additional space to achieve a certain look. You could tab the text, or as you'll learn in this lesson, you can insert white space.

Figure 24 A text frame on a master page containing an auto page number character

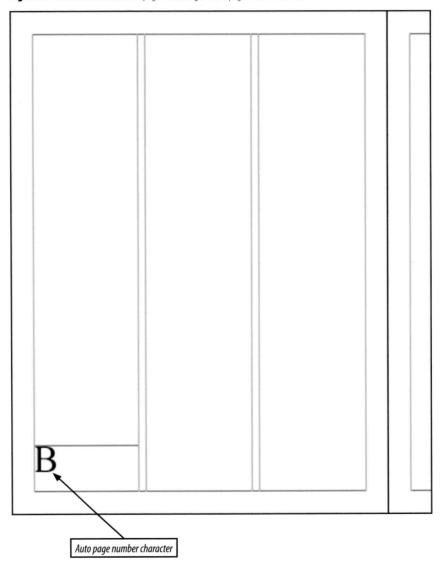

Auto page number character

The Type menu contains commands for inserting white space between words or characters. The two most-used white spaces are em space and en space. The width of an **em space** is equivalent to that of the lowercase letter m in the current typeface at that type size. The width of an **en space** is narrower—that of the lowercase letter n in that typeface at that type size. Use these commands—not the space bar—to insert white space. To insert an em space or an en space, click Type on the menu bar, point

to Insert White Space, then click either Em Space or En Space. Figure 25 shows an em space between a page number placeholder and a word.

Inserting Em Dashes and En Dashes

Sometimes you'll want to put a dash between words or characters, and you'll find that the dash created by pressing the hyphen key is not wide enough. That's because hyphens are shorter than dashes.

InDesign offers two types of dashes to insert between words or characters—the em dash and the en dash. The width of an em dash is equivalent to that of the lowercase letter m in the current typeface at that type size. The width of an en dash is narrower—that of the lowercase letter n in that typeface at that type size. To insert an em dash or an en dash, click Type on the menu bar, point to Insert Special Character, point to Hyphens and Dashes, then click either Em Dash or En Dash. Figure 26 shows an example of an en dash.

Figure 25 Identifying an em space

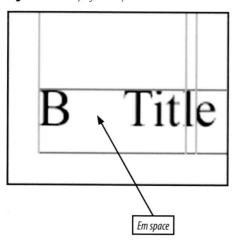

Em space

Figure 26 Identifying an en dash

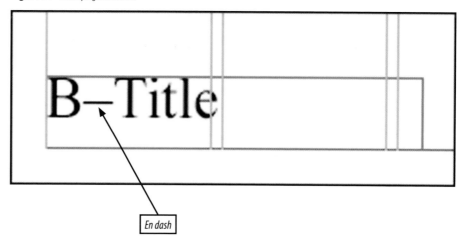

En dash

Sometimes, with certain layouts, not all your content will be right side up on your page spread. For example, you might be designing a poster that will fold four ways, so when the poster is laid out flat in your InDesign document, some of the content will be rotated on its side—or maybe even upside down! Whatever the case, when you're working with these types of layouts, you don't need to lie on your side or do a headstand to see your work right side up. Instead, use the Rotate Spread View command on the Pages panel (it's a submenu of Page Attributes) or the Rotate Spread command on the View menu. These commands rotate the view of the spread so you can work right side up. They don't affect the content on the page—just the view.

Creating a New Master Page Based on Another Master Page

Imagine that you've created a master page for a magazine layout. The master contains master items for the headline, the body copy, and the page number. It also contains master items for pictures that will appear on the page. Now imagine that you need to create another master page that will be identical to this master page, with the one exception that this new master will not contain frames for graphics. You wouldn't want to duplicate all the work you did to create the first master, would you?

To avoid repeating efforts and to create consistency between masters, you can create a new master page based on another master page. The new master would appear identical to the first. You would then modify only the elements that you want to change on the new master, keeping all the elements that you don't want to change perfectly consistent with the previous one.

Basing a new master on another master is not the same thing as duplicating a master. Duplicating a master creates a copy, but the original and the copy have no relationship.

When you base a new master on another, any changes you make to the first master will be updated on masters based on it. Think of how powerful this is. Let's say that your editor tells you to change the type size of the page numbers. Making a change in only one place offers you a substantial savings in time and effort and provides you with the certainty that the page numbers will be consistent from master to master.

Remember that all master items on new master pages will also be locked by default. To unlock a master item, you must press and hold or [shift] [command] (Mac) or [Shift] [Ctrl] (Win) to select those objects on the new master. InDesign does this so you don't accidentally move or delete objects from the new master or the original master.

Add placeholders for headlines

1. Verify that the **fill and stroke** on the toolbar are both set to **[None]**.

2. Click the **Type tool** T, then drag a **small rectangle** anywhere in the two rightmost columns above the two text frames already there.

3. Click the **Selection tool** ▶, then drag the **left handle** of the frame so it snaps to the red vertical guide.

4. Drag the **right handle** of the frame so it snaps to the right edge of the document.

   The Width text box on the Control panel should read 4.15 in.

5. Click the **bottom-center reference point** on the Control panel, then enter **1.35** in the **Y text box**.

   The text frame moves to align its bottom edge to the Y coordinate.

6. On the Control panel, change the **Height value** to **1.2**.

7. Click the **Type tool** T, click **inside the new frame**, then type **LOCATION** in all caps.

8. On the Control panel, click the **Align center button** ≡ to center the text.

9. Select the **text**, set the **typeface** to **Hobo Std Medium**, set the **Font Size** to **60 pt.**, then set the **Horizontal Scale** to **75%**.

10. Enter **[command] [B] (Mac)** or **[Ctrl] [B] (Win)** to open the **Text Frame Options dialog box**, click the **Align list arrow**, click **Bottom**, then click **OK**.

11. Deselect, then compare your text to Figure 27.

12. Click the **Selection tool** ▶ , press and hold **[shift] [option] (Mac)**, or **[Shift] [Alt] (Win)**, then drag and drop a **copy of the text frame** anywhere straight down below the original.

13. Click the **Type tool** T , select the **duplicated text**, reduce the **Font Size** to **24 pt.**, then type **day/date** in all lowercase letters.

14. Click the **Selection tool** ▶ , then verify that the **bottom-center reference point** on the Control panel is selected.

15. Type **1.75** in the **Y text box**, type **.35** in the **Height text box**, then compare your layout to Figure 28.

16. Save your work, then continue to the next set of steps.

You created and positioned two text frames on the master page, then formatted text in each.

Figure 27 Formatted headline on a master page

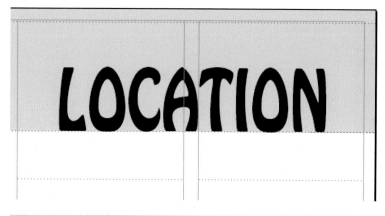

Figure 28 Formatted sub-headline on a master page

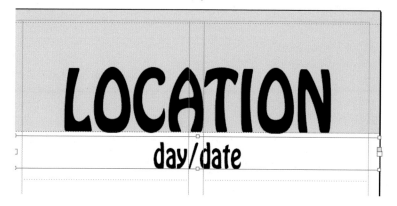

Create automatic page numbering and insert white space between characters

1. Click the **Type tool** T , draw a **text frame** anywhere in the **lower-right corner** of the spread, set its **Width** to **1.25"**, then set its **Height** to **.25"**.

2. Position the **text frame** in the **lower-right corner** inside the margin guide.

3. Type **City** in the text frame with no space after the word, choose any typeface and size you like, then verify that the text cursor is blinking to the right of the word.

4. Click **Type** on the menu bar, point to **Insert Special Character**, point to **Markers**, then click **Current Page Number**.

   The letter A appears in the text frame because this is the A-Master Page. This letter A will change on document pages to reflect the current document page. For example, on page 4, the A will appear as the number 4.

5. Click the **cursor between the y and the A**, click **Type** on the menu bar, point to **Insert White Space**, then click **Em Space**.

6. On the Control panel, set the **text** to **Align Right,** click **Object** on the menu bar, click **Text Frame Options**, then set the **Vertical Justification** to **Bottom.**

   Your text box should resemble Figure 29.

7. Copy the **selected text frame,** paste it in place, click the **bottom-left reference**

point on the Control panel, then change the **X value** to **.125**.

   The text frame moves to the left page, inside the margin guide.

8. Reformat the text so the copied text frame resembles Figure 30.

TIP You copy and paste the em space just like any other character.

9. Save your work, then continue to the next set of steps.

You created automatic page numbering on the right and left pages of the master page and inserted em spaces.

Figure 29 Formatted text on the right-hand page

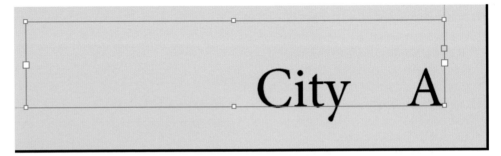

Figure 30 Reformatted text on the left-hand page

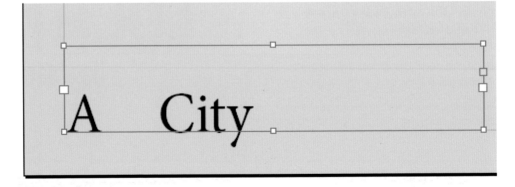

Create a new master page spread based on another master page spread

1. Expand the Pages panel, if necessary, click the **Pages panel menu button** ≡ , then click **New Master**.

2. Enter the settings shown in Figure 31, then click **OK**.

    The B-Master page icons are added to the Pages panel. Note that the B-Master icons on the Pages panel show an A because the B-Master is based on A-Master.

3. Double-click **B-Master** on the Pages panel to view the B-Master master page.

    B-Master is identical to A-Master, except that the automatic page number reads B rather than A.

4. Hide the guides.

5. Click the **Selection tool** ▶ , then try to select objects on the page.

    Objects on a master page based on another master cannot be selected in the standard way.

6. Press and hold **[shift] [command] (Mac)** or **[Shift] [Ctrl] (Win)**, then drag a **marquee** to select the elements shown in Figure 32.

TIP Make sure you start dragging on the pasteboard and not on the document or else you might accidentally select and move an object on the master.

Continued on next page

Figure 31 Settings for a new master page based on the A-Master

Figure 32 Selecting specific page elements

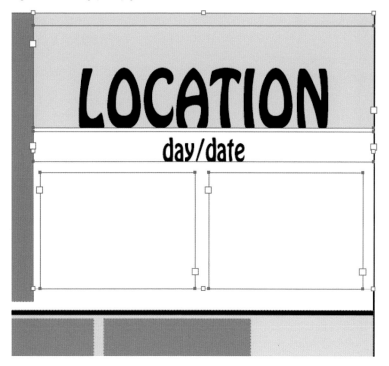

7. On the Control panel, click the **middle-left reference point**, then set the **X value** to **0**.

8. Select the **large blue frame**, click the **middle-right reference point** on the Control panel, then set the **X value** to **12.5**.

   Your B-Master spread should resemble Figure 33.

9. Save your work, then continue to the next set of steps.

You created a new master spread based on the A-Master spread. You modified the location of elements on the new master to differentiate it from the original.

Create a new blank master page spread

1. Click the **Pages panel menu button** , then click **New Master**.

2. Click the **Based on Master list arrow**, then verify that **None** is selected so your New Master dialog box resembles Figure 34.

3. Click **OK**.

   C-Master appears as two blank page thumbnails on the Pages panel.

4. Double-click the words **A-Master** in the top part of the Pages panel to view the A-Master spread, select all, then copy.

Figure 33 Five frames centered horizontally on the spread

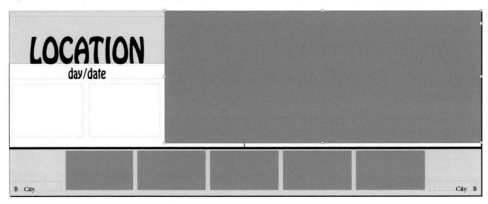

Figure 34 Creating a new master page not based on any other master

5. Double-click **C-Master** to view the C-Master spread, click **Edit** on the menu bar, click **Paste in Place,** then deselect all.

The A-Master layout is pasted into the C-Master spread. The only change is that the automatic page numbering reads C.

6. Click the **Selection tool** 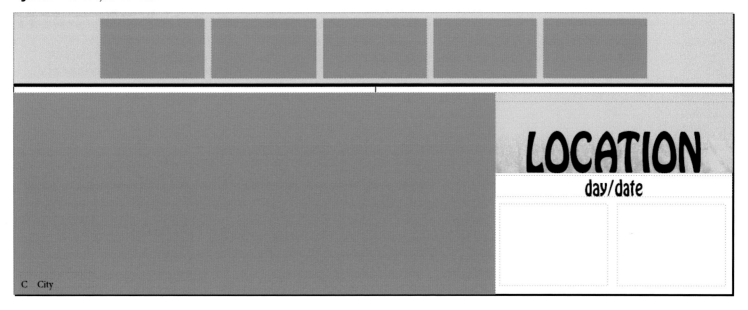, if necessary, then select the **five blue frames** at the bottom of the page as well as the **yellow frame** behind them.

Because C-Master is not based on A-Master, the items are not locked.

TIP Be sure you don't select either of the two automatic page number text boxes.

7. On the Control panel, click the **top-center reference point**, then set the **Y value** to **0**.

8. Click **Object** on the menu bar, then click **Hide**.

9. Select **all the objects above the horizontal black line**, click the **bottom-center reference point** on the Control panel, then set the **Y value** to **4.75**.

10. Delete the **automatic numbering text frame** at the bottom of the right-hand page.

Pages based on the C-Master will have page numbers only on the left page of the spread.

11. Show the **hidden frames**, then deselect all.

TIP To show the hidden frames, click Object on the menu bar, then click Show All on Spread.

12. Select the **large yellow frame** at the top of the page, click the **bottom-center reference point** on the Control panel, then note the **Y value**.

13. Select the **horizontal black line,** then set the **Y value** to be the same Y value you just noted.

Your C-Master spread should resemble Figure 35.

14. Save your work, then continue to the next lesson.

You created a new blank master spread not based on any other master. You modified the location of elements on the new master to differentiate it from the original.

Figure 35 Modified layout in C-Master

LOCATION
day/date

C   City

APPLY MASTER PAGES TO DOCUMENT PAGES

▶ *What You'll Do*

In this lesson, you will apply master pages to document pages.

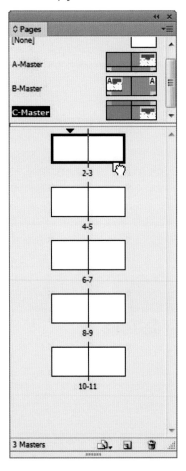

Applying Master Pages to Document Pages

Once you have created master pages, you then use the Pages panel to apply them to the document pages. One method for applying master pages is the drag-and-drop method. Using this method, you drag the master page icon or the master page name, in the top section of the Pages panel, down to the page icons in the lower section of the Pages panel. To apply the master to a single page, you drag the master onto the page icon. To apply the master to a spread, you drag the master onto one of the four corners until you see a dark border around both pages in the spread.

When you apply a master page to a document page, the document page inherits all the layout characteristics of the master.

> **TIP** You can apply the default None master page to a document page when you do not want the document page to be based on a master.

A second method for applying master pages to document pages is to use the Apply Master to Pages command on the Pages panel menu. The Apply Master dialog box allows you to specify which master you want to apply to which pages. What's great about this method is that you can apply a master to any page in the document—even inconsecutive pages—in one move. If you want to apply a master to multiple pages, use the Apply Master dialog box; it's faster than dragging and dropping.

Apply master pages to document pages

1. Click the **Pages panel menu button** ≡ , then click **Panel Options.**

2. In the **Pages section** at top, change the **Size** to **Extra Large**, then click **OK**.

   The page icons on the Pages panel are enlarged. Because the three master pages are similar in color, having larger page thumbnails will make it easier to see which masters have been applied to which spreads.

3. Scroll through the document and note that the A-Master has been automatically applied to all the pages in the document.

4. On the Pages panel, drag **B-Master by its name** to the **upper-left corner of spread 4–5** until a frame appears around the spread, as shown in Figure 36, then release the mouse button.

5. Using the same method, apply the **C-Master** to **spread 6–7**.

6. Click the **Pages panel menu button** ≡ , then click **Apply Master to Pages**.

Continued on next page

Figure 36 Applying the B-Master to the 4–5 spread

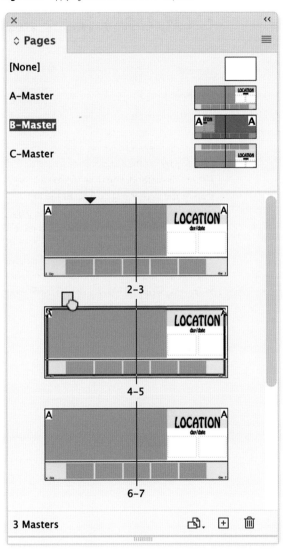

7. Click the **Apply Master list arrow**, then click **B-Master**.

8. Type **10–11** in the **To Pages text box**, then click **OK**.

   The master is applied to the spread. Your Pages panel should resemble Figure 37.

9. Navigate to **page 2**, then switch to **Presentation mode**.

10. Navigate through the spreads to see the masters applied and the automatic page numbering.

11. Exit **Presentation mode**, then save your work.

12. Continue to the next lesson.

You applied master spreads to document spreads using the drag-and-drop method and the Apply Master to Pages command.

Figure 37 Pages panel reflecting applied masters

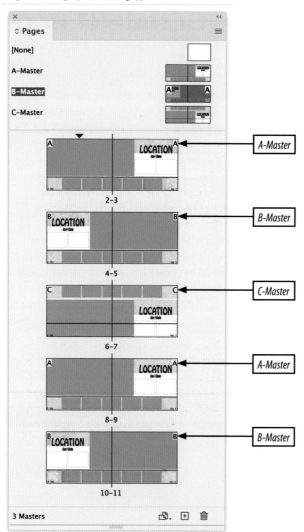

MODIFY MASTER PAGES AND DOCUMENT PAGES

▶ *What You'll Do*

In this lesson, you will make modifications to both master pages and document pages and explore how each affects the other.

Modifying Master Pages

When you modify a master item on a master page, that modification will be reflected on all document pages based on that master page. This is a powerful option. Let's say that you have created a layout for a 36-page book, and you decide that you want to change the typeface of all the headlines. If they were created on master pages, you could simply reformat the headline in the text frame placeholder on the master pages, and every document page in the book based on it would be updated.

Overriding Master Items on Document Pages

Master pages are designed to allow you to lay out the basic elements for a page that will be used repeatedly throughout a document. In most cases, however, you will want to make modifications to the document page once it is created—you might even want to delete some objects on the document page that were created on the master page.

Master page items on document pages are fixed objects and cannot be selected with normal methods.

You can modify a master page item on a document page, however, by overriding. You override a master item by pressing and holding [shift] [command] (Mac) or [Shift] [Ctrl] (Win), then clicking a master item. This makes the item selectable.

You might find that fixed master items on document pages are annoying! Long after the master page has served its purpose, you will find—especially with long documents—that the inability to just simply select master items with the Selection tool impedes your progress. You can quickly override all master items on a targeted document page by clicking Override All Master Page Items on the Pages panel menu.

Making changes to a document page is often referred to as making a local change. When you override a master item, that item nevertheless maintains its status as a master item and will still be updated with changes to the master page. For example, if you resize a master item on a document page, but you do not change its color, it will retain its new size, but if the color of the master item is changed on the master page, the master item's color will be updated on the document page.

Once a master item has been released from its fixed position, it remains selectable. You can return a master item on a document page back to its original state by selecting the item, clicking the Pages panel menu button, then clicking Remove Selected Local Overrides.

Detaching Master Items

When you are sure you no longer want a master item to be affected by updates made to the associated master page, you can detach a master item. To detach a master item, you must first override it by pressing and holding [shift] [command] (Mac) or [Shift] [Ctrl] (Win) while selecting it. Next, click the Pages panel menu button, point to Master Pages, then click Detach Selection from Master.

That's the official move. Note, though, that when you modify text in a text frame on a document page, the relationship between the text on the document page and the text on the master page tends to detach automatically. Therefore, when it comes to text, it's a smart idea to use master pages for the placement of text frames on the page but use character and paragraph styles for global formatting of the text itself.

Override master items on a document page

1. Verify that the document has been saved.

2. Double-click the **page 3 icon** on the Pages panel, click the **Selection tool** ▶, then try to select any of the objects on the page.

   Because all objects on page 3 are master items, they're fixed and cannot be selected with standard methods.

3. Press and hold **[shift] [command] (Mac)** or **[Shift] [Ctrl] (Win)**, then click the word **LOCATION**.

4. Click the **Type tool** T , select the **text**, type **MANAROLA**, then click the **pasteboard** to deselect.

5. Save your work, then continue to the next set of steps.

You overrode a master item on a document page.

Modify master items on a master page

1. Double-click the **right-hand page in the A-Master**, select the word **city**, the **em space**, and the **automatic page icon**, then set the **Font Size** to **12 pt.** and the **typeface** to **Times New Roman Regular**.

   This typeface is commonly available, but if you don't have it, use a similar serif face like Times, Garamond, or Baskerville.

2. Select only the word **City**, then change its **typeface** to **Times New Roman Italic**.

3. Make the same changes to the text on the bottom of the left-hand page of the spread.

   All the changes you are making to the A-Master are automatically updated on the B-Master but not on the C-Master.

4. Double-click the word **LOCATION** to select it, click the **Swatches panel**, then click **[Paper]**.

   The fill color of the text changes to white.

5. Click the **Selection tool** ▶ , select the **two yellow frames** on the page, then change their **fill color** to **green**.

6. Select the **black horizontal line**, then change its **stroke color** to **red**.

   Your A-Master should resemble Figure 38.

7. Double-click **B-Master**.

   All the changes you made to A-Master, except one, are reflected on B-Master because B-Master was created based on A-Master. Note, however, the headline on B-Master is still black. Type tends to behave unpredictably on master pages. The fact that this frame has been relocated from its original position might explain why it didn't update.

8. Double-click **C-Master** to view the spread.

   None of the changes from A-Master affect C-Master.

9. View **spread 8–9**.

   All the changes you made on the master page, including the white headline, are reflected on the spread.

10. View **spread 2–3**.

    All the changes you made on the master page, except the white headline, are reflected on the spread. This is because you formatted the headline locally on the page itself. The change on the master page after the fact did not override the formatting you applied on the page.

11. Save your work, then continue to the next set of steps.

You modified elements on the A-Master and noted how those modifications affected B-Master, C-Master, and the pages in the document.

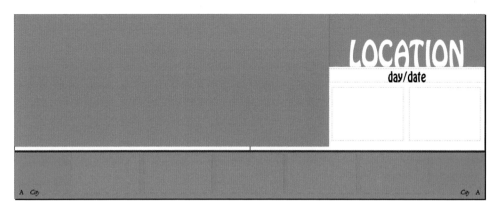

Figure 38 A-Master modifications

Remove local overrides and detach master items

1. View **spread 10–11**, then select the **large blue frame**.

2. Click the **Pages panel menu button** ☰, point to **Master Pages**, then click **Detach Selection from Master**.

3. Double-click **B-Master**, then change the **fill color** on the **large blue frame** to **red**.

4. Scroll through the document to note the changes.

   The change is reflected on spread 4–5, but not on spread 10–11.

5. Navigate to **page 3** in the document, click the **Selection tool** ▶, then select the **text frame of MANAROLA**.

6. Click the **Pages panel menu button** ☰, point to **Master Pages**, then click **Remove Selected Local Overrides**.

7. Save your work, then close the Setup document.

You detached a frame from its master. You then modified the master, noting that the change did not affect the detached frame. You selected a modified master item on a document page, then used the Remove Selected Local Overrides command to restore the item's relationship to its master.

PLACE AND THREAD TEXT

▶ *What You'll Do*

In this lesson, you will place text, thread text from frame to frame, then view text threads.

MANAROLA
tuesday august 9

Lorem ipsum dolor sit amet, consect etuer adipiscing elit, sed diam no nummy nibh euismod tincidunt ut laoreet dolore magna aliquam volutpat. Ut wisi enim ad veniam, quis nostrud exerci ullamcorper suscipit lobortis n aliquip ex ea commodo consec Duis autem vel eum iriure dolor i hendrerit in vulputate velit esse molestie consequat, vel illum dolore

Placing Text

Once you have created a text frame—either on a master page or on a document page—you can type directly into the frame, or you can place text from another document into it. When creating headlines, you usually type them directly into the text frame. When creating body copy, however, you will often find yourself placing text from another document, usually a word processing document.

Placing text in InDesign is simple and straightforward. Click the Place command on the File menu, which opens the Place dialog box. Find the text document that you want to place, then click Open.

The pointer changes to the loaded text icon. With a loaded text icon, you can drag to create a text frame or click inside an existing text frame. When you position the loaded text icon over an existing text frame, the icon appears in parentheses, as shown in Figure 39. The parentheses indicate that you can click to place the text into the text frame. Do so, and the text flows into the text frame, as shown in Figure 40.

| **TIP** The loaded text icon displays a thumbnail image of the first few lines of text that is being placed. This helps to make sure you are placing the correct file.

Figure 39 Loaded text icon positioned over a text frame

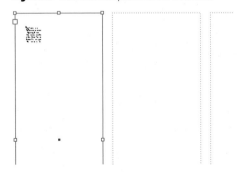

Figure 40 Text placed into a text frame

Text placed in text frame

Threading Text

InDesign provides many options for **threading** text—linking text from one text frame to another. Text frames have an in port and an out port. The **in port** is a small box in the upper left corner of a text frame that you can click to flow text from another text frame. The **out port** is a small box in the lower right corner of a text frame that flows text out to another text frame when clicked.

When threading text, you use the text frame ports to establish connections between the text frames.

In Figure 41, the center text frame is selected, and the in port and out port are identified.

The in port represents where text would flow into the text frame, and the out port represents from where text would flow out.

In the same figure, note that the out port on the first text frame is red and has a plus sign in its center. This indicates the presence of **overset text**—more text than can fit in the frame.

To thread text manually from the first text frame to the second, first click the Selection tool, then click the frame with the overset text so the frame is highlighted. Next, click the out port of the text frame. When you position your cursor over the next text frame, the cursor changes to the link icon, as shown in Figure 42. Click the link icon, and the text flows into the frame, as shown in Figure 43. When the Show Text Threads command on the View menu is activated, a blue arrow appears between any two text frames that have been threaded, as shown in Figure 44.

Figure 41 Identifying in ports and out ports

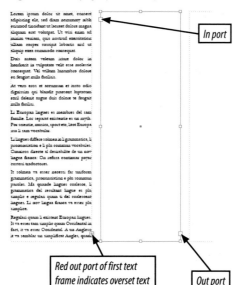

In port

Red out port of first text frame indicates overset text

Out port

Figure 42 Link icon

Link icon positioned over text frame

Figure 43 Threading text between frames

Figure 44 Showing text threads

Text thread between frames

Place text on document pages

1. Open ID 3-2.indd, then save it as **Wraps and Sections**.

   This data file has the same parameters as the document you created at the start of this chapter. The only changes are that the local document pages have been colorized and the headlines and dates have been filled in. Also, small blue circle or square frames are positioned on each spread.

2. Click the **workspace switcher**, then click **Typography**.

3. Double-click the **page 3 icon** on the Pages panel.

4. Click **File** on the menu bar, click **Place**, navigate to the drive and folder where your Chapter 3 Data Files are stored, then double-click **Greek text**.

5. Position the **cursor** over the **interior of the left text frame**.

As shown in Figure 45, the loaded text icon appears in parentheses, signaling that you can insert the loaded text into the text frame.

6. Click the **loaded text icon** in the **left text frame**.

   Text flows into the frame. The red out port with the plus sign indicates there is overset text—more text than can fit in the text frame.

7. Click the **Type tool** T , click **any word** five times to select all the text in the frame, set the **typeface** to **Times New Roman Regular**, set the **Font Size** to **8 pt.**, set the **Leading** to **9 pt.**, then set the **alignment** to **Justify with last line aligned left**.

   TIP Clicking five times selects even the text that is not currently visible in the frame. If you just click and drag to select the text that is visible, only that text will be affected by your format change.

8. Click the **Selection tool** ▶ , click the **red out port**, then position the **loaded text icon** over the **right text frame**.

   As shown in Figure 46, a link icon appears in the loaded text icon, indicating you are about to flow text from one frame to another. The red out port turns blue when you click it.

   TIP To unlink text frames, double-click the blue out port.

9. Click inside the **right text frame**.

   The text flows into the right text frame, and a new red out port appears at the bottom right of the right frame.

10. Save your work, then continue to the next set of steps.

You used the Place command to load text into a text frame, then threaded text from that frame into another.

Figure 45 Loaded text icon

Figure 46 Loaded text icon with a link icon

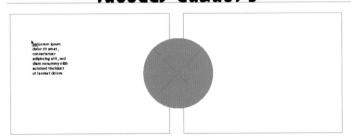

USING SMART TEXT REFLOW

Smart Text Reflow is a feature that adds pages automatically when needed to accommodate text overflow. Let's say you create a single-page document with a single text frame and begin typing. If you type so much that you get to the end of the available space in the text frame, Smart Text Reflow will automatically add a new page with a new frame so you can continue typing. This also works in reverse: If you delete the overflow text, the new page will be deleted. To work with Smart Text Reflow, open the Type Preferences dialog box, then verify that the Smart Text Reflow check box is checked. This preference works especially well with primary text frames. When you create a new document, the New Document dialog box offers you the option to create a primary text frame, which is essentially a text frame that appears automatically when you create a page—as though you had a text frame on a master page. In addition to checking the Smart Text Reflow option, verify that the Limit to Primary Text Frames check box is also checked. When this option is checked, reflow will only occur when you max out a primary text frame.

Thread text through multiple text frames

1. Click **View** on the menu bar, point to **Extras**, then click **Show Text Threads**.

   With the Show Text Threads command activated, blue arrows appear between threaded text frames when they are selected.

2. Reduce the view of the document so you can see more than one spread on your monitor.

3. Click the **Selection tool** ▶ , then click the **out port** of the right text frame.

   The loaded text icon appears.

4. Scroll so you can see both **pages 3 and 4** in the monitor window.

5. Press and hold **[option] (Mac)** or **[Alt] (Win)**, and position the **loaded text icon** over the **left text frame on page 4**.

6. Click, but do not release, **[option] (Mac)** or **[Alt] (Win)**.

   With the [option] (Mac) or [Alt] (Win) key pressed, the loaded text icon remains active. This means you won't have to click the out port of the left text frame to thread to the right text frame.

Continued on next page

7. Position the **pointer over the right text frame**, then click.

As shown in Figure 47, the text is threaded through both frames on page 4.

8. Using the same process, thread text through the remaining pages of the document.

Note that when you're done threading, you will still have loaded text.

9. Save your work, then continue to the next lesson.

You threaded text between multiple text frames on multiple pages.

Figure 47 Text threads showing text flowing from one spread to another

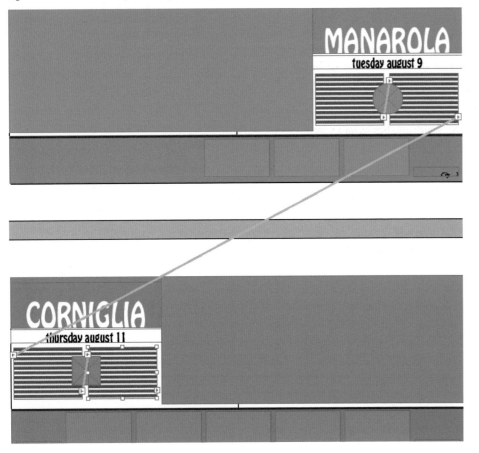

MAPPING STYLE NAMES WHEN IMPORTING WORD OR RTF FILES

When you place a Word document or RTF text in InDesign, you have many options to choose from regarding how text is imported. After you click Place on the File menu and find the Word or RTF document that you want to place, click the Show Import Options check box, then click Open. The Import Options dialog box opens. In this dialog box, you can choose to include or not include footnotes, endnotes, table of contents text, and index text. You can also choose to remove any previous styles applied to text and any table formatting. Conversely, you can opt to retain styles and table formatting applied to incoming text. You can import styles automatically by clicking the Import Styles Automatically option button and then tell InDesign how to deal with conflicts when incoming styles have the same names as existing styles in InDesign. Finally, you can map style names from the placed text file to specific styles in InDesign by clicking the Customize Style Import option button and then clicking the Style Mapping button. The Style Mapping dialog box allows you to choose which InDesign style to map to each incoming text style. For example, you can specify that the Normal style in Word is mapped to the [Basic Paragraph] style in InDesign.

CREATE NEW SECTIONS AND WRAP TEXT

▶ ***What You'll Do***

In this lesson, you will create two different numbering sections and create two text wraps around graphics frames.

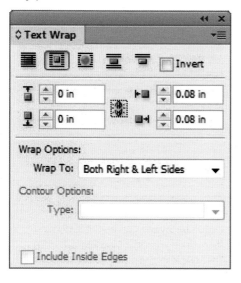

Creating Sections in a Document

A **section** is a group of pages in a document with distinct page numbering from other groups of pages. For example, sometimes in the front pages of a book, such as in the introduction or the preface, the pages will be numbered with lowercase Roman numerals, then normal page numbering will begin with the first chapter. Or in a cookbook with different courses, the "Soup" section might run from pages 1–35 and be followed by the "Salad" section, which also begins on a page 1.

You can create as many sections in a document as you wish. You determine the page on which the new section will start by clicking that page icon on the Pages panel. Choose the Numbering & Section Options command on the Pages panel menu, which opens the New Section dialog box, shown in Figure 48.

> **TIP** The first time you choose a type of page numbering for a document, the Numbering & Section Options dialog box opens instead of the New Section dialog box.

Figure 48 New Section dialog box

Wrapping Text Around a Frame

When you position a text frame or a graphics frame over another frame that contains text, you can apply a text wrap to the overlapping frame to force the underlying text to wrap around it. The Text Wrap panel offers many options for wrapping text around a frame.

Figure 49 shows a blue rectangular frame using the No text wrap option on the Text Wrap panel. Because there is no text wrap, the blue frame blocks the text behind it.

Figure 50 shows the same frame using the Wrap around bounding box option on the Text Wrap panel.

TIP To turn off text wrap in a text frame, select the text frame, click Object on the menu bar, click Text Frame Options, click the Ignore Text Wrap check box, and then click OK.

When you choose the Wrap around bounding box option, you can control the **offset**—the distance that text is repelled from the frame—by entering values in the Top, Bottom, Left, and Right Offset text boxes on the panel. The frame in Figure 50 has a 1.875" offset.

Figure 49 The blue frame has no text wrap and hides the text beneath it

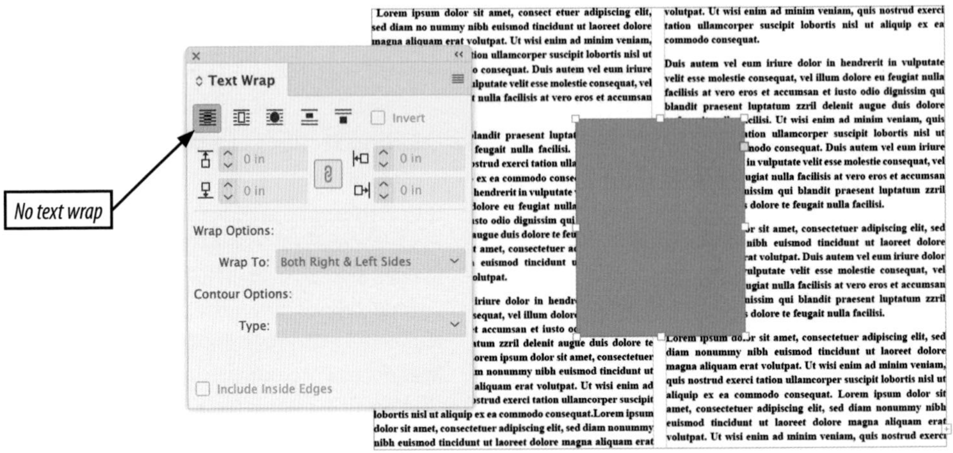

Figure 50 The frame has a 1.875" text wrap

Formatting a Text Frame to Ignore a Text Wrap

There will be times when you will want text in a frame to be immune to a text wrap in another frame. For example, let's say you have an image in a square frame and you have added a text wrap so the body copy on the page wraps around the frame. Now let's say that you want to position a caption in another text frame under the image. You'll run into a problem because the text wrap on the image will repel the caption text in the separate text frame.

At any time, you can select a text frame, open the Text Frame Options dialog box on the Object menu, then click Ignore Text Wrap. With this activated, the selected text frame will be immune to any text wrap applied to any other frames.

Create sections in a document

1. Double-click the **page 8 icon** on the Pages panel.

   The document has been designed so page 8 represents a new section in the document. The color theme changes to red and blue, and the city is Firenze.

2. Click the **Pages panel menu button** ☰ , then click **Numbering and Section Options**.

   The New Section dialog box opens.

3. Verify that the **Start Section check box** is **checked**.

4. Click the **Start Page Numbering at option button**, then type **2**.

   Your dialog box should resemble Figure 51. With these choices, you are starting a new section at page 8, renumbered as page 2.

5. Click **OK**.

   The pages are renumbered. On the Pages panel, spread 8–9 is now spread 2–3.

   TIP If a warning appears, alerting you a page number in this section already exists in another section, click OK.

6. Save your work, then continue to the next set of steps.

You used the New Section dialog box to change the sequence of the automatic page numbering in the document.

Figure 51 Renumbering the document

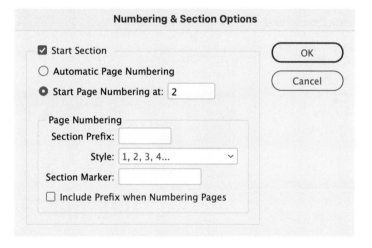

Wrap text around a frame

1. Double-click the **first page 3 icon** on the Pages panel, click the **Selection tool** ▶, then select the **small blue circle frame**.

2. Show the **Text Wrap panel**.

3. On the Text Wrap panel, click the **Wrap around bounding box button** ▣ .

   The text wraps around the rectangular bounding box, not the circle shape.

4. On the Text Wrap panel, click the **Wrap around object shape button** ▣, then type **.125** in the **Top Offset text box**.

   The text wraps around the ellipse, as shown in Figure 52.

5. Navigate to **page 4**, select the **small blue rectangular frame**, then click the **Wrap around bounding box button** ▣ on the Text Wrap panel.

6. Click the **Make all settings the same button** ⌀ to deactivate it if necessary.

7. Enter the settings in Figure 53 on the Text Wrap panel.

   The text is offset at different amounts top and bottom versus right and left. You will use the space created below the rectangle to position caption text in the next set of steps.

8. Save your work, then continue to the next set of steps.

You used the Text Wrap panel to flow text around an object's shape and around a bounding box.

Figure 52 Text wraps around object shape

Wrap around object shape

Figure 53 Formatting different offsets for the text wrap

Offset textboxes are not linked

Format a text frame to ignore a text wrap

1. Find the **text frame** on the pasteboard **to the left of page 4** in the document.

   The text frame has 8 pt. bold text that reads, "Caption goes here in this box."

2. Move the **text frame** onto **page 4** and position it **below the blue rectangle**.

   Some or all the caption text disappears because it is being repelled by the text wrap on the blue rectangle.

3. With the **small text frame** still selected, click **Object** on the menu bar, then click **Text Frame Options**.

4. Click the **Ignore Text Wrap check box**, then click **OK**.

   As shown in Figure 54, the caption text is positioned under the blue rectangle and is not affected by the text wrap.

5. Save your work, then close the Wraps and Sections document.

You applied the Ignore Text Wrap feature to a text box, so it was not affected by the text wrap.

Figure 54   The caption text box set to ignore the text wrap

CORNIGLIA

thursday august 11

esse molestie consequat, vel illum dolore eu feugiat nulla facilisis at vero eros et accumsan et iusto odio dignissim qui blandit praesent luptatum zzril delenit augue duis dolore te feugait nulla facilisi. Lorem ipsum dolor sit amet, consectetuer adipiscing elit, sed diam nonummy nibh euismod tincidunt ut laoreet dolore magna aliquam erat volutpat. Duis autem vel

Caption goes here in this text box.

eum iriure dolor in hendrerit in vulputate velit esse molestie consequat, vel illum dolore eu feugiat nulla facilisis at vero eros et accumsan et iusto odio dignissim qui blandit praesent luptatum zzril delenit augue duis dolore te feugait nulla facilisi. Lorem ipsum dolor sit amet, consectetuer adipiscing elit, sed diam nonummy nibh euismod

Text frame ignores text wrap

Create a new document and set up a master page

1. Start Adobe InDesign.
2. Without creating a new document, click InDesign (Mac) or Edit (Win) on the menu bar, point to Preferences, then click Guides & Pasteboard.
3. In the Guide Options section, click the Guides in Back check box to select, if necessary. Then click Units & Increments in the Preferences list on the left side of the dialog box, verify that the Horizontal and Vertical ruler units are set to Inches, then click OK.
4. Click File on the menu bar, point to New, then click Document.
5. In the New Document dialog box, name the document **Skills Review**.
6. Type **8** in the Number of Pages text box, press [tab], then verify that the Facing Pages check box is checked.
7. Type **5** in the Width text box, press [tab], then type **5** in the Height text box.
8. Using [tab] to move from one text box to another, type **1** in the Columns text box.
9. Type **.25** in the Top, Bottom, Inside, and Outside Margins text boxes.
10. Click Create.
11. Click the workspace switcher on the menu bar, then click Advanced, if necessary.
12. Double-click the words A-Master on the Pages panel to center both pages of the master in your window.
13. Click Window on the menu bar, point to Object & Layout, then click Transform.
14. Click the Selection tool, press and hold [command] (Mac) or [Ctrl] (Win), create a guide across the spread using the horizontal ruler, releasing the mouse pointer when the Y Location on the Transform panel reads 2.5 in.
15. Create a guide on the left page using the vertical ruler, releasing the mouse pointer when the X Location on the Transform panel reads 2.5 in.
16. Click InDesign (Mac) or Edit (Win) on the menu bar, point to Preferences, click Units & Increments, click the Origin list arrow, click Page, then click OK.
17. Create a vertical guide on the right page, releasing the mouse pointer when the X Location on the Transform panel reads 2.5 in.
18. Verify that the fill and stroke buttons on the toolbar are set to [None], click the Rectangle Frame tool, then draw a rectangle anywhere on the left page.
19. Click the top-left reference point on the Transform panel.
20. With the rectangle frame selected, type **0** in the X Location text box on the Transform panel, type **0** in the Y Location text box, type **5** in the Width text box, type **5** in the Height text box, then press [return] (Mac) or [Enter] (Win).
21. Using the same method, create an identical rectangle on the right page.
22. If necessary, type **0** in the X Location text box on the Transform panel, type **0** in the Y Location text box, then press [return] (Mac) or [Enter] (Win).

23. Click the Pages panel menu button, then click New Master.
24. Type **Body** in the Name text box, click the Based on Master list arrow, click A-Master, then click OK.
25. Click the Selection tool, press and hold or [shift] [command] (Mac) or [Shift] [Ctrl] (Win), select both rectangle frames, then delete them.
26. Double-click B-Body on the Pages panel to center both pages of the master in your window.
27. Click Layout on the menu bar, then click Margins and Columns.
28. Type **2** in the Number text box in the Columns section, then click OK.

Create text on master pages

1. Click the Type tool, create a text frame of any size anywhere in the right column on the left page, then click the Selection tool.
2. Verify that the top-left reference point is selected on the Transform panel, type **2.6** in the X Location text box, type **.25** in the Y Location text box, type **2.15** in the Width text box, type **4.5** in the Height text box, then press [return] (Mac) or [Enter] (Win).
3. Click Edit on the menu bar, click Copy, click Edit on the menu bar again, then click Paste in Place.
4. Press and hold [shift], then drag the copy of the text frame onto the right page, releasing the mouse button when it snaps into the left column on the right page.
5. Click the Type tool, then draw a small text box anywhere on the left page of the B-Body master.
6. Select the text frame and verify that the top-left reference point is selected on the Transform panel, type **.25** in the X Location text box, type **4.5** in the Y Location text box, type **1.65** in the Width text box, type **.25** in the Height text box, then press [return] (Mac) or [Enter] (Win).
7. Select the Type tool, click in the text frame, click Type on the menu bar, point to Insert Special Character, point to Markers, then click Current Page Number.
8. Click Type on the menu bar, point to Insert Special Character, point to Hyphens and Dashes, then click En Dash.
9. Type the word **Title**.
10. Click the Selection tool, select the text frame, if necessary; click Edit on the menu bar, click Copy, click Edit on the menu bar again, then click Paste in Place.
11. Press and hold [shift], then drag the copy of the text frame so it is positioned in the lower-right corner of the right page of the master page.
12. Open the Paragraph panel, click the Align right button, then delete the B and the dash after the B.

TIP Switch your workspace to Typography to access the Paragraph panel if necessary.

13. Click after the word Title, click Type on the menu bar, point to Insert Special Character, point to Hyphens and Dashes, then click En Dash.
14. Click Type on the menu bar, point to Insert Special Character, point to Markers, then click Current Page Number.

Apply master pages to document pages

1. Double-click the page 2 icon on the Pages panel.
2. Drag the B-Body master page title to the bottom-left corner of the page 2 icon until you see a black rectangle around the page 2 and 3 icons, then release the mouse button.
3. Drag the word B-Body from the top of the Pages panel to the bottom-left corner of the page 4 icon until you see a black rectangle around the page 4 icon, then release the mouse button.
4. Click the Pages panel menu button, then click Apply Master to Pages.
5. Click the Apply Master list arrow; click B-Body, if necessary, type **6–8** in the To Pages text box, then click OK.
6. Double-click the page 2 icon on the Pages panel.
7. Hide guides.

Place and thread text

1. Click File on the menu bar, click Place, navigate to the drive and folder where your Chapter 3 Data Files are stored, then double-click Skills Review Text.
2. Click anywhere in the text frame in the right column on page 2.
3. Click View on the menu bar, point to Extras, then click Show Text Threads.
4. Click the Selection tool, then click the out port of the text frame on page 2.
5. Click the loaded text icon anywhere in the text frame on page 3.

Modify master pages and document pages

1. Double-click the page 6 icon on the Pages panel.
2. Click the bottom-middle reference point on the Transform panel.
3. Click the Selection tool, press and hold or [shift] [command] (Mac) or [Shift] [Ctrl] (Win), then click the large text frame.
4. Type **.3** in the Height text box on the Transform panel, then press [return] (Mac) or [Enter] (Win).
5. Double-click A-Master in the top section of the Pages panel, then select the graphics placeholder frame on the left page.
6. Click the center reference point on the Transform panel.
7. On the Transform panel, type **3** in the Width text box, type **3** in the Height text box, then press [return] (Mac) or [Enter] (Win).

8. Double-click the right page icon of the A-Master on the Pages panel, then select the graphics placeholder frame on the right page.
9. On the Transform panel, type **2** in the Width text box, type **4** in the Height text box, then press [return] (Mac) or [Enter] (Win).
10. View the two right-hand pages on the Pages panel that are based on the A-Master right-hand page to verify that the modifications were updated.
11. Double-click B-Body on the Pages panel, click the Rectangle Frame tool, then create a frame anywhere on the left page of the B-Body master page.
12. Click the center reference point on the Transform panel, then type **2** in the X Location text box, type **2.6** in the Y Location text box, type **2.25** in the Width text box, type **1.5** in the Height text box, then press [return] (Mac) or [Enter] (Win).

Create new sections and wrap text

1. Double-click the page 1 icon on the Pages panel, click the Pages panel menu button, then click Numbering & Section Options.
2. In the Page Numbering section, click the Style list arrow, click the lowercase style letters (a, b, c, d), click OK, then note the changes to the pages on the Pages panel and in the document.

3. Double-click the page e icon on the Pages panel, click the Pages panel menu button, then click Numbering & Section Options.
4. In the Page Numbering section, click the Start Page Numbering at option button, type **5** in the text box, then verify that the Style text box in the Page Numbering section shows ordinary numerals (1, 2, 3, 4). (If it does not, click the Style list arrow, and select that style.)
5. Click OK, then view the pages in the document, noting the new style of the page numbering on the pages and on the Pages panel.
6. Double-click the page b icon on the Pages panel, click the Selection tool, press and hold [shift] [command] (Mac) or [Shift] [Ctrl] (Win), then select the rectangular graphics frame.
7. Click Window on the menu bar, then click Text Wrap.
8. Click the Wrap around bounding box button on the Text Wrap panel.
9. Type **.125** in the Right Offset text box on the Text Wrap panel, then press [return] (Mac) or [Enter] (Win).
10. Click View on the menu bar, click Fit Spread in Window, then click anywhere to deselect any selected items.
11. Compare your screen to Figure 55, save your work, then close the Skills Review document.

Figure 55 Completed Skills Review

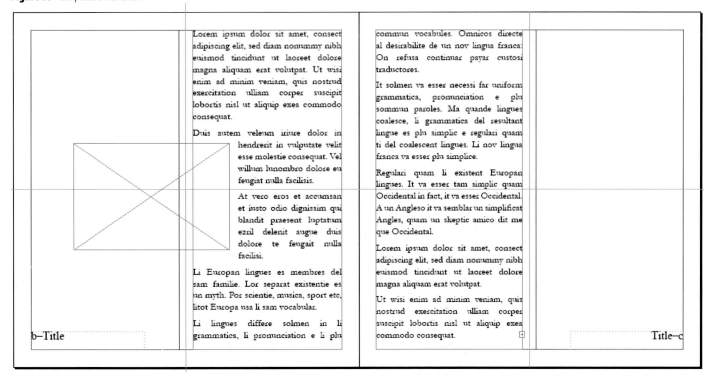

You are a graphic designer working out of your home office. A local investment company has contracted you to design its monthly 16-page newsletter. You've sketched out a design and created a new document at the correct size, and now you need to add automatic page numbering to the document.

1. Open ID 3-3.indd, then save it as **Newsletter**.
2. Double-click A-Master on the Pages panel.
3. Click the Type tool, then draw a text frame about one inch tall and one column wide.
4. Position the text frame at the bottom of the center column, being sure that the bottom edge of the text frame snaps to the bottom margin of the page.
5. Set the Preference settings so the guides are sent to the back of the layout—so all four sides of the text frame are visible.
6. Click the Type tool, then click inside the text box.
7. Click Type on the menu bar, point to Insert Special Character, point to Hyphens and Dashes, then click Em Dash.
8. Click Type on the menu bar, point to Insert Special Character, point to Markers, then click Current Page Number.
9. Click Type on the menu bar, point to Insert Special Character, point to Hyphens and Dashes, then click Em Dash.
10. Select all three text elements, and change their font size to 20 pt.
11. Click the Align center button on the Paragraph panel.
12. Click the dark blue swatch on the Swatches panel.
13. Click the Selection tool, click the bottom-center reference point on the Transform panel, double-click the Height text box on the Transform panel, type **.25**, then press [return] (Mac) or [Enter] (Win).
14. Double-click the page 5 icon on the Pages panel, compare your page 5 to Figure 56, save your work, then close the Newsletter document.

Figure 56 Completed Project Builder 1

PROJECT BUILDER 2

You work in the design department for a bank, and you are responsible for creating a new weekly bulletin, which covers various events within the bank's network of branches. You have just finished creating three master pages for the bulletin, and now you are ready to apply the masters to the document pages.

1. Open ID 3-4.indd, then save it as **Bulletin Layout**.
2. Apply the B-Master to pages 2 and 3.
3. Click the Pages panel menu button, then click Apply Master to Pages.
4. Apply the C-Master to pages 4 through 6, then click OK.
5. Place Bulletin text.doc in the text frame on page 1.
6. Select the text frame, click the out port on the text frame, double-click page 2 on the Pages panel, then click anywhere in the text frame on page 2.
7. Thread the remaining text through each page up to and including page 6 in the document.
8. Click the Preview button, deselect any selected items, then compare your page 6 to Figure 57.
9. Save your work, then close the Bulletin Layout document.

Figure 57 Completed Project Builder 2

In this project, you're going to work on a fun puzzle that will test your problem-solving skills when using X and Y locations. You will open an InDesign document with two pages. On the first page are four 1-inch squares at each corner of the page. On the second page, the four 1-inch squares appear again—this time forming a large red square that is positioned at the exact center of the 7.75-inch × 7.75-inch document page. Looking at the second page, your challenge will be to write down the X and Y coordinates of each of the four boxes at the center of the page. Then, you will test out your answers with the boxes on the first page.

Setup

1. Open ID 3-5.indd, then save it as **Center Squares**.
2. On page 1, verify that each red square is 1" × 1", then deselect all.
3. Go to page 2, then press [tab] to hide all panels.
4. Do not select any of the squares at the center.
5. Write down what you think is the X/Y coordinate of the top-left point of the top-left square.
6. Write down what you think is the X/Y coordinate of the top-right point of the top-right square.
7. Write down what you think is the X/Y coordinate of the bottom-right point of the bottom-right square.
8. Write down what you think is the X/Y coordinate of the center point of the bottom-left square.
9. Press [tab] to show all hidden panels.

10. Go to page 1, select the top-left square, then click the top-left reference point on the Transform panel.
11. Enter the X/Y coordinates that you wrote down for this point, then press [return] (Mac) or [Enter] (Win).

12. Using the same method, test out the X/Y coordinates you wrote down for the other three squares.

TIP Be sure to click the appropriate reference point on the Transform panel for each of the three remaining squares.

13. When you are done, does your page 1 match page 2 exactly as shown in Figure 58?

Figure 58 Completed Project Builder 3

This Design Project is based on the layouts you worked with in this chapter. This is your opportunity to create your own five-page layout of a five-city tour, similar to the one you created in this chapter.

1. Use Figure 12 in this chapter as a reference for the document you will create.
2. Choose five cities from anywhere in the world to profile in your document.
3. Go online and search for images that you can work with. For each city, find one photo that you can use as the large, dominant image for its page, then find at least three images you can use as smaller, secondary or support images.
4. Decide what your five-page document is. Is it a brochure, a magazine, a series of postcards, a five-page website?
5. Decide the shape and trim size of your document. Is it wider than it is tall or taller than it is wide? Or is it square? Decide the exact size for the finished document.
6. Create a new five-page document, then name it **Five Cities**.
   Note that for this project you will work with five single pages as opposed to five two-page spreads.
7. Using the skills you learned in the chapter, build a master page for your first layout.
8. Choose typefaces you want to use for your headlines, body copy, and captions.
9. Layout frames for your dominant image and for your supporting images.
10. Layout text frames for your headlines, body copy, and captions.
11. Create blocks of color for the page.
12. Use automatic page numbering for each page design.
13. Create at least two new master page versions of the layout based on the first master you designed.
14. Apply different masters to the five-page document.
15. When you are done, you should have your own original design based on the file named "Setup" that you created in the chapter.
16. Save your work, then close the Five Cities document.

Flowers
of the Desert

Lorem ipsum dolor sit amet, consect adipiscing elit, sed diam nonummy nibh euismod tincidunt ut laoreet dolore magna aliquam erat volutpat. Ut wisi enim ad minim veniam, quis nostrud exercitation ulliam corper suscipit lobortis nisl ut aliquip exea commodo consequat.

Duis autem veleum iriure dolor in hendrerit in vulputate velit esse molestie consequat. Vel willum lunombro dolore eu feugiat nulla facilisis. At vero eros et accumsan et iusto odio dignissim qui blandit praesent luptatum ezril delenit augue duis dolore te feugait nulla facilisi.

Li Europan lingues es membres del sam familie. Lor separat existentie es un myth. Por scientie, musica, sport etc, litot Europa usa li sam vocabular. Li lingues differe solmen in li grammatica, li pronunciation e li plu commun vocabules. Omnicos directe al desirabilite de un nov lingua franca: On refusa continuar payar custosi traductores.

At solmen va esser necessi far uniform grammatica, pronunciation e plu sommun paroles. Ma quande lingues coalesce, li grammatica del resultant lingue es plu simplic e regulari quam ti del coalescent lingues. Li nov lingua franca va esser plu simplice.

Regulari quam li existent Europan lingues. It va esser tam simplic quam Occidental in fact, it va esser Occidental. A un Angleso it va semblar un simplificat Angles, quam un skeptic

amico dit me que Occidental.

Lorem ipsum dolor sit amet, consect adipiscing elit, sed diam nonummy nibh euismod tincidunt ut laoreet dolore magna aliquam erat volutpat. Ut wisi enim ad minim veniam, quis nostrud exercitation ulliam corper suscipit lobortis nisl ut aliquip exea commodo consequat. Duis autem veleum iriure dolor in hendrerit in vulputate velit esse molestie consequat. Vel willum lunombro dolore eu feugiat nulla facilisis.

At vero eros et accumsan et iusto odio dignissim qui blandit praesent luptatum ezril delenit augue duis dolore te feugait nulla facilisi. Li lingues differe solmen in li grammatica, li pronunciation e li plu commun vocabules. Omnicos directe al desirabilite de un nov lingua franca: On refusa continuar payar custosi traductores.

A windmill garden is a kite flyer's dream come true.

Et solmen va esser necessi far uniform grammatica, pronunciation e plu sommun paroles. Ma quande lingues coalesce, li grammatica del resultant lingue es plu simplic e regulari quam ti del coalescent lingues. Li nov lingua franca va esser plu simplice. Regulari quam li existent Europan lingues. It va esser tam simplic quam Occidental in fact, it va esser Occidental. A un Angleso it va semblar un simplificat Angles, quam un skeptic amico dit me que Occidental.

Lorem ipsum dolor sit amet, consect adipiscing elit, sed diam nonummy nibh euismod tincidunt ut laoreet dolore magna aliquam erat volutpat. Ut wisi enim ad minim veniam, quis nostrud exercitation ulliam corper suscipit lobortis nisl ut aliquip exea commodo consequat.

Source: cengage/shutterstock/topics/free

CHAPTER **4**

WORKING WITH FRAMES

1. Align and Distribute Objects on a Page
2. Stack and Layer Objects
3. Work with Graphics Frames
4. Work with Text Frames

Adobe Certified Professional in Print & Digital Media Publication Using Adobe InDesign

1. Working in the Design Industry
This objective covers critical concepts related to working with colleagues and clients as well as crucial legal, technical, and design-related knowledge.

1.4 Demonstrate knowledge of key terminology related to publications.
    C Understand and use key terms related to multipage layouts.

2. Project Setup and Interface
This objective covers the interface setup and program settings that assist in an efficient and effective workflow, as well as knowledge about ingesting digital assets for a project.

2.4 Import assets into a project.
    B Place assets in an InDesign document.
2.5 Manage colors, swatches, and gradients.
    A Set the active fill and stroke color.

3. Organizing Documents
This objective covers document structure such as layers, tracks, and managing document structure for efficient workflows.

3.1 Use layers to manage design elements.
    A Use the Layers panel to modify layers.
    B Manage and work with multiple layers in a complex project.

4. Creating and Modifying Document Elements
This objective covers core tools and functionality of the application, as well as tools that affect the visual appearance of document elements.

4.1 Use core tools and features to lay out visual elements.
    A Create frames using a variety of tools.
    B Manipulate graphics in frames.
4.2 Add and manipulate text using appropriate typographic settings.
    E Manage text flow across multiple text areas.
    F Use tools to add special characters or content.
4.3 Make, manage, and edit selections.
    A Make selections using a variety of tools.
    B Modify and refine selections using various methods.
4.4 Transform digital graphics and media within a publication.
    A Modify frames and frame content.
    B Rotate, flip, and transform individual frames or content.
4.5 Use basic reconstructing and editing techniques to manipulate document content.
    C Use the Story Editor to edit text within a project.

ALIGN AND DISTRIBUTE OBJECTS ON A PAGE

▶ *What You'll Do*

In this lesson, you will explore various techniques for positioning objects in specific relationships to one another.

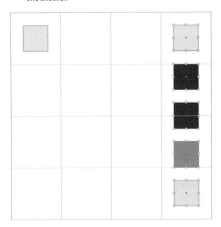

Applying Fills and Strokes

A **fill** is a color you apply to the inside of an object. A **stroke** is a color that you apply to the outline of an object. Figure 1 shows an object with a blue fill and a yellow stroke.

InDesign offers you many options for filling and stroking objects. The simplest and most direct method for doing so is to select an object and then pick a color from the Swatches panel. The color that you choose on the Swatches panel will be applied to the selected object as a fill or as a stroke, depending on whether the fill or the stroke button is activated on the toolbar.

Figure 1 An object with a fill and a stroke

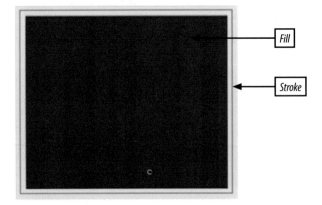

Fill

Stroke

To activate either the fill or the stroke button, click it once on the toolbar. The fill button is activated when it is in front of the stroke button, as shown in Figure 2. When the fill button is activated, clicking a swatch on the Swatches panel applies that swatch color as a fill to the selected object(s). When the stroke button is activated, as shown in Figure 3, the swatch color is applied as a stroke.

Once a stroke is applied, you can modify the **stroke weight**—how heavy the outline appears—using the Stroke panel. The Stroke panel is command central for all the modifications you can apply to a stroke, including making dotted and dashed strokes and varying stroke styles.

The Align Stroke section of the Stroke panel is critical for determining *where* on the object the stroke is applied. By default, a stroke is aligned to the center of the object's perimeter. This means that it's centered on the edge, halfway inside and halfway outside the object. For example, if you apply a 10 pt. stroke to a rectangle, five points of the stroke will be inside the object, and five points will be outside.

Figure 2 Fill is activated

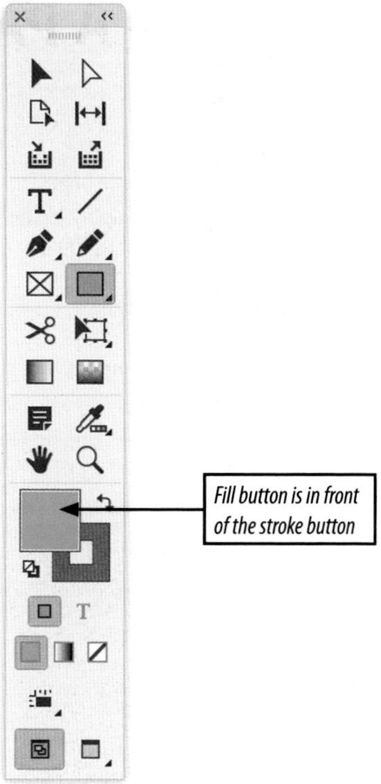

Fill button is in front of the stroke button

Figure 3 Stroke is activated

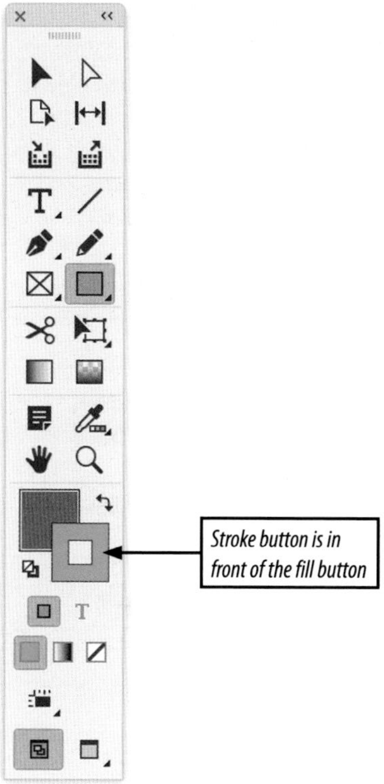

Stroke button is in front of the fill button

The Stroke panel offers three Align Stroke options: Align Stroke to Center, Align Stroke to Inside, and Align Stroke to Outside. Figure 4 shows three 2" × 2" frames with three different 10 pt. stroke alignments. Note that the object is different sizes in all three. In the first, the 2" × 2" frame is increased by 0.5 pt. on all sides because the stroke is centered. In the second, the frame with the 10 pt. stroke is 2" × 2" because the stroke is aligned to the inside. The third is the largest object, a 2" × 2" frame increased by 10 points on all sides, because the stroke is aligned to the outside.

Using the Step and Repeat Command

Many times, when laying out a page, you will want to create multiple objects that are evenly spaced in lines or in grids. InDesign offers many great utilities for accomplishing this, one of which is the Step and Repeat dialog box, as shown in Figure 5.

Figure 4 A 10 pt. stroke with three different alignments

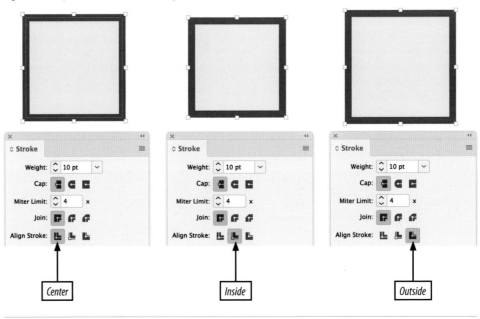

Center | Inside | Outside

Figure 5 Step and Repeat dialog box

Before you choose the Step and Repeat command, you need to decide which objects you want to copy and how many copies of it you want to create. After selecting the object, choose Step and Repeat on the Edit menu. In the Step and Repeat dialog box, you choose the number of copies. You also specify the offset value for each successive copy. The **offset** is the horizontal and vertical distance the copy will be from the original.

TIP Click the Preview check box to see transformations before you execute them.

Figure 6 shows an original 1-inch square frame and three copies created using the Step and Repeat command. The horizontal offset is two inches, and the vertical offset is two inches. Thus, each copy is two inches to the right and two inches down from the previous copy.

Note that positive and negative offset values create copies in specific directions. On the horizontal axis, a positive value creates copies to the right of the original; a negative value creates copies to the left of the original. On the vertical axis, a positive value creates copies *below* the original; a negative value creates copies above the original. Figure 7 is a handy guide for remembering the result of positive and negative offset values.

Figure 6 Copying a frame with the Step and Repeat dialog box

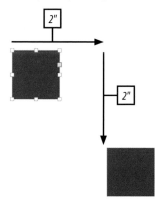

Figure 7 Understanding positive and negative offset values

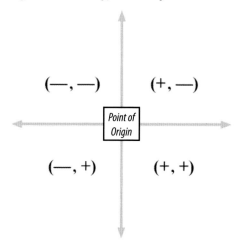

Use the vertical ruler on the left side of the document page to remember positive and negative values on the vertical axis. You are used to thinking of positive as up and negative as down, but remember that in InDesign, the default (0, 0) coordinate is in the top-left corner of the page. On the ruler, positive numbers *increase* as you move *down* the ruler.

Aligning Objects

The Align panel offers quick and simple solutions for aligning and distributing multiple objects on a page. To **align** objects is to position them by their tops, bottoms, left sides, right sides, or centers. To **distribute** objects is to space them equally on a page horizontally, vertically, or both. Using the top section of the Align panel, you can choose from six alignment buttons, shown in Figure 8.

Each option includes an icon that represents the resulting layout of the selected objects, after the button has been clicked. Figure 9 shows three objects placed randomly on the page. Figure 10 shows the same three objects after clicking the Align left edges button. Note that only the red and green boxes moved to align with the blue object. This is because the blue object was originally the leftmost object. Clicking the Align left edges button aligns all selected objects with the leftmost object.

Figure 11 shows the original three objects after clicking the Align top edges button. The red and yellow boxes move up so their tops are aligned with the top of the blue box.

TIP The Align panel has four choices for aligning objects. In addition to aligning objects using the boundaries of the selection, you can also align one or more objects to the page, margins, or spread.

Figure 8 Align Objects section of the Align panel

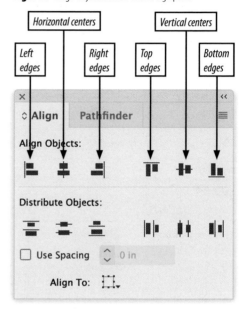

Figure 9 Three objects not aligned

Figure 10 Objects aligned with the Align left edges button

Figure 11 Objects aligned at their top edges

Distributing Objects

You use the Distribute Objects section of the Align panel to distribute objects. To distribute objects is to space them equally in relation to one another.

Figure 12 shows three objects that are not distributed evenly on either the horizontal or vertical axis. Figure 13 shows the same three objects after clicking the Distribute horizontal centers button. Clicking this button means that— on the horizontal axis— the distance between the center point of the first object and the center point of the second object is the same as the distance between the center point of the second object and the center point of the third object.

Figure 14 shows the same three objects after clicking the Distribute vertical centers button. Clicking this button means that—on the vertical axis—the distance between the center points of the first two objects is the same as the distance between the center points of the second and third objects.

Figure 12 Three objects randomly positioned

Figure 13 Horizontal centers distributed evenly

Figure 14 Horizontal and vertical centers distributed evenly

Using the Live Distribute Technique

When you select multiple objects, a bounding box appears around the objects. As you already know, you can drag the handles of that bounding box to transform all the selected objects. The Live Distribute option offers a different behavior. Instead of resizing the objects, you can use the Live Distribute option to proportionally resize the *space between* the objects.

To access the Live Distribute option, select multiple objects, start dragging a bounding box handle and then hold [space bar] as you drag. The spaces between the objects will be resized, and the alignment of the objects will change depending on where and in what direction you drag.

Figure 15 shows 20 frames aligned in a grid. Figure 16 shows the same 20 frames modified with the Live Distribute option. Note that the frames haven't changed size—only the space between them has changed.

Figure 15 Twenty frames

Images courtesy of Chris Botello

Figure 16 Space between frames increased proportionately with the Live Distribute option

Using the Gap Tool

When you're working with multiple objects, the Gap tool offers a quick way to adjust the size of the gaps between them. It also allows you to resize several items that have commonly aligned edges at once while maintaining the size of the gaps between them. Think of it this way: the Gap tool moves the gap.

Figure 17 shows a grid of 12 frames with the Gap tool positioned over the center gap. The shaded area indicates the length of the gap that will be modified by the tool. Figure 18 shows the result of dragging the Gap tool to the left. Note that only the gap moved; the size of the gap didn't change. The width of the associated frames changed.

You can use the Gap tool while pressing and holding various keys to perform other tasks as well, as shown in Table 1.

Figure 17 Gap tool positioned over a grid of frames

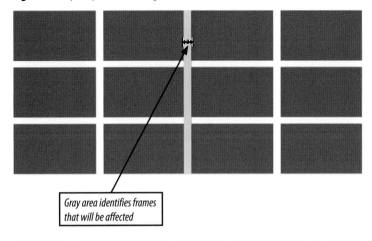

Gray area identifies frames that will be affected

Figure 18 Result of dragging the Gap tool to the left

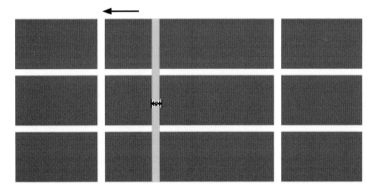

TABLE 1: GAP TOOL BEHAVIORS AND KEYBOARD COMBINATIONS		
Mac	**Win**	**Behavior**
[shift]	[Shift]	Affects the gap only between the two items nearest to the cursor
[command]	[Ctrl]	Increases the width and height of the gap
[option]	[Alt]	Moves the items with the gap instead of resizing the items

Align a stroke on an object

1. Open ID 4-1.indd, then save it as **Orientation**.

2. Verify that **guides** are showing.

3. Click the **workspace switcher list arrow** on the menu bar, then click **[Advanced]**.

4. Click the **Rectangle tool** ▢, then click anywhere on the page.

TIP When a shape tool is selected on the toolbar, clicking the document window opens the tool's dialog box, where you can enter values that determine the size of the resulting object.

5. Type **2** in the **Width text box**, type **2** in the **Height text box**, then click **OK**.

    A 2" square appears on the page.

6. Switch to the **Selection tool** ▶.

7. Fill the **square** with **Green**.

8. Stroke the **square** with **Brick Red**.

9. On the Stroke panel, type **6** in the **Weight text box**, then press **[return] (Mac) or [Enter] (Win)**.

10. Click the **Align Stroke to Outside button** ▣.

    Note on the Control panel that adding the stroke has changed the width and height measurements of the 2" square. It is now 2.1667" because of the 6 pt. stroke positioned outside of the original frame.

11. Click the **Align Stroke to Inside button** ▣.

    The dimension of the square is once again 2" because the stroke is completely inside the frame.

12. Click the **Align Stroke to Center button** ▣.

The dimension of the square changes to 2.0833.

13. Click the **top-left reference point** on the Control panel, type **0** in the **X** and **Y text boxes**, then press **[return] (Mac)** or **[Enter] (Win)**.

    The top-left corner of the square with the red stroke is positioned at the top-left corner of the artboard.

14. Save your work, then continue to the next set of steps.

You created a square using the Rectangle dialog box. You then used the Swatches panel to choose a fill color and a stroke color for the square frame. You chose a weight for the stroke and tested three options for aligning the stroke, noting that the positioning of the stroke changed the dimensions of the square. Finally, you used the Control panel to position the square at the top-left corner of the page.

Use the Step and Repeat command

1. Make sure the **green square** is still selected, then change the **stroke color** to **[None]**.

   With the stroke removed, the green square is no longer exactly at the 0X/0Y coordinate at the top-left corner of the artboard.

2. Use the Control panel to position the **top-left corner of the frame** at the **0X/0Y coordinate**.

3. Click **Edit** on the menu bar, then click **Step and Repeat**.

4. Verify that the **Horizontal** and **Vertical text boxes** are set to **0** on the Control panel, type **3** in the **Repeat Count text box**, type **2** in the **Vertical Offset text box**, type **2** in the **Horizontal Offset text box**, then click **OK**.

   Three new squares are created, each one 2" to the right 2" down from the previous one, as shown in Figure 19.

5. Click the **Selection tool** ▶ , then click anywhere on the pasteboard to deselect.

6. Select the **top two squares,** click **Edit** on the menu bar, then click **Step and Repeat**.

7. Type **1** in the **Repeat Count text box**, type **0** in the **Vertical Offset text box**, type **4** in the **Horizontal Offset text box**, then click **OK**.

8. Select the **bottom two squares** on the page, click **Edit** on the menu bar, then click **Step and Repeat**.

9. Type **1** in the **Repeat Count text box**, type **0** in the **Vertical Offset text box**, type **–4** in the **Horizontal Offset text box**, then click **OK**.

10. Click anywhere to deselect the new squares, then compare your page to Figure 20.

11. Save your work, then continue to the next set of steps.

You used the Step and Repeat command to create a checkerboard pattern, duplicating a single square seven times.

Figure 19 Viewing results of the Step and Repeat command

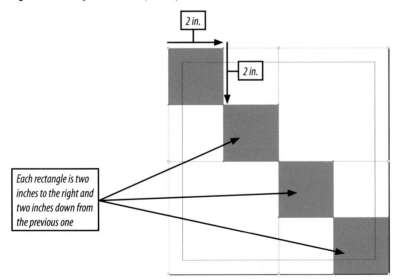

2 in.

2 in.

Each rectangle is two inches to the right and two inches down from the previous one

Figure 20 Checkerboard created using the Step and Repeat command

Use the Live Distribute technique

1. Select all, copy, then paste in place.

2. Click the **center reference point** on the Control panel, type **90** in the **Rotation Angle text box** on the Control panel, then press **[return] (Mac)** or **[Enter] (Win)**.

3. Verify that the **fill button** is in front on the toolbar, click **Dark Blue** on the Swatches panel, then compare your screen to Figure 21.

4. Select all, press and hold **[shift] [option] (Mac)** or **[Shift] [Alt] (Win)**, then click and drag the **upper-right handle of the bounding box** toward the center of the page, releasing the mouse button when your checkerboard resembles Figure 22.

   The objects are scaled from their center point.

5. Click and drag the **upper-right corner of the bounding box** toward the **upper-right corner of the document**; then, while you are still dragging, press and hold **[space bar]**.

   When you press [space bar] while dragging, the Live Distribute option is enabled. The space between the objects is modified—larger or smaller—depending on the direction in which you drag.

6. With the **[space bar]** still pressed, drag the **handle** in different directions on the document.

   Regardless of the direction you drag, the frames do not change size or shape—only the space between the frames changes.

7. With the **[space bar]** still pressed, press and hold **[shift] [option] (Mac)** or **[Shift] [Alt] (Win)**, then drag the **handle** to the **upper-right corner of the document** and release the mouse button.

   Pressing and holding [space bar] [shift] [option] (Mac) or [space bar] [Shift] [Alt] (Win) when dragging enlarges the space between the frames in proportion from the center. Your page should resemble Figure 23.

Figure 21 Viewing the complete checkerboard

Figure 22 Scaling the checkerboard in a standard manner

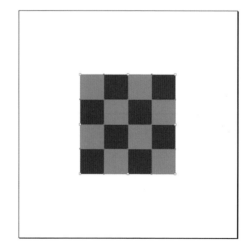

Figure 23 Expanding the space between frames with Live Distribute

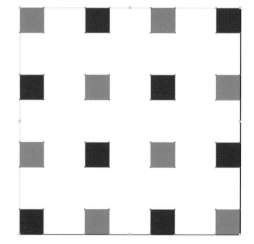

8. Begin dragging the **upper-right handle** of the bounding box slowly toward the **center of the document**.

9. As you're dragging, press **[space bar]** to activate Live Distribute, then press **[shift] [option] (Mac)** or **[Shift] [Alt] (Win)** and continue dragging toward the **center** until your artwork resembles Figure 24.

10. Deselect all, then save your work.

11. Continue to the next set of steps.

You pasted and rotated a copy of the squares to create a complete checkerboard. You selected all the frames, then dragged a bounding box handle to reduce all the objects in a standard manner. You then used the Live Distribute technique to modify the space between the objects.

Use the Gap tool

1. Click the **Gap tool** |↔| on the toolbar.

2. Position the **Gap tool** |↔| over the **middle-vertical gap**, then click and drag left so your grid resembles Figure 25.

3. Position the **Gap tool** |↔| over the **bottom-horizontal gap**, then click and drag up so your grid resembles Figure 26.

4. Position the **Gap tool** |↔| over the **gap between the top two frames in the upper-right corner**, press and hold **[shift]**, then click and drag to the left so your grid resembles Figure 27.

Continued on next page

Figure 24 Reducing the space between frames with Live Distribute

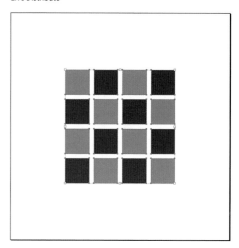

Figure 25 Moving the vertical gap

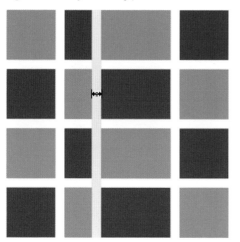

Figure 26 Moving the horizontal gap

Figure 27 Moving the gap only between two rectangles

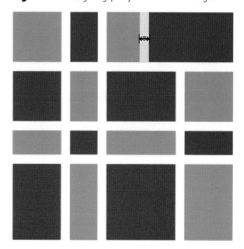

5. Press and hold **[command] (Mac)** or **[Ctrl] (Win)** then click and drag the **left edge** of the grid to the left.

 The width of the four frames on the left is increased.

6. Press and hold **[option] (Mac)** or **[Alt] (Win)** to position the **Gap tool** |↔| over the **bottom-horizontal gap**, then click and drag down.

 As shown in Figure 28, the frames on both sides of the gap move. Neither the frames nor the gap are resized—only relocated.

7. Save your work, then close the Orientation document.

You used the Gap tool with various key combinations to affect the gaps in a grid of frames.

Align objects

1. Open ID 4-2.indd, then save it as **Alignment**.

2. Click **Window** on the menu bar, point to **Object & Layout,** then click **Align**.

 The Align panel opens.

3. Press **[command] [A] (Mac)** or **[Ctrl] [A] (Win)** to select all **three objects** on the page, then click the **Align left edges button** |≡| in the Align Objects section of the Align panel.

The frames are aligned to the leftmost of the three.

4. Click **Edit** on the menu bar, then click **Undo Align**.

5. Click the **Align top edges button** |⊤| on the Align panel.

 As shown in Figure 29, the top edges of the three frames are aligned to the topmost of the three.

6. Undo the previous step, then click the **Align horizontal centers button** |≑| .

7. Click the **Align vertical centers button** |≣| .

 The three frames are stacked, one on top of the other, their center points are aligned both horizontally and vertically.

8. Save your work, then close the Alignment document.

You used the buttons in the Align Objects section of the Align panel to reposition frames with various alignments.

Figure 28 Moving frames with the Gap tool

Figure 29 Aligning three objects by their top edges

Distribute objects

1. Open ID 4-3.indd, then save it as **Distribution**.

2. Verify that **guides** are showing.

3. Select the **top two yellow squares** and the **two red squares,** then click the **Align top edges button** 🔲 in the Align Objects section of the Align panel.

   The four objects are aligned by their top edges.

4. Click the **Distribute horizontal centers button** ▮▮ in the Distribute Objects section of the Align panel.

The center points of the two red squares are distributed evenly on the horizontal axis between the center points of the two yellow squares, as shown in Figure 30.

5. Click **Edit** on the menu bar, click **Deselect All**, select the **top-left yellow square**, select the **two red squares**, then select the **bottom-right yellow square**.

6. Click the **Distribute vertical centers button** 🔲, then compare your screen to Figure 31.

7. Select the **green square**, the **two red squares**, and the **bottom yellow square**, then click the **Align right edges button** 🔲.

8. Press and hold **[shift]**, then click the **top-right yellow square** to add it to the selection.

9. Click the **Distribute vertical centers button** 🔲.

   The center points of the five squares are distributed evenly on the vertical axis, as shown in Figure 32.

10. Save your work, then close the Distribution document.

You spaced objects evenly on the horizontal and vertical axes.

Figure 30 Distributing objects evenly on the horizontal axis

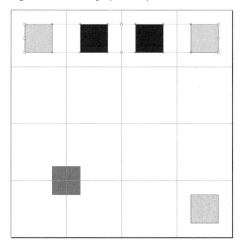

Figure 31 Distributing 4 objects evenly on the vertical axis

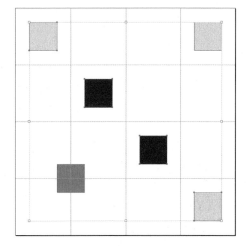

Figure 32 Distributing 5 objects evenly on the vertical axis

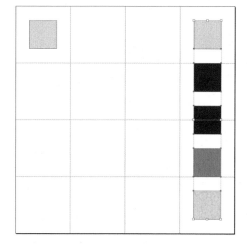

STACK AND LAYER OBJECTS

▶ What You'll Do

In this lesson, you will manipulate the stacking order of objects on the page, and you'll use the Layers panel to control how objects are layered.

Understanding the Stacking Order

The **stacking order** refers to how objects are arranged in hierarchical order. When you create multiple objects, it is important for you to remember that every object is on its own level. For example, if you draw a square frame, and then draw a circle frame, the circle frame is automatically created one level in front of the square, whether or not they overlap. If they did overlap, the circle would appear in front of the square.

> **TIP** Use the word "level" when discussing the hierarchy of the stacking order, not the word "layer," which has its own specific meaning in InDesign.

You control the stacking order with the four commands on the Arrange menu. The Bring to Front command moves a selected object to the front of the stacking order. The Send to Back command moves a selected object to the back of the stacking order. The Bring Forward command moves a selected object one level forward in the stacking order, and the Send

Backward command moves a selected object one level backward in the stacking order.

Using these four commands, you can control and arrange how every object on the page overlaps other objects.

Understanding Layers

The Layers panel is a smart solution for organizing and managing elements of a layout. The Layers panel in InDesign is very similar to the Layers panel in Adobe Illustrator. It includes options for locking and hiding individual objects on a layer.

By default, every document you create in InDesign has one layer. You can create new layers and give them descriptive names to help you identify a layer's content. For example, if you were working on a layout that contained both text and graphics, you might want to create a layer for all the text frames called Text and create another layer for all the graphics called Graphics.

Why would you do this? Well, for one reason, you can lock layers on the Layers panel. Locking a layer makes its contents non-editable until you unlock it. In the example, you could lock the Text layer while you work on the graphic elements of the layout. By doing so, you can be certain that you won't make any inadvertent changes to the text elements. Another reason is that you can hide layers. You could temporarily hide the Text layer, thus providing yourself a working view of the graphics that is unobstructed by the text elements.

You can also duplicate layers. You do so by clicking the Duplicate Layer command on the Layers panel menu or by dragging a layer on top of the Create new layer icon on the Layers panel. When you duplicate a layer, all the objects on the original layer are duplicated and will appear in their same locations on the new layer.

Layers are a smart, important solution for organizing your work and improving your workflow, especially for complex layouts. Invest some time in learning layers—it will pay off with lots of saved time and fewer headaches.

Working with Layers

You can create as many layers on the Layers panel as you need to organize your work. Figure 33 shows the Layers panel with three layers. Notice the lock icon on Layer 2. The lock icon indicates that this layer cannot be edited. All objects on Layer 2 are locked. Clicking the lock icon will unlock the layer, and the lock icon will disappear.

Think of layers on the Layers panel as being three-dimensional. The topmost layer is the front layer; the bottommost layer is the back layer. Therefore, it follows logically that objects on the topmost layer are *in front* of objects on any other layer. Layers themselves are transparent. If you have a layer with no objects on it, you can see through the layer to the objects on the layers behind it.

Note that each layer contains its own stacking order. Let's say that you have three layers, each with five objects on it. Regardless of the stacking order of the top layer, all the objects on that layer are in front of any objects on the other layers. In other words, an object at the back of the stacking order of the top layer is still in front of any object on any layer beneath it.

Figure 33 Layers panel with three layers

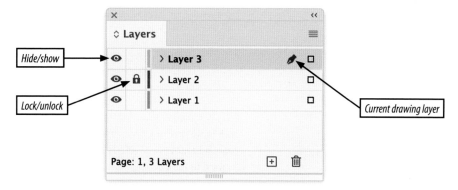

One great organizational aspect of layers is that you can assign a selection color to a layer. When you select an object, its bounding box and selection marks appear in the selection color of the layer on which it is placed, as shown in Figure 34.

You determine a layer's selection color by selecting the layer, clicking the Layers panel menu button, clicking Layer Options for the name of the selected layer, then choosing a new color from the Color menu. When you are working with a layout that contains numerous objects, this feature is a great visual aid for keeping track of objects and their relationships to other objects.

Manipulating Layers and Objects on Layers

Once you have created layers in a document, you have many options for manipulating objects on the layers and the layers themselves. You can move objects between layers, and you can reorder the layers on the Layers panel.

Clicking a layer on the Layers panel to select it is called **targeting** a layer. The layer you click is called the **target layer**. When you create a new object, the object will be added to whichever layer is targeted on the Layers panel. The pen tool icon next to the layer name is called the Current drawing layer icon. This icon will help remind you that anything placed or drawn will become part of that layer.

Figure 34 The selection color for objects on the layer

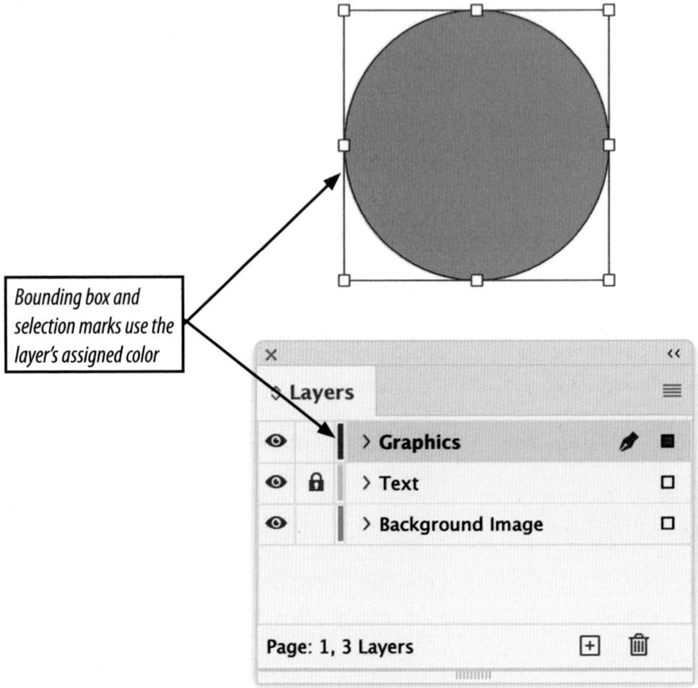

Bounding box and selection marks use the layer's assigned color

You can select any object on the page, regardless of which layer is targeted. When you select the object, the layer that the object is on is automatically targeted on the Layers panel.

When one or more objects are selected, a small, square icon on the far right of a layer on the Layers panel fills with color to show that items on the layer are selected as shown in Figure 35. The selected items button represents the selected objects. When you click and drag the selected items button and move it to another layer, the selected objects move to that layer. Therefore, you should never feel constrained by the layers you have chosen for objects; it's easy to move them from one layer to another.

You can also change the order of layers on the Layers panel by dragging a layer up or down on the panel. As you drag, a heavy black line indicates the new position for the layer when you release the mouse button.

Selecting Artwork on Layers

Let's say you have three layers in your document, each with six objects. That means your document has a total of 18 objects. If you apply the Select All command on the Edit menu, all 18 objects will be selected, regardless of which layer is targeted on the Layers panel.

In many situations, you'll want to select all the objects on one layer only. The easiest way to do this is with the selected items button. Even when nothing is selected, the button is available

Figure 35 The selected items button

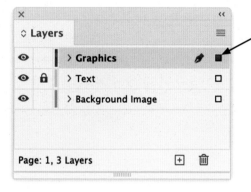

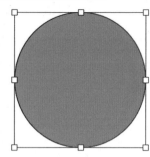

Indicates that items on this layer are selected

on every layer—as a hollow square. Click that button, and all objects on that layer will be selected. This is a powerful and useful option—make note of it.

Selecting Objects Behind Other Objects

When you have multiple overlapping objects on a page, objects behind other objects can sometimes be difficult to select. Pressing and holding [command] (Mac) or [Ctrl] (Win) allows you to "click through the stacking order" to select objects behind other objects. Simply click the top object, press and hold [command] (Mac) or [Ctrl] (Win), then click the top object again; this will select the object immediately behind it. Click the top object again, and the next object down in the stacking order will be selected.

Use the Arrange commands to change the stacking order of objects

1. Open ID 4-4.indd, then save it as **Stack and Layer**.

2. Press **[V]** to access the **Selection tool** ▶, then click the **yellow rectangle**.

3. Click **Object** on the menu bar, point to **Arrange**, then click **Bring Forward**.

   The yellow rectangle moves forward one level in the stacking order.

4. Click the **red square**, click **Object** on the menu bar, point to **Arrange**, then click **Bring to Front**.

5. Select both the **yellow rectangle** and the **blue circle,** click **Object** on the menu bar, point to **Arrange**, then click **Bring to Front**.

   Both objects move in front of the red square, as shown in Figure 36.

6. Click the **green circle**, click **Object** on the menu bar, point to **Arrange**, then click **Bring to Front**.

7. Select all, then click the **Align horizontal centers button** ≑ on the Align panel.

   The blue circle is completely behind the green circle.

8. Deselect all, then click the **center of the green circle**.

9. Press and hold **[command] (Mac)** or **[Ctrl] (Win)**, then click the **center of the green circle** again.

   The blue circle behind the green circle is selected.

10. Click **Object** on the menu bar, point to **Arrange**, then click **Bring Forward**.

As shown in Figure 37, the blue circle moves forward one level in the stacking order, in front of the green circle.

11. Deselect all, select the **blue circle,** press and hold **[command] (Mac)** or **[Ctrl] (Win)**, then click the **blue circle center** again to select the green circle behind it.

12. Still pressing and holding **[command] (Mac)** or **[Ctrl] (Win)**, click the **blue circle center** again

to select the yellow rectangle, then click the **blue circle center** once more to select the red square.

TIP Commit this selection technique to memory, as it is useful for selecting overlapping objects.

13. Save your work, then close the Stack and Layer document.

You used the Arrange commands to manipulate the stacking order of four objects.

Figure 36 Using the Bring to Front command with two objects selected

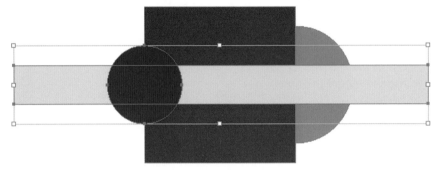

Figure 37 Sending the green circle backward one level in the stacking order

Create new layers on the Layers panel

1. Open ID 4-5.indd, save it as **Layers Intro,** then click **Layers** in the stack of collapsed panels to open the Layers panel.

   The Layers panel has one default layer named Layer 1. All the objects on the spread are on Layer 1.

2. Double-click **Layer 1** on the Layers panel.

   The Layer Options dialog box opens. In this box, you can change settings for Layer 1, such as its name and selection color.

3. Type **Tints** in the Name text box, then click **OK**.

4. Click the **Create new layer button** [+] on the Layers panel, then double-click **Layer 2**.

5. Type **Images** in the Name text box, click the **Color list arrow**, click **Orange**, then click **OK**.

6. Click the **Layers panel menu button** ☰ , then click **New Layer**.

7. Type **Text** in the Name text box, click the **Color list arrow**, click **Purple**, then click **OK**.

   Your Layers panel should resemble Figure 38.

8. Save your work, then continue to the next set of steps.

You renamed Layer 1, then created two new layers on the Layers panel.

Figure 38 Layers panel with three layers

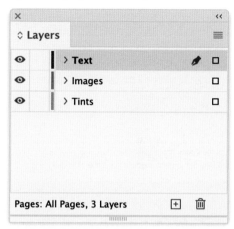

Position objects on layers

1. Press **[V]** to access the **Selection tool** ▶, then select all **seven images** on the spread.

   The Tints layer on the Layers panel is highlighted, and the selected items button ☐ appears next to the layer name.

2. Click and drag the **selected items button** ☐ from the **Tints layer** up to the **Images layer**.

   The seven images are moved to the Images layer. As shown in Figure 39, the selection edges around the frames are now orange, the color assigned to the Images layer.

3. Click the **eye icon** 👁 on the **Images layer** to hide that layer.

4. Select the **four text frames** on the left page, then drag the **selected items button** ☐ up to the Text layer.

   The text frames are moved to the Text layer and the selection marks are now purple. Be sure to note that the text wrap is still affecting the text, even though the image frame is on the Images layer and the Images layer is hidden.

5. Show the **Images layer**.

Figure 39 Seven images moved to the Images layer

6. Click the word **Text** on the **Text layer**, click the **Rectangle tool** 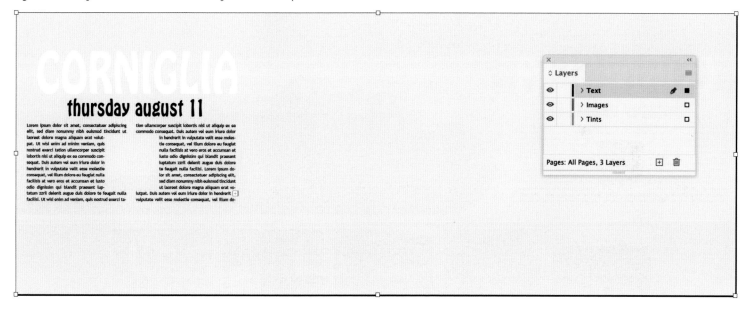, then draw a **small rectangle** anywhere on the page.

   Because the Text layer was selected on the Layers panel, the new rectangle is positioned on the Text layer.

7. Fill the **rectangles** with the **Tan swatch** on the Swatches panel.

8. Click the **top-left reference point** on the Control panel, enter **0** in the **X text box**, enter **0** in the **Y text box**, enter **12.5** in the **W text box**, then enter **4.75** in the **H text box**.

The rectangle covers the entire spread. Because the rectangle is the newest object created, it is at the top of the stacking order on the Text layer.

9. Click **Object** on the menu bar, point to **Arrange**, click **Send to Back**, then compare your spread to Figure 40.

Continued on next page

Figure 40 Rectangle moved to the bottom of the stacking order on the Text layer

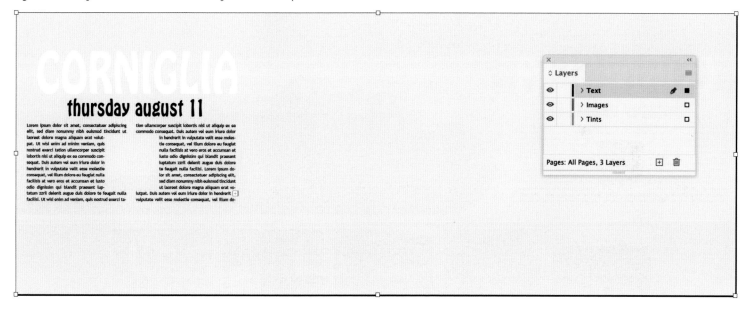

The rectangle is at the back of the stacking order of the Text layer. Because the Text layer is at the top of the Layers panel, the rectangle is in front of all images and all tints on the layers below.

10. Drag the **selected items button** ☐ down to the **Tints layer**.

The rectangle is moved to the Tints layer. It is at the top of the stacking order on the Tints layer, so the green tints are not visible.

11. Click **Object** on the menu bar, point to **Arrange**, then click **Send to Back**.

As shown in Figure 41, the tan rectangle is at the bottom of the stacking order on the Tints layer.

12. Save your work, then continue to the next set of steps.

You used the Layers panel to move selected objects from one layer to another. You targeted a layer, then created a new object, which was added to that layer. You then pasted objects into a targeted layer.

Figure 41 Rectangle moved to the bottom of the stacking order on the Tints layer

Change the order of layers on the Layers panel

1. Switch to the **Selection tool** ▶ , deselect all, then click and drag the **Tints layer** to the top of the Layers panel.

   A thick line appears, indicating where the layer will be positioned when dragged.

2. Drag the **Text layer** to the top of the Layers panel.

3. Drag the **Images layer** to the top of the Layers panel.

4. Click the **empty square** next to the **Text layer name** to lock the layer, then compare your Layers panel to Figure 42.

   The lock icon 🔒 appears when it is clicked, indicating the layer is now locked.

5. Save your work, then continue to the next set of steps.

You changed the order of layers and locked the Text layer.

Figure 42 Text layer locked

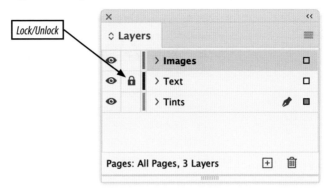

Group items on layers

1. Click the **expand button** > next to **Images** on the Layers panel.

   Expanding the layer shows the objects on the layer. The seven frames are listed on the layer with the name of the images pasted into them.

2. Select the **first four small frames** at the bottom of the layout on the page, starting with the leftmost frame.

   The selected items button □ becomes activated for each individual object that is selected.

3. Click **Object** on the menu bar, then click **Group**.

The four selected objects are moved into a folder named <group>.

4. Click the **expand button** > to expand the <group> folder.

5. Select the **fifth thumbnail frame** on the layout, which is named Three Houses.tif.

   The selected items button □ is activated beside the fifth thumbnail layer on the Layers panel. Because this image is not part of the group, it is not within the <group> folder.

6. Click and drag the **fifth thumbnail layer** into the middle of the <group> folder.

   As shown in Figure 43, Three Houses.tif is now with the other four images in

the <group> folder and is grouped with them.

7. Deselect all.

8. Lock the <group> folder so your Layers panel resembles Figure 44.

   When you expand a layer, you can lock and hide individual objects on a layer. In this example, the Images layer has seven images on it, but only five of them are locked.

9. Save your work, then close the Layers Intro document.

You modified a group using layers. You grouped four of five frames. You then added the fifth frame to the group by dragging the fifth frame into the <group> folder on the Layers panel.

Figure 43 Moving the image into the <group> folder

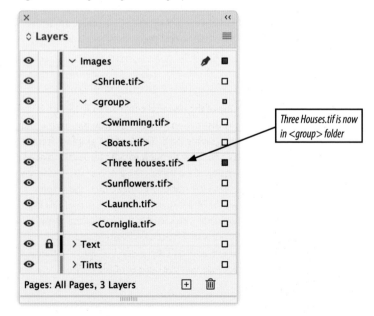

Three Houses.tif is now in <group> folder

Figure 44 Locking the <group> folder locks only the images in the folder

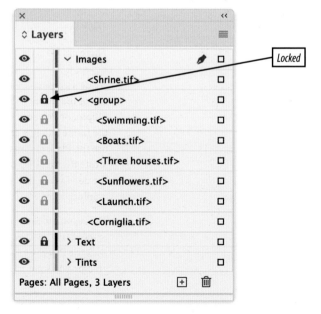

Locked

WORK WITH GRAPHICS FRAMES

▶ *What You'll Do*

In this lesson, you will create graphics frames, resize them, and manipulate graphics that you import into them.

Placing Graphics in a Document

The term graphic is quite broad. In its most basic definition, a **graphic** is an element on the page that is not text. A simple square with a fill color could be called a graphic. However, when you are talking about placing graphics in an InDesign document, the term "graphic" usually refers to bitmap images or vector graphics. **Bitmap graphics** are images that consist of pixels. They are created in a program like Adobe Photoshop, scanned in, or downloaded from the Internet or a digital camera. **Vector graphics** are artwork composed of geometrically defined paths and curves, usually illustrations created and imported from drawing programs such as Adobe Illustrator.

There are two essential methods for placing a graphic in a document. The first is to create a graphics placeholder frame using any of the InDesign's shape tools—Rectangle, Ellipse, or Polygon. Once you have created the frame and it is selected on the page, you use the Place command on the File menu to locate the graphic you want to import into the document. The graphic will appear in the graphics frame.

The second method is to place a graphic without first creating a graphics frame. If you click the Place command and then locate the graphic you want to import, your cursor will change to the loaded graphics icon, which is a thumbnail-size image of the image you chose.

Click the loaded graphics icon on the page to place the graphic. The graphic will be placed on the page in a graphics frame whose top-left corner will be positioned at the location where you clicked the loaded graphics icon.

Which is the better method? It depends on what you want to do with the graphic. If the size and location of the graphics frame is important, it's probably better to create and position the frame first, then import the graphic and make it fit into the frame. If the size and location of the frame are negotiable, you might want to place the graphic anywhere in the layout and then modify its size and location.

The Graphic vs. the Graphics Frame

One of the essential concepts in InDesign is the distinction between the graphics frame and the graphic itself. Think of the graphics frame as a window through which you see the placed graphic. Sometimes, the graphic will fit entirely within the frame. At other times, the graphic will be larger than the frame that contains it. In that case, you see only the part of the graphic that fits in the frame. The other areas of the graphic are still there; you just can't see them because they are outside of the frame.

Selecting Graphics and Frames

The difference between the graphics frame and the graphic itself is reflected on the toolbar. Anything you want to do to a graphics frame, you do with the Selection tool. Anything you want to do to the contents—to a graphic itself—you do with the Direct Selection tool. This concept is the key to manipulating graphics within a graphics frame.

Figure 45 shows a graphics frame selected with the Selection tool. The Transform panel shows the X and Y locations of the frame and the width and height of the frame. In this figure, the Transform panel shows no information about the actual placed image inside the frame.

Figure 45 Transform panel shows position info of the selected frame

tsuneomp/Shutterstock; Songquan Deng/Shutterstock

Transform panel showing info about the frame

Transform

X: 3 in   W: 2 in
Y: 2 in   H: 3 in

100%   0°
100%   0°

Figure 46 shows the same object, but this time it has been selected with the Direct Selection tool. The image itself is selected. The selection frame is brown, which is the default color for a selected graphic. This frame is called the bounding box. The **bounding box**—always rectangular—is the frame that defines the horizontal and vertical dimensions of the graphic itself—not the graphics frame. Finally, note that there are parts of the graphic that you can't see. That's because the graphic is being cropped by the graphics frame.

It's important to note that the information on the Transform panel is rendered differently. The + signs beside the X and Y text boxes are a visual indication that the Transform panel is now referring to the graphic, not the frame. The X and Y values are *in relation to the top-left corner of the frame.* Let's explore this: The upper-left reference point on the Transform panel is selected. The X/Y coordinates on the Transform panel refer to the location of the upper-left corner of the graphic. The upper-left corner of the graphic is –0.0076" left and –0.0908" above the top-left corner *of the frame.*

You will seldom be concerned with the actual X/Y coordinates of a placed graphic. In most cases, you will instead place the image in the frame at a size and position that you like and not even note what the X/Y coordinates are.

Figure 46 Transform panel shows position info of the placed image

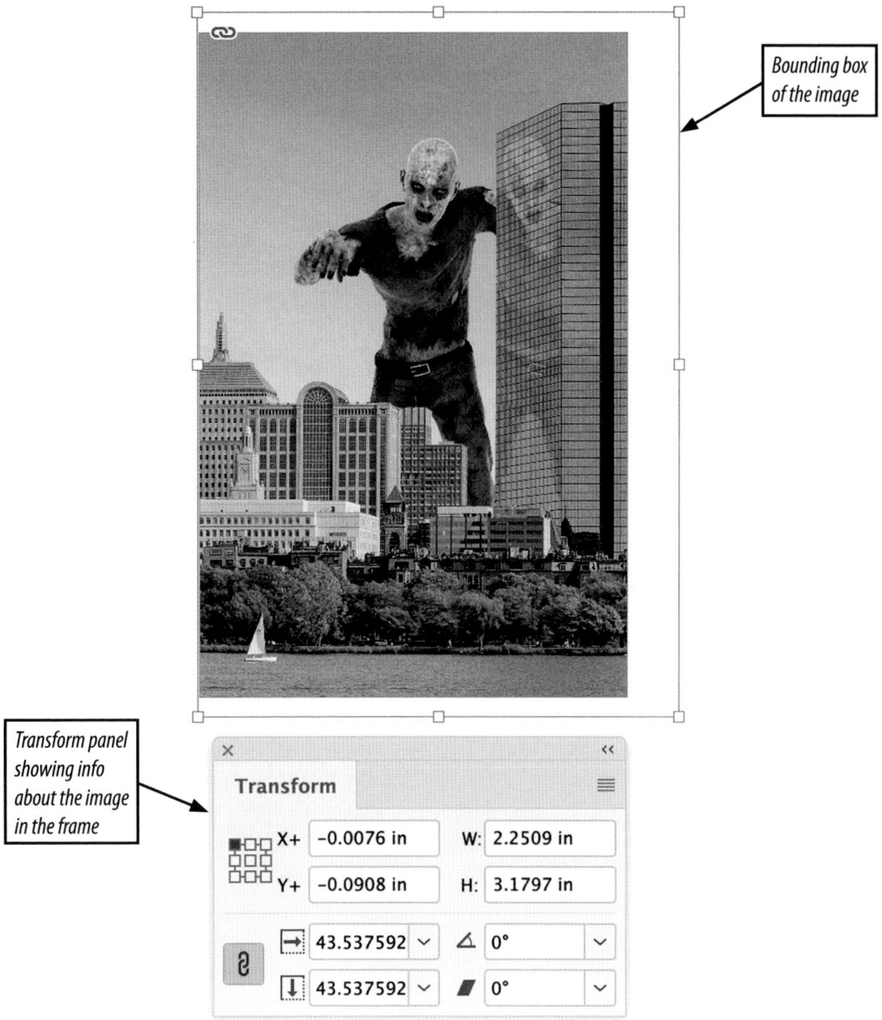

Bounding box of the image

Transform panel showing info about the image in the frame

Using the Content Indicator

When you're working with lots of graphics in lots of frames, you'll want a quicker solution for selecting graphics and frames. The quickest and easiest solution is to double-click the image. Double-clicking the image toggles between the frame and the graphic being selected.

The content indicator is a donut-shaped circle that's available whenever you float over a graphic placed in a frame. If you click the content indicator with the Selection tool, the graphic will be selected. Thus, the content indicator allows you to select the graphic with the Selection tool without having to switch to the Direct Selection tool.

You'll just need to make sure that when you intend to select a frame, you don't accidentally select the content indicator and, thus, the graphic.

Moving a Graphic Within a Frame

When you want to move a graphic within a frame, select the graphic by any method you prefer, then click and drag it. You can also move the selected graphic using the arrow keys on the keypad. When you click and drag the graphic to move it, you see a ghosted image of the areas that are outside the graphics frame. The ghosted image is referred to as a **dynamic preview**.

Once you release the mouse button, the graphic will be repositioned within the frame.

Using the Paste Into Command to Copy and Paste a Graphic

When designing layouts, you'll often find that you want to copy and paste a graphic from one frame to another. This is easy to do. First, select the graphic (not the frame), then copy it. Select the frame in which you want to paste the copy, then choose the Paste Into command on the Edit menu.

Resizing a Graphic

When you select a graphic with the Direct Selection tool, you can then resize the graphic within the frame. Changes that you make to the size of the graphic do not affect the size of the graphics frame.

CREATING A CAPTION BASED ON METADATA

Metadata is text-based information about a graphics file. For example, you can save a Photoshop file with metadata that lists information such as the image's filename, file format, and resolution. When the file is placed in an InDesign layout, you can specify that InDesign automatically generates a caption listing the metadata. These types of captions would be useful if you were creating a contact sheet of photography, for example, that listed important information about a bunch of photos on a DVD or server.

InDesign offers several methods for generating captions of placed images. The most exciting one is Live Caption. Simply click to select a frame containing an image, click the Object menu, point to Captions, then click Generate Live Caption. InDesign creates a text box immediately below the selected frame listing the metadata saved with the image—which is, at minimum, the filename. Here's the "Live" part: if you move that text frame to touch another frame containing a placed image, the text in the frame will update automatically to list the metadata information of the new image. To customize the data or formatting of the caption, click the Object menu, point to Captions, then click Caption Setup.

You can scale a selected graphic by dragging its handles or changing values in the Scale X Percentage and the Scale Y Percentage text boxes on the Transform or Control panels, as shown in Figure 47. You can also use the Transform/Scale command on the Object menu to scale the graphic. Remember, when the graphic is selected with the Direct Selection tool, only the graphic will be scaled when you use the Transform/Scale command.

Using the Fitting Commands

While it's not difficult to select a graphic with the Direct Selection tool and then scale it using the Transform panel, there are a lot of steps in the process.

For a quick solution, you can use the Fitting commands, located on the Object menu.

Figure 47 Scale X and Scale Y Percentages on the Control panel

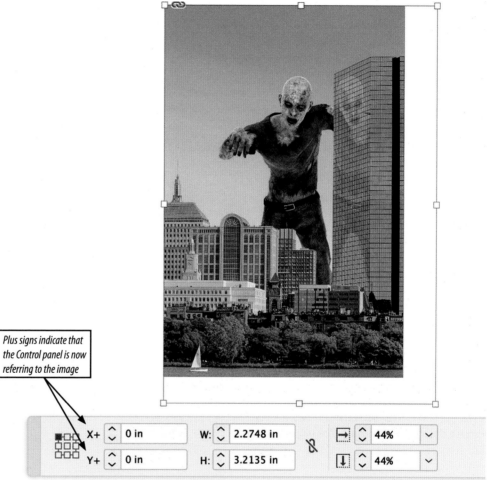

Plus signs indicate that the Control panel is now referring to the image

The Fitting commands offer different options for positioning the graphic in the frame. These commands are smart and useful, but beware—they're easy to confuse with one another. It's important that you keep each command straight in your head, because one of the commands distorts the image to fit the frame. See Table 2.

Of all the fitting commands, the Fill Frame Proportionally command is the one you're likely to use most often, because it resizes the placed graphic to a size that is guaranteed to fit the frame, with no negative space in the frame. This means that some of the graphic may not be visible if it exceeds the size of the frame, but you can be confident that it will not be distorted to fit the frame.

Wrapping Text Around Graphics with Clipping Paths

In Chapter 3, you learned how to use the Text Wrap panel to wrap text around a bounding box using the Wrap around bounding box button. You can also wrap text around a graphic inside the frame, as shown in Figure 48.

The Text Wrap panel offers many methods for doing so. In this chapter, you will focus on wrapping text around an image that was saved with a named clipping path in Photoshop. Figure 49 shows a Photoshop image with a clipping path drawn around a man. A **clipping path** is a graphic drawn in Photoshop that outlines the areas of the image you want to show when the file is placed in a layout program such as InDesign.

TABLE 2: FITTING COMMANDS		
Command	**Result**	**Proportion Issues**
Fill Frame Proportionally	The graphic is scaled proportionally to the minimum size required to fill the entire frame.	No proportion issues. The graphic is scaled in proportion.
Fit Content Proportionally	The graphic is scaled proportionally to the largest size it can be without exceeding the frame. Some areas of the frame may be empty.	No proportion issues. The graphic is scaled in proportion.
Fit Frame to Content	The frame is resized to the exact size of the graphic.	No proportion issues. The graphic is not scaled.
Fit Content to Frame	The content is resized to the exact size and shape of the frame.	The content will almost always be distorted with this fitting command.
Center Content	The center point of the graphic will be aligned with the center point of the frame.	No proportion issues. The graphic is not scaled.

Figure 48 Wrapping text around a graphic

The text is able to enter the graphics frame to wrap around the picture

Figure 49 A Photoshop image with a clipping path

Image courtesy of Chris Botello

Clipping path created in Photoshop

When you save the Photoshop file, you name the clipping path and save it with the file. When you place a graphic that has a named clipping path saved with it into your layout, InDesign recognizes the clipping path. With the graphic selected, click the Wrap around object shape button on the Text Wrap panel, click the Type list arrow in the Contour Options section of the panel, and then choose Photoshop Path, as shown in Figure 50. When you do so, the Path menu will list all the paths that were saved with the graphic file. (Usually, you will save only one path with a file.) Choose the path that you want to use for the text wrap.

TIP To define the way text wraps around a graphic, click the Wrap To list arrow in the Wrap Options section, then choose one of the available presets. Remember, in every case, you can manually adjust the resulting text wrap boundary. Though the clipping path is created in Photoshop, the text wrap itself is created in InDesign—and it is editable. As shown in Figure 51, you can relocate the path's anchor points using the Direct Selection tool. You can also use the Add Anchor Point and Delete Anchor Point tools to add or delete points to the path as you find necessary. Click the Add Anchor Point tool anywhere on the path to add a new point and increase your ability to manipulate the path. Click any anchor point with the Delete Anchor Point tool to remove it. Changing the shape of the path changes how text wraps around the path.

Figure 50 Choosing a path from Photoshop for a text wrap

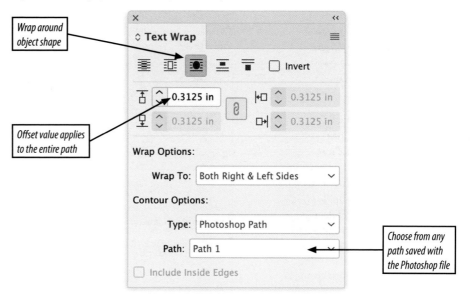

Figure 51 Manipulating the text wrap path

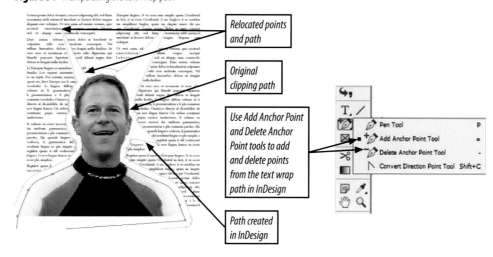

Place graphics in a document

1. Open ID 4-6.indd, then save it as **Flowers**.

2. On the Layers panel, lock the **Text layer**.

TIP When a layer is locked, the contents of the layer cannot be selected or modified; this is a smart way to protect the contents of any layer from unwanted changes.

3. Click the **Background layer** to target it, click the **Rectangle tool** , then draw a **graphics frame** in the center of the page that is approximately 3" × 3".

   The frame should have no fill or stroke. The bounding box of the frame is orange because orange is the selection color applied to the Background layer.

4. Click **File** on the menu bar, click **Place**, navigate to the drive and folder where your Chapter 4 Data Files are stored, then double-click **Windmills Ghost.psd**.

   Because the frame was selected, the graphic is placed automatically into the frame, as shown in Figure 52.

5. Click the **Selection tool** , click anywhere to deselect the frame, click the **eye icon** on the **Background layer** to hide it, then click the **Images layer** to target it on the Layers panel.

Figure 52 Viewing the placed graphic

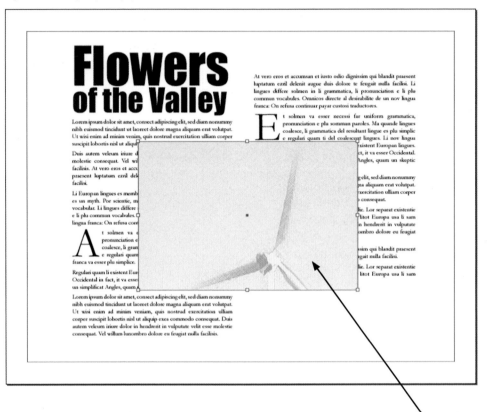

Placed graphic

6. Click **File** on the menu bar, click **Place,** navigate to the drive and folder where your Chapter 4 Data Files are stored, click **Girl at Windmills.psd**, then click **Open.**

TIP You can also access the Place command by pressing [command] [D] (Mac) or [Ctrl] [D] (Win).

7. Position the **pointer** over the **document**.

The pointer changes to the loaded graphics icon and shows a thumbnail of the graphic.

8. Click the **loaded graphics icon** on the **F** in the word **Flowers**.

As shown in Figure 53, the graphic is placed in a new graphics frame whose top-left corner is located where the loaded graphics icon was clicked.

9. Save your work, then continue to the next set of steps.

You imported two graphics using two subtly different methods. You created a graphics frame and then used the Place command to place a graphic in that frame. You used the Place command to load a graphic file and then clicked the loaded graphics icon to create a new frame for the new graphic.

Figure 53 Clicking to place a loaded graphic

sirtravelalot/Shutterstock.com

USING THE STORY EDITOR

InDesign has a feature called the Story Editor that makes it easier to edit text in complex documents. Imagine that you are doing a layout for a single magazine article. The text for the article is flowed through numerous text frames across 12 pages. Now imagine that you want to edit the text. Maybe you want to proofread it or spell-check it. Editing the text within the layout might be difficult—you'd have to scroll from page to page. Instead, you could use the Edit in Story Editor command on the Edit menu. This opens a new window, which contains all the text in a single file, just like a word processing document. Any changes that you make in the Story Editor window will be immediately updated to the text in the layout. It's a great feature!

Move a graphic in a graphics frame

1. Hide the **Images layer**.

2. Show and target the **Background layer**, click the **Selection tool** ▶ , then click the **Windmills Ghost image** in the layout.

3. Click the **top-left reference point** on the Transform panel.

4. Click the **Direct Selection tool** ▷ , then click the **image**.

   As soon as you position the Direct Selection tool ▷ over the graphic, the pointer becomes a hand pointer. The X and Y text boxes on the Transform panel change to X+ and Y+, indicating that the graphic—not the frame—is selected.

5. Note the width and height of the graphic, as listed on the Transform panel.

   The graphic is substantially larger than the frame that contains it; thus, there are many areas of the graphic outside the frame that are not visible through the frame.

6. Press and hold the **hand icon** on the graphic until the hand icon changes to a black arrow; then drag **inside the graphics frame**, releasing the mouse button when the **windmill is centered** in the frame, as shown in Figure 54.

   The graphic moves within the frame, but the frame itself does not move. Note that the blue bounding box, now visible, is the bounding box for the graphic within the frame.

Figure 54 Viewing the graphic as it is moved in the frame

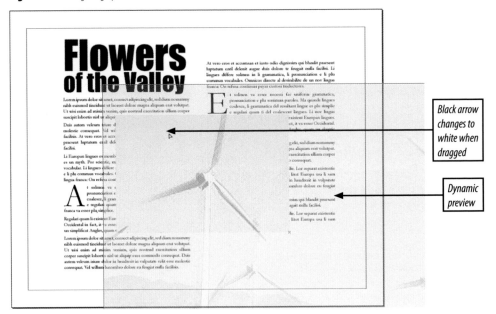

Black arrow changes to white when dragged

Dynamic preview

7. Click the **Selection tool** ▶, then click the **image**.

The orange graphics frame appears, and the blue bounding box of the graphic disappears. Note that the values on the Transform panel are again specific to the frame only.

8. Click and drag the **top-left selection handle of the graphics frame** so it is aligned with the **top-left corner of the document page**.

The graphic within the frame does not change size or location when you drag a handle on the frame.

9. Drag the **bottom-right corner of the graphics frame** so it is aligned with the **bottom-right corner of the document page**.

As the frame is enlarged, more of the graphic within the frame is visible.

10. Click the **Direct Selection tool** ▷, click the **graphic**, type **0** in the X+ text box on the Transform panel, type **0** in the Y+ text box, then press **[return] (Mac)** or **[Enter] (Win)**.

As shown in Figure 55, the top-left corner of the graphic is aligned with the top-left corner of the frame.

11. Save your work, then continue to the next set of steps.

You used the Direct Selection tool and X+ and Y+ values on the Transform panel to move a graphic within a graphics frame.

Figure 55 Viewing the entire graphic in the enlarged frame

Resize graphics frames and graphics

1. Drag the **Background layer** below the **Text layer** on the Layers panel.

2. Show and target the **Images layer**.

3. Press the **letter [A]** to access the **Direct Selection tool** ▷ , then click the **Girl at Windmills image** in the layout.

4. Verify that the **Constrain proportions for scaling button** ⓔ is activated on the Transform panel.

   The Constrain proportions for scaling button ⓔ is activated by default. If you click it, you will deactivate this feature and see a broken link icon ⓧ .

5. Type **50** in the **Scale X Percentage text box** on the Transform panel, as shown in Figure 56, then press **[return] (Mac)** or **[Enter] (Win)**.

   Because the Constrain proportions for scaling button ⓔ is activated, the graphic is scaled 50% horizontally and 50% vertically.

   The size of the graphics frame was not affected by scaling the graphic inside.

6. Deselect.

7. Press the **letter [V]** to access the **Selection tool** ▶ , then click the **image**.

8. Click **Object** on the menu bar, point to **Fitting**, then click **Fit Frame to Content**.

9. Click the **top-left reference point** on the Transform panel if it is not already selected.

Figure 56 Using the Transform panel to scale the image

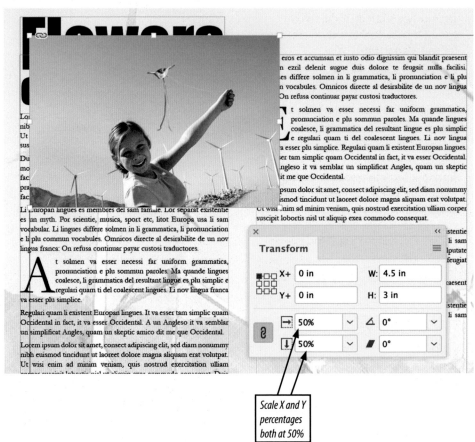

Scale X and Y
percentages
both at 50%

10. With the **frame** still selected, type **4.5** in the **X Location text box**, type **3** in the **Y Location text box**, type **3.32** in the **Width text box**, type **2.125** in the **Height text box**, then press **[return] (Mac)** or **[Enter] (Win)**.

TIP When you resize a graphics frame using the Width and Height text boxes on the Transform panel, the graphic is not resized with the frame. In other words, this graphic is still at 50%.

11. Click **Object** on the menu bar, point to **Fitting**, then click **Fit Content Proportionally**.

The graphic is scaled proportionately to fit the resized frame. Note that on the right side of the image, the frame extends the actual image. This is not a problem, but some designers like to be very precise in their work and have all frames aligned with the graphic inside them.

12. Click **Object** on the menu bar, point to **Fitting**, then click **Fit Frame to Content**.

The right edge of the frame moves left to fit to the right edge of the graphic. Your image and Transform panel should match Figure 57.

13. Deselect all, save your work, then continue to the next set of steps.

You scaled a graphic using the Transform panel, noting that the graphics frame did not change with the scale. You then scaled the graphics frame with the Transform panel, noting the graphic itself was not scaled. Lastly, you used the Fit Frame to Content command to fit the graphic proportionally to the new frame size.

Figure 57 The frame is fit to the content

Wrap text around a graphic

1. Verify that the **center image of the girl** is selected.

2. Click the **Wrap around bounding box button** 🔲 on the Text Wrap panel.

3. Verify that the **Make all settings the same button** 🔗 is active, type **.125** in the **Top Offset text box**, then press **[return] (Mac)** or **[Enter] (Win)**.

   Your page and Text Wrap panel should resemble Figure 58.

4. Deselect all.

5. Press **[command] [D] (Mac)**, or **[Ctrl] [D] (Win)**, navigate to the drive and folder where your Chapter 4 Data Files are stored, then double-click **Windmills Silhouette.psd**.

6. Click the **loaded graphics icon** on the **F** in the word **Flowers**.

   Windmills Silhouette.psd was saved with a clipping path named "Path 1" in Photoshop. It has the same sketchy texture as the windmills in the background image.

7. Click the **Wrap around object shape button** 🔲 on the Text Wrap panel, click the **Type list arrow**, click **Photoshop Path**, then note that **Path 1** is automatically listed in the Path text box.

8. Type **.14** in the **Top Offset text box**, then press **[return] (Mac)** or **[Enter] (Win)**.

   The text wraps around the windmill's shape, as defined by the path created in Photoshop plus the 0.14" offset you specified.

9. Deselect all.

Figure 58 Text wraps on all four sides

10. Click the **Selection tool** ▶, then click the **windmill image** to select the frame.

11. Type **−1.25** in the **X Location text box** on the Transform panel, type **3.8** in the **Y Location text box**, then press **[return] (Mac)** or **[Enter] (Win)**.

    As shown in Figure 59, because of the shape of the path around the graphic, a couple of words appear in an odd position near the graphic.

12. In the Wrap Options section on the Text Wrap panel, click the **Wrap To list arrow**, click **Right Side**, then deselect the graphic.

    The words are moved to the right because the wrap option forces all items to wrap against the right edge of the graphic.

TIP Whenever you have a stray word or a stubborn area after applying a text wrap, you can fine-tune the text wrap using the Delete Anchor Point tool ✎ to remove unwanted anchor points along the path. You can also move anchor points along the path using the Direct Selection tool ▷.

13. Show the **Caption layer**.

    The text on the caption layer is meant to be positioned under the center image. However, you know the text wrap on the center image will "bump" the caption, so you must set the caption frame to ignore the text wrap.

14. Select the **frame** that contains the **caption text**, press **[command] [B] (Mac)** or **[Ctrl] [B] (Win)**, click **Ignore Text Wrap**, then click **OK**.

15. Center the **text under the center image**.

16. Click the **pasteboard** to deselect the frame.

17. Press **[W]** to change to **Preview**, then compare your work to Figure 60.

18. Save your work, then close the Flowers document.

You wrapped text around a graphic, specified an offset value, then specified wrap options.

Figure 59 Noting a minor problem with the wrap

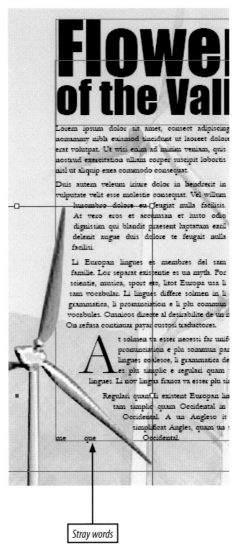

Stray words

Figure 60 The completed layout

Flowers
of the Desert

Lorem ipsum dolor sit amet, consect adipiscing elit, sed diam nonummy nibh euismod tincidunt ut laoreet dolore magna aliquam erat volutpat. Ut wisi enim ad minim veniam, quis nostrud exercitation ulliam corper suscipit lobortis nisl ut aliquip exea commodo consequat.

Duis autem veleum iriure dolor in hendrerit in vulputate velit esse molestie consequat. Vel willum lunombro dolore eu feugiat nulla facilisi. At vero eros et accumsan et iusto odio dignissim qui blandit praesent luptatum ezril delenit augue duis dolore te feugait nulla facilisi.

Li Europan lingues es membres del sam familie. Lor separat existentie es un myth. Por scientie, musica, sport etc, litot Europa usa li sam vocabular. Li lingues differe solmen in li grammatica, li pronunciation e li plu commun vocabules. Omnicos directe al desirabilite de un nov lingua franca: On refusa continuar payar custosi traductores.

A t solmen va esser necessi far uniform grammatica, pronunciation e plu sommun paroles. Ma quande lingues coalesce, li grammatica del resultant lingue es plu simplic e regulari quam ti del coalescent lingues. Li nov lingua franca va esser plu simplice.

Regulari quam li existent Europan lingues. It va esser tam simplic quam Occidental in fact, it va esser Occidental. A un Angleso it va semblar un simplificat Angles, quam un skeptic

amico dit me que Occidental.

Lorem ipsum dolor sit amet, consect adipiscing elit, sed diam nonummy nibh euismod tincidunt ut laoreet dolore magna aliquam erat volutpat. Ut wisi enim ad minim veniam, quis nostrud exercitation ulliam corper suscipit lobortis nisl ut aliquip exea commodo consequat. Duis autem veleum iriure dolor in hendrerit in vulputate velit esse molestie consequat. Vel willum lunombro dolore eu feugiat nulla facilisi.

A windmill garden is a kite flyer's dream come true.

At vero eros et accumsan et iusto odio dignissim qui blandit praesent luptatum ezril delenit augue duis dolore te feugait nulla facilisi. Li lingues differe solmen in li grammatica, li pronunciation e li plu commun vocabules. Omnicos directe al desirabilite de un nov lingua franca: On refusa continuar payar custosi traductores.

E t solmen va esser necessi far uniform grammatica, pronunciation e plu sommun paroles. Ma quande lingues coalesce, li grammatica del resultant lingue es plu simplic e regulari quam ti del coalescent lingues. Li nov lingua franca va esser plu simplice. Regulari quam li existent Europan lingues. It va esser tam simplic quam Occidental in fact, it va esser Occidental. A un Angleso it va semblar un simplificat Angles, quam un skeptic amico dit me que Occidental.

Lorem ipsum dolor sit amet, consect adipiscing elit, sed diam nonummy nibh euismod tincidunt ut laoreet dolore magna aliquam erat volutpat. Ut wisi enim ad minim veniam, quis nostrud exercitation ulliam corper suscipit lobortis nisl ut aliquip exea commodo consequat.

WORK WITH TEXT FRAMES

What You'll Do

In this lesson, you will explore options for autoflowing text through a document. You will also learn how to add column breaks to text.

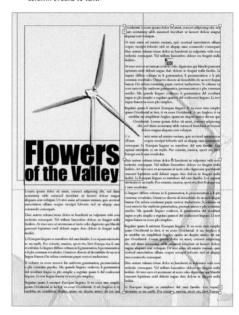

Semi-Autoflowing Text

In Chapter 3, you learned how to thread text manually—to make it flow from text frame to text frame. When you click the out port of one text frame with the Selection tool, the pointer changes to the loaded text icon. When you click the loaded text icon in another text frame, text flows from the first frame to the second frame—and the pointer automatically changes back to the Selection tool. That's great, but what if you wanted to keep threading text? Would you need to repeat the process over and over again?

This is where semi-autoflowing text comes in handy. **Semi-autoflowing** text is a method for manually threading text through multiple frames. When you are ready to click the loaded text icon in a text frame where you want text to flow, press and hold [option] (Mac) or [Alt] (Win), then click the text frame. Text will flow into the text frame, but the loaded text icon will remain active; it will not automatically revert to the Selection tool. You can then thread text into another text frame.

Autoflowing Text

You can also **autoflow** text, or automatically thread text through multiple text frames. This is a powerful option for quickly adding text to your document. Let's say you create a six-page document and you specify that each page has three columns. When you create the document, the pages have no text frames on them—they're just blank, with columns and margin guides. To autoflow text into the document, you click the Place command and choose the text document that you want to import. Once you choose the document, the pointer changes to the loaded text icon. Press and hold [shift], and the loaded text icon becomes the autoflow loaded text icon. When you click the autoflow loaded text icon in a column, InDesign creates text frames within column guides on that page and all subsequent pages and flows the text into those frames. Because you specified that each page has three columns when you created the document, InDesign will create three text frames in the columns on every page into which the text will flow.

If you autoflow more text than the document size can handle, InDesign will add as many pages as necessary to autoflow all the text. If your document pages contain objects such as graphics, the text frames added by the autoflow will be positioned in front of the graphics already on the page.

As you may imagine, autoflowing text is a powerful option, but don't be intimidated by it. The text frames that are generated are all editable. You can resize them or delete them. Nevertheless, you should take some time to practice autoflowing text to get the hang of it. Like learning how to ride a bicycle, you can read about it all you want, but actually doing it is where the learning happens.

Inserting a Column Break

When you are working with text in columns, you will often want to move text from the bottom of one column to the top of the next. You do this by inserting a column break. A **column break** is a typographic command that forces text to the next column. The Column Break command is located within the Insert Break Character command on the Type menu.

In Figure 61, the headline near the bottom of the first column would be better positioned at the top of the next column. By inserting a column break, you do exactly that, as shown in Figure 62.

Figure 61 Viewing text that needs a column break

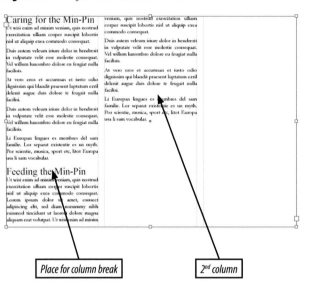

Place for column break 2nd column

Figure 62 Viewing text after inserting a column break

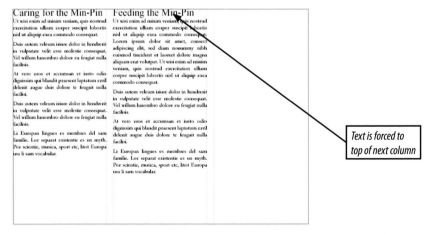

Text is forced to top of next column

Inserting a "Continued on page ..." Notation

When threading text manually or autoflowing text, you will get to a point where text has filled all the text frames on the page and continues to another page. Usually, the text continues onto the very next page—but not always. In many cases, the next page will be reserved for pictures or other publication elements, such as tables or graphs. When readers get to the bottom of the page of text, they need to know on which page the text is continued. You can insert a "Continued on page ..." notation to let the reader know where to go to continue reading.

If you've ever read a magazine or newspaper article, you are familiar with "Continued on page ..." notations. In InDesign, a page continuation is formatted as a special character. Simply create a text frame, then type the words "Continued on page X." Select the X, then apply the Next Page Number command. The X changes to the page number of the page that contains the text frame into which the text flows. If, for any reason, you move pages within the Pages panel and page numbers change, the Next Page Number character will automatically update to show the page number where the text continues.

The Next Page Number command is located within the Insert Special Character command under Markers on the Type menu.

There's one important point you need to note when creating a "Continued on page ..." notation. Below the text frame on the page of the text you are flowing, you will need to create another text frame to contain the "Continued on page ..." notation. In order for the notation to work—for it to list the page where the text continues—the top edge of the text frame that contains the notation must be touching the frame that contains the body copy that is to be continued.

PARAGRAPHS THAT SPAN OR SPLIT COLUMNS

Imagine having one text box that contains five paragraphs, with the fourth needing to be split into two columns within the text box. Or imagine that you have a single text frame with three columns, and you want to run a headline across all three columns. With InDesign, you can format text to span multiple columns or split into columns within a single text frame. Not only is this feature unprecedented; it's remarkably easy to use. Simply click your cursor in the paragraph you want to modify. Choose the Span Columns command from the Paragraph panel menu, then select to split the paragraph or span the paragraph.

Autoflow text

1. Open ID 4-7.indd, save it as **Autoflow**, then look at each page in the document.

   Other than the text frame that holds the headline on page 1, there are no text frames in the document.

2. Click the **Selection tool** ▶ double-click the **page 1 icon** on the Pages panel, click **File** on the menu bar, click **Place,** navigate to the drive and folder where your Chapter 4 Data Files are stored, then double-click **Windmill text.doc**.

   The pointer changes to the loaded text icon.

3. Drag a **text frame** in the position shown in Figure 63.

   Note that once you have drawn the frame, the loaded text icon automatically changes back to the Selection tool ▶ .

4. Click the **out port** of the text frame, then position the **loaded text icon** over the **right column on the page**.

5. Press and hold **[option] (Mac)** or **[Alt] (Win)** so the pointer changes to the semi-autoflow loaded text icon.

Figure 63 Creating a text frame using the loaded text icon

Text frame aligned with intersection of margin and guide

Out port

6. Still pressing and holding **[option] (Mac)** or **[Alt] (Win)**, click the **top-left corner of the right column** so a **new text frame** is created, then release **[option] (Mac)** or **[Alt] (Win)**.

Because you used the semi-autoflow loaded text icon, the pointer remains as a loaded text icon and does not revert back to the Selection tool ▶, as shown in Figure 64.

7. Double-click the **page 2 icon,** then click the **top-left corner of the left column** on the page.

A new frame is created, and text flows into the left column.

8. Click the **out port** of the **new text frame on page 2**, then position the **pointer** over the **right column on page 2**.

9. Press and hold **[shift]**, note the change to the loaded text icon, then click the **top-left corner of the second column**.

Because you were pressing [shift], InDesign created text frames within column guides on all subsequent pages. InDesign has added new pages to the document to accommodate the autoflow.

10. Save your work, then continue to the next set of steps.

You placed text by clicking and dragging the loaded text icon to create a new text frame. You flowed text using the semi-autoflow loaded text icon and the autoflow loaded text icon.

Figure 64   Flowing text with the semi-autoflow loaded text icon

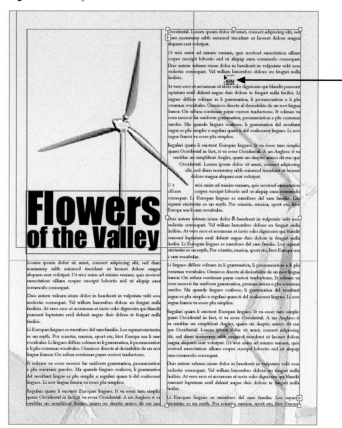

Pointer remains as loaded text icon after text has been flowed

Reflow text

1. Double-click the **page 4 icon** on the Pages panel, then create a **horizontal guide** at **5.875 in**.

2. Click the **left text frame** to select it, drag the **bottom-middle handle** of the text frame's bounding box up until it snaps to the guide, then do the same to the right text frame, so your page resembles Figure 65.

   The text is reflowed in the document.

3. Double-click the **numbers 2-3** on the Pages panel to center the spread in the document window, click **View** on the menu bar, point to **Extras**, click **Show Text Threads**, then click the **right text frame on page 2**.

Figure 65 Resizing text frames

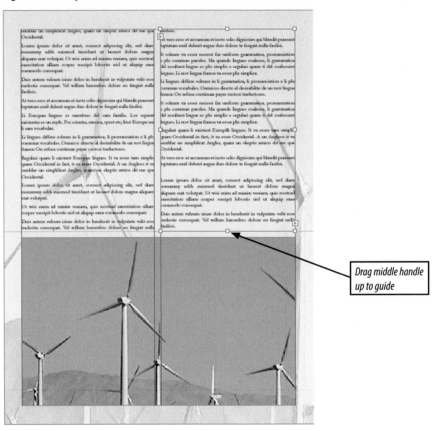

Drag middle handle up to guide

4. With the **right frame on page 2** still selected, press **[delete]**, then click the **text frame** remaining on **page 2**.

   As shown in Figure 66, the text is reflowed from the first text frame on page 2 to the first text frame on page 3.

5. Press **[command] [D] (Mac)** or **[Ctrl] [D] (Win)**, navigate to the drive and folder where your Chapter 4 Data Files are stored, then double-click **2 Windmills.psd**.

6. Click the **top-left corner of the right column on page 2**.

7. Create a **horizontal guide** at **5.375 in**.

8. Click the **text frame on page 2**, then click the **out port**.

9. Click the **intersection** between the guide you created and the **left edge of the right column**, beneath the graphic.

   As shown in Figure 67, text is now threaded through the new text frame.

10. Save your work, then continue to the next set of steps.

You resized two text frames, noting text was reflowed through the document. You deleted a text frame, then created a text frame, noting text continued to flow through the document.

Figure 66 Flowing text after deleting a text frame

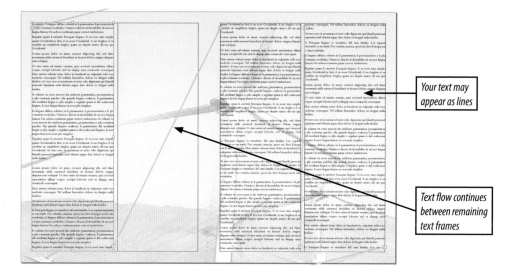

Your text may appear as lines

Text flow continues between remaining text frames

Figure 67 Threading text to a new text frame

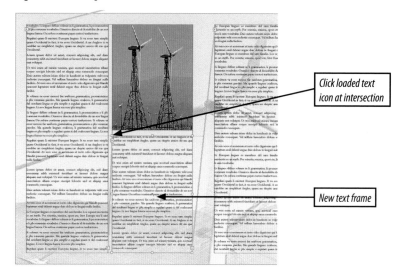

Click loaded text icon at intersection

New text frame

Add a column break

1. Double-click the **page 5 icon** on the Pages panel, then delete the **two text frames on page 5**.

2. Click **Layout** on the menu bar, click **Margins and Columns**, change the **number of columns** to **3**, then click **OK**.

3. Press **[command] [D] (Mac)** or **[Ctrl] [D] (Win)**, navigate to the drive and folder where your Chapter 4 Data Files are stored, then double-click **Sidebar copy.doc**.

4. Drag the **loaded text icon** to create a text frame, as shown in Figure 68.

5. Click **Object** on the menu bar, click **Text Frame Options**, change the **number of columns** to **3**, then click **OK**.

6. Click the **Type tool** $\boxed{T}$, then click to place the **pointer before the Windmill Speeds headline**.

Figure 68   Creating a text frame with the loaded text icon

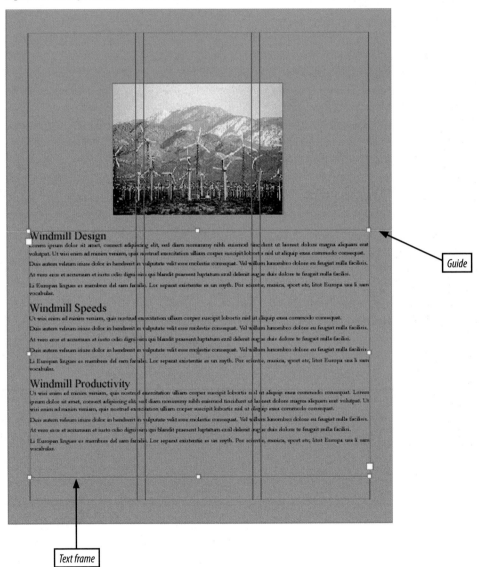

Guide

Text frame

7. Click **Type** on the menu bar, point to **Insert Break Character**, then click **Column Break**.

The Windmill Speeds text is forced into the second column.

8. Click before the **W** in the **Windmill Productivity headline**, click **Type** on the menu bar, point to **Insert Break Character**, then click **Column Break**.

Your page should resemble Figure 69.

9. Save your work, then continue to the next set of steps.

You deleted two text frames on a page and then changed the number of columns on that page. You then placed text, formatted the text frame to have three columns, and, finally, used the Column Break command to create two new column breaks.

Figure 69 Viewing the text frame with column breaks

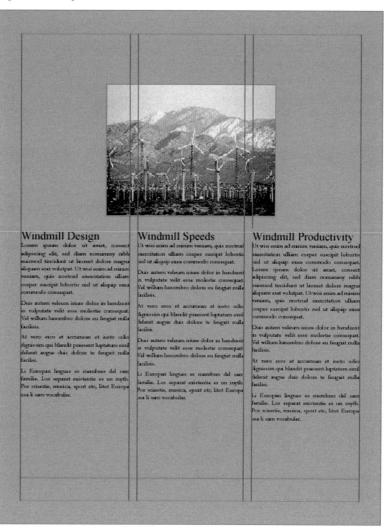

Insert a page continuation notation

1. Double-click the **page 4 icon** on the Pages panel, then create a **horizontal guide** at **5 in**.

2. Click the **Selection tool** ▶, click the **text frame in the right column**, then drag the **bottom-middle bounding box handle** up until it snaps to the guide at **5 in**.

3. Click the **Type tool** T, then create a **text frame** between the two guides, as shown in Figure 70. The edges of the two text frames should overlap slightly at the guide, which is critical for page continuation notation to work.

4. Click **Object** on the menu bar, click **Text Frame Options**, change the **Vertical Justification** to **Center**, then click **OK**.

Figure 70 Creating a text frame for the page continuation notation

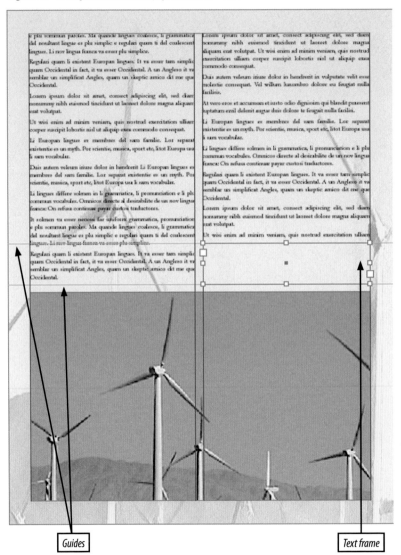

Guides

Text frame

5. Click the **Type tool** T inside the new text box, type **(Continued on page X)**, click **anywhere within the (Continued on page X) text**, show the **Paragraph Styles panel**, then click the style named **Continued**.

6. Select the **letter X**, click **Type** on the menu bar, point to **Insert Special Character**, point to **Markers**, then click **Next Page Number**.

   The text now reads (Continued on page 6), as shown in Figure 71.

   TIP You can use the Previous Page Number command along with "Continued from page . . ." text to indicate that a story is continued from a previous page.

7. Click the **Selection tool** ▶, click the **text frame** above the "Continued" text frame, then follow the text thread to verify that the text does indeed continue on page 6.

8. Save your work, then close the Autoflow document.

You inserted a page continuation notation in the document.

Figure 71 Viewing the page continuation notation

Notation

Align and distribute objects on a page

1. Open ID 4-8.indd, then save it as **Dog Days**.
2. Click the workspace switcher list arrow on the menu bar, then click Advanced or Reset Advanced if Advanced is already checked.
3. Click the Type tool, then drag a text frame that fills the left column on the page.
4. Click the Selection tool, press and hold [shift] [option] (Mac) or [Shift] [Alt] (Win), then drag a copy of the text frame and position it in line with the right column.
5. Click the Rectangle Frame tool, click anywhere on the page, type **1.5** in both the Width and Height text boxes, then click OK.
6. Click the top-left reference point on the Transform panel, type **0** in the X Location text box, type **0** in the Y Location text box, then press [return] (Mac) or [Enter] (Win).
7. Verify that the frame has no fill and no stroke.
8. Click Edit on the menu bar, click Step and Repeat, type **1** in the Repeat Count text box, type **9.5** in the Horizontal Offset text box, type **0** in the Vertical Offset text box, then click OK.
9. Select both graphics frames, click Edit on the menu bar, click Step and Repeat, type **1** in the Repeat Count text box, type **0** in the Horizontal Offset text box, type **7** in the Vertical Offset text box, then click OK.

10. Click the Rectangle Frame tool, click anywhere in the left column, type **3** in both the Width and Height text boxes, click OK, then verify that the frame has no fill or stroke.
11. Click the Selection tool, press and hold [shift], click the top-left graphics frame, then click the top-right graphics frame so three frames are selected.

12. Click Window on the menu bar, point to Object & Layout, click Align, then click the Distribute horizontal centers button on the Align panel.
13. Deselect all, select the top-left and bottom-left graphics frames and the 3" × 3" frame, click the Distribute vertical centers button on the Align panel, then compare your page to Figure 72.

Figure 72 *Completed Skills Review, Part 1*

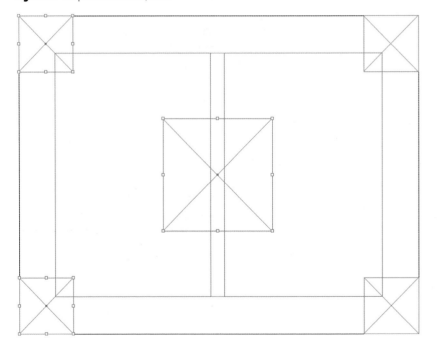

Stack and layer objects

1. Display the Layers panel.
2. Double-click Layer 1, type **Background Graphic** in the Name text box, then click OK.
3. Click the Create new layer button on the Layers panel, double-click the new layer, type **Dog Pics** in the Name text box, then click OK.
4. Click the Layers panel menu button, click New Layer, type **Body** in the Name text box, then click OK.
5. Click the Selection tool, select the five graphics frames, then drag the selected items button from the Background Graphic layer up to the Dog Pics layer.
6. Select the two text frames, then drag the selected items button from the Background Graphic layer up to the Body layer.
7. Verify the Body layer is selected, select only the left text frame, click File on the menu bar, click Place, navigate to the drive and folder where your Chapter 4 Data Files are stored, then double-click Skills Text.doc.
8. Click any word five times to select all the text, then format the text as Garamond 12-point font size with 14-point leading.
9. Click the Selection tool, click the out port of the left text frame, then click the loaded text icon anywhere in the right text frame.
10. On the Layers panel, drag the Body layer down below the Dog Pics layer.
11. Save your work.

Work with graphics frames

1. Click the Selection tool, select the top-left graphics frame, press [command] [D] (Mac) or [Ctrl] [D] (Win), navigate to the drive and folder where your Chapter 4 Data Files are stored, then double-click Red 1.psd.
2. Select the top-right graphics frame, press [command] [D] (Mac) or [Ctrl] [D] (Win), navigate to the drive and folder where your Chapter 4 Data Files are stored, then double-click Black 1.psd.
3. Select the bottom-left graphics frame, press [command] [D] (Mac) or [Ctrl] [D] (Win), navigate to the drive and folder where your Chapter 4 Data Files are stored, then double-click Red 2.psd.
4. Select the bottom-right graphics frame, press [command] [D] (Mac) or [Ctrl] [D] (Win), navigate to the drive and folder where your Chapter 4 Data Files are stored, then double-click Black 2.psd.
5. Select the top two graphics frames, click Object on the menu bar, point to Fitting, then click Fit Content to Frame.
6. Deselect all, click the Direct Selection tool, press and hold the mouse pointer on the bottom-left graphic, then drag until the dog's nose is at the center of the frame.
7. Click the center reference point on the Transform panel, type **40** in both the Scale X Percentage and Scale Y Percentage text boxes, then click and drag to center the dog's head in the frame.
8. Deselect all, click the Selection tool, select the four corner graphics frames, click the Wrap around bounding box button on the Text Wrap panel, then type **.125** in all four of the Offset text boxes.
9. Select the center graphics frame, press [command] [D] (Mac) or [Ctrl] [D] (Win), navigate to the drive and folder where your Chapter 4 Data Files are stored, then double click Dog Silo.psd.
10. Click the Direct Selection tool, click the new graphic, then click the Wrap around object shape button on the Text Wrap panel.

(continued)

11. Click the Type list arrow in the Contour Options section, choose Same as Clipping, type **.15** in the Top Offset text box, then press [return] (Mac) or [Enter] (Win).

12. Press [W] to switch to Preview, deselect all, compare your page to Figure 73, save your work, then close the Dog Days document.

Work with text frames

1. Open ID 4-9.indd, click Update Links, then save it as **Dog Days Part 2**.

2. Click the Selection tool, click the right text frame on page 1, then click the out port of the text frame.

3. Double-click page 2 on the Pages panel, position the loaded text icon over the left column, press and hold [shift], then click the top-left corner of the left column.

4. Click View on the menu bar, point to Extras, click Show Text Threads, double-click page 3 on the Pages panel, then click the eye icon in the Dog Pics layer on the Layers panel to hide it temporarily.

TIP Autoflowing the text created two text frames on page 3, but they weren't visible because the Body Copy layer is behind the Dog Pics layer.

Figure 73 Completed Skills Review, Part 2

Lorem ipsum dolor sit amet, consect adipiscing elit, sed diam nonummy nibh euismod tincidunt ut laoreet dolore magna aliquam erat volutpat. Ut wisi enim ad minim venim, quis nostrud exercitation ulliam corper suscipit lobortis nisl ut aliquip exea commodo consequat.

Duis autem veleum iriure dolor in hendrerit in vulputate velit esse molestie consequat. Vel willum lunombro dolore eu feugiat nulla facilisis. At vero eros et accumsan et iusto odio dignissim qui blandit praesent luptatum eznl delenit augue duis dolore te feugait nulla facilisi.

Li Europan lingues es membres del sam familie. Lor separat existentie es un myth. Por scientie, musica, sport etc, litot Europa usa li sam vocabular. Li lingues differe solmen in li grammatica, li pronunciation e li plu commun vocabules. Omnicos directe al desirabilite de un nov lingua franca: On refusa continuar payar custosi traductores.

At solmen va esser necessi far uniform grammatica, pronunciation e plu sommun paroles. Ma quande lingues coalesce, li grammatica del resultant lingue es plu simplic e regulari quam ti del coalescent lingues. Li nov lingua franca va esser plu simplice.

Regulari quam li existent Europan lingues. It va esser tam simplic quam Occidental in fact, it va esser Occidental. A un Angleso it va semblar un simplificat Angles, quam un skeptic amico dit me que Occidental.

Lorem ipsum dolor sit amet, consect adipiscing elit, sed diam nonummy nibh euismod tincidunt ut laoreet dolore magna aliquam erat volutpat. Ut wisi enim ad minim veniam, quis nostrud exercitation ulliam corper suscipit lobortis nisl ut aliquip exea commodo consequat. Duis autem veleum iriure dolor in hendrerit in vulputate velit esse molestie consequat. Vel willum lunombro dolore eu feugiat nulla facilisis.

At vero eros et accumsan et iusto odio dignissim qui blandit praesent luptatum eznl delenit augue duis dolore te feugait nulla facilisi. Li lingues differe solmen in li grammatica, li pronunciation e li plu commun vocabules. Omnicos directe al desirabilite de un nov lingua franca: On refusa continuar payar custosi traductores.

Solmen va esser necessi far uniform grammatica,

Images courtesy of Chris Botello

5. Verify that the Body Copy layer is selected, delete both text frames on page 3, then click the eye icon on the Dog Pics layer so the layer is visible again. The text now ends on page 2.
6. Go to page 2, click the Selection tool, click the right text frame on the page, then click the out port of the text frame.
7. Go to page 4, then click and drag the loaded text icon to create a text box across both columns on the page. The text now flows from page 2 to page 4.
8. Double-click page 2 on the Pages panel, select the right text frame, then drag the bottom-middle handle of the right text frame up so it slightly overlaps the top edge of the small text frame at the bottom of the column.
9. Click the Type tool, click the small text frame at the bottom of the right column, then type **Continued on X**.
10. Click the Continued style on the Paragraph Styles panel, then select the letter X.
11. Click Type on the menu bar, point to Insert Special Character, point to Markers, then click Next Page Number.
12. Deselect all, compare your page 2 to Figure 74, save your work, then close the Dog Days Part 2 document.

Figure 74 Completed Skills Review, Part 3

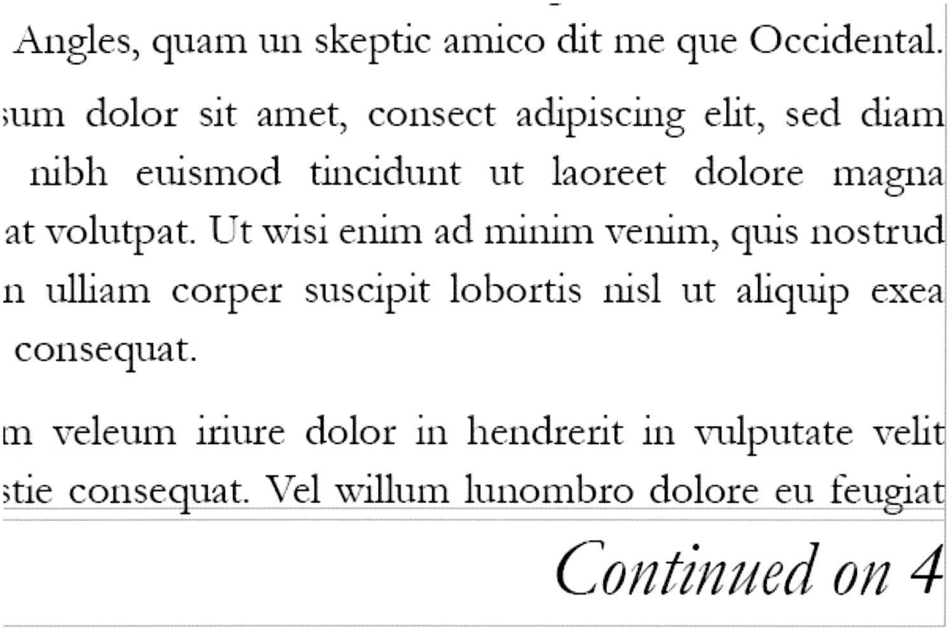

Angles, quam un skeptic amico dit me que Occidental.

:um dolor sit amet, consect adipiscing elit, sed diam nibh euismod tincidunt ut laoreet dolore magna at volutpat. Ut wisi enim ad minim venim, quis nostrud n ulliam corper suscipit lobortis nisl ut aliquip exea consequat.

m veleum iriure dolor in hendrerit in vulputate velit stie consequat. Vel willum lunombro dolore eu feugiat

Continued on 4

You work for a design firm, and you are creating a logo for a local shop that sells vintage board games. You decide to create an 8" × 8" checkerboard, which you will later incorporate into your logo.

1. Open ID 4-10.indd, then save it as **Checkerboard**.
2. Click the Rectangle Frame tool, create a 1" square frame anywhere on the board, fill it with black and no stroke, then position it so its top-left corner has a (0, 0) coordinate.
3. Use the Step and Repeat command to make one copy, one inch to the right of the original square.
4. Select the new square, if necessary, change its fill color to Brick Red, then select both squares.
5. Use the Step and Repeat command again, type **3** in the Repeat Count text box, type **0** in the Vertical Offset text box, type **2** in the Horizontal Offset text box, then click OK.
6. Verify that all squares are still selected, use the Step and Repeat command again, type **1** in the Repeat Count text box, type **1** in the Vertical Offset text box, type **0** in the Horizontal Offset text box, then click OK.
7. Deselect all, select the eight squares in the second row, click the center reference point on the Transform panel, then change the Rotation Angle text box to 180°.
8. Select all, use the Step and Repeat command again, type **3** in the Repeat Count text box, type **2** in the Vertical Offset text box, type **0** in the Horizontal Offset text box, then click OK.
9. Press [W] to switch to Preview, deselect all, then compare your work to Figure 75.
10. Save your work, then close the Checkerboard document.

Figure 75 Completed Project Builder 1

You are a designer at a design firm that specializes in travel. A client sends you a layout she created in InDesign. She wants you to use it as a template for future layouts. You open the file and decide it's best to move the basic elements onto layers.

1. Open ID 4-11.indd, then save it as **Brochure Layers**.
2. On the Layers panel, rename Layer 1 as **Background Colors**.
3. Create a new layer, then name it **Pictures**.
4. Create a new layer, then name it **Text**.
5. Select the four graphics frames, then move them onto the Pictures layer.
6. Select the two text frames, then move them onto the Text layer.
7. Use the Layers panel to select all the frames on the Pictures layer, then compare your work to Figure 76.
8. Save your work, then close the Brochure Layers document.

Figure 76 Completed Project Builder 2

Images courtesy of Chris Botello

You lead the layout team for a design firm. Your client has delivered you a Photoshop file with a clipping path. He wants you to use it in the layout he has supplied. He tells you he wants the graphic placed in the middle of the page with text wrapping around it on all four sides. You import the graphic and realize you will need to modify the path that controls the wrap in InDesign.

1. Open ID 4-12.indd, then save it as **Four Leg Wrap**.
2. Click File on the menu bar, click Place, navigate to the drive and folder where your Chapter 4 Data Files are stored, then double-click Red Silo.psd.
3. Click the loaded graphics icon anywhere on the page, click the Selection tool, then center the graphic on the page.
4. Verify that you can see the Transform panel, press and hold or [command] [shift] (Mac) or [Ctrl] [Shift] (Win), then drag the top-left corner of the frame toward the center of the frame, reducing the frame until the Width text box on the Transform panel reads approximately 5 inches.
5. Click the center reference point on the Transform panel, type **4.25** in the X Location text box, type **4.2** in the Y Location text box, then press [return] (Mac) or [Enter] (Win).
6. Click the Direct Selection tool, click the graphic, click the Wrap around object shape button on the Text Wrap panel, then adjust the offset so it is visually pleasing.
7. Draw a graphics frame in the position shown in Figure 77, being sure the bottom edges of the two graphics frames are aligned.

Figure 77 Positioning the graphics frame

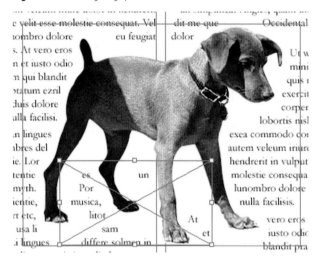

8. With only the lower graphics frame selected, click the Wrap around bounding box button on the Text Wrap panel. Adjust the new frame as necessary to move any stray text.
9. Deselect all, press [W] to switch to Preview, then compare your work to Figure 78.
10. Save your work, then close the Four Leg Wrap document.

Figure 78 Completed Design Project

Lorem ipsum dolor sit amet, consect adipiscing elit, sed diam nonummy nibh euismod tincidunt ut laoreet dolore magna aliquam erat volutpat. Ut wisi enim ad minim veniam, quis nostrud exercitation ulliam corper suscipit lobortis nisl ut aliquip exea commodo consequat.

Duis autem veleum iriure dolor in hendrerit in vulputate velit esse molestie consequat. Vel willum lunombro dolore eu feugiat nulla facilisis. At vero eros et accumsan et iusto odio dignissim qui blandit praesent luptatum ezril delenit augue duis dolore te feugait nulla facilisi.

Li Europan lingues es membres del sam familie. Lor separat existentie es un myth. Por scientie, musica, sport etc, litot Europa usa li sam vocabular. Li lingues differe solmen in li grammatica, li pronunciation e li plu commun vocabules. Omnicos directe al desirabilite de un nov lingua franca: On refusa continuar payar custosi traductores.

It solmen va esser necessi far uniform grammatica, pronunciation e plu sommun paroles. Ma quande lingues coalesce, li grammatica del resultant lingue es plu simplic e regulari quam ti del coalescent lingues. Li nov lingua franca va esser plu simplice.

Regulari quam li existent Europan lingues. It va esser tam simplic quam Occidental in fact, it va esser Occidental. A un Angleso it va semblar un simplificat Angles, quam un skeptic amico dit me que Occidental. Lorem ipsum dolor sit amet.

Ut wisi enim ad minim veniam, quis nostrud exercitation ulliam corper suscipit lobortis nisl ut aliquip exea commodo consequat. Duis autem veleum iriure dolor in hendrerit in vulputate velit esse molestie consequat. Vel willum lunombro dolore eu feugiat nulla facilisis.

At vero eros et accumsan et iusto odio dignissim qui blandit praesent luptatum ezril delenit augue duis dolore te feugait nulla facilisi. Li lingues differe solmen in li grammatica, li pronunciation e li plu commun vocabules. Omnicos directe al desirabilite de un nov lingua franca:

On refusa continuar payar custosi traductores. It solmen va esser necessi far uniform grammatica,

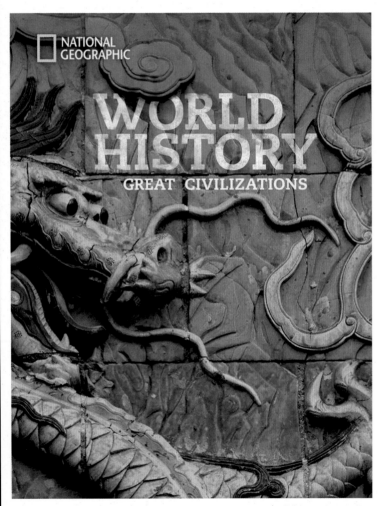

© Cengage Learning, Inc.

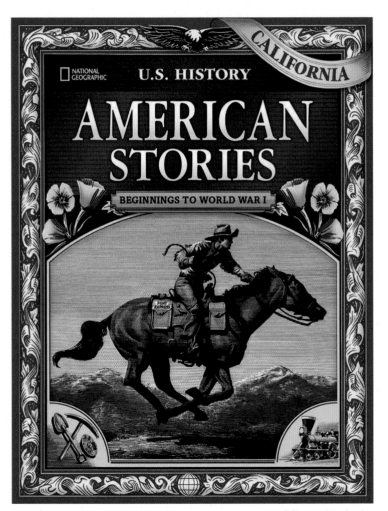

© Cengage Learning, Inc.

| NATIONAL GEOGRAPHIC **LEARNING** | SCOTT BAKER **MANAGING ART DIRECTOR** |

As a child, Scott Baker enjoyed creating comic books with his brother. Seeing their passion for art, their mother enrolled them in art classes. From an early age, Scott learned the importance of finding a creative mentor—and he has had many throughout his life. When it came time for college, Scott worked toward his BFA and Associate Degree in Illustration. After graduation, however, he wasn't sure of his career direction, so he traveled to London and worked as a freelancer for several music and fashion magazines. Those experiences opened many doors in the publishing industry upon his return to the states.

As Managing Art Director at National Geographic Learning, Scott manages a team of designers, and works to keep projects on time and within budget. In doing so, he places importance on the planning process. Scott suggests asking questions before starting work in order to establish the goal of the project and to understand the client's needs. He also values communication, both with colleagues and clients. He shares, "A big part of my job is not just creating effective designs but selling ideas, so having a good design vocabulary is extremely important."

This design vocabulary often helps Scott interpret criticism creatively. For example, if marketing requests a larger logo, Scott looks for a more elegant way to draw attention to the logo instead of simply enlarging it.

Although he has a variety of projects in his portfolio, Scott has always enjoyed designing book covers. He shares, "A cover creates a reader's first impression and sets the tone for the entire book." Creativity isn't just something Scott values while at work; it spills over into his free time as well. He enjoys drawing, writing, and painting, as well as growing fruits and vegetables in his backyard garden. Scott shares, "It's important for me to unplug whenever possible and just find time to do something more hands-on."

PROJECT DESCRIPTION

In this project, you will redesign the cover of your favorite book. You have complete creative freedom over the direction of the design. Think about the characters and events in the book. What stands out to you most? Explore all of your ideas and design a cover that will convey the feel of the book. The goal of this project is to give future readers visual insight into what the book is about.

QUESTIONS TO CONSIDER

What are the important events in the book?

What colors and images capture the tone of the book?

What is important to convey on the book cover?

GETTING STARTED

A book cover should allude to the plot or overarching theme of the book. From a design perspective, it should also stand out on a bookshelf and capture the reader's attention, making them want to open the cover and read more. Book covers take on a different tone, depending on the genre. If your chosen book is nonfiction—biography, how-to, historical, or commentary—it will carry a different feel than if it is a young adult novel or other fictional book.

Conduct an Internet search on book covers in your chosen book's genre. Compare the images. Pay close attention to the composition. Does the cover have a full illustration, photo, or graphic with the title and author's name centered, or does the text play a greater role, with a small abstract design in the corner? Look also at font choices and color choices. Then recall the events in your chosen book. Which elements from your Internet search would best convey the author's tone? Experiment with ideas and layouts until you create a cover that best represents the plot or theme of the book.

OAHU living

FALL 2015 • $4.95

A•MAZE•ING
get lost in a pineapple maze

TWIST & SHOUT
boogie-boarding daredevils stare down the north coast waves

MAVERICK
a sizzling interview with Chef Mavro

CHAPTER 5

WORKING WITH COLOR

1. Work with Process Colors
2. Apply Color
3. Work with Spot Colors
4. Work with Gradients

CERTIFIED PROFESSIONAL

Adobe Certified Professional in Print & Digital Media Publication Using Adobe InDesign

1. Working in the Design Industry

This objective covers critical concepts related to working with colleagues and clients as well as crucial legal, technical, and design-related knowledge.

1.4 Demonstrate knowledge of key terminology related to publications.

   B Demonstrate knowledge of how color is created in publications.

2. Project Setup and Interface

This objective covers the interface setup and program settings that assist in an efficient and effective workflow, as well as knowledge about ingesting digital assets for a project.

2.5 Manage colors, swatches, and gradients.

   A Set the active fill and stroke color.

   B Create and customize gradients.

   C Create, manage, and edit swatches and swatch libraries.

3. Organizing Documents

This objective covers document structure such as layers, tracks, and managing document structure for efficient workflows.

3.1 Use layers to manage design elements.

   A Use the Layers panel to modify layers.

4. Creating and Modifying Document Elements

This objective covers core tools and functionality of the application, as well as tools that affect the visual appearance of document elements.

4.6 Modify the appearance of design elements by using effects and styles.

   A Use effects to modify images or frames.

WORK WITH PROCESS COLORS

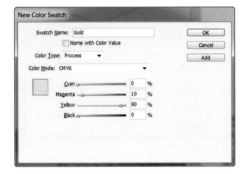

▶ What You'll Do

In this lesson, you will create new process colors and a tint swatch.

Understanding Process Colors

Process colors are colors that are created (and eventually printed) by mixing varying percentages of cyan, magenta, yellow, and black (CMYK) inks. CMYK inks are called **process inks**. Lighter colors are produced with smaller percentages of ink, and darker colors with higher percentages. By mixing CMYK inks, you can produce a large variety of colors, and you can even reproduce color photographs. Think about that for a second—when you look at any magazine, most if not all the color photographs you see are created using only four colors!

In Adobe InDesign, you create process colors by creating a new swatch on the Swatches panel or in the New Color Swatch dialog box. You then mix percentages of CMYK to create the color. Figure 1 shows the New Color Swatch dialog box, where you name and define a color. You can choose Process or Spot as your type of color using the Color Type list arrow in the New Color Swatch dialog box.

Figure 1 New Color Swatch dialog box

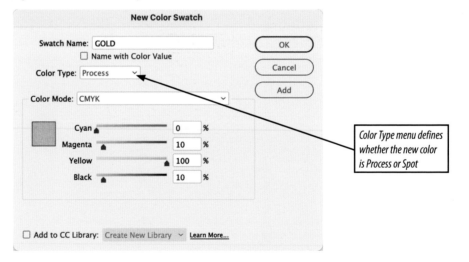

Color Type menu defines whether the new color is Process or Spot

Choosing Process defines the swatch as a process swatch, meaning that it is created with percentages of CMYK ink. Any color you create in this manner is called a **named color** and is added to the Swatches panel, as shown in Figure 2. You can choose to have the color's name defined by CMYK percentages, as shown in the figure, or you can give it another name, if you prefer.

One major benefit of working with named colors is that you can update them. For example, let's say you create a color that is 50% cyan and 50% yellow and you name it warm green. Let's say you fill 10 objects on 10 different pages with warm green, but your client tells you she prefers the objects to be filled with a darker green. You could simply modify the warm green color—change the cyan value to 70% for example—and every object filled with warm green would automatically update to show the darker green.

Figure 2 Swatch added to the Swatches panel

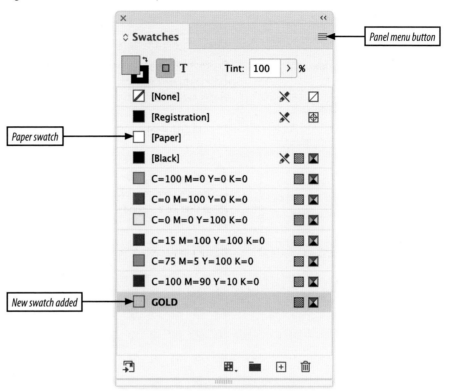

Panel menu button

Paper swatch

New swatch added

Understanding Tints

In the print world, the term "tint" is used to refer to many things. For example, some print professionals refer to all process colors as tints. In Adobe InDesign, however, the term **tint** refers specifically to a lighter version of a color.

Figure 3 shows four squares at the top. The first is filled with 100% cyan, the second is filled with a 50% tint of cyan, the third a 25% tint, and the fourth a 10% tint. Note the variations in color.

Here's the key to understanding tints—the four squares are all filled with the same cyan ink. The only difference is, in the lighter squares, the cyan ink is not solid; it does not cover the square entirely. Instead, some of the white paper is not covered, thus creating the appearance that the square is a lighter tint of cyan.

This is a key concept in printing, and the best way to keep it clear in your mind is to think of a checkerboard. In the figure, the 50% tint is enlarged. You can see it's a checkerboard pattern. 50% of the square is covered with cyan ink, and 50% is the white paper. Thus, the 50% square at the top appears significantly lighter than the 100% square. In the enlargement of the 25% tint, note that the cyan squares are all reduced in size. The square is 25% cyan ink and 75% paper.

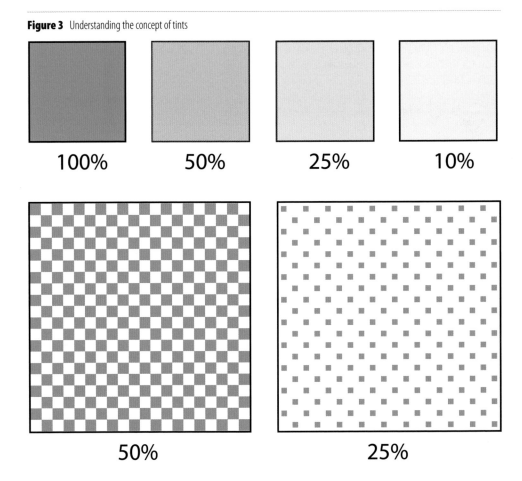

Figure 3 Understanding the concept of tints

Tints can also be created from more complex process colors. Figure 4 shows a process color that is C16 M100 Y100. It follows logically that the 50% tint of the color is C8 M50 Y50. A tint of any process color is created by multiplying each of the original colors' CMYK values by the desired tint percentage.

Creating Tint Swatches

Like process colors, you use the Swatches panel to create tint swatches. You can select a swatch on the Swatches panel, and then create a tint based on that original swatch by clicking the Swatches panel menu button, clicking New Tint Swatch, and then dragging

the Tint slider to the desired percentage. The resulting tint swatch is given the same name of the color on which it was based, along with the tint percentage next to it, as shown in Figure 5.

If you modify the original swatch, any tint swatch that is based on the original

will automatically update to reflect that modification.

For example, if your client says she wants that warm green color to be darker, then any modifications you make to warm green will affect all objects filled with tints of warm green.

Figure 4 A red process color and a 50% tint of that color

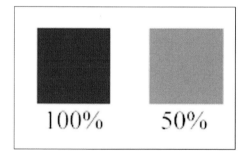

Figure 5 Tint swatch

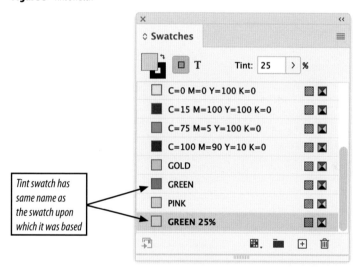

Tint swatch has same name as the swatch upon which it was based

Working with Unnamed Colors

It is not a requirement that you create named swatches for every color you want to use in your layout. Many designers prefer to use the Color panel, shown in Figure 6, to mix colors and apply them to objects. Using the Color panel, you can apply a color to an object by selecting it, then dragging the sliders on the Color panel until you are happy with the new color. As you drag the sliders, the color is continually updated in the selected object. In this way, you can experiment with different colors and allow the document's color scheme to evolve.

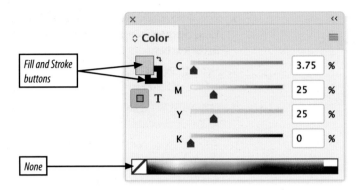

Figure 6   Color panel

When you create colors using the Color panel, those colors are not saved anywhere. Any colors you create that aren't saved to the Swatches panel are called **unnamed colors**.

There's nothing wrong, per se, with working with unnamed colors. You can mix a color on the Color panel, then apply it to an object. No problem. But it's important to understand that the color is not saved anywhere. This can result in problems later on. For example, let's say you mix a royal blue color and apply it to a document, then you show the document to

your client who says he'd prefer it to be green. So you mix a new green color. Then the client says he prefers the royal blue after all. If you didn't write down the CMYK values of that royal blue, you are out of luck because InDesign does not retain a record of it for you.

Other problems can develop too. Let's say you used that royal blue to fill multiple objects throughout the document. If you wanted to modify the color, you would need to modify each individual usage of the color. This could get very time consuming.

Does this mean you'd be smart not to use the Color panel to mix colors? Not at all. Once you've decided on a color, simply save it on the Swatches panel. It couldn't be easier. Just drag the fill (or stroke) button from the toolbar or the Color panel into the Swatches panel. You can even drag the fill (or stroke) button from the top of the Swatches panel down into the Swatches panel. The swatch will instantly be added to the Swatches panel as a process color, and its CMYK values will be used as its name.

Create process color swatches

1. Open ID 5-1.indd, then save it as **Oahu Magazine Cover**.

2. Display the Swatches panel.

3. Click the **Swatches panel menu button** ≡, then click **New Color Swatch**.

4. Verify that the **Color Type text box** displays **Process** and that the **Color Mode text box** displays **CMYK**.

5. Remove the check mark in the **Name with Color Value check box**, then type **Gold** in the **Swatch Name text box**.

6. Type **0**, **10**, **90**, and **0** in the **Cyan**, **Magenta**, **Yellow**, and **Black text boxes**, as shown in Figure 7.

7. Click **OK**, click the **Swatches panel menu button** ≡, then click **New Color Swatch**.

8. Remove the check mark in the **Name with Color Value check box**, then type **Blue** in the **Swatch Name text box**.

9. Type **85**, **10**, **10**, and **0** in the **Cyan**, **Magenta**, **Yellow**, and **Black text boxes**, then click **OK**.

10. Create a **new process color** named **Pink**, type **20** in the **Magenta text box**, type **0** in the **Cyan**, **Yellow**, and **Black text boxes**, then click **OK**.

    Your Swatches panel should resemble Figure 8.

11. Save your work, then continue to the next set of steps.

You created three new process color swatches.

Figure 7 Creating a process color swatch

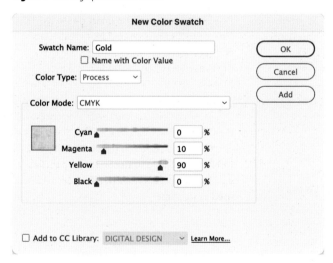

Figure 8 Three new process swatches

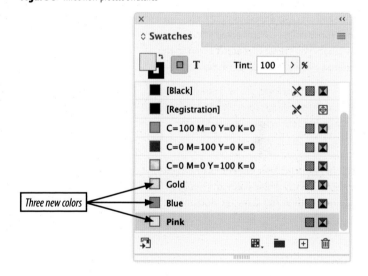

Create a tint swatch and modify the original color swatch

1. Click **Blue** on the Swatches panel, click the **Swatches panel menu button** ≡ , then click **New Tint Swatch**.

2. Drag the **Tint slider** to **25%**, then click **OK**.

   A new 25% tint swatch named Blue 25% appears on the Swatches panel.

3. Double-click the **original Blue swatch** that you created on the Swatches panel.

4. Rename it by typing **Green** in the **Swatch Name text box**, drag the **Yellow slider** to **100%**, then click **OK**.

   As shown in Figure 9, the blue swatch is renamed Green and the 25% tint swatch is renamed Green 25%.

5. Click **File** on the menu bar, then click **Save**.

   Be sure to save your work at this step, as you will later revert to this point in the project.

6. Continue to the next set of steps.

You created a new tint swatch. You then modified the original swatch on which the tint swatch was based, noting that the tint swatch was automatically updated.

Figure 9 Two swatches updated and renamed

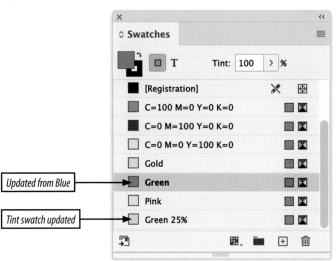

Updated from Blue

Tint swatch updated

Use the Color panel

1. Verify that the **fill button** on the toolbar is activated.

2. Click the **Selection tool** ▶, click the **Cyan-filled frame** that surrounds the image on the page, then display the **Color panel**.

3. Click the **Color panel menu button** ≡, then click **CMYK**.

4. Drag the **Magenta slider** on the Color panel to **50%**, then drag the **Cyan slider** to **50%**, as shown in Figure 10.

   The fill color of the selected frame changes to purple.

TIP When you create a new color on the Color panel, it becomes the active fill or stroke color on the toolbar, depending on which button is active.

5. Drag the **Yellow slider** to **100%**, then drag the **Cyan slider** to **0%**.

   The purple color that previously filled the frame is gone because you never

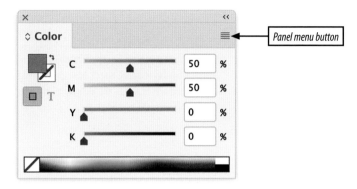

Figure 10 Color panel

actually saved the purple color on the Swatches panel.

TIP Colors that you mix on the Colors panel are not automatically saved on the Swatches panel.

6. Click the **green area** of the **CMYK spectrum** on the Color panel.

7. Drag the **Cyan slider** to **70%**, drag the **Magenta slider** to **20%**, then drag the **Yellow** and **Black sliders** to **0%**.

8. Save your work, then continue to the next set of steps.

You selected an object, then used the Color panel to change its fill to a variety of process colors, none of which were saved on the Swatches panel.

Save an unnamed color on the Swatches panel

1. Drag the **fill color** from the **Color panel** into the Swatches panel.

A new color is created on the Swatches panel, named with the CMYK percentages.

2. Drag the **Tint slider** on the Color panel to **45%**.

3. Save the new color as a swatch by dragging the **fill button** from the **top of the Swatches panel** to the **bottom of the list of swatches on the Swatches panel**.

Your Swatches panel should resemble Figure 11.

4. Double-click the **darker blue swatch** on the Swatches panel, remove the check mark in the **Name with Color Value check box**, type **Purple** in the Name text box, drag the **Magenta slider** to **100%**, then click **OK**.

As shown in Figure 12, the darker blue swatch becomes purple, and the tint swatch based on the darker blue swatch is also updated.

5. Click **File** on the menu bar, click **Revert**, then click **Revert (Mac)** or **Yes (Win)** in the dialog box that follows.

6. Continue to the next lesson.

The document is reverted to its status when you last saved. The new color swatches you created are no longer on the Swatches panel.

You saved an unnamed color on the Swatches panel, created a tint swatch based on that swatch, then reverted the document.

Figure 11 Adding a tint swatch to the Swatches panel

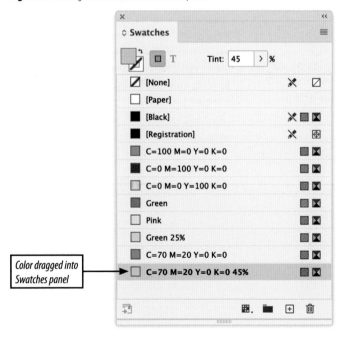

Figure 12 Two swatches updated with a modification

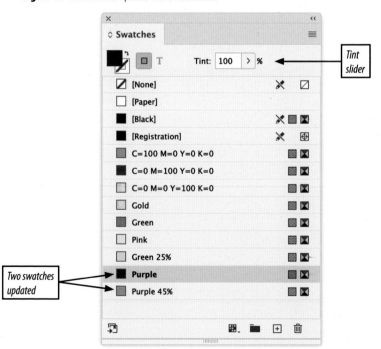

APPLY COLOR

▶ *What You'll Do*

In this lesson, you will explore various techniques for applying and modifying color swatches.

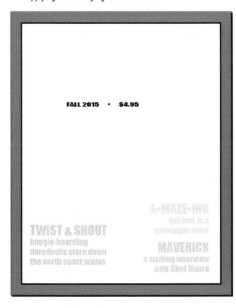

FALL 2015 · $4.95

A-MAZE-ING
get lost in a
pineapple maze

MAVERICK
a sizzling interview
with Chef Mavro

TWIST & SHOUT
boogie-boarding
daredevils stare down
the north coast waves

Applying Color to Objects

InDesign offers many options for applying fills and strokes to objects. The most basic method is to select an object, activate either the fill or the stroke button on the toolbar, then click a color on the Swatches panel or mix a color on the Color panel.

Both the Color panel and the Swatches panel have fill and stroke buttons that you can click to activate rather than having to always go back to the toolbar. When you activate the fill or stroke button on any panel, it will be activated in all the panels that have fill and stroke buttons.

Keyboard shortcuts also offer useful options. Pressing the letter [X] toggles between fill and stroke. In other words, if the stroke button is activated and you press the letter [X], the fill button will be activated. Make a note of this. It's useful and practical and allows you to avoid always having to move the mouse pointer to a panel to activate the fill or the stroke.

Dragging and dropping is also useful. You can drag a swatch from the Swatches panel onto an object and apply the swatch as a fill or a stroke. Drag a swatch over the interior of an object and the swatch will be applied as a fill. If you position the pointer precisely over the object's edge, it will be applied as a stroke. What's interesting about the drag-and-drop method is that the object does not need to be selected for you to apply the fill or the stroke. You can use the drag-and-drop method with any panel that has fill and stroke buttons.

The toolbar offers useful buttons for working with color, as shown in Figure 13. The Default Fill and Stroke button reverts the fill and stroke buttons to their default colors—no fill and a black stroke. Clicking this button will apply a black stroke and no fill to a selected object. The Swap Fill and Stroke button swaps the fill color with the stroke color.

Finally, the three "Apply" buttons on the toolbar are useful for speeding up your work. The Apply Color and Apply Gradient buttons display the last color and gradient that you've used. This makes for quick and easy access when you are using the same color or gradient repeatedly. The Apply None button is available for removing the fill or stroke from a selected object, depending on which button (fill or stroke) is active on the toolbar.

TIP If you are viewing the toolbar as a single column, you will not see all three of these buttons. Press and hold the current button on the toolbar, then click the desired button.

Understanding the Paper Swatch

If you were given a white piece of paper and a box of crayons and asked to draw a white star against a blue background, you would really have no other option than to color all of the page blue except for the star shape, which you would leave blank. The star would appear as white because the paper is white. The Paper swatch, shown in Figure 14, is based on this very concept. Use the Paper swatch whenever you want an object to have a white fill or stroke.

Figure 13 Useful color buttons on the toolbar

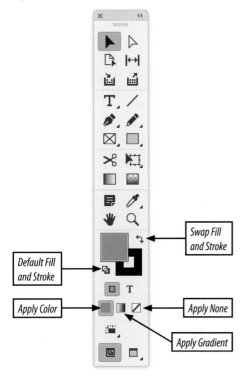

Swap Fill and Stroke

Default Fill and Stroke

Apply Color

Apply None

Apply Gradient

Figure 14 Paper swatch

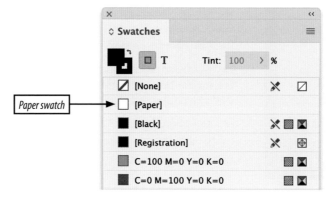

Paper swatch

Don't confuse a Paper fill with a None fill.
When you fill a frame with Paper, it is filled
with white. When you fill it with None, it
has no fill—its fill is transparent. Figure 15
illustrates this distinction. In the figure, two
text frames are positioned in front of a frame
with a yellow fill. The text frame on the left
has None as its fill; therefore, the yellow
frame behind the text frame is visible. The
text frame on the right has Paper as its fill.
If you were to print Figure 15, no ink would
be used in the area with the Paper fill. The
area would be white because the white paper
would be visible.

Figure 15 Understanding a Paper fill

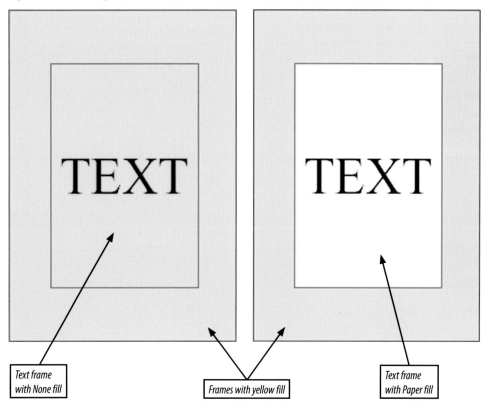

Text frame
with None fill

Frames with yellow fill

Text frame
with Paper fill

Applying Color to Text

Applying color to text is easy. There are two different methods for applying color to text, depending on whether you are using the Type tool or the Selection tool to select the text.

When you select text with the Type tool, the fill and stroke buttons on the toolbar display the letter T, as shown in Figure 16. This is a visual indication that you are filling or stroking text. Click a swatch on the Swatches panel or mix a color on the Color panel, and the text will be filled or stroked with that color.

TIP The color of the T on the Fill and Stroke buttons is always the same color as the selected text.

When you select a text frame with the Selection tool, you need to tell InDesign what you want to do—apply a fill or stroke to the frame itself or apply a fill or stroke to the text inside the frame. If you want to apply color to the text, click the Formatting affects text button on the Swatches panel, identified in Figure 17. If you want to apply color to the frame, click the Formatting affects container button. It's that simple. Note that the two buttons can also be found on the toolbar and Color panel.

Figure 16 When text is selected, fill and stroke buttons display the letter T

Figure 17 Color formatting buttons

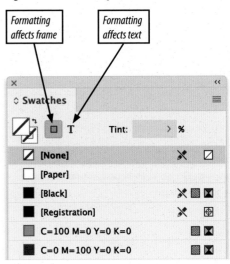

Creating Black Shadow Text

When you position text against a background color or against a photographic image, sometimes it's not easy to see the text, as shown in Figure 18. To remedy this, many designers use the classic technique of placing a black copy of the text behind the original text, as shown in Figure 19. This trick adds much-needed contrast between the text and the image behind it.

TIP Placing a black copy of text behind original text produces a different effect than using InDesign's Drop Shadow command.

Figure 18 Text positioned against an image

Image courtesy of Chris Botello

Figure 19 Text with a black copy behind it

Black text placed behind purple text

Modifying and Deleting Swatches

Once you've created a swatch or added a swatch to the Swatches panel, it is a named color and will be saved with the document. Any swatch can be modified simply by double-clicking it, which opens the Swatch Options dialog box. Any modifications you make to the swatch will be updated automatically in any frame that uses the color as a fill or a stroke.

You can also delete a swatch from the Swatches panel by selecting the swatch, then clicking the Delete selected swatch/groups button on the Swatches panel or clicking the Delete Swatch command on the Swatches panel menu. If you are deleting a swatch that is used in your document, the Delete Swatch dialog box opens, shown in Figure 20.

You use the Delete Swatch dialog box to choose a color to replace the deleted swatch. For example, if you've filled (or stroked) many objects with the color warm green and then you delete the warm green swatch, the Delete Swatch dialog box wants to know what color those objects should be. You choose another named color that is already on the Swatches panel by clicking the Defined Swatch list arrow, clicking a color, and then clicking OK. When you do so, all the objects with a warm green fill or stroke will change to the named color you chose. Note that this can be a very quick and effective method for changing the fill (or stroke) color of multiple objects simultaneously.

If you click the Unnamed Swatch option button in the Delete Swatch dialog box, all the objects filled or stroked with the deleted color will retain their color. However, since that color is no longer on the Swatches panel, those objects are now filled with an unnamed color.

Figure 20 Delete Swatch dialog box

Drag and drop colors onto objects

1. Click **View** on the menu bar, point to **Extras,** then click **Hide Frame Edges**.

2. Drag and drop the **Green swatch** on top of the **blue frame**, then release the mouse button.

3. Click the **eye icon** 👁 on the **Photo layer** on the Layers panel to hide the background image.

   Your artboard should resemble Figure 21. The frame with the black stroke does not have

a fill, so the larger frame with the green fill shows behind it.

4. Click to select the **frame with the black stroke**.

5. Click **Paper** on the Swatches panel to fill the selected frame.

   The frame is filled with white, as shown in Figure 22.

6. Save your work, then continue to the next set of steps.

You dragged and dropped a color from the Swatches panel to change the fill color of an object on the artboard. You applied the Paper swatch to fill a frame.

USING THE COLOR PICKER

In addition to using the toolbar and the Swatches panel to apply colors, you can use the Color Picker to choose and mix colors. Select the object you want to fill, then double-click the fill or stroke button on the toolbar to open the Color Picker. In the color spectrum, click or drag to select a color, drag the color slider triangles, or type values in the text boxes. To save the color as a swatch, click Add CMYK Swatch, Add RGB Swatch, or Add Lab Swatch. The color appears on the Swatches panel, displaying its color values as its name.

Figure 21 Selected frame has a black stroke and no fill

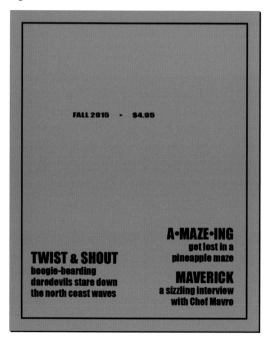

Figure 22 Viewing an object with a Paper fill color

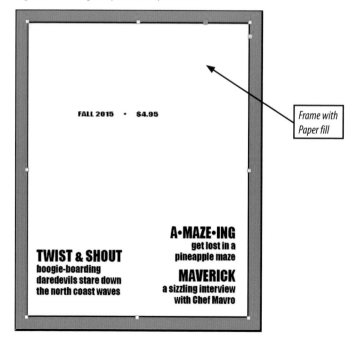

Frame with Paper fill

Apply color to text

1. Click the **Selection tool** , click the **TWIST & SHOUT text frame**, then click the **Formatting affects text button** T on the toolbar.

   As shown in Figure 23, the fill and stroke buttons display the letter T, indicating that any color you click on the Swatches panel will affect the text in the selected frame, not the frame itself.

2. Click **Gold** on the Swatches panel.

3. Click the **A·MAZE·ING text frame**, then note that the **Formatting affects container button** ☐ is active on the toolbar because you have selected a frame.

4. Click the **Type tool** T, then select **all the text in the A·MAZE·ING text frame**.

   TIP When you select text with the Type tool T, the Formatting affects text button T on the toolbar is automatically activated.

5. Click **Pink** on the Swatches panel.

6. Click the **Selection tool** ▸, click the **MAVERICK text frame**, then click the **Formatting affects text button** T on the Swatches panel.

7. Click the **Green 25% swatch** on the Swatches panel so that your document resembles Figure 24.

You explored two methods for applying color to text. In the first, you selected text with the Selection tool, clicked the Formatting affects text button, then chose a new color. In the second, you selected text with the Type tool, then chose a new color.

Figure 23 Fill and stroke buttons with selected text

Figure 24 Viewing the colors applied to text

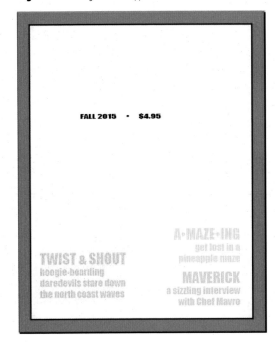

Create black shadow text

1. Show the **Photo layer** on the Layers panel, and then assess the legibility of the text in the three text frames against the background graphic.

   The text on the right is perfectly legible, but the text on the left is difficult to distinguish from the bright and busy background. You will add black shadow text to try to improve legibility.

2. Click the **Original Black Text layer** on the Layers panel, click the **Layers panel menu button** ≡ , then click **Duplicate Layer "Original Black Text."**

3. Double-click the **Original Black Text copy layer** on the Layers panel to open the Layer Options dialog box.

4. Type **Color Headlines** in the Name text box, click the **Color list arrow**, then click **Orange** so your Layer Options dialog box resembles Figure 25.

5. Click **OK**, then hide the **Original Black Text layer**.

6. With the **Color Headlines layer** still selected, delete the **Fall 2015 text frame** on the Color Headlines layer since you will not need a duplicate of this text.

7. Hide the **Color Headlines layer**, then show the **Original Black Text layer**.

8. Click the **selected items button** ☐ on the **Original Black Text layer** to select all the objects on the layer.

9. Click the **Formatting affects text button** T on the Swatches panel, then apply a **100% Black fill** to all the text.

   You will need to use the Tint slider on the Swatches panel to make all the text 100% black.

10. Deselect all.

11. Show the **Color Headlines layer**, then click the **selected items button** ☐ to select all objects on the layer.

12. Press the **up arrow** on your keypad two times, then press the **right arrow** two times.

    Your work should resemble Figure 26. The black shadow goes far toward improving legibility. The gold text on the left is easier to read against the background, but it's not nearly as legible as the text on the right. You will take a different approach to improving its legibility later in this chapter.

13. Save your work, then continue to the next set of steps.

You duplicated a layer containing text. You changed the fill color of the text on the lower layer to black, then repositioned the colored text on the upper layer so that the black text acts as a shadow. By doing so, you added contrast to the colored text, making it more legible against the picture on the Photo layer.

Figure 25 Layer Options dialog box

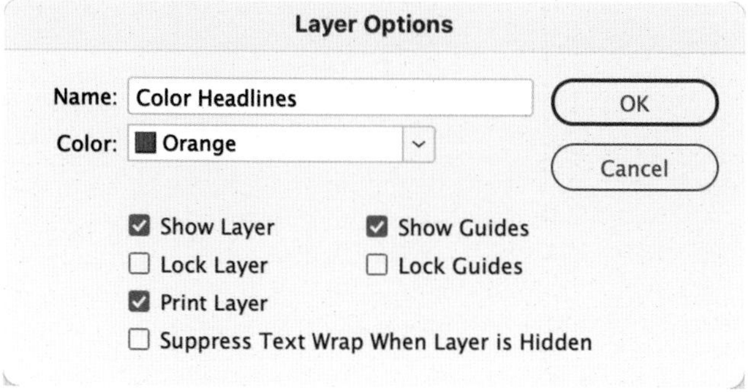

Figure 26 Using black shadow text to improve legibility

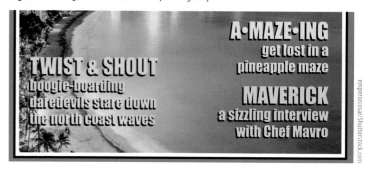

Modify and delete swatches

1. Deselect all, then drag the **Gold swatch** onto the **green frame** to change the green frame to gold.

2. Double-click the **Gold swatch** on the Swatches panel.

3. Activate the Preview option, if necessary; drag the **Black slider** to **5%**; then drag the **Magenta slider** to **100%**.

4. Click **OK**.

All usages of the Gold swatch—the frame and the "Twist & Shout" text—are updated with the modification to red.

5. Drag the **Gold swatch** to the **Delete selected swatch/groups button** 🗑 on the Swatches panel.

6. Click the **Defined Swatch list arrow** in the Delete Swatch dialog box, click **Pink**, as shown in Figure 27, then click **OK**.

As shown in Figure 28, all usages of the Gold swatch in the document are replaced by the Pink swatch.

7. Save your work, then continue to the next lesson.

You modified a swatch and noted that it updated throughout the document. You then deleted the swatch, replacing all its usages with a different swatch.

Figure 27 Delete Swatch dialog box

Figure 28 Gold colors replaced by pink colors

WORK WITH SPOT COLORS

▶ *What You'll Do*

In this lesson, you will create and apply spot colors, and import graphics that contain spot colors.

Understanding Spot Colors

Spot colors are non-process inks that are manufactured by companies. They are special pre-mixed inks that are printed separately from process inks. Though printing is based on the four process colors, CMYK, it is not limited to them. It is important to understand that although combinations of CMYK inks can produce a wide variety of colors—enough to reproduce any color photograph quite well—they can't produce every color. For this reason and others, designers often turn to spot colors.

Imagine you are an art director designing the masthead for the cover of a new magazine. You have decided that the masthead will be electric blue—vivid and eye-catching. If you were working with process tints only, you would have a problem. First, you would find that the almost-neon blue you want to achieve is not within the CMYK range; it can't be printed. Even if it could, you would have a bigger problem with consistency issues. You would want that blue to be the same blue on every issue of the magazine, month after month. But offset printing is never perfect; variations in dot size are factored in. As the cover is printed, the blue color in the masthead will certainly vary, sometimes drastically.

Designers and printers use spot colors to solve this problem. The color range of spot colors far exceeds that of CMYK. Spot colors also offer consistent color throughout a print run.

The design and print worlds refer to spot colors by a number of names:

- Non-process inks: Refers to the fact that spot colors are not created using the process inks—CMYK.
- Fifth color: Refers to the fact that the spot color is often printed in addition to the four process inks. Note, however, that a spot color is not necessarily the "fifth" color. For example, many "two-color" projects call for black plus one spot color.
- PANTONE color: PANTONE is a manufacturer of non-process inks. PANTONE is simply a brand name.
- PMS color: An acronym for PANTONE Matching System.

A good way to think of spot colors is as ink in a bucket. With process inks, if you want red, you must mix some amount of magenta ink with some amount of yellow ink. With spot colors, if you want red, you pick a number from a chart, open the bucket, and there's the red ink—pre-mixed and ready to print.

Creating Spot Color Swatches

You create spot color swatches in Adobe InDesign using the New Color Swatch dialog box. Instead of choosing CMYK values, as you would when you create a process color, you choose Spot from the Color Type list, then choose a spot color system from one of 30 systems in the Color Mode list. After you choose a system, the related library of spot colors loads into the New Swatch dialog box, allowing you to choose the spot color you want. Figure 29 shows the PANTONE+ Solid Coated color system.

Importing Graphics with Spot Colors

When you create graphics in Adobe Illustrator or Adobe Photoshop, you can create and apply spot colors in those applications as well. For example, you can create a logo in Adobe Illustrator and fill it with a spot color.

Because InDesign, Illustrator, and Photoshop are all made by Adobe, InDesign recognizes the spot colors applied to graphics created in those applications. In the previous example, when you place the graphic from Illustrator, InDesign identifies the spot color that was used and adds it to the InDesign Swatches panel. If you double-click the swatch on the Swatches panel, you will see that the swatch is automatically formatted as a spot color.

Figure 29 Creating a spot color swatch

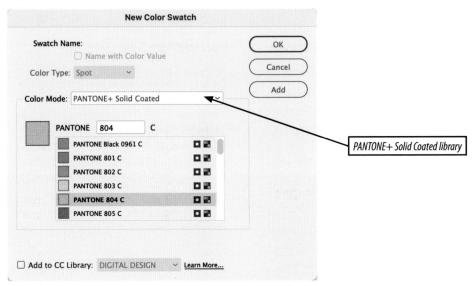

Create a spot color swatch

1. Click the **Swatches panel menu button** 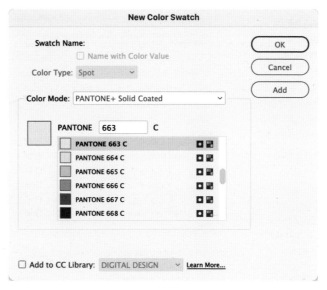, then click **New Color Swatch**.

2. Click the **Color Type list arrow**, then click **Spot**.

3. Click the **Color Mode list arrow**, then click **PANTONE+ Solid Coated**.

4. Type **663** in the PANTONE text box so your New Color Swatch dialog box resembles Figure 30.

5. Click **OK**.

   The PANTONE swatch appears on the Swatches panel. As shown in Figure 31, the icons on the right are different from the process tints shown on the other colors.

6. Change the **fill of the pink frame** to **PANTONE 663**.

7. Change the **fill of the TWIST & SHOUT text** to **PANTONE 663**.

8. Save your work, then continue to the next set of steps.

You created a spot color swatch and then applied it to elements in the layout.

Figure 30 Creating a spot color

Figure 31 PANTONE swatch on the Swatches panel

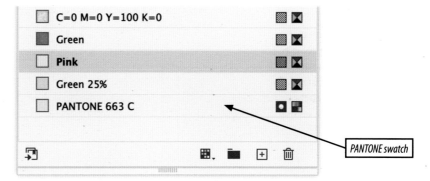

Import graphics with spot colors

1. Click the **Imported Graphics layer** on the Layers panel to target it, click the **Selection tool** ▶, then select the **frame** shown in Figure 32.

TIP Clicking in the general area of the selected frame shown in Figure 32 will select the frame.

2. Click **File** on the menu bar, click **Place**, navigate to the drive and folder where your Chapter 5 Data Files are stored, click **Living Graphic.ai**, then click **Open**.

3. Click **Object** on the menu bar, point to **Fitting**, then click **Center Content**.

   The graphic that is placed in the frame was created in Adobe Illustrator and was filled in Illustrator with PANTONE 159 C. Note that PANTONE 159 C has been automatically added as a spot color to the Swatches menu in InDesign.

TIP When you place graphics that are filled with spot colors, InDesign automatically adds those spot colors to the Swatches panel.

4. Select the **frame** shown in Figure 33.

5. Click **File** on the menu bar, click **Place**, navigate to the drive and folder where your Chapter 5 Data Files are stored, then double-click **OAHU graphic.ai**.

   OAHU graphic.ai is an Adobe Illustrator file. The fill color of O, A, H, and U is PANTONE 663—the same PANTONE 663 color that you created in InDesign. For this reason, PANTONE 663 does not need to be added to the Swatches panel.

6. Click **Object** on the menu bar, point to **Fitting,** then click **Center Content**.

7. Deselect all, then compare your document with Figure 34.

8. Save your work, then close the OAHU Magazine Cover document.

You imported a graphic that was created with a spot color in another application, then noted that the spot color was automatically added to the Swatches panel. Next, you imported a graphic that was filled with the same spot color that you had already created in InDesign.

WORKING WITH MIXED INK SWATCHES

When you are creating a two-color job—let's say, black and PMS 100—you will want to work with more than just 100% black and 100% PMS 100. You'll want to work with tints, such as a 70% black and 20% PMS 100 mix. These are called mixed swatches. A **mixed ink group** is a group of many mixed ink swatches you can generate automatically based on the two or more inks in a color job.

You create a mixed ink group by clicking the New Mixed Ink Group command on the Swatches panel menu, which opens the New Mixed Ink Group dialog box. Use this dialog box to specify the inks involved for the mixed ink group, the initial mixture, and the increments (percentages) at which new tint swatches will be generated. All the swatches will appear on the Swatches panel.

Figure 32 Selecting a frame for a graphic

Figure 33 Selected frame

Figure 34 Magazine cover with all elements in place

WORK WITH GRADIENTS

Creating Gradients

A **gradient** is a graduated blend of two or more colors. Every gradient must have at least two colors, which are commonly referred to as the **starting** and **ending colors** of the gradient. You can add more colors to a gradient—colors that come between the starting and ending colors. The colors that you add between the starting and ending colors are called **color stops**.

In InDesign, you create gradients by clicking New Gradient Swatch on the Swatches panel menu. This opens the New Gradient Swatch dialog box, shown in Figure 35. In this dialog box, you define all the elements of the gradient. You use the Gradient Ramp to define the starting and ending colors, as well as any intermediary colors for your gradient. You can choose your colors from a list of existing swatches, or you can mix colors using sliders.

Figure 35 New Gradient Swatch dialog box

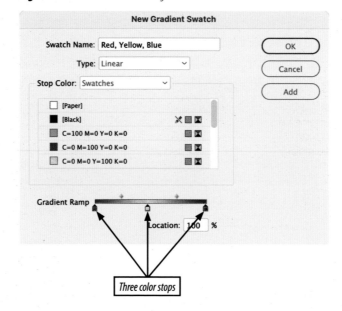

In this dialog box, you also choose whether your gradient will be radial or linear using the Type list arrow. You can think of a **radial gradient** as a series of concentric circles. With a radial gradient, the starting color appears at the center of the gradient, then radiates out to the ending color. You can think of a **linear gradient** as a series of straight lines that gradate from one color to another (or through multiple colors). Figure 36 shows a linear and a radial gradient, each composed of three colors.

Figure 37 shows the dialog box used to create the linear gradient in Figure 36. The Gradient Ramp shows the three colors in the gradient, and the yellow color stop is selected. The sliders show the CMYK values that make the yellow tint.

When you close the New Gradient Swatch dialog box, the new gradient swatch appears on the Swatches panel.

TIP On the Swatches panel, you can choose to view only swatches, only gradients, or only color groups by clicking the Swatch Views button ⊞. on the Swatches panel and choosing Show Color Swatches, Show Gradient Swatches, or Show Color Groups. To view all swatches, choose Show All Swatches.

Figure 36 A linear and a radial gradient

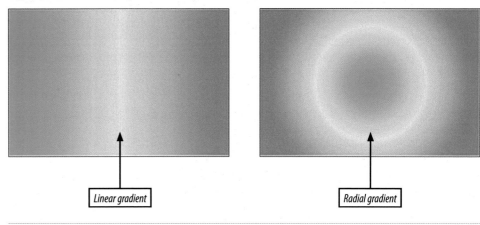

Linear gradient

Radial gradient

Figure 37 Cyan, Yellow, Green gradient settings

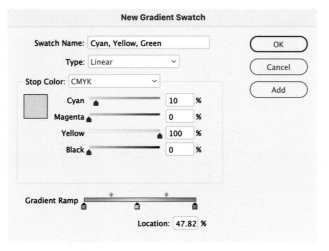

Applying Gradients

You apply a gradient to an object the same way you apply a color to an object. Simply select the object, then click the gradient on the Swatches panel. A gradient swatch can be applied as a fill or as a stroke.

If you use a gradient to fill an object, you can further control how the gradient fills the object using the Gradient Swatch tool. The Gradient Swatch tool allows you to change the length and/or direction of a linear or radial gradient.

To use the Gradient Swatch tool, first select an object with a gradient fill, then drag the Gradient Swatch tool over the object. For both linear and radial gradients, where you begin dragging and where you stop dragging determine the length of the gradient, from starting color to ending color. For linear gradients, the direction in which you drag the Gradient Swatch tool determines the angle that the gradient fills the object.

Figure 38 shows a rainbow gradient applied to objects in different ways. In the top row, the rainbow gradients fill each of the six boxes separately. In the second row, the Gradient Swatch tool is dragged across all six boxes, so the gradient itself extends across all six boxes. The black lines in the remaining four examples show how the Gradient Swatch tool was dragged across each row.

Figure 38 Using the Gradient Swatch tool

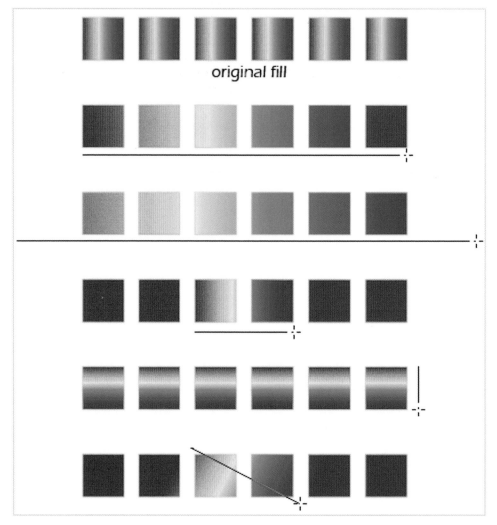

original fill

Modifying a Gradient Fill Using the Gradient Panel

Like color swatches, gradients can be modified. When you modify a gradient, all instances of the gradient used in the document will be automatically updated. Let's say you create a gradient and use it to fill 10 objects. Then you decide that in only one of those 10 objects, you want to modify the gradient by removing one color. What do you do? If you modify the gradient swatch by removing a color stop, it's going to affect all usages of the gradient. You could duplicate the gradient swatch, remove the unwanted color stop, then apply the new gradient

to the single object. But there's a better way. You can use the Gradient panel, shown in Figure 39.

When you select an object with a gradient fill, the Gradient panel shows the Gradient Ramp you used to create the gradient in the New Gradient Swatch dialog box. You can manipulate the Gradient Ramp on the Gradient panel. You can add, move, and delete color stops. You can also select color stops and modify their color using the Color panel. Here's the great part—the modifications you make on the Gradient panel only affect the gradient fill of the selected object(s).

Figure 39 Gradient panel

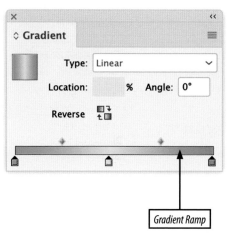

Gradient Ramp

Using the Gradient Feather Tool

The **Gradient Feather tool** causes a fill color to fade gradually to transparent. For example, if you have a frame filled with cyan and you drag the Gradient Feather tool from left to right over the width of the frame, the cyan color will fade from 100% cyan to 0% cyan.

From left to right, the cyan color will become increasingly transparent.

Figure 40 shows an image in a frame and an identically sized frame filled with black. Note that the text is difficult to read over the busy stripes in the image. In Figure 41, the Gradient Feather tool has been used to fade the black so it

appears only at the bottom of the frame. When the black frame is positioned over the image, as shown in Figure 42, the effect is that of shadow that fades up from the bottom. It's a great effect, and it can be very useful for hiding problem areas of an image or, as in this case, for making text stand out better against a busy background.

Figure 40 Text over the image is difficult to read

Figure 41 Black fill fades with the Gradient Feather tool

Fades upward to None

Figure 42 Black fade makes text more legible and adds a visually interesting effect

CALL ME

Create a linear gradient swatch

1. Open ID 5-2.indd, then save it as **Making the Gradient**.
2. Click the **Swatches panel menu button** ≡, then click **New Gradient Swatch**.
3. In the Swatch Name text box, type **Blue/Gold/ Red Linear**.
4. Click the **left color stop** on the Gradient Ramp, click the **Stop Color list arrow**, then click **Swatches** so your dialog box resembles Figure 43.

When you choose Swatches, all the colors on the Swatches panel become available for the gradient.

5. Click the **swatch** named **Blue**.

    The left color stop on the Gradient Ramp changes to blue.

6. Click the **right color stop** on the Gradient Ramp, click the **Stop Color list arrow**, click **Swatches**, then click the swatch named **Red**.

7. Click directly **below the Gradient Ramp** to add a new color stop.

    TIP Click anywhere to add the new color stop. You can adjust the location using the Location text box.

8. Type **50** in the Location text box, then press **[tab]**.

    The new color stop is located at the exact middle of the Gradient Ramp.

9. Click the **Stop Color list arrow**, click **Swatches**, then click the **swatch** named **Gold** so your New Gradient Swatch dialog box resembles Figure 44.

    The new gradient swatch is added to the Swatches panel.

10. Click **OK**, save your work, then continue to the next set of steps.

You created a three-color linear gradient swatch using three named colors.

Figure 43 New Gradient Swatch dialog box

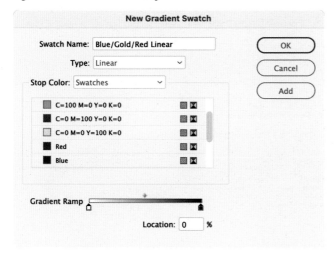

Figure 44 Adding a color stop

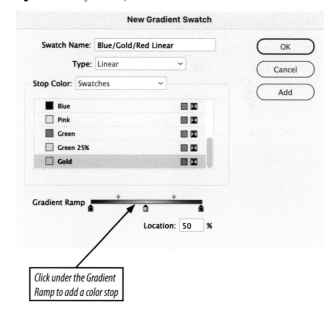

Click under the Gradient Ramp to add a color stop

Create a radial gradient swatch

1. Click the **Swatches panel menu button** ☰ , then click **New Gradient Swatch**.

   The New Gradient Swatch dialog box opens with the settings from the last created gradient.

2. In the Swatch Name text box, type **Cyan Radial**.

3. Click the **Type list arrow**, then click **Radial**.

4. Click the **center color stop**, then drag it straight down to remove it from the Gradient Ramp.

5. Click the **left color stop** on the Gradient Ramp, click the **Stop Color list arrow**, then click **CMYK**.

6. Drag **each slider** to **0%**.

7. Click the **right color stop** on the Gradient Ramp, click the **Stop Color list arrow**, then click **CMYK**.

8. Drag the **Cyan slider** to **100%**, then drag the **Magenta**, **Yellow**, and **Black sliders** to **0%** so your dialog box resembles Figure 45.

9. Click **OK**, save your work, then continue to the next set of steps.

   The new gradient swatch is added to the Swatches panel.

You created a two-color radial gradient swatch using CMYK values.

Figure 45 Settings for a radial gradient

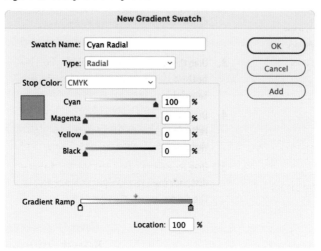

Apply gradient swatches and use the Gradient Swatch tool

1. Click the **Selection tool** ▶, select the **top frame**, then fill it with the **Blue/Gold/Red Linear gradient** from the Swatches panel.

TIP Make sure you are in Normal view and that you are viewing frame edges.

2. Click the **Gradient Swatch tool** 🔲 on the toolbar. Then, using Figure 46 as a guide, place the mouse pointer anywhere on the **top edge of the rectangular frame**, click and drag down, and release the mouse button at the bottom edge of the frame.

Your result should resemble Figure 47.

TIP Pressing and holding [shift] while dragging the Gradient Swatch tool 🔲 constrains the movement on a horizontal or vertical axis.

3. Drag the **Gradient Swatch tool** 🔲 from the **bottom-middle handle** of the frame to the **top-right handle**.

4. Drag the **Gradient Swatch tool** 🔲 from the **left edge of the document window** to the **right edge of the document window**.

5. Drag the **Gradient Swatch tool** 🔲 a **short distance from left to right in the center of the frame**, as shown in Figure 48.

6. Click the **Selection tool** ▶, click the **edge of the circular frame**, then click **Cyan Radial** on the Swatches panel.

7. Click the **Gradient Swatch tool** 🔲, press and hold **[shift]**, then drag the **Gradient Swatch tool** 🔲 from the **center point of the circle** up to the **bottom edge of the center rectangle above the circle** so your document resembles Figure 49.

8. Save your work, then continue to the next set of steps.

You filled two objects with two different gradients, and you used the Gradient Swatch tool to manipulate how the gradients filled the objects.

Figure 46 Dragging the Gradient Swatch tool straight down

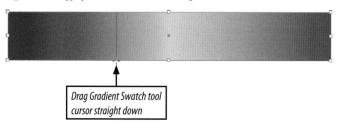

Drag Gradient Swatch tool cursor straight down

Figure 47 Linear gradient applied vertically to the frame

Figure 48 Dragging the Gradient Swatch tool from left to right

Figure 49 Gradients applied to two objects

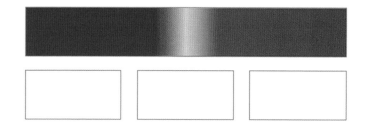

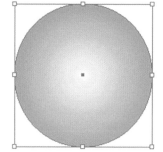

Use the Gradient Swatch tool to extend a gradient across multiple objects

1. Click **Window** on the menu bar, point to **Color**, then click **Gradient** to open the Gradient panel.

2. Deselect all, click the **Selection tool** ▶, then select the **three rectangular frames above the circle**.

3. Click **Blue/Gold/Red Linear** on the Swatches panel.

   As shown in Figure 50, the gradient fills each frame individually.

4. With the **three objects** still selected, click the **Gradient Swatch tool** 🔲, then drag it from the **left edge of the leftmost frame** to the **right edge of the rightmost frame**.

   As shown in Figure 51, the gradient gradates across all three selected objects.

5. Click the **Selection tool** ▶, then click the **rectangular frame at the top of the document window**.

6. Drag the **Gold color stop** on the Gradient Ramp straight down to remove it.

   The gold color is only removed from the gradient fill in the *selected* frame. The original gradient on the Swatches panel (Blue/Gold/Red Linear) is not affected.

7. Save your work, then close the Making the Gradient document.

You selected three objects, applied a gradient to each of them, then used the Gradient Swatch tool to extend the gradient across all three selected objects. You then modified the gradient fill of a selected object by removing a color stop from the Gradient Ramp.

Figure 50 A gradient fill applied individually to three objects

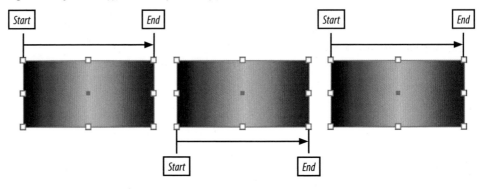

Figure 51 A gradient fill gradating across three objects

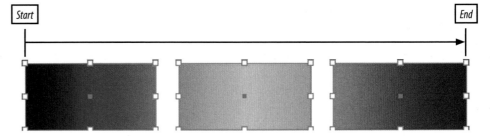

Fade color with the Gradient Feather tool

1. Open ID 5-3.indd, then save it as **Oahu Magazine Cover Final**.

   This file is at the same stage as it was when you completed Lesson 3 in this chapter.

2. Click the **Selection tool** , then click the **image** to select it.

3. Click **Edit** on the menu bar, click **Copy**, click **Edit** again, then click **Paste in Place**.

   A copy of the frame with the image is placed in the exact same location, above the original.

4. Click **Object** on the menu bar, point to **Transform**, then click **Move**.

5. Enter the settings shown in Figure 52, then click **OK**.

6. Deselect.

7. Click the **Direct Selection tool** , click the **center of the image** once to select it, then press **[delete]** on your keypad.

   The image is deleted and all that's left is the frame.

Continued on next page

Figure 52 Moving the copy 8" to the right

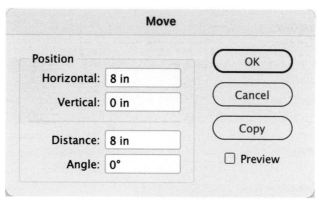

8. Fill the **frame** with the **100% Cyan** and **85% Magenta**, as shown in Figure 53.

9. Click the **Gradient Feather tool** .

10. Drag the **Gradient Feather tool** from the **bottom edge of the frame straight up**, and release it approximately one-third of the height of the frame.

   Use Figure 54 as a guide.

11. Use the **Move dialog box** to move the frame **8" to the left**.

   Your artwork should resemble Figure 55. The beach image behind the text on the left is now behind the blue fade. The beach image is still visible, but it's substantially more muted. As a result, the text on the left is now completely legible.

12. Save your work, then close the Oahu Magazine Cover Final document.

You duplicated the frame that contained the image, moved it exactly 8" to the right, then deleted the image. You filled the frame with blue, then faded it using the Gradient Feather tool. You then moved the frame to the left the exact same distance, using the blue fade to mute the background image and help the text on the left to be more legible.

Figure 53 Filling the frame with blue

Figure 54 Fading the blue fill with the Gradient Feather tool

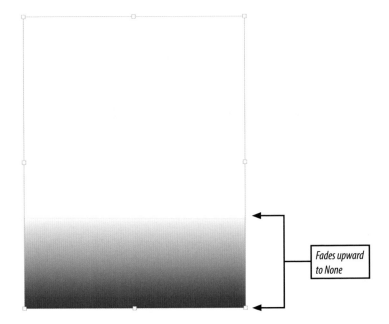

Fades upward to None

Figure 55 The final magazine cover with the text fully legible against the background image

Work with process colors

1. Open ID 5-4.indd, then save it as **LAB cover**.
2. Verify that the Swatches panel is open, click the Swatches panel menu button, then click New Color Swatch.
3. Verify that Process is chosen in the Color Type text box and that CMYK is chosen in the Color Mode text box.
4. Remove the check mark in the Name with Color Value check box, then type **Pink** in the Swatch Name text box.
5. Type **15** in the Cyan text box, press [tab], type **70** in the Magenta text box, press [tab], type **10** in the Yellow text box, press [tab], type **0** in the Black text box, press [tab], then click OK.
6. Display the Color panel if necessary.
7. Click the Color panel menu button, click CMYK, then verify that the fill button is activated.
8. Drag the Cyan slider on the Color panel to 50%, drag the Magenta slider to 10%, then drag the Yellow and Black sliders to 0%.
9. Drag the color from the fill button on the Color panel to the Swatches panel.
10. Verify that the C = 50 M = 10 Y = 0 K = 0 swatch is still selected on the Swatches panel, click the Swatches panel menu button, then click New Tint Swatch.
11. Drag the Tint slider to 35%, then click OK.

Apply color

1. Duplicate the Text layer, then rename it **Colored Text**.
2. Click View on the menu bar, point to Extras, then click Hide Frame Edges.
3. Drag and drop C = 50 M = 10 Y = 0 K = 0 from the Swatches panel to the outermost, black-filled frame.
4. Click the Selection tool, click the BRUSH UP text frame, then click the Formatting affects text button on the toolbar.
5. Click the C = 5 0 M = 10 Y = 0 K = 0 swatch on the Swatches panel.
6. Click the Holiday Issue text frame in the lower-left corner of the cover, click the Formatting affects text button on the Swatches panel, then click the Paper swatch on the Swatches panel.
7. Click the Type tool, select all the text in the PUPPY LOVE text frame, then click Pink on the Swatches panel.
8. Select all the text in the FETCH text frame, then click the C = 50 M = 10 Y = 0 K = 0 35% tint swatch on the Swatches panel.
9. Click the selected items button on the Colored Text layer to select all the items on the layer.
10. Click Object on the menu bar, point to Transform, then click Move.
11. Verify that there is a check mark in the Preview check box, type **−.03** in the Horizontal text box, type **−.03** in the Vertical text box, click OK, then deselect all.

Work with spot colors

1. Click the Swatches panel menu button, then click New Color Swatch.
2. Click the Color Type list arrow, then click Spot.
3. Click the Color Mode list arrow, then click PANTONE+ Solid Coated.
4. Type **117** in the PANTONE text box, then click OK.
5. Change the fill on the C = 50 M = 10 border to PANTONE 117 C.
6. Click the Imported Graphics layer on the Layers panel to target it, click the Selection tool, then click between the dog's eyes to select the frame for placing a new image.

7. Click File on the menu bar, click Place, navigate to the drive and folder where your Chapter 5 Data Files are stored, click LAB.ai, then click Open.

TIP LAB.ai is an Adobe Illustrator graphic filled with PANTONE 117 C.

8. Click the Photo layer on the Layers panel, click the dog graphic in the document window, click Edit on the menu bar, click Copy, click Edit on the menu bar, then click Paste in Place.

9. On the Layers panel, drag the selected items button from the Photo layer up to the Imported Graphics layer.

10. Click File on the menu bar, click Place, navigate to the drive and folder where your Chapter 5 Data Files are stored, then double-click Wally Head Silo.psd.

TIP Wally Head Silo.psd is identical to the dog photo, with the exception that it was saved with a clipping path around the dog's head to remove the red background.

11. Deselect all, then compare your work to Figure 56.

12. Save your work, then close the LAB cover document.

Figure 56 Completed Skills Review, Part 1

Work with gradients

1. Open ID 5-5.indd, then save it as **Gradient Skills Review**.
2. Click the Swatches panel menu button, then click New Gradient Swatch.
3. In the Swatch Name text box, type **Red/Golden/ Green Linear**.
4. Click the left color stop on the Gradient Ramp, click the Stop Color list arrow, then click Swatches.
5. Click the Red swatch.
6. Click the right color stop on the Gradient Ramp, click the Stop Color list arrow, click Swatches, then click the Green swatch.
7. Click immediately below the Gradient Ramp to add a third color stop.
8. Type **50** in the Location text box, then press [tab].
9. Click the Stop Color list arrow, choose Swatches, click the Gold swatch, then click OK.
10. Click the Selection tool, select the border of the top rectangular frame, verify that the fill button is activated on the toolbar, then click Red/Golden/ Green Linear on the Swatches panel.
11. Click the Gradient Swatch tool, then drag from the top-middle handle of the rectangular frame down to the bottom-right handle.
12. Display the Gradient panel if necessary.
13. Click the Selection tool, deselect the top rectangular frame, then select the three lower rectangular frames.
14. Click Red/Golden/Green Linear on the Swatches panel.
15. Click the Gradient Swatch tool, and with all three objects still selected, drag the Gradient Swatch tool from the left edge of the leftmost frame to the right edge of the rightmost frame.
16. Deselect all, then compare your work to Figure 57.
17. Save your work, then close the Gradient Skills Review document.

Figure 57 Completed Skills Review, Part 2

PROJECT BUILDER 1

You are a freelance graphic designer. You have recently been contracted to design a postcard that will be sent out in a mass mailing for the launch of a new fragrance. This is part of a larger worldwide campaign, and you are asked to work with only the colors from the bottle. The postcard will be printed with only four colors, so any tints you create must be process tints. You are told that no type can be white, because that is the color of the name on the bottle, and it should be the brightest type on the postcard.

1. Open ID 5-6.indd, then save it as **Swerve Postcard**.
2. Click the Eyedropper tool, then click the center of the perfume bottle to sample the color.
   The foreground color changes to the sampled color.
3. Open the Color panel, then set its sliders to CMYK so you can see the breakdown of the color, as shown in Figure 58.
4. Create a new Swatch named **Swerve Tan**, based on the values in Figure 58.
5. Create at least two tint swatches based on Swerve Tan.

Figure 58 Process tint breakdown on the Color panel

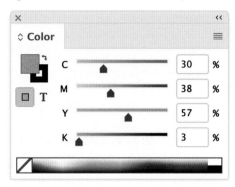

(continued)

6. Colorize the magenta text and the promo label as you like with the new colors you've created. Figure 59 shows one result.

7. Save your work, then close the Swerve Postcard document.

Figure 59 One version of the postcard

You are a freelance graphic designer. You have recently been contracted to create a cover for LAB magazine. The magazine is usually published with only one color—in black and white—but the publishers have some extra money for this issue. They want you to create a design for this cover so it will print as a two-color job. It will be printed with black and one spot color. They provide you with the black and white version of the cover. You are free to choose the spot color and apply it in whatever way you think is best.

1. Open ID 5-7.indd, then save it as **2 Color Cover**.
2. Click the Swatches panel menu button, then click New Color Swatch.
3. Click the Color Type list arrow, then choose Spot.
4. Click the Color Mode list arrow, then choose PANTONE + Solid Coated.
5. Choose PANTONE 195 C, then click OK.
6. Click the Swatches panel menu button, then click New Tint Swatch.
7. Drag the Tint slider to 25%, then click OK.
8. Change the fill of the outermost frame that is filled with black to PANTONE 195 C.
9. Click the inner white border that is filled with Paper and stroked with Black, then change its fill color to PANTONE 195 C 25%.
10. Change the fill color on the three white headlines to PANTONE 195 C 25%.
11. Compare your cover to Figure 60, save your work, then close the 2 Color Cover document.

Figure 60 Completed Project Builder 2

Figure 61 Completed Design Project 1

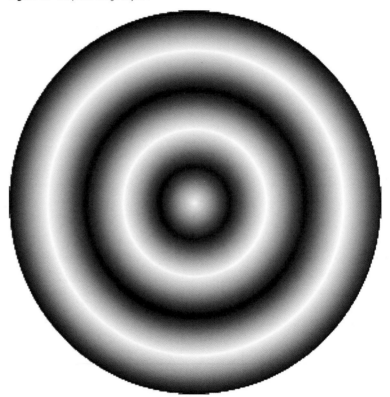

You have recently been contracted to create a logo for the Illusionists Foundation. A representative from the organization tells you that he wants the logo to be a circle filled with a radial gradient. Starting from the inside of the circle, the colors should go from white to black to white to black to white to black. He tells you that he wants each color to be very distinct. In other words, he doesn't want the white and black colors to blend into each other and create gray areas in the logo.

1. Open ID 5-8.indd, then save it as **Concentric Circle Gradient**.
2. Click the Swatches panel menu button, then click New Gradient Swatch.
3. Create a radial gradient named **Six Ring Radial**.
4. Add four new color stops to the Gradient Ramp, then position them so that they are equally spaced across the ramp.
5. Format the first, third, and fifth color stops as 0% CMYK (white).
6. Format the second, fourth and sixth color stops as 100% black.
7. Close the New Gradient Swatch dialog box, then apply the new gradient to the circle.
8. Hide the frame edges, then compare your work to Figure 61.
9. Save your work, then close the Concentric Circle Gradient document.

This project will strengthen your familiarity with process colors. You will open an InDesign document that shows 12 process colors. Each process color is numbered from 1 to 12. All 12 are very basic mixes. None of the twelve is composed of more than two process inks. Some are just one. The inks used to create the twelve colors are used at either 100% or 50%. Your challenge is to guess the CMYK components of each color.

1. Open ID 5-9.indd, then save it as **Guess the Tints**. The color squares are shown in Figure 62.
2. Write your answers on a sheet of paper numbered 1–12. For example, you could write **#3 = 100% Magenta**.
3. When you're finished, double-click each color on the Swatches panel to reveal the actual CMYK mix.
4. Tally your total number of correct answers, save your work, then close the Guess the Tints document.

Figure 62 Completed Design Project 2

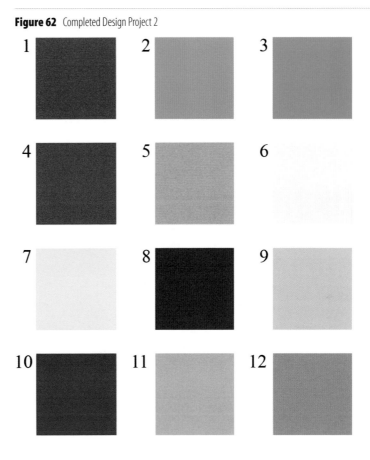

THE SUN IS STILL HIGH
IN THE ALASKAN
SUMMER SKY
WHEN THE CALL
COMES IN AT
9:47 P.M.

SIRENS WAIL, AND EIGHT SMOKEJUMPERS race to the suit-up racks. Already in logger's boots, dark green pants, and bright yellow shirts, each man practically leaps into his Kevlar jumpsuit.

"First load to the box!" a voice blares over the intercom. Itchy, Bloemker, O'Brien, Dibert, Swisher, Koby, Swan, Karp, and Cramer are the men at the top of the jump list. All evening they've mostly been hanging around the operations desk at their base at Fort Wainwright, cracking jokes and razzing each other, anxiously and excitedly waiting for their turn to leap out of a plane to fight a backcountry forest fire.

Now they have exactly two minutes to suit up and be on the plane. It's a much practiced routine: Their hands fly nimbly around their bodies, strapping on kneepads and shin guards, zipping into jumpsuits, and buckling into heavy nylon harnesses. The jumpsuits are prepacked with gear—a cargo pocket on one pant leg is stuffed with a solar panel and raincoat. The pocket on the other leg holds energy bars and a 150-foot rope, plus a rappel device in case of a treetop landing. An oversize butt pouch contains a tent and a stuff sack for the parachute.

Other smokejumpers quickly surround them, helping the men put on their main parachutes and reserve chutes. Then each man grabs his jump helmet—fitted with a cage-like mask to protect his face during a descent through branches—and his personal gear bag, which holds a liter of water, leather gloves, hard hat, flares for lighting backfires, knife, compass, radio, and special aluminum sack that serves as a last-resort fire shelter.

Two minutes after the siren, they are waddling onto the tarmac, each laden with nearly a hundred pounds of equipment and supplies. Fully dressed, they appear awkwardly overstuffed, but every man carries a carefully curated, time-tested kit of the essential items a smokejumper needs to fight and survive a fire in some of the world's most remote and rugged forests.

Photographed by team member Mike McMillan, one of the crew aims for a landing near the tail of the fire—where it started close to a group of cottages. The billowing smoke column signals a rapidly spreading "gobbler," a wildfire that's "off to the races," McMillan says.

126 NATIONAL GEOGRAPHIC

Layout/design by Tim Parks. From "Into the Fire." *National Geographic Magazine*, Vol. 235, No. 5, May, 2019

248

PROJECT DESCRIPTION

In this project, you will explore the relationship between imagery and text using a model spread from *National Geographic*. You will then study the differences between various magazine spread layouts and work with a peer to create the layout for your own spread. Your group will choose an impactful photograph and write accompanying text to describe it. The goal of this project is to create a layout that is balanced in its imagery and text placement.

SKILLS TO EXPLORE

• Format Text

• Format Paragraphs

• Create and Apply Styles

• Edit Text

• Create Bulleted and Numbered Lists

• Create a New Document and Set Up a Master Page

• Create Text on Master Pages

• Apply Master Pages to Document Pages

• Modify Master Pages and Document Pages

SOFT SKILLS CHALLENGE

In print publishing, a "Wall Walk" is an opportunity to view all pages of a product before it goes to print. During this event, large format, full-color spreads are taped to the wall, so team members can view all pages in the book or magazine in one plane and discuss changes that need to be made to the design or layout.

In this challenge, you and your partner will engage in a Wall Walk. The goal of this project is to help refine your idea of what a balanced spread looks like. To prepare, look through old magazines or conduct an Internet search. Do not choose the first spreads you see. Instead, allow yourself to peruse different styles. Look for layouts, images, text placements, and font changes that capture your eye. Then select four or more full-color spreads that grab your attention. Lay the spreads on a table or tape them to the wall.

Then observe each element of the spreads carefully. Notice the details that differentiate the spreads from one another. During your Wall Walk, discuss the relationship between text and imagery, changes in font size or style, use of white space, and the balance on each of the spreads.

WALL WALK CHECKLIST

1. Partner

2. Four or more magazine spreads

3. Safe space to facilitate respectful conversation

◀ Alaskan smokejumpers parachute into remote forested areas to fight fires.

GETTING STARTED

As you prepare to create your own layout, compare the spreads you chose for your Wall Walk to the sample spread from *National Geographic*. Discuss ways these spreads are alike and different and point out your favorite elements in each of the spreads. Be sure to note the overall composition of the spread: How much real estate does the image take up? How is the spread divided? What plays a more prominent role: text or image?

1. Create a list of the various elements that call out to you and decide which of these you would like to use in your layout. For example, would it be more impactful to show a colorful photo, a black and white photo, or a design element? In terms of font, should all of the text be the same size, or would varied fonts and sizes make the layout more interesting? Are captions necessary?

The students created a list of design elements to use in their project.

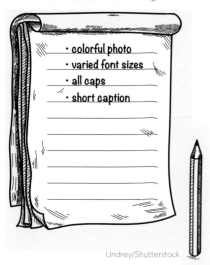

- colorful photo
- varied font sizes
- all caps
- short caption

Undrey/Shutterstock

2. Create a sketch of your layout to get a feel for how the photo and text might work together to tell a story. Ensure that all elements from your list are considered. Don't worry about the actual fonts or sizes at the moment. This part of the project focuses on the composition itself. Place your image and text blocks. How does the page feel? If necessary, add other elements, or change up the text to make it more visually interesting.

After considering many elements, the student sketched a sample magazine layout.

Creaktiva/Shutterstock

These sample magazine layouts show multiple layout options for the spread.

zeber/Shutterstock

INTO
THE
FIRE

EACH SUMMER, ELITE TEAMS KNOWN AS SMOKEJUMPERS PARACHUTE
INTO ALASKA'S BACKCOUNTRY IN A DANGEROUS RACE TO FIGHT REMOTE FIRES.

BY MARK JENKINS
PHOTOGRAPHS BY
MARK THIESSEN

120

Layout/design by Tim Parks. From "Into the Fire." *National Geographic Magazine*, Vol. 235, No. 5, May, 2019

PROJECT DESCRIPTION

In this project, you will create a comprehensive spread based on the layout from your Design Project. Consider experimenting with font size and style, and using text elements such as bulleted lists, numbered lists, or captions. Play with graphic and text frames, and add color as you see fit. The goal of this project is to create a magazine-style spread that engages the reader using a balance of imagery and text.

SKILLS TO EXPLORE

- Place and Thread Text
- Create New Sections and Wrap Text
- Align and Distribute Objects on a Page
- Stack and layer Objects
- Work with Graphics Frames
- Work with Text Frames
- Working with Color
- Work with Process Colors

SOFT SKILLS CHALLENGE

Working with a partner in a creative project can present its challenges. Often, both people bring differing views and perspectives to the project. In order to create a project you are both proud of, you will need to work together. Be honest as you discuss your strengths and weaknesses with each other. Decide how to break up the work. Will you make every decision together, or will each partner have the opportunity to use their own creative skills? Look over your layout and the Skills to Explore. Work together to come up with a list of tasks for each person in your group. Practice your speech so you are confident while presenting. You want your audience to view you as an expert on the topic.

GETTING STARTED

It's often challenging to start with a blank screen. Allow your Design Project to guide you.

1. Look at the balance on your page. Should the image take up the whole spread with just a bit of text? Or would it make more sense to have a single-page image with text on either the right or the left? Should the text come before the image, or the image before the text? These small decisions greatly influence the visual feel of the spread.

2. Compare the two *National Geographic* spreads. Both use a feature image to capture the reader's attention, but one has much more text than the other. Which one are you more drawn to and why? Think about how you might have designed these spreads differently. For example, imagine the "Into the Fire" spread had more text. What would be lost? How might this impact the spread as a whole?

3. Challenge yourself to enhance the layout with text and graphic frames. Link text blocks together in interesting ways and experiment with placing text in different positions on the page. Think outside the box by arranging the text in a way that shows its importance. For example, you may be able to reduce a larger text block to three sentences and instead use small caps to convey the importance of the words.

4. Think about how best to include color in your spread, either through font, background, or a feature callout. Remember, the text and images should work together for the ultimate visual impact.

◀ Alaskan smokejumpers parachute into remote forested areas to fight fires.

IMPRINTS OF A WATERY PAST

Early visions of alien-made canals turned out to be fantasy, but Mars does boast geologic features such as river channels and deltas that hint at a wet history. Now, after more than 40 years of exploration, scientists have a deeper understanding of the planet's surface—and how parts of the landscape were transformed by flowing water some three and a half billion years ago.

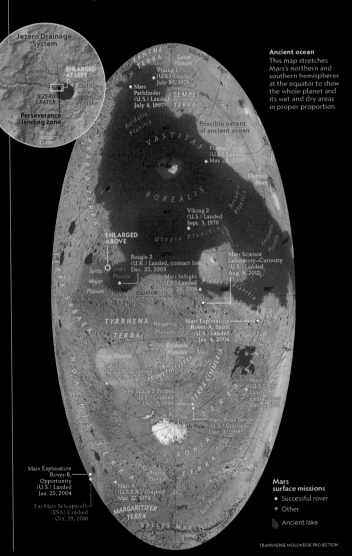

Jezero Drainage System

Inlet valley

ENLARGED AT LEFT

Inlet valley

JEZERO CRATER

Outflow valley

Ancient lake

Perseverance landing zone

25 mi
25 km

XANTHE TERRA

300°

Lunae Planum

EQUATOR

Viking 1 (U.S.) Landed July 20, 1976

Mars Pathfinder (U.S.) Landed July 4, 1997

210°

TEMPE TERRA

30°N

Ancient ocean
This map stretches Mars's northern and southern hemispheres at the equator to show the whole planet and its wet and dry areas in proper proportion.

Acidalia Planitia

VASTITAS

60°

Possible extent of ancient ocean

North Pole

Phoenix (U.S.) Landed May 25, 2008

Olympus Mons

BOREALIS

Arcadia Planitia

ARABIA TERRA

Viking 2 (U.S.) Landed Sept. 3, 1976

Utopia Planitia

240°

ENLARGED ABOVE

Beagle 2 (U.K.) Landed, contact lost Dec. 25, 2003

30°N

Mars Science Laboratory–Curiosity (U.S.) Landed Aug. 6, 2012

Syrtis Major Planum

Isidis Planitia

Mars InSight (U.S.) Landed Nov. 26, 2018

Elysium Planitia

330°

TERRA SABAEA

EQUATOR

TYRRHENA TERRA

Hesperia Planum

Mars Exploration Rover-A, Spirit (U.S.) Landed Jan. 4, 2004

ELYSIUM

Eridania Planitia

30°S

TERRA CIMMERIA

Helas Planitia

Mars 2 (U.S.S.R.) Crashed Nov. 27, 1971

PROMETHEI TERRA

Deep Space 2 Probes (U.S.) Crashed Dec. 3, 1999

Mars 3 (U.S.S.R.) Landed, contact lost Dec. 2, 1971

NOACHIS TERRA

Planum Australe

South Pole

Mars Polar Lander (U.S.) Crashed Dec. 3, 1999

AONIA TERRA

Mars Exploration Rover-B, Opportunity (U.S.) Landed Jan. 25, 2004

Argyre Planitia

Mars 6 (U.S.S.R.) Crashed Mar. 12, 1974

ExoMars Schiaparelli (ESA) Crashed Oct. 19, 2016

30°S

Solis Planum

MARGARITIFER TERRA

VALLES MARINERIS

300°

Mars surface missions
◆ Successful rover
◆ Other
Ancient lake

TRANSVERSE MOLLWEIDE PROJECTION

WARM AND WET

Warmer weather, closer to Earth's average of 57°F, would have allowed for running water and even rain. Storms might have cleared the air of most dust to create bluer skies. The wet and rocky Martian landscape could not have supported vegetation.

COLD AND ICY

Temperatures colder than Antarctica would have kept any surface water frozen, with ice and snow at high elevations. Volcanic lava and steam might have briefly warmed some regions. Ancient Mars would have appeared more gray; today oxidized iron gives its soil a ruddy hue.

ANCIENT HORIZONS

In 2003 a rover found evidence that water once flowed on Mars, but early climatic conditions on the red planet are still up for debate. Models suggest two extremes that would have allowed some liquid to exist on the surface, illustrated here; scientists suspect Mars may have cycled between both states.

MANUEL CANALES AND MATTHEW W. CHWASTYK, NGM STAFF; ALEXANDER STEGMAIER. ART: ANTOINE COLLIGNON
SOURCES: ASHLEY PALUMBO, BROWN UNIVERSITY; ROBIN WORDSWORTH, HARVARD UNIVERSITY; NASA

Scientific illustrations suggest what the surface of Mars may have looked like in the ancient past. Restrained use of typography and graphic elements allow the illustrations to be the focal point.

From "Our Obsession with Mars." *National Geographic Magazine*, Vol. 239, No. 3, March, 2021

MANAROLA

tuesday august 9

Lorem ipsum dolor sit amet, consectetuer adipiscing elit, sed diam nonummy nibh euismod tincidunt ut laoreet dolore magna aliquam erat volutpat. Ut wisi enim ad minim veniam, quis nostrud exerci tation ullamcorper suscipit lobortis nisl ut aliquip ex ea commodo consequat. Duis autem vel eum iriure dolor in hendrerit in vulputate velit esse molestie consequat, vel illum do-

lore eu feugiat nulla facilisis at vero eros et accumsan et iusto odio dignissim qui blandit praesent luptatum zzril delenit augue duis dolore te feugait nulla facilisi. Ut wisi enim ad minim veniam, quis nostrud exerci tation ullamcorper suscipit lobortis nisl ut aliquip ex ea commodo consequat. Duis autem vel eum iriure dolor in hendrerit in vulputate velit esse molestie consequat,

precedente

sequente

④

FIRENZE

tuesday august 16

Lorem ipsum dolor sit amet, consectetuer adipiscing elit, sed diam nonummy nibh euismod tincidunt ut laoreet dolore magna aliquam erat volutpat. Ut wisi enim ad minim veniam, quis nostrud exerci tation ullamcorper suscipit lobortis nisl ut aliquip ex ea commodo consequat. Duis autem vel eum iriure dolor in hendrerit in vulputate velit esse molestie consequat, vel illum do-

lore eu feugiat nulla facilisis at vero eros et accumsan et iusto odio dignissim qui blandit praesent luptatum zzril delenit augue duis dolore te feugait nulla facilisi. Ut wisi enim ad minim veniam, quis nostrud exerci tation ullamcorper suscipit lobortis nisl ut aliquip ex ea commodo consequat. Duis autem vel eum iriure dolor in hendrerit in vulputate velit esse molestie consequat,

precedente

sequente

⑧

CHAPTER 6

WORKING WITH PLACED IMAGES

1. Place Multiple Graphics
2. Use the Links Panel
3. Explore Image Resolution Issues
4. Place Vector Graphics
5. Interface InDesign with Photoshop
6. Use CC Libraries

CERTIFIED PROFESSIONAL

Adobe Certified Professional in Print & Digital Media Publication Using Adobe InDesign

1. Working in the Design Industry

This objective covers critical concepts related to working with colleagues and clients as well as crucial legal, technical, and design-related knowledge.

1.4 Demonstrate knowledge of key terminology related to publications.
  C Understand and use key terms related to multi-page layouts.

2. Project Setup and Interface

This objective covers the interface setup and program settings that assist in an efficient and effective workflow, as well as knowledge about ingesting digital assets for a project.

2.1 Create a document with the appropriate settings for web, print, and mobile.
  A Set appropriate document settings for printed and onscreen images.
  B Create a new document preset to reuse for specific project needs.

2.3 Use nonprinting design tools in the interface to aid in design or workflow.
  D Use views and modes to work efficiently.

2.4 Import assets into a project.
  B Place assets in an InDesign document.

4. Creating and Modifying Document Elements

This objective covers core tools and functionality of the application, as well as tools that affect the visual appearance of document elements.

4.1 Use core tools and features to lay out visual elements.
  B Manipulate graphics in frames.

4.2 Add and manipulate text using appropriate typographic settings.
  E Manage text flow across multiple text areas.

4.3 Make, manage, and edit selections.
  A Make selections using a variety of tools.

4.4 Transform digital graphics and media within a publication.
  A Modify frames and frame content.

4.5 Use basic reconstructing and editing techniques to manipulate document content.
  B Evaluate or adjust the appearance of objects, frames, or layers using various tools.

5. Publishing Digital Media

This objective covers saving and exporting documents or assets within individual layers or selections.

5.1 Prepare documents for publishing to web, print, and other digital devices.
  A Check document for errors and project specifications.

PLACE MULTIPLE GRAPHICS

▶ **What You'll Do**

In this lesson, you will use the Place command and Adobe Bridge to place multiple images into a layout.

Placing Multiple Images with the Place Command

The Place command on the File menu is the basic command used for placing graphics into an InDesign layout. In Chapter 4, you used the Place command to navigate to a single file, select it, then place it in a layout. You can also use the Place command to import multiple image files simultaneously. This is a great feature that offers substantial time savings when working with multiple images.

To place multiple images, click the Place command and navigate to the location where the graphics are stored. Select as many graphic files as you want to place, then click Place. The Place command will then display the **place thumbnail**, shown in Figure 1. The place thumbnail features a small, low-resolution thumbnail of a loaded image. When you've loaded multiple images, the thumbnail showing is the current loaded image, and the small number in the upper-left corner indicates how many total images are loaded. Use the right arrow and left arrow keys to scroll through all the loaded images. Click the place thumbnail on the page or in a frame and the current loaded image will be placed.

Figure 1 Place thumbnail icon

Image courtesy of Chris Botello

Number indicates the number of images loaded in the place thumbnail

When you place an image, you always have three options for how it's placed:

- Click the place thumbnail in an already existing frame, and the image will be placed into the frame.
- Click the place thumbnail on the page, InDesign will create a frame for the placed image. By default, the frame will be sized to display the entire image at 100%. In other words, the frame will be the same size as the image itself.
- Click and drag the place thumbnail to create a frame at the size that you want, and the image will be placed into that frame.

When placing graphics into frames, be aware the size at which the graphic is being placed. When you create a new frame and then place a graphic into that frame, the graphic will be placed at 100% by default—even if the graphic is larger than the frame itself. However, if you place a graphic into a "used" frame, the rules can change. For example, let's say you have a frame that contains an image, and that image has been resized to 74%. If you click the Place command and place a different image into the frame, the new image will be placed at 74%. In other words, when placing a graphic into a used frame, the new graphic is placed at the same size as the previous graphic.

Setting Frame Fitting Options

The Fitting command on the Object menu contains a submenu with many commands that affect how graphics fit into frames.

See Figure 2. Generally speaking, you'll find that the Fill Frame Proportionally and Fit Content Proportionally commands are the ones you'll use most often. The Fill Frame Proportionally command does just that: it scales the graphic so it fills the entire frame—without distorting the graphic. The Fit Content Proportionally command scales a placed graphic so the entire graphic is visible in the frame.

When you're placing many graphics into a layout, you will find it tiring to have to select the same fitting command over and over for each graphic. To alleviate this, you can set up options in the Frame Fitting Options dialog box. This dialog box allows you to define a specific fitting option for all graphics you place. If you apply settings in the Frame Fitting Options dialog box with a document open and no frames selected, the options will apply to all frames you create in that document only. If you apply frame fitting options to a selected frame, the options affect only that frame.

If you want the options applied to all frames you create in all future documents, set the frame fitting options with no documents open. By doing so, the frame fitting options you choose will be applied to all frames you create when you open a document.

TIP You can also use the Frame Fitting Options dialog box to specify the reference point for the alignment of the image in the frame.

Figure 2 Fitting commands

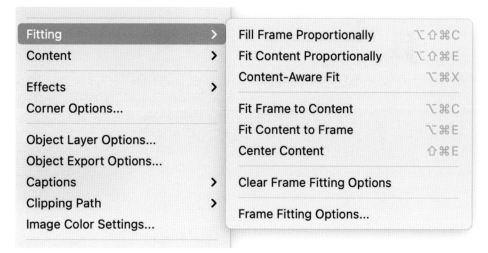

Working with Adobe Bridge

Adobe Bridge is a freestanding **content management application**.

What is content management? Imagine that you are designing a 200-page catalog, such as the quarterly catalog for L.L.Bean or IKEA. Think about the hundreds of images that you'll need to import to complete your layout. Now consider that those images—the ones that are actually used in the catalog—are only a subset of the thousands of product shots the photographers deliver after the photo shoot.

Adobe Bridge, shown in Figure 3, is designed to help you manage this content.

Let's say you have a folder with 500 image files. If you view that folder using Adobe Bridge as the interface, Bridge will show you a thumbnail of each file. You can choose the size of the thumbnail, enabling you to sample and preview each image quickly.

Adobe Bridge also allows you to apply color labels and text data to images to help you categorize them. Using the previous example of an L.L.Bean catalog, the photography team could apply the tag "shoes" to all shoe products they shoot, and "sweaters" to every sweater. Then you, the designer, could use Bridge to sort through the images to show only the shoe or sweater photographs.

You can access Adobe Bridge quickly and easily in InDesign. Just click Browse in Bridge under the File menu, and Bridge will launch.

Figure 3 Adobe Bridge interface

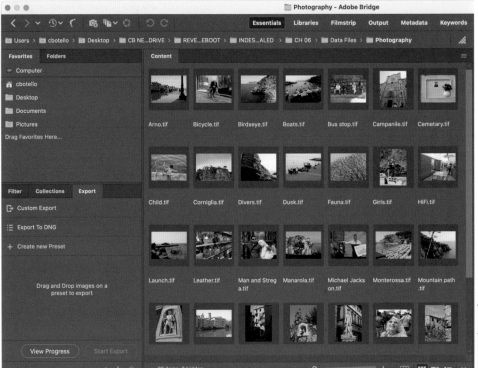

Images courtesy of Chris Botello

Using the Link Badge

When you place an image, the link badge appears at the upper-left corner of the image, as shown in Figure 4. If you hover over the link badge, the name of the placed file appears. Because it remains visible even when the frame is not selected, the link badge is useful, especially when you have a document that contains many placed images. You can simply mouse over the link badge and know immediately the name of the placed file.

If you press and hold [option] (Mac) or [Alt] (Win) and click the link badge, the Links panel will open with that image highlighted in the panel. This, too, is especially useful when you're working with many placed images.

To hide or show the link badge, click View on the menu bar, point to Extras, then click the Hide/Show Link Badge command.

Figure 4 Link badge

Link badge

Place multiple images with the Place command

1. Click **View** on the menu bar, point to **Extras**, then click **Hide Content Grabber**.

   For this chapter, you will double-click the image to toggle between selecting the frame and the image in the frame.

2. Click **View** on the menu bar, point to **Extras**, then verify that the **Link Badge** is not showing.

   For this chapter, you will access the Links panel directly.

3. Open ID 6-1.indd, then save it as **Multiple Placements**.

4. Click the **Selection tool** ▶, then select the **large blue frame** on pages 2-3.

5. Click **File** on the menu bar, click **Place**, navigate to the folder where your Chapter 6 Data Files are stored, open the **Photography folder**, then click the file **Corniglia** once to select it.

6. Press and hold **[command] (Mac)** or **[Ctrl] (Win)**, then click the following files in this order: **Townsfolk**, **Divers**, **Sheets**, **Fauna**, and **Dusk**.

7. Click **Open**.

   As shown in Figure 5, the place thumbnail is loaded, showing the Corniglia graphic and the number 6, indicating that six files are loaded.

Figure 5 Place thumbnail icon

Six images loaded

Image courtesy of Chris Botello

8. Press the **right arrow key** [→] on your keypad repeatedly to see all the files loaded in the place thumbnail.

Despite the order in which you selected them when you chose them, the files are loaded alphabetically: Corniglia, Divers, Dusk, Fauna, Sheets, and Townsfolk.

9. Press the **right arrow key** [→] repeatedly until the **Corniglia image** is the visible loaded file.

10. Click the **place thumbnail** on the **large blue frame**.

As shown in Figure 6, the Corniglia image fills the frame, and the place thumbnail now shows the next file in line.

11. Place the **remaining five loaded images** into the **five frames** at the bottom of the page in any order that you wish.

12. Select all **six frames**, click **Object** on the menu bar, point to **Fitting**, then click **Fill Frame Proportionally**.

13. Position the **images** in the frames (scale them if you like) so your page resembles Figure 7.

14. Save your work, then continue to the next set of steps.

You used the Place command to select six files to be placed, then used the arrow key to view those six files in the place thumbnail. You then placed the files and applied a fitting command to all the frames to verify that they were consistent.

Figure 6 Placing the Corniglia image

Place thumbnail and five loaded images

Figure 7 Six images loaded and fitted

Place multiple images with Adobe Bridge

1. Navigate to **spread 4-5**.

2. Click **File** on the menu bar, then click **Browse in Bridge**.

   Adobe Bridge launches and opens.

3. Navigate to the location where you store your Chapter 6 Data Files, then open the **Photography folder**.

4. Drag the **scale slider** at the bottom of the panel right to enlarge the thumbnails so only three thumbnails are visible left to right, as shown in Figure 8.

   The interface in the figure is set to charcoal; the thumbnail images tend to stand out better against a darker background.

5. Drag the **scale slider** left so nine thumbnails are visible in the panel.

6. Use the **scrollbar** on the right of the panel to scroll through all the thumbnails.

7. Click the file named **Manarola**, then note what the image looks like so you'll remember it.

8. Press and hold **[command] (Mac)** or **[Ctrl] (Win)**, then click the following five files: **Birdseye**, **Boats**, **Launch**, **Three Houses**, **Window**.

Figure 8 Bridge interface with enlarged thumbnails

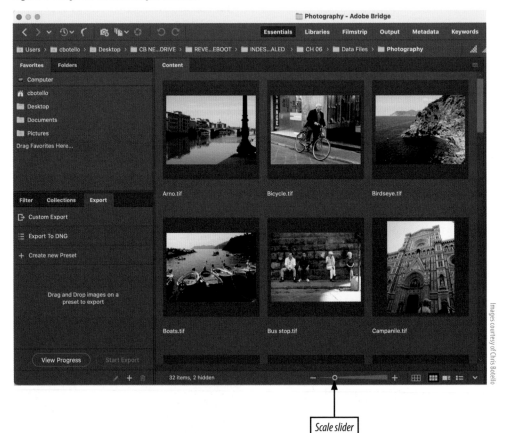

Images courtesy of Chris Botello

Scale slider

9. Click **File** on the menu bar, point to **Place**, then click **In InDesign**.

   The interface switches to InDesign, and the place thumbnail is loaded with the number 6, indicating that six files are loaded.

10. Press → to scroll through the loaded thumbnails, then scroll to the Manarola thumbnail.

11. Click in the **large blue frame** with the place thumbnail.

The Manarola image is placed into the frame.

12. Place the **remaining five loaded images** into the five frames at the top of the page in any order that you wish.

13. Select **all six frames**, click **Object** on the menu bar, point to **Fitting**, then click **Fill Frame Proportionally**.

14. Reposition any images in their frames as you like, then compare your result to Figure 9.

15. Save your work, then close the Multiple Placements document.

You previewed files on your computer using Adobe Bridge. You viewed and selected multiple files in Bridge and then placed them in an InDesign layout.

Figure 9 Placing and positioning six images

USE THE LINKS PANEL

▶ *What You'll Do*

In this lesson, you will use the Links panel to manage links to imported graphics.

Understanding Preview Files

When you use the Place command to place a graphic file, the image you see in the graphics frame in InDesign is a **preview file**; it is *not* the graphic itself. Why does InDesign work this way? Because of file size considerations.

Remember that many graphics files—especially those of scanned photos or other digital images—have very large file sizes. Some of them are enormous. For example, if you had an 8" × 10" scanned photo that you wanted to use in a layout for a magazine, that graphic would be approximately 21 megabytes, at minimum. If you placed that graphic in your InDesign layout, your InDesign file size would increase dramatically. Now imagine placing 10 of those graphics!

The preview is a low-resolution version of the placed graphic file. As such, its file size is substantially smaller than the average graphics file. The role of the preview file in the layout is ingenious. As a proxy for the actual graphic, it allows you to see a representation of the graphic in your layout without having to carry the burden of the graphic's full file size.

Using the Links Panel

You can think of the Links panel, shown in Figure 10, as command central for managing the links to placed graphics. The Links panel lists all the graphics files that you place into an InDesign document. By default, text that you place in InDesign is not linked to the original text file and therefore not listed on the Links panel.

Also by default, graphics files are listed with a thumbnail of the graphic. Next to each listing is the page number on which the file is located. The Links panel menu offers options for sorting this list. For example, you can sort the list alphabetically or by page number.

You can use the Links panel to locate a placed file in your document quickly. If you select a file on the Links panel and then click the Go to Link button on the panel, InDesign will go to the page where the placed file is located and automatically select its frame. Conversely, when you select a placed file on the document, the file's listing is automatically highlighted on the Links panel.

Figure 10 Links panel

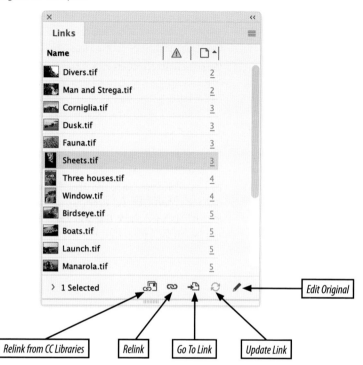

Viewing the Link Info Section of the Links Panel

Double-clicking a filename on the Links panel displays the Link Info section of the Links panel. Shown in Figure 11, the Link Info section displays important information about the placed file, including its file size, resolution, the date it was last modified, the application that created it, and its file format. The file format identifies what type of file it is, such as a Photoshop or an Illustrator file.

TIP You can also click the Show/Hide Link Information triangle to show this section of the panel.

It's always good to know the file format of a graphic and the application that created it in case you wish to edit the original. The Links panel is a big help in this regard. Click the Edit Original button on the panel, and the selected graphic will open in its original application (that is, if you have that application installed on your computer). For photographs, the original application will usually be Adobe Photoshop. For illustrations, it will usually be Adobe Illustrator.

Generally speaking, you will find the default information listed in the Link Info section of the panel to be more than satisfactory for your work. It might even be too much information. You can specify the categories of information you want to see listed in the Link Info section, by clicking the Links panel menu button, clicking Panel Options, then selecting only the check boxes of the categories you want to view.

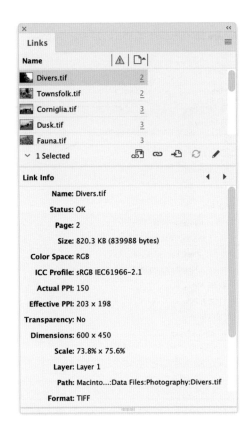

Figure 11 Link Info section of Links panel

Placing Text Files

When you place text in InDesign, the text is usually from a word processing program such as Microsoft Word. By default, when you place text in InDesign, the text is not linked to the original text file, and the placed text does not appear on the Links panel. The formatting changes you apply in InDesign don't affect the original text file, and more importantly, any changes that you may make to the original text file don't affect the formatting of the text in InDesign. You can override the default and link text you place in InDesign to the original text document. If you select the Create Links When Placing Text And Spreadsheet Files option in the File Handling preferences before you place a file, the name of the text file appears on the Links panel.

When text is linked to its original file in this manner, you can use the Links panel to update and manage the file. But beware—when you update a linked text file, any editing or formatting changes that you applied in InDesign are lost. That's why placed text in InDesign isn't linked by default: it's too risky. Even when you override the default and link text to its original file, text files in the InDesign document are not automatically updated when the original file is edited and saved. You must manually update the linked file using the Links panel.

Managing Links to Placed Graphics

When you place a graphic file, InDesign establishes a link between the graphics frame and the placed file. That link is based on the location of the file. When you first place the graphic, you must navigate through the folder structure on your computer to locate the file. You may navigate to a folder on your computer's hard drive, external drive, or network. In either case, InDesign remembers that navigation path as the method for establishing the location of the placed file.

The Links panel uses icons to alert you to the status of a placed file. The Missing icon appears beside the file's name when the established link no longer points to the file. In other words, if you move the file to a different folder (or delete it), *after* you place it in InDesign, the file will be listed as Missing on the Links panel. The Missing icon is a white question mark inside a red circle.

The Modified icon is a black exclamation point in a yellow triangle. A placed file's status is noted as Modified when the original file has been edited and saved *after* being placed in InDesign. For example, if you place a Photoshop graphic in InDesign and then open the graphic in Photoshop, edit it, and save changes, the graphic you placed in InDesign is no longer the most up-to-date version of the graphic. If you have the InDesign document open when you save the Photoshop file, InDesign automatically updates the graphic in the layout. Otherwise, the Links panel displays the Modified icon beside the file. Figure 12 shows files on the Links panel with the Missing and Modified icons.

The OK status does not have an icon. The OK status means that the established link still points to the location of the placed graphic, and the graphic itself has not been modified since being placed.

TIP If a linked or embedded file contains metadata, you can view the metadata using the Links panel. Select a file on the Links panel, click the Links panel menu button, click Utilities, then click XMP File Info.

Figure 12 Missing and Modified icons on the Links panel

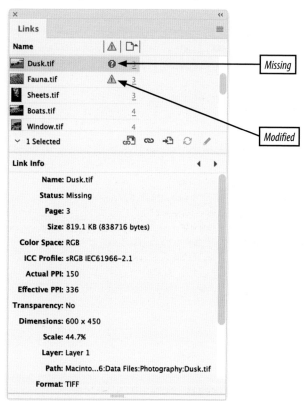

Updating Missing and Modified Files

When the Links panel displays Modified and Missing icons, those links need to be updated, meaning you need to reestablish the connection between the preview file and the graphic file that has been moved or edited.

It's easy to update modified files on the Links panel. To do so, you click the filename on the Links panel, then click the Update Link button on the panel. The link will update to the newest saved version of the file, and the status of the file will change to OK.

Files that have the Missing status need to be relinked to the graphic. To do so, you click the filename on the Links panel, click the Relink button, then navigate to the new location of the graphic file. Once the link is reestablished, the status of the file changes to OK.

When you reestablish a link, none of the formatting that you did to the graphic when you placed it the first time is lost. If, for example, you scaled a placed graphic to 35% and centered it proportionally in the graphics frame, those modifications will still be in place when you reestablish the link.

Embedding Files

InDesign allows you to embed a placed file into the InDesign document. When you embed a placed file, the file literally becomes part of the InDesign document; it no longer links to a source file.

You would embed images for one reason: to have a self-contained InDesign document without the need for supporting files. Rather than having to package an InDesign document with all its supporting files, an InDesign document with embedded graphics offers you the simplicity of having to work with only a single document.

To embed a placed graphic file, select it on the Links panel, click the Links panel menu button, then click Embed Link. The file will continue to be listed on the Links panel, but it will appear with the Embedded icon beside its name.

To relink an embedded file to its original file on your computer, click the file on the Links panel, click the Links panel menu button, then click Relink. You'll be prompted to navigate to the location of the source file to reestablish the link. The file will then be linked, not embedded.

Because an embedded file is part of the InDesign document, embedded files increase the file size of the InDesign document substantially, and this can lead to a slowdown in InDesign's performance. For this reason, you may want to avoid embedding files in InDesign and work with the standard methodology of linking to graphics.

CREATING AND USING SNIPPETS

In the same way that libraries let you store page elements for reuse, snippets let you export any elements from a document for reuse in other documents or in an object library. A **snippet** is an XML file with an .inds file extension that contains complete representation of document elements, including all formatting tags and document structure. To create a snippet, use the Selection tool to select the frames you want to reuse, click File on the menu bar, click Export, then choose InDesign Snippet from the Save as type list arrow. Remember that you can create a single snippet from multiple objects. For example, you can select all the objects on a page and create one snippet from everything on the page. (It's a good idea to group the elements before exporting the snippet.) An even easier method is to drag selected items onto the desktop, into Adobe Bridge, a Library panel, or an email message, each of which automatically creates a snippet file. To use a snippet in another file, you can use the Place command or just drag the snippet from the desktop into an InDesign document.

EXPORTING XML

XML is a versatile language that describes content—such as text, graphics, and design elements—in a format that allows that content to be output in a variety of ways. Like HTML, XML uses coded information, called "tags," to identify and organize content. Unlike HTML, XML does not describe how the information will appear or how it will be laid out on a page. Instead, XML creates an identity for the content.

XML can distinguish and identify such elements as chapter titles, headlines, body copy, an author's name, or numbered steps. Here's the hook: XML information is not specific to any one kind of output, so you can use that same information to create different types of documents, just as you can use the English alphabet to speak and write other languages.

For example, many designers work in XML to generate catalogs, books, magazines, or newspapers, all from the same XML content. The Tags panel and the Structure pane, which are two XML utilities in InDesign, interface smoothly with XML code and allow you to organize content and list it in a hierarchical order, which is essential to XML.

Before items can be exported to an XML file, they must be tagged, using the Tags panel. You can also apply an autotag to an item using the Autotag command on the Tags panel menu. When you do so, InDesign applies the default tag for that item type defined in the Tagging Preset Options dialog box. You can change the default tag settings in this dialog box by clicking the Tags panel menu button and then clicking Tagging Preset Options. All tagged items appear in the Structure pane. You can opt to show or hide tagged frames as well as tag markers using the Structure commands on the View menu. To export an XML file, click Export, then choose XML from the Format list menu.

Because XML tags are data descriptions and carry no formatting instructions, you will need to format XML content when you import it to a layout. A smart solution for doing that quickly and with consistency is to map XML tags to paragraph, character, table, or cell styles. As with all solutions involving styles, mapping tags to predefined styles makes formatting imported XML content easier and less time consuming.

To map XML tags to various styles, choose Map Tags to Styles from the Tags panel menu or the Structure pane menu. This opens the Map Tags to Styles dialog box, where you can choose an XML tag and apply a style to it.

Use the Links panel to update modified and missing graphics

1. Open ID 6-2.indd, then compare the warning dialog box you see to Figure 13.

   Your dialog box might differ from the figure.

2. Click **Don't Update Links**, then save the file as **Update Links**.

   Normally you would click Update Links and the modified links would be updated. The missing links wouldn't be updated because they are missing. For this lesson, you are instructed to not update links so you can do so manually on the Links panel.

3. Open the **Links panel**.

4. Scroll through the Links panel to view the list of the placed graphics.

   All the placed files in this document—except two—are located in the Photography folder in the Chapter 6 Data Files folder. Two files have been moved out of the Photography folder and into the Move Files folder to make them "missing" for this lesson.

   TIP Your Links panel might show all files as modified (an exclamation point in a yellow triangle). They are not really modified. This happens if you download the files to your computer.

5. Click the **Woman in Window.tif link** on the Links panel, then click the **Go to Link button** 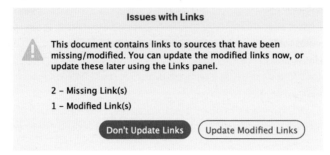.

   As shown in Figure 14, the status of the Woman in Window.tif link is listed on the Links panel as Modified. This means that it has been modified in another program (in this case, Photoshop) after it was placed into this file.

Figure 13 Issues with Links dialog box

Issues with Links

⚠ This document contains links to sources that have been missing/modified. You can update the modified links now, or update these later using the Links panel.

2 – Missing Link(s)
1 – Modified Link(s)

(Don't Update Links)   (Update Modified Links)

Figure 14 Modified image on the Links panel

Images courtesy of Chris Botello

6. Click the **Update Link button** ↻ .

   As shown in Figure 15, the link is updated, and the status of the graphic is OK.

7. If necessary, select any other **graphic files that show the Modified icon**, then click the **Update Link button** ↻ .

8. Note that both the **Hat** and **Duomo graphics** are listed as Missing.

9. Click the **Hat graphic** on the Links panel, then click the **Go to Link button** ⤓ .

   The image is selected.

10. Click the **Relink button** ∞ .

11. Navigate to the **Moved Files folder** where you store your Chapter 6 Data Files, click **Hat**, then click **Open**.

    An Information dialog box, shown in Figure 16, appears, indicating that one file has been found and relinked. This refers to the Duomo file. When you showed InDesign where the Hat file was located, InDesign also found Duomo and relinked it.

12. Click **OK**, then note on the Links panel that both missing files have been relinked.

13. Save your work, then continue to the next lesson.

You used the Links panel to update modified links, then you updated two missing links simultaneously.

Figure 15 Updated link on the Links panel

Figure 16 InDesign finds and relinks another missing graphic

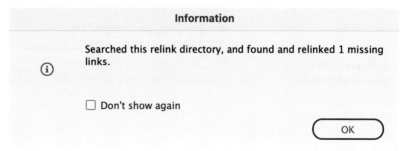

EXPLORE IMAGE RESOLUTION ISSUES

What You'll Do

In this lesson, you will learn about effective image resolution in an InDesign layout and how to modify image resolution in Adobe Photoshop.

Understanding Bitmap Graphics

Photographic images are created on computers using a rectangular grid of colored squares called **pixels**. Because pixels (a contraction of "picture elements") can render subtle gradations of tone, they are the most common medium for continuous tone images—what you perceive as a photograph on your computer. Graphics created from pixels are called **bitmap graphics**.

All scanned images and digital "photos" are composed of pixels. Figure 17 shows an example of a bitmap image. The enlarged section shows you the pixels that compose the image.

Understanding Image Resolution

The number of pixels in a given inch is referred to as the image's **resolution**. To be effective, pixels must be small enough to create an image with the illusion of continuous tone. The standard resolution for images for the web is 72 pixels per inch (ppi). For images that will be professionally printed, the standard resolution is 300 pixels per inch (ppi).

The term **effective resolution** refers to the resolution of a placed image based on its size in the layout. Effective resolution is a critical consideration whenever you're working with placed bitmap images.

Figure 17 Bitmap graphic

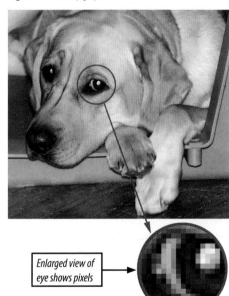

Enlarged view of eye shows pixels

The important thing to remember about bitmap images in relation to InDesign is that the size of the image placed in the InDesign layout has a direct effect on the image's resolution. Think about it—if you enlarge a placed image in InDesign, the pixels that make up the image are spread out over a larger area. Thus, the effective resolution of the image goes down because there are now fewer pixels per inch. This decrease in resolution will have a negative impact on the quality of an image when it is printed.

Therefore, enlarging an image in InDesign usually creates a problem with effective resolution: the greater the enlargement, the lower the effective resolution of the image.

| **TIP** The Link Info section in the Links panel, lists the effective resolution for all placed graphics.

Let's use a clear example to illustrate this. For a professionally printed bitmap image, the target resolution is 300 pixels per inch.

Let's say you have a Photoshop image that is 1" × 1" at 300 ppi. Since the image is at a resolution of 300 pixels per inch, it meets the target resolution and will print high-quality.

The image contains a total of 90,000 pixels (300 × 300 = 90,000).

Now, let's say you place the same image into a 2" × 2" frame and use the Fitting commands to enlarge the image 200% to fill the frame. Those same 90,000 pixels are now spread out to fill a 2" × 2" frame. Thus, the effective resolution is 150 ppi—too low for professional printing.

Figure 18 illustrates this example. Spend as much time considering this information as you need to thoroughly understand the concept of effective resolution. The main point is that the resolution of the original image is not the only consideration. Just as important is the size that it's used in InDesign. If it has been enlarged in InDesign, the effective resolution goes down.

Figure 18 Illustration of effective resolution

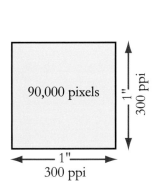

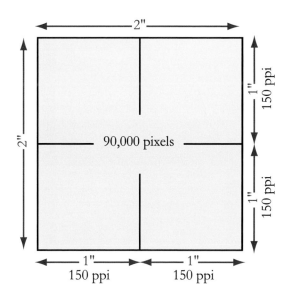

Enlarging a Graphic in Adobe Photoshop

Photoshop is the best-selling pixel-based image manipulation software application by Adobe Systems, the same company that produces InDesign. It's important to understand that scaling a graphic in Photoshop is different from scaling a graphic in InDesign. When you scale a graphic in InDesign, it either spreads the existing pixels over a larger area (enlargement) or squeezes them into a smaller area (reduction). Photoshop, because it specializes in image manipulation, allows you to actually change the number of pixels when you scale a graphic.

Let's continue with the same example from before. If you have a 1" × 1" graphic at 300 ppi, it has a total of 90,000 pixels. If you enlarge it in Photoshop to a 2" × 2" graphic, Photoshop offers you the ability to maintain the image resolution. Thus, after the scale, the image will still be 300 ppi, meaning the 2" square image will be 600 pixels wide and 600 pixels tall, for a total of 360,000 pixels. But from where do those extra 270,000 pixels come?

When enlarging a graphic in Photoshop, Photoshop creates the new pixels necessary to maintain an image's resolution by a process called **interpolation**. The color of the new pixels is based on the color information of the original pixels in the image. Thus, in the preceding example, the colors of the 270,000 new pixels are created based on the 90,000 original pixels.

TIP To be an effective designer in InDesign, you need to understand effective resolution issues and be able to work in Photoshop to modify an image's resolution.

Enlarging a bitmap graphic always results in a loss of quality—even if you do it in Photoshop. That's because interpolated data is only duplicated data—inferior to the original data that you get from a scan or a digital image that you download from your digital camera.

In a nutshell, you should try your best to create all bitmap graphics in Adobe Photoshop at both the size and resolution that they will be used at the final output stage. You then import the graphic into InDesign and leave its size alone.

If you find that you need to enlarge the graphic substantially (more than 10%), remember that all resizing of bitmap graphics should be done in Photoshop, not in InDesign. Use InDesign simply to place the graphics in a layout, create text wraps, and perform other layout-related tasks.

Is there any leeway here? Yes. If you need to reduce the size of a placed bitmap graphic in InDesign, you can do so without worrying about it too much. Reducing a bitmap graphic in InDesign is not a problem, because you *increase* the effective resolution of the bitmap graphic (the same number of pixels in a smaller area means more pixels per inch). If you need to enlarge a graphic slightly in InDesign, you can feel comfortable enlarging it up to 110%. For anything larger, enlarge it in Photoshop.

TIP Remember, nothing in this discussion applies to vector graphics. Vector graphics are resolution independent. You can feel free to enlarge and reduce placed vector graphics in InDesign to your heart's content.

Change the resolution of a placed graphic

1. Double-click **Dusk** on the Links panel, then click the **Go to Link button** ⊕ .

2. Compare your screen to Figure 19.

   The Link Info section shows that the Actual PPI of the image is 150, but the Effective PPI of the placed image is 336, making it high enough to print with quality. Because the image was placed at 44%, the effective resolution is more than double the actual resolution.

3. Double-click the **Corniglia link** on the Links panel, then click the **Go to Link button** ⊕ .

   The Actual PPI of the image is 150, and the Effective PPI is 144, which is too low for quality printing.

4. Click the **Edit Original button** ✎ on the Links panel.

   The image opens in Adobe Photoshop. You will need to have Adobe Photoshop installed on your computer to complete this lesson.

TIP Placed .PSD files will automatically open in Photoshop. Other formats, such as .TIF, must be specified in your computer's preferences to open by default in Photoshop.

Continued on next page

Figure 19 Viewing resolution info for Dusk

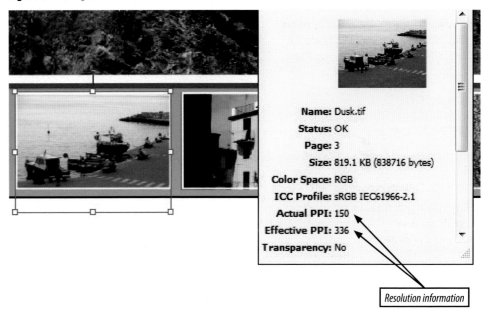

Name: Dusk.tif
Status: OK
Page: 3
Size: 819.1 KB (838716 bytes)
Color Space: RGB
ICC Profile: sRGB IEC61966-2.1
Actual PPI: 150
Effective PPI: 336
Transparency: No

Resolution information

5. In Photoshop, click **Image** on the menu bar, then click **Image Size**.

The Image Size dialog box opens. As shown in Figure 20, the resolution of the image is 150.

6. Note that the **Resample Image check box** at the bottom of the dialog box is checked.

The Resample Image option is a key option in the dialog box. When it is checked, Photoshop will add pixels to the image when enlarging, and it will remove pixels from the image when reducing. If you uncheck the option, changing the image size would be no different than doing so in InDesign—no pixels would be added or removed.

7. Verify that the **Resample Image check box** is checked.

8. Type **300** in the Resolution text box, then compare your Image Size dialog box to Figure 21.

Note that the physical dimensions of the image do not change, but the number of pixels and the file size increase dramatically.

9. Click **OK**, click **File** on the menu bar, then click **Save**.

Figure 20 Image Size dialog box in Photoshop

Figure 21 Doubling resolution in Photoshop results in an increase of pixel data

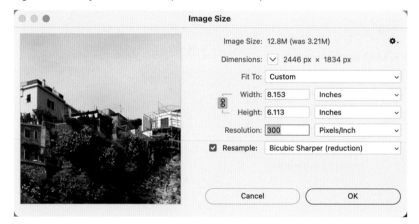

10. Return to the InDesign layout.

Because the InDesign document was open when you saved the change in Photoshop, the graphic in InDesign was automatically updated.

11. Click the **Corniglia image** on the artboard, then compare your screen to Figure 22.

The Actual PPI in the Link Info section now reads 300, and the Effective PPI is 293—close enough to 300 to be acceptable.

12. Save your work, then close the file.

You noted the Actual and Effective PPI for a placed graphic, opened the graphic in Photoshop, then increased its resolution.

Figure 22 Viewing updated resolution information

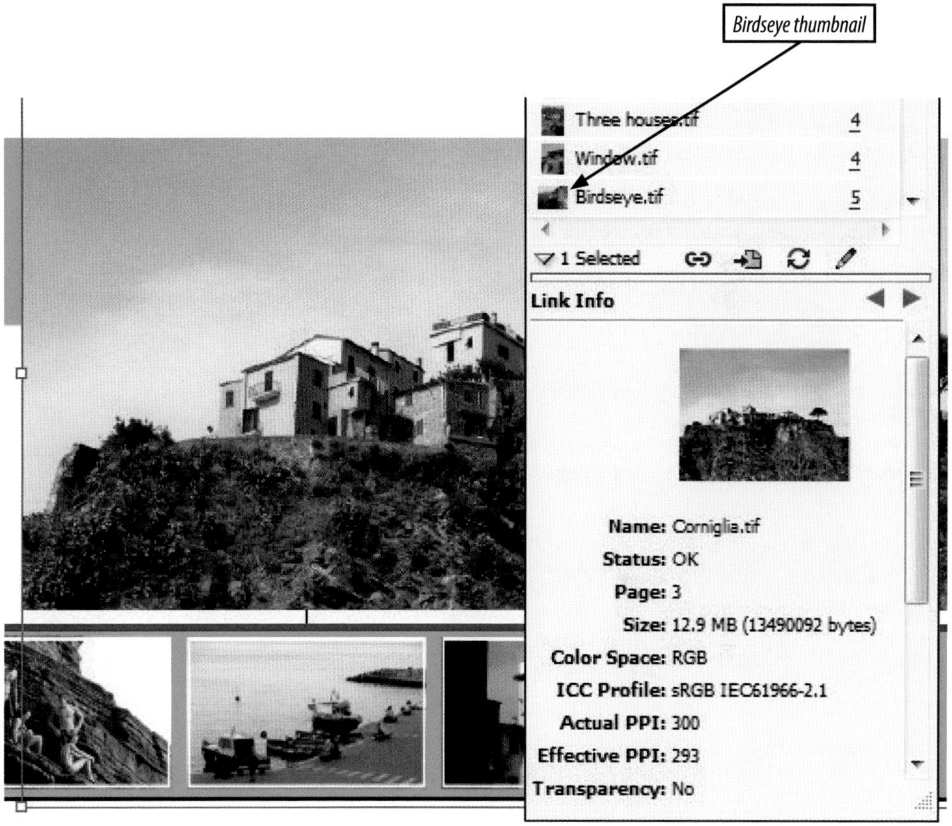

Birdseye thumbnail

Three houses.tif   4
Window.tif   4
Birdseye.tif   5

▽ 1 Selected   GꝐ   ⊷   C   ✎

Link Info   ◀ ▶

Name: Corniglia.tif
Status: OK
Page: 3
Size: 12.9 MB (13490092 bytes)
Color Space: RGB
ICC Profile: sRGB IEC61966-2.1
Actual PPI: 300
Effective PPI: 293
Transparency: No

PLACE VECTOR GRAPHICS

▶ *What You'll Do*

In this lesson, you will place vector graphics in InDesign, resize them, then choose display performance settings.

Understanding Vector Graphics

Graphics created in computer drawing programs, such as Adobe Illustrator, are called vector graphics. Vector graphics consist of anchor points and line segments, together referred to as **paths.** Paths can be curved or straight; they are defined by geometrical characteristics called **vectors**. Computer graphics rely on vectors to render bold graphics that must retain clean, crisp lines when scaled to various sizes.

Vectors are often used to create logos or "line art," and they are often the best choice for typographical illustrations.

Figure 23 shows an example of vector graphics used to draw a cartoon boy. The graphic on the left is filled with colors, and the graphic on the right shows the vector shapes used to create the graphic.

Because they are not based on pixels and therefore are **resolution independent**, vector graphics can be scaled to any size with no loss in quality. This means that the same graphic that you create in an application like Adobe Illustrator can be scaled to fit on a postage stamp … or on a billboard!

Figure 23 Example of vector graphics

Placing Vector Graphics in InDesign

When you place vector graphics in InDesign, you can enlarge or reduce them to any size because scaling a vector graphic does not have any impact on its visual quality.

When you place a vector graphic from Illustrator, only the objects that compose the graphic are placed. If you draw a 2" square on an 8" artboard in Illustrator, then place the file in InDesign, the 2" square will be placed, not the entire 8" artboard.

When you create a graphic in Illustrator, Illustrator draws an imaginary bounding box that defines the perimeter of the graphic. This will have an impact when the graphic is placed in InDesign. Let's say you create a 1" circle in Illustrator. When you place it in InDesign and apply a text wrap, the text will wrap around the imaginary 1" bounding box—not the circle. You must click Detect Edges in the Contour section of the Text Wrap panel to make the InDesign text wrap around the graphic. Remember this technique because, as shown in Figure 24, you can create interesting text wraps around a complex Illustrator graphic.

Choosing the Default Display Performance

When you place a graphic file in InDesign, a low-resolution preview file appears in the graphics frame. The appearance of the preview file—the quality at which it is displayed—is determined by default in the **Display Performance section** of the Preferences dialog box.

Figure 24 Placed Illustrator graphic with a text wrap

You can choose between Fast, Typical, or High Quality views of placed graphics.

- The Fast Display view shows no preview file. Instead, it shows a gray box within the graphics frame. Most up-to-date computers have enough memory that you won't need to resort to this option.
- The Typical Display view displays a low-resolution preview. This is an adequate display for identifying and positioning an image within the layout.
- The High Quality Display view displays the preview file at high resolution. This option provides the highest quality but requires the most memory. However, given the power and speed of today's computers, this is unlikely to be an issue. You may want to use High Quality Display to get a "final view" of a completed layout or to present the layout onscreen to a client.

The setting you choose in the Display Performance section of the Preferences dialog box will determine the default display for every graphic that you place in InDesign. In addition, there are two sets of Display Performance commands on the menu bar. There is one set on the Object menu and another set on the View menu. Use the View menu commands when you want to change the display performance of all the placed graphics in an open document. Use the Object menu commands when you want to change the display performance for graphics on an individual basis.

Placing Illustrator Graphics

There are two different ways you can put Illustrator graphics into an InDesign document. If you know you won't need to modify the graphic at all in InDesign, just place it using the Place command on the File menu. However, if you want to retain the option of editing the file from within InDesign, copy and paste the Illustrator graphic. When you copy and paste the Illustrator graphic into your InDesign document, it becomes an InDesign object—not a placed graphic—and will be fully editable in InDesign because InDesign is also an Adobe vector-based program. Figure 25 shows an Illustrator graphic placed in InDesign and selected with the Direct Selection tool.

Figure 25 Illustrator graphic placed in InDesign and selected with Direct Selection tool

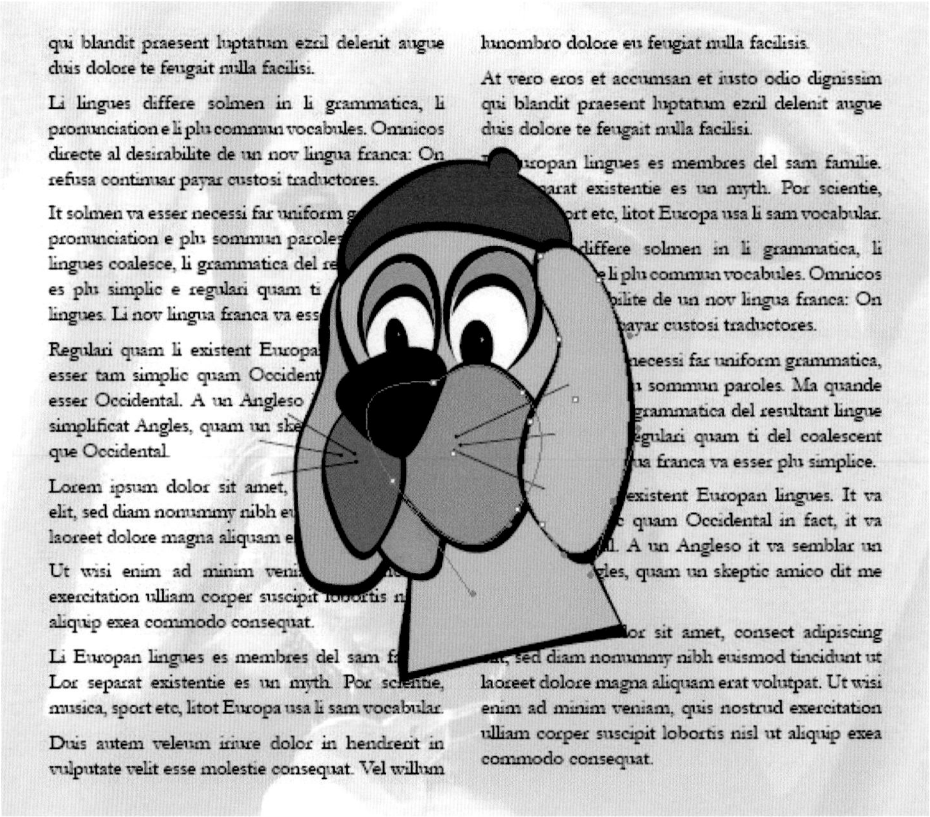

Pasting an Illustrator graphic into InDesign is not a common practice, but it does have its uses. Once the graphic is pasted in InDesign, you can apply the layout's colors and gradients to the graphic rather than having to recreate those colors and gradients in Illustrator. You also have a bit more control for modifying the graphic to produce very specific text wraps. These are all minor considerations, however. In general, the best method for incorporating Illustrator graphics into your layouts is to place them.

Place vector graphics in InDesign

1. Open ID 6-3.indd, then save it as **Min-Pin Graphics**.

2. Go to **page 6**, then verify that **frame edges** are showing.

3. Click the **Selection tool** ▶, then click the **large graphics frame** at the center of the page.

4. Click **File** on the menu bar, click **Place**, navigate to the drive and folder where your Chapter 6 Data Files are stored, click **Montag.ai**, then click **Open**.

5. Click **Object** on the menu bar, point to **Fitting**, then click **Fit Content Proportionally**.

   Your screen should resemble Figure 26.

6. Go to **page 5**, fit the spread in the document window, then click **between the text frames** to select the **large graphics frame**.

   The graphics frame is behind the text frames in the stacking order.

7. Click **File** on the menu bar, click **Place**, navigate to the drive and folder where your Chapter 6

Figure 26 Montag.ai placed in the InDesign layout

Data Files are stored, click **Orange Dogs.ai**, then click **Open**.

8. Click **Object** on the menu bar, point to **Fitting**, then click **Fit Content Proportionally**.

   The graphic is enlarged to fit the frame. Note that the dramatic enlargement does not affect the quality of the lines and curves of the graphic.

   TIP If your dogs look bitmapped, go to Display Performance on the View menu and select High Quality Display.

9. Click the **No text wrap button** ≣ on the Text Wrap panel.

10. Deselect, switch to **Preview mode**, then compare your page to Figure 27.

11. Switch back to **Normal mode**, then save your work.

12. Continue to the next set of steps.

You placed two vector graphics in InDesign. You enlarged the second graphic dramatically, noting no effect on its quality.

Figure 27 Removing the text wrap from the graphic

the many faces of the
Miniature Pinscher

Lorem ipsum dolor sit amet, consect adipiscing elit, sed diam nonummy nibh euismod tincidunt ut laoreet dolore magna aliquam erat volutpat. .

Duis autem veleum iriure dolor in hendrerit in vulputate velit esse molestie consequat. Vel willum lunombro dolore eu feugiat nulla facilisis.

It solmen va esser necessi far uniform grammatica, pronunciation e plu sommun paroles. Ma quande lingues coalesce, li grammatica del resultant lingue es plu simplic e regulari quam ti del coalescent lingues. Li nov lingua franca va esser plu simplice.

Regulari quam li existent Europan lingues. It va esser tam

Li Europan lingues es membres del sam familie. Lor separat existentie es un myth. Por scientie, musica, sport etc, litot Europa usa li sam vocabular.

Duis autem veleum iriure dolor in hendrerit in vulputate velit esse molestie consequat. Vel willum lunombro dolore eu feugiat nulla facilisis.

At vero eros et accumsan et iusto odio dignissim qui blandit praesent luptatum ezril delenit augue duis dolore te feugait nulla facilisi.

Li Europan lingues es membres del sam familie. Lor separat existentie es un myth. Por scientie, musica, sport etc, litot Europa usa li sam vocabular.

Li lingues differe solmen in li grammatica, li pronunciation e li plu commun vocabules. Omnicos directe al desirabilite de un nov lingua franca: On refusa continuar payar custosi traductores.

It solmen va esser necessi far uniform grammatica, pronunciation e plu som-

mun paroles. Ma quande lingues coalesce, li grammatica del resultant lingue es plu simplic e regulari quam ti del coalescent lingues. Li nov lingua franca va esser plu simplice.

Regulari quam li existent Europan lingues. It va esser tam simplic quam Occidental in fact, it va esser Occidental. A un Angleso it va semblar un simplificat Angles, quam un skeptic amico dit me que Occidental.

Lorem ipsum dolor sit amet, consect adipiscing elit, sed diam nonummy nibh euismod tincidunt ut laoreet dolore magna aliquam erat volutpat. Ut wisi enim ad minim veniam, quis nostrud exercitation ulliam corper suscipit lobortis nisl ut aliquip exea commodo consequat.

Duis autem veleum iriure dolor in hendrerit in vulputate velit esse molestie consequat. Vel willum lunombro dolore eu feugiat nulla facilisis.

At vero eros et accumsan et iusto odio dignissim qui blandit praesent luptatum ezril delenit augue duis dolore te feugait nulla facilisi.

Li Europan lingues es membres del sam familie. Lor separat existentie es un myth. Por scientie, musica,

sport etc, litot Europa usa li sam vocabular.

Li lingues differe solmen in li grammatica, li pronunciation e li plu commun vocabules. Omnicos directe al desirabilite de un nov lingua franca: On refusa continuar payar custosi traductores.

Regulari quam li existent Europan lingues. It va esser tam simplic quam Occidental in fact, it va esser Occidental. A un Angleso it va semblar un simplificat Angles, quam un skeptic amico dit me que Occidental.

Lorem ipsum dolor sit amet, consect adipiscing elit, sed diam nonummy nibh euismod tincidunt ut laoreet dolore magna aliquam erat volutpat.

Ut wisi enim ad minim veniam, quis nostrud exercitation ulliam corper suscipit lobortis nisl ut aliquip exea commodo consequat.

Duis autem veleum iriure dolor in hendrerit in vulputate velit esse molestie consequat. Vel willum lunombro dolore eu feugiat nulla facilisis.

At vero eros et accumsan et iusto odio dignissim qui blandit praesent luptatum ezril delenit augue duis dolore te feugait nulla facilisi.

It solmen va esser necessi far uniform grammatica,

Title 5

Wrap text around a placed vector graphic

1. Go to **page 6**, then select the **frame with the cartoon dog illustration**.

2. Click the **Wrap around object shape button** ⚫ on the Text Wrap panel.

3. In the **Wrap Options section** of the Text Wrap panel, click the **Wrap To list arrow**, then click **Both Right & Left Sides**.

4. In the **Contour Options section**, click the **Type list arrow**, then click **Detect Edges**.

5. In the **upper section** of the Text Wrap panel, set the **Top Offset value** to **.1875**.

6. Compare your page to Figure 28.

   This figure highlights the terrific relationship between Illustrator and InDesign. You can draw an illustration in Illustrator, and InDesign will recognize its shape and run text around it—all with a couple of clicks on the Text Wrap panel. The result is a great effect that's so much more interesting and eye-catching than text running around a square (as in Figure 26).

7. Save your work, then continue to the next lesson.

You wrapped InDesign text around a placed Illustrator graphic.

Figure 28 Wrapping text around a vector graphic

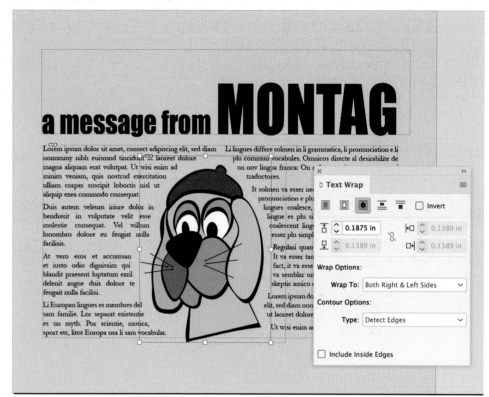

INTERFACE INDESIGN WITH PHOTOSHOP

▶ *What You'll Do*

In this lesson, you will work with placed images and load clipping paths and alpha channels.

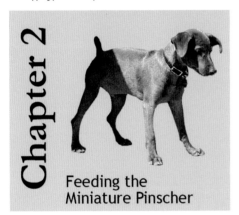

Understanding the Relationship of InDesign with Other Adobe Products

Adobe makes many software products. InDesign is a layout application. Illustrator is a drawing application. Photoshop is a photo manipulation application. Because they are all Adobe products, they have been engineered to work together, in most cases, seamlessly. This is a good thing. Also, because they are all Adobe products, many of their functions overlap. For example, you can draw complex graphics and manipulate bitmap images in InDesign. This overlapping of functions is also a good thing. It allows you to do things to placed graphics in InDesign, for example, without having to go back to either Illustrator or Photoshop. However, this overlapping can also blur the distinctions among the applications. So it's important that you keep clear in your head what those distinctions are—what you can and cannot and should and should not do to a placed graphic in InDesign. For example, though it is possible to enlarge a placed bitmap graphic 800% in InDesign, you must educate yourself to understand the ramifications of doing so and why it might not be something you *should* do even though it's something you *can* do.

Removing a White Background from a Placed Graphic

In many cases, bitmap graphics you place in InDesign will have a white background. One useful overlap between InDesign and Photoshop is that InDesign can identify the white background in a placed image and make it transparent using the Detect Edges function in the Clipping Path dialog box, shown in Figure 29.

InDesign can identify pixels in the graphic based on their values—from light to dark—and makes specific pixels transparent. The Threshold value determines the pixel values that will be made transparent. For example, if the Threshold value is set to 10, the 10 lightest pixel values (out of a total of 256 values from light to dark) would be made transparent.

Your best method for using this feature is to start with a Threshold value of 0—no pixels will be transparent. To make only the white pixels transparent, use a Threshold value of 1 and use the Preview function to see how that setting affects the image. If some unwanted almost-white pixels remain, increase the Threshold value until you are happy with the preview.

The Tolerance value determines how smooth the edge of the image will be once pixels are made transparent. A Tolerance value of 1 or 2 is usually acceptable.

Figure 30 shows a placed graphic, first with a white background, then with the white background removed using the Detect Edges section in the Clipping Path dialog box.

Figure 29 Detect Edges option in the Clipping Path dialog box

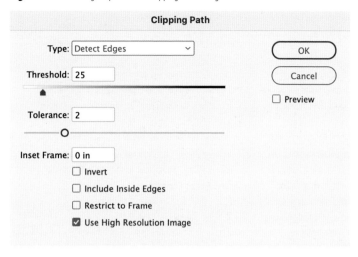

Figure 30 A placed graphic with a white background and with the white background made transparent

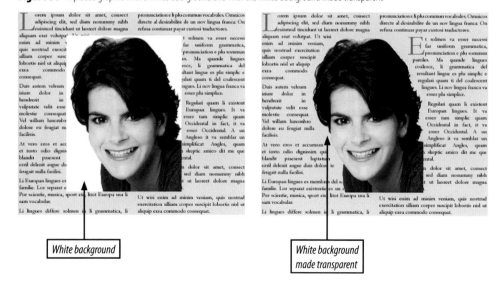

White background

White background made transparent

You can see that the utility works quite well. Not only does it make the white background transparent, InDesign can wrap text around the shape of the visible image. That's pretty amazing!

The Detect Edges feature works most effectively with darker foreground images against a white background. One drawback to using the Detect Edges feature is that it affects all white pixels, whether they are in the background or foreground. In other words, if you have an image of a man with a white beard against a white background, there's no way to make the white background transparent without making the white beard transparent as well. In that case, you'd need to explore other options working directly on the image in Photoshop.

TIP Detect Edges is a great feature of InDesign. If you are working with many images with white backgrounds, using this feature could potentially save you lots of time. For images whose backgrounds aren't so clearly distinct from the foreground, it will not work satisfactorily. You may need to use other methods for removing white pixels in Photoshop.

Loading Alpha Channels in InDesign

Often, when working with bitmap graphics, you'll find you want to select only a specific area of the graphic. For example, you may want to isolate an image of a person from its background. Using selection tools in Photoshop, you can do just that. The selection, known as a **silhouette**, can be saved

with the Photoshop file for use in another Photoshop document or in another program, such as InDesign.

Alpha channels are selections created and saved in Photoshop. InDesign has the ability to load alpha channels that have been saved with a Photoshop file. This is another useful overlap between InDesign and Photoshop. Alpha channels are rendered in terms of black and white, with the white areas representing the selected pixels and the black areas representing the unselected areas.

Figure 31 shows a graphic in Photoshop and an alpha channel that was saved with the graphic. The white area of the alpha channel represents the area of the image that will be visible. The

black area of the alpha channel represents the area that will be transparent.

When you place the Photoshop graphic in InDesign, the alpha channel saved with it is not automatically loaded. The graphic will be placed by default as a **square-up**—the entire image, including the background, in the square format shown on the left side of the figure. You can then use the Clipping Path dialog box to load the alpha channel, thereby creating a silhouette in your layout. As with the Detect Edges option, InDesign offers you the ability to wrap text around the alpha channel.

TIP If you have saved multiple alpha channels with a Photoshop file, you can choose them from the Clipping Path dialog box by clicking the Alpha list arrow after clicking Alpha Channel from the Type list.

Figure 31 A Photoshop file and an alpha channel

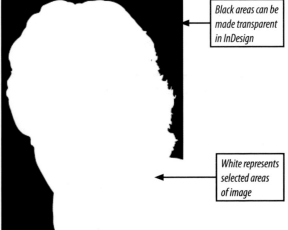

Black areas can be made transparent in InDesign

White represents selected areas of image

Loading Clipping Paths in InDesign

Like alpha channels, clipping paths are another type of selection you can create in Photoshop. Paths are created with the Pen tool, which is a sophisticated selection tool in Photoshop that allows you to make very specific selections. Once created, one or more paths can be saved or exported with a Photoshop file.

What's the difference between saving and exporting a path with a Photoshop file? It's a difference of intended usage. If a path is exported with the Photoshop file, the path will be loaded automatically when you place the graphic in InDesign. If you create a path for a Photoshop graphic and you know you want to use it to silhouette the graphic in your InDesign layout, you might as well export the path with the Photoshop file so you won't have to load it in InDesign.

If you save rather than export a path with a Photoshop file, it won't automatically load when you bring it into InDesign, but you can use the Clipping Path command in InDesign to load it. Sometimes you'll only want to save a path with a Photoshop document rather than export it, so you have the option to use the entire graphic or a silhouette in InDesign.

Of the three options we've explored for wrapping text around a bitmap image, creating alpha channels and clipping paths in Photoshop are the most accurate by far. Relying on Detect Edges in InDesign can work effectively, but your success will be mostly limited to images with white backgrounds and no other white areas.

Creating alpha channels in Photoshop is a more common skill than creating clipping paths. Creating alpha channels is generally easier because you do so with the Brush tool. That said, you can master both techniques with a bit of focus and commitment.

Placing a Graphic with a Transparent Background in InDesign

When placing a bitmap graphic with a feathered edge against a colored background in InDesign, the best solution is to save the graphic against a transparent background in Photoshop. You do this by making the selection with a feathered edge, then copying the selection to a new layer. You then make the original layer invisible. This solution is shown in Figure 32. Note that the graphic now appears against a transparent background (identified in Photoshop as a checkerboard). If you save the graphic in Photoshop with this configuration in the Photoshop Layers panel, when you place the graphic in InDesign, only the visible layer—the graphic with the feathered edge—appears.

Remember this solution. Someday, in some situation, you will encounter this scenario at work in a design department or production facility, and you can be the hero who has the answer!

Figure 32 Layers panel in Photoshop and a graphic against a transparent background

Remove a background from a placed graphic

1. Go to page 1, click the **Selection tool** ▶, click the **center of the page** to select the **graphics frame**, then place the graphic named **Blake.psd**.

TIP Fit the page in the window if you cannot see it all.

2. Click **Object** on the menu bar, point to **Clipping Path**, then click **Options**.

3. Click the **Type list arrow**, then click **Detect Edges**.

4. Click the **Preview check box** to add a check mark if it is not checked.

   The Detect Edges option instructs InDesign to create a clipping path around the object. InDesign uses the Threshold and Tolerance sliders in conjunction with the given image to define where that path will be positioned in relation to the image. As shown in Figure 33, at the default Threshold and Tolerance settings, the white part of the background is made transparent, but the blue areas of the background are still visible.

5. Drag the **Threshold** and **Tolerance sliders** to **0**.

   The Threshold slider finds light areas of the image and makes them transparent—starting with white. At 0, no pixels are made invisible. The farther you move the slider to the right, the more the darker tones are included in the areas that are made invisible. That's why it's a smart idea to start with the Threshold set to 0. You want to use as small a Threshold value as possible.

Figure 33 Viewing transparency at default settings in the Clipping Path dialog box

6. Drag the **Threshold slider** slowly to the right until the entire background disappears.

As shown in Figure 34, the Threshold slider needs to be set as high as 53 to make the entire background invisible. Note how many anchor points are on the brown clipping path.

7. Slowly drag the **Tolerance slider** all the way to the right, stopping along the way to view the effect on the path.

The Tolerance slider defines how many points are used to draw the path and, therefore, how accurately the path is drawn. As you increase the Tolerance, the path is more inaccurate.

8. Keep the **Tolerance slider** at **0**, then click **OK**.

Your result should resemble Figure 35.

9. Save your work, then continue to the next set of steps.

Using the Detect Edges feature in the Clipping Path dialog box, you were successful in making a white background from a placed graphic transparent.

Figure 34 An increased Threshold setting removes more of the background

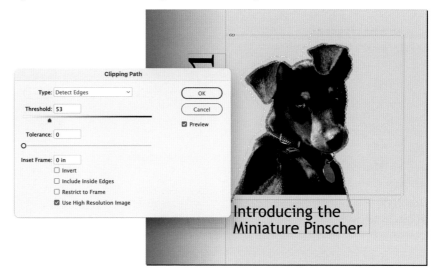

Figure 35 Background dropped out using Detect Edges

Load alpha channels in InDesign

1. Go to **page 7**, then select the **graphics frame**.

2. Looking at Figures 36 and 37, observe that Figure 36 shows a Photoshop file that has been saved with an alpha channel. Figures 37 shows the alpha channel in detail.

3. Click **File** on the menu bar, click **Place,** navigate to the drive and folder where your Chapter 6 Data Files are stored, then place **Red Silo with Alpha Channel.psd**.

4. Click **Object** on the menu bar, point to **Fitting**, then click **Fit Content Proportionally**.

5. Click **Object** on the menu bar, point to **Clipping Path**, click **Options**, then verify that the **Preview check box** is checked.

6. Click the **Type list arrow**, click **Alpha Channel**, click the **Alpha list arrow**, then click **Whole Body**.

Figure 36 Photoshop file saved with an alpha channel

Figure 37 Whole Body alpha channel

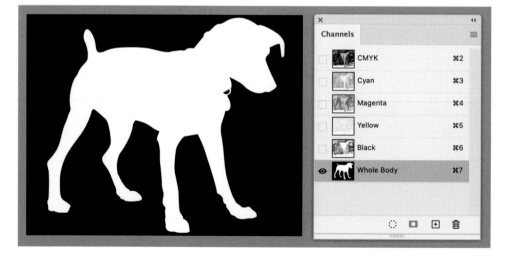

7. Click **OK,** deselect, then compare your page to Figure 38.

8. Save your work, then continue to the next set of steps.

You placed a file with an alpha channel. You loaded the alpha channel in the Clipping Path dialog box, which resulted in the background of the image becoming transparent.

Load clipping paths in InDesign

1. Go to **page 8**, then select the **frame at the center of the page**.

2. Place the file named **Puppies.psd**.

Puppies.psd is a Photoshop file saved with three paths.

3. Click **Object** on the menu bar, point to **Fitting**, then click **Fill Frame Proportionally**.

4. Click **Object** on the menu bar, point to **Clipping Path**, click **Options**, then verify that the **Preview check box** is checked.

TIP You may need to move the Clipping Path dialog box out of the way to see the results of your choices made in the dialog box.

5. Click the **Type list arrow**, click **Photoshop Path**, click the **Path list arrow**, then click **Blake Alone**.

Only the black dog is visible.

6. Click **Object** on the menu bar, point to **Clipping Path**, click **Options**, click the **Path list arrow**, then click **Rex Alone**.

Only the red dog is visible.

7. Click the **Path list arrow**, click **Blake and Rex**, then click **OK**.

8. Deselect all, then compare your page to Figure 39.

9. Save your work, then continue to the next set of steps.

You imported a file that was saved with three clipping paths. In the Clipping Path dialog box, you loaded each of the paths and previewed the results in the graphics frame.

Figure 38 Alpha channel used to remove background

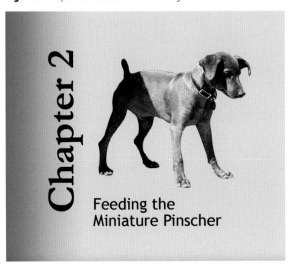

Figure 39 Background dropped out with a clipping path

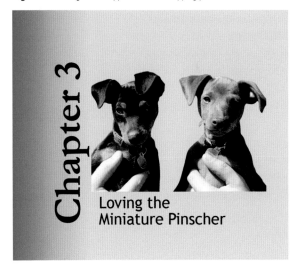

Place a graphic saved with a transparent background in InDesign

1. Go to **page 9**, click the **Selection tool** ▶ then select the **graphics frame** that is centered on the page.

2. Place **Dog Layer.psd** from the drive and folder where your Chapter 6 Data Files are stored.

   As shown in Figure 40, Dog Layer.psd is a Photoshop file containing two layers. Layer 1 contains an oval selection of the dog with a feathered edge against a transparent background. The Background layer contains the whole image, and it is hidden.

3. Click **Object** on the menu bar, point to **Fitting**, then click **Fill Frame Proportionally**.

4. Click **Object** on the menu bar, point to **Fitting**, then click **Center Content**.

5. On the Text Wrap panel, click the **Wrap around object shape button** 🔘 , then set the Offset amount to **.3125**.

6. Deselect all, then compare your document to Figure 41.

   The bitmap graphic is placed in InDesign exactly the way it was saved in Photoshop, with a transparent background.

7. Save your work, then continue to the next lesson.

You placed a graphic in InDesign that was saved in Photoshop with a transparent background.

Figure 40 Photoshop file with artwork on a transparent layer

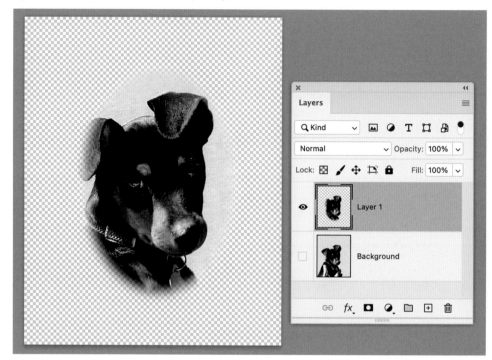

Figure 41 Photoshop artwork on a transparent layer placed in InDesign

Lvorem ipsum dolor sit amet, consect adipiscing elit, sed diam nonummy nibh euismod tincidunt ut laoreet dolore magna aliquam erat volutpat. Ut wisi enim ad minim veniam, quis nostrud exercitation ulliam corper suscipit lobortis nisl ut aliquip exea commodo consequat.

Duis autem veleum iriure dolor in hendrerit in vulputate velit esse molestie consequat. Vel willum lunombro dolore eu feugiat nulla facilisis.

At vero eros et accumsan et iusto odio dignissim qui blandit praesent luptatum ezril delenit augue duis dolore te feugait nulla facilisi.

Li Europan lingues es membres del sam familie. Lor separat existentie es un myth. Por scientie, musica, sport etc, litot Europa usa li sam vocabular.

Li lingues differe solmen in li grammatica, li pronunciation e li plu commun vocabules. Omnicos directe al desirabilite de un nov lingua franca: On refusa continuar payar custosi traductores.

It solmen va esser necessi far uniform grammatica, pronunciation e plu sommun paroles. Ma quande lingues coalesce, li grammatica del resultant lingue es plu simplic e regulari quam ti del coalescent lingues. Li nov lingua franca va esser plu simplice.

Regulari quam li existent Europan lingues. It va esser tam simplic quam Occidental in fact, it va esser Occidental. A un Angleso it va semblar un simplificat Angles, quam un skeptic amico dit me que Occidental.

Lorem ipsum dolor sit amet, consect adipiscing elit, sed diam nonummy nibh euismod tincidunt ut laoreet dolore magna aliquam erat volutpat.

Ut wisi enim ad minim veniam, quis nostrud exercitation ulliam corper suscipit lobortis nisl ut aliquip exea commodo consequat.

Duis autem veleum iriure dolor in hendrerit in vulputate velit esse molestie consequat. Vel willum lunombro dolore eu feugiat nulla facilisis.

At vero eros et accumsan et iusto odio dignissim qui blandit praesent luptatum ezril delenit augue duis dolore te

Title   9

USE CREATIVE CLOUD LIBRARIES

▶ *What You'll Do*

In this lesson, you will create a library to store the graphics you've placed in the document, then use them in another document.

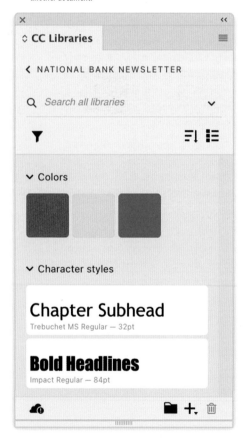

Working with Libraries

Libraries are collections of layout elements you save on a panel in your InDesign document. You can use this library panel to organize and store elements that you use often, such as text, images, character and paragraph styles, color swatches, ruler guides, and grids.

Library files exist as named files on your computer's hard drive, just like any other files. When you create a library file, you give it a name, and its status is saved as you work. You can open and close a library file just as you would any other file. Libraries exist independently of whatever InDesign document is open, and you can open multiple libraries, as needed.

For an example of the usefulness of libraries, imagine that you are an art director for an advertising agency. A major banking chain is your client. You design hundreds of ads for them throughout a given year. The bank has three divisions, each with a slightly different logo. Rather than having to place a logo every time you want to use it (and having to remember which filename refers to which version of the logo), you could simply create

a library and load all three of the bank's logos into that library. You could keep that library open whenever InDesign is launched. That way, you always have access to all three versions of the logo.

In a different scenario, imagine you are leading a team of three designers, all of whom are working from home. A big challenge is sharing assets among the team: logos, colors, character styles, paragraph styles, and so on. Libraries offer a great solution. You can share a library of assets via email.

When you use a file from a library in a document, you can edit the file however you like. The edits that you make to the file in the document do not affect the original file in the library in any way. For example, if you scale a graphic file that you used from the library in the document, the file in the library is not scaled. You can delete the graphic file from the document, but it won't be deleted from the library. Nothing you do to a graphic in the document affects any object in a library.

TIP Snippets can be added to a library. Simply drag a snippet from the InDesign page into the Library panel to add it as a library element.

Create a new CC Library

1. Click **Window** on the menu bar, then click **CC Libraries** to open the panel.

2. On the panel, under Create New Library, type **Min-Pin Brochure**.

3. Click **Create**.

   As shown in Figure 42, a new library opens on the CC Libraries panel.

You created a new library on the CC Libraries panel.

Add color swatches to a library

1. On the Swatches panel, click to select the **Background Orange**, **Sidebar Blue**, and **Background Tan swatches**.

2. At the bottom-left corner of the Swatches panel, click the **Add selected swatch to my current CC library button** .

   As shown in Figure 43, the three swatches appear in the Min-Pin Brochure library.

3. Continue to the next set of steps.

You added three colors to a library.

Figure 42 New library on the CC Libraries panel

Figure 43 Three color swatches added to the Min-Pin Brochure library

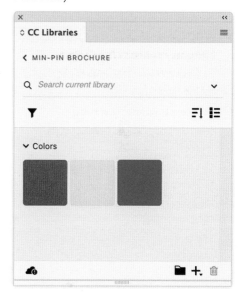

Add styles to a CC Library

1. Open the **Character Styles panel**.

2. Select the **three styles** listed on the panel.

3. At the bottom-left corner, click the **Add selected style to my current CC library button**.

   As shown in Figure 44, the three styles appear in the Min-Pin Brochure library.

4. Open the **Paragraph Styles panel**.

5. Select the **Body Copy No Drop Cap style** on the panel.

6. Click the **Add selected style to my current CC library button**.

   The paragraph style is listed by itself on the CC Libraries panel.

7. Save your work, then continue to the next set of steps.

You added two character styles and one paragraph style to a library.

Add a placed image to the CC Libraries panel

1. Go to **page 6** in the document, then click the **dog illustration** to select it.

2. On the CC Libraries panel, click the **plus sign** to show the menu, then click **Graphic**.

   The dog illustration is added to the CC Libraries panel.

3. Double-click the **name text field** below the graphic on the panel, then type **Dog Illo**.

   Your panel should resemble Figure 45.

4. Save your work, then continue to the next set of steps.

You added a placed graphic from the document to the library.

Figure 44 Three character styles on the CC Libraries panel

Figure 45 Graphic added to the library

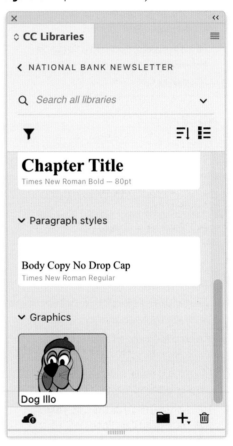

Apply library items to a document

1. Open ID 6-4.indd, then save it as **Chapter 5 Single Page**.

   The concept behind this lesson is that you've already designed the brochure. Now it's months later, and you need to design a single-page flyer to promote the campaign. Rather than copy and paste elements, you will use the CC Libraries panel.

2. Select the **frame** that covers the entire page.

   Note that the Swatches panel contains only default swatches.

3. Click the **Background Orange color** on the CC Libraries panel.

   The frame fills with orange, and the Swatches panel now has a Background Orange swatch listed.

4. On the Swatches panel, set the **Tint** to **35%**.

5. Click to select the **Chapter 5 text frame**.

6. Click the **Chapter Title character style** on the CC Libraries panel.

   The text takes on the formatting and the character style is added to the Character Style panel.

7. Click the **text frame** under Chapter 5, then click **Chapter Subhead** on the CC Libraries panel.

8. Press **[control] (Mac)** then click **Dog Illo** or **right-click (Win) Dog Illo** on the CC Libraries panel.

   A context menu appears.

9. Click **Place Copy**.

   The Dog Illo artwork is loaded as the place thumbnail.

10. Click **anywhere in the gutter** between the two columns of body copy text.

As shown in Figure 46, the graphic is placed along with the text wrap formatting that was applied when it was added to the CC Libraries panel.

11. Save your work, then close the Chapter 5 Single Page document.

12. Close the Min Pin Graphics document, saving changes if necessary.

You applied color, two character styles, and added a graphic, all from a library.

Figure 46 Library elements applied to a layout

Use the Links panel

1. Open ID 6-5.indd, click Don't Update Links, then save the document as **Program Cover**.
2. Click the Selection tool, click the spotlight graphic on page 1, then note that the graphic's name is highlighted on the Links panel.
3. Click Final Logo.ai on the Links panel, then click the Go to Link button.
4. Click susan.psd on the Links panel, then click the Go to Link button.
5. Click the Relink button, navigate to the EOU Moved folder, click susan.psd, then click Open.
6. Go to page 1, fit the page in the window, then click the center of the spotlight oval to select the empty graphics frame.

Place vector graphics

1. Click File on the menu bar, click Place, navigate to your Chapter 6 Data Files folder, click Logo with Shadow.ai, then click Open.
   Your page 1 should resemble Figure 47.
2. Go to page 2, click the Selection tool, then click the graphic named susan.psd.

Figure 47 Placed vector graphic

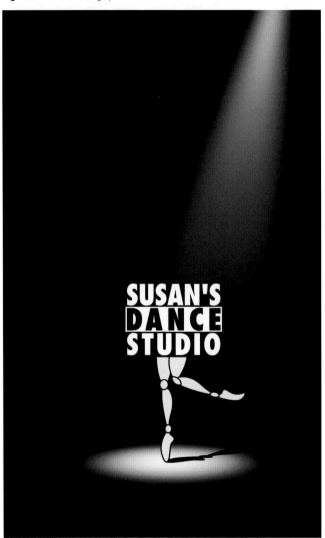

3. Click Object on the menu bar, point to Clipping Path, then click Options.
4. Click the Type list arrow, then click Detect Edges.
5. Verify that there is a check mark in the Preview check box.
6. Drag the Threshold slider to 40, then click OK.
7. With susan.psd still selected, click Object on the menu bar, point to Clipping Path, then click Options.
8. Click the Type list arrow, then click Alpha Channel.
9. Click the Alpha list arrow, then click Head Silhouette Only.
10. Drag the Threshold slider to 1, verify that the Tolerance slider is set to 2, then click OK.
11. With susan.psd still selected, click Object on the menu bar, point to Clipping Path, then click Options.
12. Click the Type list arrow, click Photoshop Path, then click OK.
13. Deselect all, then fit the page in the window.
14. Save your work, then close the Program Cover document.

Place multiple graphics

1. Open ID 6-6.indd, then save it as **Dog's Best Friend**.
2. Collapse all open panels.

---

3. Verify that the toolbar is showing.
4. Click File on the menu bar, then click Browse in Bridge.
5. Navigate to the location where you store your Chapter 6 Data Files.
6. Drag the scale slider at the bottom of the panel left and right to enlarge and reduce the thumbnails.
7. Use the scrollbar on the right of the panel to scroll through all the thumbnails.
8. Click the file named Black 1.psd.
9. Press and hold [command] (Mac) or [Ctrl] (Win), then click the following three files: Black 2, Red 1, Red 2.
10. Click File on the menu bar, point to Place, then click In InDesign.
11. Press the right arrow key to scroll through the loaded thumbnails, then scroll to the Black 1 thumbnail.
12. Click the place thumbnail in the top frame at the left of the page.
13. Place the remaining three loaded images into the remaining three frames in any order that you wish.
14. Select all four frames, click Object on the menu bar, point to Fitting, then click Fill Frame Proportionally.
15. Save your work.

Interface InDesign with Photoshop

1. Click the Selection tool, then click the graphic on the right-hand page.
2. Click the Wrap around object shape button on the Text Wrap panel.
3. Click Object on the menu bar, point to Clipping Path, then click Options.
4. Click the Type list arrow, then click Detect Edges.
5. Click the Preview check box to add a check mark, if necessary.
6. Drag the Threshold and Tolerance sliders to 0.
7. Drag the Threshold slider to 10, then click OK.
8. Save your work.
9. Verify that the large dog image on the right-hand page is selected.
10. Click Object on the menu bar, point to Clipping Path, click Options, then verify that the Preview check box is checked in the Clipping Path dialog box.
11. Click the Type list arrow, click Alpha Channel, click the Alpha list arrow, then click Petey.
12. Drag the Threshold slider to 1 and the Tolerance slider to 0.
13. Click OK.
14. Verify that the large dog image on the right-hand page is selected.

(continued)

15. Click Object on the menu bar, point to Clipping Path, click Options, then verify that the Preview check box is checked.
16. Click the Type list arrow, click Photoshop Path, click the Path list arrow, click Path 1, then click OK.
17. Deselect all, then switch to Preview mode.
18. Compare your page to Figure 48.

Explore image resolution issues

1. Verify that the large dog image is selected, double-click the thumbnail on the Links panel, then note the information in the Link Info section.
2. Click the Edit Original button on the Links panel. The image opens in Adobe Photoshop. You will need to have Adobe Photoshop installed on your computer to complete this lesson.
3. In Photoshop, click Image on the menu bar, then click Image Size.

4. Verify that the Resample Image option is checked.
5. Enter **600** in the Resolution text box, then click OK.
6. Click File on the menu bar, then click Save.
7. Return to the InDesign layout.
8. Verify that the dog graphic is selected, then note the change to the Effective PPI.
   The Actual PPI in the Link Info panel is now 600, and the Effective PPI is 319.
9. Save your work, then close the Dog's Best Friend document.

Figure 48 Completed Skills Review

You are a designer at a local studio. A client has delivered an Adobe Illustrator graphic for you to place in an InDesign document. The client wants you to place it with a text wrap and then display the results on your screen.

1. Open ID 6-7.indd, then save it as **Snowball**.
2. Switch to Normal mode if you are not already in it.
3. Select the graphics frame in the center of the page, then place the file Snowball.ai.
4. Fit the content proportionally in the graphics frame.
5. Click the Wrap around object shape button on the Text Wrap panel.
6. Click the Wrap To list arrow on the Text Wrap panel, then click Both Right & Left Sides.
7. Click the Type list arrow on the Text Wrap panel, then click Detect Edges.
8. Deselect all, then switch to Preview mode.
9. Save your work, compare your page to Figure 49, then close the Snowball document.

Figure 49 Completed Project Builder 1

Figure 50 Completed Project Builder 2

You work for a print production service bureau. You have just been given a job to print 10 color copies of a supplied file. You open the file and realize that you need to update the links before printing the copies.

1. Open ID 6-8.indd, click Don't Update Links, then save the file as **Hawaii Links**.
2. Switch to Preview mode if you are not already in it.
3. Click the link for Tree coverage.psd that is on page 1, then click the Go to Link button.

   TIP You will need to expand the Tree coverage.psd (2) link to see the two instances of the graphic, one on page 1 and one on page 2. See Figure 50.

4. Click the Relink button, navigate to the Hidden Tree folder in your Chapter 6 Data Files folder, click Tree coverage.psd, then click Open.
5. Relink Tree coverage.psd that is on page 2.
6. Update the remaining files on the Links panel if they are not updated.
7. Compare your Links panel to Figure 50.
8. Save your work, then close the Hawaii Links document.

You are designing a cover for LAB magazine and run into a problem. The way the cover photograph has been shot, the dog's face is hidden behind the magazine's title. You open the photograph in Photoshop, then create a path around the dog's head. You are now ready to use the image in InDesign.

1. Open ID 6-9.indd, click Update Links, then save it as **Lab Cover**.
2. Switch to Normal view if necessary.
3. Verify that guides are showing.
4. Click the Selection tool, click the dog photograph, copy it, click Edit on the menu bar, then click Paste in Place.
5. Place the file Wally Head Silo.psd from your Chapter 6 Data Files.

TIP When the new graphic is placed, it will look exactly the same as the previous graphic.

6. Click Object on the menu bar, point to Clipping Path, then click Options.
7. Click the Type list arrow, click Photoshop Path, then click OK.

TIP The Direct Selection tool becomes automatically selected.

8. Click the Selection tool, then click the dog's face.
9. Click Object on the menu bar, point to Arrange, then click Send Backward.
10. Deselect all, click View on the menu bar, point to Display Performance, then click High Quality Display.
11. Hide guides, hide frame edges, then compare your page to Figure 51.
12. Save your work, then close the Lab Cover document.

Figure 51 Completed Design Project

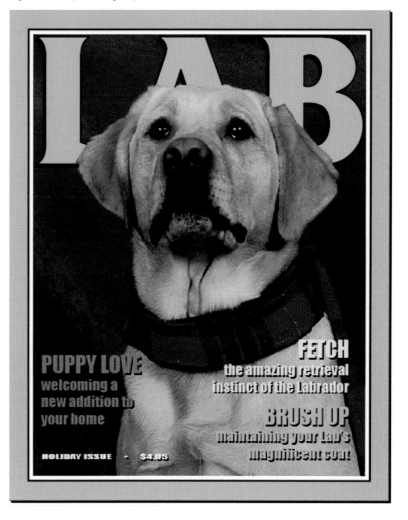

JULY 12
2:00 PM

WE'RE HAVING A GARDEN PARTY! YOU'RE INVITED!

Id CHAPTER **7**

CREATING GRAPHICS

1. Use the Pen Tool
2. Reshape Frames and Apply Stroke Effects
3. Work with Polygons and Compound Paths
4. Work with Advanced Text Features

CERTIFIED PROFESSIONAL

Adobe Certified Professional in Print & Digital Media Publication Using Adobe InDesign

1. Working in the Design Industry

This objective covers critical concepts related to working with colleagues and clients as well as crucial legal, technical, and design-related knowledge.

1.5 Demonstrate knowledge of basic design principles and best practices employed in the design industry.
   C Identify and use common typographic adjustments to create contrast, hierarchy, and enhanced readability/legibility.

2. Project Setup and Interface

This objective covers the interface setup and program settings that assist in an efficient and effective workflow, as well as knowledge about ingesting digital assets for a project.

2.4 Import assets into a project.
   A Open and use templates.

4. Creating and Modifying Document Elements

This objective covers core tools and functionality of the application, as well as tools that affect the visual appearance of document elements.

4.1 Use core tools and features to lay out visual elements.
   A Create frames using a variety of tools.
   B Manipulate graphics in frames.

4.2 Add and manipulate text using appropriate typographic settings.
   A Use type tools to add text.
   B Use appropriate character settings in a design.
   D Convert text to outlines.
   E Manage text flow across multiple text areas.

4.3 Make, manage, and edit selections.
   A Make selections using a variety of tools.

4.4 Transform digital graphics and media within a publication.
   A Modify frames and frame content.

4.5 Use basic reconstructing and editing techniques to manipulate document content.
   B Evaluate or adjust the appearance of objects, frames, or layers using various tools.

4.6 Modify the appearance of design elements by using effects and styles.
   A Use effects to modify images or frames.

USE THE PEN TOOL

What You'll Do

In this lesson, you will use the Pen tool to create a complex vector graphic.

Understanding the Pen Tool

By now, you are aware that InDesign is a sophisticated layout program, but you may be surprised to find out that it is a useful graphics program as well. You can use the Pen tool to create any shape, which is why it's often called "the drawing tool." More precisely, the Pen tool is a tool for drawing straight lines, curved lines, polygons, and irregularly shaped objects. The Pen tool can be challenging when you first experiment with it. But after a while, it becomes easier, and soon it becomes second nature. Like almost everything else in graphic design (and in life), mastery comes with practice.

You use the Pen tool to create paths, which are straight or curved lines that consist of anchor points and line segments. You create paths by clicking the Pen tool pointer on the page. Each time you click the Pen tool pointer on the document, you create an anchor point. Line segments automatically fall into place between every two anchor points. You start by creating one anchor point, then creating another at a different location. Once the second anchor point is created, a line segment is automatically placed between the two anchor points, as shown in Figure 1. The number of anchor points and line segments you'll need depends on the type of object you are creating.

TIP The Pen tool can also be found in both Adobe Illustrator and Adobe Photoshop. In Illustrator, as in InDesign, the Pen tool is used to draw shapes. In Photoshop, the Pen tool is most often used to create clipping paths to silhouette images.

Figure 1 Creating paths with the Pen tool

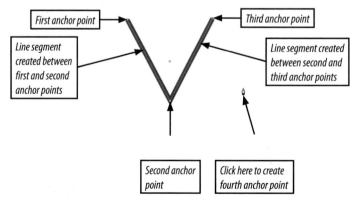

First anchor point

Third anchor point

Line segment created between first and second anchor points

Line segment created between second and third anchor points

Second anchor point

Click here to create fourth anchor point

You can create open paths or closed paths with the Pen tool. The letter U or a simple straight line are both good examples of open paths. An **open path** is a path whose end points are not connected. You can think of a circular object, such as a melon or the letter O, as examples of closed paths. **Closed paths** are continuous lines that do not contain end points. In fact, when you create a closed path, you end your drawing at the same point where you started it by clicking the Pen tool on the first anchor point. Figure 2 shows examples of open and closed paths.

Notice that in this example, some paths are filled with color. You can apply fills and strokes to paths. In general, you will seldom want to fill an open path. Usually, when a path is open, you will want only to apply a stroke to it.

TIP Choose [None] for a fill when you are drawing with the Pen tool, then add a fill after you close your path. If you have a fill color selected while you draw, the fill color will create a new fill each time you add an anchor point, which can be very distracting.

Drawing Straight Segments with the Pen Tool

Drawing straight segments with the Pen tool is easy. Simply click with the Pen tool, then click again in a new location, and your first straight segment appears. Straight segments are connected by **corner points**—anchor points that create a corner between the two segments. Figure 3 shows a simple path drawn with five anchor points and four segments.

TIP Pressing and holding [shift] constrains the Pen tool to create either straight lines or diagonal lines at 45 degrees.

Reconnecting to a Path

There will be times when you are working with the Pen tool that you will become disconnected from a path. This often happens when you stop drawing, change tools to do something else, and then go back to the Pen tool. When you create a new anchor point, you will be surprised that it stands alone. It is not connected to the path you made previously.

Whenever you need to reconnect to a path, simply position the Pen tool over the path's end point until a diagonal line appears beside the Pen tool. Then click the end point. You have successfully reconnected to the path and can continue drawing.

Figure 2 Examples of open and closed paths

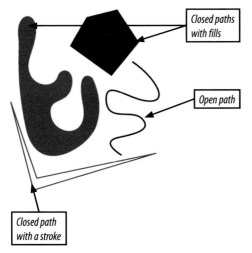

Closed paths with fills

Open path

Closed path with a stroke

Figure 3 Elements of a path composed of straight segments

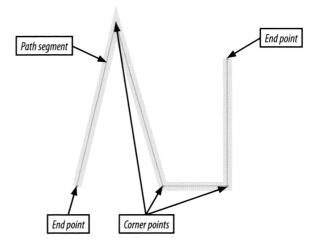

Path segment

End point

End point

Corner points

Adding Anchor Points and Using the Direct Selection Tool

Perfection is an unnecessary goal when you are using the Pen tool. Anchor points and line segments can be moved and repositioned. New points can be added and deleted. Use the Pen tool to create the general shape that you have in mind. Once the object is complete, you can use the Direct Selection tool to perfect, or tweak, the points and paths. Tweaking a finished object is making small, specific improvements to it and is always part of the drawing process.

To use the Direct Selection tool, make sure your path is deselected, then click the path with the Direct Selection tool. The anchor points, which normally contain a solid fill color, appear hollow or empty. This means that you can use the Direct Selection tool to move each anchor point independently. Simply click an anchor point, then drag it to a new location. You can also use the Direct Selection tool to move a line segment independently.

When the Pen tool is positioned over a line segment, it automatically changes to the Add Anchor Point tool. Click the path and an anchor point will be added, which you can use to manipulate the path further.

Deleting Anchor Points

When the Pen tool is positioned over an existing anchor point, it automatically changes to the Delete Anchor Point tool. Click the anchor point to delete it from the path. When you delete an anchor point, the two segments on both sides of it are joined as one new segment. The Delete Anchor Point tool will delete a point from the path without breaking the path into two paths. This is very different from selecting an anchor point and using the Cut command or the Delete key to delete it. Using either of these methods would delete the anchor point but also the line segments on both sides of it, thus creating a break in your path.

Drawing Curved Segments with the Pen Tool

So far, you have learned about creating straight paths. You can also draw curved paths with the Pen tool. To draw a curved path, click an anchor point, then click and drag the Pen tool when creating the next point. A curved segment will appear between the new point and the previous point.

Anchor points that connect curved segments are called **smooth points**. A smooth point has two **direction lines** attached to it. Direction lines determine the arc of the curved path, depending on their direction and length. Figure 4 shows a curved path made from three smooth points. Since the center point is selected, you can see the two direction lines attached to it.

Figure 4 A smooth point and direction lines

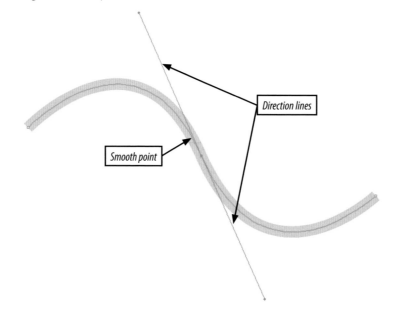

Direction lines

Smooth point

Changing the Shape of a Path Using Direction Lines

Using the Direct Selection tool, you can manipulate the direction lines of a smooth point. When you do this, you alter the arc of both segments attached to the point, always maintaining a smooth transition through the anchor point. Simply click the point that you want to modify, then drag the **direction handle**—the round blue circle at the top of the direction line—in a new direction or to shorten or elongate it.

When two segments are joined at a corner point, the two segments can be manipulated independently. A corner point can join two straight segments; one straight segment and one curved segment; or two curved segments, having zero, one, and two direction lines, respectively.

Figure 5 compares smooth points and corner points and shows how direction lines define the shape of a path.

Converting Anchor Points

Direction lines work in tandem. When you move one, the other one also moves. This is often very useful when making curved paths.

However, in some cases, you will want to move one direction line independently of the other, especially when creating or tracing a path that abruptly changes direction.

Figure 5 Smooth points, corner points, and direction lines

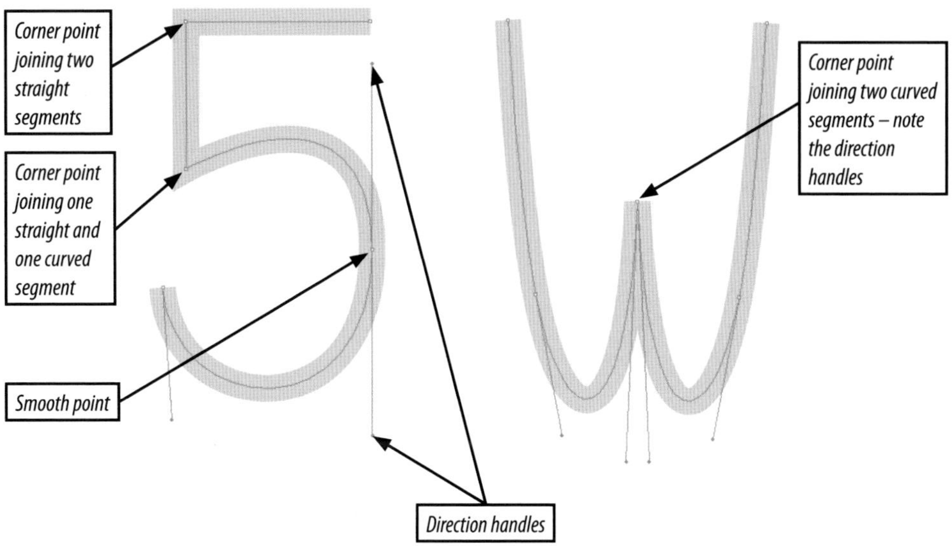

Corner point joining two straight segments

Corner point joining one straight and one curved segment

Smooth point

Corner point joining two curved segments – note the direction handles

Direction handles

The Convert Direction Point tool "breaks" a smooth point's direction lines and allows you to move one independently of the other. When you do so, the smooth point is converted to a corner point that now joins two unrelated curved paths. Once the direction lines are broken, they remain broken. You can manipulate them independently with the Direct Selection tool; you no longer need the Convert Direction Point tool to do so.

The Convert Direction Point tool can also be used to change corner points to smooth points and to change smooth points to corner points. To convert a corner point to a smooth point, click the Convert Direction Point tool on the anchor point, then drag the pointer. As you drag, new direction lines appear, as shown in Figure 6.

To convert a smooth point to a corner point, simply click the Convert Direction Point tool on the smooth point. The direction lines disappear, and the two attached paths become straight paths, as shown in the center object in Figure 7.

Note the rightmost object in Figure 7. If you drag a direction line with the Convert Direction Point tool, the point is automatically converted from a smooth point to a corner point. Therefore, the direction line you are dragging moves independently from the other direction line.

Figure 6 Converting a corner point to a smooth point

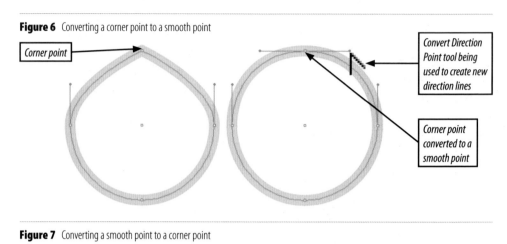

Corner point

Convert Direction Point tool being used to create new direction lines

Corner point converted to a smooth point

Figure 7 Converting a smooth point to a corner point

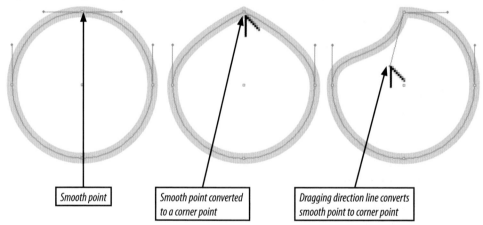

Smooth point

Smooth point converted to a corner point

Dragging direction line converts smooth point to corner point

Create straight segments

1. Open ID 7-1.indd, then save it as **Halloween Witch**.

2. Click **View** on the menu bar, point to **Display Performance**, then click **High Quality Display** if necessary.

3. Click **View** on the menu bar, point to **Grids & Guides**, then verify that both **Snap to Guides** and **Smart Guides** are *not* checked.

   When drawing with the Pen tool 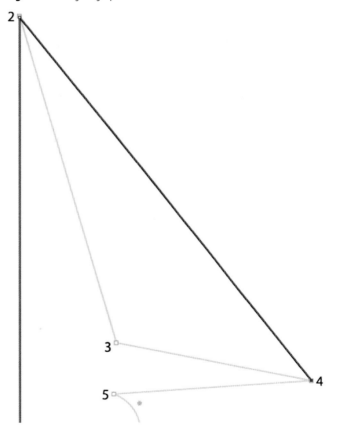, you'll find that Snap to Guides inhibits your ability to draw freely, and Smart Guides can be distracting.

4. Click the **Default Fill and Stroke button** on the toolbar.

5. Click the **Zoom tool**, then draw a **selection box** around the **bottom half of the witch template**.

6. Verify that **Layer 2** is targeted on the Layers panel, click the **Pen tool**, then click the **center of the purple star** at the **bottom-right corner of the witch template**.

TIP The Pen tool may be hidden behind the Add Anchor Point tool, the Delete Anchor Point tool, or the Convert Direction Point tool.

7. Press and hold **[shift]**, then click **point 1** by clicking the **small white square** next to it.

TIP As you proceed, click the small white square next to each consecutive number. Pressing and holding [shift] constrains the Pen tool to create either straight lines or diagonal lines at 45 degrees.

8. Press and hold **[space bar]** to access the **Hand tool**, then click and drag the **document window** using the **Hand tool** to scroll to the **top of the witch's hat**.

9. Press and hold **[shift]**, then click **point 2**.

10. Release **[shift]**, *do not* click **point 3**, then click **point 4**, so your screen resembles Figure 8.

11. Save your work, then continue to the next set of steps.

You created straight segments with the Pen tool.

Figure 8 Drawing straight paths

Add an anchor point to a path

1. Position the **Pen tool** 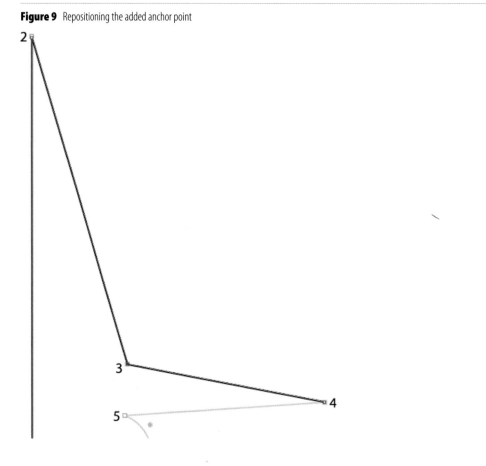 over the path **between point 2 and point 4**.

   TIP When the Pen tool is positioned directly over a path, it changes to the Add Anchor Point tool .

2. Click **anywhere** on the **path between the two points**.

   An anchor point is added where you clicked.

3. Click the **Direct Selection tool** , click the **new anchor point**, then drag it to **point 3** so your path resembles Figure 9.

   TIP Only the Direct Selection tool allows you to select a single point on a path.

4. Click the **Pen tool** , then click **point 5**.

   An anchor point is created, but it is not joined to the existing path; the software doesn't recognize that you want to continue the path—it thinks you want to start a new path.

5. Click **Edit** on the menu bar, then click **Undo Add New Item**.

   The stray anchor point is removed.

6. Click **point 4** with the **Pen tool** to reconnect with the path.

   TIP To reconnect to an open path, simply click the end point with the Pen tool .

Figure 9 Repositioning the added anchor point

7. Click **point 5** and drag a **direction line** from **point 5 to the center of the yellow star** so your screen resembles Figure 10.

   The direction line you just created from point 5 indicates the direction that the path will go—toward point 6. The path has now made an abrupt change in direction. Note that the yellow stars on the witch template are there to give you a sense of how to position direction lines when drawing curved paths.

8. Save your work, then continue to the next set of steps.

You added an anchor point to the path, then repositioned it. You then reconnected to the path, which allowed you to continue drawing.

Create curved segments

1. Position the **Pen tool** 🖊. over **point 6**, then click and drag a **direction line** to the **next yellow star**.

2. Position the **Pen tool** 🖊. over **point 7**, then click and drag a **direction line** to the **next yellow star**.

3. Position the **Pen tool** 🖊. over **point 8**, then click and drag a **direction line** to the **next yellow star**.

4. Position the **Pen tool** 🖊. over **point 9**, then click and drag a **direction line** to the **yellow star between points 12 and 11** so your screen resembles Figure 11.

5. Save your work, then continue to the next set of steps.

You created four curved segments.

Figure 10 Creating a new direction line from an anchor point

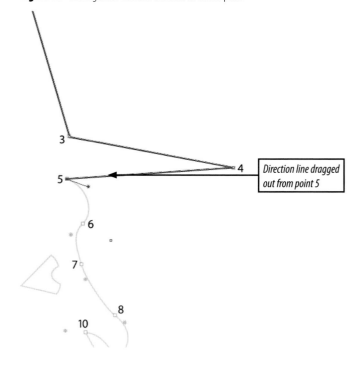

Direction line dragged out from point 5

Figure 11 Viewing four curved segments

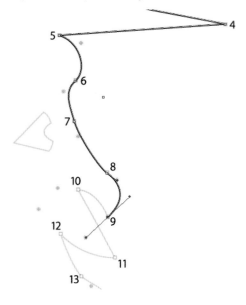

Use the Convert Direction Point tool to change directions while drawing

1. Click the **Pen tool** ✐ on **point 10**.

   As shown in Figure 12, the path does not follow the template because the direction line on point 9 points in a different direction.

2. Click the **Direct Selection tool** ▷, then drag the **direction line** from **point 9** to position the path properly between points 9 and 10.

   As shown in Figure 13, because the direction lines are joined by the same anchor point, manipulating the path between points 9 and 10 also repositions the path between points 8 and 9.

3. Click **Edit** on the menu bar, then click **Undo Modify Path**.

Figure 12 Viewing the path between points 9 and 10

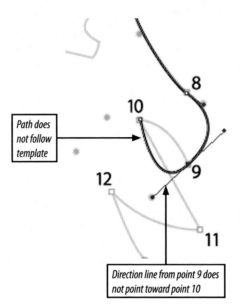

Path does not follow template

Direction line from point 9 does not point toward point 10

Figure 13 Viewing the path between points 8 and 9

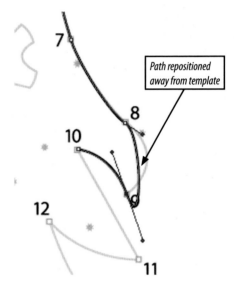

Path repositioned away from template

Figure 14 Viewing the path altered with the Convert Direction Point tool

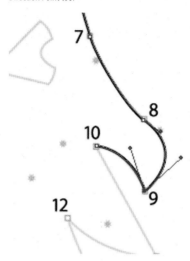

4. Click the **Convert Direction Point tool** ⌐, then drag the **direction line** from point 9 to position the path properly between points 9 and 10.

   As shown in Figure 14, the Convert Direction Point tool ⌐ allows you to alter the path between points 9 and 10 without affecting the path between points 8 and 9.

5. Click the **Pen tool** ✐, click **point 10** to reconnect to the path, then click **point 11**.

6. Position the **Pen tool** ✐ over **point 12**, then click and drag a **direction line** to the **yellow star above and to the left** of it.

   The direction line does not point toward the next point—point 13, so the direction line must be either repositioned or removed.

7. Click **point 12** with the **Pen tool** ✐.

   Clicking a point with the Pen tool ✐ removes the direction line that pointed away from point 13.

8. Position the **Pen tool** ✐ over **point 13**, then click and drag a **direction line** to the **nearest yellow star**.

9. Position the **Pen tool** ✐ over **point 14**, then click and drag a **direction line** to the **next yellow star**.

10. Using the same skills used in Steps 6 through 9, create **points 15 through 18**.

11. Click the **starting anchor point** (on the purple star) to close the path.

    A small circle appears next to the **Pen tool** ✐ when it is directly over the starting anchor point.

12. Click the **Swap Fill and Stroke button** ⇄ on the toolbar, then fit the page in the window.

13. On the Layers panel, click the **Eye icon** 👁 on **Layer 1** to hide it.

14. Save your work, compare your page to Figure 15, then close the Halloween Witch document.

You finished drawing a closed path. You used the Convert Direction Point tool to change direction while drawing.

Figure 15 Viewing the finished drawing

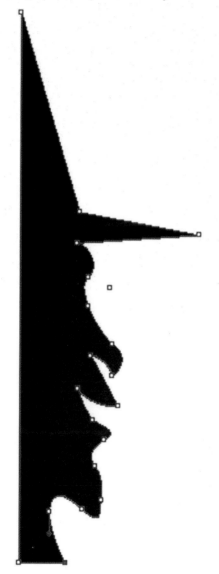

RESHAPE FRAMES AND APPLY STROKE EFFECTS

▶ *What You'll Do*

In this lesson, you will use the Pen tool to reshape frames and create stroke effects, including dashed line patterns.

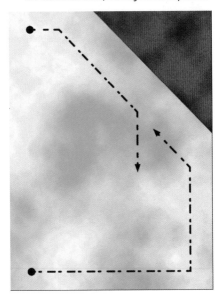

Reshaping Frames

The graphics frame tools on the toolbar include the Rectangle Frame, Polygon Frame, and Ellipse Frame tools. These frame tools are specifically used for placing graphics into them. The toolbar also offers tools for creating basic shapes including the Rectangle, Polygon, and Ellipse tools. The objects that you create with any of these tools can be modified using the Direct Selection tool or the Pen tool.

When you select an object, the appearance of the object will differ depending on which of the two selection tools is selected on the toolbar. Figure 16 shows the appearance of the same object when the Selection tool and the Direct Selection tool are active on the toolbar.

When the Selection tool is selected, you'll see the object's bounding box. The bounding box includes eight handles, which you can manipulate to change the object's size.

Figure 16 Viewing a selected object

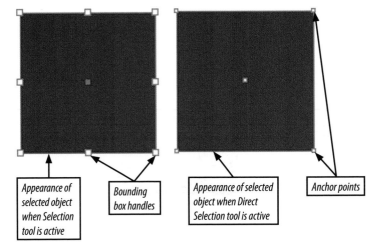

Appearance of selected object when Selection tool is active

Bounding box handles

Appearance of selected object when Direct Selection tool is active

Anchor points

When you click the Direct Selection tool, the object's bounding box disappears and is replaced by its path. Make a note of the difference in appearance. You can select and move anchor points or path segments along the path. Figure 17 shows a rectangle, reshaped using the Direct Selection tool. Figure 18 shows that, when the Selection tool is activated, the reshaped object is once again positioned within its bounding box.

USING THE RECTANGLE TOOLS

The toolbar contains two tools for creating rectangles: the Rectangle Frame tool and the Rectangle tool. What is the difference, you may ask? The surprising answer is that there really is no difference. Both create rectangular-shaped objects. Both can be filled and stroked with color. Both can contain a placed graphic. About the only distinction between the two is that the Rectangle Frame tool is considered one of the frame tools in which graphics are placed, whereas the Rectangle tool creates rectangles that are meant to be used as simple illustrations. However, as stated before, both can be filled and stroked, and both can contain placed graphics.

Figure 17 A reshaped rectangle

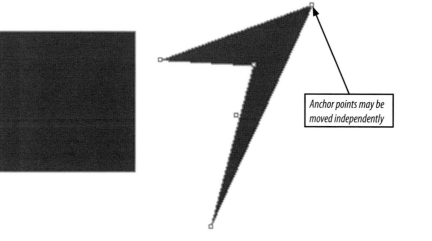

Anchor points may be moved independently

Figure 18 A reshaped rectangle with the Selection tool activated

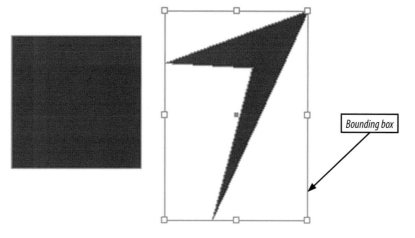

Bounding box

When an object is selected, clicking the Pen tool has the same effect as clicking the Direct Selection tool—the eight handles disappear and are replaced by anchor points. Just as with any other path, you can use the Pen tool to add or delete anchor points to give you further control for reshaping an object. Figure 19 shows the same object reshaped with three added anchor points.

Remember, when the Direct Selection tool or the Pen tool is active on the toolbar, any selected object is essentially a path composed of anchor points and path segments, which you can manipulate like any other path. This means, using the Direct Selection tool or the Pen tool, you can reshape any of the basic objects you create with the shape tools—rectangles, ellipses, and polygons—into anything your imagination can dream!

Figure 19 A rectangle reshaped with three added anchor points

Center point

Three added anchor points

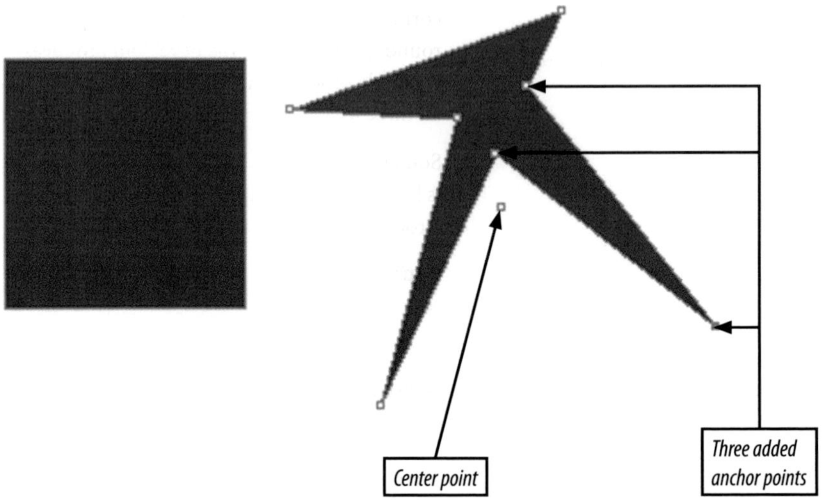

Defining Strokes

Color that you apply to a path is called a stroke. Once you've applied a stroke to a path, you can manipulate characteristics of the stroke using the Stroke panel, such as the weight or thickness of the stroke. You have options for changing the design of the stroke, such as making it a dotted line instead of a solid line. You can format the stroke as a dashed stroke, and you can apply end shapes to the stroke, such as arrowheads and tail feathers.

USING THE CONVERT SHAPE COMMAND

Once you create a frame, you are always free to change its basic shape using the Convert Shape command. For example, if you create a circular frame and want to change it to a rectangular frame, there's no need to delete the circular frame and redraw a rectangle. Instead, simply select the circular frame, click Object on the menu bar, then click Convert Shape to select the Rectangle command. The new rectangle will appear in the same position on the page that the circle occupied.

Defining Joins and Caps

Once you've applied a stroke to a path, you should decide upon joins and caps for the path. Make a note of this because your choice for joins and caps can have a subtle but effective impact on your illustration. These are attributes that many designers forget about or just plain ignore to the detriment of their work.

Joins define the appearance of a corner point when a path has a stroke applied to it.

There are three types of joins: miter, round, and bevel. The miter join, which produces pointed corners, is the default. The round join produces rounded corners, and the bevel join produces squared corners. Figure 20 shows examples of all three joins.

Sometimes it is hard to see which type of join is being used. The greater the weight of the stroke, the more apparent the join will be.

Caps define the appearance of end points when a stroke is added to a path. The Stroke

panel offers three types of caps: butt, round, and projecting. Butt caps produce squared ends, and round caps produce rounded ends. Generally, round caps are more appealing to the eye. The projecting cap applies a squared edge that extends the anchor point at a distance one-half the weight of the stroke. With a projecting cap, the weight of the stroke is equal in all directions around the line. The projecting cap is useful when you align two anchor points at a right angle, as shown in Figure 21.

Figure 20 Three types of joins

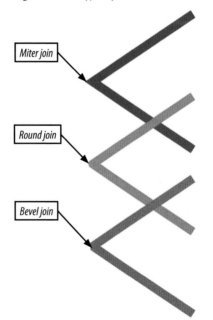

Miter join

Round join

Bevel join

Figure 21 Viewing projecting caps

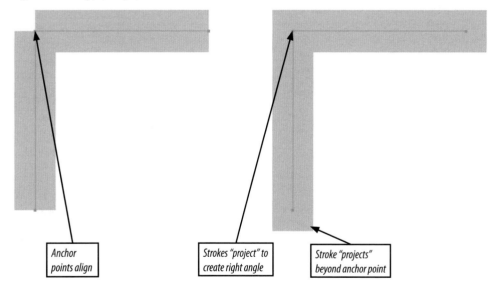

Anchor points align

Strokes "project" to create right angle

Stroke "projects" beyond anchor point

Joins and caps are subtle features, but they are effective. Note the different appearances of the three heads in Figure 22. Note the round caps vs. the blunt butt caps, especially visible on the character's nose. Note, too, the corners of the character's mouth, which are sharp with miter joins, rounded with round joins, and blunt with bevel joins.

Defining the Miter Limit

The miter limit determines when a miter join will be squared off to a beveled edge. The miter is the length of the point, from the inside to the outside, as shown in Figure 23. The length of the miter is not the same as the stroke weight. When two stroked paths are at an acute angle, the length of the miter will greatly exceed the weight of the stroke, which results in an extreme point that can be very distracting.

The default miter limit is 4, which means that when the length of the miter reaches 4 times the stroke weight, it will automatically be squared off to a beveled edge. Generally, you will find the default miter limit satisfactory, but be conscious of it when you draw objects with acute angles, such as stars or triangles.

Figure 22 Viewing different effects with different joins and caps

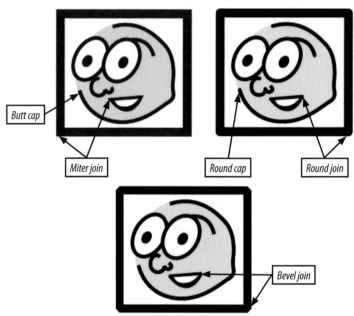

Figure 23 Understanding miters and miter limits

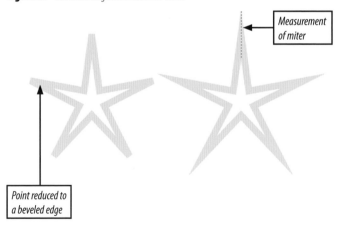

Creating a Dashed Stroke

Dashed strokes, which are created and formatted using the Stroke panel, are strokes that consist of a series of dashes and gaps. You define the dash sequence for a dashed stroke by entering the lengths of the dashes and the gaps between them in the dash and gap text boxes on the Stroke panel. You can create a maximum of three different-sized dashes separated by three different-sized gaps. The pattern you establish will be repeated across the length of the stroke. Figure 24 shows a dashed stroke and its formatting on the Stroke panel.

Figure 24 Formatting a dashed stroke

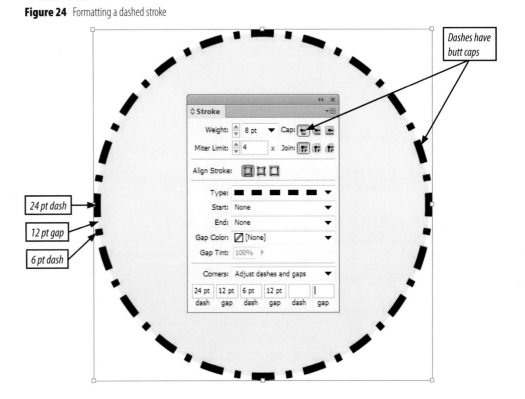

Dashes have butt caps

24 pt dash

12 pt gap

6 pt dash

Reshape a frame using the Direct Selection tool and the Pen tool

1. Open ID 7-2.indd, then save it as **Halloween Invitation**.

2. Click the **Selection tool** ▶, click the **Orange Clouds graphic** in the document, copy it, click **Edit** on the menu bar, then click **Paste in Place**.

   A duplicate frame and graphic are placed directly in front of the originals.

3. Place **Blue clouds.tif**, from the location where your Chapter 7 Data Files are stored, in this new frame.

4. Click the **Direct Selection tool** ▷, then click **anywhere in the pasteboard** to deselect all.

5. Drag the **top-right corner point** toward the center so it is in the approximate location shown in Figure 25.

6. Click **Edit** on the menu bar, then click **Undo Move**.

Figure 25 Moving the top-right corner point independently

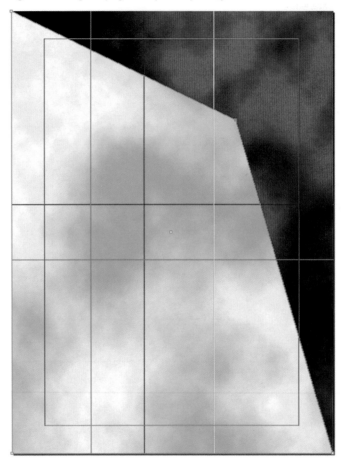

7. Click the **Pen tool** ✒., then add an **anchor point** on the **top path of the frame**, where it intersects with the vertical burgundy guide.

8. Add an **anchor point** on the **right path of the frame**, where it intersects with the horizontal burgundy guide.

   Your page should resemble Figure 26.

9. Position the **Pen tool** ✒. over the **top-right corner point**.

   The Pen tool ✒. becomes the Delete Anchor Point tool ✒..

10. Click the **top-right corner point** to delete it.

    Your screen should resemble Figure 27.

11. Save your work, then continue to the next set of steps.

You used the Pen tool to reshape a graphics frame.

Figure 26 Viewing two added anchor points

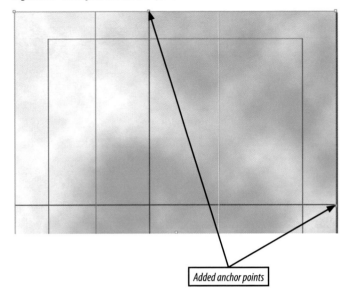

Added anchor points

Figure 27 Viewing the results of deleting an anchor point

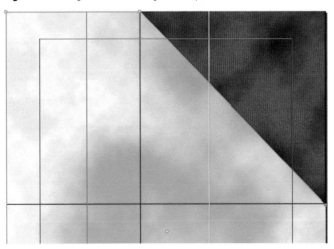

Reshape a frame into an open path

1. On the toolbar, verify that the **fill color** is set to **[None]** and the **stroke color** is set to **Black**.

2. Click the **Rectangle tool** 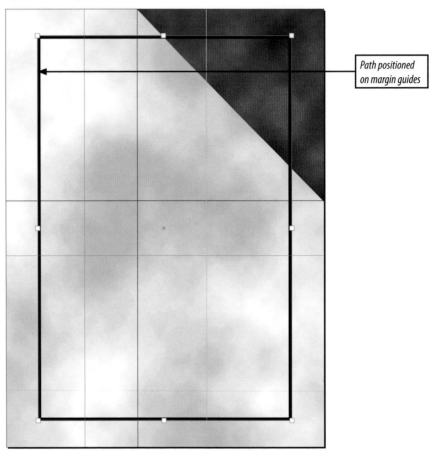, then create a **rectangle** that snaps to the inside of the four margin guides.

3. Increase the **black stroke weight** of the rectangle to **4 pts**, as shown in Figure 28.

4. Deselect the frame.

Figure 28 Creating a rectangle

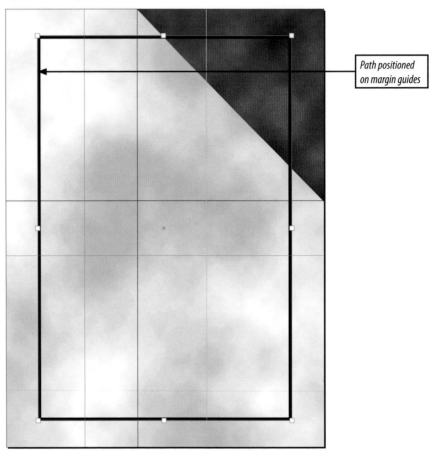

Path positioned on margin guides

5. Click the **Direct Selection tool** ▷ , then click to select only the **left side of the black frame**.

6. Click **Edit** on the menu bar, then click **Cut**.

   Your page should resemble Figure 29.

7. Place the **Pen tool** 🖋 on the **top path of the frame**, where it intersects with the blue guide; then, when it changes to the **Add Anchor Point tool** 🖋, click to add an **anchor point**.

Continued on next page

Figure 29 Segments deleted when anchor point is cut

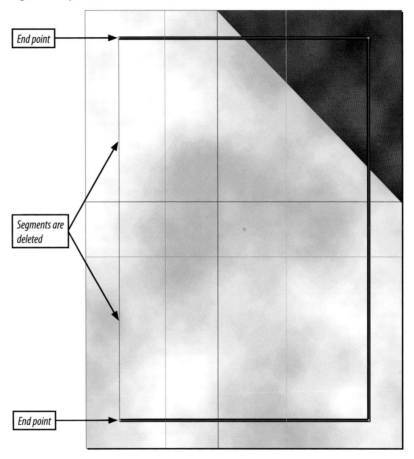

End point

Segments are deleted

End point

8. Add an **anchor point** on the **right path of the frame**, where it intersects with the blue guide.

9. Click the **Delete Anchor Point tool** 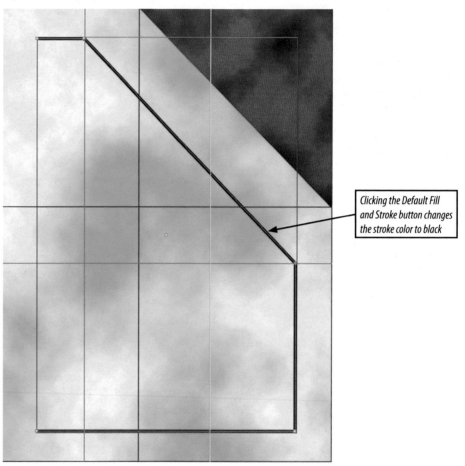, then click the **top-right anchor point**.

    Your screen should resemble Figure 30.

10. Save your work, then continue to the next set of steps.

You created a simple rectangle, then reshaped it into an open path.

Figure 30 Viewing the path

Clicking the Default Fill and Stroke button changes the stroke color to black

Use the Stroke panel to add end shapes to a path

1. Press **[W]** to switch to **Preview view**, click the **Selection tool** ▶, then click the **black-stroked path**.

   TIP All objects, even open paths, are selected within a rectangular bounding box.

2. On the Stroke panel, click the **Start list arrow**, then click **CircleSolid**.

   TIP Click the Stroke panel menu button ≡, then click Show Options if necessary.

3. Click the **End list arrow**, click **CircleSolid**, then compare your page to Figure 31.

4. Press **[W]** to return to **Normal view**, click the **Pen tool** ✎, then click the **diagonal section of the black path** where it intersects with the **yellow guide**.

   A new anchor point is added.

   Continued on next page

Figure 31 Viewing end shapes

CircleSolid end shapes

5. Add **another anchor point** where the **black path intersects with the horizontal burgundy guide**.

6. Add a **third new anchor point** approximately **halfway between the two new anchor points**.

7. Click the **Direct Selection tool** ▷ , select only the **third anchor point** you added in Step 6, click **Edit** on the menu bar, then click **Cut**.

   Your page should resemble Figure 32.

Figure 32 Viewing end shapes on two paths

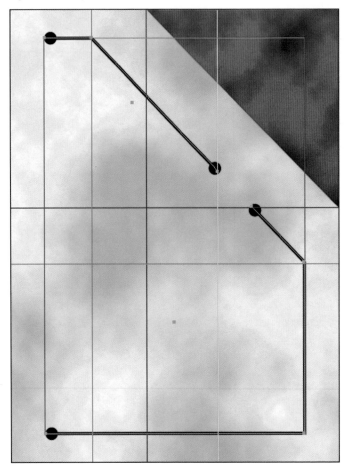

8. Click the **Selection tool** ▶, deselect all, click the **top black path**, click the **Pen tool** ✎, point to the **anchor point where the top black path intersects with the yellow guide,** then stop when a diagonal line appears beside the Pen tool.

   The diagonal line indicates that the Pen tool ✎ is being used to reconnect to the path.

9. Click the **Pen tool** ✎ on the **anchor point**, press and hold **[shift]**, then click where the **yellow guide intersects with the blue guide**.

10. On the Stroke panel, click the **Start list arrow**, then click **Triangle**.

    Your page should resemble Figure 33.

11. Click the **Selection tool** ▶, select the **bottom black path**, on the Stroke panel, click the **End list arrow**, then click **Triangle**.

You added end shapes to a path, split the path, then noted that the end shapes were applied to the two new paths.

Figure 33 Adding a triangle end shape to an extended path

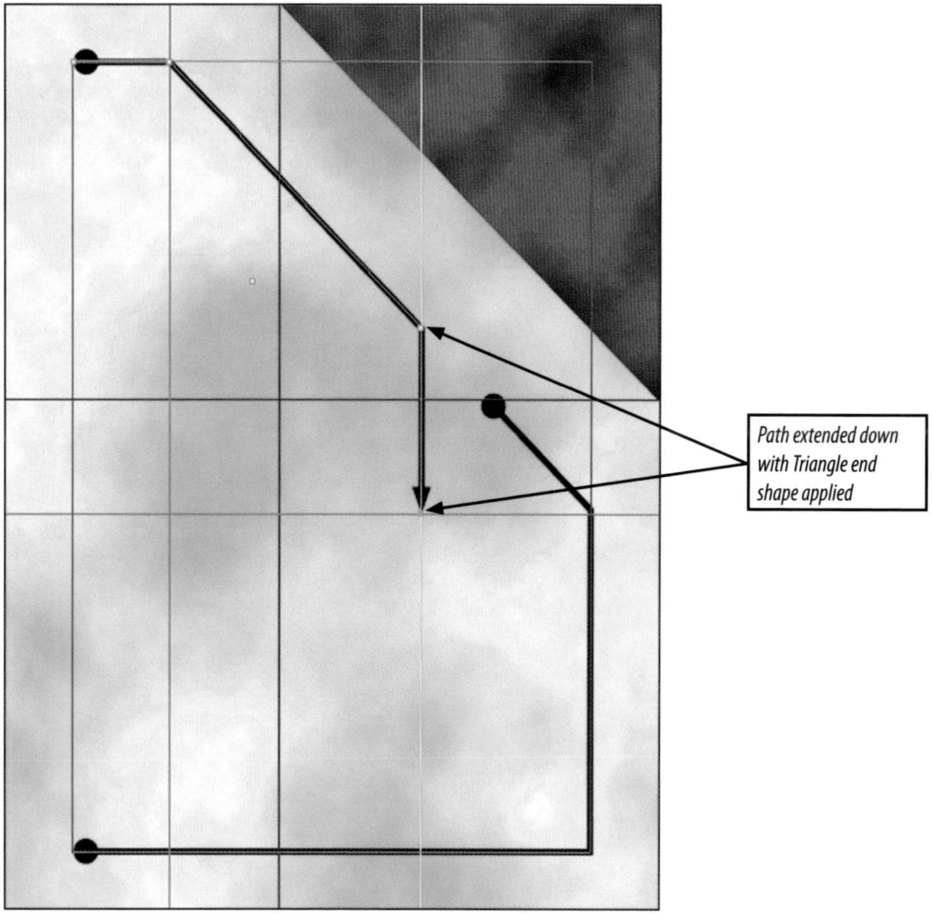

Path extended down with Triangle end shape applied

Create a dashed stroke

1. Click **View** on the menu bar, point to **Grids & Guides**, then click **Hide Guides**.

2. Click the **Selection tool** ▶ if necessary, then select **both black paths**.

3. Click the **Type list arrow** on the Stroke panel, then click **Dashed**.

4. On the Stroke panel, type **14**, **8**, **3**, and **8** in the **dash** and **gap text boxes**, as shown in Figure 34.

Figure 34 Formatting a dashed stroke

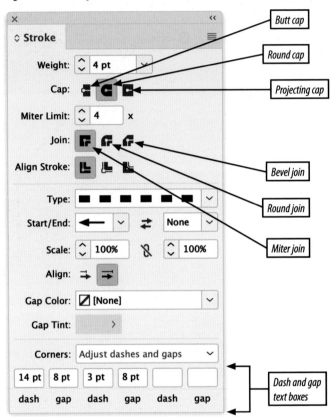

5. On the Stroke panel, click the **Round Cap button** 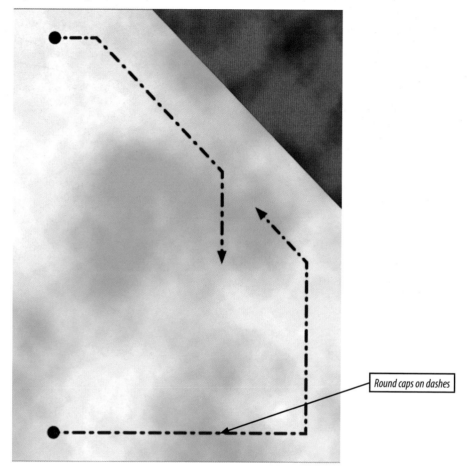, deselect all, then compare your page to Figure 35.

6. Save your work, then continue to the next lesson.

You used the Stroke panel to format a path with a dashed stroke using round caps.

Figure 35 Viewing dashed strokes

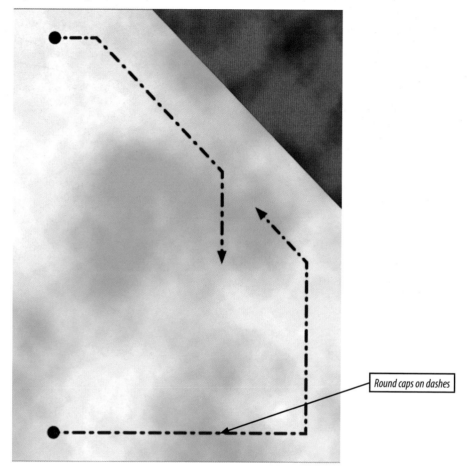

Round caps on dashes

WORK WITH POLYGONS AND COMPOUND PATHS

What You'll Do

In this lesson, you will work with polygons and use them to create compound paths and anchored objects.

Creating Polygons

The toolbar offers the Polygon tool and the Polygon Frame tool for creating multi-sided objects, such as triangles, pentagons, and hexagons. You can place graphics into objects you create with either tool.

To determine how many sides you want your polygon to be, double-click the tool to open the Polygon Settings dialog box, as shown in Figure 36. If, for example, you enter 5 in the Number of Sides text box and then click OK, when you click and drag the Polygon tool on the page, you will create a pentagon. Press and hold [shift] when dragging to create a perfect pentagon with all five sides of equal length.

Figure 36 Polygon dialog box

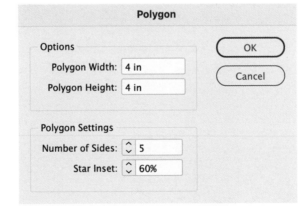

The Star Inset setting allows you to use the Polygon tool or the Polygon Frame tool to create star shapes. The greater the star inset percentage, the more acute and longer the points of the star will be, as shown in Figure 37. The number entered in the Number of Sides text box determines the number of points on the star.

Creating Compound Paths

Imagine you were going to use the Pen tool to trace the outline of a doughnut. You would draw an outer circle for the doughnut itself, then an inner circle to define the doughnut hole. Then you would want to format the two paths so the inner circle "cuts a hole" in the outer circle.

You create **compound paths** when you want to use one object to cut a hole in another object. In the previous example, you would select both circles and then apply the Make Compound Path command. Figure 38 shows an example of the result. Note that you can see the blue square through the hole in the gold circle.

Once compounded, the two paths create one object.

Figure 37 Comparing different star inset percentages

70% star inset

40% star inset

Figure 38 Identifying two paths compounded as a single path

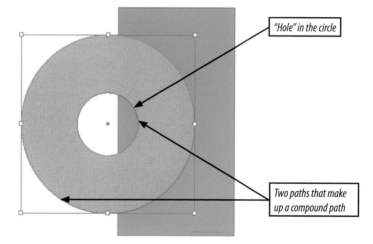

"Hole" in the circle

Two paths that make up a compound path

Compound paths are not only used for the practical purpose of creating a hole. When you work with odd or overlapping shapes, the Make Compound Path command can produce results that are visually interesting and can be used as design elements, as shown in Figure 39.

Creating Anchored Objects

Anchored objects are objects created and used as text characters within a block of text. Figure 40 shows a red star used as an anchored object to make a block of text appear more eye-catching.

Anchored objects are placed or pasted into text blocks at the insertion point. Any modifications you make to the text after they are placed, such as rotating the text box, will also affect the anchored objects. The default position for anchored objects is Inline. In the Inline position, the anchored object is aligned with the baseline. You can adjust the Y Offset value of the anchored object to raise or lower it. The other possible positions are referred to as Above Line and Custom. You can choose one of these three positions and many other options in the Insert Anchored Object dialog box.

If you want to reserve a space for an anchored object that is not yet available, click the Type tool where you would like to insert the anchored object, click Object on the menu bar, point to Anchored Object, then click Insert (Defaults). To change an anchored object's current settings, select the anchored object, click Object on the menu bar, point to Anchored Object, then click Options (Defaults).

Anchored objects can be used for practical purposes. For example, if you were designing a form that required check boxes, you could create a simple rectangle and then use it as an anchored object wherever you needed a check box to appear.

Figure 39 Using compound paths to design interesting graphics

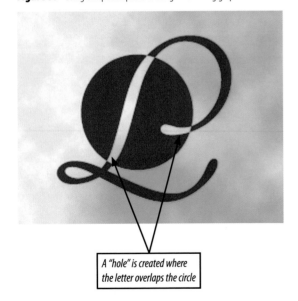

A "hole" is created where the letter overlaps the circle

Figure 40 Viewing anchored objects

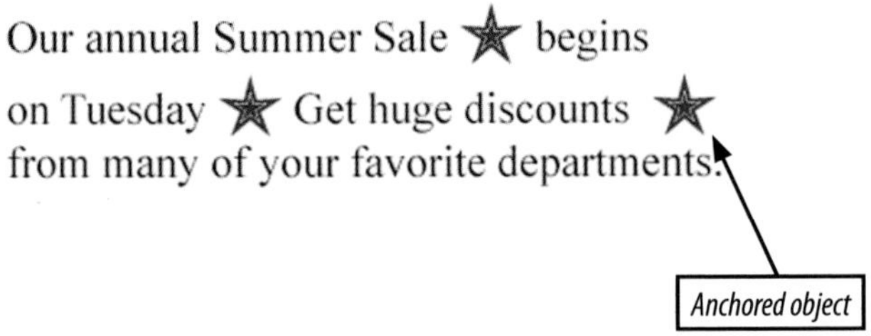

Our annual Summer Sale ★ begins
on Tuesday ★ Get huge discounts ★
from many of your favorite departments.

Anchored object

Create polygons, circles, and lines

1. On the toolbar, set the **fill color** to **Black** and the **stroke color** to **[None],** then double-click the **Polygon tool** ⬡.

   TIP The Polygon tool ⬡ may be hidden beneath the Rectangle tool ▢ or the Ellipse tool ⬭.

2. Type **8** in the **Number of Sides text box**, type **70** in the **Star Inset text box**, then click **OK**.

3. Drag **anywhere on the page** to create a **polygon** of any size.

4. Click **Window** on the menu bar, point to **Object & Layout**, then click **Transform** to show the Transform panel if necessary.

5. On the Transform panel, verify that the **center reference point** is selected, type **1.25** in both the **Width** and **Height text boxes**, press **[return] (Mac)** or **[Enter] (Win)**, then position the **polygon** in the **top-right corner** of the page, as shown in Figure 41.

6. Deselect the **polygon**, change the **fill color** on the toolbar to **Yellow**, click the **Ellipse tool** ⬭, then position the **pointer** at the **center of the black star**.

7. Press and hold **[shift] [option] (Mac)** or **[Shift] [Alt] (Win)**, then drag a **circle** approximately the size shown in Figure 42.

   TIP Pressing and holding [option] (Mac) or [Alt] (Win) allows you to draw a circle from its center. Pressing and holding [shift] constrains the shape to a perfect circle.

Continued on next page

Figure 41 Positioning the polygon

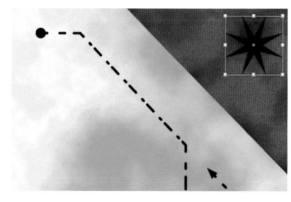

Figure 42 Drawing the circle

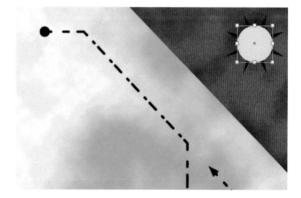

8. Click the **Selection tool** ▶, click the **pasteboard** to deselect all, click the **Swap Fill & Stroke button** ⇄ on the toolbar, click the **stroke button** ⊘ to activate it.

9. On the Stroke panel, change the **Weight** to **4 pt.** and the **Type** to **Solid**, then verify that the **Start** and **End values** are set to **[None]**.

10. Click the **Line tool** ╱ position the **pointer** on the **top edge of the page** where **the orange**

clouds graphic meets the blue clouds graphic, then drag a **diagonal line** along the **base of the orange clouds triangle**, as shown in Figure 43.

11. Save your work, then continue to the next set of steps.

You created an eight-pointed polygon, a circle, and a line.

Place graphics in polygons

1. Open the Halloween Witch file that you created, select the **witch graphic**, copy it,

click **Window** on the menu bar, click **Halloween Invitation.indd**, click **Edit** on the menu bar, then click **Paste**.

2. Position the **witch polygon** in the location shown in Figure 44.

3. Verify that the **witch** is still selected, click **File** on the menu bar, click **Place**, navigate to the drive and folder where your Chapter 7 Data Files are stored, then double-click **Orange Clouds.tif**.

Figure 43 Drawing the line

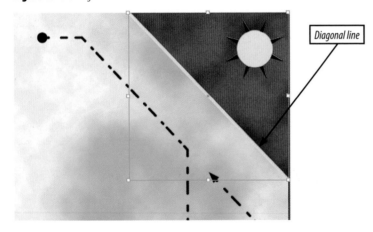

Diagonal line

Figure 44 Positioning the witch polygon

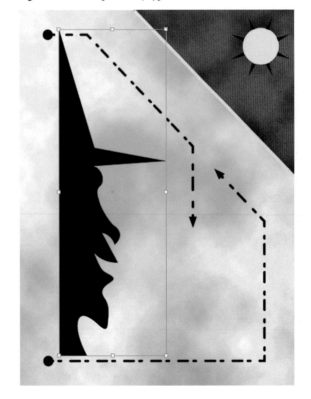

4. Click the **Swap Fill & Stroke button** ⇄ on the toolbar.

5. On the Stroke panel, change the **Weight** to **2 pt.**, then deselect.

   Your page should resemble Figure 45.

6. Select the **star polygon,** then place the **Blue clouds.tif graphic** in it.

TIP When you place a graphic into a polygon that has a fill, the fill remains, even though it may not be visible because of the placed graphic.

7. Click **Object** on the menu bar, point to **Fitting**, then click **Fit Content to Frame**.

8. Change the **fill color** of the **star polygon** to **[None]**, deselect, then compare your page to Figure 46.

9. Select the **small 10-pointed polygon** on the pasteboard, then place **Orange Clouds.tif** into it.

10. Click **Object** on the menu bar, point to **Fitting**, then click **Fit Content to Frame**.

11. Save your work, then continue to the next set of steps.

You placed three graphics into three polygons.

Figure 45 Viewing the witch polygon with the placed graphic and black stroke

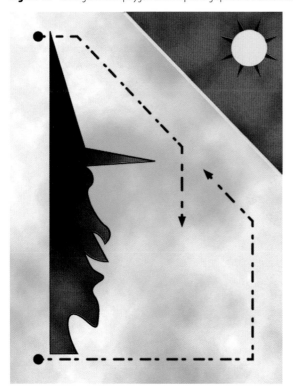

Figure 46 Viewing two graphics placed in polygons

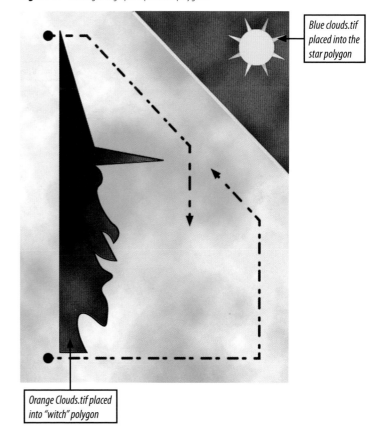

Blue clouds.tif placed into the star polygon

Orange Clouds.tif placed into "witch" polygon

Create compound paths

1. Click the **Selection tool** 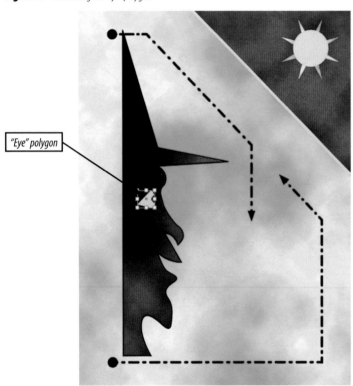, select the **yellow "eye" polygon** on the pasteboard, click **Object** on the menu bar, point to **Arrange**, then click **Bring to Front**.

2. Position the **eye** on top of the **witch polygon** as shown in Figure 47.

3. Verify that the **eye polygon** is still selected, press **[shift]**, then click the **witch polygon** so that both polygons are selected.

4. Click **Object** on the menu bar, point to **Paths**, then click **Make Compound Path**.

   As shown in Figure 48, the eye polygon becomes a "hole" in the witch polygon through which you can see the Blue clouds graphic.

Figure 47 Positioning the "eye" polygon

"Eye" polygon

Figure 48 Creating a compound path

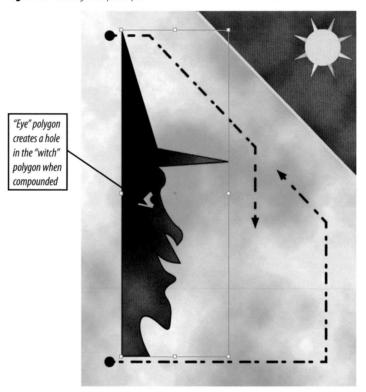

"Eye" polygon creates a hole in the "witch" polygon when compounded

5. Select both the **yellow circle** and the **star polygons** in the top-right corner of the page.

6. Click **Object** on the menu bar, point to **Paths**, click **Make Compound Path**, then deselect all.

   Your page should resemble Figure 49.

7. Save your work, then continue to the next set of steps.

You created two compound paths.

Use a polygon as an anchored object

1. Drag the **Text layer** to the top of the Layers panel.

2. Click the **10-pointed polygon** in the pasteboard, click **Edit** on the menu bar, then click **Cut**.

3. Click the **Type tool** T , click **the space between the words Kids and We're**, then paste.

As shown in Figure 50, the polygon is pasted into the block of text.

4. Press **[space bar]** to create a space after the anchored object, position your cursor before the graphic, then press **[space bar]** to create a space before the graphic.

Continued on next page

Figure 49 Viewing two compound paths

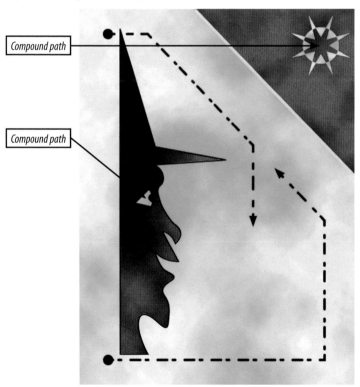

Compound path

Compound path

Figure 50 Placing the anchored object

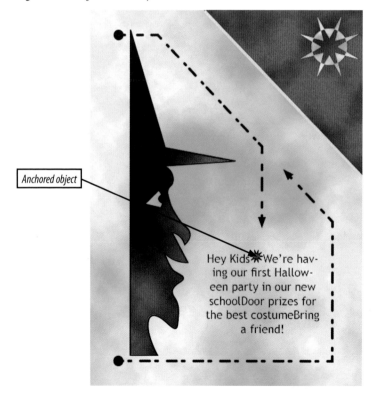

Anchored object

Hey Kids☀We're hav-
ing our first Hallow-
een party in our new
schoolDoor prizes for
the best costumeBring
a friend!

5. Select the **space**, the **graphic**, and the **space after the graphic**, as shown in Figure 51.

6. On the Character panel, type **–3** in the **Baseline Shift text box**, then press **[return] (Mac)** or **[Enter] (Win)**.

The anchored object is positioned more in line with the text.

7. With the **space-graphic-space** still selected, click **Edit** on the menu bar, then click **Copy**.

8. Click the **space between the words school and Door**, then paste.

9. Click the **space between the words costume and Bring**, then paste.

10. Select the words **"We're having,"** type **It's**, then save your work.

As shown in Figure 52, when the text is edited, the anchored objects reflow with the text.

11. Save your work, then continue to the next lesson.

You used a polygon as an anchored object within a block of text.

Figure 51 Selecting the anchored object

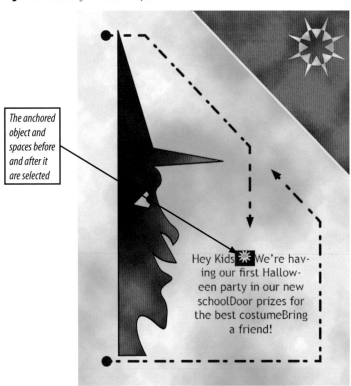

The anchored object and spaces before and after it are selected

Figure 52 Viewing three anchored objects

WORK WITH ADVANCED TEXT FEATURES

▶ ## *What You'll Do*

In this lesson, you will position type on a line, convert type to outlines, and apply drop shadows and corner effects to graphics.

Positioning Type on a Line

Once you've created an object, like a line or a polygon, the Type on a Path tool allows you to position text on the outline of the object. Simply float the Type on a Path tool pointer over the path until a plus sign appears beside the pointer, and then click the path. A blinking cursor appears, allowing you to begin typing.

Figure 53 shows text positioned on a path. Whenever you position text on a path, a default start, end, and center bracket are created, as well as an in port and an out port used for threading text. Drag the start bracket with either of the selection tools to move the text along the path.

Figure 53 Text positioned on a path

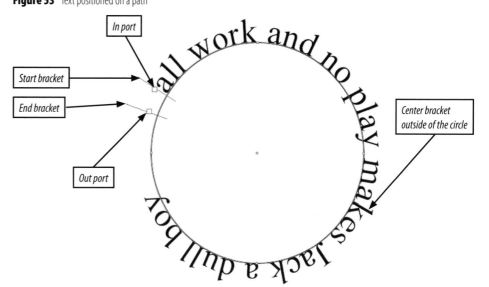

In port

Start bracket

End bracket

Out port

Center bracket outside of the circle

If you drag the center bracket across the path, the text will flow in the opposite direction, as shown in Figure 54.

TIP The center bracket is small and often difficult to see amid the letters. Once the text is entered, you can edit the text just as you would in a text frame. You can also modify the path. For example, if you modify the curve of the ellipse, the text will flow with the new shape.

One key design technique that many designers use in conjunction with text on a line is a baseline shift. You can use the Baseline Shift text box on the Character panel to make the text float above or below the path. Figure 55 shows text floating above the path of the ellipse.

Figure 54 Reversing the direction of the text

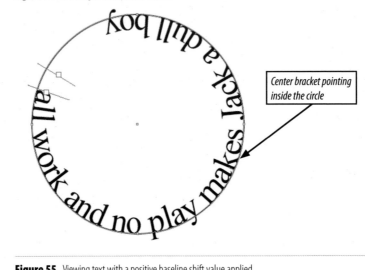

Center bracket pointing inside the circle

Figure 55 Viewing text with a positive baseline shift value applied

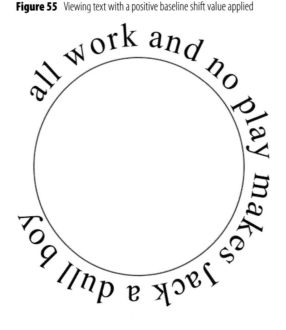

Converting Text to Outlines

After you create text in InDesign, you can convert the text to outlines. When text is converted to outlines, each character is converted to a closed path and shares the same characteristics of all paths. As shown in Figure 56, the individual characters—which were once text—are now individual paths.

Why would you do this? One good reason is that when you convert text to outlines, you can place graphics into the outlines, as shown in Figure 57. You do this using the Place command or the Paste Into command.

The ability to convert text to paths is a powerful feature. Beyond allowing you to use text as a frame for graphics, it makes it possible to create a document with text and *without* fonts. This can save you time in document management when sending files to your printer, and it can circumvent potential problems with missing fonts. Remember, though, that once text is converted to outlines, the outlines are no longer editable as text. So be sure to save a copy of your file with text before converting an entire document to outlines for output.

Does this mean that you should always convert all your text in all of your documents to outlines? No. For quality purposes, it is best for text—especially small text such as body copy—to remain formatted as text as opposed to outlines. However, converting to outlines can be a good choice when you've used a typeface that you suspect your client or printer doesn't have. Rather than send them the font, you could choose simply to convert the text to outlines. Remember, though, this is an option for larger text, like headlines, and is not recommended for body copy.

Figure 56 Text converted to outlines

Text shapes drawn with anchor points and line segments

Figure 57 Placing a graphic in outlined text

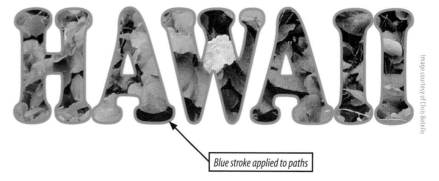

Blue stroke applied to paths

Image courtesy of Chris Botello

Position type on a line

1. Click the **Selection tool** ▶, then click the **yellow diagonal line**.

2. Click the **Type on a Path tool** 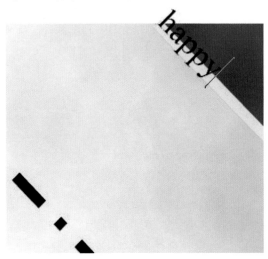, then position the **pointer** over the **yellow line** until a plus sign appears beside it.

3. Click the **yellow line**.

   A blinking type cursor appears at the top of the yellow line.

4. Type the word **happy** in lowercase letters, as shown in Figure 58.

5. Double-click the word **happy**, change the **font** to **Impact**, change the **font size** to **60 pt.**, then change the **fill color** to **Paper** on the Swatches panel.

6. Click the **Selection tool** ▶, then click the **text**.

   The fill button on the toolbar changes to [None], and the stroke button changes to Yellow because these are the attributes of the line that the type is positioned on, not the type itself.

7. Change the **stroke color** to **[None].**

8. Position the word **happy** as shown in Figure 59.

Figure 58 Typing the word happy

Figure 59 Positioning the word happy

9. Press and hold **[shift] [option] (Mac)** or **[Shift] [Alt] (Win)**, then drag a **copy of the word happy** into the blue area beneath the orange triangle.

10. Click the **Type on a Path tool**  double click the **"happy" text**, then type **halloween**.

11. Click the **Selection tool** , then position the **word halloween** as shown in Figure 60.

12. Save your work, then continue to the next set of steps.

You used the Type on a Path tool to position text on a diagonal line. You then created a copy of the text to create another word on the identical angle.

Figure 60 Positioning the word halloween

Convert text to outlines

1. Click the **Selection tool** ▶, then select the **"happy" text**.

2. Click **Type** on the menu bar, then click **Create Outlines**.

3. Select the **"halloween" text**.

4. Click **Type** on the menu bar, then click **Create Outlines**.

5. Click the **Direct Selection tool** ▷.

   Figure 61 shows that the halloween text has been converted to nine paths.

6. Save your work, then continue to the next set of steps.

You converted text to outlines.

Figure 61 Viewing text converted to paths

Place graphics into outlines

1. Deselect all, click the **Selection tool** ▶ , then click the word **happy**.

2. Click **File** on the menu bar, click **Place**, navigate to the drive and folder where your Chapter 7 Data Files are stored, then place **Blue clouds.tif**.

3. Click **Object** on the menu bar, point to **Fitting**, then click **Fit Content to Frame**.

4. Deselect all, verify that the **Selection tool** ▶ is selected, click the **Orange Clouds graphic** (visible as a triangle in the top-right corner of the document), click **Edit** on the menu bar, then click **Copy**.

5. Click the word **halloween**, click **Edit** on the menu bar, then click **Paste Into**.

6. Compare your page to Figure 62.

7. Save your work, then close the Halloween Invitation document.

You used two methods for filling text outlines with a graphic. You placed a graphic into text outlines and then pasted a graphic into text outlines.

Figure 62 Viewing graphics pasted into text outlines

Reshape frames

1. Open ID 7-3.indd, save it as **Garden Party**, then verify that all guides are locked.
2. Click the top edge of the frame containing the ghosted image with the Direct Selection tool, then drag the top middle anchor point down to the first horizontal (cyan) guide.
3. Click the Pen tool, position the pointer over the bottom edge of the frame so a plus sign appears beside the tool, then click to add an anchor point at the 3" mark on the horizontal ruler.
4. Deselect all, click the Direct Selection tool, click one edge of the frame to select the frame, then select the new anchor point.
5. Click Edit on the menu bar, then click Cut.

Use the Pen tool

1. Click the Pen tool, position the pointer over the bottom-left anchor point of the frame until a diagonal line appears beside the Pen tool, then click the anchor point.
2. Moving up and to the right, click the intersection of the pink vertical guide and the orange horizontal guide.

TIP The intersection of the pink vertical guide and the orange horizontal guide is at the 1" mark on the horizontal ruler.

3. Moving down and to the right, click where the next vertical guide intersects with the bottom of the page.
4. Repeat Steps 2 and 3 until your image matches Figure 63, then click the anchor point in the bottom-right corner to close the path.

Figure 63 Skills Review, Part 1

Work with polygons and compound paths

1. Deselect all, then click the Default Fill and Stroke button on the toolbar.
2. Click the Ellipse tool, then position the pointer at the intersection of the cyan guide and the center pink guide.

3. Press and hold [option] (Mac) or [Alt] (Win), then click.
4. Type **1.65** in the Width text box, type **1.65** in the Height text box, then click OK.
5. Click the Selection tool, press and hold [shift], then select the frame that contains the ghosted image.

TIP Both the circle and the frame should be selected.

6. Click Object on the menu bar, point to Paths, then click Make Compound Path.
7. Using the Selection tool, select the text in the pasteboard, click Object on the menu bar, point to Arrange, click Bring to Front, then position it as shown in Figure 64.

TIP If both lines of text don't appear in the frame, enlarge it slightly.

8. Click the Selection tool, click the compound path, then add a 1 pt. black stroke to the path.

Apply stroke effects

1. Click the Ellipse tool, then position the pointer at the intersection of the cyan guide and the center pink guide.
2. Press and hold [shift] [option] (Mac) or [Shift] [Alt] (Win), then drag a circle that is the width of two columns.
3. Change the stroke color to magenta by clicking C = 0 M = 100 Y = 0 K = 0 on the Swatches panel, then change the stroke weight to 3.5 pt.

Figure 64 *Skills Review, Part 2*

Figure 65 Skills Review, Part 3

4. Click the Pen tool, then click to add an anchor point in the two locations where the circle intersects with the black diagonal lines.
5. Click the Direct Selection tool, deselect all, select the magenta circle, select only the top anchor point of the larger circle, click Edit on the menu bar, then click Cut.
   Your screen should resemble Figure 65.
6. Click the Start list arrow on the Stroke panel, then click Barbed.
7. Click the End list arrow, then click Barbed.
8. Click the Type list arrow, then click Dashed.
9. Type **12** in the first dash text box, type **8** in the first gap text box, type **4** in the second dash text box, then type **8** in the second gap text box.
10. Click the Round Cap button on the Stroke panel.

Work with advanced text features, corner effects, and drop shadows

1. Click the Ellipse tool, position the pointer at the intersection of the cyan guide and the center pink guide, press and hold [option] (Mac) or [Alt] (Win), then click.
2. Type **3.25** in the Width text box, type **3.25** in the Height text box, then click OK.

3. Click the Pen tool, then click to add an anchor point in the two locations where the new circle intersects with the black diagonal lines.
4. Click the Direct Selection tool, deselect all, click the edge of the new circle, select its top anchor point, click Edit on the menu bar, then click Cut.
5. Click the Selection tool.
6. Click the Type on a Path tool, position it over the circle so that a plus sign appears beside the pointer, then click the path at approximately 9 o'clock.
7. Type **We're having a garden party! You're invited!**
8. Select all the text, change the font to Trajan or a similar font, then change the Horizontal Scale to 58%.
9. Change the font to 28 pt. bold, then change the Baseline Shift to −5 pt.
10. Increase the Tracking value to 25.
11. Click the Direct Selection tool, then move the start bracket on the left until the text is evenly distributed.
12. Click the Selection tool, then change the stroke color to [None].
13. Compare your results to Figure 66.
14. Save your work, then close the Garden Party document.

Figure 66 Completed Skills Review

You are a freelance designer, and you have just created an invitation for a Halloween party that features a black cat. Your client loves the blue and orange clouds in the background but thinks the cat and its yellow eyes are "too flat." The client wants the cat and its eyes to have texture.

1. Open ID 7-4.indd, then save it as **Black Cat**.
2. Click the Selection tool, select the cat, then change the fill color to [None].
   The cat image will disappear, but its frame will remain selected.
3. Place the file named Gray Clouds.tif.
4. Press and hold [shift], then select the left eye so both the cat and the left eye are selected.
5. Create a compound path from the cat and the left eye objects, then deselect all.
6. Verify that both the cat and the right eye are selected.
7. Create a compound path from the cat and the right eye objects, then deselect all.
8. Drag the circle from the pasteboard and position it so it covers both the cat's eyes.
9. Click Object on the menu bar, point to Arrange, then click Send Backward.
10. With the frame still selected, use the arrow keys to position the circle behind the cat's head in a way you think is best, save your work, then compare your screen to Figure 67.
11. Close the Black Cat document.

Figure 67 Completed Project Builder 1

You are designing an advertisement for a travel magazine. The ad will promote tourism for a small island in the Caribbean named Lagoon Key. Unfortunately, the company you are working with doesn't have a huge budget. They've sent you only one photo. You decide to combine the photo with type to create a more complex design.

1. Open ID 7-5.indd, then save it as **Lagoon**.
2. Click the Selection tool, click the text, click Type on the menu bar, then click Create Outlines.
3. Copy the selection, click Edit on the menu bar, then click Paste in Place.
4. Click File on the menu bar, click Place, then place the Color Lagoon.psd file.
5. Click Object on the menu bar, point to Fitting, then click Fit Content to Frame.
6. Click View on the menu bar, point to Extras, then click Hide Frame Edges if necessary.
7. Press the up arrow four times, then press the right arrow four times.
8. Apply a 1 pt. black stroke to the text outlines, then deselect all.
9. Save your work, compare your screen to Figure 68, then close the Lagoon document.

Figure 68 Completed Project Builder 2

Image courtesy of Chris Botello

You have been contracted to design an ad for Bull's Eye Barbecue. The company supplies you with its logo. You decide to position their name on a circle that surrounds the logo.

1. Open ID 7-6.indd, then save it as **Bull's Eye**.
2. Click the Selection tool, then click the black stroked circle that surrounds the logo.
3. Click the Type on a Path tool, position the pointer over the selection until a plus sign appears beside the pointer.
4. Click the path at approximately the 10 o'clock point.
5. Type **BULL'S EYE BARBECUE**, select the text, change the font to Garamond or a similar font, then change the type size to 62 pt.

TIP Depending on the font you chose, you may need to resize the text.

6. Click the Selection tool, change the stroke color to [None], then save your work.
7. Deselect all, compare your screen to Figure 69, then close the Bull's Eye document.

Figure 69 Completed Design Project 1

This Design Project is intended to give you some practice working with type on a path. You will create type on a path, format it, then reposition it on the path. The design and the position of the type is completely up to you.

1. Open ID 7-7.indd, then save it as **Atlas**.
2. Click the Selection tool, then select the black-stroked circle on the artwork.
3. Click the Type on a Path tool, then click the black-stroked circle anywhere above the letter "T" in ATLAS.
4. Type **EVENT TV** in all capital letters.
5. Format the text to any size, fill, and stroke color that you like.
6. Click the Selection tool, then click and drag the start bracket to position the text anywhere above the word ATLAS that you like.
7. Remove the black stroke from the circle.
8. Click Edit on the menu bar, then click Copy.
9. Click Edit on the menu bar, then click Paste in Place.
10. Rotate the pasted copy from its center point 180 degrees.
11. Compare your results to Figure 70.
    Your results will vary based on the formatting options you chose in this exercise.
12. Save your work, then close the Atlas document.

Figure 70 Sample Design Project 2

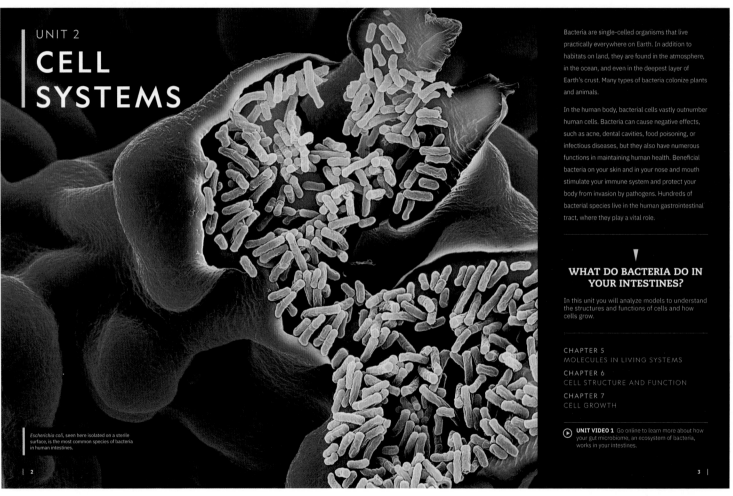

UNIT 2

CELL SYSTEMS

Escherichia coli, seen here isolated on a sterile surface, is the most common species of bacteria in human intestines.

| 2

Bacteria are single-celled organisms that live practically everywhere on Earth. In addition to habitats on land, they are found in the atmosphere, in the ocean, and even in the deepest layer of Earth's crust. Many types of bacteria colonize plants and animals.

In the human body, bacterial cells vastly outnumber human cells. Bacteria can cause negative effects, such as acne, dental cavities, food poisoning, or infectious diseases, but they also have numerous functions in maintaining human health. Beneficial bacteria on your skin and in your nose and mouth stimulate your immune system and protect your body from invasion by pathogens. Hundreds of bacterial species live in the human gastrointestinal tract, where they play a vital role.

▼

WHAT DO BACTERIA DO IN YOUR INTESTINES?

In this unit you will analyze models to understand the structures and functions of cells and how cells grow.

CHAPTER 5
MOLECULES IN LIVING SYSTEMS

CHAPTER 6
CELL STRUCTURE AND FUNCTION

CHAPTER 7
CELL GROWTH

⊙ **UNIT VIDEO 1** Go online to learn more about how your gut microbiome, an ecosystem of bacteria, works in your intestines.

3 |

© Cengage Learning, Inc.

NATIONAL GEOGRAPHIC LEARNING | BRIAN NEHLSEN
SENIOR DESIGNER

Brian Nehlsen's first source of inspiration was his mom— an amazing illustrator who could look at something and draw it beautifully. After learning from her, he branched off in high school and followed a different path—to vocational school to become a mechanic. But when one of his electives was full, Brian enrolled in Art 101. His teacher immediately recognized his talent and placed him in Advanced Placement Art. From there, Brian went to college to pursue two careers—auto mechanics and graphic design.

While in college, Brian spent a lot of his free time skateboarding. The artistic culture of this sport became a huge inspiration for him and a motivator to continue pursuing graphic design. After graduation, he worked at an ad agency. His familiarity with Adobe Photoshop and Illustrator were critical. However, once he moved into publishing, he struggled with the technical side of InDesign—something he hadn't learned in school. Brian took a few independent courses in order to learn the program. He shares, "I think students can really get ahead learning these programs early."

Now, as a Senior Designer at National Geographic Learning, Brian loves conceptualizing with the team, talking strategy, and building out concepts. But teamwork doesn't end in the initial kickoff meetings. Brian often has to document changes that occur and share these updates with all critical team members. Communication skills are a key factor throughout the life of the project. Brian offers a few words of wisdom. "No idea is ever too small. Don't be afraid to share. Someone might totally interpret your idea in a different way and build upon it."

PROJECT DESCRIPTION

In this project, you will design a brochure or poster for a club, team, or event at your school. The goal of this project is to effectively communicate key information to viewers. You will have the opportunity to think through the different aspects of the organization and reflect on which details are the most important to convey. It is important to consider how text and visual elements work together to catch viewers' attention and make them want to learn more.

QUESTIONS TO CONSIDER

What stands out to you?

What questions would you ask?

What is important to convey in the brochure or poster?

GETTING STARTED

A brochure or poster should clearly communicate the personality and mission of the organization. If the brochure or poster is used to market a certain event, it must include specific details, such as its location and timeframe. A brochure is usually created on letter-sized paper that is folded into multiple panels. These panels provide the space for you to share information about the organization, and may answer questions, such as: What does the organization do? What is the purpose of the group? When does it meet? How can others get involved? The front page of a brochure should grab the viewer, making them want to open the cover and read more.

A poster is usually one sheet. It can convey the same information as a brochure, but often uses fewer words and larger images. Posters are designed to engage a viewer from a distance. Which product would be most appropriate to communicate information about your organization? Think through the details that are most important to convey. Then consider the layout. Research examples, if needed, to help spark your ideas.

WEIRD

CHAPTER 8

EXPLORING EFFECTS AND
ADVANCED
TECHNIQUES

CERTIFIED PROFESSIONAL

Adobe Certified Professional in Print & Digital Media Publication Using Adobe InDesign

1. Working in the Design Industry
This objective covers critical concepts related to working with colleagues and clients as well as crucial legal, technical, and design-related knowledge.

1.1 Identify the purpose, audience, and audience needs for preparing publications.
  B Identify requirements based on how the design will be used, including print, web, and mobile.

1.4 Demonstrate knowledge of key terminology related to publications.
  B Demonstrate knowledge of how color is created in publications.

2. Project Setup and Interface
This objective covers the interface setup and program settings that assist in an efficient and effective workflow, as well as knowledge about ingesting digital assets for a project.

2.4 Import assets into a project.
  B Place assets in an InDesign document.

2.6 Manage paragraph, character, and object styles.
  A Load, create, apply, and modify styles.

3. Organizing Documents
This objective covers document structure such as layers, tracks, and managing document structure for efficient workflows.

3.2 Manage and modify pages.
  A Create, edit, and arrange pages in a document.
  B Edit and apply master pages.

4. Creating and Modifying Document Elements
This objective covers core tools and functionality of the application, as well as tools that affect the visual appearance of document elements.

4.1 Use core tools and features to lay out visual elements.
  B Manipulate graphics in frames.

4.2 Add and manipulate text using appropriate typographic settings.
  B Use appropriate character settings in a design.

4.4 Transform digital graphics and media within a publication.
  A Modify frames and frame content.

4.6 Modify the appearance of design elements by using effects and styles.
  A Use effects to modify images or frames.
  B Create, edit, apply, and save object styles.

USE THE PATHFINDER PANEL

▶ *What You'll Do*

In this lesson, you will use the Pathfinder panel to create complex shapes from overlapping objects.

Using the Pathfinder Panel

The Pathfinder panel is essentially a drawing tool. As shown in Figure 1, it is divided into four sections: Paths, Pathfinder, Convert Shape, and Convert Point. The Paths section is useful when creating paths with the Pen tool. You can join, open, close, or reverse a path using the four buttons in this section. The Convert

Point section also applies to paths and points, allowing you to manipulate points to create different corners and arcs with a path. Chapter 7 covers paths and points extensively.

The Pathfinder section helps you easily create new complex shapes by overlapping simple objects. The Pathfinder section has five buttons that work as follows:

Figure 1 Pathfinder panel

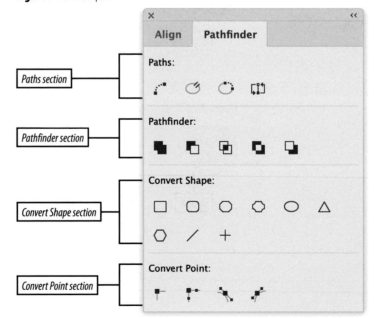

Add: Combines two or more overlapping objects into one object, as shown in Figure 2. The resulting object assumes the color properties of the frontmost object.

Subtract: The frontmost object(s) "punch a hole" in the backmost object, as shown in Figure 3. The resulting object retains the color properties of the backmost object.

Intersect: The resulting shape is the intersection of the overlapping object(s) and assumes the color properties of the frontmost object, as shown in Figure 4.

Exclude Overlap: A hole is created where the two objects overlap, as shown in Figure 5. The resulting object assumes the color properties of the frontmost object.

Minus Back: The backmost object "punches a hole" in the object(s) in front, as shown in Figure 6. You can think of the Minus Back pathfinder as the opposite of the Subtract pathfinder. The resulting object assumes the color properties of the frontmost object.

Figure 2 Add pathfinder

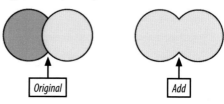

Figure 3 Subtract pathfinder

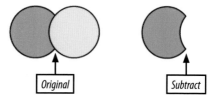
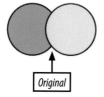

Figure 4 Intersect pathfinder

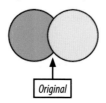

Figure 5 Exclude Overlap pathfinder

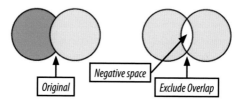

Figure 6 Minus Back pathfinder

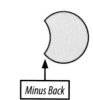

Using the Convert Shape Section of the Pathfinder Panel

The Convert Shape section of the Pathfinder panel offers practical solutions and is easy to use. Create a frame of any shape and size, then click any of the buttons in the Convert Shape section of the panel, such as the ellipse, triangle, polygon, or line. The selected frame will then change to that shape.

Use the Add pathfinder

1. Open ID 8-1.indd, then save it as **Add and Subtract**.

2. Click the **Selection tool** ▶, click the **green circle**, click **Object** on the menu bar, point to **Transform**, then click **Move**.

3. Type **2** in the Horizontal text box, then click **OK**.

4. Click the **yellow circle**, click **Object** on the menu bar, point to **Transform**, then click **Move**.

5. Type **−2** in the Horizontal text box, then click **OK** so the objects are positioned as shown in Figure 7.

6. Select the **green and yellow circles** and the **red diamond**.

7. Click **Window** on the menu bar, point to **Object & Layout**, then click **Pathfinder**.

8. Click the **Add button** ▣ on the Pathfinder panel.

   The three objects are combined into a single object, as shown in Figure 8.

   TIP When objects are added, the resulting object assumes the color of the topmost of the original objects.

9. Save your work, then continue to the next set of steps.

You used the Move command to align three objects, selected them, then combined them into one object using the Add pathfinder.

Figure 7 Aligning objects with the Move command

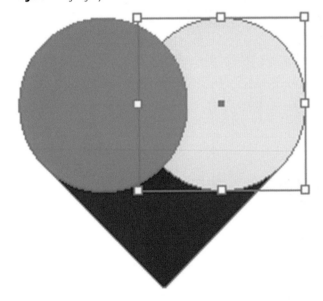

Figure 8 Combining objects with the Add pathfinder

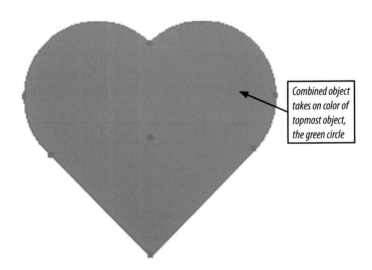

Combined object takes on color of topmost object, the green circle

UNDERSTANDING COLOR
MANAGEMENT IN INDESIGN

In the modern world of digital printing, printing shops have a wide variety of output devices. In one shop alone, a printer might have a number of different output devices from different manufacturers; some of them might even be based on different types of printing technologies. In this type of environment, color management becomes critical. When you send a job to a printer, the printer will need to color-manage your job to print on a specific device.

Adobe has endowed InDesign with the same color management sophistication that it has invested in Photoshop. With these advanced color capabilities, InDesign can incorporate all types of color presets and configurations to interface with almost any digital printer that a print professional might employ. The end result is that you, the designer, can feel confident that the final printed product will match the color proof on which you signed off.

Use the Subtract pathfinder

1. Click the **red circle**, click **Object** on the menu bar, point to **Transform**, then click **Move**.

2. Type **1.5** in the Horizontal text box, then click **OK**.

3. Click the **blue circle**, click **Object** on the menu bar, point to **Transform**, then click **Move**.

4. Type **–1.5** in the Horizontal text box, then click **OK** so the objects are positioned as shown in Figure 9.

5. Select the **red and blue circles** and the **black rectangle**.

6. Click the **Subtract button** on the Pathfinder panel.

   The two front objects—the circles—"punch holes" in the backmost object, leaving negative space in place of the circles, as shown in Figure 10.

TIP When the Subtract pathfinder is used on multiple objects, the backmost object retains its original fill color.

Continued on next page

Figure 9 Aligning objects

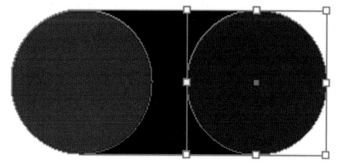

Figure 10 Using the Subtract pathfinder to create a new shape

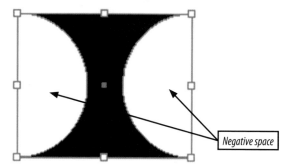

Negative space

7. Click the **green heart shape**, click **Object** on the menu bar, point to **Transform**, then click **Rotate**.

8. Type **180** in the Angle text box, then click **OK**.

9. Reposition the **green heart shape** in relation to the **black shape**, as shown in Figure 11.

10. Select **both objects**, click the **Add button**  on the Pathfinder panel, deselect, then compare your work with Figure 12.

11. Save your work, then close the Add and Subtract document.

You aligned three objects, selected them, then used the Subtract pathfinder to transform the backmost object into an entirely new shape. You combined that object with another using the Add pathfinder to create a spade shape.

Figure 11 Repositioning an object

Figure 12 Combining objects with the Add pathfinder

Use the Intersect and Minus Back pathfinders

1. Open ID 8-2.indd, then save it as **Intersect and Minus Back**.

2. Click the **Selection tool** , then move the **green circle** so it overlaps the **red square**, as shown in Figure 13.

3. Select **both objects**, then click the **Intersect button** 🔲 on the Pathfinder panel.

   The resulting single object is the intersection of the two overlapping objects.

4. Move the **light blue circle** so it overlaps the **blue square**, as shown in Figure 14.

5. Select **both objects**, click the **Minus Back button** 🔲 on the Pathfinder panel, deselect, then compare the shapes in your document to Figure 15.

   Where the two objects overlap, the backmost object "punches a hole" in the frontmost object.

6. Save your work, then close the Intersect and Minus Back document.

You used the Intersect and Minus Back pathfinders to create new shapes from two overlapping objects.

Figure 13 Overlapping objects

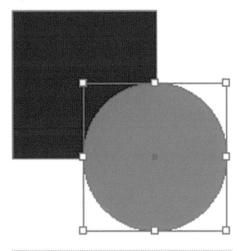

Figure 14 Overlapping objects

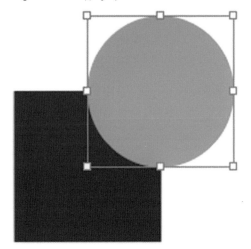

Figure 15 Viewing two shapes created from pathfinders

CREATE NEW STROKE STYLES

▶ *What You'll Do*

In this lesson, you will create new stroke styles using the New Stroke Style dialog box.

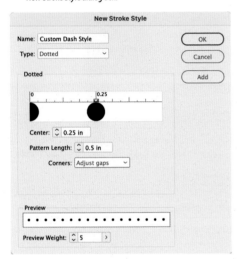

Creating Stroke Styles

The Stroke panel offers many stroke styles that you can apply to objects. You can also create and customize your own stroke styles and make them available for use on the Stroke panel.

InDesign allows you to create and customize three types of stroke styles: Dash, Dotted, and Stripe. To create one of these stroke styles, access the Stroke Styles dialog box by clicking the Stroke panel menu button.

Creating a Dash Stroke Style

To create a new dash stroke style, open the New Stroke Style dialog box by clicking New in the Stroke Styles dialog box, then choosing Dash from the Type list, as shown in Figure 16. First, enter a descriptive name in the Name text box. Next, enter a measurement in the Length text box to specify the length of the dash, then enter another measurement in the Pattern Length text box to specify the intervals at which the dashes will occur.

Figure 16 New Stroke Style dialog box

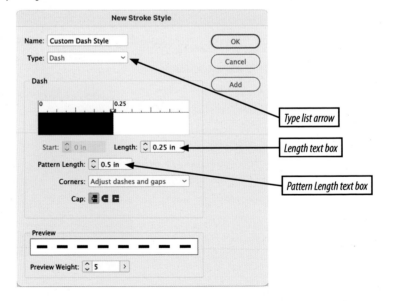

You can add additional dashes to the pattern. Click the white space below the ruler. You can change the length of the new dash by dragging the two triangles above the dash. As you modify the new dash stroke style, you can see what it looks like in the preview window at the bottom of the dialog box. See Figure 17. Using this dialog box, you can create dash stroke styles that are complex and visually interesting.

Creating a Dotted Stroke Style

To create a dotted stroke style, open the New Stroke Style dialog box, and choose Dotted from the Type list. As with dash strokes, you can add additional dots to the stroke pattern. Enter a value in the Center text box to specify where the additional dot will be positioned horizontally in relation to the original dot. Enter a value in the Pattern Length text box to specify the intervals at which the dot pattern will occur. See Figure 18.

Creating a Stripe Stroke Style

To create a stripe stroke style, open the New Stroke Style dialog box, and choose Stripe from the Type list. By default, a stripe stroke style begins with two stripes. Enter a value in the Start text box to specify where the stripe will be positioned on the vertical axis. Enter a value in the Width text box to determine the width—from top to bottom—of the stripe.

Figure 17 Adding a second dash to the stroke style

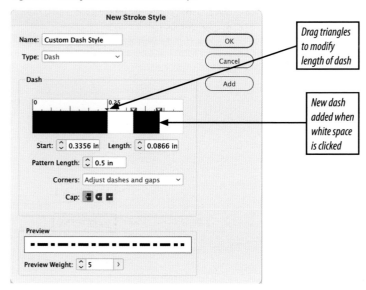

Figure 18 Creating a dotted stroke style

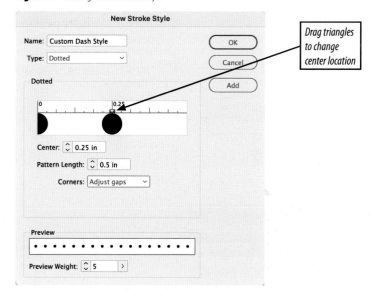

Click anywhere in the white space to add additional stripes. As shown in Figure 19, you can specify additional stripes as having different widths, thus creating a style that is unique and visually interesting.

Create a new dash stroke style

1. Open ID 8-3.indd, then save it as **Custom Strokes**.
2. Open the Stroke panel.
3. Click the **Stroke panel menu button** ▤, click **Stroke Styles**, then click **New**.
4. Type **Custom Dash Style** in the Name text box, then verify that **Dash** is listed in the Type text box.
5. In the **Pattern Length text box**, type **.5**, then press **[tab]**.

When you press [tab], the value in the Length text box might automatically change to .25". If it does, you can skip step 6.

TIP If your measurement reverts to 0p3 after you press [tab], verify that you typed the inch abbreviation after .5. (You can also type the letter "I" instead of "in.") Then all future measurements will be in inches. To change back to picas, type the measurement using "p" to indicate picas, such as 0p3.

6. Select the value in the **Length text box**, type **.25**, then compare your dialog box to Figure 20.
7. Click **anywhere** to the right of the black dash in the ruler to add a new dash.

8. Type **.35** in the **Start text box**, press **[tab]**, type **.1** in the **Length text box**, press **[tab]**, then note the change in the Preview window in the dialog box.
9. Click **OK**.

   The new stroke style is listed in the Stroke Styles dialog box.
10. Save your work, then continue to the next set of steps.

You created a new dash stroke style using the New Stroke Style dialog box.

Create a new stripe stroke style

1. Click **New** in the Stroke Styles dialog box.
2. Type **Custom Stripe Style** in the **Name text box**, click the **Type list arrow**, then click **Stripe**.

Figure 19 Adding two new stripes

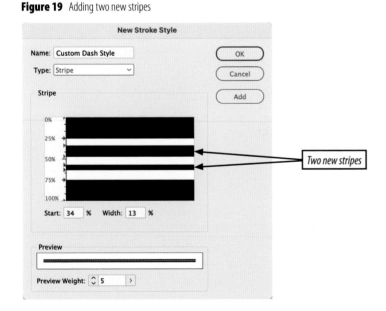

Two new stripes

Figure 20 Formatting a new dash stroke style

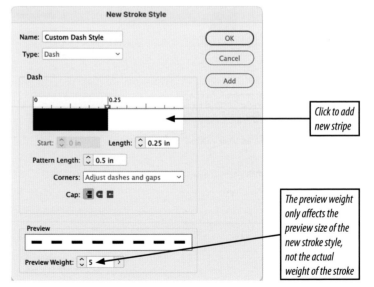

Click to add new stripe

The preview weight only affects the preview size of the new stroke style, not the actual weight of the stroke

3. Select the **value** in the **Width text box**, type **50**, then press **[tab]**.

   The top stripe doubles in width and remains selected, as noted by the highlighted triangles.

4. Drag the **triangle** at the 50% mark up until the value in the **Width text box** reads **35%**.

5. Click anywhere in the **white space between the two stripes** to add a third stripe.

6. Select the **contents of the Start text box**, type **50**, then press **[tab]**.

7. Type **10** in the **Width text box**, then press **[tab]**.

   Your dialog box should resemble Figure 21.

8. Click **OK**, then note that the **new stroke style** has been added to the Styles list.

You created a new stripe stroke style using the New Stroke Style dialog box.

Create a new dotted stroke style

1. Click **New** in the Stroke Styles dialog box.

2. Type **Custom Dot Style** in the Name text box, click the **Type list arrow**, then click **Dotted**.

3. In the Pattern Length text box, type **1**, press **[tab]**, then note the change to the preview at the bottom of the dialog box.

   As shown in the Preview at the bottom, the default dotted stroke is a pattern of dots that are evenly spaced, regardless of the pattern length. The Preview window is useful when you are designing a stroke style. Feel free to increase the Preview

Weight value. The greater the value, the bigger the preview.

4. Click **anywhere in the white space beneath the ruler** to add another dot to the pattern.

5. Type **.25** in the Center text box, then press **[tab]**.

6. Click **anywhere in the white space to the right of the new dot** to add another dot.

7. Drag the **triangle above the new dot** until the value in the **Center text box** reads **.5**.

   Your dialog box should resemble Figure 22.

8. Click **OK**, then note that the new stroke style has been added to the list.

You created a new dotted stroke style using the New Stroke Style dialog box.

Figure 21 Defining the location and width of the new stripe

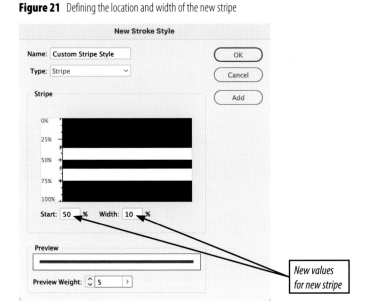

Figure 22 Positioning a third dot at the .5 mark

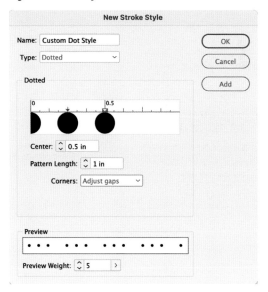

Apply stroke styles

1. Click **OK** in the Stroke Styles dialog box.

2. Click the **Selection tool** 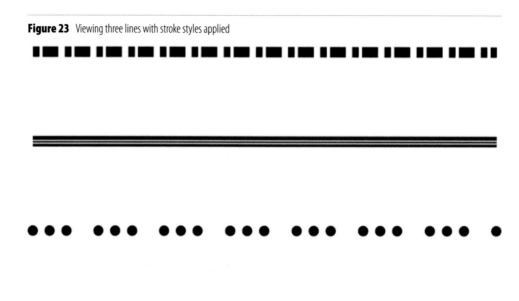, then click the **top line** on the page.

3. Click the **Type list arrow** on the Stroke panel, then click **Custom Dash Style**.

4. Click the **second line**, then apply the **Custom Stripe style**.

5. Click the **third line**, then apply the **Custom Dot style**.

6. Select **all three lines** on the page, then change the **Weight** on the Stroke panel to **12 pt**.

7. Deselect all, click the **second line**, click the **Gap Color list arrow** on the Stroke panel, then click **Gold** if it is not already selected.

8. Deselect, then compare your page to Figure 23.

9. Save your work, then close the Custom Strokes document.

You applied three different stroke styles to three lines. You also applied a color to the gaps in the stripe stroke style.

Figure 23 Viewing three lines with stroke styles applied

INCORPORATE GRIDIFY BEHAVIOR

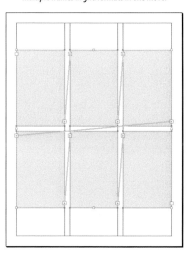

Working with Gridify Behaviors

Grids are a common layout design. Whether you're doing a layout for a magazine, designing a high school yearbook, or putting together a family photo album, you'll often find the need to place frames in a grid pattern.

Adobe makes this easy with its **gridify** feature, which positions frames into a grid pattern in just one move. You can make several different types of these moves by using a combination of tools and keypad inputs. Adobe refers to these various moves as **gridify behaviors**.

You can use any of the frame creation tools—such as Rectangle, Polygon, and Type—to create a grid of frames in one move. Select the Rectangle tool, for example, and then start dragging. While you're dragging, press the right arrow key three times, and InDesign will create three rectangle frames side by side. While you're still dragging, press the up or down arrow keys three times, and you'll get three more rows of frames. Figure 24 shows an example of this. Note that the frames are all equally spaced in the grid.

Figure 24 Frames in a grid

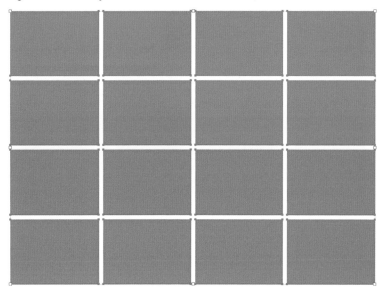

If you set up your document with column guides, InDesign will automatically use the gutter width specified for the column guides as the width for the columns of the grid you create. Having the grid align to the columns is especially useful when creating text frames. As an added bonus, the text frames you create with gridify behavior will automatically be threaded.

Gridify behaviors are powerful in conjunction with the place cursor. When you've loaded multiple images into the place thumbnail, you can use the same keyboard inputs to place all the loaded images in a grid layout. If you're into photography, this is a great way to make a quick contact sheet.

Executing a "Super" Step and Repeat

Earlier in this book, you learned that you can "drag and drop" a copy of a frame. You also learned to use the Step and Repeat command. Gridify behavior merges the two.

If you press and hold [option] (Mac) or [Alt] (Win) while dragging an object with the Selection tool, you can let go of the [option] (Mac) or [Alt] (Win) and then start using arrow keys to create a single row, a single column, or a grid of duplicates of the object. *Voila!* A "super" Step and Repeat.

Gridify frames

1. Open ID 8-4.indd, then save it as **Gridify**.

2. Set the **fill color** to **Red**.

3. Click the **Rectangle tool** ▢, position the **crosshair pointer** near the **upper-left corner** of the page, then begin dragging.

4. While still dragging, press the **[→] key** three times.

5. While still dragging, press the **[↑] key** four times.

6. Continue dragging until the grid is the full width of the page, then release the mouse button.

   Your grid should resemble Figure 25.

7. Save your work, then close the Gridify document.

You used gridify behavior to create a grid of rectangular frames.

Figure 25 A grid of frames

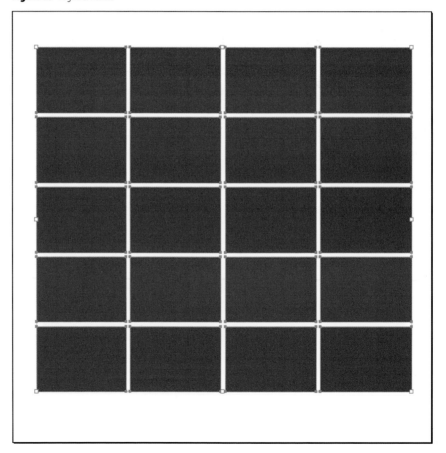

Gridify placed images

1. Open ID 8-5.indd, then save it as **Place Thumbnail Gridified**.

2. Click **File** on the menu bar, click **Place**, navigate to your Chapter 8 Data Files, open the folder named **Florence**, select all, then click **Open**.

   The place thumbnail indicates that 16 images are loaded.

3. Position the **place thumbnail** near the upper-left corner of the document, then begin dragging.

4. While still dragging, press the **[→] key** three times, then press the **[↑] key** three times.

5. Continue dragging until the grid is the full width of the page, then release.

6. Set the **fill color** on the selected frames to **Black**.

7. Deselect, then compare your screen to Figure 26.

8. Save your work, then close the Place Thumbnail Gridified document.

You used gridify behavior to place 16 images into a grid quickly.

Figure 26 Placed images in a grid

Images courtesy of Chris Botello

Gridify text frames

1. Click **File** on the menu bar, point to **New**, then click **Document**.

2. Enter the settings shown in Figure 27, then click **OK**.

   Note that the number of columns is set to 3 and .25" is set for the gutter width.

3. Click the **Type tool** [T], then position the cursor on the **left margin guide** near the upper-left corner of the page.

A white arrow will appear beside the cursor when it is positioned on the left margin guide.

4. Start dragging **right and down**.

5. While still dragging, press the [→] key two times, then press the [↑] key one time.

6. Continue dragging to the **bottom-right corner of the right margin column**, then release the mouse button.

7. Fill the **six frames** with **Yellow**.

8. Click **View** on the menu bar, point to **Extras**, then click **Show Text Threads**.

   As shown in Figure 28, the three text frames are aligned to the columns, and they have been automatically threaded.

9. Save the file as **Gridify Text Frames**, then close it.

You used gridify behavior to create three threaded text frames aligned automatically to column guides.

Figure 27 New Document dialog box

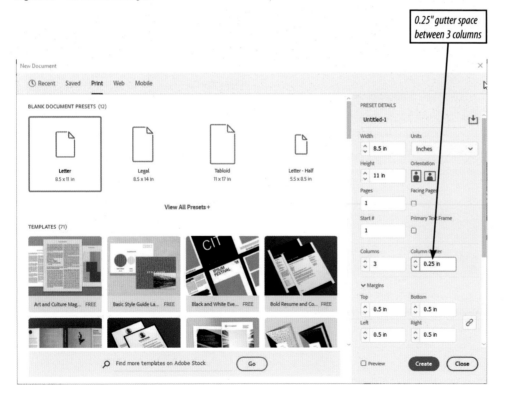

0.25" gutter space between 3 columns

Figure 28 Six frames threaded

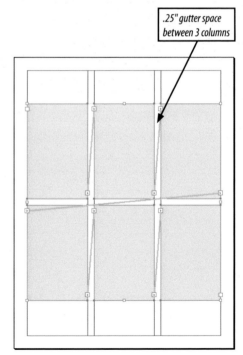

.25" gutter space between 3 columns

Execute a "super" step and repeat

1. Open ID 8-6.indd, then save it as **Super Step and Repeat**.

2. Click the **Selection tool** 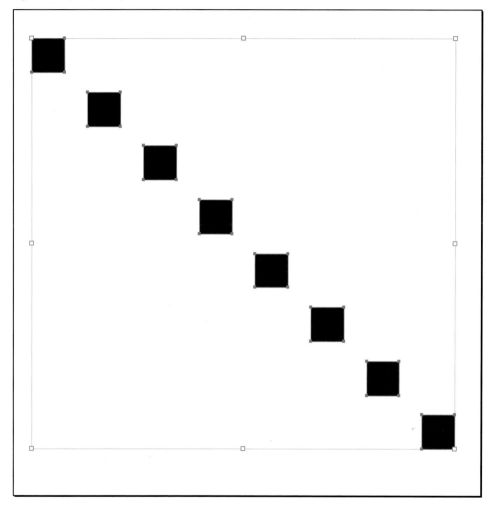, then select the **blue square**.

3. Press and hold **[option] (Mac)** or **[Alt] (Win)**, then begin dragging to the right.

4. While still dragging right, release **[option] (Mac)** or **[Alt] (Win)**, then press the **[→] key** six times, but *do not* release the mouse button when you are through.

   With each press of the [→] key, a copy is added between the original and the dragged copy.

5. Drag down to the **lower-right corner**, release the mouse button, then compare your result to Figure 29.

6. Save your work, then close the Super Step and Repeat document.

You used gridify behavior to do a "super" step and repeat.

Figure 29 Super step and repeat

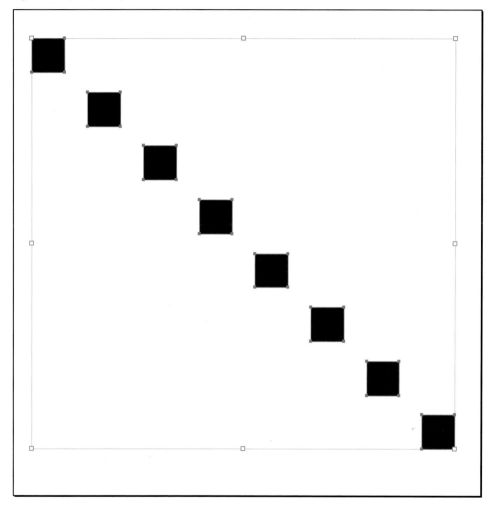

WORK WITH NESTED STYLES

▶ **What You'll Do**

In this lesson, you will use nested styles to format a block of text.

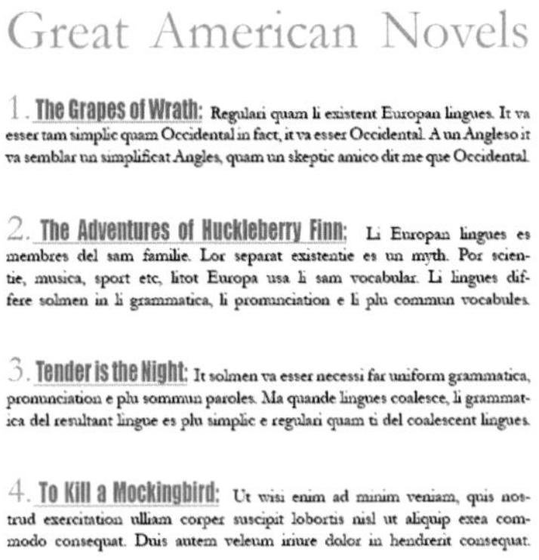

Great American Novels

1. **The Grapes of Wrath:** Regulari quam li existent Europan lingues. It va esser tam simplic quam Occidental in fact, it va esser Occidental. A un Angleso it va semblar un simplificat Angles, quam un skeptic amico dit me que Occidental.

2. **The Adventures of Huckleberry Finn:** Li Europan lingues es membres del sam familie. Lor separat existentie es un myth. Por scientie, musica, sport etc, litot Europa usa li sam vocabular. Li lingues differe solmen in li grammatica, li pronunciation e li plu commun vocabules.

3. **Tender is the Night:** It solmen va esser necessi far uniform grammatica, pronunciation e plu sommun paroles. Ma quande lingues coalesce, li grammatica del resultant lingue es plu simplic e regulari quam ti del coalescent lingues.

4. **To Kill a Mockingbird:** Ut wisi enim ad minim veniam, quis nostrud exercitation ulliam corper suscipit lobortis nisl ut aliquip exea commodo consequat. Duis autem veluem iriure dolor in hendrerit consequat.

Understanding Nested Styles

The term nested styles is based on real-world objects. If you like to cook, you've probably seen "nested" mixing bowls. These are mixing bowls of different sizes. For storage, you set the smallest one inside the next-largest one, then you set those two in the next-largest one, until all the bowls are "nested" in the largest bowl. This metaphor is also used for end tables, in which one small table slides underneath a taller table, and both of those slide underneath an even taller table. These are called "nested" tables.

In InDesign, a **nested style** is a paragraph style that contains two or more character styles. In other words, two or more character styles are "nested" within the paragraph style.

In Figure 30, each paragraph contains elements that were formatted with character styles.

Figure 30 A document with multiple character styles

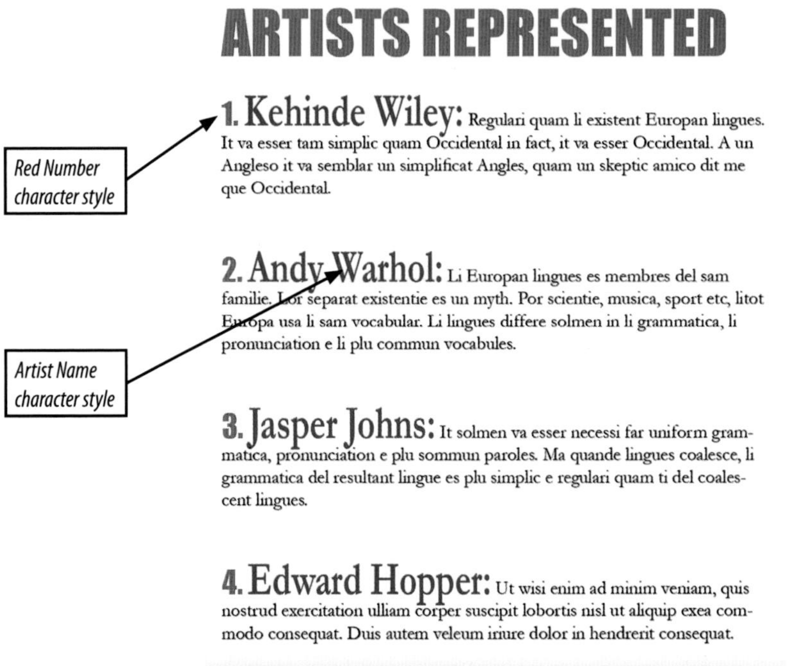

ARTISTS REPRESENTED

1. Kehinde Wiley: Regulari quam li existent Europan lingues. It va esser tam simplic quam Occidental in fact, it va esser Occidental. A un Angleso it va semblar un simplificat Angles, quam un skeptic amico dit me que Occidental.

Red Number character style

2. Andy Warhol: Li Europan lingues es membres del sam familie. Lor separat existentie es un myth. Por scientie, musica, sport etc, litot Europa usa li sam vocabular. Li lingues differe solmen in li grammatica, li pronunciation e li plu commun vocabules.

Artist Name character style

3. Jasper Johns: It solmen va esser necessi far uniform grammatica, pronunciation e plu sommun paroles. Ma quande lingues coalesce, li grammatica del resultant lingue es plu simplic e regulari quam ti del coalescent lingues.

4. Edward Hopper: Ut wisi enim ad minim veniam, quis nostrud exercitation ulliam corper suscipit lobortis nisl ut aliquip exea commodo consequat. Duis autem veluem iriure dolor in hendrerit consequat.

The numbers were formatted with a character style named Red Number, and the blue names were formatted with a character style named Artist Name.

Without nested styles, you would need to apply the character styles one at a time. For example, in the first paragraph, you'd need to select the number 1 and the period that follows it, then apply the Red Number character style. Then you'd select "Pablo Picasso:" and apply the Artist Name character style. Then you'd need to do the same for the next paragraphs. Imagine if your document profiled 100 artists!

With nested styles, you would format the entire block of text with a single paragraph style. That paragraph style would contain both the Red Number and the Artist Name character styles. They would be "nested" within the paragraph style and formatted in such a way that the first would format the number and the period and the second would format the artist's name. Then, because it's a paragraph style, the formatting would be reapplied after every paragraph break.

Applying Nested Styles

Nested styles are useful in specific situations, especially for blocks of text that contain

repeating formatting at the beginning of each paragraph. Figure 31 shows how nested styles were applied to the text in Figure 30.

In the Nested Styles section, two character styles were loaded—Red Number and Artist Name. The values entered for Red Number translate as follows: the Red Number character style will be applied to each paragraph through the first (1) period, and the Artist Name character style will be applied to each paragraph through the first em space.

If you regard the text in Figure 30 with this in mind, you see that the Red Number character is indeed applied up to and including the first period. An em space has been inserted after each artist's name, and the Artist Name character style has been applied up to that em space. If you wanted, you could also have, instead, specified that the character style be applied up to and including the colon after each artist's name. They are just two different ways of indicating where you want the formatting to stop.

Figure 31 Formatting nested styles

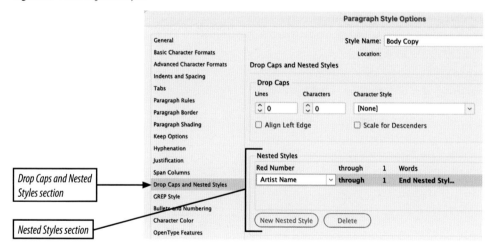

Drop Caps and Nested Styles section

Nested Styles section

Using the End Nested Style Here Command

Clearly, implementing nested styles requires a bit of forethought when formatting paragraphs. You must have characters that you can use to identify where a nested style ends. Periods, colons, and em or en spaces can be entered in the paragraph style to mark where a nested style should end.

But what if your layout doesn't call for periods, colons, or em spaces? No problem. Simply insert a special character using the End Nested Style Here command. This command is located within the Insert Special Character command on the Type menu—the same list you use to insert automatic page numbers on master pages or em dashes in body copy.

When you format the nested style in the Paragraph Style dialog box, you can specify that the nested style ends at the End Nested Style Here insertion. You do this by choosing End Nested Style Character in the Nested Styles section of the Paragraph Style Options dialog box, as shown in Figure 32.

Figure 32 Formatting a nested style using the End Nested Style Character command

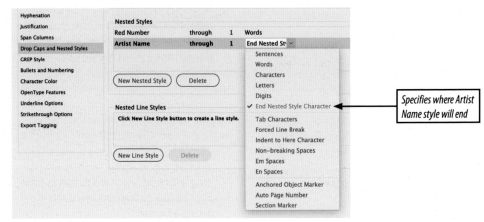

Specifies where Artist Name style will end

Apply character styles using the Character Styles panel

1. Open ID 8-7.indd, then save it as **Nested Styles**.

2. Open the Paragraph Styles panel, click the **Type tool** T, select all the **black text**, then note the **paragraph style** highlighted on the Paragraph Styles panel.

   All the black text has the Body Copy paragraph style applied to it.

3. Deselect all, select the **number 1 and the period that follows it**, then click **Number** on the Character Styles panel.

4. Select **The Grapes of Wrath** and the **colon** that follows it, then click **Title** on the Character Styles panel.

5. Deselect, then compare your page to Figure 33.

   To format the remainder of the list, you would need to select each number and apply the Number character style, then select each title, and apply the Title character style. That would be a lot of work, especially if this list had, let's say, 100 titles. Nested styles offer a solution.

6. Click **File** on the menu bar, click **Revert**, then click **Revert (Mac)** or **Yes (Win)** in the dialog box that follows.

7. Save your work, then continue to the next set of steps.

You used the Character Styles panel for applying character styles to text in a document.

Apply nested styles

1. Click the **Type tool** T, click to the **immediate right of the colon** after the word Wrath, click **Type** on the menu bar, point to **Insert Special Character**, point to **Other**, then click **End Nested Style Here**.

   The special character is invisible, so you won't see any change to the text.

2. Using the same method, insert the **End Nested Style Here special character** after the **colons in items 2–4**.

3. Double-click **Body Copy** on the Paragraph Styles panel to open the Paragraph Style Options dialog box, then click the **Preview check box** in the bottom-left corner.

4. Click **Drop Caps and Nested Styles** on the left, then click the **New Nested Style button**.

5. Click **[None]** in the Nested Styles section to highlight it, click the **[None] list arrow**, then click **Number**.

6. Double-click to select the word **Words**, then type a **period (.)** to replace Words, so your dialog box resembles Figure 34.

   The Number character style will be applied through the first period in each entry. Because the Preview option is activated, you can see the format changes to the text on the page as you work in the dialog box.

Continued on next page

Figure 33 Two character styles applied to text

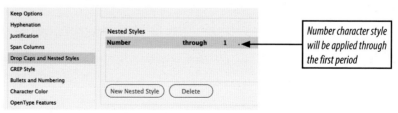

Number character style

Title character style

Figure 34 Formatting a nested style

7. Click the **New Nested Style button**, click the **[None] list arrow**, then click **Title**.

8. Click the word **Words** once, then note the format changes to the text on the page.

TIP The Title character style is applied to the first word only.

9. Click the **Words list arrow**, click **End Nested Style Character**, press **[return] (Mac)** or **[Enter] (Win)** to execute the change, then click **OK**.

As shown in Figure 35, the Title character style is applied to all the words up to the End Nested Style Character insertion.

10. Save your work, then close the Nested Styles document.

You applied two character styles to four paragraphs simultaneously by using nested styles.

Figure 35 Formatting a nested style through to the End Nested Style Character

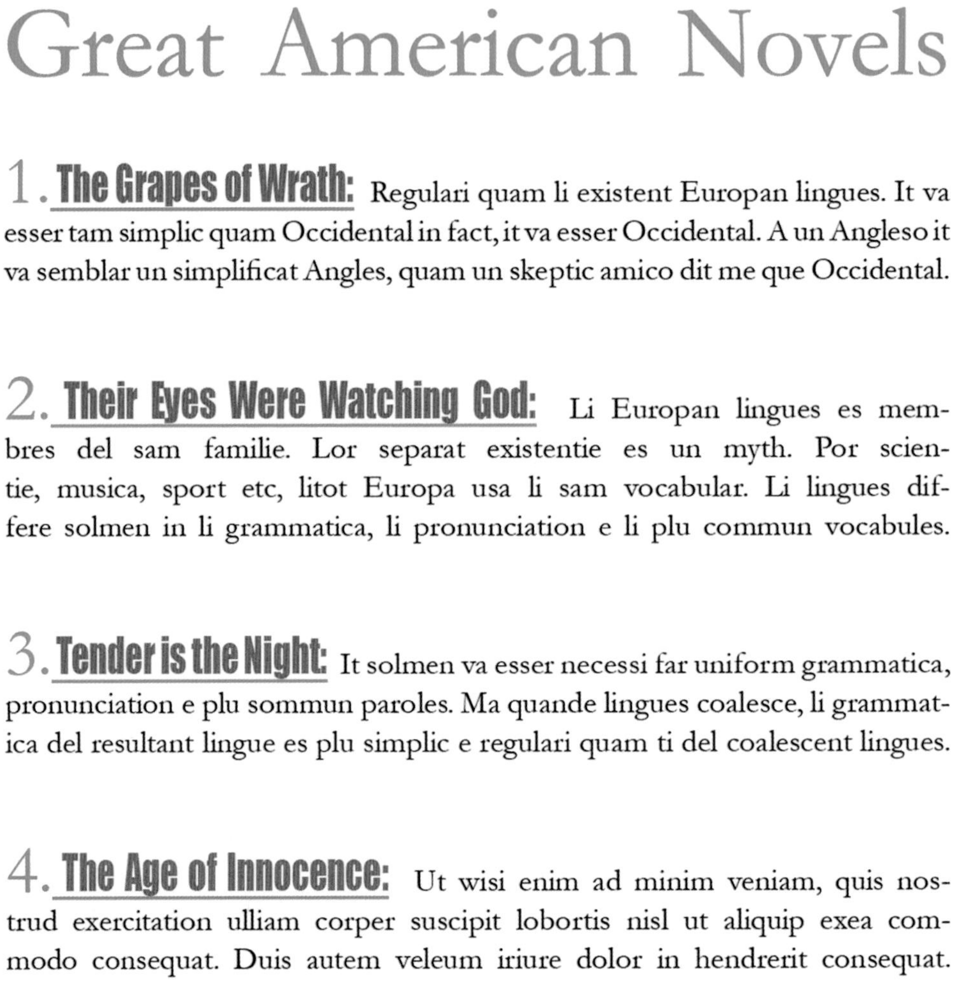

Great American Novels

1. **The Grapes of Wrath:** Regulari quam li existent Europan lingues. It va esser tam simplic quam Occidental in fact, it va esser Occidental. A un Angleso it va semblar un simplificat Angles, quam un skeptic amico dit me que Occidental.

2. **Their Eyes Were Watching God:** Li Europan lingues es membres del sam familie. Lor separat existentie es un myth. Por scientie, musica, sport etc, litot Europa usa li sam vocabular. Li lingues differe solmen in li grammatica, li pronunciation e li plu commun vocabules.

3. **Tender is the Night:** It solmen va esser necessi far uniform grammatica, pronunciation e plu sommun paroles. Ma quande lingues coalesce, li grammatica del resultant lingue es plu simplic e regulari quam ti del coalescent lingues.

4. **The Age of Innocence:** Ut wisi enim ad minim veniam, quis nostrud exercitation ulliam corper suscipit lobortis nisl ut aliquip exea commodo consequat. Duis autem veleum iriure dolor in hendrerit consequat.

APPLY LIVE CORNER EFFECTS

In this lesson, you'll use Live Corner Effects to change the appearance of corners on frames.

Applying Live Corner Effects

As noted earlier, InDesign is a frame-based application. Everything goes in a frame—images, text, and even rules. From a design perspective, too many rectangular frames can make your layouts look "boxy."

Live Corner Effects alleviate this issue by offering an interactive interface to apply different corner styles to a frame. Figure 36 shows the five styles available with Live Corner Effects.

Figure 36 Viewing corner effects

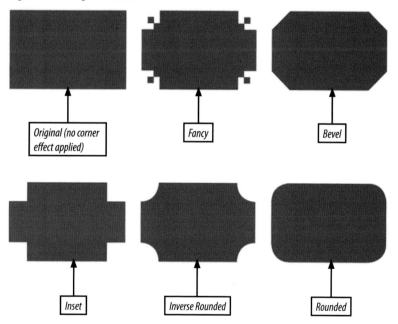

What's great about the Live Corner Effects utility is that it allows you to click and drag to specify the extent of an effect. For example, with Round Corners, you click and drag to increase the radius of the corner. You can also apply an effect to a single corner, and you can apply multiple effects to a single frame.

To use the Live Corner Effects utility, select a frame with the Selection tool. A yellow square appears on the frame, as shown in Figure 37. Click the yellow square to activate Live Corner Effects. Four yellow diamonds appear—one at each corner. If you click and drag any one of the diamonds, round corners

will be applied to all four corners, as shown in Figure 38. If you press [shift] and click and drag a corner, only that corner will be affected. The ability to apply different effects to different corners offers the opportunity to create interesting frame shapes, as shown in Figure 39.

Figure 37 Click the yellow square to activate Live Corner Effects

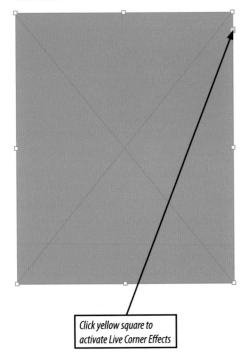

Click yellow square to activate Live Corner Effects

Figure 38 Applying the same effect to four corners

Figure 39 Applying one effect to different degrees to two corners

Shift-drag to modify a single corner

Round Corners is the default effect that is applied when you first drag the yellow diamond. To access the other effects shown in Figure 36, press and hold [option] (Mac) or [Alt] (Win), then click one of the diamonds repeatedly to cycle through the effects. When you do so, all the corners with effects applied will take on the current style. To cycle through effects on only one corner of the frame, press and hold [shift] [option] (Mac) or [Shift] [Alt] (Win), then click the diamond repeatedly. Figure 40 shows the Inset effect applied to the left side of the frame, the Fancy effect applied to the right, and an image placed into the frame.

TIP As an alternative to using Live Corner Effects, you can use the Corner Options dialog box on the Object menu.

Figure 40 Two effects applied and an image placed into the frame

Inset corner effect

Fancy corner effect

Apply round corners with Live Corner Effects

1. Open ID 8-8.indd, then save it as **Advanced Techniques**.

2. On page 1, click the **Selection tool** ▶, select the **green frame behind the title CORNIGLIA**, then click the **yellow square** on the frame.

   Four yellow diamonds appear at the corners of the frame.

3. Click and drag the **top-left diamond** straight down until the frame resembles Figure 41.

   When you click and drag a diamond, all four corners are transformed simultaneously.

4. Press and hold **[shift]**, then drag the **lower-left corner diamond** straight down.

   Pressing and holding [shift] when dragging a diamond affects only that corner.

5. Press and hold **[shift]**, then drag the **upper-right corner diamond** straight up.

   Your frame should resemble Figure 42.

Figure 41 Four rounded corners

Dragging one diamond affects all four corners

Figure 42 Modifying only two corners

Press [shift] and drag

6. Using the same methodology, apply **Live Corner Effects** so the bottom of your page 1 resembles Figure 43.

7. Using the same methodology, apply **Live Corner Effects** so your page 2 resembles Figure 44.

Continued on next page

Figure 43 Round corners on page 1

Figure 44 Round corners on page 2

8. Apply **Live Corner Effects** so your page 3 resembles Figure 45.

9. Save your work, then continue to the next set of steps.

You created round corners on frames using Live Corner Effects.

Cycle through Live Corner Effects

1. Verify that you are on **page 3**, select the **large image** with the **Selection tool** ▶, then click the **yellow square**.

2. Click and drag the **top-right diamond** to the left until the pop-up measurement box reads **1"**, as shown in Figure 46.

Figure 45 Round corners on page 3

Image courtesy of Chris Botello

Figure 46 Modifying the Live Corner Effect

Pop-up measurement box

3. Press and hold **[option] (Mac)** or **[Alt] (Win)**, then click any of the **yellow diamonds** one time.

   As shown in Figure 47, all four corners of the frame change to the Fancy corner effect.

4. Press and hold **[option] (Mac)** or **[Alt] (Win)**, then click any of the **yellow diamonds** two times slowly.

5. Press and hold **[shift] [option] (Mac)** or **[shift] [Alt] (Win)**, click the **top-left yellow diamond** one time, then click the **bottom-left diamond** one time.

   Your screen should resemble Figure 48.

6. Press and hold **[option] (Mac)** or **[Alt] (Win)**, then click any of the **yellow diamonds**.

   All four corners are restored to right angles because you have cycled through all the corner effects.

7. Save your work, then continue to the next lesson.

You cycled through Live Corner Effects, applying them to all four corners and to individual corners.

Figure 47 Fancy corner effects on all four corners

Figure 48 Two different Live Corner Effects

WORK WITH EFFECTS AND OBJECT STYLES

▶ *What You'll Do*

In this lesson, you'll apply various effects to type and objects, and you'll use the Object Styles panel and the New Object Style dialog box to format and apply object styles to type and frames.

Understanding Effects

The Effects dialog box, shown in Figure 49, offers a number of effects that you can apply to objects to make your layouts more visually interesting. All the available effects are listed on the left side of the dialog box, and settings for each effect become available on the right side of the dialog box when you click the name of the effect on the left. You can apply multiple effects to a single object.

Figure 49 Effects dialog box

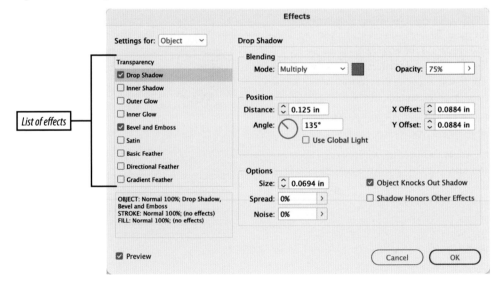

Figure 50 shows text with a bevel and emboss effect and a pink drop shadow.

InDesign effects, such as glows, shadows, bevels, embosses, and feathers, are all **nondestructive**, which means they are not necessarily permanent. At any time, you can apply, remove, or modify them. In other words, they don't permanently alter or "destroy" the object to which they're applied.

When you select a frame, the Effects panel lists information about any effects applied to the frame or to contents of the frame. When you have applied effects, the Add object effect icon *fx.* appears beside the word Object in the panel. The Add object effect icon *fx.* also appears at the bottom of the panel. If you click the Add object effect icon *fx.*, a menu will appear, showing the effects that have been applied, as shown in Figure 51.

You apply an effect to an object or text by first selecting the frame or text frame with the Selection tool, then clicking the Effects command on the Object menu. This opens the Effects dialog box, where all effects are applied and modified. Once you have applied effects, you can double-click the Add object effect icon *fx.* on the Effects panel to reopen the Effects dialog box if you want to modify or remove effects. This is an alternative to using the menu command. To remove an effect, simply uncheck the effect on the left side of the dialog box.

Figure 50 Text with two effects applied

Figure 51 Applied effects listed on Effects panel menu

Copying Effects Between Objects

You can also copy effects between objects on the Effects panel. Select any object that has an effect applied to it, then drag the Add object effect icon *fx.* to another object in the document. The effects applied to the first object will be applied to the second.

Note that when you copy effects from one object to another, no relationship is created between the objects. If you modify the effects on one object, the other object won't be affected by the change.

Working with Object Styles

A lot of the work you do in InDesign is essentially formatting. As you learned in Chapter 2, you can save all the formatting you do to text as a character style or a paragraph style, then use those styles to format other text.

Object styles follow the same logic. They are styles saved for formatting. Let's say you want to put a 1.5" black stroke and a white drop shadow effect on every picture frame in a document. It would be highly illogical to apply that formatting repeatedly to every picture frame. Not only would it be repetitive, but it would

become extremely time consuming if tomorrow you wanted to make a change. Instead, save the formatting as an object style, then apply it to other objects. Any modification you make to the object style will update automatically to any object that uses the object style.

The New Object Style dialog box allows you to specify a variety of formatting choices for graphics frames and text frames. At first glance—wow—there's a lot of information there. But you'll find that the New Object Style dialog box is straightforward, intuitive, and easy to incorporate into your day-to-day work with InDesign.

You can create a new object style from scratch in the New Object Style dialog box. First, create and name a new style. Then, specify formats for that style using the categories listed on the left.

You're likely to find that a more practical way to make a new object style is to first format an object on the page, then save the formatting as an object style. This method allows you to incorporate some trial and error while you're formatting the object on the page. Once you've got it where you want it, click the Object Styles

panel menu button, then click New Object Style. When the dialog box opens, all the formatting you applied to the object will be activated in the dialog box, ready to be saved as a style and applied to other objects.

Applying and Editing Object Styles

Once you've created an object style, the named style is listed on the Object Styles panel. Select an object on the page, such as a text frame, graphics frame, or shape that you created with the Pen tool, then click the object style on the panel that you want to use. All the formatting that is specified as the style will be applied to the selected object.

The power of object styles is not limited simply to applying them to objects. In many ways, they are even more powerful when you want to edit effects. Editing object styles couldn't be easier. Simply double-click the style you want to edit on the Object Styles panel. This will open the Object Style Options dialog box, where you can make as many changes to the style as you like. It's when you click that OK button that the magic happens. With that one click, every object in your document using that style will update to reflect the changes you made.

Apply and copy an Inner Shadow effect

1. Navigate to page 1, click the **Selection tool** ▶, then select the **large image**.

2. Click **Object** on the menu bar, point to **Effects**, then click **Inner Shadow**.

   The Effects dialog box opens with Inner Shadow checked on the left and Inner Shadow settings on the right.

   TIP Move the dialog box to see as much of the selected image as possible.

3. Enter the settings shown in Figure 52, then click **OK**.

   Your result should resemble Figure 53.

4. With the **large image** still selected, open the **Effects panel**, then click the **Add object effect button** _fx._ on the Effects panel.

   The menu lists the Inner Shadow effect with a check box, indicating it has been applied to the image.

5. Select the **five small frames** at the bottom of the layout, then set the **stroke color** to **[None]**.

Continued on next page

Figure 52 Settings for an Inner Shadow

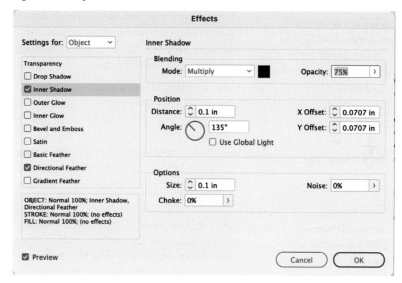

Figure 53 Inner Shadow effect applied

6. Select the **large image on the page**, then drag the **Add object effect icon** _fx._ from the **highlighted Object line** on the Effects panel to the **leftmost small frame**, as illustrated in Figure 54.

   The Inner Shadow effect is applied to the small frame. The large frame remains selected.

7. Drag the **Add object effect icon** _fx._ to the other four small frames on the page, then deselect all.

8. Save your work, then continue to the next set of steps.

You applied an Inner Shadow effect to a frame with a placed graphic, then copied the effect to five other frames.

Apply a Bevel and Emboss and a Drop Shadow effect

1. Use the **Selection tool** ▶ to select the **CORNIGLIA text frame**.

2. Click **Object** on the menu bar, point to **Effects**, then click **Bevel and Emboss**.

3. Enter the settings shown in Figure 55, but *don't click OK* when you're done.

Figure 54 Copying an effect from one image to another

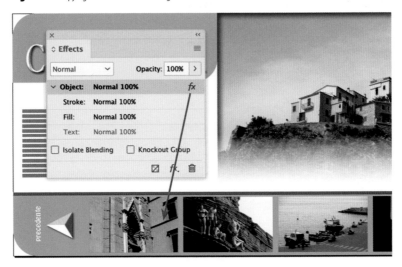

Figure 55 Settings for a Bevel and Emboss effect

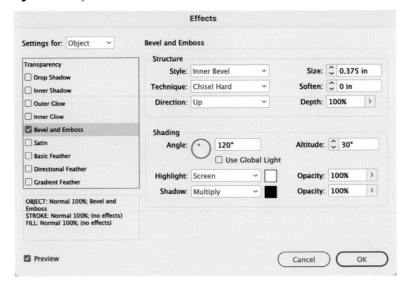

4. Click the words **Drop Shadow** on the left side of the dialog box, then enter the settings shown in Figure 56.

5. Click **OK**, then compare your text to Figure 57.

6. Save your work, then continue to the next set of steps.

You applied two effects to text: a Bevel and Emboss and a Drop Shadow.

Figure 56 Settings for a Drop Shadow effect

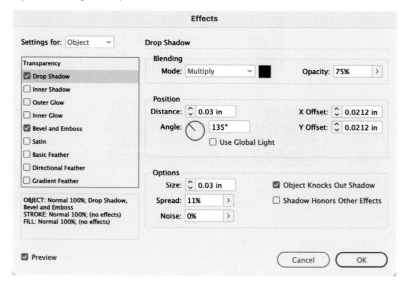

Figure 57 Text with two effects applied

By default, if you overlap one object with another, the bottom object will be hidden behind the top object where they overlap. One option for manipulating this relationship is to apply a blending mode to the top object. **Blending modes** allow you to create different transparency and color effects where two or more objects overlap.

The Effects panel lists 15 blending modes. Some blending modes, such as Screen, are very practical and can be used to produce common effects. Others, such as Difference, produce more extreme effects and are therefore not used as often.

Blending modes work by comparing the colors in the overlapping graphics and then running those colors through a mathematical algorithm to produce an effect. They are almost always used on an experimental basis. Just try out different effects until you find one that works well with the objects you are blending.

Of the 15 blending modes, one in particular deserves special attention because of its usefulness—Multiply. Be sure to familiarize yourself with it. When **Multiply** is applied to an object, the object becomes transparent but retains its color. You can think of the effect as that of overlapping colors drawn by magic markers. Two important features to memorize about the Multiply blending mode are that any white areas of a graphic become transparent, and any black areas remain black.

Create and apply an object style

1. Verify that the **CORNIGLIA text frame** is selected.

2. Click **Window** on the menu bar, point to **Styles**, then click **Object Styles**.

3. Click the **Object Styles panel menu button** 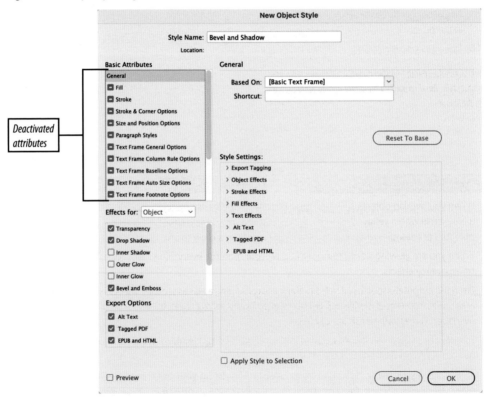, then click **New Object Style**.

   The New Object Style dialog box opens.

4. Type **Bevel and Shadow** in the Style Name text box, then note in the lower-left section that the Bevel and Emboss and Drop Shadow effects are checked.

5. Uncheck all the attributes in the **Basic Attributes section**.

UNDERSTANDING GLOBAL LIGHT

Global Light is a setting that applies a uniform lighting angle to three InDesign effects that deal with shadows and transparency: Drop Shadow, Inner Shadow, and Bevel and Emboss. When you apply one of these effects to an InDesign object, you will see the Use Global Light check box in the corresponding dialog box. When checked, InDesign applies the global light settings defined in the Global Light dialog box. To set global lighting, click the Effects panel menu button, then click Global Light. You can experiment with different values in the Angle and Altitude check boxes and preview them before you close the dialog box.

Your dialog box should resemble Figure 58. You will use this object style to apply the Bevel and Emboss and the Drop Shadow effects to other objects. The basic attributes that you unchecked were those of the CORNIGLIA text, such as the fill color, stroke color, and text wrap. You did not want to save these attributes with this object style, so you unchecked them.

6. Click **OK**.

   Note that the Bevel and Shadow object style is listed on the Object Styles panel.

Figure 58 New Object Style dialog box

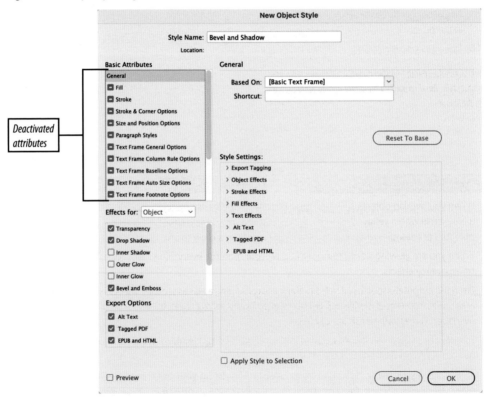

7. Use the **Selection tool** ▶ to select the **white triangle** to the left of the small images, then click **Bevel and Shadow** on the Object Styles panel.

   As shown in Figure 59, the Bevel and Shadow object style is applied to the triangle.

8. Apply the **Bevel and Shadow object style** to the **other triangle**.

9. Apply the **Bevel and Shadow object style** to the **two other headlines** and **four other triangles** in the layout.

10. Save your work, then continue to the next set of steps.

You selected text with two effects applied, then created a new object style. You then applied the object style to other objects in the layout.

Figure 59 Bevel and Shadow style applied to triangle shape

APPLYING TRANSPARENCY TO OBJECTS

When you manipulate an object's transparency, you are not limited to changing the opacity of the entire object. In fact, you can change the opacity of just the fill, just the stroke, or just the text. When you select an object that you want to modify, click the expand arrow next to Object on the Effects panel, then click Fill, Stroke, or Text. For example, if you click Stroke and then change the opacity to 50%, only the stroke of the selected object will be 50% transparent. The object's fill will remain unchanged. You can also achieve the same results by selecting an object, clicking the Apply Effect to Object button on the Control panel, then clicking Fill, Stroke, or Text. When Object is selected, both the fill and the stroke of the selected object will change.

MANAGING COLOR WITH EFFECTS AND TRANSPARENT OBJECTS

When you overlap objects, InDesign allows you to create transparency effects, as though you are seeing one object through another. For example, if you overlap a blue circle with a yellow circle with a transparency effect, the overlapped area will appear green. Transparency also comes into play when you apply effects to objects. For example, when you apply a drop shadow or a glow to an object, those effects are transparent by definition.

When you are viewing transparency effects on your monitor, everything looks great. It's when you print a document that unexpected colors can result from transparency effects.

From the output perspective, it helps to think of overlapping areas as separate shapes with their own fills. To use the previous example, think of the green overlapped area not as a section of the blue object overlapped by the yellow object but as a separate object with a green fill. That's how InDesign, on the code level, manages overlapped areas with transparency effects.

For example, when you flatten a document (remove its layers) for output, InDesign creates multiple objects from overlapping objects and assigns them their own colors to mimic transparency effects.

To avoid unexpected shifts in color, when you're outputting your document, you should assign a "color space" for InDesign to use when assigning colors to overlapped areas. If you are outputting for the Web or for an on-screen presentation, choose the RGB color space. If you are outputting for print, choose the CMYK color space.

To assign a color space for transparency, click the Edit menu, point to Transparency Blend Space, then click Document RGB or Document CMYK. The blending space you choose is applied only to those spreads that contain transparency.

Remove an object style from an object

1. Navigate to **page 3**, then select the **MANAROLA headline** with the Bevel and Shadow object style.

2. Note the **Add object style icon** _fx._ in the highlighted Object line on the Effects panel.

3. Drag the **Add object style icon** _fx._ to the **Delete selected style icon** 🗑 on the Effects panel.

   Both effects are removed.

4. Save your work, then continue to the next set of steps.

You removed effects from text.

Apply feathering effects

1. Select the **blue oval** on page 1.

2. Click **Object** on the menu bar, point to **Effects**, then click **Basic Feather**.

3. Enter the settings shown in Figure 60, then click **OK**.

4. Click **File** on the menu bar, click **Place**, navigate to the **Photography folder** where your Chapter 8 Data Files are stored, then choose the file named **Girls**.

5. Fit the image so that your frame resembles Figure 61.

   When you place an image into a frame with a Feather effect, the image takes on the effect.

6. Navigate to **page 2**, select the **large image** on the page, then click the **Gradient Feather tool** 🖼 on the toolbar.

   The Gradient Feather tool 🖼 is a freehand tool. The feather is applied as an effect and can be modified or removed like any other effect.

Figure 60 Settings for a Basic Feather effect

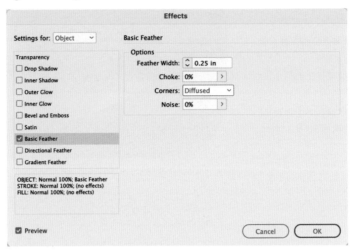

Figure 61 Image placed in a feathered frame

Image courtesy of Chris Botello

7. Position the **Gradient Feather tool** over the **left green shutter** in the image, click and drag to the **left edge of the image**, release the mouse button, then deselect.

   As shown in Figure 62, the image gradually fades to white. The length of the fade is the length that you dragged the Gradient Feather tool.

8. Navigate to **page 1**, then select the **large image**.

9. Click **Object** on the menu bar, click **Effects**, then click the words **Directional Feather** in the column on the left.

10. Set the **Bottom text box** to **1"** so your dialog box resembles Figure 63.

11. Click **OK**, deselect, then compare your page 1 to Figure 64.

12. Save your work, then close the Advanced Techniques document.

You applied three feather effects, including a basic feather, gradient feather, and directional feather.

Figure 62 Gradient feather effect

Figure 63 Directional Feather settings

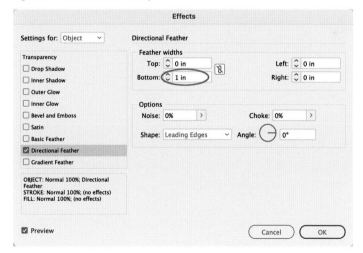

Figure 64 Final layout with the directional feather

CORNIGLIA

thursday august 11

Lorem ipsum dolor sit amet, consect etuer adipiscing elit, sed diam no nummy nibh euismod tincidunt ut laoreet dolore magna aliquam erat volutpat. Ut wisi enim ad minim veniam, quis nostrud exerci tation ullam corper sus cipit lobortis nisl ut aliquip ex ea commodo consequat. Duis autem vel eum iriure dolor in hendrerit in vulputate velit esse molestie consequat, vel illum dolore eu feugiat nulla facilisis at vero eros et accumsan et iusto odio dignissim qui

blandit praesent luptatum zzril delenit augue duis dolore te feugait nulla facilisi. Ut wisi enim ad minim veniam, quis nostrad exerci tation ullamcorper suscipit lobortis nisl ut aliquip ex ea commodo consequat. Duis autem vel eum iriure dolor in hendrerit in vulputate velit esse molestie consequat, vel illum dolore eu feugiat nulla facilisis at vero eros et accumsan et iusto odio dignissim qui blandit praesent luptatum zzril delenit augue duis dolore te feugait nulla

precedente

seguente

WORK WITH MULTIPLE PAGE SIZES

▶ **What You'll Do**

In this lesson, you will specify three different page sizes in a single document.

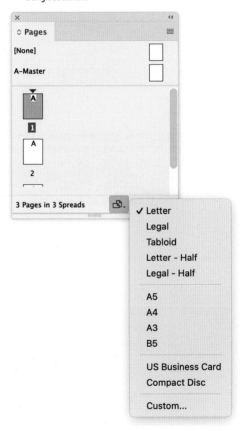

Working with Multiple Page Sizes

Imagine you're a designer and your boss tells you that you need to create layouts for a new client, including letterhead, a business card, and a 4" × 6" postcard. Each piece will contain the same elements—the client's logo, contact information, and a background pattern placed from Photoshop. What do you do? In earlier versions of InDesign, you would create three separate documents. You'd need to copy and paste the elements from one document to another. Then, if you needed to make any changes, you'd have to do so in all three documents.

Some designers thought up a work-around solution. In the above case, they'd create one really big document—say 18" × 18"—then they'd position all three elements in that large space. The problem with that is that the document size has no relationship to the artwork. You would need to manually create and position crop marks for each of these three elements.

Fortunately, InDesign has evolved over the years. Now you can work with multiple page sizes in a single document. Sticking with the same scenario, you could start by creating a letter-sized document for the letterhead. Create the document with three pages. Then, for the business card, select one of the page thumbnails on the Pages panel, and click the Edit page size button on the panel, identified in Figure 65. When you do so, a submenu appears, listing numerous standard-size choices, which you can apply to the selected page. If none of those is what you want, you can simply click Custom Page Size and enter specific page dimensions.

Working in this manner, you can change the size of any and every page on the Pages panel. Then, let's say you print the document—in this case, all three pages—with crop marks. InDesign will print unique crop sizes for each page to match the dimensions of that page. How cool is that? Figure 66 shows a PDF file of three different page sizes from one document, each with its own set of crops.

Figure 65 Edit page size button

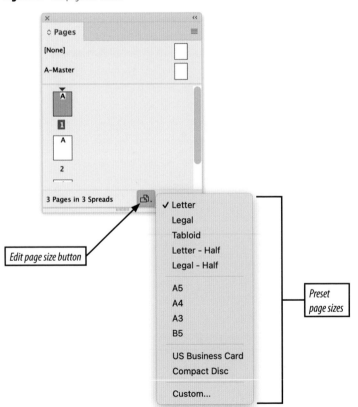

Edit page size button

Preset page sizes

Figure 66 Three page sizes output to PDF

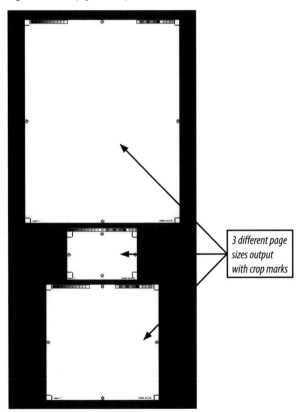

3 different page sizes output with crop marks

Working with Multiple Size Master Pages

The new multiple page size feature also works with master pages.

Imagine that you customize all the stationery for the employees at your company. All employees get their own stationery, business cards, and business envelopes customized with their name. You could create a single document with three master pages—one for the letterhead, one for the business cards, and one for the envelopes.

You could then apply the master to any page in the document. For example, a document page might be letter size, but if you drag your business card master to that page, it will be resized to 2" × 3.5". Think about it—in this scenario, you could keep customized stationery, business cards, and envelopes for every employee in a single document!

Create multiple page sizes in a single document

1. Click **File** on the menu bar, point to **New**, then click **Document**.

2. Enter the values shown in Figure 67, then click **Create**.

   The document is a three-page, letter-size document with a .5" margin.

Continued on next page

Figure 67 New Document dialog box

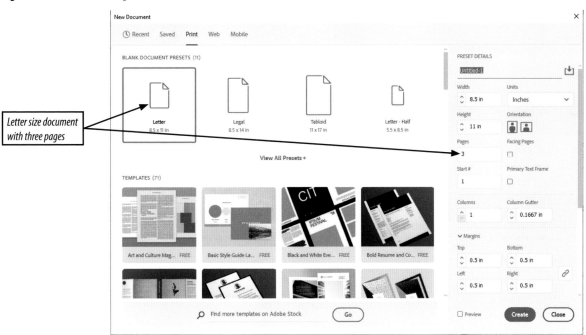

Letter size document with three pages

3. Open the **Pages panel**, then double-click the **page 2 thumbnail**.

4. Click the **Edit page size button** 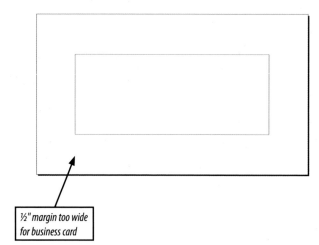. on the Pages panel, then click **US Business Card**.

As shown in Figure 68, the page size changes to 2" × 3.5"—the standard size of a US business card. Note that the 0.5" margin, which worked for the letter size page, is impractically large for a business card layout.

5. With **page 2** still targeted on the Pages panel, click **Layout** on the menu bar, click **Margins and Columns**, set the **four Margins** to **.125**, then click **OK**.

The margin width is reduced. The change to the margins affected only page 2. Pages 1 and 3 retain the 0.5" margins.

6. Double-click **page 3** on the Pages panel.

7. Click the **Edit page size button** 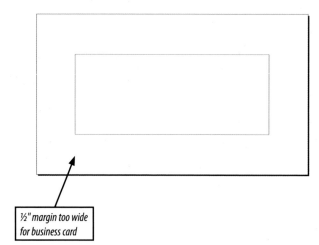. on the Pages panel, then click **Custom**.

The Custom Page Size dialog box opens.

8. Type **4 × 6 Postcard** in the Name text box, set the **Width** to **4**, then set the **Height** to **6**.

9. Click **Add**.

4 × 6 Postcard is added to the list. 4 × 6 Postcard will now be available in the Edit page size menu if you want to use it again.

10. Click **OK**, then save the file as **Multiple Page Sizes**.

11. Save your work, then continue to the next set of steps.

You specified two different page sizes in a single document.

Figure 68 Standard US business card size

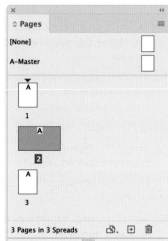

½" margin too wide for business card

Create a master page of a different size in a document

1. Click the **Pages panel menu button** ☰, click **New Master**, then click **OK** in the New Master dialog box.

   A new master page, named B-Master, is created and targeted on the Pages panel. The B-Master is created at 8.5" × 11"—the document size specified when the document was created.

2. Click the **Edit page size button** 🗐. on the Pages panel, then click **Tabloid**.

   Only the B-Master changes to the Tabloid size of 11" × 17".

3. On the Pages panel, drag the **B-Master icon** to the **page 1 thumbnail**.

   TIP If the Master Page Size Conflict warning appears, click the Use master page size button.

4. Double-click the **page 1 thumbnail**, then compare your screen to Figure 69.

   Page 1, originally letter size, is now tabloid size.

5. Save your work, then close the Multiple Page Sizes document.

You created a new master page, then changed its page size. You then applied that master page to a document page, noting the change in size of the document page when the master was applied.

Figure 69 Tabloid master applied

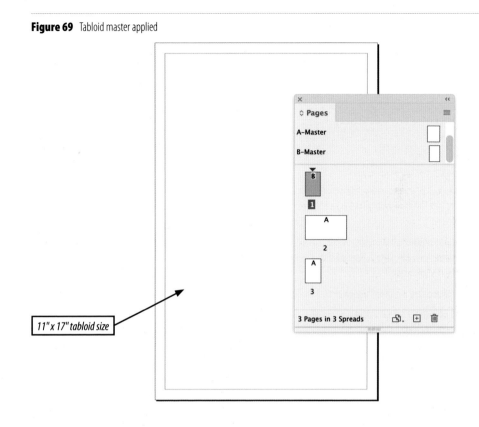

11" x 17" tabloid size

DESIGN WITH MULTIPLE DOCUMENTS

▶ *What You'll Do*

In this lesson, you will explore various options for working with multiple documents.

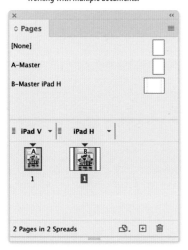

Working with Multiple Layouts

Multiple layouts have always played a role in graphic design. Long before the personal computer came into the game, graphic designers were creating letterhead, envelopes, and business cards for clients. In today's media space, there's a great demand for creating and working effectively with multiple layouts such as these. One relatively small advertising campaign might have a poster, various-sized print ads for various-sized magazines, a web page layout, and perhaps a layout for the iPad.

The Content Collector panel, shown in Figure 70, is a shuttle for moving objects between documents. The panel has two tools: the Content Collector tool and the Content Placer tool. The Content Collector tool takes objects—frames, text, and placed images—from a document and puts them into the Content Collector panel. The Content Placer tool places those objects into another document. The Content Collector tool and the Content Placer tool are also available on the toolbar. The panel offers three Place option buttons, also identified in Figure 70.

Figure 70 Content Collector panel

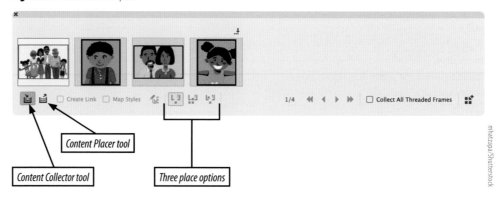

Content Placer tool

Content Collector tool

Three place options

The Content Collector panel is more than just a glorified cut-and-paste utility. It allows you to create links between the objects. If you collect a text frame in the Content Collector panel, you can click the Create Link option then place the text in a second document. The text in the second document is now "linked" to the text in the first document and is listed in the Links panel. If you make changes to the parent text frame in the first document, the Links panel in the second document will identify that the child text frame can be updated with those changes. This offers you significant time savings and is a method you can rely on to maintain consistency between multiple documents.

Rather than creating and saving multiple documents, you can work with multiple layouts within a single document using the Create Alternate Layout command. With alternate layouts, you could have a layout for a letter-size piece of letterhead, a 2" × 3.5" business card, and a 4" × 9" envelope all in one document. Figure 71 shows the Pages panel with exactly those three layouts in one document. Note that a master page exists for each of the three layouts.

When you create an alternate layout, all the objects from the original layout are automatically copied to the alternate layout, and you will have the option to link all the text from the parent to the child.

Figure 71 Alternate layout thumbnails on the Pages panel

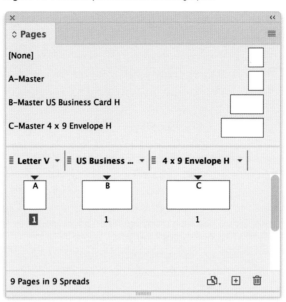

Use the Content Collector tool

1. Open ID 8-9.indd, then save it as **iPad V**.

   The file is 768 pixels × 1024 pixels, the standard size of a tablet device like the iPad.

2. Click **File** on the menu bar, point to **New**, then click **Document**.

   The New Document dialog box opens.

3. Click **Mobile** at the top of the New Document dialog box.

4. Enter the settings shown in Figure 72.

   These settings are standard for an iPad held horizontally. Note that the page size reads iPad, and the Orientation is set to Portrait.

   TIP If you do not see the iPad preset, click the View All Presets + button in the middle of the New Document dialog box.

5. Click **Create**.

6. Save the new document as **iPad H**, then return to the **iPad V (vertical) document**.

7. Click the **Content Collector tool** 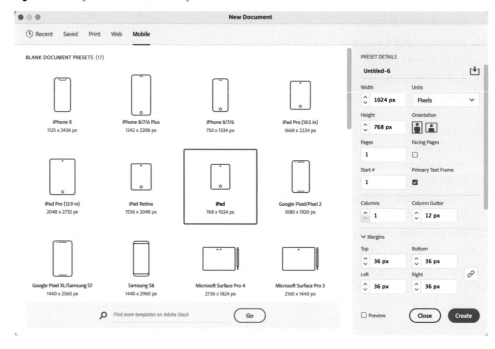 on the toolbar.

   The Content Collector panel, shown in Figure 73, opens. Note the two tools at the lower-left corner: the Content Collector tool and the Content Placer tool. The Content Collector tool should be the active tool.

8. Click the **large image of the family** on the page.

   The large image of the family is added to the Content Collector panel.

9. Moving left to right, click the **three thumbnail images** at the bottom of the page.

Figure 72 Settings in the New Document dialog box

Figure 73 Content Collector panel

Content Placer tool

Content Collector tool

As shown in Figure 74, the four images are positioned in the Content Collector panel in the order that you clicked them.

10. Switch to the **iPad H document**, then click the **Content Placer tool** ⬛ .

11. Verify that the **Create Link** and **Map Styles check boxes** are *not* checked on the Content Collector panel.

12. Float your cursor anywhere over the document.

The place thumbnail appears showing a thumbnail of the image that will be placed with the Content Placer tool ⬛ . The number 4 on the place thumbnail indicates that four images are loaded in the Content Collector panel.

13. Press the **→ key** on your keypad repeatedly.

When you press the → key, the next image in the sequence becomes the loaded image.

14. Press the **→ key** until the **family photo** is the loaded image.

15. Click anywhere on the **document page**.

The image is placed on the page and is removed from the Content Collector panel.

16. Click the **page** three more times to place the remaining **three collected images**.

As shown in Figure 75, all three images are placed on the page and the Content Collector panel is empty.

17. Save your work, then close the iPad H document.

18. Keep the **iPad V document** open, then continue to the next set of steps.

You used the Content Collector tool to copy images from one document to another. You explored options for choosing different images as the loaded image, then you added all the images from the Content Collector panel to the second document.

Figure 74 Four images in the Content Collector panel

Figure 75 Four images added to the second document

Link text and objects between documents

1. Open ID 8-10.indd, then save it as **iPad H Linked**.
2. Go to the **iPad V document** and verify that nothing is selected.
3. Click the **Content Collector tool** 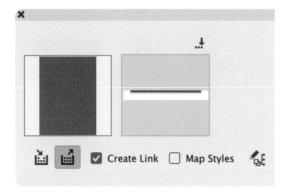 on the toolbar, then click the **large red frame** on the page.

    The large red frame is added to the Content Collector panel.
4. Click the **Love Phoenix ... text** under the large image.
5. Switch to the **iPad H Linked document**, then click the **Content Placer tool** on the Content Collector panel.

    The red frame is the loaded image.
6. Click the **Create Link check box** on the Content Collector panel to activate it.

    Your Content Collector panel should resemble Figure 76.
7. Click **anywhere** on the document page.

    The red frame is placed on the page, and the Love Phoenix ... text is loaded in the Content Collector panel.
8. Click **anywhere on the pasteboard** to the left of the document page.

    TIP When placing text through the Content Collector panel, it's a good idea to place the text on the pasteboard. If you click on the page and there's a frame on the page, you will often unintentionally place the text into the frame.
9. Redesign the page elements as necessary so your page resembles Figure 77.

Figure 76 Activating the Create Link option

Figure 77 Positioning the red frame and the text

10. Switch to the **iPadV document**, then click the **Selection tool** ▶.

11. Select the **gray-filled frame**, click **Edit** on the menu bar, then click **Place and Link**.

    The Content Collector panel opens, the gray frame is automatically added, and the Create Link option is automatically checked.

12. Click the **Selection tool** ▶ on the toolbar.

13. Click the **Happy Holidays text** to select it.

14. Click **Edit** on the menu bar, then click **Place and Link**.

    The Happy Holidays text is added to the Content Collector panel.

15. Go to the **iPad H Linked document**.

16. Use the **Content Placer tool** 🗒 to place the **gray frame** and the **Happy Holidays text** on the page.

17. Position the **two new elements** so your page resembles Figure 78.

18. Save your work, then continue to the next set of steps.

You created linked content using two methods. First you used the Create Link option in the Content Collector panel, then you used the Place and Link command in the Edit menu, resulting in four items—two frames and two text boxes—linked between two documents.

Figure 78 Positioning the gray frame and headline text

Modify and update linked text and objects between documents

1. Go to the **iPad V document**.

2. Select the **large red frame**.

3. On the Swatches panel, change its **fill color** to **Pantone 300**.

4. Select the **smaller gray frame**, then change its **fill color** to **Pantone 2975**.

5. Change the **Happy Holidays headline fill** to **[Paper]** (white).

6. In the type under the main photo, change **Lillian** to **Grandma**, **Ronna** to **Mom**, **Malcolm** to **Dad**, and **James** to **Pops**.

7. Save your work, then switch to the **iPad H Linked document**.

8. In the **iPad H Linked document**, open the **Links panel**.

   As shown in Figure 79, the Links panel shows four items that can be updated. This represents the changes made to the four items in the iPad V document. Note that two of the items have a Text icon beside them.

9. Update each link, then compare your layout to Figure 80.

   As shown in the figure, the two text updates were successful. However, when the two colored frames were updated, the changes you made resizing them were lost.

Figure 79 Linked items that can be updated

Figure 80 Four updated links; resize changes to two frames were lost

Frames are returned to original size with the update

10. Resize the two frames so your layout resembles Figure 81.

11. Save your work, then close the iPad H Linked document.

12. Save the iPad V document, and keep it open for the next set of steps.

You made edits to two frames and two text boxes in the vertical document. You noted that the text edits were updated successfully in the horizontal document. Though the frame edits did update, changes made to resize the frames in the horizontal document were lost with the update.

Figure 81 Alternate layout finalized

Create an alternate layout

1. Verify that the **iPad V document** is the only open document.

2. Compare your **Pages panel** to Figure 82.

   Because this document was created as a Mobile document with iPad as its page size, the Pages panel identifies the layout as standard for a vertical iPad. Thus, the Pages panel lists iPad V above the page thumbnail.

3. Click **Layout** on the menu bar, then click **Create Alternate Layout**.

4. Compare your Create Alternate Layout dialog box to Figure 83.

The Create Alternate Layout function is somewhat intuitive: The new layout is automatically named iPad H, and the page orientation is set to Landscape. The size of this document will be the same as the vertical document, but in the alternate layout, the longer side is the width.

Figure 82 Pages panel

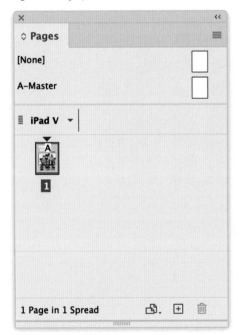

Figure 83 Create Alternate Layout dialog box

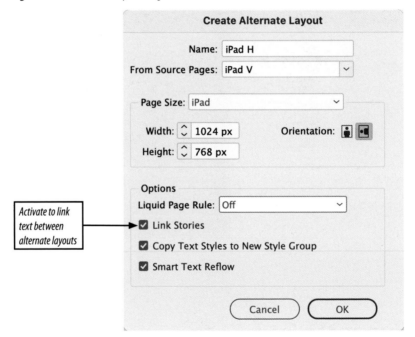

Activate to link text between alternate layouts

5. Verify that **Liquid Page Rule** is set to **Off**.

Liquid Page Rule, if activated, provides options that will attempt to intuitively reposition items in an alternate layout.

6. Verify that the **Link Stories check box** is checked, then click **OK**.

A new section named iPad H is added to the panel with a new thumbnail.

7. Double-click the **thumbnail under iPad H**, then compare your screen to Figure 84.

The alternate layout is created with all the elements from the vertical layout positioned

on the alternate layout. The text frames in the alternate layout are linked to the vertical layout because the Link Stories option was checked when the alternate was created.

8. Save your work, then close the iPad V document.

You created an alternate document using the Link Stories option.

Figure 84 Artwork in the alternate layout

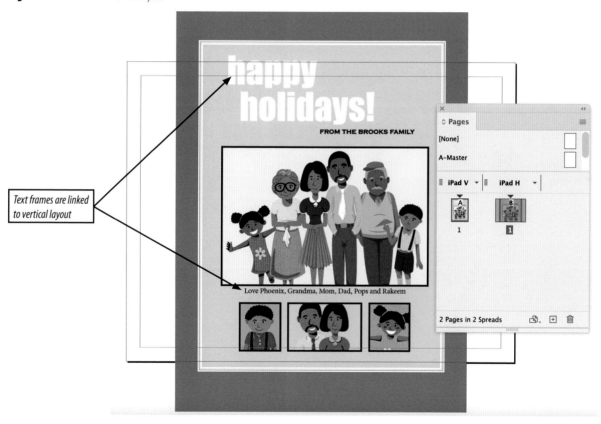

Text frames are linked to vertical layout

Use the Pathfinder panel

1. Open ID 8-11.indd, then save it as **Pathfinder and Strokes Review**.
2. Click the Selection tool, then move the objects on the page so you can see how the graphic is built.
3. Revert the file to return the layout to its original state.
4. Display the Layers panel, then verify that only Layer 1 is visible and targeted.
5. Select all, then click the Subtract button on the Pathfinder panel.
6. Click Edit on the menu bar, click Copy, click Edit on the menu bar, click Paste in Place, then change the fill color to PANTONE 1797 C.
7. Make Layer 2 visible and active, press and hold [shift], then click the yellow star to add it to the selection.
8. Click the Exclude Overlap button on the Pathfinder panel.
9. Click PANTONE Reflex Blue C on the Swatches panel.

Create new stroke styles

1. Deselect all.
2. Click the Stroke panel menu button, then click Stroke Styles.
3. Click New, then type **New Dash** in the Name text box.
4. Verify that Dash is listed in the Type text box.

5. Select the value in the Length text box, then type **.125 in**.
6. Click the white space to the right of the dash to add a new dash.
7. Select the value in the Start text box, type **.19 in**, press [tab], type **.01** in the Length text box, then press [tab].
8. Click OK.

9. Note the New Dash stroke in the Stroke Styles dialog box, then click OK.
10. Select the circle, click the Type list arrow on the Stroke panel, then click New Dash.
11. Change the stroke color to PANTONE Reflex Blue C, then compare your work to Figure 85.
12. Save your work, then close the Pathfinder and Strokes Review document.

Figure 85 *Skills Review, Parts 1 and 2 completed*

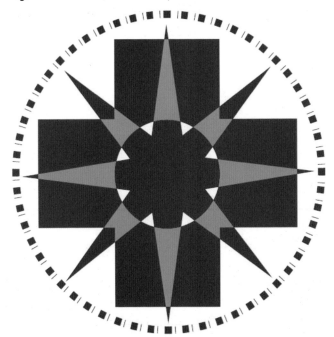

Work with nested styles

1. Open ID 8-12.indd, then save it as **Nested Styles Skills**.

2. Click the Type tool, click to the immediate right of the colon after the word Wiley, click Type on the menu bar, point to Insert Special Character, point to Other, then click End Nested Style Here.

3. Using the same method, insert the End Nested Style Here special character after the colons in items 2–4.

4. Double-click Body Copy on the Paragraph Styles panel, then click the Preview check box in the bottom-left corner to select it if it is not already selected.

5. Click Drop Caps and Nested Styles in the box on the left, then click New Nested Style.

6. Click the [None] list arrow, click Red Number, then press [return] (Mac) or [Enter] (Win) to execute the change.

7. Click New Nested Style, click [None] to highlight it if it is not already, click the [None] list arrow, then click Artist Name.

8. Click Words once, click the Words list arrow, click End Nested Style Character, then press [return] (Mac) or [Enter] (Win) to execute the change.

9. Click OK, compare your work to Figure 86, save your work, then close the Nested Styles Skills document. Your screen may look different if your computer substituted fonts.

Figure 86 Skills Review, Part 3 completed

ARTISTS REPRESENTED

1. Kehinde Wiley: Regulari quam li existent Europan lingues. It va esser tam simplic quam Occidental in fact, it va esser Occidental. A un Angleso it va semblar un simplificat Angles, quam un skeptic amico dit me que Occidental.

2. Andy Warhol: Li Europan lingues es membres del sam familie. Lor separat existentie es un myth. Por scientie, musica, sport etc, litot Europa usa li sam vocabular. Li lingues differe solmen in li grammatica, li pronunciation e li plu commun vocabules.

3. Jasper Johns: It solmen va esser necessi far uniform grammatica, pronunciation e plu sommun paroles. Ma quande lingues coalesce, li grammatica del resultant lingue es plu simplic e regulari quam ti del coalescent lingues.

4. Edward Hopper: Ut wisi enim ad minim veniam, quis nostrud exercitation ulliam corper suscipit lobortis nisl ut aliquip exea commodo consequat. Duis autem veleum iriure dolor in hendrerit consequat.

SKILLS REVIEW

(continued)

Incorporate gridify behavior

1. Open ID 8-13.indd, then save it as **Gridify Skills**.
2. Set the fill color to Red.
3. Click the Ellipse tool, position the crosshair near the upper-left corner of the page, then begin dragging.
4. While still dragging, press the → key three times.
5. While still dragging, press the [↑] key four times.
6. Continue dragging until the grid is the full width of the page, then release the mouse button.
   Your grid should resemble Figure 87.
7. Save your work, then close the Gridify Skills document.

Figure 87 Skills Review, Part 4 completed

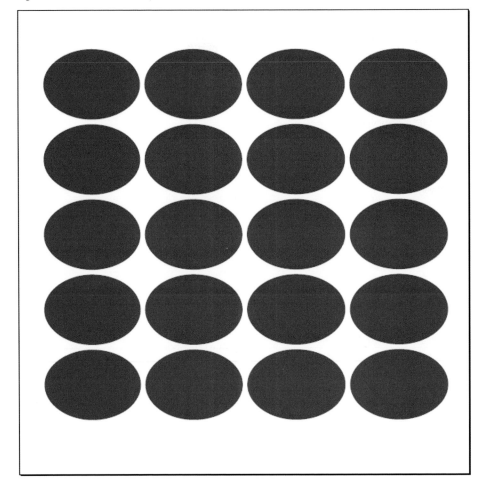

Execute a super step and repeat

1. Open ID 8-14.indd, then save it as **Super Step and Repeat Skills**.
2. Click the Selection tool, then select the blue circle.
3. Press and hold [option] (Mac) or [Alt] (Win), then begin dragging to the right.
4. While still dragging right, release [option] (Mac) or [Alt] (Win), then press the ➝ key six times, but do not release the mouse button.
5. Drag down to the lower-right corner, release the mouse button, then compare your result to Figure 88.
6. Save your work, then close the Super Step and Repeat Skills document.

Figure 88 Skills Review, Part 5 completed

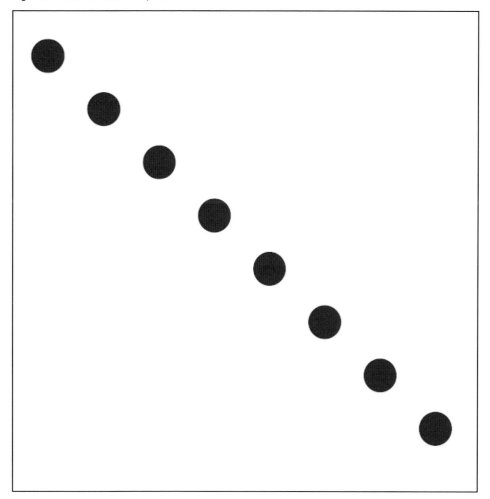

(continued)

Apply Live Corner effects

1. Open ID 8-15.indd, then save it as **Effects Skills**.
2. Navigate to page 2, select the image, then click the small yellow square.
3. Drag the top-right diamond left inward approximately 0.25" to round all four corners.
4. Do the same to the images on pages 3, 4, and 5.
5. Select the image on page 2, click the yellow square, press and hold [option] (Mac) or [Alt] (Win), then click any of the yellow diamonds one time to change all four corners of the frame to the Fancy corner effect.

6. Select the image on page 3, click the yellow square, press and hold [option] (Mac) or [Alt] (Win), then click any of the yellow diamonds two times.
   All four corners of the frame change to the Bevel corner effect.
7. Select the image on page 4, click the yellow square, press and hold [option] (Mac) or [Alt] (Win), then click any of the yellow diamonds three times to change all four corners of the frame to the Inset corner effect.
8. Select the image on page 5, click the yellow square, press and hold [option] (Mac) or [Alt] (Win), then click any of the yellow diamonds four times so all four

corners of the frame change to the Inverse Rounded corner effect.
9. Compare your spread to Figure 89.
10. Navigate to page 1, then select all four frames on the page.
11. Click Object on the menu bar, then click Corner Options.
12. Verify that the Make All Settings the Same button ⚙ is activated.
13. Enter **.1** in any of the four text boxes, then press [tab].
14. Click any of the four shape list arrows, then click Rounded.
15. Click OK, then save your work.

Figure 89 Live Corner Effects reviewed

as with all true beauty
the flowers require no flattery

· · ·

they are confident
in their grace

the water moves
and rolls and crashes

· · ·

the trees listen
and observe

Images courtesy of Chris Botello

Work with effects and object styles

1. On page 1, select the second image from the left.
2. Click Object on the menu bar, point to Effects, then click Inner Shadow.
3. Enter the settings shown in Figure 90, but do *not* click OK.
4. Click the words Drop Shadow on the left side of the Effects dialog box, then enter the settings shown in Figure 91.
5. Click OK.
6. With the image still selected, open the Effects panel, then click the Add object effect icon on the panel to see which effects are checked in the pull-down menu.
7. Drag the Add object effect icon from the Effects panel beside Object: Normal 100% to the image of the flower to the right.
8. Save your work.
9. With the second frame still selected, click Window on the menu bar, point to Styles, then click Object Styles.

Figure 90 Inner Shadow settings

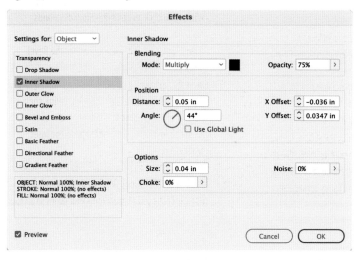

Figure 91 Drop Shadow settings

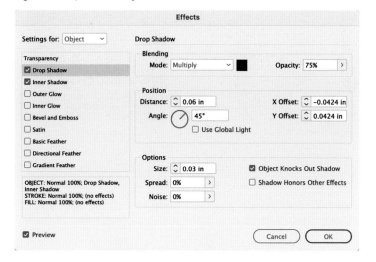

10. Click the Object Styles panel menu button, then click New Object Style.
11. Type **Inner and Drop Shadow** in the Style Name text box, then make sure in the lower-left section that the Inner Shadow and Drop Shadow effects are checked.
12. Uncheck all the attributes in the General section.
13. Click OK.
14. Use the Selection tool to select the leftmost image, then click Inner and Drop Shadow on the Object Styles panel.
15. Apply the Inner and Drop Shadow object style to all the other frames in the document, then compare your page 1 layout to Figure 92.
16. Save your work, then close the **Effects Skills** document.

Figure 92 Object styles reviewed

The Road to Hana

a visual journey through Maui

Images courtesy of Chris Botello

Work with multiple page sizes

1. Click File on the menu bar, point to New, then click Document.
2. Enter the values shown in Figure 93, then click OK.
3. Open the Pages panel, then double-click the page 2 thumbnail.
4. Click the Edit page size button on the Pages panel, then click Compact Disc.
5. With page 2 still targeted on the Pages panel, click Layout on the menu bar, click Margins and Columns, set the four Margins text boxes to .125, then click OK.
6. Double-click page 3 on the Pages panel.
7. Click the Edit page size button on the Pages panel, then click Custom.
   The Custom Page Size dialog box opens.
8. Type **3 × 5 Envelope** in the Name text box, set the Width to 5, then set the Height to 3.
9. Click Add.
10. Click OK, then save the file as **Multiple Page Size Skills**.
11. Close the Multiple Page Size Skills document.

Figure 93 New Document dialog box

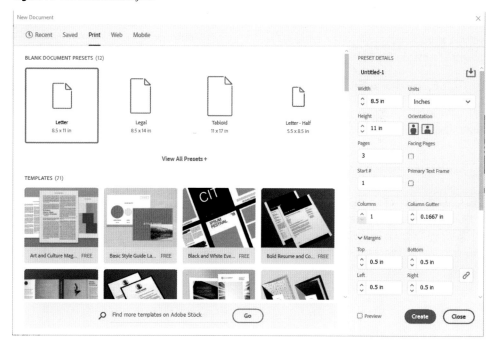

A new magazine named *WEIRD* is courting you with the idea of hiring you in its art department. The company has asked you to submit a sample of a cover design. You are an avid fan of the magazine, and you know that every month the designers do something interesting with the title artwork. You decide to use a customized stroke style to create a '70s look.

1. Open ID 8-16.indd, then save it as **Weird**.
2. Open the Stroke Styles dialog box, click New, type **Vibe** in the Name text box, click the Type list arrow, then click Stripe.
3. Click the bottom stripe, then drag the top triangle down until the Start value reads 85.
4. Click the top stripe, then drag the bottom triangle up until the Width value reads 15.
5. Add a new stripe between the two stripes, change the Start value to 30, change the Width value to 42, then click OK twice.
6. Click the Direct Selection tool, then click the W to select all of the letters.
7. Set the fill color to [None], then add a 6 pt. black stroke.
8. On the Stroke panel, change the Type to Vibe.
9. Deselect, compare your work to Figure 94, save your work, then close the WEIRD document.

Figure 94 Completed Project Builder 1

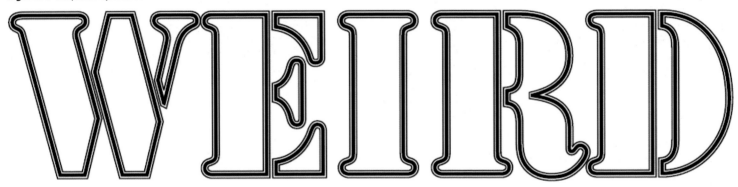

You run a small graphics business out of your home. A friend comes to you with an old photo of her grandmother. She wants to put it in a 3.5" × 5" frame and asks you to create a soft oval effect for the photo.

1. Open ID 8-17.indd, then save it as **Vignette**.
2. Click the Selection tool, select the frame, then fill it with the Tan swatch.
3. With the frame still selected, click the Ellipse tool, position the pointer over the center point of the selected frame, press and hold [option] (Mac) or [Alt] (Win), then click.
4. Type **3** in the Width text box, type **4.5** in the Height text box, then click OK.
5. Verify that the ellipse you just created has no fill or stroke.
6. Click the Add object effect icon *fx.* on the Effects panel, then click Basic Feather.
7. Click the Basic Feather check box, type **.75** in the Feather Width text box, then click OK.
8. Place the file named Portrait.psd from the drive and folder where your Chapter 8 Data Files are stored.
9. Click the Direct Selection tool, then center the woman's face in the oval.
10. Click View on the menu bar, point to Extras, click Hide Frame Edges if it is not already selected, deselect all, then compare your work to Figure 95.
11. Save your work, then close the Vignette document.

Figure 95 Completed Project Builder 2

Image courtesy of Chris Botello

Your client has opened a coffee shop near your home office. She doesn't have a big budget for purchasing artwork, so she's asked you to create some digital art to hang on her walls. She gives you an old photo and tells you she wants you to use it to create "something old and modern at the same time."

1. Open ID 8-18.indd, then save it as **Granny Warhol**.
2. Make the Photos layer visible, then select the top-left graphics frame using the Selection tool.
3. Click the Blending mode list arrow on the Effects panel, then select Multiply.
4. Select the top-right graphics frame, then change the blending mode to Screen.
5. Select the bottom-left graphics frame, then change the blending mode to Hard Light.
6. Select the bottom-right graphics frame, drag the Opacity slider to 30%, then deselect all.
7. Press and hold [option] (Mac) or [Alt] (Win), then click the Background layer on the Layers panel to select the four colored squares behind the photos.
8. Verify that the center reference point on the Transform panel is selected.
9. Double-click the Rotate tool, type **90** in the Angle text box, then click OK.
10. Save your work, deselect all, compare your work to Figure 96, then close the Granny Warhol document.

Figure 96 Completed Design Project

DESIGN PROJECT 2

This project is designed to challenge your ability to recognize and distinguish pathfinders visually.

1. Open ID 8-19.indd or refer to Figure 97.
2. On a piece of paper write the numbers 1 through 5 for recording answers to this project.
3. Identify the pathfinder used in each of the numbered examples shown in the file and Figure 97, and write your answers on your numbered piece of paper.

Figure 97 Design Project Challenge

Original

1.

2.

3.

4.

5.

THE DARWIN
BICENTENNIAL
PART TWO
—

MODERN
DARWINS

THE FATHER OF EVOLUTION WOULD BE THRILLED TO SEE THE SCIENCE HIS THEORY HAS INSPIRED.

ONE LIGHT, ONE DARK: THESE TWO MICE ARE THE SAME
SPECIES, AND PARTICIPANTS IN GROUNDBREAKING
SCIENCE EXPLORING HOW NATURAL SELECTION ACTS
ON GENES, CREATING A WORLD OF DIVERSITY.

Layout/design by Elaine Bradley. From "The Darwin Bicentennial: Part Two–Modern Darwins." *National Geographic Magazine*, Vol. 215, No. 2, February, 2009

PROJECT DESCRIPTION

In this project, you will explore ways in which graphic designers use a photo to inspire their layout. You will focus on color and different design elements that interact with each other on a comprehensive spread. The goal of this project is to create a layout that incorporates an image and simple blocks of text inspired by a photo.

SKILLS TO EXPLORE

- Apply Color
- Work with Spot Colors
- Work with Gradients
- Working with Placed Images

- Place Multiple Graphics
- Use the Links Panel
- Explore Image Resolution Issues
- Place Vector Graphics

SOFT SKILLS CHALLENGE

Learning to pay attention to details is critical in graphic design. Regardless of your project's composition, noticing the smaller details shows that you are tuned in to the nuances of your project and understand the importance of creating balance on the page. The goal of this project is to compare printed advertisements in order to train your eye to notice details.

In this challenge, you and two partners will scour magazines or newspapers and choose 10–12 advertisements to compare. Lay the advertisements side-by-side and take note of the following: details that were included to enhance the overall feel of the advertisement as well as details that were overlooked. In this second category, you might include a misaligned text box, misspelling, or color-matching issue, among others. Discuss your findings with your partners.

◀ A researcher studies two mice of the same species to show how Darwin's theory of natural selection creates genetic diversity.

GETTING STARTED

Challenge yourself to see beyond the visible image.

1. Look over the *National Geographic* spread "Modern Darwins". Notice the simplicity in the layout. Envision a different title treatment by placing "Modern" in landscape mode. How does this small change impact the left-facing page and the spread as a whole? With the title taking up less real estate on the spread, would you need additional text to fill the white space?

2. Pay careful attention to the color choice. The designer chose to pick up the blue from the glove to use in two text elements. In this way, the color helps connect the image and the text. Why were those text elements chosen? Would you have selected others? How might the left-facing page look different if all the text were black?

3. Using a photograph that calls out to you, experiment with image and text placement. Practice layering objects by placing a drawn image behind the photo. If the photo is hard to distinguish from the background, adjust the color or create a drop shadow. Pull a color or colors from the photograph to use in your background and be selective with how and where the color(s) are used.

AMAZING NYC
1 2 3 4
AN OTHER DAY IN NEW YORK CITY
BRIDGE
BROOKLYN
BKLYN
LIMITED
BIG APPLE   Yuliya Evstratenko/Shutterstock

THE DARWIN
BICENTENNIAL
PART TWO

MODERN
DARWINS

THE FATHER OF EVOLUTION WOULD BE THRILLED TO SEE THE SCIENCE HIS THEORY HAS INSPIRED.

ONE LIGHT, ONE DARK, THESE TWO MICE ARE THE SAME SPECIES, AND PARTICIPANTS IN GROUNDBREAKING SCIENCE EXPLORING HOW NATURAL SELECTION ACTS ON GENES, CREATING A WORLD OF DIVERSITY

56 NATIONAL GEOGRAPHIC • FEBRUARY 2009

Layout/design by Elaine Bradley. From "The Darwin Bicentennial: Part Two-Modern Darwins." *National Geographic Magazine*, Vol. 215, No. 2, February, 2009

PROJECT DESCRIPTION

In this project, you will focus on hierarchy of elements and the ways in which imagery and text complement each other to build upon the layout you created in your Design Project. The goal of this project is to create a simple yet comprehensive spread utilizing color and attention to detail.

SKILLS TO EXPLORE

- Interface InDesign with Photoshop
- Use Creative Cloud Libraries
- Use the Pen Tool
- Reshape Frames and Apply Stroke Effects
- Work with Polygons and Compound Paths
- Work with Advanced Text Features
- Use the Pathfinder Panel
- Create New Stroke Styles

SOFT SKILLS CHALLENGE

Communication is a key skill for many careers and is especially important in the design world. Often, designers put their heads together to brainstorm ideas or concepts for a project. These ideas need to be communicated, not only amongst the group, but with clients and other members of the team.

In this challenge, you will work with a group of two or more peers to communicate your design approach. Share your photo and explain the reasons for your layout and composition. Allow your peers time to ask questions and offer their suggestions and feedback. Then invite your peers to present their ideas as well. The goal of this challenge is to think through your concept and communicate your ideas intelligently to others.

GETTING STARTED

As you begin to create your comprehensive spread, keep simplicity in mind. Often the most impactful images and layouts are those that are easiest for the reader to track.

1. Find the focal point. Look back at the model spread. Notice how the blue hand holding the mouse is the focal point of the image. The mouse is pointing down, just as the word "Modern" is set in portrait mode. Now look at your chosen photo. What is the focal point of your image? How might you incorporate that into your text formatting?

2. Focus on hierarchy. Which elements are most important in your design? Font choice and font size are not the only ways to convey importance. Color and placement are other ways to highlight important elements for the reader.

3. Be creative. The gloved hand looks as if it is forming an "o" with its fingers. Perhaps that is the reason the artist chose to make the "o" in "Modern" the same shade of blue as the glove. Notice how the designer placed the "o" both in text and image on the same plane. Allow yourself room to add your own creative flair to your spread.

4. Use supporting elements. While the eye is initially drawn to the gloved hand holding the mouse, a second mouse helps to "anchor" the image. The designer chose to mirror its placement with the word "Darwins" to create balance on the spread. In addition, the placement of the caption provides additional information without detracting from the image itself.

BY
CRAIG WELCH

PHOTOGRAPHS BY
BRIAN SKERRY

Secrets of the Whales

WE'RE LEARNING THAT
SOME GROUPS OF WHALES
AND DOLPHINS HAVE THEIR
OWN DIALECTS, DIETS,
AND ROUTINES—CULTURAL
DIFFERENCES ONCE THOUGHT
TO BE UNIQUE TO HUMANS.

KILLER FEAST

A killer whale, or
orca, chases herring
in a Norwegian fjord.
Groups of killer whales
(which are technically
part of the dolphin
family) have distinct
eating habits. Some
corral schooling fish.
Others hunt sharks or
seals, while some feast
almost exclusively on
salmon. These habits
are partly cultural—
learned behaviors
passed down through
generations.

A killer whale corrals an army of herring. Effective use of typography, scale, color, and white space work in harmony with the scale and movement found in the photograph.

Photograph by Brian Skerry. From "Secrets of the Whales." *National Geographic Magazine*, Vol. 239, No. 5, May, 2021

restaurant	signature	chef	review	hours	info
SHAME ON THE MOON		Bill Carter	*"The fish selection is imaginitive and varied. Be sure to sample from the chef's seafood tasting menu on Thursday nights."*	5-10	
BLAME IT ON MIDNIGHT		Ann Mahoney	*"The pasta menu is Mahoney's secret weapon. The fettucine en brodo is rivaled only by the tortellini, which was simply a marvel."*	3-11	
THE BLACK SWAN		Kelli Jacob	*"With all of the incredible seafood specialty dishes, you might overlook the succulent beef and veal selections. That would be a tragedy."*	4-11	
CHEZ BLAKE		Tim Chen	*"The juxtaposition of textures is stunning. My favorite was a crunchy crab salad served on a smooth lime gelee."*	4-10	
THE GROOVE POD		Peter Pardon	*"Peter Pardon is a culinary master of the unexpected."*	5-11	

key

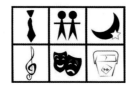

 = DRESS TO IMPRESS   = ENTERTAINMENT, DANCING, ETC.

= CHILDREN'S MENU   = PRE-THEATER MENU

= LATE-NIGHT MENU   = TAKE-OUT

CHAPTER **9**

WORKING WITH TABS & TABLES

1. Work with Tabs
2. Create and Format a Table
3. Format Text in a Table
4. Place Graphics in a Table

Adobe Certified Professional in Print & Digital Media Publication Using Adobe InDesign

2. Project Setup and Interface

This objective covers the interface setup and program settings that assist in an efficient and effective workflow, as well as knowledge about ingesting digital assets for a project.

2.1 Create a document with the appropriate settings for web, print, and mobile.
  A Set appropriate document settings for printed and on-screen images.

2.3 Use nonprinting design tools in the interface to aid in design or workflow.
  B Use rulers.
  C Use guides and grids.

2.4 Import assets into a project.
  B Place assets in an InDesign document.

4. Creating and Modifying Document Elements

This objective covers core tools and functionality of the application, as well as tools that affect the visual appearance of document elements.

4.1 Use core tools and features to lay out visual elements.
  B Manipulate graphics in frames.

4.2 Add and manipulate text using appropriate typographic settings.
  B Use appropriate character settings in a design.
  C Use appropriate paragraph settings in a design.

4.4 Transform digital graphics and media within a publication.
  A Modify frames and frame content.

4.5 Use basic reconstructing and editing techniques to manipulate document content.
  C Use the Story Editor to edit text within a project.

4.8 Create and edit tables.
  A Create a table to display data.
  B Edit tables and cells.

WORK WITH TABS

▶ **What You'll Do**

In this lesson, you will use the tab ruler to position text at specific horizontal positions within a frame.

Dancewear Sales				
Product	**# Purchased**	**# Sold**	**Best Color**	**Profit**
T-Shirts	50	45	White	$950.00
Sweatshirts	100	100	Navy	$1500.00
Leotards	200	150	White	$725.00
Tap Shoes	20	2	n/a	$60.50

Using Tabs

Tabs are used to position text at specific horizontal locations within a text frame. Figure 1 shows a simple layout created using tabs. The heading "Column 2" and the five items beneath it are all aligned with the left-justified tab shown in the Tabs panel.

Note that the left edge of the tab ruler in the Tabs panel is aligned with the left edge of the text frame. This alignment occurs by default when you select a text frame and open the Tabs panel. The alignment of the text frame with the tab ruler makes it easier to note the horizontal position of text within a frame. For example, in the same figure, you can see at a glance that Column 2 is positioned two inches in from the left edge of the text frame.

If you scroll up or down, or resize the page or the text frame, the text frame will no longer be aligned with the tab ruler. To realign the two, simply click the Position Panel above Text Frame button on the Tabs panel. The tab ruler will move to realign itself with the text frame.

Figure 1 Tabs panel

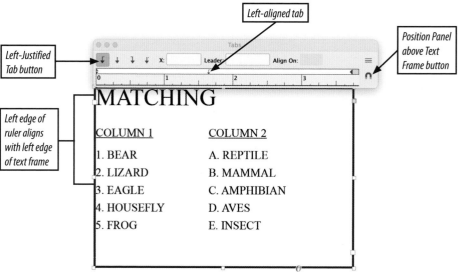

Left-aligned tab

Position Panel above Text Frame button

Left-Justified Tab button

Left edge of ruler aligns with left edge of text frame

MATCHING

COLUMN 1	COLUMN 2
1. BEAR	A. REPTILE
2. LIZARD	B. MAMMAL
3. EAGLE	C. AMPHIBIAN
4. HOUSEFLY	D. AVES
5. FROG	E. INSECT

Once text has been aligned on a tab, moving the tab moves the text as well. In Figure 2, the tab has been moved right to 2.5", and the left edge of the text is also aligned at that position. The text does not need to be selected to be moved. Simply moving the tab moves the text.

To delete a tab from the tab ruler, simply drag it off the tab ruler.

Using Different Tab Alignments

The Tabs panel offers four types of tab buttons for aligning text—Left-Justified Tab, Center-Justified Tab, Right-Justified Tab, and Align to Decimal Tab. To create a tab in the tab ruler, you click a tab button, then click a location in the tab ruler or click a tab button, then enter

a location in the X text box in the Tabs panel.

In Figure 3, the second column of text is aligned with a left-justified tab. Note that the tab is selected in the tab ruler—it is highlighted with blue. When a tab is selected, its horizontal location is indicated in the X text box. This tab is positioned at the 2.25" mark.

Figure 2 Moving a tab

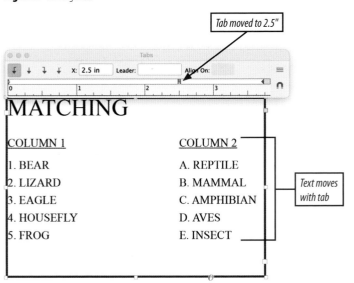

Figure 3 Using the Left-Justified Tab button

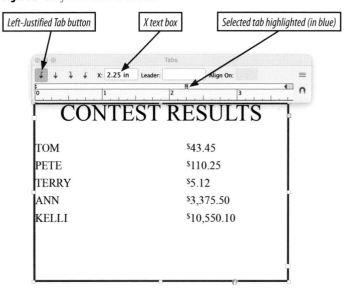

In Figure 4, the tab of the second column has been changed to a center-justified tab.

Its horizontal location remains unchanged; however, now the center points of the text are aligned at the 2.25" mark.

TIP You change a tab from one type to another by clicking the tab in the tab ruler, then clicking a different type of tab button.

In Figure 5, the position of the right-column tab has not changed, but its alignment has changed to a right-justified tab. Notice that the lines of text are all aligned on the right.

Figure 4 Using the Center-Justified Tab button

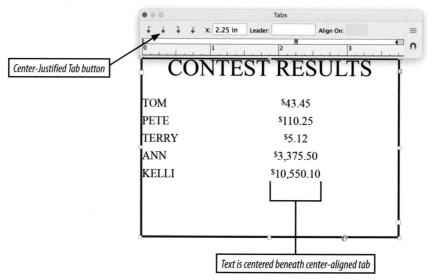

Center-Justified Tab button

Text is centered beneath center-aligned tab

Figure 5 Using the Right-Justified Tab button

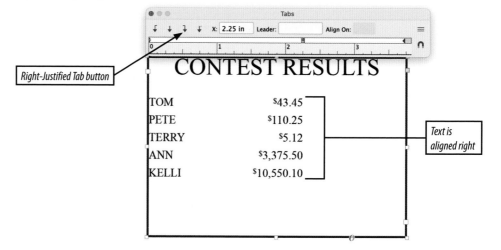

Right-Justified Tab button

Text is aligned right

In Figure 6, the tab alignment has been changed to an align-to-decimal tab. The decimal points of each number in the column are aligned at the 2.25" mark. This tab is a good choice when working with numbers.

When you use an align-to-decimal tab, you can align text with characters other than a decimal point, such as an asterisk or a dollar sign. As shown in Figure 7, by clicking the Align to Decimal Tab button, then typing a $ in the Align On text box, the column is aligned on the dollar sign.

Figure 6 Using the Align to Decimal Tab button

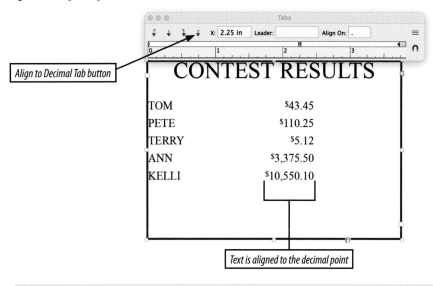

Align to Decimal Tab button

Text is aligned to the decimal point

Figure 7 Using the Align On text box

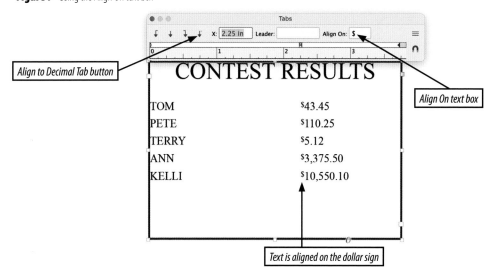

Align to Decimal Tab button

Align On text box

Text is aligned on the dollar sign

Using Text Insets

When you enter text in a text frame, a **text inset** determines how far from the edge of the frame the text is positioned, or *inset,* into the frame. Text insets can be entered for all four sides of a text frame—top and bottom, left and right. For example, a .5" text inset means that text will be inset one-half inch on all four sides of a frame.

In Figure 8, a heavy black stroke has been added to the text frame. The addition of the stroke makes the position of the text visually unpleasing—the text is too close to the top and the left edges of the frame.

Text inset values are entered in the Text Frame Options dialog box. In Figure 9, a .25" text inset has been added to the top and left sides of the frame. Note the light blue line that indicates the top and left margins of the text within the text frame.

| **TIP** When you use tabs in a text frame that has a text inset, the tab ruler aligns itself with the light blue text inset line, not the left edge of the text frame.

Figure 8 Applying a rule creates the need for a text inset

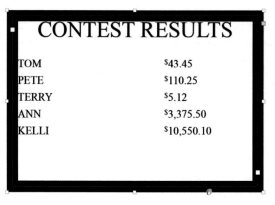

Figure 9 Applying a text inset

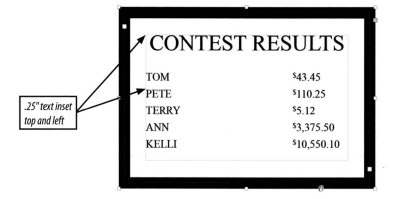

.25" text inset top and left

Adding Rules Above or Below Paragraphs

Many times, you will want to add a horizontal rule above or below a line or more of text. InDesign regards rules above and below text as paragraph attributes—in other words, they are part of the text formatting. If you resize the text—let's say you make it larger—the rule increases however much is necessary to continue underlining the text. If you move the text, the rule moves with it.

Rules for text are defined in the Paragraph Rules dialog box, shown in Figure 10. This dialog box allows you to specify a number of attributes for the rule, including its color and its weight. This is where you also specify whether the rule is positioned above or below the text.

When you apply a rule below text, the rule is positioned by default at the baseline of the text. Often, you will find this to be visually unpleasing. Figure 11 shows text with a rule positioned at its baseline.

Generally speaking, a rule below looks best when it is slightly below the baseline. Use the Offset text box in the Paragraph Rules dialog box to accomplish this. When the rule is defined as a Rule Below, a positive offset value moves the rule *down* from the baseline.

Figure 10 Paragraph Rules dialog box

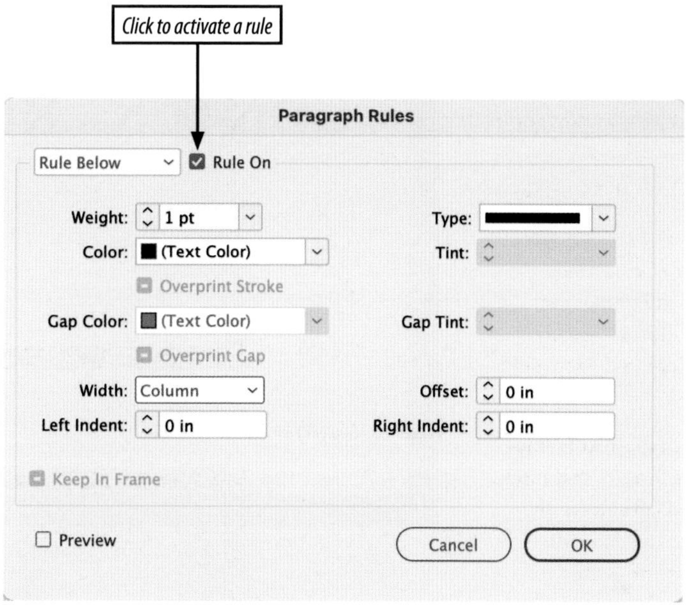

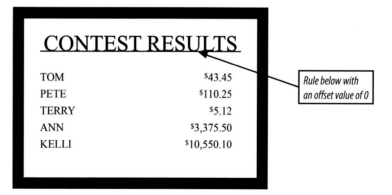

Figure 11 Rule below with 0 pt. offset value

Rule offsets are best specified in points. A **point** is 1/72 of an inch. This small increment allows you to be very specific when positioning a rule. For a rule below, a two- or three-point offset value is usually best. Figure 12 shows the same rule with a three-point offset.

TIP If your ruler units are set to inches, you can still enter values as points. Simply type p before a value to specify it as points. For example, if you want to specify a six-point offset value, type p6 in the Offset text box.

Set a text inset and insert tabs

1. Open ID 9-1.indd, then save it as **Tabs**.

2. Click the **Selection tool** ▶, click the **blue text**, click **Object** on the menu bar, then click **Text Frame Options**.

3. Disable the **Make all settings the same feature** 🔗 if necessary.

4. In the Inset Spacing section, type **.25** in the **Top text box**, type **.125** in the **Left text box**, then click **OK**.

   The text is inset inside the frame.

5. Click **Type** on the menu bar, then click **Tabs**.

   As shown in Figure 13, the left edge of the tab ruler is automatically aligned with the left edge of the text inset so the measurements in the ruler match the text exactly.

Figure 12 Rule below with 3 pt. offset value

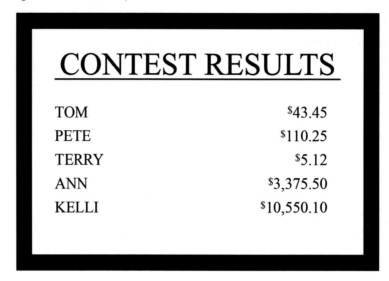

Figure 13 Tabs panel

Left edge of tab ruler aligns with left edge of text inset

6. Click the **Type tool** $\boxed{T}$, select **all the text** in the frame, then click the **Left-Justified Tab button** ↧ on the Tabs panel.

7. Position the pointer in the space **just above the numbers**—in the top third of the tab ruler— then click and drag until the **X text box** reads **1 in**, as shown in Figure 14.

8. Click to create a **second tab** at **2"**.

9. Click **anywhere in the tab ruler** to the right of the second tab to add a **third tab**.

   The third tab remains selected, and its horizontal location is displayed in the X text box.

10. Double-click the **value** in the **X text box**, type **3**, then press **[return] (Mac)** or **[Enter] (Win)**.

The third tab is moved to the 3" mark.

11. Using either of the two methods from the above steps, add a **new tab at 4"**, then compare your work to Figure 15.

12. Save your work, then continue to the next set of steps.

You inset text from the top and left margins in the Text Frame Options dialog box. You then selected all the text in the frame and set four left-justified tabs at 1" intervals.

Figure 14 Adding a tab to the tab ruler

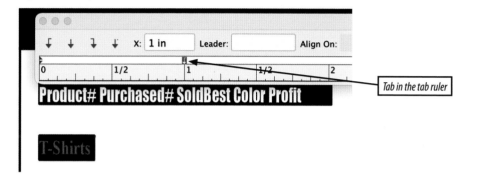

Tab in the tab ruler

Figure 15 Adding a fourth tab

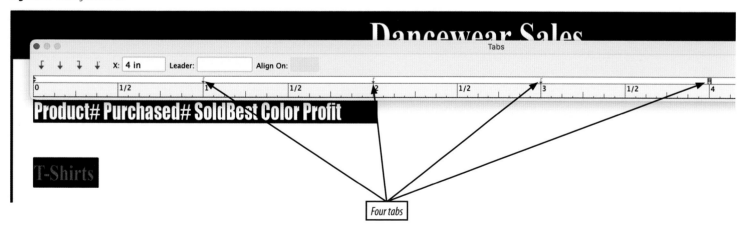

Four tabs

Enter text using tabs

1. Click the **Type tool** T , click to the **left of the first # sign** in the first line of text, then press **[tab]**.

2. Tab the remaining text in the first line so your page resembles Figure 16.

3. Click to the **right of the word T-Shirts**, press **[tab]**, then type **50**.

4. Press **[tab]**, type **45**, press **[tab]**, type **White**, press **[tab]**, then type **$950**.

5. Using the same method, enter the information shown in Figure 17 so your page matches the figure.

   Now that the text is entered, note that the text is not centered in the frame—there is a large gap of space to the right of the last column.

6. Select all the text, then press and hold **[command] [B] (Mac)** or **[Ctrl] [B] (Win)** to open the Text Frame Options dialog box.

7. Change the **Left Inset Spacing value** to **.5**, then click **OK**.

   Everything shifts to the right and the tabs remain spaced at 1" intervals. Note that the left edge of the tab ruler is no longer aligned with the left edge of the text inset.

8. Click in the **text** to deselect it, then click the **Position Panel above Text Frame button** n on the Tabs panel.

   The left edge of the tab ruler realigns itself with the left edge of the text inset.

9. Save your work, then continue to the next set of steps.

You used tabs to enter text at specific horizontal locations. You modified the left text inset value, noting that the 1" tab intervals were not affected.

Figure 16 Tabbing the top line of text

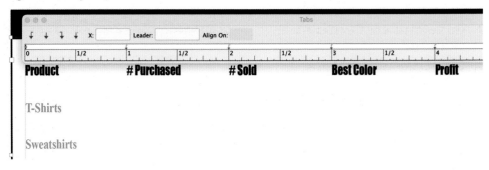

Figure 17 Entering values in each column

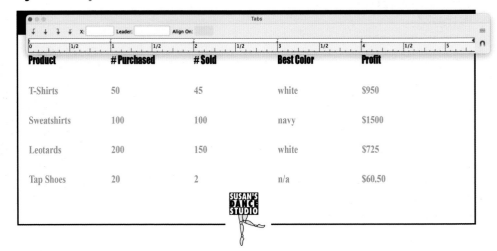

Change the type and location of tabs

1. Select **all the blue text**.

2. Click the **first tab** at the **1" location** in the tab ruler to select it.

3. Click the **Center-Justified Tab button** ↓ .

   The tab changes to a center-justified tab and the first column of text is now centered at the 1" mark.

4. With the **first tab** in the tab ruler still highlighted, select the **value in the X text box**, type **1.3**, then press **[return] (Mac)** or **[Enter] (Win)**.

   The first column is now centered in relation to the # Purchased column headline.

5. Click the **second tab** to highlight it, click the **Center-Justified Tab button** ↓ , then relocate the tab to **2.3"**.

6. Click the **third tab** to highlight it, click the **Center-Justified Tab button** ↓ , then relocate the tab to **3.25"**.

7. Click the **fourth tab** to highlight it, click the **Align to Decimal Tab button** ↓ , then relocate the tab to **4.15"**.

8. Select only the **"# Sold" text** in the top row, then relocate its tab to **2.15"**.

9. Type **.00** after $950, $1500, and $725.

10. Click **Edit** on the menu bar, click **Deselect All**, save your work, then compare your page with Figure 18.

11. Save your work, then continue to the next set of steps.

TIP Be sure to save your work because you will revert to this stage of the exercise in the next set of steps.

You selected tabs, changed them to different types of tabs, then moved tabs in the tab ruler.

Figure 18 Reformatted tabs

Dancewear Sales

Product	# Purchased	# Sold	Best Color	Profit
T-Shirts	50	45	white	$950.00
Sweatshirts	100	100	navy	$1500.00
Leotards	200	150	white	$725.00
Tap Shoes	20	2	n/a	$60.50

Apply tab leaders and rules

1. Select all the **blue text**, then click the **first tab** in the tab ruler to highlight it.

2. Type a **period (.)** in the **Leader text box** in the Tabs panel, press **[return] (Mac)** or **[Enter] (Win)**, then deselect all.

    As shown in Figure 19, the period is used as a character that connects the product listings to the first tab.

3. Select all the **blue text**, click the **second tab** in the tab ruler, type a **period (.)** in the **Leader text**

box, press **[space bar]**, then press **[return] (Mac)** or **[Enter] (Win)**.

   Using the space creates a dot pattern that has more space between each dot.

4. Click the **third tab** in the tab ruler, type an **asterisk (*)** in the **Leader text box**, then press **[return] (Mac)** or **[Enter] (Win)**.

5. Click the **fourth tab** in the tab ruler, type a **hyphen (-) followed by a space** in the **Leader text box**, press **[return] (Mac)** or **[Enter] (Win)**, deselect, then compare your work to Figure 20.

6. Click **File** on the menu bar, click **Revert**, then click **Revert (Mac)** or **Yes (Win)**.

7. Select **all the text** in the frame.

   Note that when you select all the text, the tab ruler shows eight tabs. These represent all the tabs applied to the selected text—four to the top row and four different tabs to the blue text.

8. Click the **Paragraph panel menu button** , then click **Paragraph Rules**.

9. Click the **list arrow** at the top of the dialog box, click **Rule Below**, then click the **Rule On check box**.

Figure 19 Using a period as a tab leader

Figure 20 Using various characters as tab leaders

Dancewear Sales				
Product	**# Purchased**	**# Sold**	**Best Color**	**Profit**
T-Shirts	50	45************** white	- - - - - - - -	$950.00
Sweatshirts	100	100 ************* navy	- - - - - - -	$1500.00
Leotards	200	150 ************* white	- - - - - - - -	$725.00
Tap Shoes	20	2 ************** n/a	- - - - - - - - - -	$60.50

10. Choose the settings for **Weight**, **Color**, **Offset**, and **Right Indent** as shown in Figure 21, click **OK**, then deselect all.

Note that in the Offset text box, the value was entered as 6 pt. When you tab from the Offset text box to the Right Indent text box, the points value is automatically converted to its equivalent in inches.

11. Select only the **top line of text in the table**, click the **Paragraph panel menu button** ≡, click **Paragraph Rules**, click the **Weight list arrow**, then click **2 pt**.

12. Click the **Type list arrow**, click **Dotted**, click the **Gap Color list arrow**, click **[Paper]**, then click **OK**.

13. Select the **bottom line of blue text**, open the **Paragraph Rules dialog box**, uncheck the **Rule On option**, then click **OK**.

14. Deselect all, save your work, compare your page to Figure 22, then close the Tabs document.

You used the Leader text box in the Tabs panel to set various characters as tab leaders. You used the Paragraph Rules dialog box to apply a rule below the rows of text in the text frame.

Figure 21 Specifying attributes for the rule below

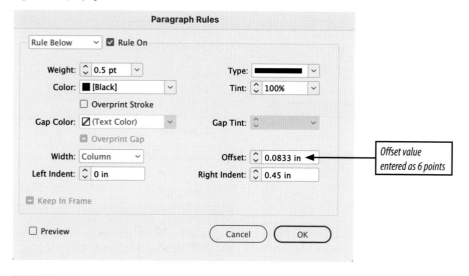

Figure 22 The finished chart

	Dancewear Sales			
Product	**# Purchased**	**# Sold**	**Best Color**	**Profit**
T-Shirts	50	45	white	$950.00
Sweatshirts	100	100	navy	$1500.00
Leotards	200	150	white	$725.00
Tap Shoes	20	2	n/a	$60.50

CREATE AND FORMAT A TABLE

▶ What You'll Do

In this lesson, you will create a table and apply fills and strokes.

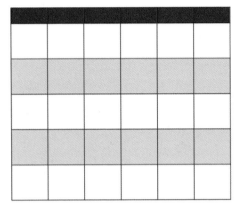

Working with Tables

As with tabs, tables are an efficient method for communicating information and an important component to any layout application. **Tables** consist of rectangles in horizontal **rows** and vertical **columns**. Each rectangle is called a **cell**. Figure 23 shows an example of a table.

The first important thing to note about tables is that InDesign regards them as text. Tables can only be created within a text frame. When you edit a table, you do so with the Type tool. If you select a table with the Selection tool, you can only modify the text frame, not the text or the formatting of the cells in the text frame.

Figure 23 An example of an InDesign table

State	Founded	Area	Capital	Pop	Flag
CONNECTICUT	1788	5,544 sq/mi	Hartford	3,405,000	
MASSACHUSETTS	1788	10,555 sq/mi	Boston	6, 349,000	
NEW HAMPSHIRE	1788	9,351 sq/mi	Concord	1,235,000	
RHODE ISLAND	1790	1,545 sq/mi	Providence	1, 048,00	
VERMONT	1791	9,615 sq/mi	Montpelier	608,000	
MAINE	1829	35,387 sq/mi	Augusta	1,274,000	

Creating Tables

The first step in creating a table is to create a text frame. Once you've created the text frame, you can specify the number of rows and columns for the table in the Insert Table dialog box, shown in Figure 24. When you create the table, it always appears in a default layout, as shown in Figure 25. Note that the default width of the cells is determined by the number of columns and the width of the text frame. In other words, the default width of the cells is the width of the text frame divided by the number of columns.

Figure 24 Insert Table dialog box

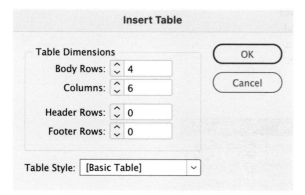

Figure 25 Default table layout

Formatting Tables

The Table panel, shown in Figure 26, is command central for manipulating a table. Even after you create the table, you can modify the number of rows and columns using the Table panel.

After you create the table, you determine the width of the columns and the height of the rows. Individual columns and rows in a table can have varying widths and heights. Column widths and row heights determine the size of any given cell in the table.

Figure 26 Table panel

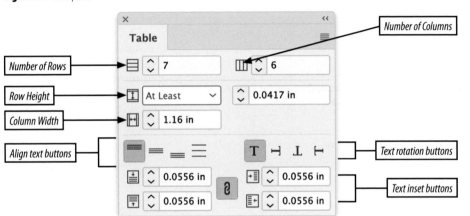

Number of Rows

Row Height

Column Width

Align text buttons

Number of Columns

Text rotation buttons

Text inset buttons

USING TABLE STYLES AND CELL STYLES

If you use tables a lot, you'll be glad to know that you can save any special formatting applied to tables or individual cells for future use by creating table styles or cell styles. This feature is especially useful if you need to create tables with identical formatting. Simply format your table with fills and strokes of your choice, select the table, click the Table Styles panel menu button, then click New Table Style. In the New Table Style dialog box, assign a descriptive name for your new style, and choose options that allow you to further define the style, such as Row Strokes, Column Strokes, and Fills. Click OK, and you'll see your new style on the Table Styles panel. Create a new table, select it, then click the style on the Table Styles panel. The same process is used to create and apply cell styles. The difference is that you only select a cell with the formatting that you wish to save as a style, instead of an entire table. You can also import table and cell styles from other InDesign documents by clicking the Table Styles panel menu button or the Cell Styles panel menu button and then clicking Load Table and Cell Styles. Open the InDesign document with the table and/or cell styles you want, and they will appear in your Table Styles and Cell Styles panels.

You can set the size of all the cells in a table simultaneously by selecting them all and entering values on the Table panel. You can also select a single column or row and specify a width just for that particular column or row.

Figure 27 shows the default table with a modified row height. The top row is 0.5" high, and the rest are all 1.625" high.

TIP You can import a table from a Microsoft Word or Excel document using the Place command. The imported data appears in an InDesign table.

Headers and footers can be specified in the Insert Table dialog box at the time that you create the table, or you can convert existing rows to header or footer rows using the Convert Rows commands on the Table menu.

Applying Strokes and Fills to a Table

Adding color to a table can do wonders for its visual interest and improve the impact of the information it contains. You can apply strokes to the cells of the table to modify the color and the weight of the lines that make up the table grid.

You apply strokes and fills to a table just as you would to other InDesign objects. You can select a single cell, multiple cells, or an entire row or column. Remember, the Type tool is used to select elements of a table. You can then use the Swatches panel to add a fill color or to apply a stroke color, and you can use the Stroke panel to modify the weight of the strokes.

You can also use the Table menu to apply fills and strokes. In addition, the Table menu provides options for alternating fills and strokes by row or column. Alternating fills is a technique that is often used to improve readability and enhance the look of a table. Figure 28 shows a table filled with two alternating colors.

TIP Long tables may continue over many pages in your document. To repeat information from the top or bottom row each time the table is divided, you can use headers or footers.

Figure 27 Modified table

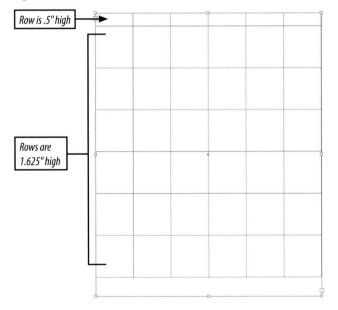

Row is .5" high

Rows are 1.625" high

Figure 28 A table with an alternating fill

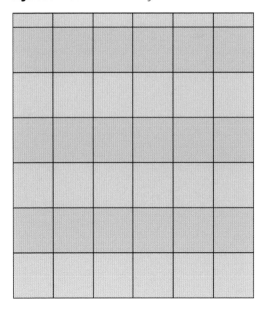

Create a table and change the number of rows

1. Open ID 9-2.indd, then save it as **Table**.

   The document is empty.

2. Close all open panels except for the toolbar, click the **Type tool** T , then create a **text frame** that snaps to all four margin guides.

3. Click **Table** on the menu bar, then click **Insert Table**.

4. Type **4** in the **Body Rows text box**, type **6** in the **Columns text box**, then click **OK**.

5. Click **Window** on the menu bar, point to **Type & Tables**, then click **Table** to show the Table panel.

6. Click the **up arrow** next to the **Number of Rows text box** three times, so there are **seven rows** in the table, as shown in Figure 29.

You created a table, then used the Table panel to increase the number of rows in the table.

Figure 29 Modifying a table with the Table panel

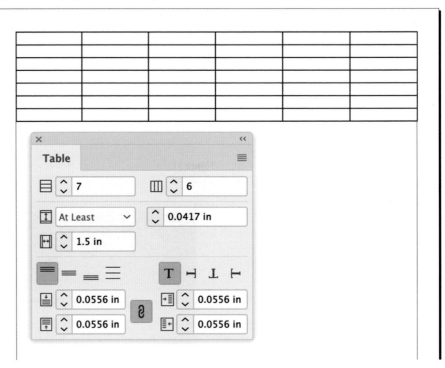

Set the size of a table

1. Position the **pointer** over the **second cell in the first column**, then click and drag to select **all the rows except the top row**, as shown in Figure 30.

2. Click the **Row Height list arrow** on the Table panel, then click **Exactly**.

3. Type **1.4** in the text box to the right of the **Row Height text box**, press **[return] (Mac)** or **[Enter] (Win)**, then compare your work to Figure 31.

4. Position the **pointer** over the **left edge of the top row**.

   When the pointer becomes a heavy black arrow, click to select the entire top row.

5. Click the **Row Height list arrow** on the Table panel, then click **Exactly**.

6. Type **.625** in the text box next to the Row Height text box, then press **[return] (Mac)** or **[Enter] (Win)**.

   The bottom row disappears, and an overset text icon appears in the bottom-right corner of the text frame, indicating that there is no longer enough room in the text frame to hold all the rows in the table.

7. Position the **pointer** over the **left edge of the second row** so the heavy black arrow appears again.

8. Click to select the **second row**, click the **Table panel menu button** ≡ , point to **Delete**, then click **Row**.

   The entire second row is deleted, and the overset text icon disappears because all six rows now fit in the text frame.

You selected six rows and entered a value for their height on the Table panel. You selected only the top row, then entered a different value for its height. You then deleted a row so all rows could fit in the text frame.

Figure 30 Selecting multiple rows

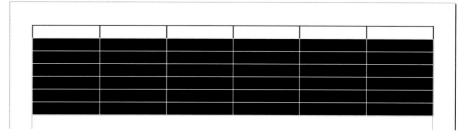

Figure 31 Formatting the height of selected rows

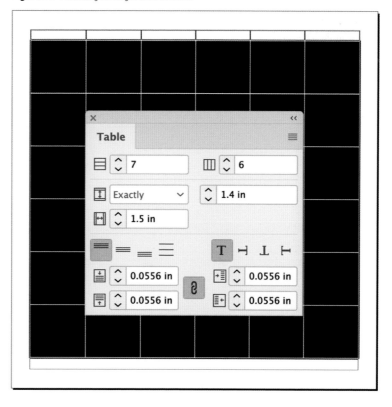

Apply strokes to a table

1. Position the **pointer** over the **top-left corner of the table** so a black diagonal arrow appears, then click to select the **entire table**.

2. Click **Table** on the menu bar, point to **Cell Options**, then click **Strokes and Fills**.

3. Click the **Weight list arrow** in the Cell Options dialog box, then click **2 pt**.

4. Click the **Color list arrow**, then click **Navy**.

5. Click **OK**, then click the **pasteboard** to deselect all.

6. Click **View** on the menu bar, point to **Grids & Guides**, click **Hide Guides**, click **View** on the menu bar again, point to **Extras**, click **Hide Frame Edges,** then compare your table to Figure 32.

You selected all the cells of the table, then applied strokes.

Figure 32 Viewing strokes applied to cells

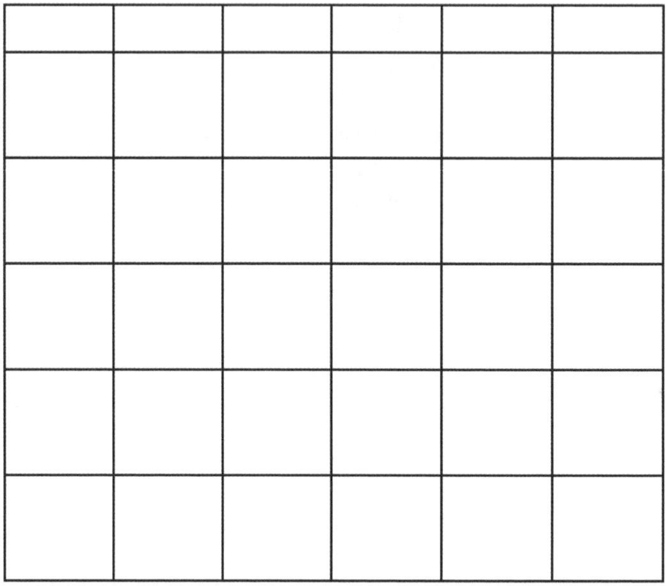

Apply fills to a table

1. Position the **pointer** over the **top-left corner of the table** so the black diagonal arrow appears, then click once to select the entire table.

2. Click **Table** on the menu bar, point to **Table Options**, then click **Alternating Fills**.

3. Click the **Alternating Pattern list arrow**, then click **Every Other Row**.

4. Click the **first Color list arrow** on the left side of the dialog box, click **Black**, type **20** in the **Tint text box**, then click **OK**.

5. Click the **pasteboard** to deselect all, then compare your table to Figure 33.

6. Select the **entire top row**, click **Table** on the menu bar, point to **Cell Options**, then click **Strokes and Fills**.

7. Click the **Color list arrow** in the **Cell Fill section** of the dialog box, click **Red**, type **100** in the Tint text box, then click **OK**.

8. Click the **pasteboard** to deselect all, then compare your table to Figure 34.

9. Save your work, then continue to the next set of steps.

You applied a fill to three rows simultaneously by using the Alternating Fills command. You then changed the fill color of the first row.

Figure 33 Applying alternating fills

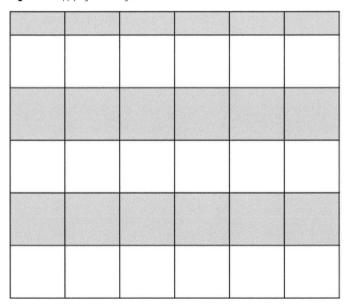

Figure 34 Changing the fill color of the first row

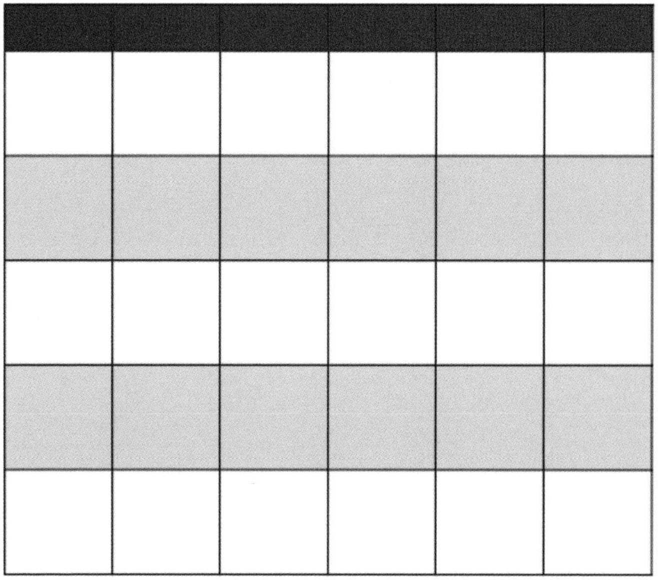

FORMAT TEXT IN A TABLE

restaurant	signature	chef	review	hours	info
SHAME ON THE MOON		Bill Cohen	*"The fish selection is imaginative and varied. Be sure to sample from the chef's seafood tasting menu on Thursday nights."*	5-10	dress to impress late night menu entertainment
BLAME IT ON MIDNIGHT		Ann Mahoney	*"The pasta menu is Mahoney's secret weapon. The fettuccine en brodo is rivaled only by the tortellini, which was simply a marvel."*	3-11	children's menu take out
THE BLACK SWAN		Kelli Jacob	*"With all of the incredible seafood specialty dishes, you might overlook the succulent beef and veal selections. That would be a tragedy."*	4-11	dress to impress entertainment pre-theater menu
CHEZ BLAKE		Tim Brodt	*"The juxtaposition of textures is stunning. My favorite was a crunchy crab salad served on a smooth lime gelee."*	4-10	children's menu
THE GROOVE POD		Peter Panik	*"Peter Panik is a culinary master of the unexpected."*	5-11	late night menu children's menu

Entering Text in a Table

Because tables are always in text frames and, as such, are regarded as text, entering text in them is simple and straightforward. With the Type tool selected, simply click in a table cell, and begin typing. Press [tab] to move from column to column. You can also use the arrow keys to move from cell to cell in any direction.

To modify selected text in a cell, use the features on the Character panel, just as you would in a regular text frame.

When you enter text in a cell, it is aligned to the left edge of the cell by default. You can select the text and change its alignment just as you would for any other text, using buttons such as Align right or Align center, on the Paragraph panel.

By default, text that is entered in a cell is also aligned vertically to the top of the cell. To modify this, use the vertical alignment buttons on the Table panel, shown in Figure 35.

Figure 35 Vertical alignment buttons

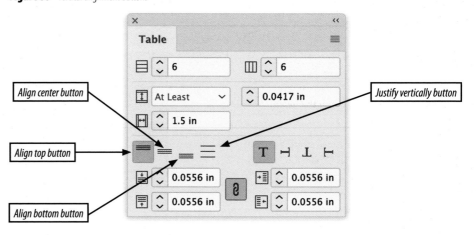

Figure 36 shows text in a table that is centered both horizontally and vertically.

Modifying a Table to Fit Text

Once you have entered text into a table, you will often find that you need to modify the table to better fit the text. Sometimes the rows will not be tall enough to contain all the text, and sometimes the columns won't be wide enough. In Figure 37, for example, the left column is too narrow for some of the state names. However, the second column is more than wide enough to contain the four-digit dates. Wouldn't it be great if you could quickly reduce the size of the second column and increase the size of the first?

Fortunately, InDesign makes it easy to modify the height of a row or the width of a column. One way to do this is to select the row or column and change the height or width value on the Table panel. Another option is simply to drag a cell border left or right to decrease or increase the width. Similarly, you can drag a cell border up or down to modify the height of a row.

The ability to change the size of cells in this manner is a powerful option. It allows you to experiment until the table looks the way you want it to look. Without this option, you would need to enter values repeatedly into the Table panel for each column and row, using trial-and-error guesswork, until you achieved a satisfactory result.

Figure 36 Text centered horizontally and vertically

MAINE	1820	35,387 sq/mi	Augusta	1,274,000

Figure 37 A column that is too narrow

State	Founded	Area	Capital	Pop
CONNECTICUT	1788	5,544 sq/mi	Hartford	3,405,000
MASSACHU-SETTS	1788	10,555 sq/mi	Boston	6, 349,000
NEW HAMP-SHIRE	1788	9,351 sq/mi	Concord	1,235,000

Too narrow →

Insetting Text Within a Cell

The cell inset text boxes at the bottom of the Table panel, shown in Figure 38, allow you to control the text inset for all four sides of the cell. With the default inset of 0.0556 in., a block of text would appear as shown in Figure 39. Note how on the left and right, the text is very close to the vertical borders of the cell, whereas there is a lot of "air" above and below. The reason the top and bottom margins are larger is because there is not enough text to take up more vertical space. The result is that the text appears to "fight" the cell, as though it doesn't fit properly.

Figure 40 shows the same block of text with the left and right inset values increased to 0.1875 in. Note the improved appearance.

Figure 38 Cell inset text boxes

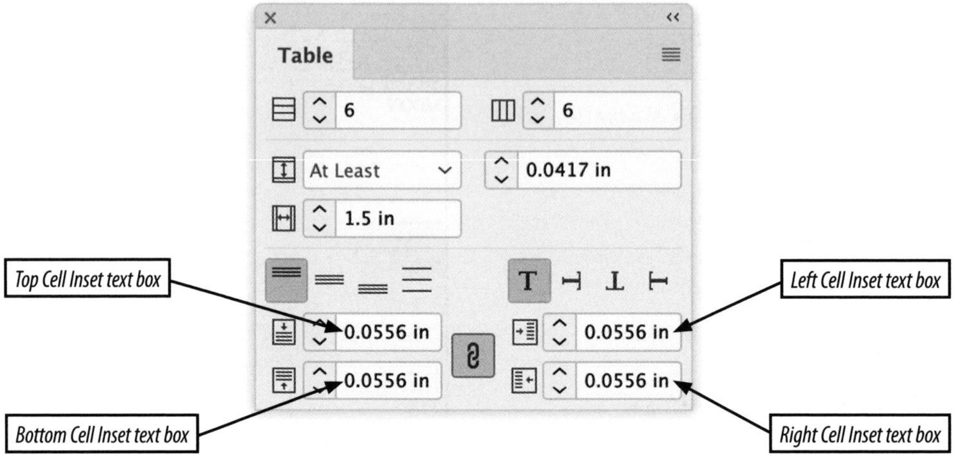

Top Cell Inset text box

Left Cell Inset text box

Bottom Cell Inset text box

Right Cell Inset text box

Figure 39 Text with a default cell inset

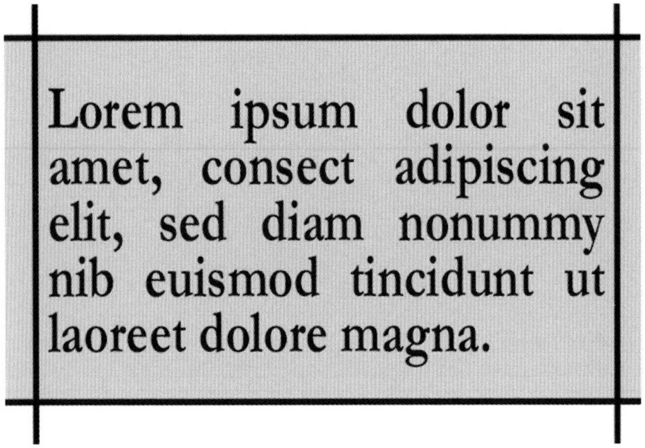

Lorem ipsum dolor sit amet, consect adipiscing elit, sed diam nonummy nib euismod tincidunt ut laoreet dolore magna.

Figure 40 Text with increased right and left cell inset values

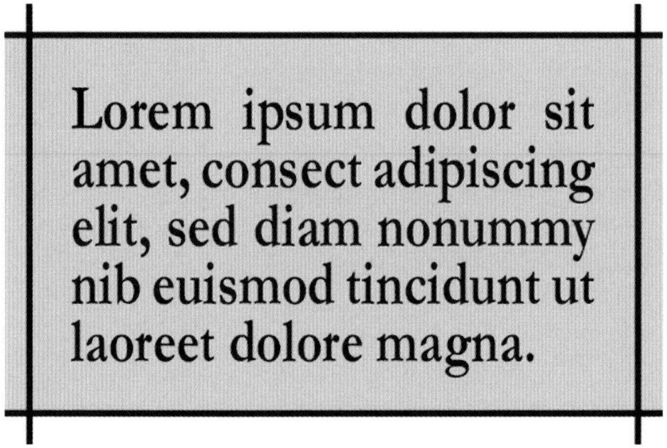

Lorem ipsum dolor sit amet, consect adipiscing elit, sed diam nonummy nib euismod tincidunt ut laoreet dolore magna.

Enter text in a table

1. Click the **Type tool** T , if necessary, click in the **top-left cell**, then type **restaurant**.

2. Press **[tab]**, then type **signature**.

3. In the **remaining four cells of the top row**, type **chef**, **review**, **hours,** and **info**.

4. Click in the **first cell of the second row**, then type **SHAME ON THE MOON** in all capital letters.

5. Press ↓ then type **BLAME IT ON MIDNIGHT** in all capital letters.

6. Press ↓, then type **THE BLACK SWAN** in all capital letters.

7. Press ↓ then type **CHEZ BLAKE** in all capital letters.

8. Press ↓, type **THE GROOVE POD** in all capital letters, then compare your table to Figure 41.

You entered text into the cells of a table.

Figure 41 Entering text into a table

restaurant	signature	chef	review	hours	info
SHAME ON THE MOON					
BLAME IT ON MIDNIGHT					
THE BLACK SWAN					
CHEZ BLAKE					
THE GROOVE POD					

Format text in a table

1. Position the **pointer** over the **left edge of the first cell in the top row** so the black arrow appears pointing right, then click once to select the row.

TIP The Type tool T must be selected in order for the black arrow to appear.

2. Show the **Swatches panel**, click the **Formatting affects text button** T , click **[Paper]**, then verify that the **stroke color** is set to **[None]**.

   The text changes to a white fill.

3. Show the **Character panel**, change the font to **Impact**, then change the **font size** to **18 pt**.

4. Click **anywhere in the first cell of the second row**, then drag down to select **all the cells in the first column (except the top cell)**.

5. Show the **Character Styles panel**, then click **Restaurant name**.

TIP If you need to substitute fonts for this exercise, your Restaurant name style may differ from that shown in the figures.

6. Position the **pointer** over the **top-left corner of the table** so the black diagonal arrow appears, then click to select the **entire table**.

7. Click the **Align center button** ≡ on the Paragraph panel.

8. Click the **pasteboard** to deselect all, then compare your table to Figure 42.

   Your text may break differently. Use soft returns to adjust line breaks on the restaurant names if necessary.

9. Save your work, then close the Table document.

You modified the font, the font size, and the alignment of text in a table. You also applied a character style to selected text in a table.

EDITING TABLES IN STORY EDITOR

You can edit tables just like text in Story Editor. Simply select the table, click Edit on the menu bar, then click Edit in Story Editor. The text in each cell is identified by a column or row number and is easily editable. After making all necessary changes, close the Story Editor window to return to the updated table in InDesign. If you have added notes to table cells, they will also appear in Story Editor.

Figure 42 Formatting text in a table

restaurant	signature	chef	review	hours	info
SHAME ON THE MOON					
BLAME IT ON MIDNIGHT					
THE BLACK SWAN					
CHEZ BLAKE					
THE GROOVE POD					

Position text vertically within a cell

1. Open ID 9-3.indd, verify that you are in **Normal view**, then save it as **Table Complete**.

   This table has the exact formatting of the table you created but has additional text, a "key" graphic placed below the table, and icons on the pasteboard.

   TIP If your computer substituted fonts when you opened ID 9-3.indd, your Restaurant name style may differ from that shown in the figures.

2. Select the **top row of cells**, then click the **Align bottom button** ≡ on the Table panel.

3. Click **anywhere** in the "**BLAME IT ON MIDNIGHT**" cell, then click the **Justify vertically button** ≡ on the Table panel.

4. Position the **pointer** over the **top-left corner of the table** until a black diagonal arrow appears, then click to select the **entire table**.

5. Click the **Align center button** ≡ on the Table panel.

6. Deselect all, then compare your work to Figure 43.

7. Save your work, then continue to the next set of steps.

You used the align buttons on the Table panel to format how text is positioned vertically within a cell.

Figure 43 Table with all text centered vertically and horizontally

restaurant	signature	chef	review	hours	info
SHAME ON THE MOON		Bill Cohen	"The fish selection is imaginitive and varied. Be sure to sample from the chef's seafood tasting menu on	5-10	dress to impress late night menu entertainment
BLAME IT ON MIDNIGHT		Ann Mahoney	"The pasta menu is Mahoney's secret weapon. The fettucine en brodo is rivaled only by the tortellini.	3-11	children's menu take out
THE BLACK SWAN		Kelli Jacob	"With all of the incredible seafood specialty dishes, you might overlook the succulent beef and	4-11	dress to impress entertainment pre-theater menu
CHEZ BLAKE		Tim Brodt	"The juxtaposition of textures is stunning. My favorite was a crunchy crab salad served on a smooth	4-10	children's menu
THE GROOVE POD		Peter Panik	"Peter Panik is a culinary master of the unexpected."	5-11	late night menu children's menu

SETTING UP A DOCUMENT GRID OR A BASELINE GRID

Grid lines are guides to which you can snap InDesign elements. Document grids are used for snapping objects, and baseline grids are used for aligning columns of text. Baseline grids look like ruled notebook paper and cover entire spreads. Document grids look more like graph paper and cover the entire pasteboard. You can view both grids by clicking View on the menu bar, pointing to Grids & Guides, then choosing Show Document Grid or Show Baseline Grid. You can change grid settings by opening the Grids Preferences dialog box. For example, you can change the color of grid lines, the vertical and horizontal space between document gridlines, and the number of subdivisions. Baseline grid preferences are set for an entire document. However, it is possible to create a baseline grid for an individual text frame. To do so, select the frame, click Object on the menu bar, then click Text Frame Options. Click the Baseline Options tab in the Text Frame Options dialog box, then choose an option for the First Baseline Offset. For example, you can choose Ascent, Cap Height, Leading, x Height, or Fixed. Click the Preview check box to see how each option affects your text. In the Baseline Grid section of the dialog box, you can customize the baseline grid for the text box.

Adjust column widths and cell insets

1. Click **View** on the menu bar, point to **Grids & Guides**, then click **Show Guides**.

2. Note the **"review" text** in the fourth column.

TIP Red circles in cells indicate that the cell content is too big to fit in the cell.

3. Position the **pointer** over the **navy blue vertical cell border** that separates the "hours" column from the "info" column so a double arrow appears, as shown in Figure 44.

4. Click and drag the **border** left, so the **vertical cell border** is aligned with the **green vertical guide**, as shown in Figure 45.

The width of the "hours" column is reduced. The width of the "info" column is not reduced; it merely moves with the "hours" column.

5. Position the **pointer** over the **navy blue vertical cell border** to the right of the "review" column so that a double arrow appears.

Figure 44 Positioning the cursor over a column rule

restaurant	signature	chef	review	hours	info
SHAME ON THE MOON		Bill Cohen	"The fish selection is imaginitive and varied. Be sure to sample from the chef's seafood tasting menu on	5-10	dress to impress late night menu entertainment
BLAME IT ON MIDNIGHT		Ann Mahoney	"The pasta menu is Mahoney's secret weapon. The fettucine en brodo is rivaled only by the tortellini.	3-11	children's menu take out
THE BLACK SWAN		Kelli Jacob	"With all of the incredible seafood specialty dishes, you might overlook the succulent beef and	4-11	dress to impress entertainment pre-theater menu
CHEZ BLAKE		Tim Brodt	"The juxtaposition of textures is stunning. My favorite was a crunchy crab salad served on a smooth	4-10	children's menu
THE GROOVE POD		Peter Panik	"Peter Panik is a culinary master of the unexpected."	5-11	late night menu children's menu

Figure 45 Reducing the width of a column

restaurant	signature	chef	review	hours	info
SHAME ON THE MOON		Bill Cohen	"The fish selection is imaginitive and varied. Be sure to sample from the chef's seafood tasting menu on	5-10	dress to impress late night menu entertainment
BLAME IT ON MIDNIGHT		Ann Mahoney	"The pasta menu is Mahoney's secret weapon. The fettucine en brodo is rivaled only by the tortellini.	3-11	children's menu take out
THE BLACK SWAN		Kelli Jacob	"With all of the incredible seafood specialty dishes, you might overlook the succulent beef and	4-11	dress to impress entertainment pre-theater menu
CHEZ BLAKE		Tim Brodt	"The juxtaposition of textures is stunning. My favorite was a crunchy crab salad served on a smooth	4-10	children's menu
THE GROOVE POD		Peter Panik	"Peter Panik is a culinary master of the unexpected."	5-11	late night menu children's menu

6. Click and drag the **arrow** right until the **right edge of the "review" column** is aligned with the **green guide**, as shown in Figure 46.

7. Select only the **five cells containing reviews**.

8. On the Table panel, increase the **Left Cell Inset value** to **.125**, then increase the **Right Cell Inset value** to **.125**.

9. Deselect all, click **View** on the menu bar, point to **Grids & Guides**, click **Hide Guides**, then compare your table to Figure 47.

10. Save your work, then continue to the next set of steps.

You decreased the width of one column and increased the width of another in order to fit text. You also increased the left and right cell insets so the text was not too close to the vertical rules.

Figure 46 Increasing the width of a column

restaurant	signature	chef	review	hours	info
SHAME ON THE MOON		Bill Cohen	"The fish selection is imaginitive and varied. Be sure to sample from the chef's seafood tasting menu on Thursday nights."	5-10	dress to impress late night menu entertainment
BLAME IT ON MIDNIGHT		Ann Mahoney	"The pasta menu is Mahoney's secret weapon. The fettucine en brodo is rivaled only by the tortellini, which was simply a marvel."	3-11	children's menu take out
THE BLACK SWAN		Kelli Jacob	"With all of the incredible seafood specialty dishes, you might overlook the succulent beef and veal selections. That would be a tragedy."	4-11	dress to impress entertainment pre-theater menu
CHEZ BLAKE		Tim Brodt	"The juxtaposition of textures is stunning. My favorite was a crunchy crab salad served on a smooth lime gelee."	4-10	children's menu
THE GROOVE POD		Peter Panik	"Peter Panik is a culinary master of the unexpected."	5-11	late night menu children's menu

Figure 47 Viewing the edited table

restaurant	signature	chef	review	hours	info
SHAME ON THE MOON		Bill Cohen	"The fish selection is imaginitive and varied. Be sure to sample from the chef's seafood tasting menu on Thursday nights."	5-10	dress to impress late night menu entertainment
BLAME IT ON MIDNIGHT		Ann Mahoney	"The pasta menu is Mahoney's secret weapon. The fettucine en brodo is rivaled only by the tortellini, which was simply a marvel."	3-11	children's menu take out
THE BLACK SWAN		Kelli Jacob	"With all of the incredible seafood specialty dishes, you might overlook the succulent beef and veal selections. That would be a tragedy."	4-11	dress to impress entertainment pre-theater menu
CHEZ BLAKE		Tim Brodt	"The juxtaposition of textures is stunning. My favorite was a crunchy crab salad served on a smooth lime gelee."	4-10	children's menu
THE GROOVE POD		Peter Panik	"Peter Panik is a culinary master of the unexpected."	5-11	late night menu children's menu

PLACE GRAPHICS IN A TABLE

In this lesson, you will insert graphics into table cells using the Place command and the Copy and Paste commands.

restaurant	signature	chef	review	hours	info
SHAME ON THE MOON		Bill Cohen	*"The fish selection is imaginitive and varied. Be sure to sample from the chef's seafood tasting menu on Thursday nights."*	5-10	
BLAME IT ON MIDNIGHT		Ann Mahoney	*"The pasta menu is Mahoney's secret weapon. The fettucine en brodo is rivaled only by the tortellini, which was simply a marvel."*	3-11	
THE BLACK SWAN		Kelli Jacob	*"With all of the incredible seafood specialty dishes, you might overlook the succulent beef and veal selections. That would be a tragedy."*	4-11	
CHEZ BLAKE		Tim Brodt	*"The juxtaposition of textures is stunning. My favorite was a crunchy crab salad served on a smooth lime pâte."*	4-10	
THE GROOVE POD		Peter Panik	*"Peter Panik is a culinary master of the unexpected."*	5-11	

Placing Graphics in a Table

InDesign makes it easy to place a graphic into a cell in a table. One simple method is to click in the cell and then use the Place command to choose and place the graphic.

Graphics that are placed in cells are treated like any other placed graphics. They appear on the Links panel and can be updated or edited, if necessary.

If the graphic you place is too large to fit in the cell, a red circle will appear in the bottom-right corner of the cell. Your only options are to increase the size of the cell or decrease the size of the graphic. Figure 48 shows a table with six graphics placed in the rightmost column.

Figure 48 Placing graphics in a table

State	Founded	Area	Capital	Pop	Flag
CONNECTICUT	1788	5,544 sq/mi	Hartford	3,405,000	
MASSACHUSETTS	1788	10,555 sq/mi	Boston	6,349,000	
NEW HAMPSHIRE	1788	9,351 sq/mi	Concord	1,235,000	
RHODE ISLAND	1790	1,545 sq/mi	Providence	1,048,00	
VERMONT	1791	9,615 sq/mi	Montpelier	608,000	
MAINE	1820	35,387 sq/mi	Augusta	1,274,000	

If you've entered text into a table, you have the option of replacing text with graphics. Remember, InDesign regards tables as text. Thus, graphics in tables function as anchored objects, just like any other text element. Many designers, when they are building tables, will simply type a graphic's name in a cell as a placeholder and place the graphics in the pasteboard for later use. Then, when they're finished editing the table, they replace the text with the graphics.

You replace text in a cell with a graphic the same way you add anchored objects to a block of text. Select the graphic on the pasteboard with the Selection tool, copy it, select the text in the cell with the Type tool, then paste the graphic. The graphic will flow with any other text that is in the cell. This is a powerful option; it allows you to place both text and graphics in a single cell!

| **TIP** If a graphic you want to insert is in a separate file, you can use the Place command to import it at the insertion point location.

Merging and Splitting Table Cells

There may be times when you would like to convert one or more table cells into one large cell, a process known as merging. Merging cells allows you to accommodate more text or larger graphics in one cell. For example, you may want to create a merged cell and place a heading in it like "Weekly Camp Activities" above a row of cells that includes the five weekdays. To merge a group of cells, select the cells, click Table on the menu bar, then click Merge Cells. Conversely, you can select one or more cells and split them horizontally

or vertically. Just click Table on the menu bar and choose Split Cells Vertically or Split Cells Horizontally.

Dragging and Dropping Rows and Columns

Rows and columns can be moved by dragging them to a new location in the table. Simply select a row or column and drag it to a new location in the table. To copy a row or column, press and hold [option] (Mac) or [Alt] (Win) while dragging the row or column to a new location. This is a great way to duplicate information in an existing row or column.

Place graphics in a table

1. Click in the **second cell of the second row**.

2. Place the file named **Sole.tif** from the location where your Chapter 9 Data Files are stored.

3. Click in the **second cell of the third row**.

4. Place the file named **Crab salad.tif**, then compare your work to Figure 49.

5. Click the **Selection tool** ▶, select the **Crab Salad.tif graphic**, click **Object** on the menu bar, point to **Clipping Path**, then click **Options**.

Continued on next page

Figure 49 Placing two graphics

restaurant	signature	chef	review	hours	info
SHAME ON THE MOON		Bill Cohen	"The fish selection is imaginitive and varied. Be sure to sample from the chef's seafood tasting menu on Thursday nights."	5-10	dress to impress late night menu entertainment
BLAME IT ON MIDNIGHT		Ann Mahoney	"The pasta menu is Mahoney's secret weapon. The fettucine en brodo is rivaled only by the tortellini, which was simply a marvel."	3-11	children's menu take out
THE BLACK SWAN		Kelli Jacob	"With all of the incredible seafood specialty dishes, you might overlook the succulent beef and veal selections. That would be a tragedy."	4-11	dress to impress entertainment pre-theater menu
CHEZ BLAKE		Tim Brodt	"The juxtaposition of textures is stunning. My favorite was a crunchy crab salad served on a smooth lime gelee."	4-10	children's menu
THE GROOVE POD		Peter Panik	"Peter Panik is a culinary master of the unexpected."	5-11	late night menu children's menu

6. Click the **Type list arrow**, click **Alpha Channel**, then click **OK**.

7. Moving **downward in the second column**, place the following graphics: **Striped bass.tif**, **Gnocchi.tif**, and **Tuna.tif**.

8. Select the **Gnocchi.tif graphic**, click **Object** on the menu bar, point to **Clipping Path**, then click **Options**.

9. Click the **Type list arrow**, click **Alpha Channel**, click **OK**, then compare your table to Figure 50.

You used the Place command to place graphics in cells.

Replace text with graphics

1. Click the **Selection tool** ▶ , click the **moon graphic** in the pasteboard, then copy it.

TIP The "moon" graphic is the top-left graphic on the pasteboard.

2. Click the **Type tool** T , then select the **"late night menu" text** in the **top cell of the info column**.

3. Click **Edit** on the menu bar, then click **Paste**.

4. Select the **"late night menu" text** in the bottom cell of the info column, click **Edit** on the menu bar, then click **Paste**.

Your table should resemble Figure 51.

TIP Press [return] (Mac) or [Enter] (Win) if "children's menu" is not on a separate line.

5. Click the **Selection tool** ▶ , click the **tie graphic** in the pasteboard, copy it, then click the **Type tool** T .

6. Triple-click **dress to impress** in the **top cell of the info column** to select the line of text, then paste.

The tie graphic replaces the text. The moon graphic and tie graphic are on the same line.

Figure 50 Placing three additional graphics

restaurant	signature	chef	review	hours	info
SHAME ON THE MOON		Bill Cohen	"The fish selection is imaginitive and varied. Be sure to sample from the chef's seafood tasting menu on Thursday nights."	5-10	dress to impress late night menu entertainment
BLAME IT ON MIDNIGHT		Ann Mahoney	"The pasta menu is Mahoney's secret weapon. The fettucine en brodo is rivaled only by the tortellini, which was simply a marvel."	3-11	children's menu take out
THE BLACK SWAN		Kelli Jacob	"With all of the incredible seafood specialty dishes, you might overlook the succulent beef and veal selections. That would be a tragedy."	4-11	dress to impress entertainment pre-theater menu
CHEZ BLAKE		Tim Brodt	"The juxtaposition of textures is stunning. My favorite was a crunchy crab salad served on a smooth lime gelee."	4-10	children's menu
THE GROOVE POD		Peter Panik	"Peter Panik is a culinary master of the unexpected."	5-11	late night menu children's menu

Figure 51 Replacing two lines of text with graphics

restaurant	signature	chef	review	hours	info
SHAME ON THE MOON		Bill Cohen	"The fish selection is imaginitive and varied. Be sure to sample from the chef's seafood tasting menu on Thursday nights."	5-10	dress to impress ☽ entertainment
BLAME IT ON MIDNIGHT		Ann Mahoney	"The pasta menu is Mahoney's secret weapon. The fettucine en brodo is rivaled only by the tortellini, which was simply a marvel."	3-11	children's menu take out
THE BLACK SWAN		Kelli Jacob	"With all of the incredible seafood specialty dishes, you might overlook the succulent beef and veal selections. That would be a tragedy."	4-11	dress to impress entertainment pre-theater menu
CHEZ BLAKE		Tim Brodt	"The juxtaposition of textures is stunning. My favorite was a crunchy crab salad served on a smooth lime gelee."	4-10	children's menu
THE GROOVE POD		Peter Panik	"Peter Panik is a culinary master of the unexpected."	5-11	☽ children's menu

7. Click the **Selection tool** ▶, click the **music graphic** in the pasteboard, copy it, click the **Type tool** T, select the **"entertainment" text** in the **top cell of the info column**, then paste.

The top cell in your info column should resemble Figure 52.

8. Using the same method, replace **all the text in the info column** with **corresponding icons** so your table resembles Figure 53.

TIP Use the key below the table to identify the icon that corresponds with the text. Each icon file

has a clipping path you can use to remove the background if necessary.

9. Save your work, then close the Table Complete document.

You replaced selected text elements with graphics.

Figure 52 Placing three graphics in a cell

Figure 53 Completing the table

restaurant	signature	chef	review	hours	info
SHAME ON THE MOON		Bill Cohen	*"The fish selection is imaginitive and varied. Be sure to sample from the chef's seafood tasting menu on Thursday nights."*	5-10	
BLAME IT ON MIDNIGHT		Ann Mahoney	*"The pasta menu is Mahoney's secret weapon. The fettucine en brodo is rivaled only by the tortellini, which was simply a marvel."*	3-11	
THE BLACK SWAN		Kelli Jacob	*"With all of the incredible seafood specialty dishes, you might overlook the succulent beef and veal selections. That would be a tragedy."*	4-11	
CHEZ BLAKE		Tim Brodt	*"The juxtaposition of textures is stunning. My favorite was a crunchy crab salad served on a smooth lime gelee."*	4-10	
THE GROOVE POD		Peter Panik	*"Peter Panik is a culinary master of the unexpected."*	5-11	

Work with tabs

1. Open ID 9-4.indd, then save it as **Tab Review**.
2. Click the Selection tool, click the text frame that contains the data, click Object on the menu bar, then click Text Frame Options.
3. In the Inset Spacing section, type **.3** in the Top text box, type **.3** in the Left text box, then click OK.
4. Click the Type tool, then select all the text.
5. Click Type on the menu bar, then click Tabs.
6. Click the Left-Justified Tab button on the Tabs panel.
7. Position the pointer in the white space in the top third of the ruler—just above the numbers—then click and drag until the X text box reads 1 in.
8. Using the same method, create a new tab at 2.25", making sure the tab is left-justified.
9. Click anywhere to the right of the second tab to add a third tab.
10. Select the measurement in the X text box, type **3,** then press [return] (Mac) or [Enter] (Win), then make sure the tab is left-justified.

11. Click the Type tool pointer to the left of the first # sign in the first line of text, then press [tab].
12. Click the Type tool pointer to the left of the second # sign, then press [tab].
13. Click the Type tool pointer to the left of the word Profit, then press [tab].
14. Using the same tabs, tab the numbers on the next four lines.

TIP Be sure to click to the immediate left of each number before pressing [tab].

15. Select all the text, click Object on the menu bar, click Text Frame Options, change the Left Inset to .5, then click OK.
16. Click the Position Panel above Text Frame button on the Tabs panel.
17. Select only the bottom four rows of text.
18. Click the first left-justified tab at 1" in the tab ruler to select it.
19. Type **1.4** in the X text box, then press [return] (Mac) or [Enter] (Win).
20. Click the second left-justified tab at 2.25" on the tab ruler to select it.

21. Type **2.5** in the X text box, then press [return] (Mac) or [Enter] (Win).
22. Click the Align to Decimal tab button on the Tabs panel.
23. Click the third left-justified tab at 3" on the tab ruler to select it.
24. Click the Align to Decimal Tab button on the Tabs panel.
25. Type **3.2** in the X text box, then press [Enter] (Win) or [return] (Mac).
26. With the four rows of text still selected, click the first tab on the tab ruler to highlight it.
27. In the Leader text box, type **a period followed by a space**, then press [return] (Mac) or [Enter] (Win).
28. Click the second tab in the tab ruler to highlight it.
29. In the Leader text box, type **a period followed by a space**, then press [return] (Mac) or [Enter] (Win).
30. Click the third tab in the tab ruler to highlight it.
31. In the Leader text box, type **a period followed by a space**, then press [return] (Mac) or [Enter] (Win).
32. Click the Paragraph panel menu button, then click Paragraph Rules.
33. Click the list arrow at the top of the dialog box, click Rule Below, then click the Rule On check box.

34. Choose the same settings shown in Figure 54 to define the rule, then click OK.
35. Deselect all, close the Tabs panel, then compare your page to Figure 55.
36. Save your work, then close the Tab Review document.

Create and format a table

1. Open ID 9-5.indd, then save it as **Table Review**.
2. Close all open panels except for the toolbar, click the Type tool, then create a text frame that snaps to all four margin guides.
3. Click View on the menu bar, point to Grids & Guides, then click Hide Guides.
4. Click Table on the menu bar, then click Insert Table.
5. Type **7** in the Body Rows text box, then type **6** in the Columns text box.
6. Click OK, click Window on the menu bar, point to Type & Tables, then click Table.
7. Position the pointer over the second cell in the first column, then click and drag to select all the rows except the top row.
8. Click the Row Height list arrow on the Table panel, then click Exactly.
9. Type **1.625** in the text box next to the Row Height text box, then press [return] (Mac) or [Enter] (Win).

Figure 54 Paragraph Rules dialog box

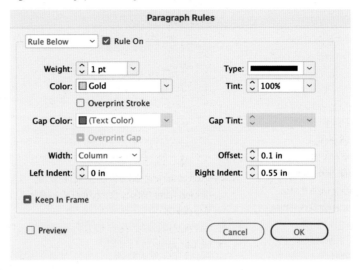

Figure 55 Completed Skills Review, Part 1

Lemonade Stand Sales

Salesperson	# Pitchers Made	# Sold	Profit
Ron	30	15	$150.00
Barbara	37	27	$270.00
Margret	20	20	$200.00
Adam	20	7	$70.00

10. Position the pointer over the left edge of the top cell in the first row so the heavy black arrow appears pointing to the right.
11. Click once to select the top row.
12. Click the Row Height list arrow on the Table panel, then click Exactly.
13. Type .5 in the text box next to the Row Height text box, then press [return] (Mac) or [Enter] (Win).
14. Position the pointer over the top-left corner of the table so the black diagonal arrow appears.
15. Click once to select the entire table.
16. Click Table on the menu bar, point to Cell Options, then click Strokes and Fills.
17. Click the Weight list arrow, then click 2 pt.
18. Click the Color list arrow, click Black, then click OK.
19. Click Table on the menu bar, point to Table Options, then click Alternating Fills.
20. Click the Alternating Pattern list arrow, then click Every Other Row.
21. Click the first Color list arrow on the left side of the dialog box, click Gold, then type 100 in the Tint text box.
22. Click the second Color list arrow on the right side of the dialog box, click Navy, type 18 in the Tint text box, then click OK.
23. Select the top row of cells, click Table on the menu bar, point to Cell Options, then click Strokes and Fills.

24. In the Cell Fill area, click the Color list arrow, click Navy, type 100 in the Tint text box, then click OK.

Format text in a table

1. Click the Type tool in the top-left text box, then type **State**.
2. Press [tab], then type **Founded**.
3. In the remaining four cells of the top row, type **Area**, **Capital**, **Pop,** and **Flag**.
4. Click in the first cell of the second row, then type **CONNECTICUT** in all capital letters.

TIP Type all the state names in capital letters.

5. Press ↓, then type **MASSACHUSETTS**.
6. Press ↓, then type **NEW HAMPSHIRE**.
7. Press ↓, then type **RHODE ISLAND**.
8. Press ↓, then type **VERMONT**.
9. Press ↓, then type **MAINE**.
10. Position the pointer over the left edge of the first cell in the top row so the black arrow appears pointing right, then click to select the entire row.
11. Show the Swatches panel, click the Formatting affects text button, then click [Paper].
12. Show the Character panel, change the font to Impact, then change the font size to 18 pt.
13. Click anywhere in the first cell of the second row, then drag down to select all the cells in the first column (except the top row).
14. Show the Character Styles panel, then click Names.

TIP If your computer substituted a different font and your state names are not all capital letters, select the state names and apply another all-capital font.

15. Position the pointer over the top-left corner of the table so a black diagonal arrow appears, then click to select the entire table.
16. Click the Align center button on the Paragraph panel, then deselect all.
17. Save your work, then close the Table Review document.
18. Open ID 9-6.indd, then save it as **Table Review Completed**.
19. Select the top row of cells, then click the Align bottom button on the Table panel.
20. Click anywhere in the "CONNECTICUT" cell, then click and drag to select the bottom six rows.
21. Click the Align center button on the Table panel.
22. Click View on the menu bar, point to Grids & Guides, then click Show Guides if necessary.
23. Position the pointer over the vertical cell border that separates the first two columns so a double arrow appears.
24. Click and drag the arrow right so the vertical cell border is aligned with the green vertical guide.
25. Position the pointer over the vertical cell border that separates the second and third columns so a double arrow appears.

26. Click and drag the arrow left so the vertical cell border is aligned with the red vertical guide.
27. Position the pointer over the vertical cell border that separates the fifth and sixth columns so a double arrow appears.
28. Click and drag the arrow left so the vertical cell border is aligned with the blue vertical guide.
29. Position the pointer over the right edge of the table, then drag right until the right edge of the table is aligned with the margin guide.

Place graphics in a table

1. Click in the sixth cell of the second row.
2. Place the file named CT State Flag.tif from the location where your Chapter 9 Data Files are stored.
3. Click in the next cell down.
4. Place the file named MA State Flag.tif.
5. Using the same method and moving downward in the column, place the following graphics: NH State Flag.tif, RI State Flag.tif, VT State Flag.tif, and ME State Flag.tif.
6. Deselect all, hide guides, then compare your table with Figure 56.

TIP Your screen may appear different if your computer substituted fonts.

7. Save your work, then close the Table Review Completed document.

Figure 56 Completed Skills Review, Part 2

State	Founded	Area	Capital	Pop	Flag
CONNECTICUT	1788	5,544 sq/mi	Hartford	3,405,000	
MASSACHUSETTS	1788	10,555 sq/mi	Boston	6, 349,000	
NEW HAMPSHIRE	1788	9,351 sq/mi	Concord	1,235,000	
RHODE ISLAND	1790	1,545 sq/mi	Providence	1, 048,00	
VERMONT	1791	9,615 sq/mi	Montpelier	608,000	
MAINE	1820	35,387 sq/mi	Augusta	1,274,000	

You are a designer at a game manufacturing company. A junior designer has emailed you a chart showing the winners of a recent promotion. You immediately notice that the chart is not well designed. You decide to make improvements before showing it to your manager.

1. Open ID 9-7.indd, then save it as **Contest Redesign**.
2. Select the headline only, then click the Align center button on the Paragraph panel.
3. Select all the text in the frame, click Object on the menu bar, then click Text Frame Options.
4. In the Inset Spacing section, type **.4** in the Top text box only, verify that the other three text boxes are set to 0, then click OK.
5. Select only the five rows of data (not the headline).
6. Click Type on the menu bar, then click Tabs.
7. Click the left-justified tab already in the tab ruler to select it, then click the Align to Decimal Tab button.
8. Select the contents of the X text box on the Tabs panel, type **2.75,** then press [return] (Mac) or [Enter] (Win).
9. Click the tab ruler approximately at the 2" mark to add a new tab.
10. Change the tab to a left-justified tab.
11. Select the contents of the X text box, type **.75,** then press [return] (Mac) or [Enter] (Win).
12. Click to the left of the first name, then press [tab].
13. Tab the remaining four names, close the Tabs panel, then compare your work to Figure 57.
14. Save your work, then close the Contest Redesign document.

Figure 57 Completed Project Builder 1

CONTEST RESULTS

T. JONES	$50.00
P. PARDON	$100.00
T. ALLEN	$8.00
A. MAHONEY	$10,000.00
K. JACOB	$3,000.00

Your company has recently held a sales contest. You are in charge of showing the contest results. One of your staff designers has emailed you a chart showing the results and says it's "ready to go." You believe the chart looks a bit stark, so you decide to add rules to it.

1. Open ID 9-8.indd, then save it as **Contest Rules**.
2. Select the five lines of data, then increase the leading to 20 pts.
3. Click the Paragraph panel menu button, then click Paragraph Rules.
4. Click the Rule On check box, type **.25** in the Left Indent text box, type **.25** in the Right Indent text box, type **p5** in the Offset text box, then click OK.
5. Select only the first row of text (T. Jones), click the Paragraph panel menu button, then click Paragraph Rules.
6. Click the Rule Below list arrow, choose Rule Above, then click the Rule On check box.
7. Type **.25** in the Left Indent text box, type **.25** in the Right Indent text box, type **p15** in the Offset text box, then click OK.
8. Deselect all, save your work, compare your chart to Figure 58, then close the Contest Rules document.

Figure 58 Completed Project Builder 2

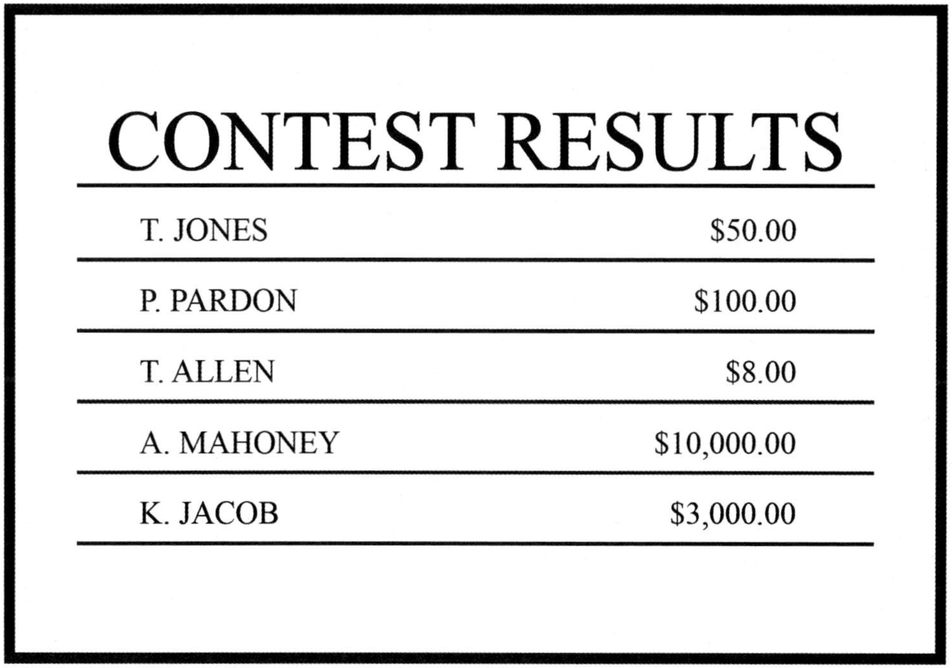

CONTEST RESULTS	
T. JONES	$50.00
P. PARDON	$100.00
T. ALLEN	$8.00
A. MAHONEY	$10,000.00
K. JACOB	$3,000.00

You are a freelance designer. Your client has given you a table created in InDesign and has asked you to "give it some life." You open the file and decide it needs color and some reformatting.

1. Open ID 9-9.indd, then save it as **Mountain Table**.
2. Select all the cells in the table, change their height to exactly .75 in, then change their width to exactly 2 in.
3. Center all the text horizontally and vertically.
4. Change the cell strokes to 2 pt. Navy.
5. Apply alternating fills of 18% Navy and 18% Green.
6. Change the fill on the top row to 100% Navy.
7. Change the top row of text to 22 pt. Impact.
8. Change the fill color of the text on the top row of text to [Paper].
9. Select all the text in rows 2 through 6, then change the type size to 22 pt.
10. Deselect all, then compare your work to Figure 59.
11. Save your work, then close the Mountain Table document.

Figure 59 Completed Design Project 1

Mountain	State	Elevation	First Scaled
Mount Jefferson	Utah	6288 ft.	1937
Mount Rustic	Colorado	7789 ft.	1933
Mount Green	Massachusetts	4953 ft.	1877
Bear Mountain	California	5784 ft.	1899
Goat Mountain	New Hampshire	6235 ft.	1910

In this project, you will build a chart from scratch, using tabs based on supplied information. You are free to choose the size of the chart and any colors, rules, tab leaders, or text formatting that might make the chart more visually pleasing. The chart will be based on the following information:

1. Create a new InDesign document, then save it as **Holiday Chart**.
   The title of the chart is **Annual Holiday Fund Raiser**.
   Five students sold five different products during the holiday raffle. The sales information is as follows:
   - Karen sold 100 lollipops at a retail cost of 35 cents per unit, for a total net revenue of $35.00.
   - Jimmy sold 45 lapel pins at a retail cost of $2 per unit, for a total net revenue of $90.00.
   - Billy sold 30 candles at a retail cost of $2.50 per unit, for a total net revenue of $75.00.
   - Susan sold 10 rolls of mints at a retail cost of 50 cents per unit, for a total net revenue of $5.00.
   - Michael sold 20 calendars at a retail cost of $10 per unit, for a total net revenue of $200.00.

2. When you finish the chart, compare your work to Figure 60.

3. Save your work, then close the Holiday Chart document.

Figure 60 Sample Design Project 2

Annual Holiday Fund Raiser

Sales Person	Product	Number Sold	Retail Cost	Net Revenue
Karen	Lollipops	100	$.35	$35.00
Jimmy	Lapel Pins	45	$2.00	$90.00
Billy	Candles	30	$2.50	$75.00
Susan	Mints	10	$.50	$5.00
Michael	Calendars	20	$10.00	$200.00

Table of Contents

CHAPTER **10**

MAKING
BOOKS, TABLES
OF CONTENTS,
AND INDEXES

1. Create a Book File
2. Organize a Book File
3. Create a Table of Contents
4. Create an Index

Adobe Certified Professional in Print & Digital Media Publication Using Adobe InDesign

1. Working in the Design Industry

This objective covers critical concepts related to working with colleagues and clients as well as crucial legal, technical, and design-related knowledge.

1.4 Demonstrate knowledge of key terminology related to publications.

   C Understand and use key terms related to multi-page layouts.

2. Project Setup and Interface

This objective covers the interface setup and program settings that assist in an efficient and effective workflow, as well as knowledge about ingesting digital assets for a project.

2.1 Create a document with the appropriate settings for web, print, and mobile.

   A Set appropriate document settings for printed and onscreen images.

4. Creating and Modifying Document Elements

This objective covers core tools and functionality of the application, as well as tools that affect the visual appearance of document elements.

4.2 Add and manipulate text using appropriate typographic settings.

   B Use appropriate character settings in a design.
   C Use appropriate paragraph settings in a design.
   F Use tools to add special characters or content.

CREATE A BOOK FILE

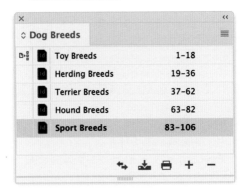

Making Books in InDesign

Imagine that you've created a lot of InDesign documents, each of which is meant to be a chapter in a book. InDesign's Book feature allows you to combine and collate multiple documents into one book with continuous pagination. Want to switch the order of chapters? Easy! The Book panel allows you to reorganize at will, and it will automatically repaginate your book every time you make a change.

This is a very helpful feature. InDesign's automatic table of contents and index features will amaze you. With a click of a button, InDesign examines all the documents on the Book panel, identifies text items you've saved with specific paragraph styles, then sorts those text items into a table of contents or an index, complete with page numbers.

Creating a Book File

In Adobe InDesign, a **book** is a collection of two or more InDesign documents that are paginated as a single book. For example, you can collect three 10-page documents as a single 30-page book.

Creating a book is similar to creating a document—use the New command on the File menu, but choose Book instead of Document. A book is an individual InDesign file, like a library file, and when opened, it appears as a panel. Figure 1 shows an open book file.

Figure 1 Open book file

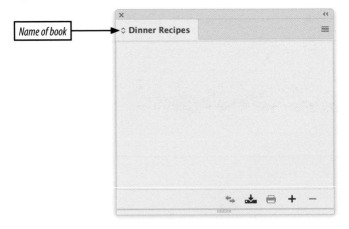

Name of book

TIP Unlike InDesign documents, which have a filename extension of .indd (InDesign document), book files have a filename extension of .indb (InDesign book).

Adding Documents to a Book Panel

To create a book, you add InDesign documents to the Book panel. When you do so, the documents are paginated as though they were one book. For example, adding five 20-page documents would create a book that is paginated as 1–100. Figure 2 shows a Book panel after four documents have been added. Note the page ranges next to each document name.

When you add documents to a Book panel, the page numbering of those documents is also changed on the Pages panel when the document is opened from the Book panel. For example, if you add two 20-page documents to the Book panel, the second document on the panel will be paginated as pages 21–40. It is important to remember that page numbering changes that occur in your book file affect the original documents as well, so always save backup copies of your original documents before adding them to a Book panel. You never know when you might need to go back to the original document.

Double-clicking a document on the Book panel opens the document. When a document is open, the Book panel shows the Document is open icon, as shown in Figure 3.

Figure 2 Viewing documents in the book file

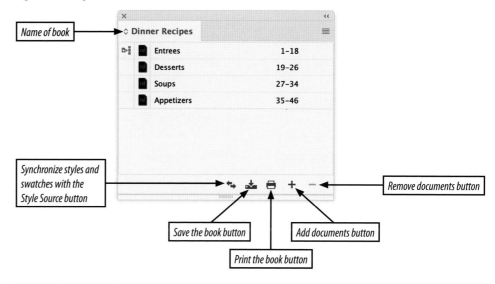

Name of book

Synchronize styles and swatches with the Style Source button

Save the book button

Print the book button

Add documents button

Remove documents button

Figure 3 Book panel showing an open document

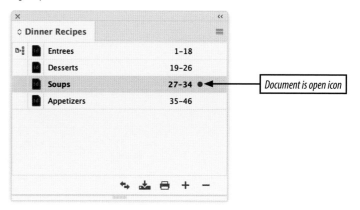

Document is open icon

Create a book file

1. Open ID 10-1.indd and click **Don't Update Links** in the Issues with Links dialog box.

TIP It is important that you click Don't Update Links in the Issues with Links dialog box for the exercises in this chapter to work correctly.

2. Note the number of pages on the Pages panel, then save it as **Toy Breeds**.

The document has 18 pages, numbered 1–18.

3. Open ID 10-2.indd and click **Don't Update Links** in the Issues with Links dialog box.

4. Note the number of pages on the Pages panel, then save it as **Herding Breeds**.

The document has 18 pages, numbered 1–18.

5. Open ID 10-3.indd and click **Don't Update Links** in the Issues with Links dialog box.

6. Note the number of pages on the Pages panel, then save it as **Terrier Breeds**.

The document has 26 pages, numbered 1–26.

7. Open ID 10-4.indd and click **Don't Update Links** in the Issues with Links dialog box.

8. Note the number of pages on the Pages panel, then save it as **Hound Breeds**.

The document has 20 pages, numbered 1–20.

9. Open ID 10-5.indd and click **Don't Update Links** in the Issues with Links dialog box.

10. Note the number of pages on the Pages panel, then save it as **Sport Breeds**.

The document has 24 pages, numbered 1–24.

11. Close all open documents.

12. Click **File** on the menu bar, point to **New**, then click **Book**.

13. Name the new file **Dog Breeds**, then click **Save**.

As shown in Figure 4, a Book panel appears with a single tab named Dog Breeds. This panel is the book file.

14. Continue to the next set of steps.

You viewed each document that will be used in the book, then created a new book file.

Figure 4 Dog Breeds Book

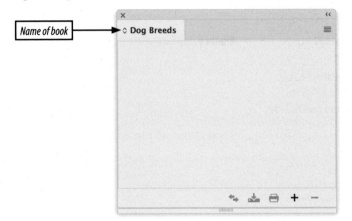

Name of book ← ◊ Dog Breeds

Add documents to a book file

1. Click the **Book panel menu button** ≡ , then click **Add Document.**

2. Navigate to the drive and folder where you saved your files from the previous set of steps, click **Toy Breeds.indd**, then click **Open**.

   As shown in Figure 5, the document is listed on the Book panel along with its page range.

3. Click the **Add documents button** + on the Book panel, then add the document named **Herding Breeds.indd**.

   The document, which was numbered 1–18 in its original file, is added to the Book panel as pages 19–36.

4. Using either of the two methods outlined before, add the following documents in the following order: **Terrier Breeds.indd**, **Hound Breeds.indd**, and **Sport Breeds.indd**.

   As shown in Figure 6, the Book panel contains five documents, and the pagination is continuous, for a total of 106 pages in the book.

5. Click the **Save the book button** ⬇ on the Book panel.

6. Continue to the next lesson.

You added five documents to the Book panel to create a book with 106 pages.

Figure 5 Adding a document to the Book panel

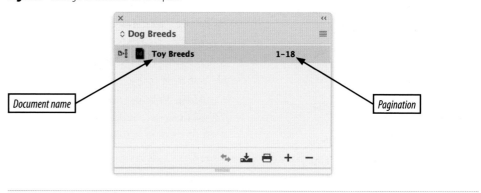

Document name | Pagination

Figure 6 Dog Breeds book with five documents added

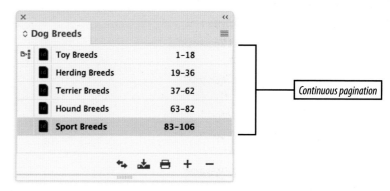

Continuous pagination

ORGANIZE A BOOK FILE

▶ *What You'll Do*

In this lesson, you will modify both the order and the page range of documents on the Book panel.

Manipulating the Order of Documents in a Book File

When you add documents to a book file, the documents are repaginated as you add them. However, you can reorder the documents at any time simply by dragging them up or down on the Book panel. Figure 7 shows four documents in the Dinner Recipes book reordered into the sequence of a meal, with appetizers first and desserts last.

When you reorder documents on the Book panel, the documents are repaginated accordingly—in both the panel and the documents themselves.

Modifying the Page Range of Documents

Typically, the documents that you add to a Book panel will start on page 1 in their original incarnation. In other words, if you add five documents, each would have originally been numbered starting with page 1. By default, page 1 is always a right-hand page.

Figure 7 Reordering documents in the Dinner Recipes book

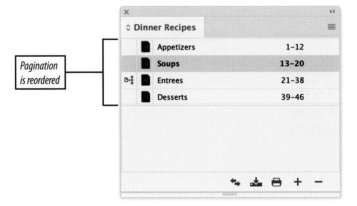

As discussed previously, documents are repaginated when added to a book file. This can create left-hand page/right-hand page issues. For example, let's say you add two documents. Originally, the first is paginated as pages 1–11. The second is paginated as pages 1–12. Therefore, each begins on a right page. However, once both are added to a book file, the second document will be paginated as pages 12–23. This means that the first page of the second document is now a left-hand page.

This may or may not be a problem for your intended book layout. If it is a problem, you will want to repaginate the document so it once again begins on a right-hand page. To do so, access the Book Page Numbering Options dialog box from the Book panel menu, as shown in Figure 8. This dialog box allows you to manipulate how documents are paginated as they are added to the book file.

In the preceding example, you would select the second document and then click the Continue on next odd page option button. This forces the next document to begin on the next odd page in the book. Thus, the second document once again begins on a right-hand page.

This method works on all documents on the Book panel except the first document, because the first document is not "continued" from any other document. In a book file, the first document starts on a right-hand page 1 by default. If you want it to start on an even-numbered left-hand page, you need to use a different method. Double-clicking the page numbers of a document on the Book panel opens both the document and the Document Numbering Options dialog box. You can use this dialog box to define the document start page as page 2, for example, as shown in Figure 9. Now the first document begins on an even-numbered left-hand page.

Figure 8 Book Page Numbering Options dialog box

Figure 9 Document Numbering Options dialog box

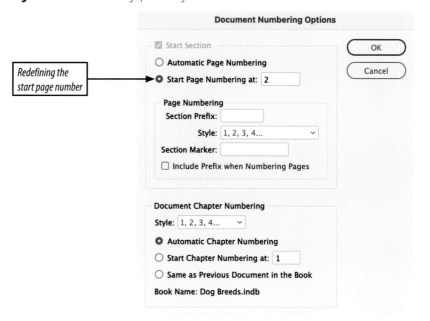

Manipulate the order of documents

1. Note the **order of documents** on the Book panel.

    For this project, each document will be a chapter in the book. You want the chapters to flow in alphabetical order.

2. Drag **Toy Breeds** down to the bottom of the list.

    As shown in Figure 10, when Toy Breeds is moved to the bottom of the list, the page range is renumbered—Toy Breeds now appears on pages 89–106.

    TIP When you move a document in the list, a thick horizontal line appears to denote its new location.

3. Rearrange the list so it is in alphabetical order, as shown in Figure 11.

4. Double-click **Toy Breeds** on the Book panel.

    TIP Double-clicking the name of a document on the Book panel opens the InDesign document. Note the Document is open icon ● next to the page numbers for Toy Breeds on the Book panel.

5. Open the Pages panel.

    Manipulating a document on the Book panel affects the actual document. The Pages panel in Toy Breeds.indd lists the document pages as 89–106.

6. Close the Toy Breeds document.

7. Continue to the next set of steps.

    You modified the order of documents on the Book panel, noting the changes in page range. You opened one of the documents and noted that the changes made on the Book panel directly affected the document.

Figure 10 Moving Toy Breeds chapter to the end of the book

Figure 11 Reordering the chapters into alphabetical order

Modify the page range of documents

1. Click the **Book panel menu button** 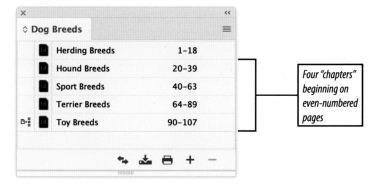, then click **Book Page Numbering Options**.

   You will designate the first page of every chapter to appear on a left page—an even page number.

2. Click the **Continue on next even page option button**, then click **OK**.

   As shown in Figure 12, all chapters except for Chapter 1 begin on an even-numbered page. Note that Chapter 1 still ends on page 18, but Chapter 2 now begins on page 20 because of this change to pagination. Page 19 will still exist in the book, but

it will be a blank page automatically inserted by InDesign. Instead, you will change Chapter 1 so it too opens on an even page number.

3. On the Book panel, double-click the **page numbers** for Herding Breeds.

   TIP Double-clicking the page numbers on the Book panel opens both the document and the Document Numbering Options dialog box. The Document is open icon ● appears beside Herding Breeds on the Book panel, indicating that the file is open.

4. Click the **Start Page Numbering at option button**, then type **2** in the text box, as shown in Figure 13.

5. Click **OK**.

6. Save the Herding Breeds file, then close it.

7. Note the **Chapter 1 page range** on the Book panel.

   The book now begins on page 2 and ends on page 107, with all chapters beginning on an even-numbered left-hand page.

8. Click the **Save the book button** on the Book panel.

9. Continue to the next lesson.

You modified the page range of the book so every chapter begins on a left-hand even-numbered page.

Figure 12 Changing the pagination of 5 chapters

Figure 13 Document Numbering Options dialog box

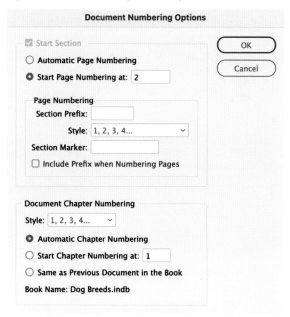

CREATE A TABLE OF CONTENTS

Creating a Table of Contents

A **table of contents (TOC)** is a list of divisions in a book and the pages on which they start. When you create a TOC for a book, it is generated from information contained within the documents that make up the book. Specifically, the entries in the TOC are text items from the documents formatted with specific paragraph styles.

Here's how it works: Let's say you've created four documents you want to collate into a recipe book. You want the title of every recipe from every document to be listed in the TOC. To make this happen, you must format the title of each recipe with the same paragraph style.

When you collate the four documents in the book file and then generate a TOC, InDesign searches through all four of the documents and locates all the text elements that were formatted with the paragraph style you have specified. In this example, that would be all the recipe titles. InDesign then copies all those text elements into a TOC format. It lists all the text elements and the pages on which they appear in the book.

Loading Paragraph Styles

Now that you understand how InDesign uses paragraph styles to create a TOC, it is important to understand how to manage paragraph styles properly. Remember, paragraph styles must be consistent for every document that has been added to the book.

The best method for assuring consistent paragraph styles is to load them between documents. This couldn't be easier. Once you've created the first document to be used in the book, create the second document, then use the Load Paragraph Styles command on the Paragraph Styles panel menu. You use this command to import the paragraph styles from the first document into the second document. Now, both documents access the same paragraph styles.

If you do this for the remaining documents for the book, all the paragraph styles will be consistent for all the documents that make up the book.

Maintaining Consistent Styles Between Documents in a Book

In Figure 14, note the Style Source icon to the left of Entrees. This means that InDesign regards the paragraph styles in the Entrees document as the master paragraph styles. In other words, the paragraph styles in the other three documents should be consistent with those in the Entrees document.

TIP By default, the first document you add to the Book file is designated as the style source.

You can select two or more documents on the Book panel and then use the Synchronize Selected Documents command on the panel menu to synchronize styles. When you do so, InDesign automatically searches all the paragraph styles in the selected files and compares them to those in the style source document. If InDesign finds paragraph styles in any of the selected documents that are not consistent with the style source document, it will modify those styles so they match, thus ensuring consistency throughout the book.

This is a great feature. However, in most cases, you should not need to use it. Creating a TOC requires foresight and planning. By the time that you add documents into a book file, if you've done your work properly, all your paragraph styles should be consistent. You should not need to rely on the Synchronize Selected Documents command.

Generating a Table of Contents

A table of contents is an individual InDesign document that you add to the Book panel to become part of the book. When creating the TOC document, it is critical that you carefully choose the same document-setup specifications that were used to create the other documents in the book, such as page size and orientation. After creating the TOC document, add it to the Book panel. Figure 15 shows a TOC document added as page 1 on the Dinner Recipes Book panel.

Figure 14 Identifying the master paragraph style

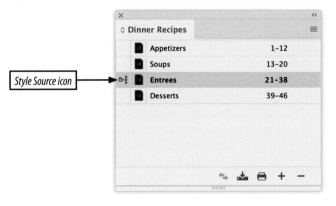

Style Source icon

Figure 15 TOC document on the Book panel

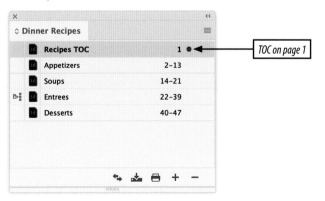

TOC on page 1

Once you've added the TOC document to the Book panel, you must then load the paragraph styles used in the other documents in the book. The only way the TOC document can access the paragraph styles necessary to create the TOC is to have those paragraph styles loaded into the TOC document itself. Simply use the Load Paragraph Styles command on the Paragraph Styles panel.

The Table of Contents dialog box, shown in Figure 16, is command central for creating a TOC. Once you have loaded the paragraph styles, they will be available in the Other Styles box. Choose which styles you want the TOC to use by adding them to the Include Paragraph Styles box.

One last thing: Be sure to check the Include Book Documents check box in the dialog box. This tells InDesign to use the documents on the Book panel as the basis for the TOC.

When you click OK, the TOC is generated. The pointer will appear as the loaded text icon. Simply click it in the TOC document, and it will flow the TOC data.

Reformatting Paragraph Styles

In most cases, the paragraph styles from which you generate your TOC will not be appropriate for the TOC layout. In the case of the recipe example, the recipe headlines were formatted as 24 pt. headlines. As shown in Figure 17, this size is too large for TOC entries.

Figure 16 Table of Contents dialog box

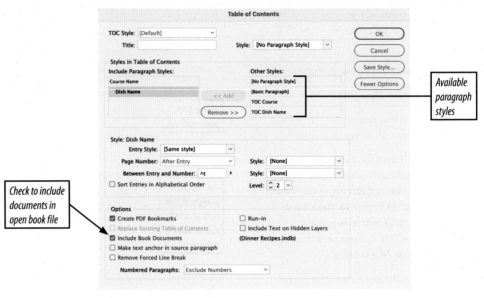

Figure 17 TOC formatted with loaded paragraph styles

You have several options for formatting TOC entries. Once you generate the TOC, you can reformat the text any way you see fit, or you can modify the paragraph styles in the TOC document only.

For another solution, you can create new paragraph styles in the TOC document that are more appropriate for the layout. Any new paragraph styles that you create will be listed in the Table of Contents dialog box.

In the Style section of the Table of Contents dialog box, you can use the new paragraph styles to modify the appearance of the loaded paragraph styles. In Figure 18, the loaded Course Name paragraph style is being modified by the TOC Course paragraph style (note the Entry Style text box).

Figure 19 shows the same data reformatted with two new paragraph styles.

Figure 18 Modifying a loaded paragraph style

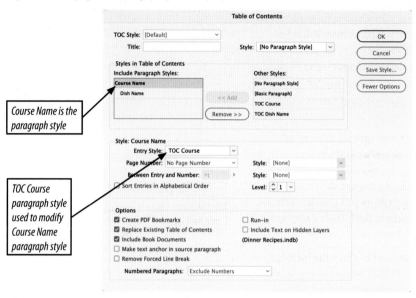

Figure 19 TOC with reformatted paragraph styles

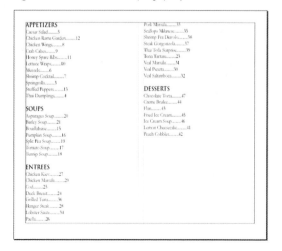

Identify and load paragraph styles for a TOC

1. Double-click **Toy Breeds** on the Book panel to open the document.

2. Open the Paragraph Styles panel.

3. Click the **Type tool** T, then click to place the pointer anywhere in the **TOY BREEDS headline** on the first page.

   The Paragraph Styles panel identifies the style applied to TOY BREEDS as Section Name.

4. Click to place the pointer in the **Silky Terrier headline** at the top of the next page.

   The Paragraph Styles panel identifies this style as Breed Name.

5. Close the Toy Breeds document.

6. Open ID 10-6.indd, then save it as **TOC**.

7. Click the **Paragraph Styles panel menu button** ≡, then click **Load Paragraph Styles**.

8. Navigate to the location where you store your files, click **Toy Breeds**, then click **Open**.

   The Load Styles dialog box appears, showing the two paragraph styles that are in the Toy Breeds file.

9. Click **OK**.

   As shown in Figure 20, the Breed Name and Section Name styles from the Toy Breeds file are added to the Paragraph Styles panel in the TOC file.

10. Click **File** on the menu bar, then click **Save**.

You opened a document and examined which text elements were formatted with paragraph styles. You then opened a document that will be used as the TOC and loaded the paragraph styles from the first document.

Create a table of contents

1. With the TOC document still open, click the **Add documents button** + on the Book panel, then add the TOC document to the book.

   The TOC document is added to the bottom of the list.

2. Drag **TOC** to the top of the list so your Book panel resembles Figure 21.

3. Click **Layout** on the menu bar, then click **Table of Contents**.

Figure 20 Loading paragraph styles

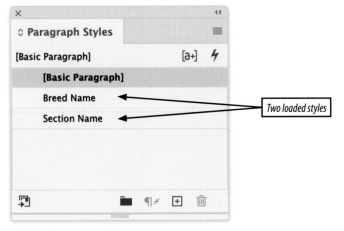

Figure 21 Moving the TOC to the top of the Book panel

4. Verify that the **Title text box** reads **Contents**, then click the **Style list arrow**.

The Breed Name and Section Name paragraph styles are in the list and available to be used.

5. Choose **TOC Title** so your dialog box resembles Figure 22.

TIP TOC Title is a blank paragraph style available by default.

6. Note that the two paragraph styles that you loaded from Toy Breeds.indd are listed in the Other Styles section.

7. Click **Section Name**, then click **Add**.

Section Name is now listed in the Include Paragraph Styles section of the dialog box.

8. Double-click **Breed Name**.

Breed Name is now listed beneath Section Name, as shown in Figure 23.

TIP Double-clicking a style is an alternative to using the Add button.

9. In the Options section, click the **Include Book Documents check box**.

This check box tells InDesign to create the TOC from the Dog Breeds book.

TIP This step is easy to forget; make a mental note of it.

10. Click **OK**.

If a dialog box appears asking if you want to include overset text, click OK.

Continued on next page

Figure 22   Table of Contents dialog box

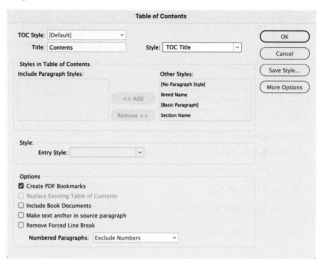

Figure 23   Adding two styles to be used in the TOC

Two styles added for use in the TOC

11. Position the **pointer** over the **top-left corner of the margin guides**, then click once.

    Your page should resemble Figure 24. InDesign has generated a table of contents based on the paragraph styles from the Toy Breeds document. Specifically, InDesign looked in the Toy Breeds document to find every instance of use of the Breeds paragraph style. The Breeds paragraph style was used on every page and applied to the name of the dog breed covered on a page. In the TOC that InDesign created, every dog breed name is listed along with the page number it appears on in the Toy Breeds document.

    Note that the paragraph styles loaded correctly, but those paragraph styles were the right size for the Toy Breeds document layout, not for this TOC layout. You will need to modify the paragraph styles in the TOC document so the fonts are smaller.

12. Continue to the next set of steps.

You specified the two paragraph styles that will be used in the TOC, then loaded the TOC into a text frame.

Create paragraph styles for a TOC

1. On the Paragraph Styles panel, click the **Paragraph Styles panel menu button** ☰, then click **New Paragraph Style**.

2. In the Style Name box, name the new style **TOC Section**.

3. Click **Basic Character Formats**, click the **Font Family list arrow**, click **Times New Roman** or a similar font, click the **Font Style list arrow**, click **Bold**, click the **Size list arrow**, click **14 pt.**, click the **Leading List arrow**, then click **24 pt.**

4. Click **OK**.

    A new paragraph style named TOC Section appears on the Paragraph Styles panel.

5. Click the **Paragraph Styles panel menu button** ☰, then click **New Paragraph Style**.

6. Name the new style **TOC Breed**, click **Basic Character Formats**, click the **Font Family list arrow**, click **Times New Roman** or a similar font, click the **Font Style list arrow**, click **Regular**, click the **Size list arrow**, click **10 pt.**, then click **OK**.

    Your Paragraph Styles panel should resemble Figure 25.

7. Save your work, then continue to the next set of steps.

You created two new paragraph styles for the TOC.

Figure 24 InDesign generates the table of contents based on layer styles applied in the source document

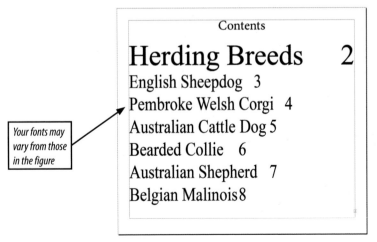

Contents

Herding Breeds 2
English Sheepdog 3
Pembroke Welsh Corgi 4
Australian Cattle Dog 5
Bearded Collie   6
Australian Shepherd 7
Belgian Malinois 8

Your fonts may vary from those in the figure

Figure 25 Two new paragraph styles

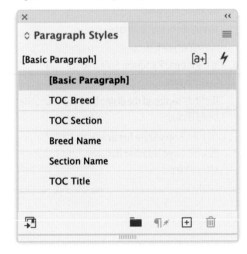

Reformat a table of contents

1. Click **Layout** on the menu bar, then click **Table of Contents**.

2. In the Include Paragraph Styles section, click **Section Name**.

    The Style section of the dialog box, directly beneath the Include Paragraph Styles box, now reads Style: Section Name.

3. Click the **Entry Style list arrow**, then click **TOC Section**.

    The Section Name paragraph style will be reformatted with the TOC Section paragraph style you just created and formatted specifically for the TOC.

4. On the **upper-right side of the dialog box**, click the **More Options button** to expand the dialog box.

5. In the **Style section of the dialog box**, click the **Page Number list arrow**, then click **No Page Number**.

    All options in your dialog box should resemble Figure 26.

6. In the Include Paragraph Styles section, click **Breed Name**.

    The Style section of the dialog box now reads Style: Breed Name.

7. Click the **Entry Style list arrow**, click **TOC Breed**, click the **Page Number list arrow**, then click **After Entry**.

Continued on next page

Figure 26 Reformatting the Section Name paragraph style with the TOC Section paragraph style

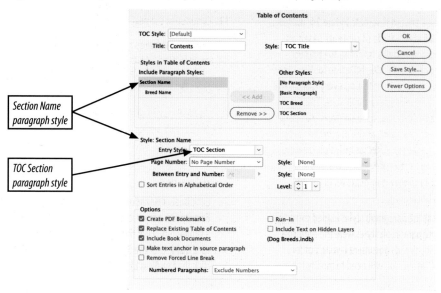

8. Select **all the text in the Between Entry and Number text box**, then type **.... (four periods)**.

9. Click the **Sort Entries in Alphabetical Order check box**.

10. Verify that the **Replace Existing Table of Contents check box** is checked.

    Your dialog box should resemble Figure 27.

11. Click **OK**.

TIP Click Yes if you see a warning box about overset text. You may see an Information dialog box stating that the table of contents has been updated successfully. If so, click OK.

12. Click the **Selection tool** ▶, select the **text frame** on the page, click **Object** on the menu bar, click **Text Frame Options**, change the **number of columns** to **4**, then click **OK**.

    Your page should resemble Figure 28.

13. Using the **Type tool** T, position the cursor **before Terrier Breeds**, click **Type** on the menu bar, point to **Insert Break Character**, then click **Column Break**.

14. Deselect all, press the **letter [W]** to hide guides, then compare your screen to Figure 29.

15. Save your work, then close the TOC document.

You reformatted the imported paragraph styles with other styles you created that were appropriate for the TOC layout.

Figure 27 Reformatting the Breed Name paragraph style with the TOC Breed paragraph style

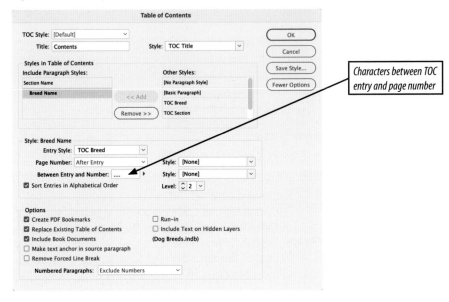

Characters between TOC entry and page number

Figure 28 Viewing the reformatted TOC

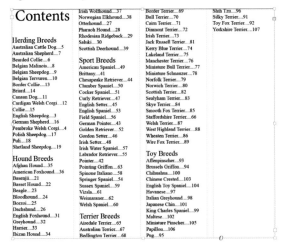

Figure 29 Viewing the final TOC

Contents

CREATE AN INDEX

▶ *What You'll Do*

In this lesson, you will create an index based on the documents in the book file.

Creating Index Entries

An **index** is an alphabetized list of terms in a book that references the page or pages on which those items are mentioned. Index entries are specified within the documents that make up the book and are saved with the documents.

Specifying index entries is easy to do. Simply select the text you want to use as an index entry, click the Create a new index entry button on the Index panel, then click OK in the New Page Reference dialog box. The selected text will be added to the Index panel, as shown in Figure 30.

Figure 30 Creating an index entry

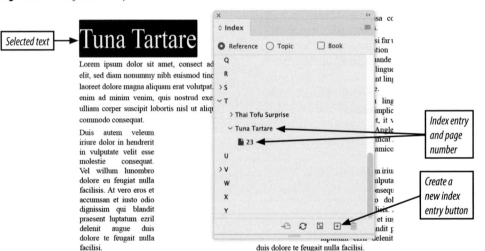

Selected text

Index entry and page number

Create a new index entry button

Generating an Index

An index is an individual InDesign document that you add to the Book panel to become part of the book. This will usually be a one- or two-page document. As with the TOC document, it is critical that you carefully choose the same document setup specifications that were used to create the other documents in the book. Once you have created the index document, add it to the Book panel.

After you've added the index document to the Book panel, click the Generate index button on the Index panel, shown in Figure 31. This opens the Generate Index dialog box, shown in Figure 32. As its name implies, this dialog box generates the index based on the index entries saved with the documents that compose the book. Be sure to check the Include Book Documents check box before clicking OK.

Figure 31 Index panel

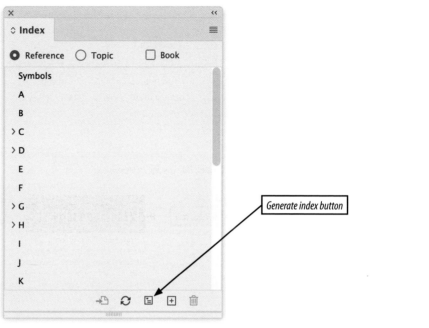

Generate index button

Figure 32 Generate Index dialog box

Generating a Cross-Reference Index Entry

Creating an index is a linguistic challenge. One of your greatest challenges will be to anticipate the way a reader will search the index for specific topics. For example, if you have written a book on recipes, you might have an index entry for Bouillabaisse. That seems pretty straightforward, but you would also need to anticipate that some of your readers would go to the F section of the index looking for bouillabaisse. Why F? F, for Fish Stew.

In this example, you could simply create an index entry for Fish Stew with the page number for Bouillabaisse. However, for consistency reasons, it would be better to create a cross-reference. You do this in the New Cross-reference dialog box, shown in Figure 33. You create this cross-reference entry in the document when you create the other index entries. When you click OK, a new entry will be created, as shown in Figure 34.

Figure 33 New Cross-reference dialog box

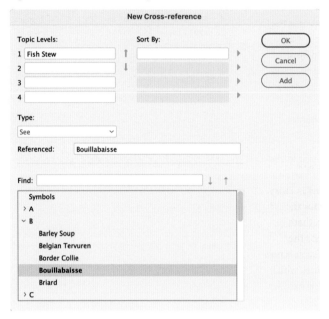

Figure 34 Cross-referenced index entry

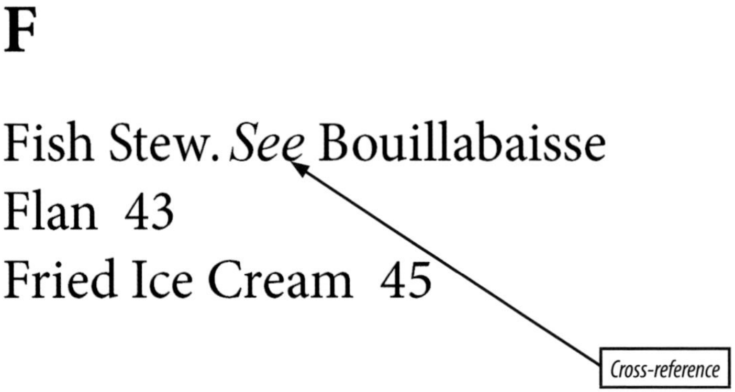

F

Fish Stew. *See* Bouillabaisse
Flan 43
Fried Ice Cream 45

Cross-reference

Sorting Index Entries

Once you've created individual index entries for specific topics in your document, you may want to sort specific entries together under a new topic. For example, you might have three separate index entries for Veal Marsala, Chicken Marsala, and Pork Marsala. However, your reader might go to the "M" section of your index looking for the word "Marsala." For that reason, you would want an index entry that reads "Marsala Dishes" and lists the three Marsala dishes and their page numbers.

To do this, you must create a new index entry for Marsala Dishes. Go to the page for the first Marsala dish—in this example, that's Chicken Marsala—then click to place the pointer in the headline. Click the Create a new index entry button on the Index panel, which opens the New Page Reference dialog box. As shown in Figure 35, Marsala Dishes is entered in the number 1 text box, and Chicken Marsala is entered in the number 2 text box.

Figure 35 New Page Reference dialog box

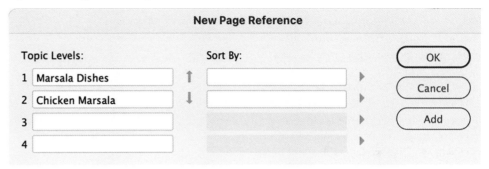

When you click OK, a new entry appears in the "M" section for Marsala Dishes with Chicken Marsala listed beneath it, as shown in Figure 36. Repeat this process for Veal Marsala and Pork Marsala, and your Index panel will resemble Figure 37.

When you save changes to the document and generate the index, the listing will appear as shown in Figure 38.

Figure 36 An original index entry duplicated as a subentry

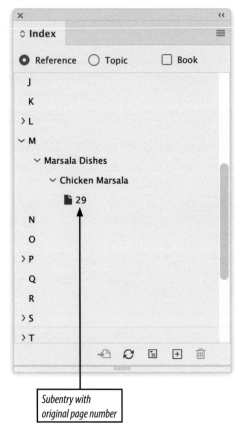

Subentry with original page number

Figure 37 Three sorted subentries on the Index panel

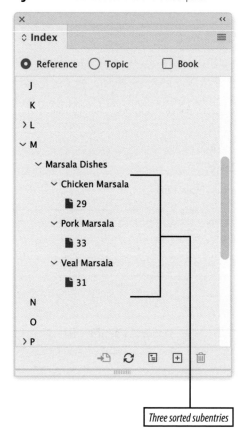

Three sorted subentries

Figure 38 Sorted subentries in an index

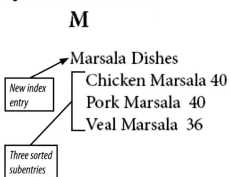

New index entry

Three sorted subentries

Create an index entry

1. On the Book panel, double-click **Toy Breeds**.

   The document opens.

2. Click **Window** on the menu bar, point to **Type & Tables**, then click **Index**.

3. On the Index panel, click each **triangle next to each alphabet letter** to view the index entries that have already been created.

   An index entry has been created for every breed in the document except the breed on page 91, Silky Terrier.

4. On the Pages panel, double-click **page 91** to center it in the window, click the **Type tool** T , then select the **Silky Terrier headline**.

   TIP Be sure that the Index panel is visible, and that you can see the "S" section.

5. Click the **Create a new index entry button** ⊞ on the Index panel.

   When text is selected, clicking this button opens the New Page Reference dialog box.

6. Note that the **Type list box** contains **Current Page** and that **Silky Terrier** is automatically listed in the **Topic Levels section**.

7. Click **OK**.

8. Expand the **Silky Terrier entry** on the Index panel, then compare your Index panel to Figure 39.

   An entry for Silky Terrier on page 91 is added to the Index panel.

9. Click **File** on the menu bar, click **Save**, then close the Toy Breeds document.

You created an index entry.

Figure 39 New entry on the Index panel

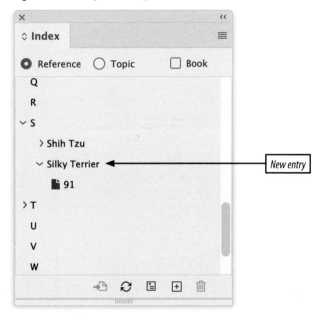

Generate an index

1. Open ID 10-7.indd, then save it as **Index**.

2. On the Dog Breeds book, click the **Add documents button** +, then add **Index**.

TIP Index should be added at the bottom of the list. If it appears elsewhere, drag it to the bottom of the list.

3. Click the **Generate index button** 🔲 on the Index panel.

The Generate Index dialog box opens.

4. Delete the **text in the Title text box**.

You don't need this dialog box to insert a title for you because the title "Index" already exists in a text frame in the Index document.

5. Remove the **check mark in the Replace Existing Index check box**, then click the **Include Book Documents check box** so your Generate Index dialog box resembles Figure 40.

6. Click **OK,** position the loaded text pointer over the **top-left corner of the text frame** on page 108, then click.

7. Adjust any bad column breaks.

8. Deselect all, hide all guides, then compare your index to Figure 41.

The index is generated based on all the index entries created in each of the five documents. Note that Silky Terrier—the entry you created—is listed on page 91 in the "S" section.

TIP If you are asked to save any of the "Breeds" documents, click Yes.

9. Click **File** on the menu bar, then click **Save**.

10. Click the **Save the book button** ⬇ on the Book panel.

11. Continue to the next set of steps.

You generated an index based on all the index entries in the five documents.

Figure 40 Generate Index dialog box

Figure 41 Generating an index

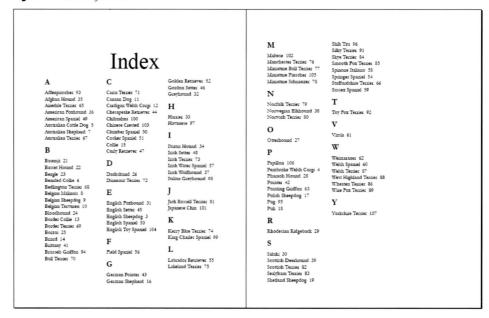

Create index cross-references

1. Double-click **Toy Breeds** on the Book panel to open the document.

2. Click the **Index panel menu button** ≡, then click **New Cross-reference**.

3. In the **Topic Levels section**, type **Min-Pin** in the **number 1 text box**.

4. Click the **Type list arrow**, then click **See**.

5. In the **large box at the bottom**, scroll to the "M" **section**, then click the **triangle** to expose the "M" index entries.

6. Drag **Miniature Pinscher** into the **Referenced text box**.

The words Miniature Pinscher should appear in the Referenced text box, as shown in Figure 42.

7. Click **OK,** then scroll to the **M section** on the Index panel.

As shown in Figure 43, a new entry for Min-Pin has been added, with the reference See Miniature Pinscher.

8. Save your work, then close the Toy Breeds document.

9. Verify that **Index.indd** is the only open document, then click the **Generate index button** 📖 on the Index panel.

10. In the **Generate Index dialog box**, check the **Replace Existing Index**

check box to replace the previous index, verify that the **Include Book Documents check box** is checked, then click **OK.**

11. Save your work, then continue to the next set of steps.

TIP If you receive a message telling you the index has been replaced successfully, click OK.

The replacement index now shows the cross-reference after the Min-Pin entry.

You created a new index entry that is cross-referenced to an existing entry.

Figure 42 Creating a cross-reference

Figure 43 Min-Pin entry on the Index panel

Sort index entries

1. Open **Sport Breeds**.

   Sport Breeds contains four pages that profile retriever breeds of dogs.

2. Click the **Type tool** T, double-click **page 44** on the Pages panel, then click **anywhere in the Chesapeake Retriever headline**.

3. Click the **Index panel menu button** ≡, then click **New Page Reference**.

4. In the Topic Levels section, type **Retrievers** in the **number 1 text box**, type **Chesapeake Retriever** in the **number 2 text box**, click **OK**, then compare your Index panel to Figure 44.

5. Double-click **page 47** on the Pages panel, click the **Type tool** T anywhere in the **Curly Retriever headline**, click the **Index panel menu button** ≡, then click

   New Page Reference on the Index Panel Options menu.

6. Type **Retrievers** in the **number 1 text box**, type **Curly Retriever** in the **number 2 text box**, then click **OK**.

7. Using **pages 52 and 55**, create new page references for the **Golden Retriever** and **Labrador Retriever**.

   Your Index panel should resemble Figure 45.

Figure 44 New index entry with a subentry cross-reference

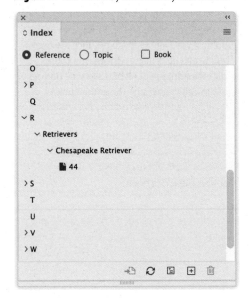

Figure 45 Four sorted subentries

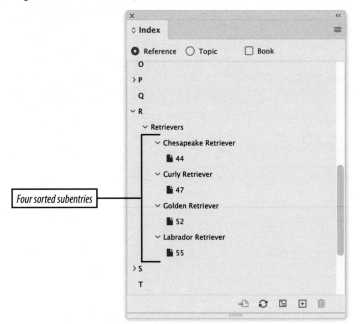

Four sorted subentries

8. Save your work, close the Sport Breeds document, verify that **Index.indd** is the only document open, then generate a **replacement index**.

   As shown in Figure 46, the new index has an entry for Retrievers with the four retriever breeds sorted beneath as subentries.

   TIP Read the sidebar on this page titled, "Exporting a Book File."

9. Save your work, close the Index document, then close the Book panel.

   TIP If you are prompted to save changes to Dog Breeds.indb before closing, click Save (Mac) or Yes (Win).

You created a new index entry, then sorted four other subentries.

Figure 46 Updated index with four sorted subentries

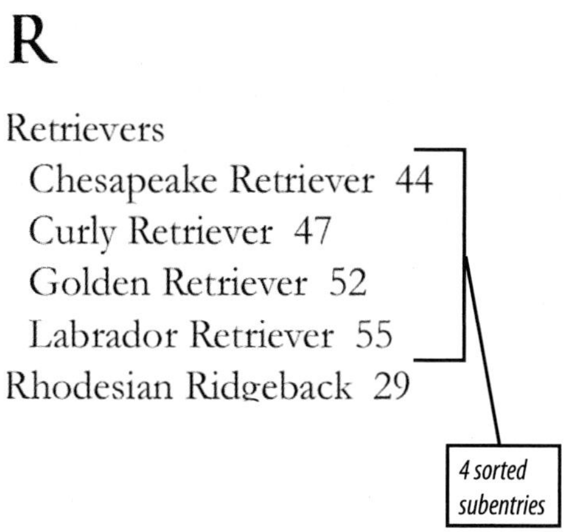

R

Retrievers
   Chesapeake Retriever 44
   Curly Retriever 47
   Golden Retriever 52
   Labrador Retriever 55
Rhodesian Ridgeback 29

4 sorted subentries

EXPORTING A BOOK FILE

It is important you understand that the book file itself is the book. For example, as a result of doing the exercises in this chapter, you have created a book file named Dog Breeds. You have determined how the sections will flow, you have determined that each section will open on a left-hand, even-numbered page, and you have added a table of contents and an index. Remember that all the work you've done on the Book panel has affected the original data files with which you started. They've been renumbered, and in some cases, pages have been moved to correspond to the changes you made on the Book panel. At this point, if you were ready to produce the book, you would have many options. You could click the Print the Book button at the bottom of the Book panel, and the entire book would print. If this were a job that was being professionally printed, you could package and send the individual InDesign files to the printer just like you would any other project. You could also export a single PDF that houses the entire book.

Create a book file

1. Open ID 10-8.indd, then save it as **Appetizers**.
2. Open ID 10-9.indd and click **Don't Update Links** in the Issues with Links dialog box.

TIP Click **Don't Update Links** in the Issues with Links dialog box for the next two documents that you open.

3. Save the file as **Soups**.
4. Open ID 10-10.indd, then save it as **Entrees**.
5. Open ID 10-11 .indd, then save it as **Desserts**.
6. Close all open documents.
7. Click File on the menu bar, point to New, then click Book.
8. Name the new file **Dinner Recipes**, then click Save.
9. Click the Book panel menu button, then click Add Document.
10. Add Entrees.indd.
11. Click the Add documents button on the Book panel, then add Desserts.indd.
12. Add the following two documents: Soups.indd and Appetizers.indd.
13. Click the Save the book button on the Book panel.

Organize a book file

1. On the Book panel, click and drag Soups to the top of the list.
2. Click and drag Appetizers to the top of the list.
3. Note that all the documents on the Book panel begin on odd page numbers.

For this project, you want each chapter to begin on an even-numbered left-hand page.

4. Click the Book panel menu button, then click Book Page Numbering Options.
5. Click the Continue on next even page option button, then click OK.
6. On the Book panel, double-click the page numbers for Appetizers.
7. Click the Start Page Numbering at option button, type **2** in the text box, then click OK.
8. Save the change, close the Appetizers document, then note the page range on the Book panel.
9. Click the Save the book button on the Book panel.

Create a table of contents

1. Open ID 10-12.indd, then save it as **Recipes TOC**.
2. Click the Paragraph Styles panel menu button, then click Load Paragraph Styles.
3. Open Appetizers.indd.
4. Click OK in the Load Styles dialog box.
5. Click File on the menu bar, then click Save.
6. With Recipes TOC.indd still open, click the Add documents button on the Book panel.
7. Add Recipes TOC.indd.
8. Drag Recipes TOC to the top of the list.
9. Click Layout on the menu bar, then click Table of Contents.
10. Delete the text in the Title text box.
11. In the Other Styles list, click Course Name, then click Add.

12. Double-click Dish Name.
13. In the Options section at the bottom of the dialog box, click the Include Book Documents check box to select it.
14. Click OK.
15. Position the pointer over the top-left corner of the margin guides on the page, then click once.
16. Click Layout on the menu bar, then click Table of Contents.
17. In the Include Paragraph Styles section, click Course Name to select it.
18. Click the Entry Style list arrow, then click TOC Course.
19. Click the Page Number list arrow, then click No Page Number.

TIP If necessary, click More Options to display the Page Number option.

20. In the Include Paragraph Styles section, click Dish Name to select it.
21. Click the Entry Style list arrow, then click TOC Dish Name, click the Page Number list arrow, then click After Entry.
22. Select the contents of the Between Entry and Number text box, then type ..... (five periods).
23. Click the Sort Entries in Alphabetical Order check box to select it, then verify that the Replace Existing Table of Contents check box is checked.
24. Click OK.
    If you see a dialog box saying that the TOC was updated successfully, click OK.

25. Click the Selection tool, select the text frame on the page, click Object on the menu bar, click Text Frame Options, change the number of columns to 2, click OK, then deselect all.
Your page should resemble Figure 47.
26. Save your work, then close the Recipes TOC document.

Create an index

1. On the Book panel, double-click Entrees to open the document.
2. Click Window on the menu bar, point to Type & Tables, then click Index.
3. On the Pages panel, double-click page 23 to center it in the window, click the Type tool, then select the Tuna Tartare headline.
4. Click the Create a new index entry button on the Index panel.
5. Click OK.
6. Click File on the menu bar, click Save, then close Entrees.
7. Open ID 10-13.indd, then save it as **Recipes Index**.
8. Click the Add documents button on the Dinner Recipes Book panel, add Recipes Index.indd, then drag it to the bottom of the Book panel.
9. Click the Generate index button on the Index panel.
10. Delete the text in the Title text box.
11. Remove the check mark in the Replace Existing Index check box, then click to select the Include Book Documents check box.
12. Click OK.

Figure 47 Completed Skills Review, Part 1

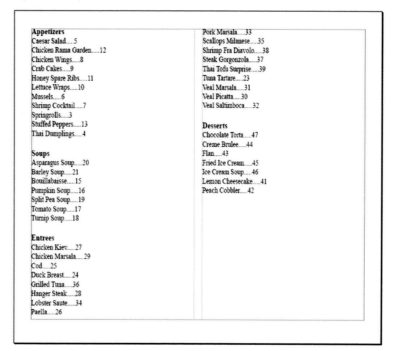

13. Position the loaded text pointer over the top-left corner of the text frame in Recipes Index.indd, then click.
14. Click File on the menu bar, then click Save.
15. Click the Save the book button on the Book panel.
16. Double-click Soups on the Book panel to open the document.
17. Click the Index panel menu button, then click New Cross-reference.
18. In the Topic Levels section, type **Fish Stew** in the number 1 text box.
19. Click the Type list arrow, then click See.
20. In the large box at the bottom, scroll to the "B" section, then click the triangle to expose the "B" index entries.

21. Drag Bouillabaisse into the Referenced text box, then release the mouse button when the plus sign appears in the pointer.

22. Click OK.

23. Save your work, then close the Soups document.

24. Verify that Recipes Index.indd is the only open document, then click the Generate index button on the Index panel.

25. In the Generate Index dialog box, check the Replace Existing Index check box, then click OK.

26. Double-click Entrees on the Book panel to open the document.
Entrees contains three Marsala dishes—Pork, Veal, and Chicken.

27. Click the Type tool, double-click page 29 on the Pages panel, then click anywhere in the headline.

28. Click the Index panel menu button, then click New Page Reference.

29. In the Topic Levels section, type **Marsala Dishes** in the number 1 text box, type **Chicken Marsala** in the number 2 text box, then click OK.

30. Double-click page 31 on the Pages panel, click anywhere in the headline, click the Index panel menu button, then click New Page Reference.

31. Type **Marsala Dishes** in the number 1 text box, type **Veal Marsala** in the number 2 text box, then click OK.

32. Double-click page 33 on the Pages panel, click anywhere in the headline, click the Index panel menu button then click New Page Reference.

33. Type **Marsala Dishes** in the number 1 text box, type **Pork Marsala** in the number 2 text box, then click OK.

34. Save your work, close the Entrees document, verify that Recipes Index.indd is the only document open, then generate a replacement index.

35. Adjust column breaks to improve the layout, deselect all, press [W] to hide guides, then compare your index to Figure 48.

36. Save your work, close the Recipes Index document, then close the Dinner Recipes book.

Figure 48 *Completed Skills Review, Part 2*

Index

A	H	T
Asparagus Soup 20	Hanger Steak 28	Thai Dumplings 4
B	Honey Spare Ribs 11	Thai Tofu Surprise 39
Barley Soup 21	**I**	Tomato Soup 17
Bouillabaisse 15	Ice Cream Soup 46	Tuna Tartare 23
C	**L**	Turnip Soup 18
Caesar Salad 5	Lemon Cheesecake 41	**V**
Chicken Kiev 27	Lettuce Wraps 10	Veal Marsala 31
Chicken Marsala 29	Lobster Saute 34	Veal Picatta 30
Chicken Rama Garden 12		Veal Saltimboca 32
Chicken Wings 8	**M**	
Chocolate Torta 47	Marsala Dishes	
Cod 25	Chicken Marsala 29	
Crab Cakes 9	Pork Marsala 33	
Creme Brulee 44	Veal Marsala 31	
D	Mussels 6	
Duck Breast 24	**P**	
F	Paella 26	
Fish Stew. *See* Bouillabaisse	Peach Cobbler 42	
Flan 43	Pork Marsala 33	
Fried Ice Cream 45	Pumpkin Soup 16	
G	**S**	
Grilled Tuna 36	Scallops Milanese 35	
	Shrimp Cocktail 7	
	Shrimp Fra Diavolo 38	
	Split Pea Soup 19	
	Springrolls 3	
	Steak Gorgonzola 37	
	Stuffed Peppers 13	

You work for a publishing company and have created an index for a book on dog breeds. Your boss comes to you and tells you that the index is not complete. You will need to sort three breeds under a new index entry.

1. Open ID 10-14.indd, then save it as **Sort Setters**.
2. Click the Type tool, double-click page 6 on the Pages panel, then click in the headline.
3. Click the Index panel menu button, then click New Page Reference.
4. In the Topic Levels section, type **Setters** in the number 1 text box, type **English Setter** in the number 2 text box, then click OK.
5. Double-click page 7 on the Pages panel, click in the headline, click the Index panel menu button, then click New Page Reference.
6. Type **Setters** in the number 1 text box, type **Gordon Setter** in the number 2 text box, then click OK.
7. Double-click page 9 on the Pages panel, click in the headline, click the Index panel menu button, then click New Page Reference.
8. Type **Setters** in the number 1 text box, type **Irish Setter** in the number 2 text box, then click OK.
9. Scroll to the S section, then compare your index to Figure 49.
10. Save your work, then close the Sort Setters document.

Figure 49 Completed Project Builder 1

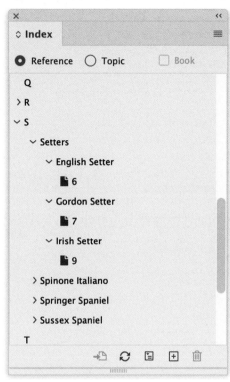

PROJECT BUILDER 2

You work for a publishing company and have created an index for a book on dog breeds. Your boss tells you the index is not complete. He wants you to create a cross-reference entry titled "Red Setter" that points to the Irish Setter page.

1. Open ID 10-15.indd, then save it as **Cross-reference Setters**.
2. Click the Selection tool.
3. Click the Index panel menu button, then click New Cross-reference.
4. In the Topic Levels section, type **Red Setter** in the number 1 text box.
5. Click the Type list arrow, then click See.
6. In the large box at the bottom, scroll to the "I" section, then click the triangle to expose the "I" index entries.
7. Drag Irish Setter into the Referenced text box, then release the mouse button when the plus sign appears in the pointer.
8. Click OK.
9. Scroll to the R section of the Index panel to view the cross-reference, then compare your Index panel to Figure 50.
10. Save your work, then close the Cross-reference Setters document.

Figure 50 Completed Project Builder 2

You are a graphic designer at a publishing company. One of your clients comes to you with an InDesign file and wants your help. The client generated a table of contents from a book file and was surprised that the paragraph styles used to create the book did not work for the layout of the TOC. When you receive the file, you note that he didn't include the book file. This means you can't regenerate a new TOC file. Therefore, you decide to reformat the layout directly in the InDesign document.

1. Open ID 10-16.indd, then save it as **TOC Redesign**.
2. On the Paragraph Styles panel, double-click Breed Name, click Basic Character Formats, change the Size to 10, then click OK.
3. Double-click Section Name, click Basic Character Formats, change the Size to 16, click Advanced Character Formats, change the Horizontal Scale to 72%, then click OK.
4. Select the text frame, open the Text Frame Options dialog box, change the number of columns to 4, then click OK.
5. Triple-click the word Contents, then delete it.
6. Delete any extra space at the top of the column, switch to the Selection tool, deselect all, press [W] to hide guides, then compare your page to Figure 51.
7. Save your work, then close the TOC Redesign document.

Figure 51 Completed Design Project

Herding Breeds
Australian Cattle Dog..........5
Australian Shepherd..........7
Bearded Collie..........6
Belgian Malinois..........8
Belgian Sheepdog..........9
Belgian Tervuren..........10
Border Collie..........13
Briard..........14
Canaan Dog..........11
Cardigan Welsh Corgi..........12
Collie..........15
English Sheepdog..........3
German Shepherd..........16
Pembroke Welsh Corgi..........4
Polish Sheepdog..........17
Puli..........18
Shetland Sheepdog..........19

Hound Breeds
Afghan Hound..........35
American Foxhound..........36
Basenji..........21
Basset Hound..........22
Beagle..........23
Bloodhound..........24
Borzoi..........25
Dachshund..........26
English Foxhound..........31
Greyhound..........32
Harrier..........33
Ibizan Hound..........34
Irish Wolfhound..........37

Norwegian Elkhound..........38
Otterhound..........27
Pharaoh Hound..........28
Rhodesian Ridgeback..........29
Saluki..........30
Scottish Deerhound..........39

Sport Breeds
American Spaniel..........49
Brittany..........41
Chesapeake Retriever..........44
Clumber Spaniel..........50
Cocker Spaniel..........51
Curly Retriever..........47
English Setter..........45
English Spaniel..........53
Field Spaniel..........56
German Pointer..........43
Golden Retriever..........52
Gordon Setter..........46
Irish Setter..........48
Irish Water Spaniel..........57
Labrador Retriever..........55
Pointer..........42
Pointing Griffon..........63
Spinone Italiano..........58
Springer Spaniel..........54
Sussex Spaniel..........59
Vizsla..........61
Weimaraner..........62
Welsh Spaniel..........60

Terrier Breeds
Airedale Terrier..........65
Australian Terrier..........67
Bedlington Terrier..........68
Border Terrier..........69
Bull Terrier..........70
Cairn Terrier..........71
Dinmont Terrier..........72
Irish Terrier..........73
Jack Russell Terrier..........81
Kerry Blue Terrier..........74
Lakeland Terrier..........75
Manchester Terrier..........76
Miniature Bull Terrier..........77
Miniature Schnauzer..........78
Norfolk Terrier..........79
Norwich Terrier..........80
Scottish Terrier..........82
Sealyham Terrier..........83
Skye Terrier..........84
Smooth Fox Terrier..........85
Staffordshire Terrier..........66
Welsh Terrier..........87
West Highland Terrier..........88
Wheaten Terrier..........86
Wire Fox Terrier..........89

Toy Breeds
Affenpinscher..........93
Brussels Griffon..........94
Chihuahua..........100
Chinese Crested..........103
English Toy Spaniel..........104

Havanese..........97
Italian Greyhound..........98
Japanese Chin..........101
King Charles Spaniel..........99
Maltese..........102
Miniature Pinscher..........105
Papillon..........106
Pug..........95
Shih Tzu..........96
Silky Terrier..........91
Toy Fox Terrier..........92
Yorkshire Terrier..........107

THE ROAD TO HANA

a visual journey through Maui

CHAPTER

11

CERTIFIED
PROFESSIONAL

PREPARING, PACKAGING, AND EXPORTING DOCUMENTS FOR PRINT AND THE WEB

1. Create Bleeds, Slugs, and Printer's Marks
2. Use the Ink Manager and Preview Color Separations
3. Preflight and Package a Document
4. Export a Document for Print and the Web

Adobe Certified Professional in Print & Digital Media Publication Using Adobe InDesign

1. Working in the Design Industry
This objective covers critical concepts related to working with colleagues and clients as well as crucial legal, technical, and design-related knowledge.

1.1 Identify the purpose, audience, and audience needs for preparing publications.
   B Identify requirements based on how the design will be used, including print, web, and mobile.

1.4 Demonstrate knowledge of key terminology related to publications.
   B Demonstrate knowledge of how color is created in publications.
   C Understand and use key terms related to multipage layouts.

2. Project Setup and Interface
This objective covers the interface setup and program settings that assist in an efficient and effective workflow, as well as knowledge about ingesting digital assets for a project.

2.1 Create a document with the appropriate settings for web, print, and mobile.
   A Set appropriate document settings for printed and on-screen images.
   B Create a new document preset to reuse for specific project needs.

2.3 Use nonprinting design tools in the interface to aid in design or workflow.
   D Use views and modes to work efficiently.

4. Creating and Modifying Document Elements
This objective covers core tools and functionality of the application, as well as tools that affect the visual appearance of document elements.

4.7 Add interactive or dynamic content or media to a project.
   A Add interactive elements and behaviors.
   B Demonstrate knowledge of how to embed rich-media objects.

5. Publishing Digital Media
This objective covers saving and exporting documents or assets within individual layers or selections.

5.1 Prepare documents for publishing to web, print, and other digital devices.
   A Check document for errors and project specifications.

5.2 Export or save documents to various file formats.
   B Save in appropriate formats for print, screen, or online.
   C Print proof copies before publishing.
   D Package an InDesign project.

CREATE BLEEDS, SLUGS, AND PRINTER'S MARKS

▶ What You'll Do

In this lesson, you will create bleed and slug areas, and then you will output a document with printer's marks.

Understanding Bleeds

Before discussing bleeds, it's important to understand trim size. Trim size is the size to which a printed document will be cut, or trimmed, when it clears the printing press. For example, an 8" × 10" magazine may be printed on a page that is 12" × 14", but it will be trimmed to 8" × 10".

Professionally printed documents are printed on paper or a "sheet" that is larger than the document's trim size. The extra space is used to accommodate bleeds, crops, and other printer's marks. **Bleeds** are areas of the layout that extend to the trim size. In Figure 1, the green background extends to the trim on all four sides; the yellow strip extends to the trim on the left and the right. Both are said to "bleed" off the edge.

It's important to understand that areas of the layout that extend to the trim—areas that are meant to bleed—must actually go beyond the trim size when the document is prepared for printing to accommodate for the margin of error in trimming.

Nothing is perfect, and this includes the cutting device used to trim printed pieces when it clears the printing press. You can target the cutting device to slice the paper exactly at the trim size, but you can never expect it to be dead-on every time. There is a margin of error, usually 1/32"–1/16".

Figure 1 Identifying areas that will bleed

Green extends to the trim size on all four sides

Yellow extends to the trim size on two sides

To accommodate for this margin of error, any item that bleeds—any item that extends to the trim size—must actually extend *beyond* the trim size in your final layout. The standard measurement a bleed item must extend beyond the trim size is 0.125".

Creating Bleeds

You define a bleed area for a document in the Bleed and Slug section of the New Document dialog box when you're creating a document. Or, if you want to define a bleed area after the document has been created, you can do this in the Document Setup dialog box, shown in Figure 2.

TIP Most designers prefer to address the issues with items that bleed after they've designed the layout.

Figure 2 shows that the trim size for the document is 6" wide by 3" in height and that a 0.125" bleed area is to be added outside the trim size. This bleed area is reflected in the document by a red guide, shown in Figure 3.

You use this guide when you extend areas that bleed beyond the trim size.

As shown in Figure 4, the green background has been extended to the bleed guide on all four sides, and the yellow strip has been extended on the left and the right. If the trimmer trims slightly outside of the trim size (the black line), the extra bleed material provides the room for that error.

Figure 2 Document Setup dialog box

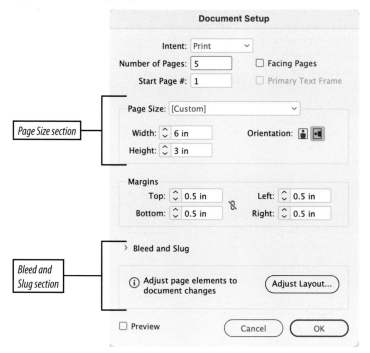

Figure 3 Identifying the bleed guide

Figure 4 Extending bleed items to the bleed guide

Creating Slugs

Often, when you output a document, you'll want to include a note on the output, referred to as a **slug**. Slugs are often notes to the printer, phone numbers to call if there are any problems, or other information related to the file.

Obviously, slugs are not meant to be part of the final trimmed document. They must be positioned outside the trim size and outside the bleed area so they will be discarded when the document is trimmed. InDesign allows you to create a **slug area** in the Bleed and Slug section of the Document Setup dialog box or the New Document dialog box, shown in Figure 5. In this figure, 0.5" has been specified for a slug area on all four sides of the document. The slug area is identified by a blue guide, shown in Figure 6. Create a text frame, position it in the slug area, then type whatever information you want to keep with the file, as shown in Figure 7.

When you create a slug, use the [Registration] swatch on the Swatches panel as the fill color for the text. When the document is color separated, anything filled with the [Registration] swatch appears on all printing plates.

Figure 5 Defining the slug area

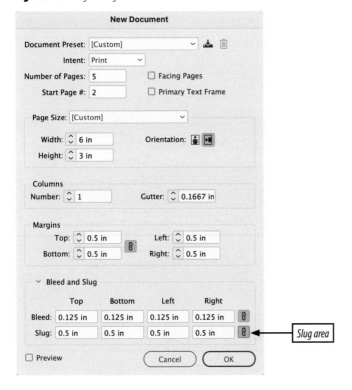

Figure 6 Identifying the slug area

Slug area identified by blue guide

Figure 7 Adding a slug

Slug contained in the slug area

Previewing Bleeds and Slugs

The bleed and slug areas are not visible in Preview mode. If you want to see a preview of the page with those areas visible, press and hold the Preview button at the bottom of the toolbar to reveal the Bleed and Slug buttons, as shown in Figure 8. Bleed mode will show you a preview with the bleed area included, and Slug mode will show you a preview with both the bleed and slug areas included.

Printing Bleeds, Slugs, and Printer's Marks

When you output a document, you can choose whether or not the bleed and slug areas will print; usually they are printed along with printer's marks. You specify these items to print in the Marks and Bleed section of the Print dialog box, shown in Figure 9. **Printer's marks** include **crop marks**, which are guidelines that define the trim size. **Bleed marks** define the bleed size. Printers use **registration marks** to align the color-separated output. **Color bars** are used to maintain consistent color on press, and **page information** includes the title of the InDesign document.

Figure 10 shows a printed document output with a bleed area and a slug area and identifies all five printer's marks.

Figure 8 View mode buttons on the toolbar

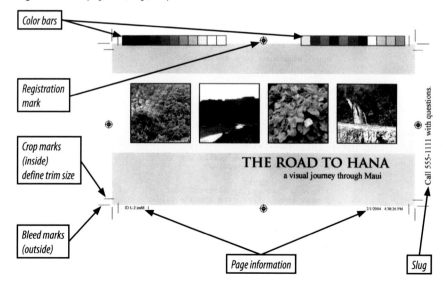

Figure 9 Marks and Bleed section of the Print dialog box

Figure 10 Identifying bleeds, slugs, and printer's marks

Create a bleed

1. Open ID 11-1.indd, then save it as **OAHU to Print**.

2. Verify that the screen mode is set to **Normal view** so guides are visible.

3. Click **File** on the menu bar, then click **Document Setup**.

   The document's size, or, the trim size, is 6" × 7.5".

4. As shown in Figure 11, type **.125** in the **Top**, **Bottom**, **Inside**, and **Outside Bleed text boxes**; click **OK**; then compare your page to Figure 12.

A bleed guide appears defining the bleed area, which is .125" outside the trim size on all four sides.

TIP Rather than enter .125 four times, click the Make all settings the same button 🔗 , type .125 once, press [tab] and the other three text boxes will automatically update.

Figure 11 Document Setup dialog box

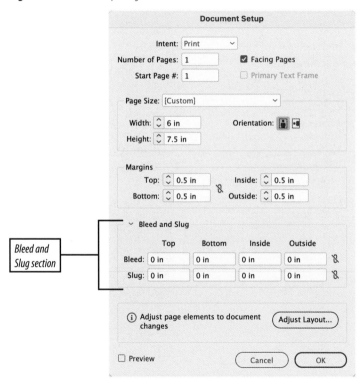

Figure 12 Bleed area

5. Click the **Selection tool** ▶, select the **blue frame**, then drag the **frame corners** to the bleed guide so that your document resembles Figure 13.

6. Save your work, then continue to the next set of steps.

You specified the bleed area in the Document Setup dialog box, then you modified an object on the page so that it will bleed on all four sides.

Create a slug

1. Click **File** on the menu bar, then click **Document Setup**.

2. Type **.5** in the **Top**, **Bottom**, **Inside**, and **Outside Slug text boxes**; click **OK**; then compare your page to Figure 14.

A slug guide appears, defining the slug area, which is 0.5" outside the trim size on all four sides.

Continued on next page

Figure 13 Modifying an object's size to bleed

Figure 14 Slug area

Slug guide

3. Drag the **text frame** from the pasteboard into the **slug area at the right of the document**, then change the **stroke color of the text frame** to **[None]**.

4. Click the **Type tool** T, then type the following in the text frame: **Printer: Any ?s call me at 800-555-1212**.

5. Click the **Selection tool** ▶, then position the **text frame** in the same location shown in Figure 15.

6. Verify that the **text frame** is still selected, then click the **Formatting affects text button** T on the Swatches panel.

7. Change the **fill color** of the text to **[Registration]**, then deselect the text frame.

   With a [Registration] fill, the slug text will appear on all printing plates if the document is color separated.

8. Save your work, then continue to the next set of steps.

You specified a slug area in the Document Setup dialog box, you typed a message for the printer in the slug area, then you filled the text with the [Registration] swatch.

Figure 15 Typing a message in the slug area

Message to printer

Preview bleeds and slugs

1. Click the **Preview button** □. on the toolbar.

   In Preview mode, neither the bleed nor the slug area is visible. Your toolbar must be set to two columns to see the Preview button □.

2. Press and hold the **Preview button** □. until you see the Bleed and Slug buttons, then click the **Bleed button** □.

   Bleed mode shows the document and the bleed area.

3. Press and hold the **Bleed button** □. , then click the **Slug button** □.

   As shown in Figure 16, in Slug mode, the bleed and slug areas are previewed along with the document.

4. Click the **Normal button** □.

5. Save your work, then continue to the next set of steps.

You viewed the layout in Preview, Bleed, Slug, and Normal modes.

Figure 16 Viewing the layout in Slug mode

Print bleeds, slugs, and printer's marks

1. Click **File** on the menu bar, then click **Print**.

2. Verify that **Copies** is set to **1** and **Pages** is set to **All**, then click **Setup** in the box on the left.

TIP Don't click the Page Setup (Mac) or Setup (Win) or button at the bottom of the dialog box.

3. Click the **Paper Size list arrow**, click **Letter**, click the **Page Position list arrow**, then click **Centered**.

   Your dialog box should resemble Figure 17.

TIP Your letter choice may be Letter (8.5 x 11 in), US Letter, or another variation of an 8.5" × 11" inch document, depending on your printer type.

4. Click the **Marks and Bleed category** in the box on the left.

5. In the Marks section, click the **All Printer's Marks check box,** then click the **Offset up arrow** until the value reads **.375 in**.

   The Offset value specifies how far outside the trim the crop and bleed marks will be positioned. This is something to consider if you have bleed elements. Let's say your bleed is .125", which is standard. Since you don't want your crop marks *inside* the bleed element, you'd set the Offset value to .25" or greater. That way, the crop marks are positioned outside the bleed.

6. In the Bleed and Slug section, verify that the **Use Document Bleed Settings check box** is checked, then click the **Include Slug Area check box**.

   Your dialog box should resemble Figure 18.

Figure 17 Setup category in the Print dialog box

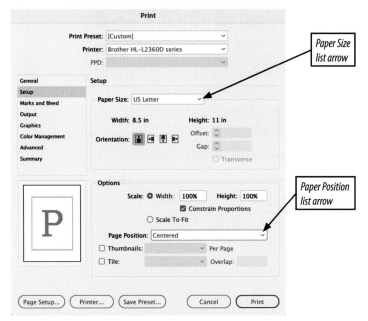

Figure 18 Activating printer's marks

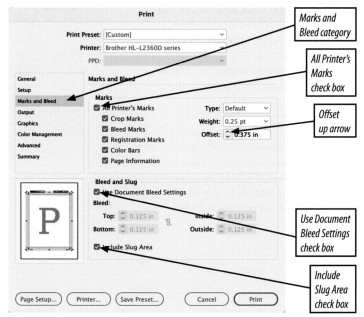

7. Click **Print**.

Compare the printer's marks in Figure 19 to your own output.

8. Save your work, then continue to the next lesson.

You opened the Print dialog box, set the paper size and page position, and activated all printer's marks, the document's bleed settings, and the slug area. You then printed the document.

UNDERSTANDING INDESIGN COMPATIBILITY

One of the most important features of Adobe InDesign is that it interfaces effectively with other Adobe products. An InDesign layout can be exported as a PDF, which means that the layout can be opened in both Adobe Photoshop and Adobe Acrobat. You can export the layout as an EPS, so it can be placed in both Adobe Photoshop and Adobe Illustrator. The relationship between the Adobe products also works when importing files into an InDesign layout. If you have a Photoshop file with many layers, you don't need to save a flattened copy for use in InDesign—InDesign will place a layered Photoshop document without any problems. Similarly, you can place Illustrator files in InDesign without saving them in the EPS format.

Figure 19 Identifying printer's marks in the printed document

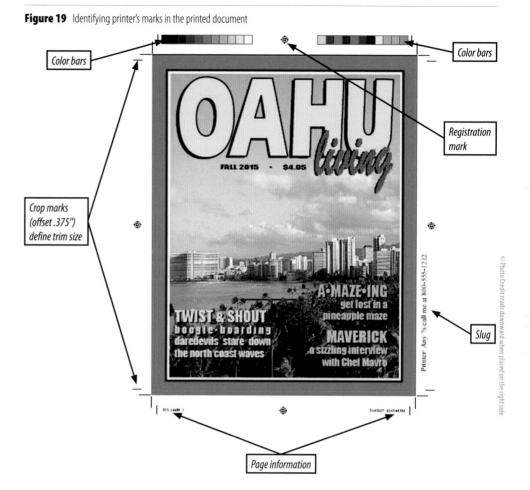

Color bars

Color bars

Registration mark

Crop marks (offset .375") define trim size

Slug

Page information

© Photo Credit reads downward when placed on the right side

USE THE INK MANAGER AND PREVIEW COLOR SEPARATIONS

▶ *What You'll Do*

In this lesson, you will use the Ink Manager to specify swatches as process or spot colors, and then you'll preview separations on the Separations Preview panel.

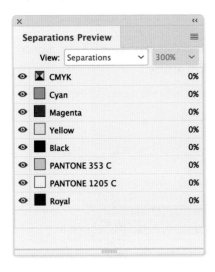

Using the Ink Manager

The Ink Manager dialog box, shown in Figure 20, gives you control over the inks that you create on the Swatches panel. One important function that the Ink Manager provides is the ability to convert spot colors easily to process inks if you should want to do so.

TIP You can access the Ink Manager from the Swatches panel menu. You may ask, "Why would you create a swatch as a spot color if you intend to output it as a process color?" Good question. You should know that many designers choose not to be too meticulous when creating swatches.

Figure 20 Ink Manager dialog box

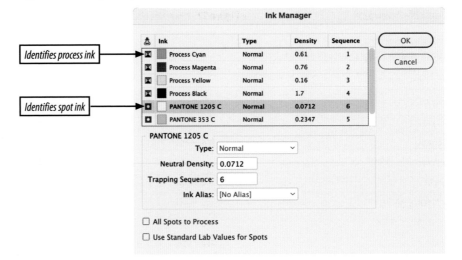

Designers will often use the PANTONE panel to create swatches without a care as to whether they are defined as spot or process. That's why many printers are seldom surprised when they open a client's document for a standard 4-Color print job and find that it has been saved with 22 spot inks!

The Ink Manager makes it easy to specify how the document will color separate. It is important to remember that using the Ink Manager is something you do at the output phase of your work with a document. The changes you make to inks in the Ink Manager only affect the output of the document, not the inks in the document. For example, you might convert a swatch from a spot ink to a process ink in the Ink Manager, but the swatch will continue to be defined as a spot ink on the Swatches panel.

Using the Separations Preview Panel

The Separations Preview panel, shown in Figure 21, is another panel that allows you to see the number of inks available for printing the document at a glance. The Separations Preview panel lists only the four process inks and any swatches that are defined as spot inks.

The Separations Preview panel is interactive. Click on an ink, and the areas of the document that use that ink will appear black. The areas not using that ink will disappear. Figure 22 shows Black selected in the panel and only the areas of the document that contain black ink being previewed in the document.

Why is this useful? It's important to note that the Separations Preview panel comes into play in the output stages, not in the design stages. But at the output stage, it is a great resource for the print professional to see how a document will color separate and to inspect each plate quickly.

Figure 21 Separations Preview panel

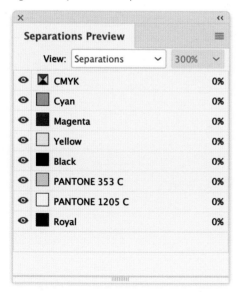

Figure 22 Viewing the black ink in the document

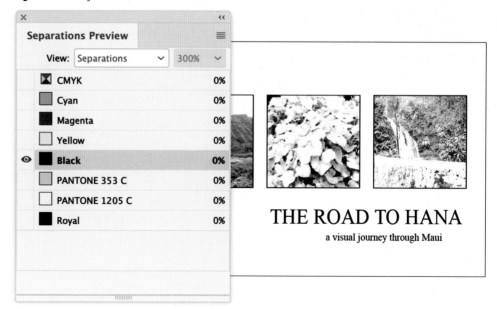

Use the Ink Manager

1. Open the Swatches panel, then note the **three PANTONE spot ink swatches**, as shown in Figure 23.

2. Click the **Swatches panel menu button** ☰, then click **Ink Manager**.

3. Scroll in the **Ink Manager dialog box** and note the inks listed.

   The list of inks in the Ink Manager window is different from the list on the Swatches panel. The Ink Manager lists the four process inks (CMYK) and the three swatches specified as spot inks. Any other process swatches are not listed because they are composed of the four process inks.

4. Click **PANTONE 427 C**, then click the **spot ink icon** ◨ to the left of PANTONE 427 C to convert it from a spot ink to a process ink, as shown in Figure 24.

   You have converted PANTONE 427 C from a spot ink to a process ink.

5. Click **PANTONE 159 C**, then click the **spot ink icon** ◨ to the left of PANTONE 159 C.

   PANTONE 159 C is converted to a process ink. The document will now output four process inks and PANTONE 2925 C as the one spot ink, for a total of five inks.

6. Click **OK**.

7. Note the **inks on the Swatches panel**.

   Changes you make using the Ink Manager affect only the output; they do not reflect how colors are defined in the document. Though PANTONE 427 C and 159 C will be output as process inks, the Swatches panel continues to show a spot ink icon beside them, because that is how they were specified when created.

Figure 23 Swatches panel with three spot inks

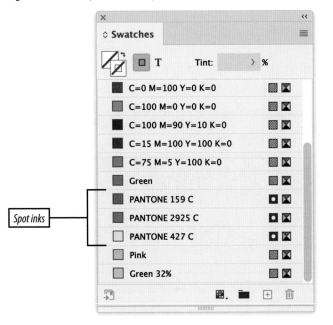

Spot inks

Figure 24 Converting a spot ink to a process ink

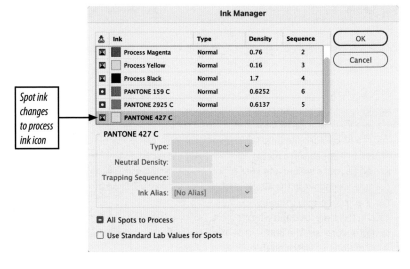

Spot ink changes to process ink icon

8. Click **File** on the menu bar, click **Print**, then click the **Output category** on the left.

   As shown in Figure 25, the Inks section of the Print dialog box specifies that the document will separate into five inks.

9. Click **Cancel**.

You used the Ink Manager to convert two spot inks to process inks. You then switched to the Output category of the Print dialog box to verify that the document would separate into five inks, as shown in the Inks section of the Print dialog box.

Figure 25 Viewing inks in the Output category of the Print dialog box

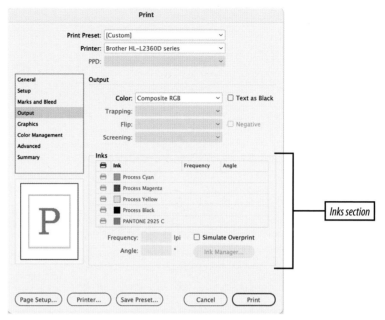

Inks section

VIDEO FILES AND THE MEDIA PANEL

You can place video files into InDesign and play them back when you export your InDesign document as an interactive PDF. When you place a video into InDesign, it appears in a media frame and in the Media panel. Media frames can be formatted just like graphics frames. You can resize them, position them, and add a stroke weight and stroke color. The Media panel allows you to play back the video and adjust its settings. You will not be able to play the video in the document window. In the Media panel, you can define the poster frame, which is the static image that will show in the exported file. The poster frame can be a frame you choose by using the Current Frame option. You can even choose a graphic file to be the poster frame. You can also choose whether the video should play on the page load and whether it should loop (play continuously until manually stopped). On the Media panel, you can create navigation points to use with button actions (see the Buttons and Forms panel). Navigation points help break up your video into sections, such as chapters in a book, and allow your viewers more options for watching the video.

Use the Separations Preview panel

1. Click **Window** on the menu bar, point to **Output**, then click **Separations Preview**.

2. Click the **View list arrow** on the Separations Preview panel, then click **Separations**.

   As shown in Figure 26, the document is specified to separate color into five inks—the four process inks plus PANTONE 2925 C, which has been specified as a spot ink in the Ink Manager dialog box.

3. Click **PANTONE 2925 C** on the Separations Preview panel.

   The areas of the document that have PANTONE 2925 C applied appear as black. Other areas are invisible.

4. Position the **pointer** over the **black border** in the document.

   100% appears beside the ink listed on the panel, indicating that this area is to be printed with 100% PANTONE 2925 C.

Figure 26 Five inks on the Separations Preview panel

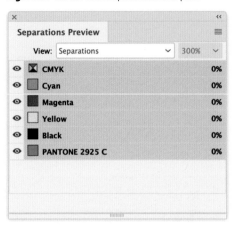

WORKING WITH EVENTS, ACTIONS, AND BOOKMARKS

InDesign offers the ability to create interactive PDFs using buttons. Just like clicking a button on a Web page to jump to a new location, you can create buttons in InDesign that will take the viewer to another location in the document. Buttons are added to a document using the Buttons and Forms panel. First select a graphic on the page, then choose an action from the Action list on the Buttons and Forms panel. An example of an action is "Go to Last Page." For an action to be triggered, it must be linked to an event. An event is the specific interactive occurrence that triggers the action of a button. A typical event is "On Click" or "On Rollover." For example, you could create a shape, attach a "Go to Last Page" action using an "On Click" event. When a viewer clicks this button in the exported PDF, they will be taken to the last page of the document. You can also create navigation in an InDesign document using bookmarks. A bookmark is a type of link made from text that also allows viewers to navigate documents exported as an Adobe PDF. Adobe Acrobat includes a Bookmark panel. InDesign bookmarks automatically appear in the PDF Bookmarks panel.

You create bookmarks by selecting text, then clicking the Create new bookmark button ⊞ on the Bookmarks panel. The new bookmark appears on the panel. To access the Bookmarks panel, click Window on the menu bar, point to Interactive, then click Bookmarks. Entries in a generated table of contents are automatically added to the Bookmarks panel.

5. Click **Cyan** on the Separations Preview panel.

   As shown in Figure 27, the areas of the document that have Cyan applied appear as black. Note that the slug message is showing because it is filled with [Registration] and thus is on every separation.

6. Move the **pointer** over the **document** and note the percentages of cyan and the other inks.

   There is 0% Cyan in the title OAHU and 0% PANTONE 2925 C anywhere except in the border.

7. Click **Magenta**, then click **Yellow**, then click **Black** to preview those inks.

8. Click **CMYK** to preview only the areas of the document that will be printed with process inks.

9. Click the **empty gray square** beside the PANTONE 2925 C ink to make the ink visible in the preview.

10. Click the **View list arrow** on the Separations Preview panel, click **Off**, then close the Separations Preview panel.

11. Save your work, then continue to the next lesson.

You used the Separations Preview panel to preview how the document will be color separated into five inks.

Figure 27 Using the Separations Preview panel to view a single ink in the document

PREFLIGHT AND PACKAGE A DOCUMENT

▶ *What You'll Do*

In this lesson, you will explore options for preflighting and packaging a document.

Preflighting a Document

Before an airplane takes off, the pilots perform a preflight check. Running down a checklist, they verify that the many controls necessary to fly a plane safely are all working properly.

In the print world, designers and printers have adopted the term **preflight** to refer to checking a document before it's released from the designer to the printer or service bureau, or before it's downloaded to an output device.

When you complete a document, it is important to find and correct any errors in the document to ensure that it prints correctly. The Preflight feature is an InDesign utility you can use to check an open document for errors such as missing fonts, missing or modified links, and overset text. Any errors that are found are listed on the Preflight panel; you can use this list to fix any problems by substituting fonts, fixing overset text issues, and/or updating missing and modified files. A green circle on the left side of the status bar, also known as Live Preflight, indicates that there are no preflight errors in a document. When the circle is red, there are errors.

UNDERSTANDING TEXT VARIABLES

Text variables are preset bits of information that you can automatically insert into your InDesign documents. Text variables—such as Running Header, Modification Date, and Chapter Number—go hand in hand with using master pages on multipage documents as well as with headers and footers. You can define a text variable by telling exactly where it should go (before an em dash, after punctuation, and so on) and then insert it on the page. To work with text variables, click Type on the menu bar, point to Text Variables, then click Define or Insert Variable. You can also create new text variables by clicking the New button in the Text Variables dialog box. Like all master page items, text variables work to ensure consistency across your publication.

The Preflight panel is shown in Figure 28. The On check box is checked because Preflight is on. The [Basic] Preflight profile—which, by default, checks for missing fonts, missing or modified links, and overset text—is selected. The Preflight all pages option button indicates that all pages in the document have been checked. You can click the Preflight specified pages option button to choose a page range to be checked. You can create customized preflight profiles in which you indicate what you would like the Preflight panel to flag as errors to be fixed. For example, you may want InDesign to flag font sizes smaller than 12 points as an error because your document cannot have them for one reason or another.

To create a custom preflight profile, click the Preflight panel menu button, then click Define Profiles. Click the New preflight profile button (plus sign) on the left, name the profile, pick and choose settings in the right pane, then click OK. Custom preflight profiles can be accessed by clicking the Profile list arrow on the Preflight panel.

Packaging a Document

Once a document has been preflighted, it's ready to be packaged. Packaging a document means getting it ready to send to a printer, a composition house, or a client for printing or archiving. Remember, a complete InDesign document is the document itself plus all placed graphics and fonts that are used. All the components are required in order to output the document successfully.

When you use the Package command, InDesign automatically creates a folder and packages a copy of the InDesign document, copies of all the placed graphics, and copies of all the fonts used. By automating the process, the Package command removes much of the potential for human error.

Figure 28 Preflight panel

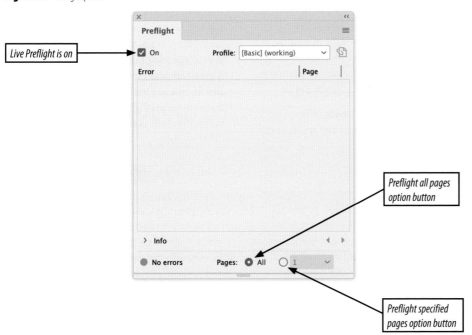

Live Preflight is on

Preflight all pages option button

Preflight specified pages option button

Preflight and package a document

1. Click **Window** on the menu bar, point to **Output**, then click **Preflight**.

   The Preflight panel opens, and no errors are listed. If there were errors, such as missing fonts or missing placed images, they would be listed here.

2. Close the **Preflight panel**.

3. Click **File** on the menu bar, then click **Save**.

   A file must be saved before it can be packaged.

4. Click **File** on the menu bar, then click **Package**.

   The Package dialog box opens, as shown in Figure 29.

5. Click **Fonts** in the box on the left.

6. Note the **two fonts** listed, then click the **Show Problems Only check box** if it is not already selected.

   If the fonts used in the document are available on your system, the two fonts listed in the window will disappear. You may have more fonts listed if you do not have the same fonts installed.

7. Click **Links and Images** on the left, note the two imported graphics listed, then note the information below the window for each selected graphic.

8. Click the **Show Problems Only check box** if it is not already selected.

   If the links to the two imported graphics have been updated, they should disappear from the window.

Figure 29 Package dialog box

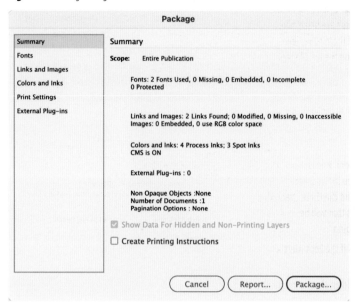

USING THE FLATTENER PREVIEW PANEL

If you prepare InDesign documents for output or prepress, you will be interested in the Flattener Preview panel. It's important to remember that InDesign is a graphic design application as well as a layout program. Designers typically create layered documents, often with blending modes between the layers to create special effects. Complex documents like these can be a challenge to print—a layered document sometimes appears differently as output than it does on the screen. The Flattener Preview panel allows you to preview how specific areas of a layout will appear when output. This panel is especially useful for previewing transparent drop shadows, objects with a feathered edge, transparent placed graphics from Illustrator or Photoshop, and the graphics that interact with the types of objects listed previously.

9. Click the **Colors and Inks category** on the left.

   Because three swatches are specified as spot inks on the Swatches panel, all three are listed here as spot inks. However, two of them have been converted to process inks using the Ink Manager dialog box, which overrides the information in this window.

10. Click **Report**, then click **Save** in the Save As dialog box.

11. Click **Package**.

   As shown in Figure 30, a folder name is automatically supplied for you in the Create Package Folder dialog box, and the three checked items at the bottom are tasks that will be performed during the packaging.

12. Click **Package**, then click **OK** if the Font Alert dialog box appears.

13. Open the **OAHU to Print Folder**, then compare its contents to Figure 31.

   The folder contains the InDesign document, the .txt instructions document, a Fonts folder, and a Links folder.

TIP If your list of files does not show the Instructions text file, click the Files of type list arrow in the bottom of the Open a File dialog box, then click All Files.

14. Return to the **OAHU to Print document** in InDesign.

15. Continue to the next lesson.

You preflighted a document, then packaged a document, noting that copies of fonts and linked graphics were stored in the delivery folder.

Figure 30 Create Package Folder dialog box

Figure 31 Contents of the OAHU to Print Folder

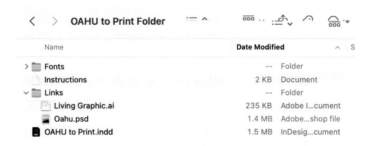

EXPORT A DOCUMENT FOR PRINT AND THE WEB

Exporting a Document

Exporting a document is a different function than saving a document or printing a document. When you export a document, the document you create is your InDesign file saved in a different file format. Figure 32 shows the Export dialog box and the available file formats for exporting.

"Why would I do this?" you may be asking. The Export command is used most often to translate a document into another format so it can be used in another application or uploaded to the Web.

Figure 32 Export dialog box

Export		
Save As:	OAHU to Print Uncompressed	
Tags:		

< | >   ☰ ∨   ▦ ∨   📁 OAHU to Print Folder   ⬍   ∧   Q Search

Name	∧	Date Modified
~oahu to print~sqznn5.idlk		Today at 1:45 PM
> 📁 Fonts		Jul 1, 2014 at 1:4
Instructions		Jul 1, 2014 at 1:4
> 📁 Links		Jul 1, 2014 at 1:4
📄 OAHU to Print.indd		Today at 8:39 AM

Format ✓ **Adobe PDF (Print)**

          Adobe Experience Manager Mobile Article
          Adobe PDF (Interactive)
          EPS
          EPUB (Fixed Layout)
          EPUB (Reflowable)
          HTML
          InDesign Markup (IDML)
          JPEG
          PNG
          XML

☐ Use InDesign Document Name

New Folder   Cancel   **Save**

Common exports of InDesign documents include the following:

EPS An EPS, or encapsulated PostScript, file can be placed as a bitmap graphic in Adobe Photoshop or Adobe Illustrator.

PDF Portable document format, or PDF, is the file format used in Adobe Reader, a free software program that allows you to view documents created from other software programs without having to have those programs installed on your computer. When an InDesign document is exported as a PDF, all fonts and placed graphics are embedded in the PDF. Thus, the PDF is a complete and self-contained export of the entire document.

JPEG A JPEG is a compressed graphic file format that has a smaller file size than other graphic formats and is ideal for graphics that will be used in layouts designed for the Internet. You can export an object or objects on an InDesign document page as JPEG files. Or you can export one page, a range of pages, or an entire InDesign document as a JPEG. Exporting InDesign objects or document pages as JPEG files is useful when you want to post a selection, page, or multiple pages as an image on the Web. To export a selected object, page, or document as a JPEG file, choose JPEG in the Save as type box in the Export dialog box.

Exporting a PDF for Print and Email

PDF is one of the most common export formats for InDesign documents. The key to the relationship between InDesign and a PDF is that, as a PDF, the InDesign document is complete and self-contained. Issues with imported graphics and fonts become nonissues. The PDF file includes all imported graphics and fonts. The recipient of the file does not need to have the document fonts loaded to view the file correctly.

The self-contained nature of PDFs, and the issues that it solves, makes PDF the format of choice for both professional printing and for emailing documents. In advertising and design agencies, it's standard procedure to export an InDesign document as a PDF to email to the client for approval. For professional printing, it's becoming more and more the case that, rather than package an InDesign document with all supporting graphics and fonts, printers ask for a single "high-res" PDF.

The two examples above convey the "low-end" and "high-end" roles of the InDesign–PDF relationship. When a layout includes placed graphics, especially high-resolution, large-file-size Photoshop images, how you export the PDF affects how the document is compressed to reduce the resulting file size.

When emailing a layout as a PDF, you will export the document with compression utilities activated to reduce the file size for email. These compression utilities will compress the file size of placed images.

When sending a layout to a printer for professional printing, you won't want the placed graphics to be compressed. In this case, you'll export the PDF with compression utilities turned off. The resulting PDF will likely be too large to email, but it will remain high quality for printing.

Export a page to EPS format

1. Click **File** on the menu bar, then click **Export**.

2. In the Export dialog box, click the **Format list arrow (Mac)** or the **Save as type list arrow (Win)**, click **EPS**, then click **Save**.

3. In the Export EPS dialog box, shown in Figure 33, note that you can choose which pages you want to export.

   Because this document is a single page, you will accept the default in the Ranges text box.

4. Click the **Color list arrow**, then select **RGB**.

   Because we are using this export to create a high-resolution image of the file that can be opened and manipulated in Photoshop, we will export in the RGB format.

5. Note that the Bleed settings are all 0.

   You want to export with a bleed only if you are sending the file to be printed and trimmed.

6. Click **Export**.

Figure 33 Export EPS dialog box

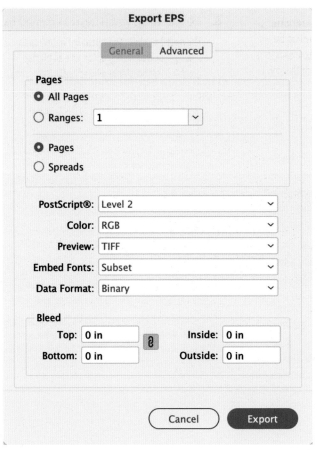

7. Open Photoshop, click **File** on the menu bar, click **Open**, then open **OAHU to Print.eps**.

The Rasterize EPS Format dialog box, shown in Figure 34, gives you options for converting the EPS to a bitmap image, including determining the resolution for the Photoshop image. At this point, you can choose between opening a high-resolution version (300 ppi), which you could use for a hi-res print, or a low-resolution version (72 ppi),

which you could use on a website or to include in an email.

8. Enter the settings shown in Figure 34, then click **OK**.

The page from InDesign opens in Photoshop as a 300 ppi RGB bitmap graphic. Like all bitmap graphics, this graphic can be edited in Photoshop.

9. Exit Photoshop without saving changes to the file, then return to the OAHU to Print document in InDesign.

10. Continue to the next set of steps.

Using the Export as EPS option, you were able to open an InDesign page in Photoshop as a bitmap graphic.

Export a compressed PDF for email

1. Click **File** on the menu bar, then click **Export**.

2. In the Export dialog box, name the file **OAHU to Email**.

3. Click the **Format list arrow (Mac)** or **Save as type list arrow (Win)**, click **Adobe PDF (Print)**, then click **Save**.

4. At the top of the Export Adobe PDF dialog box, click the **Adobe PDF Preset list arrow**, then click **[Smallest File Size]**.

The presets in the list are standard settings that you can use as a starting point for exporting a PDF. For example, Smallest File Size is preset with compression settings that will reduce the size of all placed graphics.

5. Verify that the **View PDF after Exporting check box** is checked.

6. Click **Compression** on the left side of the dialog box.

The settings in this dialog box reflect the Smallest File Size preset.

Continued on next page

Figure 34 Rasterize EPS Format dialog box

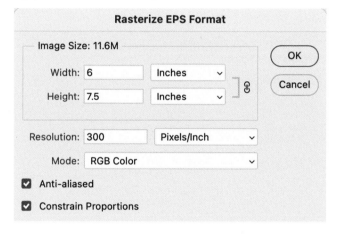

7. Enter the settings shown in Figure 35.

The settings indicate that for both color and grayscale images, InDesign will use JPEG compression with Maximum image quality to reduce the file size. The settings also indicate that InDesign will use Bicubic Downsampling (standard pixel interpolation) to reduce to 72 pixels per inch any color or grayscale graphics that are greater than 72 pixels per inch. Downsampling refers to reducing the resolution of a bitmap image. Thus, a 300-pixel-per-inch PSD graphic in the layout will be reduced to a 72-pixel-per-inch JPEG with Maximum quality in the PDF.

TIP You should always use Maximum as your setting for JPEG quality. Modern day Internet speeds can easily traffic images, especially low-resolution images, so there's never a need to choose anything less than the best quality setting.

8. Click **Marks and Bleeds** on the left side of the dialog box and verify that nothing is checked.

Note that the word (modified) now appears beside Smallest File Size at the top of the dialog box. This indicates that the Smallest File Size preset has been modified because you changed the compression settings.

9. Click the **Save Preset button** in the lower-left corner, type **My Email Export** in the Save Preset As text box in the Save Preset dialog box, then click **OK**.

These new settings are now saved and will be available in the Preset list for any future PDFs that you want to email.

10. Click **Export**.

The PDF will open in Acrobat for you to view. The exported PDF file size is less than 1 MB.

11. Continue to the next set of steps.

You exported the OAHU to Print document as an Adobe PDF file with a file size small enough to email. You entered settings for JPEG compression and for reducing the resolution of placed images. You then saved a preset for the settings you entered.

Figure 35 Settings for a low-resolution and compressed PDF

Export an uncompressed PDF for professional offset printing

1. Click **File** on the menu bar, then click **Export**.

   Note that if you were exporting this file as a PDF for professional printing, you would first place a CMYK version of the large cityscape image in your layout before exporting the PDF from InDesign. Because CMYK is a far smaller color space than RGB, many designers save a CMYK copy of the original RGB images, thus preserving the RGB originals for other uses. For example, if you were producing the same layout for print and for the Internet, the Internet uses the RGB color space, so you would want those original RGB images for your web layout.

2. In the Export dialog box, name the file **OAHU to Print Uncompressed**.

3. Click the **Format list arrow (Mac)** or the **Save as type list arrow (Win)** to select **Adobe PDF (Print)**, then click **Save**.

4. In the Export Adobe PDF dialog box, click the **Adobe PDF Preset list arrow**, then click **[High Quality Print]**.

   Note that the My Email Export you created in the last set of steps is listed as a preset.

5. Verify that **View PDF after Exporting** is checked.

6. Click **Compression** on the left side of the dialog box.

7. Enter the settings shown in Figure 36.

   The settings indicate that no compression or downsampling will be applied to any of the images in the layout. Thus, if this document were built for professional printing with high-resolution images, the images would not be affected.

Continued on next page

Figure 36 Compression and downsampling deactivated

8. Click **Marks and Bleeds** on the left side of the dialog box, then enter the settings shown in Figure 37.

   Printer's marks include crop marks and color bars.

9. Make sure that the **Use Document Bleed Settings** and **Include Slug Area check boxes** are checked.

   These settings will be represented in the final PDF.

10. Note that the word (modified) now appears beside High Quality Print at the top of the dialog box.

11. Click the **Save Preset button** in the lower-left corner, type **Output for Hi-Res Printing** in the Save Preset As text box in the Save Preset dialog box, then click **OK**.

   These new settings are now saved and will be available in the Preset list for any future PDFs that you want to export with no compression.

12. Click **Export**.

   The PDF will open in Acrobat as shown in Figure 38, with trim marks, bleed marks, a bleed and a slug area, and color bars at the top.

13. Continue to the next set of steps.

You exported the OAHU to Print document as an Adobe PDF file with no compression for professional printing.

Figure 37 Marks and Bleeds category

Figure 38 Exported PDF with no compression and with printer's marks and bleed and slug area

Export an interactive PDF for the Web

1. Click **File** on the menu bar, then click **Export**.

   Note that if you were exporting this file as a PDF for the Internet, you would use an RGB version of the cityscape image.

2. In the Export dialog box, name the file **OAHU Interactive PDF**.

3. Click the **Save as type list arrow**, click **Adobe PDF (Interactive)**, then click **Save**.

4. In the General section of the dialog box, enter the settings shown in Figure 39.

   Note in the Viewing section that you can specify that the image fits on-screen when it opens and opens in Full Screen Mode.

5. In the **Compression section** of the dialog box, enter the settings shown in Figure 40.

   For any on-screen image, 72 ppi is all that is necessary for resolution. The default is 144 ppi. The image at this resolution will still have a small file size, especially with the JPEG compression, and will download quickly with no problems.

6. Click **Export**.

   The document opens in Acrobat on your screen and in Full Screen Mode.

7. Close all open PDFs in Acrobat.

8. In InDesign, save the Oahu to Print document, then close it.

You exported an InDesign document as a compressed interactive PDF ready to be used on the Web.

Figure 39 General settings for exporting the interactive PDF

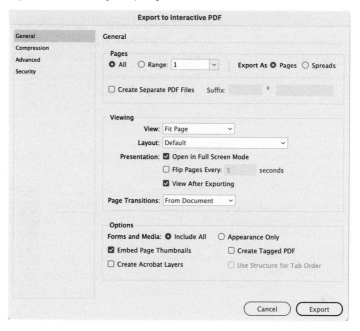

Figure 40 Compression settings for exporting the interactive PDF

Create bleeds, slugs, and printer's marks

1. Open ID 11 -2.indd, then save it as **Hana**.
2. Verify that guides are showing.
3. Click File on the menu bar, then click Document Setup.
4. Click the More Options button if necessary to display the Bleed and Slug section of the dialog box.
5. Type **.125** in the Top, Bottom, Left, and Right Bleed text boxes, then click OK.
6. Click the Selection tool, select the green frame on page 1, then drag the frame's corners to the bleed guide on all four sides.
7. Select the yellow frame on page 1, then drag the left and right sides of the frame to the left and right edges of the bleed guide.
8. Using the same methodology, create bleeds for the green and yellow frames on pages 2-5.
9. Press and hold the Normal button on the toolbar, then click the Preview button.
10. Press and hold the Preview button, then click the Bleed button.
11. Click the Normal button.
12. Click File on the menu bar, then click Print.
13. Verify that Copies is set to 1 and Pages is set to All, then click the Setup category in the box on the left.
14. Verify that Paper Size is set to Letter, click the leftmost Orientation icon, click the Page Position list arrow, then click Centered.

15. Click the Marks and Bleed category on the left.
16. In the Marks section, click the All Printer's Marks check box, then set the Offset value to .385 in.
17. In the Bleed and Slug section, verify that the Use Document Bleed Settings check box is checked.
18. Click Print.

Use the Ink Manager and preview color separations

1. On the Swatches panel, note that three swatches are specified as spot inks.
2. Click the Swatches panel menu button, then click Ink Manager.
3. Scroll in the Ink Manager and note the inks listed.
4. Click Royal, then click the spot ink icon to the left of Royal to convert it to a process ink.
5. Click PANTONE 1205 C, then click the spot ink icon to the left of PANTONE 1205 C to convert it to a process ink.
6. Click OK.
7. Click Window on the menu bar, point to Output, then click Separations Preview.
8. Click the View list arrow on the Separations Preview panel, then click Separations.
9. Move the Separations Preview panel to the side so that you can see the entire document.
10. Click PANTONE 353 C on the Separations Preview panel.
11. Click Cyan on the Separations Preview panel.
12. Move the pointer over the document and note the percentages of Cyan and the other inks.

13. Click Magenta, then click Yellow, then click Black to preview those inks.
14. Click CMYK to preview only the areas of the document that will be printed with process inks.
15. Click the empty gray square beside the PANTONE 353 C ink to make the ink visible in the preview.
16. Click the View list arrow, click Off, then close the Separations Preview panel.

Preflight and package a document

1. Click the Preflight menu arrow on the status bar, then click Preflight Panel.
2. Close the Preflight panel.
3. Click File on the menu bar, then click Package.
4. Click the Fonts category on the left.
5. Verify that the Show Problems Only check box is not checked.
6. Note the font listed.
7. Click the Links and Images category on the left, verify that the Show Problems Only check box is not checked, note the imported graphics listed, then note the information below the window for each selected graphic.
8. Click the Show Problems Only check box.
9. Click Report, use the filename given, then click Save.
10. Click Package, then click Save.
11. Type **Instructions** in the File name text box if the filename is not already there.
12. Click Create Package Folder dialog box (Mac) or Continue to open the Package Publication dialog box (Win).

13. Note that a folder name has been supplied for you, then note the three checked items to the left.
14. Click Package.
15. Click OK in the Font Alert dialog box that follows.
16. Minimize InDesign, go to where you saved your Hana Folder, then open it.
17. Open the Links folder to view its contents.
18. Return to the Hana document in InDesign.

Export a document

1. Click File on the menu bar, then click Export.
2. In the Export dialog box, name the file **Hana to Print Compressed**.
3. Click the Format list arrow (Mac) or the Save as type list arrow (Win), click Adobe PDF (Print), then click Save.
4. In the Export Adobe PDF dialog box, click the Adobe PDF Preset list arrow, then click [Smallest File Size].
5. Verify that All is selected in the Pages section and that View PDF after Exporting is checked.
6. Click Compression on the left side of the dialog box.
7. Enter the settings shown in Figure 41.
8. Click Marks and Bleeds on the left side of the dialog box and verify that nothing is checked.
9. Note that the word (modified) now appears beside Smallest File Size at the top of the dialog box.
10. Click the Save Preset button in the lower-left corner, type **Hana Email Export** in the Save Preset As text box in the Save Preset dialog box, then click OK.
11. Click Export.

12. Click File on the menu bar, then click Export.
13. In the Export dialog box, name the file **Hana to Print Uncompressed**.
14. Click the Format list arrow (Mac) or the Save as type list arrow (Win), click Adobe PDF (Print), then click Save.

15. In the Export Adobe PDF dialog box, click the Adobe PDF Preset list arrow, then click [High Quality Print].
16. Verify that View PDF after Exporting is checked.
17. Click Compression on the left side of the dialog box.

Figure 41 Compression settings for the PDF

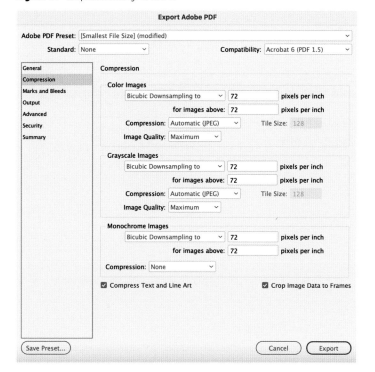

(continued)

18. Enter the settings shown in Figure 42.
19. Click Marks and Bleeds on the left of the dialog box, then enter the settings shown in Figure 43.
20. Note that the word (modified) now appears beside High Quality Print at the top of the dialog box.
21. Click the Save Preset button in the lower-left corner, type **My No Compression** in the Save Preset As text box in the Save Preset dialog box, then click OK.
22. Click Export, then compare the first page of your PDF file to Figure 44.
23. Save the file, then close the Hana document.

Figure 42 Compression settings for the PDF

Figure 43 Marks and Bleeds settings

Figure 44 Completed Skills Review

THE ROAD TO HANA

a visual journey through Maui

Hana.indd   1

10/2/21   8:17 PM

As part of your job at a prepress service company, you open customers' documents, preflight them, then output them. Starting on a new project, you open the customer's InDesign layout and note that the job ticket says the page is to be printed at letter size. You notice immediately that the document has been built to letter size, but the customer failed to create bleeds.

1. Open ID 11-3.indd, then save it as **Multiple Bleeds**.
2. Verify that guides are showing.
3. Open the Document Setup dialog box.
4. Type **.125** in all four Bleed text boxes, then click OK.
5. Click the Selection tool, select the large background graphic, then drag the frame's four corners to the bleed guide on all four sides.
6. Click Object on the menu bar, point to Fitting, then click Fit Content to Frame.
7. Select the Windmill Silhouette graphic in the bottom-left corner, then drag the left and bottom sides of the frame to the left and bottom sides of the bleed guide.
8. Select the Windmills Color graphic on the right side of the layout, then drag the right side of the frame to the right side of the bleed guide.
9. Deselect all, compare your work to Figure 45, save your work, then close Multiple Bleeds.

Figure 45 Completed Project Builder 1

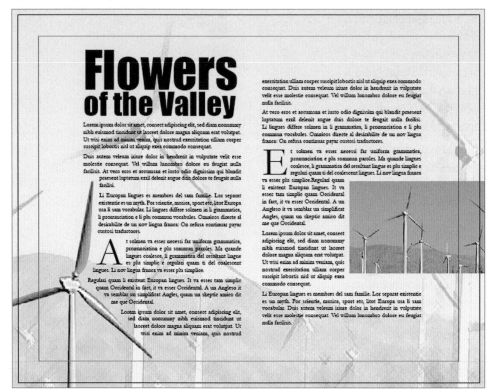

You work for a prepress service bureau, opening customers' documents, preflighting them, then outputting them to film. You've just opened the file for the cover of a monthly dog magazine. The job ticket says that it will print with five colors—CMYK + PANTONE 117 C. You decide to check that the customer specified inks properly.

1. Open ID 11-4.indd, then save it as **Lab Separations**.
2. Open the Separations Preview panel, turn separations on, then note that the document is currently specified to separate into seven colors.
3. Click the Swatches panel menu button, then click Ink Manager.
4. Convert PANTONE 183 C and PANTONE 2706 C to process inks, then click OK.
5. On the Separations Preview panel, verify that the document will now separate into five colors. PANTONE 183 and 2706 are not listed on the Separations Preview panel because they have been converted to process inks.
6. Click PANTONE 117 C on the Separations Preview panel to preview where the spot ink will print, then compare your screen to Figure 46.
7. Turn separations off on the Separations Preview panel, then close the Separations Preview panel.
8. Save your work, then close the Lab Separations document.

Figure 46 Completed Project Builder 2

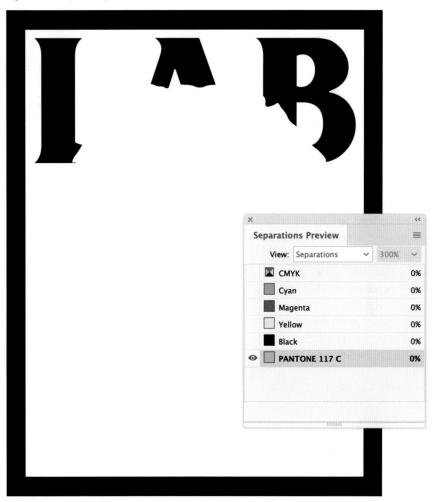

DESIGN PROJECT 1

You are the webmaster at *LAB* magazine. Every month, you update the website with the contents from the current issue. The art director from the print department has sent you the InDesign layout for this month's cover. You will need to resize it to 50% of its original size, then upload it to the website. But first, you need to export it from InDesign so that you can manipulate it in Photoshop. Note: If you do not have Photoshop, end the exercise after Step 5.

1. Open ID 11-5.indd, then save it as **Lab Web Cover**.
2. Click File on the menu bar, then click Export.
3. Export the file in EPS format, then click Save.
4. In the Export EPS dialog box, click the Color list arrow, then click RGB.

TIP Color bitmap graphics for the Web are saved in RGB mode.

5. Click Export.
6. Open Photoshop, click File on the menu bar, click Open, then open Lab Web Cover.eps.
7. In the Rasterize EPS Format dialog box, verify that the Mode text box reads RGB Color, then click OK.
8. Compare your Photoshop file to Figure 47.
9. Close the Photoshop file without saving changes, then close Photoshop.
10. Return to InDesign, then close Lab Web Cover.indd.

Figure 47 Completed Design Project 1

This project is designed to challenge you to figure out how to create a bleed for a tricky document. Finch Design has sent an InDesign file to be printed as a business card. Its main graphic is a large letter F, which has been specified in the Impact font. The top and bottom of the letter F must bleed. Enlarging the letter F to create the bleed is not an option; the client has noted that the relationship between the letter F and the company name (finch design) must not be altered in any way.

The challenge is to figure out the best way to create the bleed at the top and bottom.

1. Open ID 11-6.indd, then save it as **Finch Bleed**.
2. Verify that guides are visible.
3. Open the Document Setup dialog box.
4. Type **.125** in the Top and Bottom Bleed text boxes, then click OK.
5. Click the Selection tool, then select the letter F text frame.
6. Create outlines.
7. Click the Direct Selection tool, then select the top two anchor points of the letter F.
8. Move the top line of the letter F up to the bleed guide.
9. Select the bottom two anchor points of the letter F, then move the bottom line of the letter F down to the bleed guide.
10. Deselect, compare your work to Figure 48, save your work, then close the Finch Bleed document.

Figure 48 Completed Design Project 2

Left Quiz

NEXT | **EXPLORERS QUIZ**

EXPLORE This quiz is the last of seven to run in 2013 to celebrate National Geographic's 125th anniversary.

COOL TOOLS FROM MOTHER NATURE

We often get our best ideas by looking out the window. What's out there in nature represents 3.8 billion years of research and development, according to biomimicry expert Janine Benyus. Ideas that failed in evolutionary product testing are now fossils. What's left are some highly instructive success stories. This is a quiz about some of the spin-offs that have come from paying attention to life right here on Earth.

1. TYPE 2 DIABETES NOW AFFECTS TENS OF MILLIONS OF PEOPLE. RESEARCHERS RECENTLY DEVELOPED A TREATMENT THAT COMES FROM WHICH **NATURAL PRODUCT?** A. The bark of the sycamore tree B. Gila monster spit C. A camel's gall bladder D. The Venus flytrap

2. WHICH ANIMAL, FIRST DISCOVERED IN THE **HUDSON RIVER VALLEY,** TURNED THE IDEA OF **EXTINCTION** FROM HERESY INTO A **FACT OF LIFE?** A. The American cheetah B. The giant ground sloth C. The American mastodon D. *Megalosaurus*

3. THE FIRST DRUG TO TURN HIV FROM A DEATH SENTENCE INTO A CONTROLLABLE DISEASE WAS BASED ON PRODUCTS FROM WHICH SPECIES? A. A marine sponge B. An immune West African monkey C. The Pacific yew tree D. A cone snail

4. WHAT **ANIMAL BEHAVIOR** IS TEACHING POWER PLANTS **A WAY TO CUT THEIR CARBON DIOXIDE EMISSIONS?** A. Tardigrade cryptobiosis B. Grizzly bear hibernation C. Albatross long-distance flight D. Coral calcification

5. BIOLOGIST AND ROBOTICS EXPERT **CLAIRE RIND** DESIGNED A COLLISION AVOIDANCE SYSTEM FOR CARS BY OBSERVING WHAT ANIMAL? A. Impala B. Mustang C. Jaguar D. Locust

6. CHARLES DARWIN SPENT YEARS STUDYING WHICH ANIMAL GROUP AS HE **DEVELOPED THE IDEA OF EVOLUTION** BY NATURAL SELECTION? A. Earthworms B. Galápagos iguanas C. Barnacles D. The peppered moth

FIND ANSWERS ON PAGE 29.

HANNAH TAK, NGM STAFF. ART: GRAFILU (PORTRAIT); NGM ART. PHOTO: STOCKBYTE/GETTY IMAGES

Right Quiz

NEXT | **EXPLORERS QUIZ**

EXPLORE This quiz is the fifth of seven to run in 2013 to celebrate National Geographic's 125th anniversary. The next quiz will appear in October.

WOMEN AND DISCOVERY

For centuries female explorers got to pursue their ambitions only in disguise or against fierce resistance. If they somehow succeeded, society often ignored them or, worse, treated them as superwomen, because that was a way, Egyptian feminist Huda Shaarawi wrote, "to avoid recognizing the capabilities of all women." With that in mind, this quiz celebrates ordinary women doing extraordinary things.

1. WHO WAS THE **FIRST WOMAN** TO CIRCUMNAVIGATE THE EARTH? A. Krystyna Chojnowska-Liskiewicz B. Naomi James C. Tania Aebi D. Jeanne Baret

2. IN 1910 A CIGARETTE COMPANY FEATURED **MISS ANNIE SMITH PECK** ON ITS TRADING CARD SERIES OF "THE WORLD'S GREATEST EXPLORERS." WHO WAS SHE? A. The first person to bring back a living electric eel from South America B. A solo traveler down the length of the Amazon C. A pioneering mountain climber D. A biologist tracking jaguars solo at night

3. MISSY MAZZOLI'S 2012 OPERA *SONG FROM THE UPROAR* IS BASED ON THE LIFE OF WHICH **FEMALE EXPLORER IN AFRICA?** A. Isabelle Eberhardt B. Mary Kingsley C. Mary Leakey D. Delia Akeley

AFRICA

4. WHICH IS THE BEST KNOWN AMONG THE FOSSILS, SHIPWRECKS, AND ARTIFACTS **SUE HENDRICKSON** HAS DISCOVERED AROUND THE WORLD? A. The keel of the *Santa Maria*, lost on Christmas Day, 1492 B. "Sue," a *Tyrannosaurus rex* C. A fossilized giant squid D. An ancient tree-dwelling horseshoe crab trapped in amber

5. THE *NEW YORK TIMES* NAMED HER **ONE OF THE LEADING WOMEN EXPLORERS IN THE WORLD.** WHO WAS SHE? A. Annie Edson Taylor B. Harriet Chalmers Adams C. Nellie Bly D. Amelia Earhart

6. AFTER RETIRING FROM HER NURSING CAREER SOME YEARS AGO, **BARBARA HILLARY** DECIDED TO TRAVEL. AT THE AGE OF 79 SHE BECAME THE **FIRST BLACK WOMAN** TO DO WHAT? A. Dive to the *Titanic* B. Visit both the North and South Poles C. Summit Everest D. Swim the English Channel

FIND ANSWERS ON PAGE 29.

HANNAH TAK, NGM STAFF. ART: MARC JOHNS; AMERICAN TOBACCO (PECK CARD); NGM ART (MASK). NGM MAPS

550

Layout/design by Hannah Tak. From "Explorers Quiz." *National Geographic Magazine*, Left/E: Vol. 224, No. 6, December 2013; Right/O: Vol. 224, No. 3, September, 2013

PROJECT DESCRIPTION

In this project, you will create a personal collage using both imagery and text. You may choose to lean more heavily on text, as in the model *National Geographic* images, varying font sizes and formatting. Or you may choose to include more imagery and use the text as a support tool. The goal of this project is to create a collage that combines text and imagery in a complementary way.

SKILLS TO EXPLORE

- Incorporate Gridify Behavior
- Work with Nested Styles
- Apply Live Corner Effects
- Work with Effects and Object Styles
- Work with Multiple Page Sizes
- Design with Multiple Documents
- Work with Tables
- Work with Tabs

SOFT SKILLS CHALLENGE

Self-expression can be defined as using a creative medium, such as art, design, photography, music, or dance, to share your thoughts and feelings. Although graphic designers are creatives, they don't always get the opportunity to fully express themselves, as much of their hired work is for clients. In this challenge, you will create a journal entry to express yourself.

In the center of the page, write down one word you would use to describe yourself. Be honest—this might be a different word than what friends might choose to describe you. Scattered around the page, add other words that give tribute to your strengths, efforts, hobbies, and emotions. Then add color. Maybe "anxious" is given a green background or the letters in "musician" are turned into black and white piano keys. Allow your personality to shine. When you are finished, share your work with a teacher or peer, if you feel comfortable doing so.

◀ Question and answer choices are contained within the letters "E" and "O", as part of a quiz feature in the magazine.

GETTING STARTED

As you begin to create your personal collage, look back at your journal entry.

1. Which words stand out to you? Which qualities are unique to you? Choose one letter to represent yourself. Maybe it's the first letter of your name or the first letter of your favorite sport. Place that letter in the center of the page.

2. Using Hannah Tak's artwork as a model, place some of the words from your journal entry inside the letter. Decide whether you'd like your collage to rely on words or images more heavily. Turn some of the words into images. For example, "athletic" could be a sketch of a foot kicking a ball. Continue to add words and images that represent you inside the letter.

Faenkova Elena/Shutterstock

3. Experiment with nesting and sizing text and images to achieve varying results. Use one common element, such as size or weight, to convey importance. Carry that element through your design so the viewer can pinpoint your values at first glance.

NEXT | EXPLORERS QUIZ

EXPLORE This quiz is the last of seven to run in 2013 to celebrate National Geographic's 125th anniversary.

COOL TOOLS FROM MOTHER NATURE

We often get our best ideas by looking out the window. What's out there in nature represents 3.8 billion years of research and development, according to biomimicry expert Janine Benyus. Ideas that failed in evolutionary product testing are now fossils. What's left are some highly instructive success stories. This is a quiz about some of the spin-offs that have come from paying attention to life right here on Earth.

1. TYPE 2 DIABETES NOW AFFECTS TENS OF MILLIONS OF PEOPLE. RESEARCHERS RECENTLY DEVELOPED A TREATMENT THAT COMES FROM WHICH **NATURAL PRODUCT?** A. The bark of the sycamore tree B. Gila monster spit C. A camel's gall bladder D. The Venus flytrap

2. WHICH ANIMAL, FIRST DISCOVERED IN THE **HUDSON RIVER VALLEY,** TURNED THE IDEA OF **EXTINCTION** FROM HERESY INTO A **FACT OF LIFE?** A. The American cheetah B. The giant ground sloth C. The American mastodon D. *Megalosaurus*

3. THE FIRST DRUG TO TURN **HIV FROM A DEATH** SENTENCE INTO **A CONTROLLABLE DISEASE** WAS BASED ON PRODUCTS FROM WHICH SPECIES? A. A marine sponge B. An immune West African monkey C. The Pacific yew tree D. A cone snail

4. WHAT **ANIMAL BEHAVIOR** IS TEACHING POWER PLANTS **A WAY TO CUT THEIR CARBON DIOXIDE EMISSIONS?** A. Tardigrade cryptobiosis B. Grizzly bear hibernation C. Albatross long-distance flight D. Coral calcification

5. BIOLOGIST AND ROBOTICS EXPERT **CLAIRE RIND** DESIGNED A COLLISION AVOIDANCE SYSTEM FOR CARS BY OBSERVING WHAT ANIMAL? A. Impala B. Mustang C. Jaguar D. Locust

6. CHARLES DARWIN SPENT YEARS STUDYING WHICH ANIMAL GROUP AS HE **DEVELOPED THE IDEA OF EVOLUTION** BY NATURAL SELECTION? A. Earthworms B. Galápagos iguanas C. Barnacles D. The peppered moth

FIND ANSWERS ON PAGE 29.

HANNAH TAK, NGM STAFF. ART: GRAFILU (PORTRAIT); NGM ART. PHOTO: STOCKBYTE/GETTY IMAGES

NEXT | EXPLORERS QUIZ

EXPLORE This quiz is the fifth of seven to run in 2013 to celebrate National Geographic's 125th anniversary. The next quiz will appear in October.

WOMEN AND DISCOVERY

For centuries female explorers got to pursue their ambitions only in disguise or against fierce resistance. If they somehow succeeded, society often ignored them or, worse, treated them as superwomen, because that was a way, Egyptian feminist Huda Shaarawi wrote, "to avoid recognizing the capabilities of all women." With that in mind, this quiz celebrates ordinary women doing extraordinary things.

1. WHO WAS THE **FIRST WOMAN** TO CIRCUMNAVIGATE THE EARTH? A. Krystyna Chojnowska-Liskiewicz B. Naomi James C. Tania Aebi D. Jeanne Baret

3. MISSY MAZZOLI'S 2012 OPERA *SONG FROM THE UPROAR* IS BASED ON THE LIFE OF WHICH **FEMALE EXPLORER IN AFRICA?**

AFRICA

A. Isabelle Eberhardt B. Mary Kingsley C. Mary Leakey D. Delia Akeley

4. WHICH IS THE BEST KNOWN AMONG THE FOSSILS, SHIPWRECKS, AND ARTIFACTS **SUE HENDRICKSON** HAS DISCOVERED AROUND THE WORLD? A. The keel of the *Santa María*, lost on Christmas Day, 1492 B. "Sue," a *Tyrannosaurus rex* C. A fossilized giant squid D. An ancient tree-dwelling horseshoe crab trapped in amber

2. IN 1910 A CIGARETTE COMPANY FEATURED **MISS ANNIE SMITH PECK** ON ITS TRADING CARD SERIES OF "THE WORLD'S GREATEST EXPLORERS." WHO WAS SHE? A. The first person to bring back a living electric eel from South America B. A solo traveler down the length of the Amazon C. A pioneering mountain climber D. A biologist tracking jaguars solo at night

5. THE *NEW YORK TIMES* NAMED HER **ONE OF THE LEADING WOMEN EXPLORERS IN THE WORLD.** WHO WAS SHE? A. Annie Edson Taylor B. Harriet Chalmers Adams C. Nellie Bly D. Amelia Earhart

6. AFTER RETIRING FROM HER NURSING CAREER SOME YEARS AGO, **BARBARA HILLARY** DECIDED TO TRAVEL. AT THE AGE OF 79 SHE BECAME **THE FIRST BLACK WOMAN TO DO WHAT?** A. Dive to the *Titanic* B. Visit both the North and South Poles C. Summit Everest D. Swim the English Channel

FIND ANSWERS ON PAGE 29.

HANNAH TAK, NGM STAFF. ART: MARC JOHNS; AMERICAN TOBACCO (PECK CARD); NGM ART (MASK). NGM MAPS

Layout/design by Hannah Tak. From "Explorers Quiz." *National Geographic Magazine,* Left/E: Vol. 224, No. 6, December 2013; Right/O: Vol. 224, No. 3, September, 2013

552

PROJECT DESCRIPTION

In this project, you will create a spread for an imagined autobiography that expands upon the collage you created for your Design Project. This spread should include text and images or graphics that represent one aspect of your life. Choose one focal point. For example, if you are "creative", you might design a colorful quilt across the majority of the spread and include a table listing your best creative assets using a variety of fonts and colors. The goal of this project is to showcase one of your interests or talents in a spread that would be appropriate for a book.

SKILLS TO EXPLORE

- Create and Format a Table
- Format Text in a Table
- Place Graphics in a Table
- Make Books, Tables of Contents, and Indexes
- Create a Book File
- Organize a Book File
- Create a Table of Contents
- Create Bleeds, Slugs, and Printer's Marks
- Use the Ink Manager and Preview Color Separation

SOFT SKILLS CHALLENGE

Critique is as much a part of the art world as the design itself. Learning to accept constructive criticism from others and using it to enhance your work is a learned skill. Also important is learning how to give appropriate feedback to others.

In this challenge, you will be sharing your Design Project with a small group of classmates. Each participant should be given the time to present their project and classmates should be given time to share their thoughts and perspectives. When giving feedback, offer one strength you see in the project, as well as one area of improvement. Be respectful in your tone of voice, and keep in mind that the presenter worked hard on this project.

When receiving feedback, keep an open mind and know that your classmates are offering suggestions to help you improve upon your skills.

After all presenters have taken their turn, take a moment to reflect on your Design Project. How might you incorporate some of the feedback you received into your Portfolio Project?

GETTING STARTED

Choosing the most important aspect of your life can be a daunting task, especially if you hold many things and people in high regard.

1. Chunk your interests into categories, as you would chapters in a book. Once you have clearly defined categories, it might be easier to choose one area to focus on.

2. Interview friends, classmates, and teammates. Ask them to define your skills and talents in just a few words. Hearing the perspective of others can sometimes open your eyes to your own hidden abilities.

3. Find your own inspiration. If you had an afternoon free, would you spend it rock climbing, baking, or practicing with your band? Allow yourself to explore what motivates and inspires you!

GLOSSARY

A

Align To position objects in specific relationship to each other on a given axis.

Alpha channels Selections made in Photoshop that have been saved with a descriptive name, and which can be loaded into an InDesign document.

Anchored objects Objects created and used as text characters within a block of text.

Autoflow The automatic threading of text through multiple text frames.

B

Baseline The invisible line on which text sits.

Bitmap graphics Images created by pixels in a program like Photoshop. Every digital image and scanned graphic is a bitmap graphic.

Bleed marks Marks that define the bleed size of a document.

Bleeds Areas of the layout that extend to the trim size.

Blending mode An InDesign feature that allows you to create different transparency and color effects in which two or more objects overlap.

Book In InDesign, a collection of two or more InDesign documents that are paginated as a single book.

Bounding box Always rectangular, the frame that defines the horizontal and vertical dimensions of the graphic.

C

Caps Define the appearance of end points when a stroke is added to a path. The Stroke panel offers three types of caps: butt, round, and projecting.

Cell A rectangle in a table row or column.

Clipping path A graphic drawn in Photoshop that outlines the areas of the image to be shown when the file is placed in a layout program such as InDesign.

Closed paths Continuous lines that do not contain end points.

Color bars Used to maintain consistent color on press.

Color stops Colors added to a gradient located between the starting and ending colors.

Column break A typographic command that forces text to the next column.

Columns Vertical page guides often used to define the width of text frames and body copy. Also, in a table, the vertical arrangement of cells.

Compound paths One or more closed paths joined to create one complete path using the Make Compound Path command. You create compound paths when you want to use one object to cut a hole in another object.

Condition set A snapshot of the current visibility of applied conditions to text; allows you to set multiple conditions simultaneously.

Content Management Application A framework to organize and access electronic content, such as Adobe Bridge.

Corner points Anchor points that create a corner between two line segments.

Crop marks Guidelines that define the trim size.

D

Dashed strokes Strokes that consist of a series of dashes and gaps, created and formatted using the Stroke panel.

Data merge When a data source containing fields and records is merged with a target document to create personalized documents.

Direction handle The round blue circle at the top of the direction line that you drag to modify a direction line.

Direction line One of two lines attached to a smooth point. Direction lines determine the arc of the curved path, depending on their direction and length.

Distribute To position objects on a page so they are spaced evenly in relation to one another.

Dock To connect the bottom edge of one panel to the top edge of another panel so both move together.

Document grid An alignment guide to which objects can be aligned and snapped.

Drop cap A design element in which the first letter or letters of a paragraph are increased in size to create a visual effect.

Dynamic preview An InDesign feature in which the entirety of a placed graphic, including areas outside a graphics frame, can be seen as the graphic is being moved.

E

Effective resolution The resolution of a placed image based on its size in the layout.

Em space A type of white space inserted into a text box. The width of an em space is equivalent to that of the lowercase letter m in the current typeface and type size.

En space A type of white space inserted into a text box. The width of an en space is equivalent to that of the lowercase letter n in the current typeface and type size.

Event The specific interactive occurrence that triggers the action of a button.

F

Facing pages Two pages in a layout that face each other, as in an open magazine, book, or newspaper.

Fields Labels in a data source that categorize information in the records of a database, which are placed in a target document to specify how to do a data merge.

Fill A color applied to the inside of an object.

Frames Rectangular, oval, or polygonal shapes that you use for a variety of purposes, such as creating a colored area on the document or placing text and graphics.

G

Glyphs Alternate versions of type characters; usually used for symbols like trademarks, etc.

Gradient A graduated blend between two or more colors.

Graphic An element on a page that is not text. In an InDesign document, a graphic refers to a bitmap or vector image.

Graphics frames Frames in which you place imported artwork.

Gridify To position frames into a grid pattern in one move, using tool and keypad combinations.

Gridify behaviors Various gridify moves accomplished using various tool and keypad combinations.

Guides Horizontal or vertical lines positioned on a page. Guides are used to help align objects on the page.

Gutter The space between two columns.

I

Index An alphabetized list of terms in a book that references the page or pages on which those items are mentioned.

In port A small box in the upper-left corner of a text frame that you can click to flow text from another text frame.

Interpolation The process by which Photoshop creates new pixels in a graphic to maintain an image's resolution.

J

Joins Define the appearance of a corner point when a path has a stroke applied to it as miter, round, or bevel.

K

Kerning The process of increasing or decreasing space between a pair of characters.

L

Leading The vertical space between lines of text.

Libraries Collections of layout elements that appear as a panel in your InDesign document for organizing and storing graphics. Also called *Object Libraries*.

Linear gradient A series of straight lines that gradate from one color to another (or through multiple colors).

M

Margin guides Page guides that define the interior borders of a document.

Master item An object on the master page that functions as a place where objects on the document pages are to be positioned.

Master pages Templates created for a page layout or for the layout of an entire publication.

Merged document A target document that has been merged with records from a data source.

Multiply A practical and useful blending mode in which the object becomes transparent but retains its color.

N

Named color Any color created in the New Color Swatch dialog box.

Nested style Paragraph style that contains two or more character styles within the paragraph style.

Nondestructive effect Applied effect such as glow, shadow, bevel, and emboss that do not permanently change the graphic to which they are applied.

Normal mode Screen mode in which all page elements—including margin guides, ruler guides, frame edges, and the pasteboard—are visible.

O

Object Text or graphic element such as an image, a block of color, or a simple line that is placed in an InDesign document.

Offset The distance text is repelled from a frame. Also, the specified horizontal and vertical distance a copy of an object will be from the original.

Open path A path whose end points are not connected.

Orphan Words or single lines of text at the bottom of a column or page that become separated from the other lines in a paragraph.

Out port A small box in the lower-right corner of a text frame that flows text out to another text frame when clicked.

Overset text Text that does not fit in a text frame.

P

Page information A type of printer's marks that includes the title of the InDesign document.

Page size The size a printed document will be cut when it clears the printing press.

Paragraph return Inserted into the text formatting by pressing [return] (Mac) or [Enter] (Win). Also called a *hard return*.

Pasteboard The area surrounding the document.

Path Straight or curved line created with vector graphics.

Pixel Short for "picture element"; a single-colored square that is the smallest component of a bitmap graphic.

Point A unit used to measure page elements equal to 1/72 of an inch.

Point of origin The location on the object from which a transform is executed.

Preflight Refers to checking a document before it's released to a printer or downloaded to an output device.

Presentation mode A screen mode in which all nonprinting elements, panels, and menu bar are invisible and the page is centered and sized against a black background so the entire document fits in the monitor window.

Preview file A low-resolution version of a placed graphic file. As such, its file size is substantially smaller than the average graphic file.

Preview mode A screen mode in which all nonprinting page elements are invisible.

Printer's marks Include crop marks, bleed marks, registration marks, color bars, and page information.

Process colors Colors that are created (and eventually printed) by mixing varying percentages of cyan, magenta, yellow, and black (CMYK) inks.

Process inks Cyan, magenta, yellow, and black ink; the fundamental inks used in printing.

Pull quote A typographical design solution in which text is used at a larger point size and positioned prominently on the page.

R

Radial gradient A series of concentric circles in which the starting color appears at the center of the gradient and then radiates out to the ending color.

Records Rows of information organized by fields in a data source file.

Registration marks Marks that align color-separated output.

Registration swatch The swatch you should use as the fill color for slug text so it appears on all printing plates.

Resolution The number of pixels in an inch in a bitmap graphic.

Resolution independent When an image has no pixels; usually refers to vector graphics.

Rows In a table, the horizontal arrangement of cells.

Ruler guides Horizontal and vertical rules you can position anywhere in a layout as a reference for positioning elements.

Rulers Measurement utilities positioned at the top and left sides of the pasteboard to help you align objects.

Rules Horizontal, vertical, or diagonal lines on the page used as a design element or to underline text.

S

Screen Modes Options for viewing documents, such as Preview, Normal, and Presentation mode.

Section A group of pages in a document with distinct page numbering from other groups of pages.

Semi-autoflowing A method for manually threading text through multiple frames.

Silhouette A selection you make in Photoshop using selection tools, such as the Pen tool.

Slug A note included on a document for a printer. A slug usually contains special instructions for outputting the document.

Slug area The area for a slug, positioned outside the document's trim size, so it will be discarded when the document is trimmed.

Smart Guides Guides that appear automatically when objects are moved in a document and provide information to help position objects precisely in relation to the page or other objects.

Smooth points Anchor points that connect curved segments.

Snippet An XML file with an .inds file extension that contains a complete representation of document elements, including all formatting tags and document structure.

Soft return In typography, using the shift key in addition to the [return] (Mac) or Enter (Win) key will move text onto the following line without creating a new paragraph.

Spot colors Non-process inks that are manufactured by companies; special pre-mixed inks that are printed separately from process inks.

Spread Two pages that face each other—a left page and a right page—in a multipage document.

Square-up The default placement of a Photoshop file in InDesign that includes the entire image with background.

Stacking order Refers to the hierarchical order of objects on a level.

Stroke A color applied to the outline of an object.

Stroke weight The thickness of a stroke, usually measured in points.

Style A group of formatting attributes that can be applied to text or objects.

T

Table of Contents (TOC) A list of divisions in a book and the pages on which they start, generated in InDesign by styles applied to headings and subheadings.

Tables Rectangles in horizontal rows and vertical columns that organize information.

Tab A command that positions text at specific horizontal locations within a text frame.

Target document An InDesign file containing text that will be seen by all recipients as well as placeholders representing fields in a data source with which it will be merged.

Target layer The layer selected on the Layers panel.

Targeting Clicking a layer on the Layers panel to select it.

Text frame Box drawn with the Type tool in which you type or place text.

Text inset In a text frame, the distance the text is from the frame edge.

Threading Linking text from one text frame to another.

Tint In InDesign, a lighter version of a given color.

Tracking Adjusting the spaces between letters in a word or paragraph.

Transform The act of moving, scaling, skewing, or rotating an object.

Trim size The size a printed document will be cut when it clears the printing press.

U

Unnamed colors Any colors you create that aren't saved to the Swatches panel.

V

Vector graphics Artwork created entirely by geometrically defined paths and curves, usually created and imported from Adobe Illustrator.

Vectors Straight or curved paths defined by geometrical characteristics, usually created and imported from a drawing program.

W

Widow Words or single lines of text at the top of a column or page that become separated from the other lines in a paragraph.

Workspace The arrangement of windows and panels on your monitor.

Z

Zero point By default, the upper-left corner of the document; the point from which the location of all objects on the page is measured.

dragging frame, 27

drawing
    changing directions, 311, 316–317
    curved segments with Pen tool, 310, 315
    tool, 307

drop caps, 53, 58–61

Drop Shadow effect, 394–395

Duplicate Layer command, 155

duplicating. *See also* copying; copying
        and pasting
    layers, 155
    master pages, 108
    text frames, 100

dynamic preview, 168

dynamic spell checking, 69

E

editing tables in Story Editor, 460

editing text
    Autocorrect feature, 69
    complex documents, 173
    Drag and Drop, 70
    dynamic spell checking, 69
    Find/Change command, 68, 70
    spell checking, 68–69, 71

Edit Original button, 268

Edit page size button, 402, 404

effect(s), 390–400
    applying, 391, 393, 395
    copying, 392, 393

managing color, 397
nondestructive, 391
and transparent objects, 397

effective resolution, 274, 275

Effects dialog box, 390, 391

Effects panel, 391, 392, 395, 397

email, exporting PDFs for, 535, 537–538

embedding files, Links panel, 270

em space, 107

ending colors, 228

End Nested Style Character, 382

End Nested Style Here command, 380

enlarging graphics
    bitmap graphics, 276
    Photoshop, 276
    vector graphics, 276

en space, 107

EPS format, 523, 535, 536
    exporting documents to, 536–537

events, 528

Excel, importing tables, 451

Exclude Overlap button, Pathfinder
        panel, 363

exporting
    book files, 505
    paths, saving *vs.*, 289
    XML, 271

exporting documents, 534–541
    to EPS format, 536–537

exporting PDFs, 535
    compressed PDFs, 537–538
    Interactive PDF, 541
    for print and email, 535
    for professional offset printing, 539–540
    uncompressed PDFs, 539–540

Eyedropper tool, 104

F

facing pages, 87, 88

feathering, applying, 398–400

fields, 62

fill(s), 140
    applying, 140–142
    applying to objects, 213–214, 219
    applying to tables, 451, 455
    Paper *vs.* None, 215

Fill button, 140–141, 213–214, 220

Fill Frame Proportionally command, 259

Find/Change command, 68, 70

Fit Content Proportionally command, 259

Fitting commands, 169–170, 259

Flattener Preview panel, 532

font(s)
    on Character panel, searching for, 46
    warnings, 10

footnotes, 61
    formatting, 49, 50
    inserting automatically, 49